THE GUINNESS BOOK OF
KINGS, RULERS & STATESMEN

For my parents

THE GUINNESS BOOK OF
KINGS, RULERS & STATESMEN

CLIVE CARPENTER

GUINNESS SUPERLATIVES LIMITED
2 CECIL COURT, LONDON ROAD, ENFIELD, MIDDLESEX

Editor: Anne Smith

Published in Great Britain by
Guinness Superlatives Limited,
2 Cecil Court, London Road,
Enfield, Middlesex

ISBN 0 900424 46 X

Telephone 0332 371931

Information processing, computer
composition & phototypesetting
by Bemrose Information Services

Printed by Bemrose & Sons Ltd, Derby
Bound by Morrison & Gibb Ltd., London and Edinburgh

Contents

Acknowledgements

Introduction

Entries arranged by state in alphabetical order

Index

Acknowledgements

Among the many people, diplomatic missions, and government and public bodies to whom I am in debt for both valuable advice and information I wish to express my gratitude to the Embassies in London of Costa Rica, Israel, Italy, The Netherlands, South Africa, Switzerland, and the United States of America, the London High Commissions of Australia, Barbados and New Zealand, the Consulate-General of Monaco, the Commonwealth Secretariat, the Polish Institute and Sikorski Museum and to the staff of Worthing Reference Library.

Introduction

This book lists chronologically the Heads of State and of Government, from the year 3000 BC to the present day, of all sovereign states of the modern world and of many nations which no longer exist as independent countries.

The records of heads of governments, of European countries in particular, have in most cases only been listed for the last half century. Due to the space available and the vast number involved, the period included was thought to be the most informative.

Wherever possible the name of each ruler is recorded either in the principal language of the country concerned or in the form used in the lifetime of the individual. English versions of these names are to be found in the index. The transliteration of personal names is a matter upon which there is little agreement and there is more than one possible version for names transliterated from Arabic, Hebrew, Far Eastern languages and those tongues which use the Cyrillic and Greek alphabets. Chinese names have been transliterated according to the Wade-Giles system.

Presentation of Information

The principal states are recorded alphabetically; minor states are noted alphabetically within the text with cross-references to the major headings under which their full entries are to be found.

For each individual the dates of his, or her, tenure of office are noted in bold type, and the dates of birth and death are included where these are known; they are indicated by a 'b' and 'd' respectively. In the case of posts which are either hereditary and/or held for life the date of death is omitted unless it differs from the date upon which the term of office ended, and the cause of death, if known, immediately follows the end of office date; such hereditary and similar positions are indicated in the text by a dagger (†). In most cases the date given for the beginning of a primeministerial term of office relates to the appointment of the individual as Premier rather than to the actual formation of a Ministry—in some states the period between assumption of office as Prime Minister and swearing in of a complete Ministry can be several weeks.

Biographical details have been included for many of the more interesting individuals. These are to be found recorded under the major period of office of a leader who has ruled more than once. Where an individual has ruled in more than one state the biographical details of that ruler are not repeated but are included in the major entry only—such major entries are cross-referenced.

Abu Dhabi *see* United Arab Emirates

Abyssinia *see* Ethiopia

Achaea

A Frankish Crusader Principality which, at its zenith, covered most of the Morea and Attica in Greece.

† Prince of the Morea

GUILLAUME I de Champlitte **1205-1209**. With Geoffroi I de Villehardouin he took southern Greece from the Byzantine Empire.

† Princes of Achaea

GEOFFROI I de Villehardouin Ruler of Achaea 1205-1209; Prince of Achaea, with Morea **1209-*c*1228.**
GEOFFROI II de Villehardouin *c*1228-1246, son of Geoffroi I.
GUILLAUME II **1246-May 1278,** son of Geoffroi II. In 1267 he became a vassal of Carlo I, King of Sicily and Naples.
CHARLES I May **1278-Jan 1285**; was also Carlo I of Naples.
CHARLES II Jan **1285-1289** waived his rights; was also Carlo II of Naples.
ISABELLE (Princess) co-ruler **1289-1297**; daughter of Guillaume II; date of death uncertain.
FLORENT (of Hainaut) co-ruler **1289-1297**, first husband of Isabelle.
CHARLES II **1297-1301**; was also Carlo II of Naples.
ISABELLE (Princess) co-ruler **1301-1307** deposed.
PHILIPPE I (of Savoy) co-ruler **1301-1307** deposed, second husband of Isabelle; date of death uncertain.
PHILIPPE II **1307-1313**, son of Charles II.
MATHILDE (Princess) **1313-1318,** daughter of Isabelle.
ROBERT I **1318-1322**; was also Roberto, King of Naples.
JEAN I **1322-1333,** son of Robert I.
ROBERT II **1333-1364,** nephew of Jean I.
MARIE de Bourbon (Princess) **1364-1370,** widow of Robert II. She disputed the throne with Philippe III.
PHILIPPE III (of Taranto) **1364-1373,** brother of Robert II. He disputed the throne with Marie de Bourbon.
JACQUES I des Baux **1373-Jul 1383,** nephew of Philippe III.
1383-1396 Upon the death of Jacques I des Baux five pretenders sought the Principality - none of them can be considered to have reigned.

† Self-Proclaimed Princes of Achaea

PEDRO BORDO de SAN SUPERANO **1396-1402.** Commander of the Navarrese in Achaea he usurped the throne.
CENTURIONE ZACCARIA **1404-1432** having lost most of Achaea to the Greeks in 1430, nephew of Pedro Bordo. Upon his death Achaea passed to the Byzantine Empire.

Afghanistan

Afghanistan was divided into small states until *c*1220, ruled by the Mongol Emperors *c*1220-mid 13th century, divided between local Mongol leaders mid 13th century-1404 and then became part of the Timurid Empire (1404-1507) before being annexed to Iran. An independent Afghan state in Qandahar (1709-1729) may be regarded as the ancestor of the Kingdom of Afghanistan, originally an Amirate. A Republic was established following a coup in 1973.

THE AFGHAN STATE IN QANDAHAR

† Khans

MIR VEYS KHAN **1709-1715.** He led the revolt against Persian rule.
MAHMUD KHAN **1715-1725,** son of Mir Veys Khan.
ASHRAF KHAN **1725-Oct 1729** assassinated, cousin of Mahmud Khan.
1729-1747 Iranian rule restored.

THE AMIRATE OF AFGHANISTAN

† Amirs of the Afghans

DURRANI DYNASTY
AHMAD SHAH DURRANI (Babu - 'Father of the nation') **1747-Oct 1773,** b (Ahmad Khan Abdali) 1722. He took advantage of Persia's weakness to seize Qandahar where he was 'elected' Amir. He freed all the Afghan lands from foreign control.
TIMUR SHAH Oct **1773-1793,** son of Ahmad Shah, b 1746.
ZAMAM MIRZA SHAH **1793-1800** deposed, fifth son of Timur; date of death of this usurper, who ended his days a captive, uncertain.
MAHMUD SHAH **1800-1803** deposed, son of Timur; date of death uncertain.
SHAH SHOJA **1803-1809** deposed, son of Timur.
MAHMUD SHAH **1809-1818** deposed and exiled.

BARAKZAI DYNASTY
DOST MOHAMMAD KHAN **1818-Aug 1839** fled, b 1793.

DURRANI DYNASTY
SHAH SHOJA   1839-early 1843 assassinated, son of Timur. He was restored by the British during the first Afghan War.

BARAKZAI DYNASTY
(AKBAR KHAN, son of Dost Mohammad, led the anti-British resistance from 1839 to 1842 but cannot be said to have reigned as Amir; d 1849.)
DOST MOHAMMAD KHAN   1843-9 Jun 1863, b 1793.
SHIR 'ALI KHAN   Jun 1863-21 Feb 1879, third son of Dost Mohammad Khan, b c 1825.
(MOHAMMAD UFZUL KHAN, half-brother of Shir 'Ali, was in revolt in 1866 but cannot be considered to have reigned.)
(MOHAMMAD AZIM KHAN, half-brother of Shir 'Ali, controlled much of the country including Kabul from 1866 to 1869 but is not regarded as having reigned as Amir.)
YA 'QUB KHAN   Feb-Oct 1879 when forced to abdicate by the British in the second Afghan War, son of Shir 'Ali, b 1849; d 15 Nov 1923.
ABDOR RAHMAN KHAN   Oct 1879-Oct 1901, grandson of Dost Mohammad, b c 1844.

THE KINGDOM OF AFGHANISTAN

† Kings of the Afghans

BARAKZAI DYNASTY
HABIBOLLAH KHAN   Oct 1901-20 Feb 1919 assassinated, eldest son of Abdor Rahman Khan, b 3 Jul 1872. Proclaimed himself to be King.
AMANOLLAH KHAN   Feb 1919-14 Jan 1929 abdicated in a coup, third son of Habibollah Khan, b 1 Jun 1892; d in exile 25 Apr 1960. A great innovator he secured recognition of Afghanistan's independence by Britain after the third Afghan War (1919-21).

USURPING KING
HABIBOLLAH (Bachech Saqow) **17 Jan-Oct 1929,** executed 3 Nov 1929.

BARAKZAI DYNASTY
MUHAMMAD NADER SHAH   Oct 1929-8 Nov 1933 assassinated, cousin of Amanollah Khan, b 10 Apr 1880.
MUHAMMAD ZAHIR SHAH   Nov 1933-17 Jul 1973 deposed in a bloodless coup, son of Muhammad Nader Shah, b 15 Oct 1914.

Prime Ministers

SARDAR MUHAMMAD HASHIM KHAN 1929-1946, brother of Nader Khan, b c 1884; d 26 Oct 1953.
Marshal **SHAH MAHMUD KHAN GAZI 1946-Sep 1953,** uncle of King Zahir Shah, b c 1887; d 27 Dec 1959.

Gen **SARDAR KHAN MOHAMMED DAOUD   30 Sep 1953-Mar 1963**; see President Mohammed Daoud.
Dr **MOHAMMED YUSSUF   9 Mar 1963-Oct 1965,** b 21 Jan 1917.
MOHAMMED HASHIM MAIWANDWAL   Oct 1965-Oct 1967, b 1921; d 1 Oct 1973 committed suicide after an attempted coup.
NOUR AHMAD ETEMADI   11 Oct 1967-Jun 1971, b 22 Feb 1921.
Dr **ABDUL ZAHIR   9 Jun 1971-Dec 1972,** b 3 May 1910.
Dr **MOHAMMED MUSA SHAFIQ   12 Dec 1972-17 Jul 1973** deposed in coup, b 1921.

THE REPUBLIC OF AFGHANISTAN

Presidents

MOHAMMED DAOUD   17 Jul 1973-27 Apr 1978 killed in a coup, cousin and brother-in-law of King Muhammad Zahir Shah, b 18 Jul 1909.
Gen **DAGARWAL ABDUL KADIR** acting President **27 Apr-1 May 1978.**
NOOR MOHAMMED TARAKI   since 1 May 1978, b 1918.

Prime Ministers

Lieut-Gen **MOHAMMED DAOUD   18 Jul 1973-27 Apr 1978** killed in a coup, also President.
Gen **DAGARWAL ABDUL KADIR** acting PM **28 Apr-1 May 1978.**
NOOR MOHAMMED TARAKI   since 1 May 1978, b 1918.

Ajman   *see* United Arab Emirates

Akkad   *see* Babylonia

Alba, Kings of   *see* Kings of Scots, United Kingdom

Albania

Albania was a province of Rome then of Byzantium before falling to the Normans, Serbs and Bulgars. The Albanians were autonomous from the mid-14th century until 1467 when, despite the efforts of Iskander Beg (Scanderbeg) who is surprisingly still a national hero in Communist Albania, the country fell to the Ottoman Turks. After the 1912 Balkan war Albania was declared independent (28 Nov 1912) - an independence confirmed by the Treaty of London (1913). The Great Powers made Albania a Principality but the state experienced several forms of government, and lack of government, until a Republic was proclaimed in 1925. A Kingdom from 1928 to 1939, Albania was annexed by Italy (1939), was liberated (Nov 1944), and became a Communist Republic in Jan 1946.

THE STATE OF ALBANIA

De Facto Ruler

1912-1914 A period of anarchy.
ESSAD PASHA   1913-Dec 1913, b 1863; d 13 Mar 1920 assassinated.

THE PRINCIPALITY OF ALBANIA

Regent

ESSAD PASHA   Dec 1913-6 Feb 1914; continued in power until the Prince arrived in Albania 7 Mar 1914.

† Prince

HOUSE OF WIED
WILHELM I   6 Feb-5 Sep 1914 *de facto* but arguably to **21 Jan 1925** when the Republic was declared *de jure,* b (a Prince of Wied) 26 Mar 1876; d 18 Apr 1945. Unable to govern owing to anarchy, and deprived of any foreign support by the outbreak of World War 1, Wilhelm left Albania but did not abdicate.

Regent

ESSAD PASHA   Oct 1914-Feb 1916; in control of part of Albania as Regent until 1919.

THE KINGDOM OF ALBANIA

† Self-Proclaimed King
(controlling only part of Albania)

HOUSE OF ESSAD
ESSAD PASHA   1919-13 Mar 1920 assassinated.

THE PRINCIPALITY OF ALBANIA

1920-Dec 1922 A period of anarchy in which no central power was effective.
Apr 1920-Jan 1925 Nominal rule by a Council of Regents.

Self-proclaimed King Zog with Queen Geraldine who is distantly related to ex-President Richard Nixon (Popperfoto)

THE REPUBLIC OF ALBANIA

President

AHMED BEY ZOGU   Jan 1925-1 Sep 1928 when he became King.

THE KINGDOM OF ALBANIA

† King of the Albanians

ZOG I SKANDERBEG III   1 Sep 1928-8 Apr 1939 *de facto* **or 2 Jan 1946** *de jure,* b (member of the family of hereditary Governors of central Albania) 8 Oct 1895; d 9 Apr 1961. The true founder of Albania as a nation, Zog was in turn Premier, President and King. Although vain and despotic, he ended the anarchy, dragging Albania into the 20th century and establishing schools, roads, police, the city of Tirane (formally a village) and even the Albanian language out of diverse local dialects. He was deposed by invading Italian forces in 1939.
(VITTORIO EMANUELE III of Italy assumed the title King of Albania on 16 Apr 1939 and renounced that style on 3 Sep 1943.)

THE PROVISIONAL GOVERNMENT

Premier

Col **ENVER HOXHA** (later Gen) **Oct 1944-11 Jan 1946.**

THE SOCIALIST REPUBLIC
(formerly the People's Republic)

Presidents

(Presidents of the Presidium of the National Assembly)
Dr **OMER NICHANI 11 Jan 1946-Jul 1953.**
Maj-Gen **HADJI LLESHI since 24 Jul 1953,** b 1913.

Prime Ministers

Col-Gen **ENVER HOXHA 11 Jan 1946-Jul 1954,** b 16 Oct 1908.
Col-Gen **MEHMET SHEHU since 20 Jul 1954,** b 10 Jan 1913.

First Secretaries of the Albanian Workers' (Communist) Party

Col-Gen **ENVER HOXHA Jan 1946-1948.**
Col-Gen **MEHMET SHEHU 1948-Jul 1953.**
Gen **ENVER HOXHA since July 1953.**

Algeria

Interior Algeria cannot be said to have been ruled by any power until the French penetrated the south between 1852 and 1891; coastal Algeria was controlled by the Carthaginians (7th century BC-202 BC), Romans (until 5th century AD), Vandals (5th century), Byzantine Empire (from 533), Arabs, Barbary pirates, Turks (c 1518-1830) and the French from 1830 until independence was granted on 3 Jul 1962.

Presidents

FERHAT ABBAS 25 Sep 1962-15 Sep 1963, b 24 Oct 1899.
AHMED BEN BELLA 15 Sep 1963-19 Jun 1965 when he was deposed in a coup, b 1918.
HOUARI BOUMEDIENNE (originally named Mohammed Brahim Boukarouba - Houari Boumedienne is a pseudonym adopted while fighting the French) President **since 10 Dec 1976;** Head of State: Chairman of the Revolutionary Council **19 Jun 1965-10 Dec 1976,** b 23 Aug 1927.

Prime Ministers

YOUSSEF BEN KHEDDA provisional Premier **3 Jul-26 Sep 1962,** b 1919.
AHMED BEN BELLA 26 Sep 1962-19 Jun 1965 when he was deposed in a coup, b 1918; also President from 15 Sep 1963.
HOUARI BOUMEDIENNE since 4 Jul 1965; also President.

Anatolia *see* Seljuq Empire

Andorra

The co-Principality of the Valleys of Andorra was founded in 1278.

Heads of State

There are two co-Princes who are not, however, of equal status: the junior Prince is the French Head of State as the successor to the Count of Foix; the senior Prince is the Bishop of Seo de Urgel. Present Senior Prince: Msgr JUAN MARTI ALANSIS, Bishop of Urgel.

(Both co-Princes are represented in Andorra by a Viguier.)

Head of Government

(The head of the administration is termed the Syndic-Général.)
JULIA REIG since Dec 1972.

Angola

The Portuguese established coastal settlements in the 16th and 17th centuries (Luanda in 1576 and Benguela in 1617) but lost them to the Dutch in 1641. Restored to Portugal in 1648, Angola consisted of little more than a littoral strip until the 1870s, and the boundaries of the colony were not settled until 1905. Independence as a Republic was granted on 11 Nov 1975.

President

Dr **AGOSTINHO NETO since 11 Nov 1975,** b 17 Sep 1922.

Prime Minister

LOPO FORTUNATO FERREIRA do NASCIMENTO since 14 Nov 1975.

Anhalt *see* Germany

Anjou *see* France

Annam *see* Vietnam

Antigonid Kingdoms *see* Asia,
Antigonid Kingdom of; and Macedonia, Greece

Antioch *see* Crusader States

Arabia *see* Saudi Arabia

Aragon *see* Spain

Ararat *see* Urartu

Argentina

Spanish from 1536, Argentina formed part of the Vice-Royalty of Peru but was later erected as a separate Vice-Royalty - that of La Plata. Independence was declared on 9 Jul 1816. From 1810 the country was called the United Provinces of La Plata, from 1825 the Argentine Confederation, and from 1853 Argentina. At times in the early history of the country, local independence has been such that the nation can scarcely be said to have existed, and upon one occasion a province (Buenos Aires) seceded as an independent Republic.

THE UNITED PROVINCES OF LA PLATA

1816-1825 A federation with no effective central government.

THE ARGENTINE CONFEDERATION

Presidents
(sometimes referred to as Governors)

BERNARDINO RIVADAVIA 1826-Jul 1827, b 20 May 1780; d 2 Sep 1845. In many ways the founder of Argentina, he achieved much in public works (particularly education) and attempted to establish a central governmental system. However, local caudillos, jealous of his intellect and for their independence, forced him into exile.
VICENTE LÓPEZ y PLANES Jul 1827-1828, b 1784; d 10 Oct 1856.
(After López, the central government virtually ceased to exist and each province functioned almost as a sovereign state.)

Dictators

Gen **JUAN MANUEL de ROSAS Dec 1829-1833;
Mar 1835-3 Feb 1852** fled, b 30 Mar 1793; d 14

President Juan Peron arm-in-arm with his wife Isabel who became the first woman Head of State of a Republic (Popperfoto)

Mar 1877. The ruler of Buenos Aires Province, this gaucho who occupied an ill-defined role as 'Supremo' of the foreign and defence affairs of the Confederation, imposed his will upon as much of the Confederation as he could. Although a ruthless tyrant - he was eventually deposed by a rising supported by armed intervention from Brazil and Uruguay - he did much to consolidate the country which was in danger of total disintegration.
JUAN RAMÓN BALCARCE 1833-Mar 1835 *de facto,* b 1773; d 12 Nov 1836.

PROVISIONAL GOVERNMENT OF THE CONFEDERATION

VICENTE LÓPEZ y PLANES Feb-May 1852 Head of Government.
Gen **JUSTO JOSÉ de URQUIZA May-Oct 1852** Director.
Dr **VALENTINO ALSINA 30 Oct-Dec 1852** Governor.
Gen **PINTO Dec 1852-Oct 1853** provisional Governor.

THE REPUBLIC OF ARGENTINA

Presidents

Gen **JUSTO JOSÉ de URQUIZA** acting President **Nov 1853-1854**; President **1854-Feb 1860**, b 1800; d Apr 1870 assassinated.

SANTIAGO DERQUI Feb 1860-Sep 1861 acting President, b 1810; d 1891.

JUAN ESTEBAN PEDERNERA acting President **Sep 1861,** b 1796; d 1886.

Gen **BARTOLOMÉ MITRE** acting President **Sep 1861-Oct 1862**; President **12 Oct 1862-Oct 1868,** b 26 Jun 1821; d 18 Jan 1906. A talented academic and soldier, he led his province, Buenos Aires, out of the Confederation but later reunited the country.

Col **DOMINGO FAUSTINO SARMIENTO 12 Oct 1868-Oct 1874,** b 13 Feb 1811; d 12 Sep 1888.

NICOLÁS AVELLANEDA 12 Oct 1874-Oct 1880, b 1 Oct 1836; d 26 Dec 1885.

Gen **JULIO A. ROCA 12 Oct 1880-Oct 1886,** b 1843; d 19 Oct 1914.

MIGUEL JUÁREZ CELMÁN 12 Oct 1886-Jul 1890, son-in-law of Gen Roca, b 29 Sep 1844; d 17 Dec 1907. He was obliged to resign in the economic chaos resulting from the collapse of the Baring financial empire.

CARLOS PELLEGRINI Jul 1890-Oct 1892, b 1847; d 17 Jun 1906.

LUIS SÁENZ PEÑA Oct 1892-Jan 1895, b 1823; d 4 Jul 1907.

Dr **JOSÉ EVARISTO URIBURU 23 Jan 1895-Oct 1898,** b 19 Nov 1831; d 23 Oct 1914.

Gen **JULIO A. ROCA Oct 1898-Oct 1904.**

MANUEL QUINTANA Oct 1904-Mar 1906, b 1835; d in office.

JOSÉ FIGUEROA ALCORTA 1906-Oct 1910, b 1860; d 1931.

ROQUE SÁENZ PEÑA Oct 1910-9 Aug 1914, son of Luis Sáenz Peña, b 19 Mar 1851; d in office. Extraordinarily able, this visionary politician laid the foundations of a democratic society which has seldom been realised.

Dr **VICTORINO de la PLAZA** acting President **9 Aug 1914-Oct 1916,** b 1840; d 29 Sep 1919.

Dr **HIPÓLITO IRIGOYEN 12 Oct 1916-Oct 1922,** b 12 Jul 1852; d 3 Jul 1933. A verbose, talented but naive democrat, he determined to establish democracy securely in Argentina, but by making the army the constitutional guarantors of free elections he opened the way to regular military intervention in government.

Dr **MARCELO TORCUATO de ALVEAR 12 Oct 1922-Oct 1928,** b 4 Oct 1868; d 25 Mar 1942.

Dr **HIPÓLITO IRIGOYEN 12 Oct 1928-6 Sep 1930** deposed in coup.

Gen **JOSÉ FELIX URIBURU 6 Sep 1930-20 Feb 1932,** b 1868; d 28 Apr 1932.

Gen **AGUSTIN PEDRO JUSTO 20 Feb 1932-Feb 1938,** b 26 Feb 1876; d 10 Jan 1943.

Dr **ROBERTO M. ORTIZ 20 Feb 1938-Jun 1942,** b 24 Sep 1886; d 15 Jul 1942.

Dr **RAMÓN S. CASTILLO 27 Jun 1942-4 Jun 1943** deposed in coup, b 20 Nov 1873; d 12 Oct 1944.

Gen **ARTURO RAWSON 5-7 Jun 1943** deposed in coup, b 1885; d 1952.

Gen **PEDRO P. RAMÍREZ 7 Jun 1943-9 Mar 1944,** b 30 Jan 1884; d 11 Jun 1962.

Gen **EDELMIRO J. FARRELL 9 Mar 1944-4 Jun 1946.**

Gen **JUAN DOMINGO PERÓN 4 Jun 1946-22 Sep 1955** deposed in coup, b 8 Oct 1895; d 1 Jul 1974 in office during second term. A charismatic personality, Perón, aided by his second wife Eva who was adored by the masses, swept to power with union and working class support for his radical policies. He became authoritarian and frittered away the Treasury in an attempt to buy continued popularity. The massive system of state ownership, pensions and welfare he instituted has proved a crippling economic burden to all subsequent Presidents. The amazing return to power in 1973 demonstrates the strength of his legend.

Gen **EDUARDO LONARDI 23 Sep-13 Nov 1955** deposed, b 15 Sep 1896; d 23 Mar 1956.

Gen **PEDRO EUGENIO ARAMBURU 13 Nov 1955-Apr 1958,** b 21 May 1903; d Jun 1970 - murdered.

Dr **ARTURO FRONDIZI 1 Mar 1958-29 Mar 1962** deposed in coup, b 28 Oct 1908.

Dr **JOSÉ MARIA GUIDO** acting President **30 Mar 1962-Oct 1963,** b 20 Aug 1910; d 13 Jun 1975.

Dr **ARTURO UMBERTO ILLIA 12 Oct 1963-Jun 1966** deposed in coup, b 4 Aug 1901.

Gen **JUAN CARLOS ONGANIA 28 Jun 1966-8 Jun 1970** deposed in coup, b 17 Mar 1914.

8-18 Jun 1970 Military junta.

Brig-Gen **ROBERTO MARCELO LEVINGSTON 18 Jun 1970-22 Mar 1971** deposed in coup, b 1 Jan 1920.

22-25 Mar 1971 Military junta.

Gen **ALEJANDRO AGUSTIN LANUSSE 26 Mar 1971-May 1973,** b 28 Aug 1918.

Dr **HECTOR JOSÉ CAMPORA 25 May-13 Jul 1973.**

Dr **RAÚL LASTIRI** acting President **14 Jul-12 Oct 1973.**

Gen **JUAN DOMINGO PERÓN 12 Oct 1973-1 Jul 1974.**

Señora **MARIA ESTELA MARTINEZ de PERON** (more commonly known as ISABEL de PERON) **1 Jul 1974-13 Sep 1975.**

ITALO ARGENTINO LUDER acting President **13 Sep-16 Oct 1975.**

Señora **MARIA ESTELA MARTINEZ de PERÓN** (more commonly known as ISABEL de PERON) **16 Oct 1975-24 Mar 1976** deposed in coup, widow of Gen Perón, b 6 Feb 1931. The first woman president in the world.

24-29 Mar 1976 Military junta.

Gen **JORGE RAFAEL VIDELA** since **29 Mar 1976,** b 1925.

THE REPUBLIC OF BUENOS AIRES
(which seceded from the Argentine Confederation on 12 Oct 1853)

Heads of Government

Pastor **OBLIGADO** Oct 1853-May 1857.
Dr **VALENTINO ALSINA** May 1857-10 Nov 1859 when Buenos Aires joined the Republic of Argentina.

Armenia

The Armenians occupied Urartu after its collapse. An independent united Armenia flourished from *c*94-*c*63 BC, but then became a vassal state of Rome and later of the Parthians. An independent Armenian Kingdom was revived in the 9th century and lasted until the 11th. Little Armenia or Cilicia was an independent unit from 1080-1375 when all Armenia passed to the Mamluks. Ottoman rule lasted from the 14th century until 1918. An Armenian state was re-established on 26 Mar 1918 but was absorbed by the Soviet Union on 3 Dec 1920.

KINGDOM OF ARMENIA

† King

TIGRAN II (or TIGRANES II) *c*94-63 BC when he became a vassal of Rome, or *c*56 BC when his reign ended. He united the Armenian states of Greater Armenia and Sophene and established an empire including most of Georgia and Syria and part of Parthia. His power waned after war against Pontus and then Rome.
63 BC-AD 395 Armenia was a client state of Rome.
***c*442-*c*631** Armenia was effectively divided between Byzantine and Persian rulers until the start of the 5th century when nearly all Armenia was under Persian control.
653 Western Armenia passed from Byzantine to Arab rule.

† Kings of the Bagratid Dynasty

ASOT I and V (or ASHOT I) Prince of Princes of Armenia from 862 as a vassal of the Arabs; independent King **885-*c*890.**
SMBAT I and IX (or SEMBAT I) **890-914 or 915,** son of Asot I.
ASOT II and VI (or ASHOT II) **914 or 915-928,** son of Smbat I.
ABAS 928-952, brother of Asot II.
ASOT III and VII (or ASHOT III) **952-977,** son of Abas, known as 'The Merciful'.
SMBAT II and X (or SEMBAT II) **977-989,** son of Asot III, known as 'The Conqueror'.

GAGIK I 989-1020, brother of Smbat II.
SMBAT III and XI (or SEMBAT III) sole ruler **1020-1021**; co-ruler **1021-1040,** son of Gagik I.
ASOT IV and VIII co-ruler **1021-1039,** brother of Smbat III.
GAGIK II 1040 or 1042-1045 deposed and imprisoned by Basil II of Byzantium, grandson of Gagik I; assassinated 1079 after a long captivity. He was defeated by and forced to cede Armenia to the Byzantine Emperor.
11th-14th centuries Armenia nominally under Byzantine rule until Ottoman rule was established.

LITTLE ARMENIA OR CILICIA

Sometimes termed 'the Armenian state in exile' Little Armenia existed as an independent unit in southern Asia Minor from 1080-1375.

THE PRINCIPALITY OF (LITTLE) ARMENIA

† Princes of the Rupenid Dynasty

ROUPEN I 1080-1095. He proclaimed the independence of Cilicia.
KONSTANTIN I 1095-1099, son of Roupen I.
THOROS I 1099 or 1100-1129, son of Konstantin I.
LEO I 1129-1138 deposed, brother of Thoros I, d 1141 a captive in exile.
1138-1145 Byzantine rule.
THOROS II 1145-1169, son of Leo I.
ROUPEN II 1169-1170 deposed, son of Thoros II; date of death uncertain.
MLEH 1170-1175 assassinated, uncle of Roupen II.
ROUPEN III 1175-1186 abdicated, nephew of Mleh, became a monk; date of death unknown.
LEO II 1186-1198 or 1199 when he became King, brother of Roupen III.

THE KINGDOM OF (LITTLE) ARMENIA

† Kings of the Rupenid Dynasty

LEO II and I Prince from 1186; King **1198 or 1199-May 1219,** brother of Roupen III.
ZABEL (or ISABEL) **May 1219-1222** deposed, daughter of Leo II; date of death uncertain.
PHILIPPE 1222-1225 deposed, husband of Zabel; date of death uncertain. A French knight from Antioch he ceased to be King when Zabel was forced to divorce him.
ZABEL (or ISABEL) **1225-1226** deposed; date of death uncertain.

† Kings of the Hetumid Dynasty

HETUM I (or HAYTON I) **1226-1269** abdicated, second husband of Zabel, d 1270 having become a Franciscan friar. Hetum was made King by his father the Regent who forced Zabel's divorce and her re-marriage to his son.

LEO III or II **1269-1289,** son of Hetum I.

HETUM II (or HAYTON II) **1289-1293** abdicated, son of Leo III, d 1308.

THOROS III or I **1293-1294** abdicated, son of Leo III, d ? 1298.

HETUM II (or HAYTON II) **1294-1296** deposed.

SMBAT **1296-1298** deposed, son of Leo III; date of death uncertain. He seized the throne, blinded Hetum II and killed Thoros III.

KONSTANTIN II or I **1298-1299** deposed, son of Leo III; date of death uncertain.

HETUM II (or HAYTON II) **1299-1305** abdicated.

LEO IV or III **1305-1308,** son of Thoros III.

OSIN (or OSHIN) **1308-1320,** son of Leo IV (III) or of Leo III (II).

LEO V or IV **1320-1341,** son of Osin, died willing the throne to Hetum II's nephew, Gui de Lusignan.

† Kings of the Lusignan and Baronial Dynasties

GUI de Lusignan **1342-1344** assassinated, nephew of Hetum II.

(JEAN de Lusignan, brother of Gui, may have proclaimed himself sovereign in 1342 as Konstantin II or III.)

KONSTANTIN III or II **1344-1363,** a usurping baron.

KONSTANTIN IV or III **1363-1373** assassinated, cousin of Konstantin III.

(PIERRE, King of Cyprus and relative of Gui de Lusignan was styled King of Armenia 1368-1369 but cannot be said to have reigned.)

LEO VI or V de Lusignan **1373-Apr 1375** when his capital was taken by the Mamluks, nephew of Gui, d 1393 in exile after being captive of the Mamluks (1375-82).

THE ARMENIAN STATE

That part of Armenia which had passed to Russia in 1813 took advantage of the Russian revolution to secede and form an independent country on 26 Mar 1918. The Soviet Army invaded in 1920 ending Armenia's brief experience of freedom on 3 Dec 1920.

Head of Government

R. KACHAZNUNI **spring 1918-Dec 1920.**

Asia, The Antigonid Kingdom of

A short lived Kingdom, including most of Asia Minor, which was founded by Antigonus I - one of the diadochoi (successors) to Alexander the Great.

† King

ANTIGONUS I (Monophthalmos - the one-eyed) Ruler in Asia Minor **323-316 BC**; Regent **316-306 BC**; King **306-spring 301 BC** when he died in battle, b 382 BC. This ruthless former general of the staff of Alexander the Great carved himself an Asian Kingdom but aimed at the entire empire. He died in his attempt to take Egypt.

Asoka Empire *see* India

Assur *see* Assyria

Assyria

For 1200 years Assyria was one of the leading powers of the Middle East. Centred upon the city of Assur, later upon Kalakh and finally upon Nineveh, Assyria became a great empire whose boundaries often stretched far beyond its native northern Mesopotamia.

† Kings of Assur

AMORITE DYNASTY OF ASSUR

SHAMSHIADAD I *c* 1800-*c* 1781 BC. With a band of followers he took the city of Assur and made himself King.

ISHMEDAGAN I *c* 1780-*c* 1755 BC when Hammurabi took Assur, son of Shamshiadad I; fate unknown.

c 1755-*c* 1700 BC Assur under Akkadian rule.

DYNASTY OF ASSUR

ADASI *c* 1700 BC.

BELBANI *c* 1692-*c* 1683 BC.

LIBAIJU *c* 1682-*c* 1666 BC.

SHARMA-ADAD I *c* 1665-*c* 1654 BC.

EN?TAR-SIN *c* 1653-*c* 1642 BC. The name of this sovereign is not known for certain.

BAZAIJU *c* 1641-*c* 1614 BC.

LULLAIJU *c* 1613-*c* 1608 BC.

SHUNINUA *c* 1607-*c* 1594 BC.

SHARMA-ADAD II *c* 1593-*c* 1591 BC.

IRISHUM *c* 1590-*c* 1578 BC.

SHAMSHIADAD II c 1577-c 1572 BC.
ISHMEDAGAN II c 1571-c 1556 BC.
SHAMSHIADAD III c 1556-c 1540 BC.
ASHURNIRARI I c 1539-c 1514 BC.
PUZURASHUR c 1513-c 1500 BC.
ENLILNASIR I c 1499-c 1487 BC.
NURILI c 1486-c 1475 BC.
c 1474 BC An unknown King.
ASHURRABI I c 1473-c 1453 BC.
ASHURNADINAHHE I c 1452-c 1433 BC.
ENLILNASIR II c 1432-c 1427 BC.
ASHURNIRARI II c 1426-c 1420 BC.
ASHURBELNISHESHU c 1419-c 1411 BC.
c 1410-c 1403 BC An unknown King.
ASHURNADINAHHE II c 1402-c 1393 BC.
ERIBA-ADAD I c 1392-c 1366 BC.
ASHURUBALLIT I c 1365-c 1330 BC. Upon the
fall of Mitanni, to which Kingdom Assur had
been a vassal, Ashuruballit created an inde-
pendent state which he termed the Kingdom of
the Land of Assur.
ENLILNIRARI c 1329-c 1320 BC, son of Ashurbal-
lit I.
ARIKDENILI c 1319-c 1308 BC.
ADADNIRARI I c 1307-c 1275 BC. Having made
himself master of Mesopotamia he modestly
styled himself 'King of All'.
SHALMANESER I c 1274-c 1245 BC, son of
Adadnirari I.
TUKULTININURTA I c 1244-c 1208 BC murdered
by his sons, son of Shalmaneser I. This King (the
Ninos of Greek myth) defeated Babylon and
wrecked her temples before installing the cult of
Marduk in Assyria - a sacrilege that his people
said merited death.
ASHURNADINAPLI c 1207-c 1204 BC, son of
Tukultininurta I.
ASHURNIRARI III c 1203-c 1198 BC deposed,
brother of Ashurnadinapli.

SECOND DYNASTY OF ASSUR
ENLILKUDURUSUR c 1197-c 1193 BC when he
fled, fate unknown. This King deposed Ashurnirari who was too pro-Babylonian for Assur, but
defeated by a Babylonian invasion he fled.

THIRD DYNASTY OF ASSUR
NINURTA-APALEKUR I c 1193-c 1180 BC.
ASHURDAN I c 1179-c 1135 BC.
NINURTATUKULTIASHUR c 1134 BC.
MUTAKKILNUSKU c 1134 BC.
ASHURRESHISHI I c 1133-c 1116 BC.
TIGLATHPILESER I (or TUKULTIAPALESHA-
RRA I) c 1115-c 1076 BC. He campaigned against
Babylon and in Syria, Kurdistan and by the
Mediterranean to build a considerable empire.
ASHARIDAPALEKUR c 1076-c 1075 BC, son of
Tiglathpileser I.
ASHURBELKALA I c 1074-c 1056 BC, son of
Tiglathpileser I.

FOURTH DYNASTY OF ASSUR
ERIBA-ADAD II c 1055-c 1054 BC deposed. A
usurper; fate unknown.

*The cruel King Ashurnasirpal II of Assur in whose
reign Assyrian culture reached its zenith* (Radio
Times Hulton Picture Library)

THIRD DYNASTY OF ASSUR
SHAMSHIADAD IV c 1053-c 1050 BC, son of
Tiglathpileser I.
ASHURNASIRPAL I c 1049-c 1031 BC, grandson
of Tiglathpileser I. An invalid King whose weak
rule hastened the collapse of the empire. A long
period of decline, until the reign of Adadnirari II,
followed.
SHALMANESER II c 1030-c 1019 BC.
ASHURNIRARI IV c 1018-c 1013 BC.
ASHURRABI II c 1012-c 972 BC.
ASHURRESHISHI II c 971-c 967 BC.
TIGLATHPILESER II (or TUKULTIAPALES-
HARRA II) c 966-c 935 BC.
ASHURDAN II c 934-c 912 BC.
ADADNIRARI II c 911-c 891 BC.
TUKULTININURTA II c 890-c 884 BC, son of
Adadnirari II.
ASHURNASIRPAL II c 883-c 859 BC, son of
Tukultininurta II. A savage fighter, he enlarged
the empire through his long campaigns which
were probably the first to use cavalry and
battering rams.
SHALMANESER III c 858-c 824 BC, son of
Ashurnasirpal II.
ASHURDANINAPAL c 824 BC deposed, elder son
of Shalmaneser III. Passed over in the suc-
cession, he seized the crown but was soon

deposed by the brother who had been willed the throne.

SHAMSHIADAD V *c*823-*c*811 BC, younger son of Shalmaneser III.

ADADNIRARI III *c*810-*c*783 BC, son of Shamshiadad V.

SHALMANESER IV *c*782-*c*773 BC, son of Adadnirari III.

ASHURDAN III *c*772-*c*755 BC.

ASHURNIRARI V *c*754-*c*746 BC deposed. Assyria had reached its nadir when this King was overthrown in a coup in which, according to some sources, all the Royal Princes were murdered.

FIFTH DYNASTY OF ASSUR

TIGLATHPILESER III (or TUKULTIAPALES-HARRA III) *c*745-*c*727 BC. The general who deposed Ashurnirari V. A very able strategist and perhaps the greatest Assyrian King, he reformed the administration and added extra provinces including Damascus and Israel.

SHALMANESER V *c*726-*c*722 BC assassinated, son of Tiglathpileser III.

SARGON II (or SHARRU-KIN II) *c*721-705 BC died in battle, probably a younger son of Tiglathpileser III (though some sources maintain he was a usurper).

SENNACHERIB (or SINAKHKHE-ERIBA) *c*704-681 BC, son of Sargon II; murdered by his sons. An extravagant builder, he erected the monumental Nineveh palace. Vengeful, he utterly destroyed Babylon (his sacrilege of wrecking the shrine of Marduk was used as a justification for his murder).

ASHURAKHEDDINA (or ESARHADDON) 680-669 BC, son of Sennacherib. A vigorous ruler, he restored Babylon and Marduk's temple and conquered Egypt - an overstretching of resources that greatly contributed to the fall of Assyria.

ASHURBANIPAL 668-630 BC, son of Ashurakheddina.

ASHURETILILANI 630-628 BC deposed, twin son of Ashurbanipal, d after 625 BC. He fought his brother for the throne, lost and fled.

SINSHARISHKUN 628-612 BC, twin brother of Ashuretililani, died by fire when Nineveh was sacked by the Medes.

614-612 BC Most of Assyria was annexed by the Medes.

ASSYRIAN DYNASTY IN HARAN

ASHURUBALLIT II 611-609 or 608 BC. A general who briefly maintained an Assyrian state independent of the Medes and based at Haran.

Asturias *see* Spain

Australia

The first permanent European settlement in Australia was in the Sydney area in 1788. On 1 Jan 1901 the colonies of New South Wales, Queensland, South Australia, Tasmania, Victoria and Western Australia were federated as states in the Commonwealth of Australia - *de facto* an independent nation. The sovereignty of Australia was confirmed by the Statute of Westminster in 1931.

Governors-General

John Adrian Louis Hope, 1st Marquess of **LINLITHGOW** (7th Earl of HOPETOUN) **Jan 1901-Jul 1902,** b 25 Sep 1860; d 29 Feb 1908.

Hallam Tennyson, 2nd Baron **TENNYSON Jul 1902-Jan 1904,** b 11 Aug 1852; d 2 Dec 1928.

Henry Stafford Northcote, 1st Baron **NORTHCOTE Jan 1904-Sep 1908,** b 18 Nov 1846; d 29 Sep 1911.

William Humble Ward, 2nd Earl of **DUDLEY Sep 1908-Jul 1911,** b 25 May 1867; d 29 Jun 1932.

Thomas Denman, 3rd Baron **DENMAN Jul 1911-May 1914,** b 16 Nov 1874; d 24 Jun 1954.

Sir **RONALD FERGUSSON** (later 1st Viscount NOVAR of Raith) **May 1914-1920,** b 6 Mar 1860; d 30 Mar 1934.

Sir Henry William Forster, 1st Baron **FORSTER** of Lepe **Oct 1920-Oct 1925,** b 31 Jan 1866; d 15 Jan 1936.

Sir John Lawrence Baird, 1st Baron **STONEHAVEN** (later 1st Viscount STONEHAVEN) **Oct 1925-Oct 1930,** b 27 Apr 1874; d 20 Aug 1941.

Arthur Herbert Tennyson Cocks, 6th Baron **SOMERS** acting Governor-General **Oct 1930-Jan 1931,** b 20 Mar 1887; d 14 Jul 1944.

Sir **ISAAC ALFRED ISAACS Jan 1931-Jan 1936,** b 6 Aug 1855; d 11 Feb 1948. The first Australian-born Governor-General, Isaacs, the son of a Jewish tailor, was an outstanding lawyer. His appointment was strongly opposed by the 'establishment'.

Brig-Gen Sir Alexander Gore Arkwright Hore-Ruthven, 1st Baron **GOWRIE** (later 1st Earl) **Jan 1936-Sep 1944,** b 6 Jul 1872; d 2 May 1955.

Sir **WINSTON J DUGAN** acting Governor-General **Sep 1944-Jan 1945,** b 8 May 1877; d 17 Aug 1951.

Prince **HENRY, DUKE OF GLOUCESTER Jan 1945-Jan 1947,** third son of King George V, b 31 Mar 1900; d 10 Jun 1974.

Sir **WINSTON J. DUGAN** acting Governor-General **Jan-Mar 1947.**

Sir **WILLIAM JOHN McKELL Mar 1947-Sep 1952,** b 26 Sep 1891.

Field Marshal Sir William Joseph Slim, 1st Viscount **SLIM Sep 1952-Feb 1960,** b 6 Aug 1891; d 14 Dec 1970.

WILLIAM SHEPHERD MORRISON (1st Viscount DUNROSSIL) **Feb 1960-2 Feb 1961,** b 10 Aug 1893; d in office.

Sir **REGINALD ALEXANDER DALLAS BROOKS** acting Governor-General **Feb-Aug 1961,** d 1966.

Sir **WILLIAM PHILIP SIDNEY** (1st Viscount DE L'ISLE, 6th Baron de L'Isle) **Aug 1961-May 1965,** b 23 May 1909.

Sir **HENRY ABEL SMITH** acting Governor-General **May-Sep 1965,** son-in-law of Princess Alice, Countess of Athlone, b 8 Mar 1900.

Sir Richard Gardiner Casey, Baron **CASEY** (Life Peer) **Sep 1965-Apr 1969,** b 29 Aug 1890; d 17 Jun 1976.

Sir **PAUL MEERNAA CAEDWALLA HASLUCK** **Apr 1969-Jul 1974,** b 1 Apr 1905.

Sir **JOHN ROBERT KERR** **Jul 1974-Dec 1977,** b 24 Sep 1914.

Sir **ZELMAN COHEN** **since Dec 1977,** b 1920.

Prime Ministers

Sir **EDMUND BARTON** **Jan 1901-Sep 1903,** b 18 Jan 1849; d 7 Jan 1920.

ALFRED DEAKIN **24 Sep 1903-Apr 1904,** b 3 Aug 1856; d 7 Oct 1919.

JOHN CHRISTIAN WATSON **Apr-Aug 1904,** b 9 Apr 1867; d 18 Nov 1941.

Sir **GEORGE HOUSTON REID** **Aug 1904-Jul 1905,** b 25 Feb 1845; d 12 Sep 1918.

ALFRED DEAKIN **5 Jul 1905-Nov 1908.**

ANDREW FISHER **13 Nov 1908-Jun 1909,** b 29 Aug 1862; d 22 Oct 1928.

ALFRED DEAKIN **Jun 1909-Apr 1910.**

ANDREW FISHER **Apr 1910-Jun 1913.**

Sir **JOSEPH COOK** **24 Jun 1913-Sep 1914,** b 6 Dec 1860; d 30 Jul 1947.

ANDREW FISHER **Sep 1914-Oct 1915.**

WILLIAM MORRIS HUGHES **27 Oct 1915-Jan 1923,** b 25 Sep 1864; d 27 Oct 1952. Perhaps the most colourful figure in Australian politics, his unpopular ideas on defence and his witty and rather pompous character led to many controversies in a career pursued in four different political parties.

STANLEY MELBOURNE BRUCE **9 Jan 1923-Oct 1929,** b 15 Apr 1883; d 25 Aug 1967.

JAMES HENRY SCULLIN **22 Oct 1929-Jan 1932,** b 18 Sep 1876; d 25 Sep 1953.

JOSEPH ALOYSIUS LYONS **6 Jan 1932-7 Apr 1939,** b 15 Sep 1879; d in office.

Sir **EARLE CHRISTMAS GRAFTON PAGE** **7-20 Apr 1939,** b 8 Aug 1880; d 20 Dec 1961.

Sir **ROBERT GORDON MENZIES** **20 Apr 1939-Aug 1941,** b 20 Dec 1894; d 15 May 1978.

Sir **ARTHUR WILLIAM FADDEN** **28 Aug-Oct 1941,** b 13 Apr 1895; d 24 Apr 1973.

JOHN JOSEPH CURTIN **3 Oct 1941-5 Jul 1945,** b 8 Jan 1885; d in office.

FRANCIS MICHAEL FORDE acting PM **6-13 Jul 1945,** b 18 Jul 1890.

JOSEPH BENEDICT CHIFLEY **13 Jul 1945-Dec 1949,** b 22 Sep 1885; d 13 Jun 1951.

Sir Robert Menzies, who was devoted to the monarchy and the British connection, held office continuously for 16 years (Radio Times Hulton Picture Library)

Sir **ROBERT GORDON MENZIES** **15 Dec 1949-Jan 1966.**

HAROLD EDWARD HOLT **20 Jan 1966-17 Dec 1967,** b 5 Aug 1908; drowned off Portsea, South of Melbourne, 17 Dec 1967.

Sir **JOHN McEWEN** acting PM **18 Dec 1967-9 Jan 1968,** b 29 Mar 1900.

JOHN GREY GORTON **9 Jan 1968-Mar 1971,** b 9 Sep 1911.

WILLIAM McMAHON **10 Mar 1971-Dec 1972,** b 23 Feb 1908.

EDWARD GOUGH WHITLAM **5 Dec 1972-Nov 1975,** b 11 Jul 1916.

JOHN MALCOLM FRASER **since 11 Nov 1975,** b 21 May 1930.

Austria

Österreich, the eastern province of the Holy Roman Empire, was founded in the 9th century. From 976 the territory was ruled by Babenberg Margraves who became Dukes from 1156. The Duchy, from 1453 Archduchy, of Austria passed to the Habsburgs in 1276 and remained in their possession until 1918. Austria proper continued to be an Archduchy until 1804 thus its rulers should be referred to as Archdukes rather than by their principal title Holy Roman Emperor. The Empire

The first Austrian Habsburgs: Duke Rudolf I (left) and Duke Albrecht I (right) in a window at St Stephen's Cathedral, Vienna (Supplied by Weidenfeld & Nicholson Ltd; copyright of Osterreichische Nationalbibliothek, Vienna)

of Austria was founded as late as 1804 and was abolished following World War I. The Republic, provisionally proclaimed in 1919, was formally inaugurated in Nov 1921 and ceased to exist when the country was annexed to Germany in 1938 (Anschluss). Although an Austrian Federal Republic was restored in 1945 the state did not regain sovereignty until 1955 when the occupation forces were withdrawn.

† Margraves

HOUSE OF BABENBERG
LEOPOLD I 976-994. Appointed Margrave by the Emperor.
HEINRICH I 994-1018, son of Leopold I.
ADALBERT 1018-1055, brother of Heinrich I.
ERNST 1055-1075 killed in battle, son of Adalbert.
LEOPOLD II 1075-1095, son of Ernst.
LEOPOLD III (St Leopold) **1095-1136,** son of Leopold II, b 1075.
LEOPOLD IV 1136-1141, nephew of Leopold III.
HEINRICH II 1141-1156 when he became Duke.

† Dukes

HOUSE OF BABENBERG
HEINRICH II Margrave from 1141; Duke **1156-13 Jan 1177,** brother of Leopold IV, b c 1114.
LEOPOLD V Jan 1177-1194, son of Heinrich II, b 1157.
FRIEDRICH I 1194-1198, son of Leopold V.
LEOPOLD VI 1198-1230, brother of Friedrich I, b 1176.
FRIEDRICH II 1230-15 Jun 1246 killed in battle by the Hungarians, son of Leopold VI, b 1211.
HERMANN 1246-1250, nephew by marriage to Friedrich II.

HOUSE OF PREMYSL
OTTOKAR 1253-1276; was also Premysl Otakar I of Bohemia.

HOUSE OF HABSBURG
The early Habsburgs frequently divided the Austrian lands amongst themselves. Co-rulers without a territorial division were also known, thus it was possible to have several Dukes at the same time. The regnal numbers of the Babenberg Dukes were ignored, the Habsburgs beginning a new series from 1276.

RUDOLF I 1276-25 Dec 1282 when he divided Austria between his sons, b 1 May 1218; d 15 Jul 1291. Ruler of a small Swiss county, Rudolf of Habsburg (Habichtsburg), one of the outstanding military strategists of the early Middle Ages, was elected Emperor. Lacking a power base he claimed Austria as a vacant Imperial fief, expelling Ottokar.
RUDOLF II co-ruler **Dec 1282-1 Jun 1283,** youngest son of Rudolf I.
ALBRECHT I co-ruler **Dec 1282-1308** murdered, eldest son of Rudolf I, b c 1250.
RUDOLF III co-ruler **?-1307,** eldest son of Albrecht I.
FRIEDRICH I co-ruler **1308-13 Jan 1330,** second son of Albrecht I, b c 1286. Friedrich disputed the Imperial throne with Louis IV by whom he was temporarily imprisoned. His voluntary return to captivity when unable to persuade his brother Leopold to accept one of the conditions of his release is often cited as an example of knightly chivalry.
LEOPOLD I co-ruler **1308-1326,** third son of Albrecht I.
ALBRECHT II co-ruler **1330-1339**; sole ruler **1339-1358,** fourth son of Albrecht I.
OTTO co-ruler **1330-1339,** youngest son of Albrecht I.
RUDOLF IV co-ruler **1358-1365,** eldest son of Albrecht II. Co-ruler with his brothers Rudolf claimed sovereign powers which led to a quarrel with the Emperor. He embellished Vienna, founding the University and St Stephen's Cathedral.
FRIEDRICH II co-ruler **1358-1362,** brother of Rudolf IV.

ALBRECHT III co-ruler **1358-1395,** brother of Rudolf IV. Falling out with Leopold III he partitioned the Habsburg lands keeping Austria proper.

LEOPOLD III co-ruler **1358-1386,** brother of Rudolf IV.

WILHELM co-ruler **1386-1398** when Austria was divided, eldest son of Leopold III.

LEOPOLD IV co-ruler **1386-1398,** second son of Leopold III.

† Dukes of Austria

Rulers of the modern provinces of Upper and Lower Austria.

ALBRECHT IV 1398-1404, son of Albrecht III.

ALBRECHT V 1404-27 Oct 1439, son of Albrecht IV, b 16 Aug 1397. A vigorous ruler who gained Bohemia, Hungary and the Imperial throne.

LADISLAUS 22 Feb 1440-23 Nov 1457, posthumous son of Albrecht V; succeeded at birth.

ALBRECHT VI Nov 1457-1463, brother of Friedrich III.

Rulers of Styria, Carinthia, Tirol and Carniola.

WILHELM co-ruler **1398-1406,** see earlier reference.

LEOPOLD co-ruler **1398-1411,** see earlier reference.

ERNST co-ruler **1406-1411;** sole ruler **1411-1424,** third son of Leopold III.

ALBRECHT VI co-ruler **1424-1463,** younger son of Ernst.

FRIEDRICH III co-ruler **1424-1453** when he became Archduke.

† Archdukes of Austria

HOUSE OF HABSBURG

FRIEDRICH III Duke from 1424; Archduke **1453-19 Aug 1493,** elder son of Ernst, b 21 Sep 1415. An indolent, weak man whose reign saw endless strife with relatives and neighbouring powers but also the reunification of Austria through the demise of others. He became Emperor and gave himself the new · title of Archduke, but lost Hungary, Bohemia and most of his worldly goods.

MAXIMILIAN I Aug 1493-12 Jan 1519, son of Friedrich III, b 22 Mar 1459. Maximilian had few resources but built an empire. He laid the foundations for Austria's greatness through marriage - the children of his first wife eventually won Spain, Burgundy and the Low Countries for the Habsburgs by marriage, while the alliances of their children added Bohemia and Hungary; his second wife, a parvenue but very wealthy Sforza, filled the Treasury with her dowry. He tried to improve the government and finances but was defeated by his extravagance.

KARL I Jan 1519-Apr 1521 when he delegated the Archduchy of Austria to his brother, better known as Emperor Charles V; was also Carlos I, King of Spain.

FERDINAND I Apr 1521-25 Jul 1564, grandson to Maximilian I; younger brother of Karl I, b 10 Mar 1503. Appointed to Austria by his illustrious brother Charles V, Ferdinand had little ambition, much temper and an underestimated intelligence. The legal heir to Hungary, he had to fight Janos Zapolya to gain half that country which had been invaded by the Turks who later beseiged Vienna forcing him to pay tribute - an act traditionally called weakness but more correctly realism.

MAXIMILIAN II Jul 1564-12 Oct 1576, eldest son of Ferdinand I, b 31 Jul 1527.

RUDOLF II Oct 1576-May 1611 when he was deposed, eldest son of Maximilian II, b 18 Jul 1552; d 20 Jan 1612. Unfit to rule, he became increasingly unbalanced and was deposed as Head of the Family and King of Hungary (1608) and as King of Bohemia and Archduke of Austria (1611), though he remained Emperor.

MATTHIAS May 1611-20 Mar 1619 though he had renounced Bohemia in 1617 and Hungary in 1618, third son of Maximilian II, b 24 Feb 1557.

FERDINAND II Mar 1619-15 Feb 1637, nephew of Maximilian II, b 9 Jul 1578.

FERDINAND III Feb 1637-2 Apr 1657, elder surviving son of Ferdinand II, b 13 Jul 1608.

LEOPOLD I Apr 1657-5 May 1705, only surviving son of Ferdinand III, b 9 Jun 1640. At the great seige of Vienna (1683), he retreated to raise fresh troops against the Turks, but the day was won by the Polish army. Surprisingly 'the little Herr in red stockings' was hailed as the saviour of Europe. Among his practical legacies were a standing army, universities, a new legal code and the first steps in the transformation of Vienna into one of Europe's most beautiful cities.

JOSEPH I May 1705-17 Apr 1711, eldest son of Leopold I, b 26 Jul 1678.

KARL II Apr 1711-20 Oct 1740, brother of Joseph I, b 1 Oct 1685.

MARIA THERESIA (Archduchess) sole ruler **Oct 1740-18 Aug 1765;** co-ruler **18 Aug 1765-29 Nov 1780,** daughter of Karl II, b 13 May 1717. Maria Theresa inherited a badly governed state that was soon treacherously attacked by Frederick II of Prussia (who seized Silesia) and then by other powers in the Austrian Succession and Seven Years' Wars. However, this attractive, inexperienced, warm-hearted woman turned out to be the founder of modern Austria, a gifted administrator with a fighting courage that inspired loyalty. The mother of 16 she found time for her family, to build the Schönbrunn and, with a genuine concern for her people, to reform Austria, developing education, taxing the nobility for the first time and establishing a freer judiciary. A good judge of character she picked able advisers, including Kaunitz - perhaps the most talented if devious statesman of the era.

HOUSE OF HABSBURG-LORRAINE

JOSEPH II co-ruler **18 Aug 1765-29 Nov 1780;** sole

Franz Joseph I who ruled an empire but lived austerely: his spartan bedroom contained only a bed and a washstand (Radio Times Hulton Picture Library)

ruler **Nov 1780-21 Feb 1790,** eldest son of Maria Theresia, b 13 Mar 1741. For 15 years Joseph ruled jointly and in conflict with his mother. It is common to picture him as a reformer frustrated by his conservative mother: the truth is many of the reforms claimed as his were hers in concept while most of his own reforms were too radical and provocative.

LEOPOLD II 21 Feb 1790-1 Mar 1792, second son of Maria Theresia, b 5 May 1747.

FRANZ II Mar 1792-11 Apr 1804 when he became Franz I, Emperor of Austria.

† Emperors

HOUSE OF HABSBURG-LORRAINE

FRANZ I Archduke from Mar 1792; Emperor **11 Apr 1804-2 Mar 1835,** eldest son of Leopold II, b 12 Feb 1768. Realism enabled Franz to survive defeat by Napoleonic France. He ended the 1000-year-old Holy Roman Empire, having taken the precaution of adopting an Austrian Imperial title; until 1809 he guided Austria without Metternich - their relationship was a more equal partnership than once imagined. The Emperor and his Minister were less reactionary than is supposed and Austria progressed socially and economically. Metternich's peace (the Vienna

Settlement ending the Napoleonic Wars) has been much maligned - although ignoring nationalist feelings, it did give modern Europe her longest period without a major war.

FERDINAND I Mar 1835-2 Dec 1848 when he abdicated, eldest son of Franz I, b 19 Apr 1793; d 29 Jun 1875.

FRANZ JOSEPH I Dec 1848-21 Nov 1916, nephew of Ferdinand I, b 18 Aug 1830. Remembered as an aged Emperor with enormous whiskers, Franz Joseph inherited an Empire on the verge of disintegration in the 1848 revolutions and left it nearly 70 years later about to collapse in the war he had stumbled into by mishandling the Serbian crisis. Austria made startling economic progress and he led the country to recovery after two wars, but be merely postponed the end of the Empire, failing to make the necessary changes, although the Dual Monarchy, giving Hungary autonomy, was inaugurated (1866).

KARL I Nov 1916-11 Nov 1918 when he renounced the government but did not abdicate, great-nephew of Franz Joseph, b 17 Aug 1887; d 1 Apr 1922.

THE FEDERAL REPUBLIC OF AUSTRIA

Presidents

Dr **KARL SEITZ** acting President **Oct-Dec 1920,** b 4 Sep 1869; d 3 Feb 1950.

Dr **MICHAEL ARTHUR JOSEF JAKOB HAINISCH 9 Dec 1920-Dec 1928,** b 15 Aug 1858; d 26 Feb 1940.

Dr **WILHELM MIKLAS 5 Dec 1928-13 Mar 1938** when Austria was forcibly annexed to Germany, b 15 Oct 1872; d 20 Mar 1956.

Chancellors (Premiers)

Dr **KARL BURESCH 20 Jun 1931-May 1932,** b 12 Oct 1878; d 16 Sep 1936.

Dr **ENGELBERT DOLLFUSS 19 May 1932-25 Jul 1934,** b 4 Oct 1892; assassinated.

Dr **KURT SCHUSCHNIGG** acting PM **25-26 Jul 1934.**

ERNST RUDIGER, Prince **STARHEMBERG 26-29 Jul 1934.**

Dr **KURT SCHUSCHNIGG 29 Jul 1934-11 Mar 1938** when German forces invaded, b 14 Dec 1897; d 18 Nov 1977.

Dr **ARTHUR SEYSS-INQUART 11-13 Mar 1938,** b 22 Jul 1892; executed as a war criminal 16 Oct 1946.

Mar 1938-May 1945 Austria included within the German Reich.

THE FEDERAL REPUBLIC OF AUSTRIA

Austria was recreated in May 1945 but remained under occupation by Britain, France, the United States and the Soviet Union until 25 Oct 1955.

Federal Presidents

Dr **KARL RENNER 20 Dec 1945-31 Dec 1950,** b 14
Dec 1870; d in office.
LEOPOLD FIGL acting President **Dec 1950-27
May 1951.**
Dr **THEODOR KÖRNER 27 May 1951-4 Jan 1957**;
from 25 Oct 1955 President of a sovereign state,
b (Theodor Körner von Siegringen - he
renounced his title) 24 Apr 1873; d in office.
Dr **JULIUS RAAB** acting President **15 Jan-5 May
1957.**
Dr **ADOLF SCHÄRF 6 May 1957-28 Feb 1965,** b 20
Apr 1890; d in office.
Dr **JOSEF KLAUS** acting President **28 Feb-9 Jun
1965.**
Dr **FRANZ JONAS 9 Jun 1965-23 Apr 1974,** b 4
Oct 1899; d in office.
Dr **BRUNO KREISKY** acting President **24 Apr-8
Jul 1974.**
Dr **RUDOLF KIRCHSCHLÄGER since 8 Jul 1974,**
b 20 Mar 1915.

Federal Chancellors
(Premiers)

Dr **KARL RENNER** Chancellor of the Provisional
Government **1 May-20 Oct 1945;** Chancellor **20
Oct-4 Dec 1945.**
LEOPOLD FIGL 4 Dec 1945-Mar 1953, b 2 Oct
1902; d 1965.
Dr **JULIUS RAAB 22 Mar 1953-Apr 1961**; from 25
Oct 1955 Chancellor of a sovereign state, b 29
Nov 1891; d 8 Jan 1964.
Dr **ALFONS GORBACH 11 Apr 1961-Apr 1964,** b
2 Sep 1898; d 31 Jul 1972.
Dr **JOSEF KLAUS 2 Apr 1964-Mar 1970,** b 15 Aug
1910.
Dr **BRUNO KREISKY since 3 Mar 1970,** b 22 Jan
1911.

Aztecs, The *see* Mexico

The Kingdoms of Babylonia or South Mesopotamia

The major powers in the lands between the Tigris
and the Euphrates from *c*2550 BC to the final
destruction of Babylon by the Persians in 482 BC
are recorded below. The earlier dates can only be
approximate and there are many variations in the
spelling of the names of the Kings. The styles
adopted by the sovereigns also give rise to
difficulties since many individuals used grandiose
terms such as 'King of the Four Quarters of the
World' or 'King of the Universe', thus more
realistic styles (eg King of Babylon), which the
Kings may not actually have used, are to be found
below.

THE KINGDOM OF LAGASH
(in eastern Sumeria)

Although the major power of its day Lagash never
united all of Sumeria.

† Kings

LUGALSHAGENGUR *c*2550 BC.

Dynasty of Urnanshe
URNANSHE after *c*2550 BC. A commoner who
founded a new dynasty.
ARKURGAL *c*2500-*c*2470 BC, son of Urnanshe.
EANNATUM *c*2470-*c*2440s? BC, son of Arkurgal.
ENANNATUM I *c*2430s BC?, brother of Eanna-
tum.
ENTEMENA *c*2420s BC, nephew of Eannatum.
ENANNATUM II ?-*c*2395 BC when Lagash was
annexed by Uruk, son of Entemena.
*c*2395-*c*2370 BC Lagash under control of the city
of Uruk.

† Rulers
(when subject to Kish)

ENETARZI *c*2370 BC. A priest who led Lagash to
independence.
LUGALANDA *c*2370-*c*2348 BC deposed; subse-
quent fate unknown.
URUKAGINA *c*2347-*c*2346 BC when he became
King.

† King

URUKAGINA Ruler from *c*2347 BC; King
*c*2346-*c*2341 BC when the city was destroyed.

KINGDOM OF UMMA
(in eastern Sumeria)

† King

LUGALZAGGISI before *c*2340-*c*2315 BC deposed, imprisoned and publicly humiliated by
Sargon of Akkad. King of Umma, Lagash and
Uruk, he called himself 'King of the Lands' and
was supreme in Sumeria until the rise of Sargon.

KINGDOM OF KISH
(in northern Sumeria)

† Kings

KUBABA (Queen) *c*2370 BC. Ex-'Madame' of a
pleasure house she led Kish's fight for
independence from Uruk.
PUZURSIN *c*2350 BC?

URZABABA ?-*c* 2331 BC when he was deposed by his cupbearer Sargon; subsequent fate uncertain.

SHARRUM-KIN (or SARGON I); see Kings of Sumer and Akkad.

KINGDOM OF AKKAD
(or Agade)

† Kings of Sumer and Akkad

SHARRUM-KIN (or SARGON I) *c* 2331-*c* 2276 BC, formerly King of Kish. Sargon founded a new capital, Akkad, around which he built up an Empire (the Akkadian Empire) which after *c* 2315 BC included all Sumeria. A figure of legend, he was said to have been found in the bulrushes (like Moses) and raised by a goddess and a gardener. Sargon modestly styled himself 'King of the Four Quarters of the World'.

RIMUSH *c* 2275-*c* 2267 BC murdered?, younger son of Sharrum-kim.

MANISHTUSU *c* 2266-*c* 2252 BC killed?, elder son of Sharrum-kim.

NARAMSIN *c* 2251-*c* 2215 BC d in battle, grandson of Sharrum-kim.

SHARKALISHARRI *c* 2214-*c* 2190 BC killed.

IGIGI *c* 2189 BC.

NANUM *c* 2189 BC.

EMI *c* 2188 BC.

ELULU *c* 2187 BC. A Gutian.

DUDU *c* 2186-*c* 2166 BC. He regained the city of Akkad from the Gutians.

SHUDURAL *c* 2165-*c* 2151 BC when the city of Akkad was so totally destroyed by the Gutians that it has never been discovered.

c 2151-*c* 2120 BC Gutian rule throughout Sumeria.

† King of Sumer and Akkad in Uruk

UTUHEGAL *de facto* King of Sumer and Akkad *c* 2120-*c* 2113 BC deposed, King of Uruk who styled himself 'King of the Four Quarters of the World'; fate unknown.

† Kings of Sumer and Akkad in Ur

URNAMMU *c* 2113-*c* 2096 BC d in battle, brother of Utuhegal whom he deposed. Took the style 'King of Sumer and Akkad' and Ur for his capital.

SHULGI *c* 2095-*c* 2049 BC, son of Urnammu.

BURSIN *c* 2048-*c* 2039 BC.

SHUSIN *c* 2038-*c* 2030 BC.

IBBISIN *c* 2030-*c* 2022 BC when Amorite invasions ended his empire or *c* 2005 BC when he was taken captive from Ur by Elamites; fate unknown.

† Kings of Sumer and Akkad in Isin
(in central Sumeria)

DYNASTY OF MARI
ISHBI-IRRA *c* 2017-*c* 1985 BC. After *c* 2005 BC he gained control of south Babylonia and took the style 'King of Sumer and Akkad'.

SHUILISHU *c* 1984-*c* 1975 BC.

IDDINDAGAN *c* 1974-*c* 1954 BC.

ISHMEDAGAN *c* 1953-*c* 1935 BC.

LIPITISHTAR *c* 1934-*c* 1924 BC. He lost supremacy to Larsa.

DYNASTY OF ISIN
URNINURTA *c* 1923-*c* 1896 BC.

BURSIN *c* 1895-*c* 1874 BC.

LIPITENLIL *c* 1873-*c* 1869 BC.

ERRAIMITTI *c* 1868-*c* 1861 BC.

ENLILBANI *c* 1860-*c* 1837 BC, adopted son of Erraimitti.

ZAMBIA *c* 1836-*c* 1834 BC.

ITERPISHA *c* 1833-*c* 1831 BC.

URDUKUGA *c* 1830-*c* 1828 BC.

SINMAGIR *c* 1827-*c* 1817 BC.

DAMIQILISHU *c* 1816-*c* 1794 BC when Isin finally fell to Larsa.

† Kings of Sumer and Akkad in Larsa

DYNASTY OF THE AMORITES
NAPLANUM *c* 2025-*c* 2005 BC.

EMISUM *c* 2004-*c* 1977 BC.

SAMIUM *c* 1976-*c* 1942 BC.

ZABAYA *c* 1941-*c* 1933 BC.

GUNGUNUM *c* 1932-*c* 1906 BC. He took Ur, the supremacy in Sumeria from Isin and the name 'King of Sumer and Akkad'.

ABISARE *c* 1905-*c* 1895 BC.

SUMUEL *c* 1894-*c* 1866 BC.

NURADAD *c* 1865-*c* 1850 BC.

SINIDINNAM *c* 1849-*c* 1843 BC.

SINERIBAM *c* 1842-*c* 1841 BC.

SINIQISHAM *c* 1840-*c* 1836 BC when Larsa was taken by the city of Kazallu; fate unknown.

c 1836-*c* 1834 BC Larsa was ruled by Kazallu.

DYNASTY OF IAMUTBAL
WARADSIN *c* 1834-*c* 1823 BC, son of Kudurmabuk.

KUDURMABUK *c* 1823 BC abdicated, father of Waradsin; date of death unknown. The ruler of Iamutbal, he overthrew Kazallu's rule in Larsa and set his son up as King.

RIMSIN *c* 1822-*c* 1763 BC deposed; restored *c* 1741-*c* 1740 BC, son of Kudurmabuk; twice deposed by Babylon he became a captive; date of death unknown.

c 1740 BC Larsa was finally annexed by Babylon.

KINGDOM OF BABYLON

† Kings

AMORITE DYNASTY
SUMUABUM *c*1894-*c*1881 BC. He established a small Kingdom round Babilu ('Gateway of God').
SUMULAEL *c*1880-*c*1845 BC, son of Sumuabum.
SABIUM *c*1844-*c*1831 BC.
APILSIN *c*1830-*c*1813 BC.
SINMUBALLIT *c*1812-*c*1793 BC.
HAMMURABI *c*1792-*c*1750 BC. Remembered chiefly for his Code of Laws (now known to be 'borrowed' from previous codes), Hammurabi should rather be recalled for his great conquests - he conquered all Mesopotamia, styled himself 'King of the Universe' and turned Akkad into Babylonia.
SAMSUILUNA *c*1749-*c*1712 BC.
ABIESHU *c*1711-*c*1684 BC.
AMMIDITANA *c*1683-*c*1647 BC.
AMMIZADUQA *c*1646-*c*1626 BC.
SAMSUDITANA *c*1625-*c*1595 BC deposed when Babylon was ravaged by the Hittites; subsequent fate unknown.

'SEALAND' DYNASTY OF SUMER.
GULKISHAR *c*1594 BC dethroned by the Kassites; fate unknown.

FIRST KASSITE DYNASTY
(The early Kings of the Kassites of the Diyala Valley in Mesopotamia before the Kassite invasion of Babylon were as follows: GANDASH, AGUM I, KASHTILIASH I, ABIRATTASH, KASHTILIASH II, URZIGURUMASH, KHARBASHIKHU, TIPTAKZI and AGUM II.)
AGUM II *c*1590-*c*1530 BC. King of the Kassites, he made himself King of Babylon.
BURNABURIASH I *c*1530-*c*1500 BC.
*c*1500-*c*1490 BC An unknown King.
KASHTILIASH III *c*1490-*c*1470 BC.
ULUMBURIASH *c*1470-*c*1460 BC, brother of Kashtiliash III.
AGUM III *c*1460-*c*1450 BC.
KADASHMANKHARBE I *c*1450-*c*1435 BC.
KARAINDASH *c*1434-*c*1418 BC.
KURIGALZU I *c*1417-*c*1400 BC.
KADASHMANENLIL I *c*1399-*c*1381 BC.
BURNABURIASH II *c*1380-*c*1350 BC.
KARAKHARDASH II *c*1349-*c*1348 BC murdered for being too pro-Assyrian, elder son of Burnaburiash II.

SECOND KASSITE DYNASTY
NAZIBUGASH *c*1347-*c*1345 BC murdered by invading Assyrians. The Kassite general who deposed Karakhardash II.

FIRST KASSITE DYNASTY
KURIGALZU II *c*1345-*c*1324 BC, younger son of Burnaburiash II.

NAZIMARUTTASH *c*1323-*c*1298 BC, son of Kurigalzu II.
KADASHMANTURGU *c*1297-*c*1280 BC, son of Nazimaruttash.
KADASHMANENLIL II *c*1279-*c*1265 BC, son of Kadashmanturgu.
KUDURENLIL *c*1264-*c*1256 BC.
SHAGARAKTISHURIASH *c*1255-*c*1243 BC.
KASHTILIASH IV *c*1242-*c*1235 BC deposed by an Assyrian invasion; subsequent fate uncertain.

ASSYRIAN DYNASTY
TUKULTININURTA I *c*1235-*c*1227 BC; was also Tukultininurta I of Assyria.

BABYLONIAN DYNASTY
ENLILNADINSHUMI *c*1227 BC taken prisoner by Elamites; fate unknown.

THIRD KASSITE DYNASTY
KADASHMANKHARBE II *c*1226-*c*1225 BC.
ADADSHUMIDDIN *c*1224-*c*1219 BC.

FIRST KASSITE DYNASTY
ADADSHUMUSUR *c*1218-*c*1189 BC, son of Kashtiliash IV.
MELISHIKHU *c*1188-*c*1174 or 1172 BC.
MARDUKAPALIDDINA I *c*1173 or 1171-*c*1161 BC.
ZABABASHUMIDDIN *c*1160 BC defeated and deposed by the Elamites; date of death unknown.

FOURTH KASSITE DYNASTY
ENLILNADINAHHE *c*1159-*c*1158 or 1157 BC deposed. A puppet of the Elamites, he turned against them and was taken captive; date of death unknown.

SECOND DYNASTY OF ISIN
MARDUKKABITAHHESHU *c*1156-*c*1139 BC. He set up a state in Isin which was free from the Elamites and regarded as the successor to the Kassite Babylonian Kingdom.
ITTIMARDUKBALATU *c*1138-*c*1131 BC.
NINURTANADINSHUM *c*1130-*c*1125 BC.
NEBUCHADNEZZAR I (or NABUKUDURRIUSUR I) *c*1124-*c*1103 BC. One of the great Kings of the ancient world, he captured Babylon, making it his capital, and crushed the Elamite state.
ENLILNADINAPLI *c*1102-*c*1099 BC, son of Nebuchadnezzar I.
MARDUKNADINAHHE *c*1099-*c*1081 BC deposed, brother of Nebuchadnezzar I; fate unknown.
MARDUKSHAPIKZERI *c*1080-*c*1068 BC when he was deposed by invading Aramaeans; date of death unknown.

ARAMAEAN DYNASTY
This is the traditional name for the dynasty though it is uncertain if the following Kings, of whom virtually nothing is known, were Aramaeans.

MARDUKAHHE-ERIBA before c 1045 BC?
MARDUK-? c 1044-c 1033 BC?

Second Dynasty of Isin
NABUSHUMILIBUR c 1032-c 1025 BC.

'Sealand' Dynasty
SIMMASHSHIHU c 1024-c 1007 BC assassinated by Eamukinshumi.
EAMUKINSHUMI c 1007 BC deposed probably murdered.
KASHUNADINAHHE c 1006-c 1004 BC.

Bazi Dynasty
EULMASHSHAKINSHUMI c 1003-c 987 BC.
NINURTAKUDURUSUR I c 986-c 984 BC.
SHIRIQTUSHUQAMUNA c 984 BC for about three months.

Elamite Dynasty
MARBITIAPALUSUR c 983-c 978 BC.

'Eighth' Dynasty of Babylon
NABUMUKINAPLI c 977-c 942 BC.
NINURTAKUDURUSUR II c 941 BC.
MARBITAHHEIDDIN c 941-c 930? BC.
SHAMASHMUDAMMIQ c 930?-c 904 BC murdered by Nabushumishkun I.
NABUSHUMISHKUN I c 904-c 888 or c 882 BC.
NABUAPALIDDIN c 887 or c 881-c 855 or c 851 BC.
MARDUKZAKIRSHUMI I c 854 or c 850-c 828 or c 822 BC. He was forced to accept Assyrian help and overlordship to put down the revolt of his younger brother Mardukbelusate.
MARDUKBELUSATE c 855 or c 851 BC, younger brother of Mardukzakirshumi I, d in battle c 853 or c 849 BC after an unsuccesful attempt on his brother's throne.
MARDUKBALATSUIQBI c 827 or c 821-c 814 BC defeated in battle by Assyria he was taken captive and deposed; date of death unknown.
BABA-AHI-IDDIN c 814-c 813 BC deposed; taken prisoner by the Assyrians and subsequent fate unknown.

'Sealand' Babylonian Dynasty
c 812-c 803 BC dates of individual reigns unknown.
NABUMUKINZERI.
MARDUKBELZERI.
MARDUKAPALIDOINA II.

Chaldean Dynasty
ERIBAMARDUK c 802-c 763 BC.
NABUSHUMISHKUN II c 762-c 748 BC.
NABUNASIR c 747-c 734 BC.
NABUNADINZERI c 733-c 732 BC assassinated, son of Nabunasir.

Second Chaldean Dynasty
NABUSHUMUKIN c 731 BC assassinated by Nabumukinzer. The general who deposed and assassinated Nabunadinzeri.

Aramaean Dynasty
NABUMUKINZER c 731-c 729 BC deposed and killed by Tiglathpileser III of Assyria.

Assyrian Dynasty
PULU (also TIGLATHPILESER III of Assyria) c 728-c 727 BC.
ULULAI (also SHALMANESER V of Assyria) c 726-c 722 BC.

Aramaean Dynasty
MARDUKAPALIDDINA II c 721-c 710 BC when he fled.

Assyrian Dynasty
SARGON II 710-705 BC; see Assyria.
SENNACHERIB 704-703 BC; see Assyria.

Babylonian Dynasty
MARDUKZAKIRSHUMI II 703 BC - for one month.

Aramaean Dynasty
MARDUKAPALIDDINA II 703-702 BC when he fled again when the Assyrians invaded; date of death unknown.

Babylonian Puppet Dynasty
BELIBNI 702-700 BC deposed. An Assyrian puppet who was deposed after he tried to be a real King.

Assyrian Dynasty
ASHURNADINSHUM 699-694 BC, son of Sennacherib of Assyria. Taken captive by Elamites; date of death unknown.

Elamite Dynasty
NERGALUSHEZIB c 693 BC deposed by Assyria, he was imprisoned then publicly humiliated by Sennacherib; date of death unknown.

Chaldean Dynasty
MUSHEZIBMARDUK 692-689 BC deposed, taken captive and publicly humiliated by Sennacherib; date of death unknown.

Assyrian Dynasty
SENNACHERIB 688-681 BC.
ESARHADDON 680-669 BC, son of Sennacherib.
ASHURBANIPAL 668-652 BC deposed; see Assyria.
SHAMASHSHUMKIN 652-648 BC committed suicide, younger brother of Ashurbanipal; committed suicide by throwing himself into the flames of his burning palace. Originally 'sub-King' in Babylon, he made an unsuccessful attempt to assert complete independence from his brother who then laid seige to Babylon.
ASHURBANIPAL 648-633 BC.

BABYLONIAN DYNASTY
KANDALANU   632-627 BC. Ashurbanipal's governor in Babylon, he declared himself sovereign anticipating his master's death.

NEO-BABYLONIAN OR CHALDEAN DYNASTY
A period sometimes referred to as the Neo-Babylonian Empire.

NABOPOLASSAR   Nov 626-Aug 605 BC. Formerly the Chaldean leader and Assyria's governor in the 'Sealands', he won Babylon and destroyed his former masters in alliance with the Medes.
NEBUCHADNEZZAR II (or NABUKUDURRIU-SUR II) **Sep 605-562 BC,** son of Nabopolassar. A ruler of great energy and ability, he built the Tower of Babel, the Hanging Gardens of Babylon and a large empire which included Syria and Palestine where he rased Jerusalem and took the Jews into exile in Babylonia.
AWIL-MARDUK (Evil-Merodach in the Bible) **562-559 BC** probably assassinated, son of Nebuchadnezzar II.
NERIGLISSAR   559-Apr 556 BC when he died in battle, brother-in-law of Awil-Marduk.
LABASHIMARDUK   May 556 BC - for two or three days; one of the shortest reigns in history, son of Neriglissar; an infant who was deposed and later assassinated.

SYRIAN OR ARAMAEAN DYNASTY OF HARAN
NABU-NA'ID (often called NABONIDUS) **summer 556-Oct 539 BC** when Babylon fell to the Persians; d c530 BC? A gifted soldier from a Syrian princely family, Nabonidus seized power in Babylon but soon offended the people by promoting the cult of his god Sin to the detriment of Babylon's god Marduk. During his long and puzzling campaign in Arabia he made his son co-ruler of the Kingdom they both lost upon the Persian invasion of Oct 539 BC.
BELSHARUSUR (Belshazzar in the Bible) co-ruler **545-Oct 539 BC** when he was killed in battle against the Persians, son of Nabu-Na'id. The King who failed to see the writing on the wall - the threat of a Persian invasion.

PERSIAN DYNASTY
CYRUS   Oct 539-summer 529 BC; was also Kurash II of Iran.
CAMBYSES   summer 529-March 522 BC; was also Kombujia II of Iran.
BARDIYA   March-autumn 522 BC; was also Bardiya of Iran.

BABYLONIAN PRETENDER
NEBUCHADNEZZAR III   Oct-Dec 522 BC killed when Darayavaush I of Persia retook Babylon, claimed to be a son of Nabu-Na'id.

PERSIAN DYNASTY
DARAYAVAUSH I   Dec 522-Sep 521 BC.

BABYLONIAN PRETENDER
NEBUCHADNEZZAR IV   Sep 521-Nov 521 BC executed, claimed to be a son of Nabu-Na'id; executed by impaling when the Persians retook Babylon following his revolt.

PERSIAN DYNASTY
DARAYAVAUSH I   Nov 521-Nov 484 BC; was also Darayavaush I of Iran.
XERXES   Nov 484-Aug 482 BC; was also Xerxes I of Iran.

BABYLONIAN PRETENDERS
BELSHIMMANI   Aug 482 BC; fate unknown.
SHAMASHERA   Sep 482 BC killed when the Persians retook the city and devastated it.
Sep 482 BC Xerxes I regained control of Babylon but did not resume use of the ancient title 'King of Babylon' which thus disappeared.

Baden *see* Germany

The Bahamas

British rule over the Bahamas began in 1670 but was not recognised by Spain (which power claimed the islands in 1492) until 1783. Independence was declared on 10 Jul 1973.

Governors-General

Sir **MILO BOUGHTON BUTLER   1973-1977,** b 11 Aug 1906.
GERALD CASH   acting Governor-General **since 1977.**

Prime Minister

LYNDEN O. PINDLING   since 10 Jul 1973, b 22 Mar 1930.

Bahmani Kingdom *see* India

Bahrain

The Persian Gulf island state of Bahrain ceased to be protected by Britain and assumed full sovereignty on 15 Aug 1971.

† Emir

ISA bin SULMAN al KHALIFAH   Ruler from 2 Nov 1961; Emir **since 15 Aug 1971,** b 3 Jul 1933.

Prime Minister

Shaikh **KHALIFA bin SULMAN al KHALIFAH since 15 Aug 1971,** brother of the Emir, b 1935.

Banda Oriental *see* Uruguay

Bangladesh

The Muslim districts of Bengal became the eastern province of Pakistan upon the creation of that country in 1947 when the British withdrew from India. East Pakistan seceded from Pakistan in Mar 1971 but cannot be said to have come into existence as a sovereign state until after the Indo-Pakistan war and the establishment of a Government in Dacca in Dec 1971.

THE PROVISIONAL GOVERNMENT

Head of State

SYED NAZRUL ISLAM acting Head of State **6-22 Dec 1971.**

Head of Government

TAJUDDIN AHMED 6-22 Dec 1971, d 1975.
22 Dec 1971 The Government of Bangladesh was formed in Dacca with international recognition.

THE REPUBLIC OF BANGLADESH

Presidents

SYED NAZRUL ISLAM acting President **22 Dec 1971-10 Jan 1972.**
Shaikh **MUJIBUR RAHMAN 10-12 Jan 1972.**
ABU SAYEED CHOWDHURY 12 Jan 1972-Dec 1973.
MUHAMMAD ULLAH 24 Dec 1973-Jan 1975, b 21 Nov 1921.
Shaikh **MUJIBUR RAHMAN 25 Jan-15 Aug 1975,** b 17 Mar 1920; d in office - murdered with his family. The leader of the East Pakistan independence movement, Shaikh Mujibur Rahman was released from gaol in West Pakistan by Ali Bhutto after the Indo-Pakistan war. He returned to become Head of Government of the country he had done much to create.
KHANDAKER MOSHTAQUE AHMED 15 Aug-3 Nov 1975 deposed in coup, b 1918.
Justice **ABUSADAT MOHAMMED SAYEM 6 Nov 1975-Apr 1977,** b 1 Mar 1916.
Maj-Gen **ZIAUR RAHMAN since 21 Apr 1977.**

Prime Ministers

TAJUDDIN AHMED acting PM **22 Dec 1971-12 Jan 1972.**
Shaikh **MUJIBUR RAHMAN 12 Jan 1972-Jan 1975.**
M. MANSOOR ALI 25 Jan-15 Aug 1975 deposed in coup.
KHANDAKER MOSHTAQUE AHMED 15 Aug-6 Nov 1975 deposed in coup.
Justice **ABUSADAT MOHAMMED SAYEM** acting PM **26 Nov 1975-Nov 1976.**
Maj-Gen **ZIAUR RAHMAN** acting PM-Chief Martial Law Administrator **29 Nov 1976-Jun 1978**; Head of civilian government since Jun 1978.

Bar *see* Lorraine, France

Barbados

British since 1605, Barbados became independent on 30 Nov 1966.

Governors-General

Sir **JOHN MONTAGUE STOW Nov 1966-1967,** b 3 Oct 1911.
Sir **WINSTON SCOTT May 1967-9 Aug 1976,** b 27 Mar 1900; d in office.
Sir **DEIGHTON WARD since 17 Nov 1976.**

Prime Ministers

ERROL WALTON BARROW 30 Nov 1966-Sep 1976, b 21 Jan 1920.
JOHN MICHAEL GODFREY ADAMS since 8 Sep 1976.

Barcid State in Iberia *see* Carthage

Basutoland *see* Lesotho

Batavian Republic *see* The Netherlands

Bavaria *see* Germany

Belgium

In feudal medieval Europe, modern Belgium was divided between several small states: the County of Flanders (the most important); the counties of Hainaut, Limburg and Namur; the Duchy of Brabant, and the Prince-Bishopric of Liège. Burgundian rule in the 14th and 15th centuries was followed by Spanish dominion from 1477-1714 when the Congress of Rastatt ceded the Spanish Netherlands to Austria against which power they revolted in 1789. The United Belgian States were established in Brabant in 1790 but were annexed by France in 1795. Placed under Dutch rule by the Congress of Vienna in 1815, Belgium rose against the Netherlands in 1830 in which year a Provisional Belgian Government was established on 4 October. The Kingdom of Belgium dates from the installation of Prince Leopold of Saxe-Coburg as King of the Belgians on 21 Jul 1831.

† Kings of the Belgians

HOUSE OF SAXE-COBOURG-GOTHA

LÉOPOLD I 21 Jul 1831-10 Dec 1865, b 16 Dec 1790. A naturalised Briton, Prince Leopold, the widower of Princess Charlotte of Wales, was Britain's candidate for the Belgian throne. In the first years of his reign King Léopold faced a Dutch invasion; later he enjoyed greater security than most continental monarchs - Belgium was practically the only European state untouched by the 1848 revolutions. An outstanding patron of science and education, the 'Nestor of Europe' was highly influential in diplomacy, giving his advice, sometimes unsought, to other sovereigns, in particular his niece Queen Victoria.

LÉOPOLD II 10 Dec 1865-17 Dec 1909, second but elder surviving son of Léopold I, b. 9 Apr 1835. He established the Congo Free State but ceded it to Belgium after the exposure of forced labour and other serious abuses in the Congo ended his personal rule of that territory.

ALBERT I 17 Dec 1909-17 Feb 1934 when he was killed in a fall while rock climbing near Namur, younger but only surviving son of Léopold II's brother Philippe, b 8 Apr 1875. King Albert, a most noble character who was universally beloved, and has been called 'the best constitutional monarch who has ever reigned on the Continent of Europe'.

LÉOPOLD III 17 Feb 1934-16 Jul 1951 when he abdicated following controversy about his war leadership and his marriage to a Flemish commoner, elder son of King Albert, b. 3 Nov 1901.

BAUDOUIN I since 16 Jul 1951, elder son of Léopold III by his first wife, Princess Astrid of Sweden, b. 7 Sep 1930.

Albert I triumphantly entering Brussels at the head of the troops he had commanded during World War I (Radio Times Hulton Picture Library)

Prime Ministers

HENRI VICTOR Count **CARTON de WIART 20 Nov 1920-Dec 1921,** b 31 Jan 1869; d 6 May 1951.

GEORGES THEUNIS 16 Dec 1921-May 1925, b 18 Feb 1873; d 21 Aug 1944.

ALOIS Burgrave **van de VIJVERE 13-22 May 1925;** acting PM **May-Jun 1925.**

PROSPER Viscount **POULLET 8 Jun 1925-May 1926,** b 5 Mar 1868; d 3 Jul 1937.

MARCEL-HENRI JASPAR 21 May 1926-Jun 1931, b 28 Jul 1870; d 15 Feb 1939.

JULES RENKIN 5 Jun 1931-Oct 1932, b 3 Dec 1862; d 16 Jul 1934.

CHARLES Count **de BROQUEVILLE 23 Oct 1932-Nov 1934,** b 4 Dec 1860, d 4 Sep 1940.

GEORGES THEUNIS 19 Nov 1934-Mar 1935.

PAUL van ZEELAND 25 Mar 1935-Oct 1937; acting PM **25-30 Oct 1937,** b 11 Nov 1893; d 22 Sep 1973.

HUBERT PIERLOT 30 Oct-Nov 1937; acting PM **Nov 1937.**

PAUL-ÉMILE JANSON 24 Nov 1937-May 1938, b 30 May 1872; d 14 Jun 1951.

PAUL-HENRI SPAAK 13 May 1938-Feb 1939.

HUBERT PIERLOT 20-27 Feb 1939; acting PM **Feb-Mar 1939;** PM **Mar 1939-Jun 1940;** PM in exile during German occupation **Jun 1940-Sep 1944;** Premier in Brussels again **8 Sep 1944-Feb 1945,** b 23 Sep 1883; d 13 Dec 1963.

ACHILLE van ACKER 6 Feb 1945-Feb 1946, b 8 Apr 1898; d 10 Jul 1975.

PAUL-HENRI SPAAK 28 Feb-21 Mar 1946; acting PM **21-27 Mar 1946.**

ACHILLE van ACKER 27 Mar-Jul 1946; acting PM 18 Jul-1 Aug 1946.

CAMILLE HUYSMANS 1 Aug 1946-Mar 1947, b 26 May 1871; d 25 Feb 1968.

PAUL-HENRI SPAAK 12 Mar 1947-Jun 1949; acting PM 27 Jun-23 Jul 1949, b 25 Jan 1899; d 31 Jul 1972. A noted international figure, Spaak was President of the Assemblies of the UNO and the Council of Europe and Secretary-General of NATO.

GASTON EYSKENS 23 Jul 1949-Mar 1950; acting PM 22 Mar-29 Apr 1950; PM 29 Apr-6 Jun 1950, b 1 Apr 1905.

Prof JEAN PIERRE DUVIEUSART 6 Jun-13 Aug 1950; acting PM 13-15 Aug 1950, b 10 Apr 1900.

JOSEPH PHOLIEN 15 Aug 1950-Jan 1952, b 28 Dec 1884; d 4 Jan 1968.

JEAN van HOUTTE 9 Jan 1952-Apr 1954, b 17 Mar 1907.

ACHILLE van ACKER 19 Apr 1954-Jun 1958.

GASTON EYSKENS 9 Jun 1958-Apr 1961.

THÉO LEFÈVRE 6 Apr 1961-Jul 1965, b 17 Jan 1914; d 18 Sep 1973.

PIERRE CHARLES JOSÉ MARIE HARMEL 28 Jul 1965-Feb 1966; acting PM 17 Feb-2 Mar 1966, b 16 Mar 1911.

PAUL VAN DEN BOEYNANTS 2 Mar 1966-Apr 1968; acting PM 22 Apr-18 Jun 1968, b 22 May 1919.

GASTON EYSKENS 18 Jun 1968-Dec 1972.

EDMOND JULES ISIDORE LEBURTON 13 Dec 1972-Jan 1974, b 18 Apr 1915.

LÉO TINDEMANS since 26 Jan 1974, b 16 Apr 1922.

COUNTY OF FLANDERS

Although nominally subject to the French King the Counts of Flanders were often able to act as virtually independent sovereigns.

† Counts

HOUSE OF FLANDERS

BOUDEWIJN I (or BAUDOUIN I) 862-879, son-in-law of Charles II of France. A leading French nobleman this very able warrior eloped with the daughter of Charles II who later granted him Flanders as a powerful buffer state against the Vikings.

BOUDEWIJN II (or BAUDOUIN II) 879-918, son of Boudewijn I.

ARNULF I (or ARNOLPHE I) 918-950 abdicated, son of Boudewijn II, d 989.

BOUDEWIJN III (or BAUDOUIN III) 950-961, son of Arnulf I.

ARNULF I (or ARNOLPHE I) 961-965 abdicated.

ARNULF II (or ARNOLPHE II) 965-989, kinsman of Boudewijn II; known as 'The Young'.

BOUDEWIJN IV (or BAUDOUIN IV) 989-1036, son of Arnulf II; known as 'Barbatus' - the bearded.

BOUDEWIJN V (or BAUDOUIN V) 1036-1067, son of Boudewijn IV; known as 'The Debonnaire'.

BOUDEWIJN VI (or BAUDOUIN VI) 1067-1070, son of Boudewijn V.

ARNULF III (or ARNOLPHE III) 1070-1071, son of Boudewijn V.

ROBERT I 1071-1093, son of Boudewijn VI, b c 1013.

ROBERT II of Jerusalem 1093-1111, son of Robert I.

BOUDEWIJN VII (or BAUDOUIN VII) 1111-1119, son of Robert II, b 1058.

KAREL I (or CHARLES I) 1119-1127 assassinated, cousin of Boudewijn VII, b 1083.

HOUSE OF NORMANDY

WILLEM I (or GUILLAUME I) 1127-1128, grandson of William I of England; known as Cliton.

HOUSE OF ALSACE

DIRK I (or THIERRY I) 1128-1168 abdicated, grandson of Robert I, b 1100; d 1177. He fought for control of Flanders against Willem I.

PHILIP I (or PHILIPPE I) 1168-1191, son of Dirk I.

MARGARETHA I (or MARGUERITE I) co-ruler 1191-1194, daughter of Dirk I.

HOUSE OF HAINAUT

BOUDEWIJN VIII (or BAUDOUIN VIII) co-ruler 1191-1194, husband of Margaretha I; d 1195.

BOUDEWIJN IX (or BAUDOUIN IX) 1194-1205 murdered, son of Margaretha I and Boudewijn VIII, b 1171; was also Baudouin, Emperor of Constantinople (Latin Empire).

JEANNE sole ruler 1205-1212; co-ruler 1212-1233, daughter of Boudewijn IX.

HOUSE OF PORTUGAL

FERDINAND co-ruler 1212-1233, husband of Jeanne, b 1186.

HOUSE OF HAINAUT

JEANNE 1233-1244.

MARGARETHA II (or MARGUERITE II) 1244-1280, daughter of Boudewijn IX, b c 1200.

HOUSE OF DAMARTIN

GUI de Dampierre 1280-1305 died in captivity having unsuccessfully attempted to throw off France's nominal sovereignty over Flanders, son of Margaretha II, b 1225.

ROBERT III 1305-1322, son of Gui, b 1240.

LOUIS I de Nevers 1322-1346 murdered, grandson of Robert III, b c 1304. The Count who presided over one of Flanders' most prosperous periods joined the anti-French forces in the Hundred Years' War and fought at Crécy.

LOUIS II 1346-1384, son of Louis I, b 1330.

MARGARETHA III (or MARGUERITE III) 1384-1405, sister of Louis I, b 1305. The wife of

Philippe of Burgundy, Flanders passed to that power upon her death.

Benin

The West African Kingdom of Dahomey became French in 1892. The Republic of Dahomey became independent on 1 Aug 1960; the name was changed to Benin on 1 Dec 1975.

Presidents

HUBERT MAGA Head of State 1 Aug-31 Dec 1960; President **31 Dec 1960-28 Oct 1963** when he was deposed in a coup, b 10 Aug 1916.
28 Oct 1963-19 Jan 1964 Presidency suspended.
SOUROU MIGAN APITHY 19 Jan 1964-29 Nov 1965, b 8 Apr 1913.
TAIROU CONGACOU 29 Nov-22 Dec 1965 when he was deposed in a coup, b 1913.
Gen **CHRISTOPHE SOGLO 22 Dec 1965-17 Dec 1967** when he was deposed in a coup, b 1909.
Maj **MAURICE KOUANDETÉ 20-21 Dec 1967,** became Prime Minister; b 1933.
Lieut-Col **ALPHONSE ALLEY 21 Dec 1967-17 Jul 1968,** b 3 Apr 1930.
Dr **EMILE DERLIN ZINSOU 17 Jul 1968-10 Dec 1969** when he was deposed in a coup, b 23 Mar 1918.
Dec 1969-Apr 1970 Presidency suspended.
Apr-1 May 1970 Presidential Council (Hubert Maga, Justin Ahomadegbé and Sourou Migan Apithy).
HUBERT MAGA 1 May 1970-7 May 1972.
JUSTIN AHOMADEGBE 7 May-26 Oct 1972 when he was deposed in a coup.
Maj **MATHIEU KEREKOU** President of the Military Revolutionary Council **27 Oct 1972-1 Dec 1975**; President of the MRC and Head of State of Benin **since 1 Dec 1975,** b 1934.

Prime Ministers

HUBERT MAGA 1 Aug 1960-28 Oct 1963; see President Maga.
Col **CHRISTOPHE SOGLO** Head of the Provisional Government **29 Oct 1963-19 Jan 1964,** b 1909.
JUSTIN AHOMADEGBÉ 25 Jan 1964-29 Nov 1965.
TAIROU CONGACOU 29 Nov-22 Dec 1965; see President Congacou.
Gen **CHRISTOPHE SOGLO 22 Dec 1965-17 Dec 1967**; see President Soglo.
17-21 Dec 1967 Revolutionary Military Committee exercised the powers of Premier.
Maj **MAURICE KOUANDETÉ 21 Dec 1967-17 Jul 1968.**
Dr **EMILE DERLIN ZINSOU 17 Jul 1968-10 Dec 1969**; see President Zinsou.

Lieut-Col **EMILE de SOUZA** Chairman of the Military Directorate **12 Dec 1969-Apr 1970.**
HUBERT MAGA 1 May 1970-7 May 1972; see President Maga.
JUSTIN AHOMADEGBÉ 7 May-26 Oct 1972; see President Ahomadegbé.
Maj **MATHIEU KEREKOU since 27 Oct 1975**; see President Kerekou.

Bernicia see Anglo-Saxon Kingdoms, United Kingdom

Bhutan

The Himalayan mountain Kingdom of Bhutan took its present form as an hereditary monarchy in the Wangchuk family in 1907.

† Kings

UGYEN WANGCHUK 1907-Aug 1926.
JIGME WANGCHUK Aug 1926-30 Mar 1952, son of Ugyen.
JIGME DORJI WANGCHUK Mar 1952-21 Jul 1972, son of Jigme, b 1929. A reformer, he renounced his absolute powers, made the first steps to Parliamentary government and built roads, schools and hospitals.
JIGME SINGHI WANGCHUK since 21 Jul 1972, son of Jigme Dorji, b 11 Nov 1955.

Bijapur see India

Birkenfeld see Oldenburg, Germany

Bithynia

A Kingdom of NW Asia Minor which became a significant power during the 3rd century BC.

† Kings of Bithynia of the Graeco-Thracian Dynasty

ZIBOETES c327-c279 BC.
NICOMEDES I c279-c250 BC, son of Ziboetes.
ZIAELAS c250-229 BC.
PRUSIAS I 229-c180 BC.
PRUSIAS II c180-149 BC murdered by Nicomedes II.
NICOMEDES II EPIPHANES 149-94 BC. Bithynia reached its zenith during the reign of this Hellenist who murdered his way to power.

NICOMEDES III EPIPHANES PHILOPATOR 94-91 BC deposed. The heirless Nicomedes III willed the state to Rome.

NICOMEDES IV (real name Socrates) **91-90 BC**, brother of Nicomedes III whom he briefly deposed; fate uncertain.

NICOMEDES III EPIPHANES PHILOPATOR 90-74 BC.

74 BC Bithynia became a Roman possession.

Boer Republics *see* South Africa

Bohemia *see* Czechoslovakia

Bolivia

Originally called Upper Peru, modern Bolivia was detached from the Spanish Vice-Royalty of Peru in the 18th century and ceded to that of La Plata. Independence was declared on 10 Jul 1825 and achieved as the Republic of Bolivia on 5 Aug 1825. From 1836-1839 the country was joined in a federation with Peru. (Bolivia is often quoted as the prime example of Latin American instability and one authoritative source states that 193 coups have occurred there. This reputation is somewhat unfair as only one in six of the 'coups' has resulted in a change of government and all but one in three have happened during the anarchy of 1840-1860.)

THE PROVISIONAL GOVERNMENT

Head

Gen **ANTONIO JOSÉ de SUCRE   10 Jul-5 Aug 1825.**

THE REPUBLIC

Presidents

Gen **ANTONIO JOSÉ de SUCRE** acting President **Aug 1825-1826**; President **Oct 1826-Apr 1828,** b 3 Feb 1795; d 4 Jun 1830 assassinated. Sucre, the liberator of Ecuador, intervened in Upper Peru at the request of Simon Bolivar, after whom he named the new state.

PEDRO BLANCO acting President **Apr-Aug 1828.**

Gen **JOSÉ MIGUEL de VELASCO** acting President **Aug 1828-Jan 1829.**

Gen **ANTONIO JOSÉ de SUCRE   Jan-Mar 1829** deposed in coup.

Marshal **ANDRÉS SANTA CRUZ   1829-1836; 1836-Jan 1839** President of Bolivia within the Confederation of Peru and Bolivia; **Jan-Feb 1839** President of independent Bolivia, b 1792; d 25

Sep 1865. An able general he created a loose uneasy federation with Peru when Bolivia was threatened by Chile.

Gen **JOSÉ MIGUEL de VELASCO   Feb 1839-Nov 1841.**

JOSÉ BALLIVÍAN   Nov 1841-Dec 1847 deposed in coup, b 1804; d 1852.

EUSEBIO GUILARTE   Jan-Dec 1848 deposed in coup.

MANUEL ISIDORO BELZÚ acting President **1848-Aug 1850**; President **Aug 1850-Aug 1855,** b 1808; d 1865.

Gen **JORGE CÓRDOBA   Aug 1855-Nov 1857** deposed in coup, b 1822; d 1861.

JOSÉ MARIA LINARES acting President **Nov 1857-16 Jan 1861** deposed in coup, b 1810; d 1861.

Jan-May 1861 A period of anarchy with no central authority.

JOSÉ MARIA d'ACHA acting President **May-Aug 1861**; President **Aug 1861-Dec 1864** deposed in coup, d 1868.

Gen **MARIANO MELGAREJO** acting President **Dec 1864-Feb 1865**; President **Feb 1865-Jun 1871** deposed in coup, b 1818; d Jun 1871 assassinated.

Col **AGUSTIN MORALES** acting President **Jan-Jun 1871**; President **Jun 1871-27 Oct 1872,** b 1810; d 27 Oct 1872 assassinated in coup.

TOMÁS FRIAS   Oct-Nov 1872.

Lieut-Col **ADOLFO BALLIVIAN   Nov 1872-4 Feb 1874** assassinated, b 1831.

TOMÁS FRIAS   Feb 1874-May 1876 deposed in coup, b 1804; d 1882.

Gen **HILARION DAZA   4 May 1876-Dec 1879** deposed in coup, b 1840; d 1894 assassinated.

Gen **NARCISO CAMPERO** acting President **Dec 1879-Jun 1880**; President **20 Jun 1880-Aug 1884,** b 1813; d 1896.

GREGORIO PACHECO   1 Aug 1884-Aug 1888.

ANICETO ARCE   1 Aug 1888-Aug 1892, b 1824; d 1906.

MARIANO BAPTISTA   1 Aug 1892-Aug 1896, b 1832; d 1907.

SERGIO FERNÁNDEZ ALONSO   1 Aug 1896-Apr 1899 deposed in civil war between Sucre and La Paz, each city claiming to be capital.

Apr-Oct 1899 Military junta.

Col **JOSÉ MANUEL PANDO   Oct 1899-Aug 1904**; murdered Jun 1917.

Gen **ISMAEL MONTES   Aug 1904-Aug 1909.**

ELIODORO VILLAZÓN   Aug 1909-Aug 1913.

Gen **ISMAEL MONTES   Aug 1913-Aug 1917.**

JOSÉ GUTIÉRREZ GUERRA   Aug 1917-12 Jul 1920 deposed in coup.

JUAN BAUTISTA SAAVEDRA Head of military junta **Jul 1920-Jan 1921**; President **28 Jan 1921-Sep 1925** deposed in coup, b 1870; d 1 Mar 1939.

FELIPE GUZMÁN acting President **Sep 1925-Jan 1926.**

HERNANDO SILES   Jan 1926-28 May 1930, b 1881; d 23 Nov 1943 in an air accident.

Col **DAVID R. TORO** Head of military junta **28 May-27 Jun 1930** deposed in coup, b 1898.

Gen **CARLOS BLANCO GALINDO** Head of military junta **27 Jun 1930-Feb 1931,** b 12 Mar 1882; d 2 Oct 1942.

DANIEL SALAMANCA acting President **Feb-Mar 1931**; President **5 Mar 1931-27 Nov 1934** deposed in coup, b 8 Jul 1869; d 17 Jun 1935. Originally an able democrat he became a ruthless dictator. He led his country, against the advice of his generals, into the Chaco War against Paraguay - a war irrationally conducted which led to appalling losses in Bolivia.

JOSÉ LUIS TEJADA SORZANO **27 Nov 1934-17 May 1936** deposed in coup, b 1881; d 1938.

Major **GERMÁN BUSCH** (later Col) Head of military junta **17-20 May 1936.**

Col **DAVID R. TORO** **20 May 1936-13 Jul 1937** deposed.

Col **GERMÁN BUSCH** **13 Jul 1937-23 Aug 1939,** b 23 Mar 1904; d in office - committed suicide.

Gen **CARLOS QUINTANILLA** acting President **23 Aug 1939-12 Mar 1940,** b 1883; d 1964.

Gen **ENRIQUE PEÑARANDA** **12 Mar 1940-20 Dec 1943** deposed in coup, b 1892.

Major **GUALBERTO VILLAROEL** **20 Dec 1943-21 Jul 1946,** b 1908; d in office - he was shot, lynched by the mob, thrown from the presidential balcony and then hanged on a lamp post.

Dr **NÉSTOR GUILLÉN** acting President **22 Jul-1 Aug 1946,** b 1890.

1-15 Aug 1946 Military junta.

Chief Justice **TOMÁS MONJE GUTIÉRREZ** **15 Aug 1946-9 Mar 1947,** b 1884; d 1954.

Dr **ENRIQUE HERTZOG** **10 Mar 1947-Oct 1949,** b 1897.

Dr **MAMERTO URRIOLAGOITIA** acting President **Oct 1949**; President **24 Oct 1949-May 1951,** b 1895.

Gen **HUGO BALLÍVÍAN ROJAS** **15 May 1951-8 Apr 1952** deposed in coup, b 1901.

Dr **HERNAN SILÉS** acting Head of State **9-16 Apr 1952.**

Dr **VICTOR PAZ ESTENSSORO** **16 Apr 1952-6 Aug 1956.**

Dr **HERNAN SILÉS** **6 Aug 1956-Aug 1960,** b 1914.

Dr **VICTOR PAZ ESTENSSORO** **6 Aug 1960-4 Nov 1964** deposed in coup, b 2 Oct 1907.

Gen **RENÉ BARRIENTOS ORTUÑO** acting President and Head of military junta **4 Nov 1964-May 1965.**

Gen **ALFREDO OVANDO CANDÍA** and Gen **RENÉ BARRIENTOS ORTUñO** co-Chairman of military junta and co-equal Heads of State **26 May 1965-4 Jan 1966.**

Gen **ALFREDO OVANDO CANDÍA** sole Head of State **4 Jan-6 Aug 1966,** b 6 Apr 1918.

Gen **RENÉ BARRIENTOS ORTUÑO** **6 Aug 1966-27 Apr 1969,** b 21 Jun 1925; d in office - in an air accident.

Dr **LUIS ADOLFO SILES SALINAS** **27 Apr-26 Sep 1969** deposed in coup, b 30 May 1919.

Gen **ALFREDO OVANDO CANDÍA** **26 Sep 1969-6 Oct 1970** deposed, b 6 Apr 1918.

Gen **JUAN JOSÉ TORRES** **7 Oct 1970-21 Aug 1971** deposed in coup, b 5 Mar 1921; d 1976 assassinated.

Col **HUGO BANZER SUARÉZ** **22 Aug 1971-21 Jul 1978,** b 10 May 1926.

Gen **JUAN PERADA ASBUN** since **22 Jul 1978,** b 1932.

Bophuthatswana *see* South Africa

Bosporus, Kingdom of *see* Pontus

Botswana

The British protectorate of Bechuanaland, established in 1885, gained independence as the Republic of Botswana on 30 Sep 1966.

President

Sir **SERETSE KHAMA** since **30 Sep 1966,** b 1 Jul 1921.

Brandenburg *see* Germany

Brazil

Discovered by the Portuguese Cabral in 1500, Brazil was organised as a 'Government General' of Portugal in 1548. In 1815 when Brazil had been the home of the Portuguese Royal House in exile for seven years the country was raised to a Kingdom with very limited autonomy. Independence was declared on 7 Sep 1822 by Pedro I, son of João VI, King of Portugal and Brazil, and on 12 Oct 1822 Brazil became an Empire. The monarchy was overthrown on 15 Nov 1889 since when the country has been a Republic.

THE KINGDOM

† Kings

HOUSE OF BRAGANCA

MARIA (Queen) **16 Dec 1815-20 Mar 1816**; was also Maria I of Portugal.

JOÃO **20 Mar 1816-12 Oct 1822**; was also João VI of Portugal.

Pedro II of Brazil who encouraged Alexander Graham Bell and was the first monarch to use the telephone (Radio Times Hulton Picture Library)

THE EMPIRE

† Emperors

HOUSE OF BRAGANCA
PEDRO I Perpetual Defender and Protector of Brazil 13 May-12 Oct 1822; Emperor **12 Oct 1822-7 Apr 1831** abdicated, elder son of João VI of Portugal, b 12 Oct 1798; d 24 Sep 1834.
PEDRO II Apr 1831-15 Nov 1889 when he was deposed, son of Pedro I, b 2 Dec 1825; d in exile 5 Dec 1891. His undeserved deposition in a coup, partly provoked by the landowners' fear of the liberal Crown Princess, ended a period of remarkable stability and economic and social progress.

THE REPUBLIC OF BRAZIL, KNOWN AS THE UNITED STATES OF BRAZIL

Presidents

Marshal **MANUEL DEODORO da FONSECA 15 Nov 1889-23 Nov 1891,** b 5 Aug 1827; d 23 Aug 1892.
Marshal **FLORIANO PEIXOTO** acting President **23 Nov 1891-15 Nov 1894,** b 1842; d 1895.
Dr **PRUDENTE de MORAES BARROS 15 Nov 1894-15 Nov 1898,** b 1841; d 3 Dec 1902.
Dr **MANUEL FERRAZ de CAMPOS SALLES 15 Nov 1898-15 Nov 1902,** b 15 Feb 1841; d 28 Jun 1913.
Dr **FRANCISCO da PAULA RODRIGUES ALVES 15 Nov 1902-15 Nov 1906,** b 7 Jun 1848; d 18 Jan 1919. Possibly Brazil's most gifted President he was responsible for great improvements in public health, for rebuilding Rio de Janeiro, and for defusing border disputes with neighbouring states.
Dr **AFFONSO AUGUSTO MOREIRA PENNA 15 Nov 1906-14 Jun 1909,** b 30 Nov 1847; d in office.
Dr **NILO PECANHA** acting President **14 Jun 1909-15 Nov 1910,** b 2 Oct 1867; d 31 May 1926.
Marshal **HERMES RODRIGUES da FONSECA 15 Nov 1910-15 Nov 1914,** nephew of Manuel Deodoro da Fonseca b 12 May 1855; d 9 Sep 1923.
Dr **WENCESLAU BRÁZ PEREIRA GOMES 15 Nov 1914-15 Nov 1918,** b 26 Feb 1868; d 15 May 1966.
Dr **DELFIM MOREIRA da COSTA RIBEIRO** acting President **15 Nov 1918-28 Jul 1919,** b 1868; d ? 1940.
Dr **EPITÁCIO da SILVA PESSOA 28 Jul 1919-15 Nov 1922,** b 23 May 1865; d 1942.
Dr **ARTUR da SILVA BERNARDES 15 Nov 1922-15 Nov 1926,** b 8 Aug 1875; d 23 Mar 1955.
Dr **WASHINGTON LUIZ PEREIRA de SOUZA 15 Nov 1926-25 Oct 1930** deposed in coup, b 26 Oct 1869; d 4 Aug 1957.
25-26 Oct 1930 Three man military junta.
Dr **GETÚLIO DORNELLES VARGAS 26 Oct 1930-29 Oct 1945** deposed in a coup, b 19 Apr 1883; d 24 Aug 1954. In his first term he inaugurated a dictatorship ('The New State') but was popular because he attacked big business, did much to modernise the country, introduced social security and reformed the tax and education systems. At the end of his second term (31 Jan 1951-24 Aug 1954) he committed suicide after revelations of extensive corruption and abuse of power.
Chief Justice Dr **JOSÉ LINHARES** provisional President **30 Oct 1945-31 Jan 1946,** b 1886; d 26 Jan 1957.
Gen **EURICO GASPAR DUTRA 31 Jan 1946-31 Jan 1951,** b 18 May 1885; d 11 Jun 1974.
Dr **GETÚLIO DORNELLES VARGAS 31 Jan 1951-24 Aug 1954.**
Dr **JOÃO CAFÉ FILHO 24 Aug 1954-8 Nov 1955,** b 3 Feb 1899; d 20 Feb 1970.
CARLOS COIMBRA da LUZ acting President **8-11 Nov 1955,** b 1894; d 1961.
NEREU de OLIVEIRA RAMOS acting President **11 Nov 1955-31 Jan 1956** deposed in coup, b 1889; d 17 Jun 1958.
JUSCELINO KUBITSCHEK de OLIVEIRA 31 Jan 1956-31 Jan 1961, b 12 Sep 1902; d 22 Aug 1976.
JÂNIO da SILVA QUADROS 31 Jan-25 Aug 1961, b 25 Jan 1917.
PASCOAL RANIERI MAZZILLI provisional President **25 Aug-7 Sep 1961,** b 17 Apr 1910; d Apr 1975.
JOÃO BELCHIOR MARQUES GOULART 7 Sep 1961-31 Mar 1964 deposed in a coup, b 1 Mar 1918.

PASCOAL RANIERI MAZZILLI acting President **2-15 Apr 1964.**

Marshal **HUMBERTO de ALENCAR CASTELO BRANCO 15 Apr 1964-15 Mar 1967,** b 20 Sep 1900; d 18 Jul 1967 in an air accident. Under a new constitution he established an authoritarian military regime greatly reducing the power of the legislature and abolishing the political parties.

Marshal **ARTUR da COSTA e SILVA 15 Mar 1967-30 Oct 1969,** b 3 Oct 1902; d 17 Dec 1969.

Gen **EMILIO GARRASTAZU 30 Oct 1969-15 Mar 1974,** b 4 Dec 1905.

Gen **ERNESTO GEISEL since 15 Mar 1974,** b 3 Aug 1907.

Brittany *see* France

Brunswick *see* Germany

Buenos Aires, Republic of *see* Argentina

Bulgaria

The Bulgars from the Caucasian Steppes and the Ukraine crossed the Danube into the Byzantine province of Moesia *c* AD 680 and founded an independent state that existed as a Khanate, an Empire and a Principality (with a couple of short interludes of Byzantine rule) until 1393 when the country was taken by the Turks. Bulgaria achieved autonomy within the Ottoman Empire on 13 Jul 1878 as a Principality and became a Sovereign Kingdom in Oct 1908. The monarchy was overthrown in 1946 and a Communist People's Republic was declared on 15 Sep 1946.

OLD GREAT BULGARIA

The name traditionally given to the Bulgarian homeland in the Caucasian Steppes and in the Ukraine.

† Sublime Khan of the Bulgarians

KHAN KUBRAT *c* 595-*c* 642. This Christian ruler united the pagan Bulgars but his extensive empire was divided between his five sons in *c* 642.

BULGARIA, THE KHANATE OF

† Khans of the Bulgarians

HOUSE OF DULO

ASPARUKH *c* 680 when he crossed into modern Bulgaria -701, third son of Khan Kubrat. The founder of the Bulgarian state.

TERVEL 701-718; with the personal title of Tsar from 705, son or grandson of Asparukh.

718-725 A Khan whose name has not survived.

SEVAR 725-740. The last known male descendant of Attila the Hun.

HOUSE OF VOKIL

KORMISOSH *c* 740-756.

VINEKH 756-761 massacred with his family, son of Kormisosh.

HOUSE OF UGAIN

TELETS 761-autumn 763 assassinated, b 731.

763-772 A period of anarchy during which Sabin, Umar, Tioktu and Pagan tried to gain the throne.

HOUSE OF TELERIG

TELERIG 772-777 when he fled; date of death unknown.

HOUSE OF KARDAM

KARDAM 777-802.

802-803 Interregnum.

HOUSE OF PANNONIA

KHAN KRUM 803-13 Apr 814.

OMURTAG Apr 814-831, son of Khan Krum. The builder of luxurious palaces and the notorious persecutor of Christians.

MALAMIR 831-836.

PRESSIAN 836-852.

BORIS I (Boris-Mihail after conversion to Christianity in 864 or 865) **852-864 or 865** when he became Chief Prince.

† Chief Princes of the Bulgarians

HOUSE OF PANNONIA

BORIS I MIHAIL Khan from 852; **864 or 865-889** when he abdicated to become a monk, d 907.

VLADIMIR 889-893 deposed and blinded, eldest son of Boris I; date of death unknown.

SIMEON I 893-925 when he became Tsar.

† Emperors (Tsars) and Autocrats of the Romans and the Bulgars

HOUSE OF PANNONIA

SIMEON I 925-27 May 927, younger son of Boris I. Intended for the Church, Simeon I proved a worldly and very ambitious Tsar under whom the First Bulgarian Empire reached its zenith.

PETUR May 927-969, son of Simeon I.

BORIS II 969-972 deposed; restored briefly *in absentia* 976, son of Petur; d accidentally from a

stray arrow. He was taken captive by the Byzantines who expelled the Russians in 971-2.
972-976 A period of Byzantine rule.

HOUSE OF THE COMITOPULI
SAMUEL Ruler **from 976**; Tsar **993-1014.** Samuel, who initially led the revolt against Byzantium in the name of Boris II, freed Bulgaria, proclaimed himself Tsar and took Macedonia.
GABRIEL RADOMIR 1014-1015 assassinated by Ivan Vladislav; son of Samuel.
IVAN VLADISLAV 1015-1018 d in battle, cousin of Gabriel Radomir.
1018-1040 A period of rule by the Byzantine Empire.
PETUR DELYAN co-ruler **1040-1041,** grandson of Samuel; date of death uncertain. Briefly re-established Bulgarian independence but failed when he fell out with his co-ruler who later blinded him.
ALUSIANUS co-ruler **late 1040-1041,** son of Ivan Vladislav; date of death unknown.
1041-1186 A period of Byzantine rule.

† Princes of the Bulgarians

HOUSE OF TARNOVO, OR ASSENID DYNASTY
PETUR ASSEN 1186-1197 assassinated. With his brothers he re-established an independent Bulgaria.
ASSEN I (sometimes referred to as Ivan Assen I) co-ruler **1186-1196** assassinated, brother of Petur Assen.
KALOYAN 1197-Nov 1204 when he was confirmed as Tsar.

† Emperors (Tsars) of the Bulgarians

HOUSE OF TARNOVO
KALOYAN Prince from 1197; Tsar **6 Nov 1204-Dec 1207** assassinated, brother of Petur Assen and Assen I.
BORIL Dec **1207-1218** deposed, nephew of Kaloyan; date of death unknown.
IVAN ASSEN II 1218-1241, son of Assen I. In a brilliant reign this Tsar annexed Albania, Epirus, Macedonia and parts of Thrace, encouraged trade and the spread of monasticism, and ruled sagely, reforming the finances of his state which dominated the Balkans.
KOLOMAN I 1241-1246.
MIHAIL II ASSEN 1246-1257.
(MICO, a usurper, may be considered to have reigned briefly in 1257.)
KONSTANTIN ASSEN TIKH 1257-1277 d in battle against Ivailo.

USURPING TSARS
IVAILO 1277-1279 deposed.
IVAN ASSEN III 1279-1280. A puppet of the Byzantine Emperor.
IVAILO 1280 assassinated.

TERTER DYNASTY
GEORGI I TERTER 1280-1292 when he fled; date of death unknown.

USURPING TSARS
SMILITZ (or SMILETS) **1292-1298**; d 1300? A puppet of the Mongols.
CAKA 1299, son-in-law of Georgi I.

TERTER DYNASTY
TODOR SVETOSLAV 1298-1322, son of Georgi I Terter.
GEORGI II TERTER 1322-1323.

SHISHMANID DYNASTY
MIHAIL SHISHMAN 1322-1330 d in battle.
IVAN ALEXANDER sole ruler **1330-1365?** co-ruler **1365?-1371,** nephew of Mihail Shishman.
IVAN SHISHMAN co-ruler **1365?-1371**; sole ruler **1371-17 Jul 1393** when his capital was taken by the Turks, son of Ivan Alexander; date of death unknown.
Jul 1393-13 Jul 1878 Bulgaria was ruled by the Ottoman Turks until it was finally granted autonomy within the Ottoman Empire.

THE PRINCIPALITY OF BULGARIA

† Princes of Bulgaria

HOUSE OF BATTENBERG
ALEXANDER I 29 Apr 1879-21 Aug 1886 deposed; restored **29 Aug-3 Sep 1886** abdicated, b (a Prince of Battenberg) 5 Apr 1857; d in exile 17 Nov 1893. After agreeing to the union of Bulgaria with Eastern Rumelia (against the terms of the Treaty of Berlin which had granted autonomy to Bulgaria), Alexander was kidnapped and forced to abdicate by Russian agents.

HOUSE OF SAXE-COBURG AND GOTHA OR WETTIN
FERDINAND I 7 Jul 1887-5 Oct 1908 when he became King.

THE KINGDOM OF BULGARIA

† Kings (Tsars) of the Bulgarians

HOUSE OF SAXE-COBURG AND GOTHA OR WETTIN
FERDINAND I Prince from 7 Jul 1887; King **5 Oct 1908-3 Oct 1918** abdicated, b (a Prince of Saxe-Coburg) 26 Feb 1861; d in exile 10 Sep 1948. He did much to develop Bulgaria and secured sovereignty for his adopted country but his longing for extra territory brought Bulgaria defeat in the Second Balkan War and World War I forcing him to abdicate.
BORIS III Oct **1918-28 Aug 1943,** elder son of Ferdinand I, b 30 Jan 1894; d under suspicious

circumstances - possibly murdered by German agents.

SIMEON II 28 Aug 1943-16 Sep 1946 when he left Bulgaria following a rigged referendum in favour of a Republic, son of Boris III, b 16 Jun 1937.

Prime Ministers

ALEKSANDR STAMBOLIYSKI Oct 1919-14 Jun 1923, b 1 Mar 1879; d 14 Jun 1923 executed immediately after deposition. A pacifist who opposed Bulgaria's alliance with Germany in World War I, he did much for the peasants but was deposed for his republicanism and anti-military sentiments.

ALEKSANDR TSANKOV Jun 1923-Jan 1926, b 21 Jun 1879; d 17 Jul 1959.

ANDREI LIAPCHEV Jan 1926-Jun 1931, b 30 Nov 1866; d 6 Nov 1933.

ALEKSANDR MALINKOV Jun-Oct 1931, b 20 Apr 1867; d 21 Mar 1938.

NIKOLAI MUSHANOV Oct 1931-19 May 1934 deposed in coup, b 2 Apr 1872; d Jul 1951.

Col **KIMON GHEORGHIEV 19 May 1934-Jan 1935.**

Gen **PENCHO ZLATEV 22 Jan-Apr 1935,** b 2 Nov 1881; d 24 Jul 1948.

ANDREI TOSHEV 20 Apr-Nov 1935, b 1867; d 10 Jan 1944.

Dr **GEORGI KIOSSEIVANOV 22 Nov 1935-Feb 1940,** b 19 Jan 1884; d 27 Jul 1960.

Prof **BOGDAN FILOV 16 Feb 1940-Sep 1943,** b 10 Apr 1883; executed as a war criminal Feb 1945.

Prof **DOBRI BOJILOV 13 Sep 1943-May 1944,** b 1884; executed as a war criminal Feb 1945.

IVAN BAGRIANOV 1 Jun-1 Sep 1944, b 1892; executed as a war criminal Feb 1945.

KOSTA MURAVIEV 2-9 Sep 1944, b 1893; d 31 Jan 1965.

Col **KIMON GHEORGHIEV 9 Sep 1944-15 Sep 1946** when he became PM of the Communist Republic, b 11 Aug 1882; d 28 Sep 1969.

THE PEOPLE'S REPUBLIC OF BULGARIA

Presidents

VASSIL KOLAROV acting President **15 Sep 1946-Dec 1947,** b 1877; d 22 Jan 1950. Virtually the founder of the Bulgarian Communist Party in 1919.

MINTSO NEITSEV Dec 1947-May 1950, b 23 Mar 1897; d 11 Aug 1956.

GEORGI DAMYANOV 27 May 1950-27 Nov 1958, b 23 May 1901; d in office.

DIMITER GANEV 30 Nov 1958-20 Apr 1964, b 28 Sep 1898; d in office.

GEORGI TRAIKOV 23 Apr 1964-Jul 1971, b 8 Apr 1898; d 1975.

TODOR ZHIVKOV since 7 Jul 1971, b 7 Sep 1911.

Ferdinand I, who being clever, witty and allegedly wily, was nicknamed 'Ferdy the Fox', was always exquisitely dressed (Radio Times Hulton Picture Library)

Prime Ministers

Col **KIMON GHEORGHIEV 15 Sep-22 Nov 1946.**

GEORGI DIMITROV 22 Nov 1946-2 Jul 1949, b 18 Jun 1882; d in office. A printer, he was court-martialled in World War I, attempted to depose Tsankov in 1923, lived in exile as a Soviet citizen until 1945 and returned with the Red Army to preside over the transformation of Bulgaria into a Communist satellite state.

VASSIL KOLAROV 2 Jul 1949-22 Jan 1950.

VALKO CHERVENKOV Jan 1950-Apr 1956, b 6 Sep 1900.

ANTON YUGOV 17 Apr 1956-Nov 1962, b 5 Aug 1904.

TODOR ZHIVKOV 19 Nov 1962-Jul 1971.

STANKO TODOROV since 7 Jul 1971, b 10 Dec 1920.

First Secretaries of the Communist Party of Bulgaria
(before 1954 Secretary-General)

VALKO CHERVENKOV 4 Dec 1947-Mar 1954.

TODOR ZHIVKOV since 8 Mar 1954.

Burgundy *see* France

Burma

Burma was united as a single Kingdom in the 16th century and again from 1757. British annexation of Burma was completed in 1885. The state gained independence as the Republic (later Socialist Republic) of the Union of Burma on 4 Jan 1948.

THE KINGDOM OF BURMA

† Kings

TOUNGOO DYNASTY
TABINSHWEHTI *c* **1540-1551.** He united the Burmese, Shan and Mon into one state.
BAYINNAUNG   1551-1581, brother-in-law of Tabinshwehti. His empire, including parts of India and Thailand, fell apart on his death.
1581-1757 Divided into several states.

KONBAUNG DYNASTY
ALAUNGPAYA   1757-1760 d of battle wounds, b 1714.
HSINBYUSHIN   1760-1782, son of Alaungpaya.
BODAWPAYA   1782-1819. Totally out of touch with reality he ordered the British to surrender what is now Bangladesh to Burma: this brought the Burmese Wars and the extinction of the Burmese Kingdom.
BAGYIDAW   1819-1837, grandson of Bodawpaya. Britain annexed most of coastal Burma in this reign
THARRAWADDY MIN   1837-1846.
PAGAN MIN   1846-1853.
MINDON MIN   1853-1878.
THIBAW   1878-1885 when all Burma was annexed by Britain, son of Mindon Min, b 1858; d 1916.
1885-1948 British rule.

THE REPUBLIC OF THE UNION OF BURMA

Presidents

SAO SHWE THAIK   6 Jan 1948-Mar 1952; d 1962.
Dr **BA U** (formerly U BA SWE) **12 Mar 1952-Mar 1957,** b 19 Apr 1915.
U **WIN MAUNG   13 Mar 1957-2 Mar 1962** deposed in coup, b 17 Apr 1916.
U **NE WIN** (formerly Gen NE WIN) Chairman of the Revolutionary Council **since 9 Mar 1962,** b 24 May 1911.

Prime Ministers

THAKIN NU (later called U NU) **4 Jan 1948-Jun 1956.**

Dr **BA U** (formerly U BA SWE) **5 Jun 1956-Mar 1957.**
U **NU   13 Mar 1957-Sep 1958,** b 25 May 1907.
Gen **NE WIN** (later U NE WIN) **27 Sep 1958-Apr 1960.**
U **NU   4 Apr 1960-2 Mar 1962** deposed in coup.
U **NE WIN** (formerly Gen NE WIN) acting PM **2-9 Mar 1962**; PM **9 Mar 1962-Mar 1974.**
U **SEIN WIN   4 Mar 1974-Mar 1977.**
U **MAUNG MAUNG KHA   since 29 Mar 1977.**

Burundi

The Tutsi Kingdom of Burundi, which may have been founded as early as the 16th century, was incorporated in German East Africa in 1890. Burundi became a Belgian Trust Territory in 1919, an independent Kingdom on 1 Jul 1962 and a Republic on 28 Nov 1966.

THE KINGDOM OF BURUNDI

† Kings

MWAMBUTSA IV   1 Jul 1962-8 Jul 1966 when he was deposed by his son in a palace coup, b 1912; d May 1977.
NTARE V   8 Jul 1966-28 Nov 1966 when he was deposed, b 1947; d 29 Apr 1972 killed during tribal unrest.

Prime Ministers

ANDRÉ MUHIRA   1 Jul 1962-Jun 1963, related to Ntare V by marriage.
PIERRE NGENDANDUMWE   Jun 1963-Apr 1964, b 1930.
ALBIN NYAMOYA   Apr 1964-11 Jan 1965, became Premier in the Republic.
PIERRE NGENDANDUMWE   11-15 Jan 1965 when he was assassinated, b 1930.
JOSEPH BAMINA   25 Jan 1965-mid Sep 1965, executed shortly after leaving term of office.
LÉOPOLD BIHA mid Sep 1965-8 Jul 1966 when he was deposed in a palace coup.
Captain **MICHEL MICOMBERO   11 Jul 1966-28 Nov 1966** when he deposed the King and established a Republic, b 1939.

THE REPUBLIC OF BURUNDI

Presidents

Captain **MICHEL MICOMBERO** (later Lieut-Gen) **29 Nov 1966-1 Nov 1976** when he was deposed in a coup.
Lieut-Col **JEAN-BAPTISTE BAGAZA   since 9 Nov 1976.**

A mosaic of the Byzantine Emperor Justinianus the Great and his court (Anderson-Giraudon)

Prime Ministers

Captain **MICHEL MICOMBERO** (later Lieut-Gen) President and Premier **29 Nov 1966-15 Jul 1972.**
ALBIN NYAMOYA 15 Jul 1972-5 Jun 1973, b 1924.
Lieut-Gen **MICHEL MICOMBERO 5 Jun 1973-1 Nov 1976** when he was deposed.
Lieut-Col **ÉDOUARD NZAMBIMANA since 11 Nov 1976.**

The Byzantine (or Eastern Roman) Empire

Upon the death of the Emperor Theodosius I in Jan 395 the Roman Empire was divided between his sons. The Eastern or Byzantine Empire initially included Macedonia, Dacia, Aegyptus, Orientis, Pontus, Thracia and Asia; for the Western Roman Empire see The Roman Empire.

† Emperors

THEODOSIAN DYNASTY
ARCADIUS co-ruler in the East **383-395;** Byzantine Emperor **Jan 395-408,** son of Theodosius I, b c 377.
THEODOSIUS II co-ruler **402-408;** sole ruler **408-28 Jul 450** d from hunting injuries, son of Arcadius, b 10 Apr 401.
PULCHERIA (Empress) co-ruler **414-c416,** sister of Theodosius II, b 19 Jan 399; d 453.

THRACIAN DYNASTY
MARCIANUS 25 Aug 450-Feb 457, husband of Pulcheria, b 396.
LEO I 7 Feb 457-3 Feb 474, kinsman of Marcianus.
LEO II co-ruler **Oct 473-Feb 474;** sole ruler **Feb-mid 474,** grandson of Leo I.
ZENO (Tarasicodissa) **mid 474-9 Apr 491,** son-in-law of Leo I and father of Leo II.
BASILISCUS co-ruler **475-476,** brother-in-law of Leo I, d 477 executed.
ANASTASIUS I Apr 491-9 Jul 518, married the widow of Zeno.

JUSTINIAN DYNASTY
JUSTINUS I Jul 518-1 Aug 527, b c450.
JUSTINIANUS I Aug 527-14 Nov 565, nephew of Justinus I, b 483. One of the most successful

Byzantine Emperors, Justinian enlarged the empire retaking north Africa and much of Italy. He was a great builder (his monuments include the Hagia Sophia) and an important reformer who recodified the law laying the foundations of modern civil codes. Although he improved the lot of slaves he was a harsh ruler who massacred thousands of rebel prisoners.

JUSTINUS II **Nov 565-4 Oct 578,** nephew of Justinianus I.

TIBERIUS II CONSTANTINUS co-ruler **26 Sep-Oct 578;** sole ruler **Oct 578-14 Aug 582,** adopted son of Justinus II.

MAURICIUS (Flavius Tiberius) co-ruler **13 Aug 582;** sole ruler **Aug 582-602** murdered by Phocas; son-in-law of Tiberius II, b c 539.

PHOCAS **602-610;** executed.

HERACLIAN DYNASTY

HERACLIUS **610-11 Feb 641,** b c 575. An important military and administrative reformer who did more than any other to lay the foundations of Byzantium's medieval greatness.

CONSTANTINUS III **Feb-May 641,** son of Heraclius, b c 610.

HERACLEONAS co-ruler **Feb-May 641;** sole ruler **May-Sep 641** banished, half-brother of Constantinus III; fate uncertain.

CONSTANS II (Pogonatus) **Sep 641-668** murdered, son of Constantinus III, b 630.

CONSTANTINUS IV co-ruler **654-668;** sole ruler **668-685,** son of Constans II, b 648.

JUSTINIANUS II **685-695** deposed, son of Constantinus IV, b c 669. An able but cruel ruler who was deposed, mutilated (his nickname Rhinometus means 'nose cut off') and banished. Restored by the Bulgars his second reign ended in assassination.

LEONTIUS **695-698** murdered.

TIBERIUS III ASPIMAR **698-705** executed.

JUSTINIANUS II **705-Dec 711.**

PHILIPPICUS **711-713** deposed; date of death unknown.

ANASTASIUS II **713-716** deposed; became a monk but was executed in 721 after attempting to regain the throne.

THEODOSIUS III **716-717** deposed; d after 717.

ISAURIAN DYNASTY

LEO III **717-18 Jun 741,** b late 670s.

CONSTANTINUS V (Copronymus) co-ruler **720-Jun 741;** sole ruler **Jun 741-14 Sep 775,** son of Leo III, b 718. He won great victories over both Arab and Bulgar and during later sieges of Constantinople the people would flock to his tomb to beg the intercession of this popular warrior.

LEO IV **Sep 775-8 Sep 780,** son of Constantinus V, b 25 Jan 749.

IRENE (Empress) **Sep 780-790** banished, wife of Leo IV, b c 752; d 9 Aug 803. Co-monarch with her son Constantinus VI, she was banished by him but returned to blind and depose him. She was canonised by the Orthodox Church for reintroducing icons.

CONSTANTINUS VI co-ruler **Sep 780-790;** sole ruler **790-Jan 792;** co-ruler **Jan 792-797** probably murdered, son of Irene, b 770.

IRENE (Empress) **Jan 792-802** deposed.

NICEPHORUS I **802-26 Jul 811** d in battle against the Bulgars.

STAURACIUS **Jul 811** - reigned a few days, mortally wounded in the battle in which his father died, son of Nicephorus I.

MICHAEL I **Jul 811-Jul 813** deposed, son-in-law of Nicephorus I; date of death uncertain.

LEO V ('The Armenian') **Jul 813-25 Dec 820** murdered.

ARMORIAN DYNASTY

MICHAEL II **Dec 820-Oct 829.**

THEOPHILUS **Oct 829-Jan 842,** son of Michael II.

MICHAEL III **Jan 842-May 867** assassinated, son of Theophilus.

MACEDONIAN DYNASTY

BASILIUS I sole ruler **May 867-870;** co-ruler **870-886.**

LEO VI co-ruler, **870-886;** sole ruler **886-912,** son of Basilius I.

CONSTANTINUS VII **912-959,** son of Leo VI, b 905.

ROMANUS I (Lecapenus) co-ruler **919 to 944,** father-in-law of Constantinus VII.

ROMANUS II **959-963,** son of Constantinus VII, b 939.

NICEPHORUS II PHOCAS **963-10 or 11 Dec 969** murdered, married the widow of Romanus II, b 912.

IOANNES I TZIMISCES **Dec 969-10 Jan 976,** married a sister of Constantinus VII.

BASILIUS II **Jan 976-1025,** son of Romanus II, b c 958. Nicknamed Bulgaroctonus ('Slayer of the Bulgars') he added the Balkans, Mesopotamia, and parts of Georgia and Armenia to the empire.

CONSTANTINUS VIII co-ruler **Jan 976-1025;** sole ruler **1025-1028,** son of Romanus II, b late 950s.

ROMANUS III (Argyrus) **1028-Apr 1034,** first husband of Zoe.

MICHAEL IV **Apr 1034-10 Dec 1041,** second husband of Zoe.

MICHAEL V (Calaphates) **Dec 1041-1042** deposed and blinded, nephew of Michael IV; date of death unknown.

ZOE (Empress) co-ruler **1042-c 1050,** daughter of Constantinus VIII.

CONSTANTINUS IX co-ruler **1042-1056,** third husband of Zoe, b c 1000.

THEODORA (Empress) co-ruler **1042-1056,** sister of Zoe.

MICHAEL VI (Stratioticus) **1056-Jun 1057** deposed; fate uncertain.

COMNENUS DYNASTY

ISSAC I COMNENUS **8 Jun 1057-25 Dec 1059** abdicated, b c 1005; d 1061.

The Byzantine Empress Theodora from a mosaic in the Basilica of San Vitale in Ravenna (Alinari-Giraudon)

DUCAS DYNASTY

CONSTANTINUS X DUCAS Dec 1059-21 May 1067.

MICHAEL VII DUCAS **May 1067-31 Mar 1078** abdicated, son of Constantinus X; d c 1079.

ROMANUS IV DIOGENES co-ruler **1 Jan 1068-1071** deposed and blinded, married the widow of Constantinus X; murdered 1072.

NICEPHORUS III BOTANEIATES co-ruler **from 7 Jan 1078**; sole ruler **Mar 1078-4 Apr 1081** abdicated; married, probably bigamously, the wife of Michael VII; d later in 1081.

COMNENUS DYNASTY

ALEXIUS I COMNENUS Apr 1081-1118, nephew of Isaac I, b 1048.

IOANNES II COMNENUS 1118-8 Apr 1143, son of Alexius I, b 1088.

EMMANUEL I COMNENUS Apr 1143-24 Sep 1180, son of Ioannes II, b c 1122.

ALEXIUS II COMNENUS Sep 1180-Nov 1183 strangled by order of Andronicus I; son of Emmanuel I, b 1169.

ANDRONICUS I COMNENUS Nov 1183-12 Aug 1185 murdered by the mob, grandson of Alexius I, b 1118.

ANGELUS DYNASTY

ISAAC II ANGELUS Sep 1185-8 Apr 1195 deposed and blinded, b c 1135; executed Feb 1204.

ALEXIUS III Apr 1195-1203 deposed, brother of Isaac II; d 1211. He usurped the throne of his brother who later deposed him. In 1203 he fled when the Crusaders threatened Constantinople taking with him much of the Treasury.

ALEXIUS IV co-ruler **1 Aug 1203-Jan 1204,** son of Issac II; strangled by Alexius V on 8 Feb 1204.

ISAAC II ANGELUS co-ruler **Aug 1203-Jan 1204** deposed.

ALEXIUS V Jan-12 Apr 1204 executed as a regicide.

1204-1261 The Crusaders established an empire of their own in Constantinople, the Latin Empire, while the Lascaris family founded a state at Nicaea which was analogous to Constantinople and was the true heir to the Byzantine Empire.

THE LATIN EMPIRE

The French and Flemish leaders of the 4th Crusade set up their state in Constantinople after Alexius IV had requested aid - the Latin Empire was a French state in spirit.

† Latin Emperors in Constantinople

BAUDOUIN I 16 May 1204-1205, son of Boudewijn V, Count of Hainaut, b 1172. Elected Emperor by the Crusaders, he was captured and killed by the Bulgars.

HENRI 1205-1216, brother of Baudouin I.

PIERRE de Courtenay 1216-1217, brother-in-law of Henri.

YOLANDE (Empress) **1217-Sep 1219,** widow of Pierre and sister of Henri.

ROBERT de Courtenay 1221-1228, son of Yolande and Pierre. An inept ruler who lost all the Empire except the city of Constantinople.

BAUDOUIN II de Courtenay 1228-25 Jul 1261 when Byzantine forces retook Constantinople, brother of Robert, b 1217; d 1273 in exile.

THE BYZANTINE EMPIRE IN NICAEA

† Emperors

LASCARIS DYNASTY

THEODORUS I LASCARIS 1206-1222, son-in-law of Alexius III, b c 1175. The founder of the Byzantine Empire in exile at Nicaea.

IOANNES III DUCAS VATATZES 1222-3 Nov 1254, son-in-law of Theodorus I, b 1193.

THEODORUS II LASCARIS Nov 1254-Aug 1258, son of Ioannes III, b 1222.

IOANNES IV LASCARIS Aug 1258-1261 deposed, blinded and imprisoned, son of Theodorus II, b 1250; fate uncertain.

THE BYZANTINE EMPIRE RESTORED TO CONSTANTINOPLE

† Emperors

PALAEOLOGUS DYNASTY

MICHAEL VIII PALAEOLOGUS co-ruler **Dec 1258-1261**; sole ruler **1261-11 Dec 1282,** b c 1224. The reign of the usurper Michael VIII was crowned by the recapture of Constantinople (Aug 1261).

ANDRONICUS II PALAEOLOGUS Dec 1282-1328 deposed, son of Michael VIII, b 1260; d 1332. Through his policy of appeasement the Byzantine state was irreversibly weakened - like most Byzantine Emperors he believed the danger to him was from the West (and the Crusaders) rather than from the Turks in the East whom he largely ignored.

ANDRONICUS III PALAEOLOGUS co-ruler ·**1325-1328**; sole ruler **1328-15 Jun 1341,** grandson of Andronicus II whom he deposed.

IOANNES V PALAEOLOGUS Jun 1341-1376 deposed, son of Andronicus III, b 1332.

CANTACUZENUS DYNASTY

IOANNES VI CANTACUZENUS co-ruler **1347-1354** when forced to abdicate, b 1292; d 15 Jun 1383. A usurper.

MATTHAEUS CANTACUZENUS co-ruler **1354,** son of Ioannes VI.

PALAEOLOGUS DYNASTY

EMMANUEL II PALAEOLOGUS co-ruler **Sep 1373-1376** deposed, son of Ioannes V, b 1350.

ANDRONICUS IV PALAEOLOGUS 1376-1379, son of Ioannes V.

IOANNES V PALAEOLOGUS 1379-1390 deposed.

EMMANUEL II PALAEOLOGUS co-ruler **1379-1390** deposed.

IOANNES VII PALAEOLOGUS 1390 - Reigned for a few months, son of Andronicus IV, b 1360; d c 1410.

IOANNES V PALAEOLOGUS co-ruler **1390-1391.**

EMMANUEL II PALAEOLOGUS co-ruler **1390-1391**; sole ruler **1391-1399**; co-ruler **1399-1402**; sole ruler **1402-1421**; co-ruler **1421-21 Jul 1425.**

IOANNES VII PALAEOLOGUS co-ruler **1399-1402.**

IOANNES VIII PALAEOLOGUS co-ruler **1421-1425**; sole ruler **Jul 1425-31 Oct 1448,** son of Emmanuel II, b 1390.

CONSTANTINUS XI PALAEOLOGUS *de jure*; **Oct 1448-early 1449**; *de facto* from **early 1449-29 May 1453** when Constantinople fell to the Turks, brother of Ioannes VIII, b 1403; almost certainly died in battle - this last Byzantine Emperor was last seen fighting in one of the gates of Constantinople as the city fell to the invading Turks.

The Caliphate of the East or The Empire of the Caliphate

Caliph means 'successor'; ie the successor to Muhammad, Seal of the Prophets. The Caliphate was intended to be a state which included all the followers of Islam, and so for a time it was, but gradually the temporal powers of the Caliphs were restricted leaving but spiritual functions.

Seal of the Prophets

MUHAMMAD exercised temporal power in Medina **from 622**; in Mecca **630-3 Jun 632,** b 571. The inspired Prophet Muhammad instituted the strongly nationalist faith of Islam which demands submission to God as revealed to him and through the Qur'an. When his prophecies met with opposition in Mecca, Muhammad fled to Medina (Sep 622 - from which date the Muslim era is reckoned). Accepted as leader in Medina, he warred against Mecca and united the Islamic community in the Hejaz into a nation.

† Caliphs
('Successors' to the Prophet)

ORTHODOX (RASHIDUN) OR PATRIACHAL CALIPHS
These are not recognised by the minority Shia Muslims.

ABU BAKR (as-Siddiq meaning 'the Upright') **Jun 632-23 Aug 634,** father-in-law of Muhammad, b c 573.
'UMAR I summer 634-644 assassinated, father-in-law of Muhammad. By means of the jihad (holy war) this strict able ruler created a Muslim empire taking Syria and Palestine, Mesopotamia, Egypt and Iran to make the Caliphate a great power.
UTHMAN ibn 'AFFAN 644-656 assassinated, son-in-law of Muhammad, b c 575. He issued the authorised version of the Qur'an but this unpopular leader was murdered by disaffected Egyptian troops while reading it.
ALI ibn ALI TALIB 656-661 assassinated, cousin of Muhammad, b c 600.
al-HASAN 661 abdicated under pressure, son of Ali, d c 670?

UMAYYAD CALIPHATE OR CALIPHS OF THE HOUSE OF THE SUFYANIDS
MU'AWIYAH I 661-680, b c 602. A Syrian general who had opposed Ali Talib, Mu'awiyah established the Caliphate as a quasi-hereditary temporal monarchy based in Damascus.

ORTHODOX OR PATRIACHAL CALIPH
al-HUSAYN 680 d in battle, brother of al-Hasan.

UMAYYAD CALIPHATE OR CALIPHS OF THE HOUSE OF THE SUFYANIDS
YAZID I 680-683, son of Mu'awiyah I.
MU'AWIYAH II 683, eldest son of Yazid I.
MARWAN I ibn al-HAKAM 684-685, distant kinsman of Mu'awiyah II.
'ABD al-MALIK ibn MARWAN 685-Oct 705, son of Marwan I, b 647. Called 'Father of Kings' this splendid warrior extended the Empire to Morocco and suppressed revolts in Iran, Iraq and the Hejaz.
al-WALID I Oct 705-715, eldest son of 'Abd al-Malik, b c 675. His reign saw the Islamic Empire at its zenith stretching from the Indus to the Pyrenees.
SULAYMAN 715-717, son of 'Abd al-Malik.
'UMAR II ibn 'Abd al-Aziz 717-720, nephew of 'Abd al-Malik.

YAZID II 720-724, son of 'Abd al-Malik.
HISHAM I 724-743, son of 'Abd al-Malik. A deceptively peaceful reign - the Caliphate, which suffered a major defeat at Tours (632), had an empire too big to be governable and too diverse to withstand the imminent revolts and secessions.
al-WALID II 743-744, son of Yazid II.
YAZID III 744, son of al-Walid II.
IBRAHIM 744, son of al-Walid I.
MARWAN II 744-749 when he fled, grandson of Marwan I; killed c 751. The Abbasids, descendants of Muhammad's uncle al-Abbas, exploited many local grievances against Marwan and toppled the Caliph in a coup.

† ABBASID CALIPHS
The Caliphs of this dynasty adopted regnal names and it is by these, often epithets, that they were known rather than by their personal names.

ABU' al-ABBAS al-SAFFAH 749-754, descendant of Mohammad's uncle al-Abbas, b c 720. He led the Abbasids in the revolt that deposed Marwan II.
ABU-DJAFAR al-MANSUR 754-775, brother of as-Saffah. This notorious miser moved his capital to Baghdad which was to remain the seat of the Caliphate.
MUHAMMAD al-MAHDI 775-785, son of al-Mansur.
MUSA al-HADI 785-786, son of al-Mahdi.
HARUN ar-RASHID 786-809, son of al-Mahdi.
MUHAMMAD al-AMIN 809-813 Western Caliph murdered, son of ar-Rashid.
ABDOLLAH al-MAMUN 809-813 Eastern Caliph; sole Caliph 813-833, son of ar-Rashid. Inheriting half an empire (the division was an attempt to govern a realm already diminished by secession and revolt; eg Spain and Tunisia), he defeated his brother to become sole sovereign.
al-MU'TASIM 833-842, son of ar-Rashid.
HARUN al-WATHIQ 842-847, son of al-Mu'tasim.
DJAFAR al-MUTAWAKKIL 847-861, son of al-Mu'tasim. The last outstanding Caliph for over two centuries he attempted to reform the government of the realm - his successors were weak and inept rulers who governed a rapidly diminishing empire.
MUHAMMAD al-MUNTASIR 861-862 deposed, son of al-Mutawakkil; date of death uncertain.
AHMAD al-MUSTA'IN 862-866 deposed, grandson of al-Wathiq; date of death uncertain.
MUHAMMAD al-MU'TAZZ 866-869 deposed, son of al-Mutawakkil; date of death uncertain.
MUHAMMAD al-MUHTADI 869-870 deposed, son of al-Wathiq; date of death uncertain.
AHMAD al-MU'TAMID 870-892, son of al-Mutawakkil.
AHMAD al-MU'TADID 892-902, nephew of al-Mu'tamid.
ALI al-MUKTAFI 902-908, son of al-Mu'tadid.
DJAFAR al-MUQTADIR 908-932, son of al-Mu'tadid.

MUHAMMAD al-QAHIR 932-934 deposed and blinded, son of al-Mu'tadid; date of death uncertain.

AHMAD ar-RADI 934-940, son of al-Muqtadir. Surrendering most of his temporal power to an Emir, ar-Radi was the last Caliph to have much effect on government.

IBRAHIM al-MUTTAQI 940-944 deposed and blinded, son of al-Muqtadir; date of death uncertain.

al-MUSTAKFI 944-945 deposed and blinded, son of al-Muktafi; date of death uncertain.

EMIR OF EMIRS OF THE DAYLAMI

AHMAD ebn BUYEH 945-946 exercised powers of Caliph during an interregnum; 'head of government' until 949. Not Caliph.

ABBASID CALIPHS

al-MUTI 946-974, son of al-Muqtadir.

al-TA'I 974-991 deposed, son of al-Muti; date of death uncertain.

al-QADIR 991-1031, grandson of al-Muqtadir.

al-QA'IM 1031-1075, son of al-Qadir.

al-MUQTADI 1075-1094, grandson of al-Qa'im. This Caliph was able to regain some of the temporal powers assumed by the Seljuq Turks who had been the real power in the land since 1055.

al-MUSTAZHI 1094-1118, son of al-Muqtadi.

al-MUSTARSHID 1118-1135 'legally' murdered, son of al-Mustazhi.

al-RASCHID 1135-1136 executed, son of al-Mustarshid.

al-MUQTAFI 1136-1160, son of al-Mustarshid.

al-MUSTANJID 1160-1170, son of al-Muqtafi.

al-MUSTADI 1170-1180, son of al-Mustarshid.

an-NASIR 1180-1225, son of al-Mustadi. An outstanding diplomat he dominated the Middle East.

az-ZAHIR 1225-1226, son of an-Nasir.

al-MUNSTANSIR 1226-1242, kinsman of an-Nasir.

al-MUSTA'SIM 1242-10 Feb 1258, kinsman of an-Nasir; kicked to death by the Mongols who sacked Baghdad in Feb 1258 bringing an end to the Caliphate of the East.

(A distant kinsman of an-Nasir was installed in Turkey as a puppet Caliph in 1265 - his line lasted until 1517 when the Ottoman Sultan adopted the style Caliph falsely claiming that the last Abbasid had willed the dignity to him. 'Ottoman Caliphs' lasted until the establishment of the Turkish Republic.)

Cambodia

A Cambodian Kingdom, formed before 598 by the merger of the Kingdoms of Funan and Chenla, existed in the 6th and 7th centuries and was revived in the 9th century. A powerful state in the 12th and 13th centuries Cambodia passed to the Thais in the 14th century. Independent again in the 16th and 17th centuries the country came under Thai and Vietnamese control until 1846. A French protectorate was proclaimed in 1863, autonomy granted after World War II and complete independence regained on 9 Nov 1953. A Republic was declared in Nov 1970 and in Apr 1975 a Communist regime was set up.

THE KINGDOM OF CAMBODIA

† Kings

BHAVAVARMAN I before 598-c600.

MAHENDRAVARMAN c600-c611, brother of Bhavavarman.

ISANAVARMAN c611-c635, son of Mahendravarman.

BHAVAVARMAN II c635-?

JAYAVARMAN I c650-c700?

c700-c802 After the death of Jayavarman I Cambodia broke up into a number of small states.

JAYAVARMAN II c802-850. The true founder of Cambodia, he reunited the Khmers in one Kingdom.

JAYAVARMAN III 850-877 possibly murdered, son of Jayavarman II.

INDRAVARMAN I 877-889, cousin of Jayavarman III.

YASOVARMAN I 889-900, son of Indravarman I.

HARSHAVARMAN I fl. early 10th century.

HARSHAVARMAN II fl. early 10th century.

RAJENDRAVARMAN I fl. 10th century.

JAYAVARMAN IV 928-942 or 944.

RAJENDRAVARMAN II 944-968.

JAYAVARMAN V 968-1001.

UDAYADITYAVARMAN I 1001-1002 deposed; date of death uncertain.

SURYAVARMAN I 1002-1050. He fought Udayadityavarman I for the Crown, built much of Angkor Wat and conquered southern Thailand and Laos.

UDAYADITYAVARMAN II 1050-1066, son of Suryavarman I.

HARSHAVARMAN III 1066-1080 deposed; d after 1080.

JAYAVARMAN VI 1080-1107. A usurper.

DHARANINDRAVARMAN I 1107-1113.

SURYAVARMAN II 1113-1150. Under this King the Khmers reached their zenith of power controlling an empire stretching from the Vietnamese coast to Malaya.

DHARANINDRAVARMAN II 1150-1160, son of Suryavarman II.

YASOVARMAN II 1160-1166 assassinated by his successor, son of Suryavarman II.

TRIBHUVANADITYAVARMAN 1166-1177 d in battle. A usurper.

JAYAVARMAN VII King from 1177 de jure; de facto 1181-c1215 or 1219, son of Dharanindravarman II, b c1120. Perhaps the greatest Khmer

King he rebuilt the Kingdom with the aid of her rivals the Cham. He constructed roads, temples and hospitals.

INDRAVARMAN II after c1215-1243.

JAYAVARMAN VIII 1243-1295. He made Buddhism rather than Hinduism the state religion.

INDRAVARMAN III 1296-1308.

INDRAJAYAVARMAN 1308-1327.

JAYAVARMAN PARAMESVARA 1327-? possibly King to 1369 when much of Cambodia was invaded by the Thais.

Mid 14th century-1516 Period of decline and subordination to the Thais.

REVIVED INDEPENDENT KINGDOM

† Kings

ANG CHAN 1516-1566. He established Khmer independence after raiding the Thai Ayutthaya capital.

BAROM REACHEA I 1566-1576.

SATHA 1576-c1594 deposed; date of death uncertain.

CHUNG PREI c1594-1597; d in battle against the Spanish whom Satha had called in to aid him.

BAROM REACHEA II 1597-1599, son of Satha.

BAROM REACHEA III 1599-1603. A usurper who fought a civil war against two other 'Kings'.

BAROM REACHEA IV (Soryopor) **1603-1618,** brother of Satha.

CHEY CHETTA II 1618-1628.

Early 17th century-1846 Cambodia ceased to exist as an independent nation and became a vassal state of the Thais and Vietnamese sometimes owing allegiance to both simultaneously.

† Independent Kings

ANG DUONG 1846-1860. He re-established Khmer independence.

NORODOM 1860-1863 when a French protectorate was established.

† Kings under French Protection

NORODOM King **since 1860; 1863-Apr 1904,** b 1834.

SISOWATH Apr 1904-9 Aug 1927, half-brother of Norodom, b Aug 1840.

MONIVONG Aug 1927-1941, son of Sisowath, b 27 Dec 1875.

NORODOM SIHANOUK 1941-16 Dec 1948 under French protection; **16 Dec 1948-9 Nov 1953** with limited independence in the French Union.

INDEPENDENT KINGDOM

† Kings

NORODOM SIHANOUK King **since 1941;** sovereign King **9 Nov 1953-2 Mar 1955** abdicated, grandson of Sisowath, b 31 Oct 1922.

NORODOM SURAMARIT 6 Mar 1955-3 Apr 1960, father of Norodom Sihanouk and son-in-law of Sisowath, b 6 Mar 1896.

6 Apr-20 Jun 1960 Council of Regency.

Heads of State

Prince **NORODOM SIHANOUK** (formerly King) acting Head of State **20 Jun 1960-18 May 1968** deposed.

(Queen KOSSOMAK, mother of Norodom Sihanouk, shared some of the duties of Head of State as 'Symbol of the Throne' .)

Prime Ministers

SAMDECH PENN NOUTH 9-15 Nov 1953.

CHANN AK 23 Nov 1953-Mar 1954, b 27 May 1892.

SAMDECH PENN NOUTH Mar 1954-Jan 1955.

LENG NGETH 24 Jan-Sep 1955.

Prince **NORODOM SIHANOUK 25 Sep 1955-Jan 1956.**

OUN CHEANG SUN 3-13 Jan 1956; acting PM **Jan-Mar 1956.**

Prince **NORODOM SIHANOUK 1-30 Mar 1956.**

KHIM TIT 2 Apr-8 Aug 1956; acting PM **8 Aug-15 Sep 1956.**

Prince **NORODOM SIHANOUK 15 Sep-15 Oct 1956.**

SAN YUN 15 Oct 1956-Mar 1957; acting PM **Mar-Apr 1957.**

Prince **NORODOM SIHANOUK 7 Apr-Jul 1957.**

SIM VAR 30 Jul 1957-Jan 1958.

SAMDECH PENN NOUTH 17 Jan-Apr 1958.

SIM VAR Apr-Jul 1958.

Prince **NORODOM SIHANOUK 14 Jul 1958-Apr 1960.**

PHO PROEUNG 13 Apr 1960-Jan 1961.

Prince **NORODOM SIHANOUK 23 Jan 1961-Oct 1962.**

Prince **NORODOM KANTOL Oct 1962-Oct 1966,** b 15 Sep 1920.

Gen **LON NOL 18 Oct 1966-Apr 1967;** acting PM **30 Apr-2 May 1967.**

SON SANN 2 May-31 Dec 1967; acting PM **Jan 1968.**

SAMDECH PENN NOUTH 30 Jan-Mar 1968.

THE STATE OF CAMBODIA

Head of State

CHENG HENG 21 Mar 1968-1 Nov 1970 when he became President.

Prime Ministers

SAMDECH PENN NOUTH   18 Mar 1968-Aug 1969.
Gen **LON NOL   12 Aug 1969-1 Nov 1970** when he became PM of the Republic.

THE KHMER REPUBLIC

Presidents

CHENG HENG   1 Nov 1970-Mar 1972, b 1916.
Gen **LON NOL   14 Mar 1972-1 Apr 1975**; fled before the Communist invasion, b 13 Nov 1913.
Maj-Gen **SAUKHAM KHOY** acting President **1-12 Apr 1975** fled.
Gen **SUTSAKHAN** acting Head of State **12-17 Apr 1975** fled.

Premiers

Gen **LON NOL   1 Nov 1970-Mar 1972.**
Lieut-Gen **SISOWATH SIRIK MATAK   11-13 Mar 1972**; executed by Communists May 1975.
Gen **LON NOL   13-18 Mar 1972.**
SON NGOC THANH   18 Mar-Oct 1972.
HANG THUN HAK   14 Oct 1972-Apr 1973; acting PM **Apr-May 1973.**
IN TAM   May-Dec 1973.
LONG BARET   26 Dec 1973-17 Apr 1975; executed by Communists May 1975.

DEMOCRATIC CAMBODIA

On 17 Apr 1975 the Communist regime was established after the fall of the capital.

Presidents

Prince **NORODOM SIHANOUK   17 Apr 1975-Apr 1976.**
KHIEU SAMPHAN   since 11 Apr 1976, b 1932.

Prime Ministers

SAMDECH PENN NOUTH   17 Apr 1975-Apr 1976, b 1 Apr 1906.
POL POT   Apr-Sep 1976.
NUON CHEA acting PM **27 Sep 1976-Sep 1977.**
POL POT   since Sep 1977.

Cameroon

The German colony of Kamerun, established in 1884, was occupied by British and French forces in 1916 and divided between those two countries as Trust Territories in 1919. The French portion gained independence as a Republic on 1 Jan 1960; the southern part of the British Cameroons joined the Republic on 1 Oct 1960 while the northern British portion voted to join Nigeria.

President

AHMADOU AHIDJO Head of State and Premier **1 Jan-5 May 1960**; President **since 5 May 1960,** b May 1924.

Prime Ministers

AHMADOU AHIDJO   1 Jan-5 May 1960; see President Ahidjo.
(The office of Premier was suspended 1960-2 Jun 1975 when the post was recreated: from 1961-1972 East and West Cameroon had state Premiers.)
PAUL BIYA   since 30 Jun 1975, b 13 Feb 1933.

Canada

French settlements in Canada began in the 1530s; English colonisation commenced in the 1580s. The French territories were ceded to Britain in 1763 but Canada remained a group of separate colonies until Confederation on 1 Jul 1867 when Quebec, Ontario, New Brunswick and Nova Scotia united to form what was *de facto* an independent nation under the terms of the British North America Act. British Columbia entered the federation in 1871; Prince Edward Island in 1873. The former lands of the Hudson's Bay Company were ceded to Canada and from these territories were formed the provinces of Manitoba (1870), Alberta and Saskatchewan (both 1905). Newfoundland joined the Confederation on 31 Mar 1949.

Governors-General

Charles Stanley, 4th Viscount **MONCK   Jul 1867-Nov 1868,** b 10 Oct 1819; d 29 Nov 1894.
John Young, 1st Baron **LISGAR   Jan 1869-May 1872,** b 31 Aug 1807; d 6 Oct 1876.
Frederick Temple Hamilton-Temple-Blackwood, 1st Marquess of **DUFFERIN and AVA   May 1872-Oct 1878,** b 21 Jun 1826; d 12 Feb 1902.
John Douglas Sutherland Campbell, Marquess of **LORNE** (later 9th Duke of ARGYLL) **Oct 1878-Aug 1883,** son-in-law of Queen Victoria, b 6 Aug 1845; d 2 May 1914.
Henry Charles Keith Petty-Fitzmaurice, 5th Marquess of **LANSDOWNE** (6th Earl of KERRY) **Aug 1883-Apr 1888,** b 14 Jan 1845; d 3 Jun 1927.
Frederick Arthur Stanley, 1st Baron **STANLEY of Preston** (later 16th Earl of DERBY) **May 1888-May 1893,** b 15 Jan 1841; d 14 Jun 1908.
Sir John Campbell Gordon, 7th Earl of **ABERDEEN** (later 1st Marquess of ABERDEEN and

TEMAIR) **May 1893-Jul 1898,** b 3 Aug 1847; d 7 Mar 1934.

Gilbert John Elliot-Murray-Kynynmound, 4th Earl of **MINTO Jul 1898-Sep 1904,** b 9 Jul 1845; d 1 Mar 1914.

Albert Henry George Grey, 4th Earl **GREY Sep 1904-Mar 1911,** b 28 Nov 1851; d 29 Aug 1917.

Prince **ARTHUR** William Patrick Albert, (Duke of CONNAUGHT and STRATHEARN) **Mar 1911-Nov 1916,** son of Queen Victoria, b 1 May 1850; d 16 Jan 1942.

Victor Christian William Cavendish, Duke of **DEVONSHIRE Nov 1916-Aug 1921,** b 31 May 1868; d 6 May 1938.

Gen Julian Hedworth George Byng, 1st Viscount **BYNG** of Vimy **Aug 1921-Aug 1926,** b 11 Sep 1862; d 6 Jun 1935. It was appropriate that Byng, whose fine tactics were responsible for the Canadian forces' capture of the Vimy Ridge in World War I, should become Governor-General of Canada.

Freeman Freeman-Thomas, 1st Viscount of **WILLINGDON Oct 1926-Feb 1931,** b 12 Sep 1866; d 12 Aug 1941.

Vere Brabazon Ponsonby, 9th Earl of **BESS-BOROUGH Apr 1931-Oct 1935,** b 27 Oct 1880; d 10 Mar 1956.

JOHN BUCHAN (1st Baron TWEEDSMUIR) **Nov 1935-12 Feb 1940,** b 26 Aug 1875; d in office. Historian, newspaper correspondent and novelist, John Buchan is best remembered as the creator of Richard Hannay.

Alexander Augustus Frederick William Alfred George, Earl of **ATHLONE Jun 1940-Apr 1946,** husband of Princess Alice of Albany, b (a Prince of Teck) 14 Apr 1874; d 16 Jan 1957.

Harold Rupert Leofric George Alexander, Field Marshal 1st Viscount **ALEXANDER** of Tunis **Apr 1946-Feb 1952,** b 10 Dec 1891; d 16 Jun 1969. A superb tactician he organised the extraordinary retreat from Dunkirk beaches (he was the last man out of 300,000 to leave), the withdrawal from Burma, and the masterly capture of Tunis and invasion of Italy.

CHARLES VINCENT MASSEY Feb 1952-Sep 1959, b 20 Feb 1887; d 30 Dec 1968.

Maj-Gen **GEORGES PHILIAS VANIER Sep 1959-5 Mar 1967,** b 23 Apr 1888; d in office.

DANIEL ROLAND MICHENER Apr 1967-Jan 1974, b 19 Apr 1900.

JULES LEGER since Jan 1974, b 4 Apr 1913.

Prime Ministers of the Confederation of Canada

Sir **JOHN ALEXANDER MacDONALD 1 Jul 1867-Nov 1873,** b 11 Jan 1815; d 6 Jun 1891.

ALEXANDER MacKENZIE 7 Nov 1873-Oct 1878, b 28 Jan 1822; d 17 Apr 1892.

Sir **JOHN ALEXANDER MacDONALD 17 Oct 1878-Jun 1891.**

Sir **JOHN JOSEPH CALDWELL ABBOTT 16 Jun 1891-Nov 1892,** b 12 Mar 1821; d 30 Oct 1893.

Sir Wilfrid Laurier - the first French-speaking Premier of the Canadian Confederation (Radio Times Hulton Picture Library)

Sir **JOHN SPARROW DAVID THOMPSON Nov 1892-12 Dec 1894,** b 10 Nov 1844; d in office.

Sir **MACKENZIE BOWELL Dec 1894-Apr 1896,** b 27 Dec 1823; d 10 Dec 1917.

Sir **CHARLES TUPPER 1 May-11 Jul 1896,** b 2 Jul 1821; d 30 Oct 1915.

Sir **WILFRID LAURIER Jul 1896-Oct 1911,** b 20 Nov 1841; d 17 Feb 1919. The first French-speaking Canadian Premier he probably did more than any other Prime Minister to establish an independent Canadian identity - in particular he resisted British attempts to subjugate the Canadian economy to the British.

Sir **ROBERT LAIRD BORDEN Oct 1911-Jul 1920,** b 26 Jun 1854; d 10 Jun 1937. By insisting on separate Canadian representation at the Versailles Peace Conference and by gaining membership of the League of Nations he won international recognition of Canada's sovereign independence.

ARTHUR MEIGHEN 10 Jul 1920-Dec 1921, b 16 Jun 1874; d 5 Aug 1960.

WILLIAM LYON MacKENZIE KING 29 Dec 1921-Jun 1926, b 17 Dec 1874; d 22 Jul 1950. The grandson of the MacKenzie King who raised the revolt against British rule in Canada (1837), he was a major influence in drawing up the Statute of Westminster - the document which contains formal recognition of the sovereignty of the Dominions.

ARTHUR MEIGHEN 26 Jun-25 Sep 1926.

WILLIAM LYON MacKENZIE KING 25 Sep 1926-Jul 1930.

RICHARD BEDFORD BENNETT (later Viscount Bennett) **30 Jul 1930-Oct 1935,** b 3 Jul 1870; d 27

Jun 1947. Through protectionism he revived the economy after the Depression.

WILLIAM LYON MacKENZIE KING 24 Oct 1935-Nov 1948.

LOUIS STEPHEN St LAURENT 15 Nov 1948-Jun 1957, b 1 Feb 1882; d 25 Jul 1973.

JOHN GEORGE DIEFENBAKER 21 Jun 1957-Apr 1963, b 18 Sep 1895.

LESTER BOWLES PEARSON 17 Apr 1963-Apr 1968, b 23 Apr 1897; d 27 Dec 1972.

PIERRE ELLIOTT TRUDEAU since 20 Apr 1968, b 18 Oct 1919.

Cape Verde Islands

Portuguese from 1461, the Cape Verde Islands were granted independence as a Republic on 5 Jul 1975.

President

ARISTIDES PEREIRA since 5 Jul 1975, b 17 Nov 1924.

Prime Minister

Major **PEDRO PIRES since 15 Jul 1975.**

Cappadocia

A Kingdom of eastern Asia Minor which was an important power during the 2nd century BC.

† Kings

FIRST DYNASTY

ARIARATHES III Epistates from 262 or 261 BC; King **after c 260-220 BC.** He made Cappadocia an independent state and himself King.

ARIARATHES IV EUSEBES 220-163 BC.

ARIARATHES V EUSEBES PHILOPATOR 163-c 130 BC d in battle.

OROPHERNES c 163-c 155 BC killed. A pretender who briefly expelled Ariarathes V with Seleucid support.

NYSA (Queen) **c 130-c 126 BC,** widow of Ariarathes V; date of death unknown. She murdered her five sons to be able to rule herself.

ARIARATHES VI c 126-111 BC assassinated.

ARIARATHES VII PHILOMETOR 111-c 100 BC murdered by Mithradates VI of Pontus; son of Ariarathes VI.

ARIARATHES EUSEBES PHILOPATOR c 100-96 BC deposed, claimed to be son of Ariarathes V - in reality a son of Mithradates VI of Pontus; date of death unknown.

ARIARATHES VIII 96-95 BC, son of Ariarathes VII.

ARIARATHES EUSEBES PHILOPATOR 95 BC.

SECOND DYNASTY

ARIOBARZANES I PHILOROMAIOS c 95-65 BC abdicated; d 62 BC. A noble chosen to be King.

ARIOBARZANES II PHILOPATOR 63-52 BC, son of Ariobarzanes I.

ARIOBARZANES III EUSEBES PHILOROMAIOS 52-42 BC, grandson of Ariobarzanes I; killed by one of Julius Caesar's assassins. His ill-advised involvement in Roman politics led to his murder and Cappadocia's loss of independence.

42-36 BC Cappadocia was occupied by the Romans.

ARCHELAUS SISINES 36 BC-AD 14 deposed by Tiberius; d AD 17. A puppet of Imperial Rome.

AD 14 After the deposition of Archelaus Sisines, Cappadocia became a Roman province.

Carthage

Archaeological evidence suggests that this Phoenician colony was founded c 800 BC, a date that ties in with the traditional year of foundation given by Timaeus - 814 BC. By the 6th century, Carthage which had received much migration from Tyre, was an independent city state. The first Carthaginian King there is evidence for is Mago whose dynasty ruled from c 550 to c 375 BC. A 'Republic' (c 373-c 339 BC) gave way to a restored monarchy which was abolished in 308 BC from which time, until the city was destroyed by Rome in the spring of 146 BC, Carthage was governed by two Suffetes who were elected annually - the kingship was not totally abandoned but was rather relegated to an obscure, probably religious, shadow existence. In the middle of the 3rd century a Carthaginian Barcid state was founded in Spain and maintained a *de facto* independence of Carthage - it was to this Iberian state ('New Carthage') and not to Old Carthage that the famous general Hannibal belonged.

THE KINGDOM OF CARTHAGE

† Kings

MAGONID DYNASTY

(MALCHUS, sometimes referred to as a King of Carthage, was almost certainly legendary.)

MAGO I c 550-c 530 BC.

HASDRUBAL I c 550-c 510 BC, probably son of Mago I.

HAMILCAR c 510-480 BC committed suicide, probably nephew of Hasdrubal I.

HANNO ('The Navigator') **480-440 BC** deposed, son of Hamilcar, b *c* 500 BC; d in exile 430 BC.

HANNIBAL   440-spring 406 BC, nephew of Hanno.

HIMILCO I   spring 406-spring 396 BC when he committed suicide; not formally declared King until 396? Son of Hanno.

MAGO II   spring 396-375 BC killed in battle by Syracusans, descendant of Mago I.

HIMILCO II   *c* 375 BC, son of Mago II; may have reigned briefly.

CARTHAGINIAN 'REPUBLIC'
(c373-c339 BC)

(The monarchy was abolished *c* 373 BC and an aristocratic 'Republic' established.)

de facto Dictator of Carthage

HANNO ('The Great') ***c* 373-between 360 and 346 BC.** Hanno, commander of the army and virtual dictator of Carthage, attempted a coup to make himself King but was frustrated in his ambition and tortured to death in 346 BC.

THE KINGDOM OF CARTHAGE

† Kings of Carthage

HANNONIAN DYNASTY
GISCO   *c* 339-? BC, son of Hanno the Great.
(HAMILCAR, probably nephew of Gisco, may have been King in the 320s BC.)
HAMILCAR   *c* 319-summer 309 BC captured by Syracusans and tortured to death, son of Gisco.
BOMILCAR   summer 309-Oct 308 BC crucified after attempting to seize complete power for the monarch.

THE CARTHAGINIAN REPUBLIC
(Oct 308-spring 146 BC)

The Republic was ruled by two Suffetes elected annually - see introduction.

THE BARCID STATE IN IBERIA

† Commanders-In-Chief and de facto Heads of State

DYNASTY OF HAMILCAR BARCA
HAMILCAR BARCA   241 or 237-winter 229 BC drowned. The very able Commander Hamilcar Barca founded an autonomous Carthaginian state in Spain to use as a base to attack Rome after the first Carthaginian War.
HASDRUBAL   winter 229-221 BC assassinated, son-in-law of Hamilcar Barca. He assumed the

Hannibal, who held no office in Carthage until old age, was Head of the Barcid State in Iberia (The Ny Carlsberg Glyptotek, Copenhagen)

role of King in all but name and founded Cartegena - 'New Carthage'.
HANNIBAL ('The Great') **221-*c* 211 BC,** son of Hamilcar Barca, b 246 BC; d (suicide) in exile 183 or 182 BC. Hannibal, who swore undying hatred for Rome as a boy of nine, used the Iberian state as a tool of war against Rome. His brilliant campaign carefully prepared with Gallic allies (but unsuccessful), his epic journey over the Alps (only three elephants survived) and his masterly tactics in the 16-year-war with Rome are famous.
HASDRUBAL II   211-203 BC voted out of office, brother of Hannibal.
HANNO   203-? BC, nephew of Hannibal.

Castile *see* Spain

Central Africa

The territory of Ubangi-Shari came under French influence in the 1880s and 1890s. It became independent as the Central African Republic on 13 Aug 1960 and on 4 Dec 1976 the country was renamed the Central African Empire when

Self-proclaimed Emperor Bokassa I whose impoverished Central African Empire witnessed a lavish coronation in 1977 (Popperfoto)

President Bokassa proclaimed himself to be Emperor of the world's newest monarchy.

THE CENTRAL AFRICAN REPUBLIC

Presidents

DAVID DACKO Head of State **13 Aug-17 Nov** 1960; President **17 Nov 1960-1 Jan 1966** when he was deposed in a coup, b 1931.
Gen **JEAN-BEDEL BOKASSA** (later Marshal) **1 Jan 1966-4 Dec 1976** when he was proclaimed first Emperor of the Central African Empire, a cousin of David Dacko whom he deposed.

Prime Ministers

DAVID DACKO 13 Aug 1960-1 Jan 1966; see President Dacko.
JEAN-BEDEL BOKASSA 1 Jan 1966-1 Jan 1975; see President Bokassa.
ÉLISABETH DOMITIEN 1 Jan 1975-7 Apr 1976, the first woman Premier in Africa.

JEAN-BEDEL BOKASSA 7 Apr-5 Sep 1976; see President Bokassa.
ANGE PATASSÉ 5 Sep-4 Dec 1976, became the first Premier of the Empire.

THE CENTRAL AFRICAN EMPIRE

† Emperor

BOKASSA I since 4 Dec 1976, formerly President Marshal Jean-Bedel Bokassa, b 22 Feb 1921.

Prime Minister

ANGE PATASSÉ since 14 Dec 1976.

Central America

The Spanish Central American possessions, claimed for Spain between 1519 and 1526, gained their independence in Sep 1821 and joined the Mexican Empire in Jan 1822. Seceding in July 1823 these territories formed the federal United Provinces of Central America which fell apart in the anarchy which began in 1836. Central America may be said to have ceased to exist by 1839.

Presidents

MANUEL JOSÉ ARCE 1825-1829 deposed; b 1787; d 1847.
JOSÉ F. BARRUNDIA provisional President **1829-1830.**
FRANCISCO MORAZÁN 1830-1836; *de facto* ruler of parts of Central America **until 1839,** b 16 Oct 1799; d 15 Sep 1842, shot after trying to recapture Costa Rica. His stormy term of office which saw endless revolts ended in the collapse of Central America into total anarchy.

Ceylon *see* Sri Lanka

Chad

The colony of Chad was created in 1922 out of territory recognised to be French in 1889. Independence was declared on 11 Aug 1960.

Presidents

NGARTA TOMBALBAYE (formerly FRANCOIS TOMBALBAYE) Head of State **11 Aug 1960-23 Apr 1962**; President **23 Apr 1962-13 Apr 1975** when he was killed in a coup, b 15 Jun 1918.

Brig-Gen **FÉLIX MALLOUM** (later Gen) President of the Supreme Military Council **since 15 Apr 1975,** b 10 Sep 1932.

Prime Ministers

NGARTA TOMBALBAYE 11 Aug 1960-13 Apr 1975; see President Tombalbaye.
FÉLIX MALLOUM since 12 May 1975; see President Malloum.

Chile

Spanish from 1541, Chile formed part of the Vice-Royalty of Peru. Independence was declared on 18 Sep 1810 but was not finally secured until after the Battle of Chacabuco (Feb 1817).

Rulers
(with no clearly defined legal position)

JOSÉ MIGUEL CARRERA 1811-1813 deposed, b 15/16 Oct 1785; d 4 Sep 1821 killed while aiding Argentinian nationalists. The rival of O'Higgins, Carrera was one of the two leaders of the Chilean independence movement - a cause which suffered through this personality clash.
Gen **BERNARDO O'HIGGINS 1813-1814,** b 20? Aug 1776; d Oct 1842. A brilliant general O'Higgins organised the forces that overthrew Spanish rule. With San Martin he won the victory at Chacabuco one of the most important battles in the Latin American Wars of Independence.
JOSÉ MIGUEL CARRERA 1814.
1814-Feb 1817 Spanish rule restored.

Directors

Gen **BERNARDO O'HIGGINS Feb 1817-Jan 1823.**
Jan 1823 Provisional triumvirate.
Gen **RAMÓN FREIRE Jan 1823-May 1827,** b 1787; d 1851.
MANUEL BLANCO ENCALADA May 1827, b 1790; d 1876.
May 1827 Provisional triumvirate.
FRANCISCO PINTO May 1827-Sep 1831, b 1785; d 1858.
Gen **JOAQUÍN PRIETO Sep 1831-May 1833,** b 1786; d 1854.

Presidents

Gen **JOAQUÍN PRIETO May 1833-Sep 1841.**
Gen **MANUEL BULNÈS Sep 1841-Sep 1851,** b 1799; d 1866.
MANUEL MONTT Sep 1851-Sep 1861, b 8 Sep 1809; d 20 Sep 1880.
JOSÉ JOAQUÍN PÉREZ Sep 1861-Sep 1871, b 1801; d 1889.

FEDERICO ERRÁZURIZ ZAÑARTU Sep 1871-Sep 1876, b 1825; d 1877.
ANIBAL PINTO Sep 1876-Sep 1881, b 1825; d 1884.
DOMINGO SANTA MARIA Sep 1881-Sep 1886, b 4 Aug 1825; d 18 Jul 1889.
JOSÉ MANUEL BALMACEDA Sep 1886-19 Sep 1891, b 19 Jul 1840; d in office, committed suicide after losing a civil war over the relative powers of President and Congress.
JORGE MONTT Sep 1891-Sep 1896, b 1847; d 7 Nov 1922.
FEDERICO ERRÁZURIZ ECHAURREN Sep 1896-12 Jul 1901, b 1850; d in office.
GÉRMAN RIESCO acting President **Jul-Sep 1901**; President **Sep 1901-Dec 1904,** b 1854; d 1916.
RAFAEL RAYES acting President **Dec 1904-Sep 1906.**
PEDRO MONTT Sep 1906-16 Aug 1910, son of Manuel Montt, b 1846; d in office.
ELIAS FERNANDEZ ALBANO acting President **16 Aug-6 Sep 1910,** b 1845; d in office.
EMILIANO FIGUEROA acting President **Sep 1910-Sep 1911.**
RAMÓN BARROS LUCO Sep 1911-Dec 1915, b 1835; d 1919.
JUAN LUIS SANFUENTES Dec 1915-Jun 1920, b 27 Dec 1858; d 27 Jul 1930.
LUIS BARROS BORGONO acting President **Jun-Dec 1920,** b 1858; d 1943.
ARTURO ALESSANDRI PALMA Dec 1920-Sep 1924 deposed, b 20 Dec 1868; d 24 Aug 1950.
Sep 1924-Jan 1925 Military junta.
ARTURO ALESSANDRI PALMA Jan-Oct 1925.
LUIS ALTAMIRANO Oct-Dec 1925; d 1936.
EMILIANO FIGUEROS LARRAIN Dec 1925-Jul 1927, b 1860; d May 1931.
Gen **CARLOS IBÁÑEZ del CAMPO Jul 1927-26 Jul 1931** fled, b 2 Nov 1877; d 28 Apr 1960.
PEDRO OPAZO acting President **26-28 Jul 1931.**
JUAN ESTEBAN MONTERO acting President **28 Jul-18 Aug 1931,** b 1879; d 25 Feb 1952.
MANUEL TRUCCO acting President **18 Aug-Nov 1931.**
JUAN ESTEBAN MONTERO 15 Nov 1931-4 Jun 1932 deposed in coup.
5 Jun-8 Jul 1932 Military junta: Carlos Dávila Espinoza; Col Marmaduke Grove and Gen Arturo Puga.
CARLOS DÁVILA ESPINOZA acting President **8 Jul-13 Sep 1932** deposed, b 15 Sep 1884; d 19 Oct 1955.
Gen **BARTOLOMÉ BLANCHE** acting President **13 Sep-1 Oct 1932.**
ABRAHAM OYANEDEL acting President **1 Oct-24 Dec 1932.**
ARTURO ALESSANDRI PALMA 24 Dec 1932-Dec 1938, b 20 Dec 1868; d 24 Aug 1950. The first working class President of Chile he made many reforms and instituted constitutional amendments which decreased the power of the legislature in favour of the President.
PEDRO AGUIRRE CERDA 24 Dec 1938-25 Nov 1941, b 29 Jun 1879; d in office.

GÉRONIMO MÉNDEZ acting President **25 Nov 1941-Apr 1942,** b 1884; d 1959.
JUAN ANTONIO RIOS 1 Apr 1942-27 Jun 1946, b 10 Nov 1888; d in office.
ALFREDO DUHALE acting President **27 Jun-3 Aug 1946,** b 1894.
Vice-Admiral **VICENTE MERINO BIELECH** acting President **3 Aug-Nov 1946.**
GABRIEL GONZÁLEZ VIDELA 3 Nov 1946-Nov 1952, b 23 Nov 1898.
Gen **CARLOS IBÁÑEZ del CAMPO 3 Nov 1952-Nov 1958.**
JORGE ALESSANDRI RODRIGUEZ 3 Nov 1958-Nov 1964, nephew of Arturo Alessandri Palma, b 19 May 1896.
EDUARDO FREI MONTALVA 3 Nov 1964-Nov 1970, b 16 Jan 1911.
SALVADOR ALLENDE GOSSENS 3 Nov 1970-11 Sep 1973 deposed in coup, b 26 Jul 1908; committed suicide as the Presidential Palace was taken.
Gen **AUGUSTO PINOCHET UGARTE** Head of Military junta and acting President **11 Sep 1973-17 Dec 1974**; President **since 17 Dec 1974,** b 25 Nov 1915.

China

Three dynasties ruled in northern China before the country was united in 221 BC, but by AD 221 that unity had been lost. Reunited by the Sui Dynasty in 581 China again split into smaller states c 907 but again formed one nation under the Sung Dynasty from 960. The invasion of the Juchen in 1226 once more divided China, but the Mongols (Yüan Dynasty) ruled all the country from 1279. The Chinese Empire was re-established under a native dynasty (the Ming) in 1368; the brief Shun Dynasty succeeded in 1644 and in the same year the Manchu Ch'ing Dynasty was installed in China - it lasted until the overthrow of the monarchy in 1912. A Provisional Republic was proclaimed in 1911 and formally established in 1912. Unsuccessful attempts to restore a monarchy occurred in 1916 and 1917 after which the south under warlords was effectively independent. The southern Kuomintang regime was from 1928 the government of most of China. Invading Japanese forces held large northern, eastern and coastal areas from the early 1930s to 1945 and set up an 'independent' state in Manchuria. After a civil war the Communists founded the People's Republic of China in Oct 1949; the Nationalists retreated to Taiwan (see Taiwan - the Nationalist Government of China).

(Note: There is no agreement as to how Chinese names should be romanised. In the following the Wade-Giles system, rather than Pin-Yin, is used.)

† EMPERORS

THE YÜ OR HSIA DYNASTY
The first Chinese dynasty ruled part of the Hwang Ho Basin c 2205-c 1766 BC. The line did exist but the names of those monarchs that are known may belong to tradition rather than fact.

THE SHANG OR YIN DYNASTY
Founded by T'ang the Shang Dynasty from eastern China ruled from c 1766-c 1112 BC. There were said to be 39 Kings in this Line.

THE CHOU DYNASTY
The Chou Dynasty divides into four periods: West Chou (c 1122-c 771 BC), East Chou (770-249 BC), the 'Spring and Autumn Period' (722-481 BC) and the warring states period (to 221 BC).

THE CH'IN DYNASTY
SHIH HUANG-TI 221-210 BC. At the cost of many lives he united China through war. He established both central and provincial administrations but this dictatorial and iconoclastic military regime ruthlessly suppressed dissent. All books were burned except those that favoured Ch'in ideals.
ERH SHIH 210-207 BC killed, son of Shih Huang-ti.
207-202 BC There followed a period of anarchy until the Han Dynasty.

THE HAN DYNASTY
KAO TSU (personal name LIU PANG) **202-195 BC.**
HUI-TI 194-188 BC, son of Kao Tsu.
LÜ (Empress) **188-179 BC** - in theory Regent, but in practice she did not use the names of the two infants for whom she governed, widow of Kao Tsu. Pictured in Chinese legend as the archetype of the evil widow she is compared today with Mme Mao.
WEN-TI (personal name LIU HENG) **179-157 BC,** son of Kao Tsu.
CHING-TI 156-141 BC.
WU-TI 140-87 BC.
CHAO-TI 86-74 BC.
HSÜAN-TI 73-49 BC.
YÜAN-TI 48-33 BC.
CH'ENG-TI 32-7 BC.
AI-TI 6-1 BC, nephew of Ch'eng-ti.
P'ING-TI 1 BC-AD 5.
YING-TI AD 6-8, b AD 4.

HSIN DYNASTY
WANG MANG AD 9-23 assassinated, brother-in-law of Yüan-ti. A usurper who justified his act by false omens. An important reformer, he redistributed land and improved the finances. He has been called a Socialist but in reality his reforms which alienated many, leading to revolts and his murder, were intended to make administration more efficient.

Han Dynasty

KUANG WU-TI (personal name LIU HSIU) **AD 25-57.**

MING-TI 58-76.

CHANG-TI 77-88.

HO-TI 88-105.

105-220 Civil wars and anarchy. During and after the reign of Ho-ti centrifugal forces destroyed the unity of the state and through civil wars many local warlords were able to establish their independence.

The Time of the 'Three Kingdoms'

The southern provinces were outside the control of the Emperors during this period. In the north were three dynasties: 221-265 Wei Dynasty; 221-265 Shu Dynasty; 265-420 Wu Dynasty (ruled part of China).

Western Tsin or Chin Dynasty

(ruled most of China)

WU-TI 265-290; ruler of most of China from 280, b Ssu-ma Yen.

HUI-TI 290-306, son of Wu-ti.

HUAI-TI 306-311 taken captive in the Hun invasion of 311; assassinated 313.

MIN-TI 313-316 when forced to surrender to the Huns; fate uncertain.

South Chinese Dynasties
(317-589)

EASTERN CHIN or TSIN DYNASTY (317-419). LIU-SUNG or SUNG DYNASTY (420-478). SOUTHERN CH'I DYNASTY (479-501). LIANG DYNASTY (502-556). CH'EN DYNASTY (557-588).

North Chinese Dynasties
(304-581)

EARLIER CHAO DYNASTY (ruled most of north China) (304-329). LATER CHAO DYNASTY (329-349). EARLIER CH'IN DYNASTY (351-394). LATER CH'IN DYNASTY (384-417). WESTERN CH'IN DYNASTY (385-431). EARLIER YEN DYNASTY (352-370). LATER YEN DYNASTY (384-409). WESTERN YEN DYNASTY (384-395). SOUTHERN YEN DYNASTY (398-410). NORTHERN YEN DYNASTY (409-436). TAI or TOBA DYNASTY (338-376). EARLIER LIANG DYNASTY (313-376). NORTHERN LIANG DYNASTY (397-439). WESTERN LIANG DYNASTY (400-421). LATER LIANG DYNASTY (386-403). SOUTHERN LIANG DYNASTY (379-414). HSIA DYNASTY (407-431). TOBA (Turkish) DYNASTY (385-550). NORTHERN CH'I DYNASTY (550-576). NORTHERN CHOU DYNASTY (557-581).

(The various states into which north and south China had subdivided were reunited into one nation under the Sui Dynasty.)

Sui Dynasty

WEN-TI (personal name YANG CHIEN) **581-604.** The power behind the throne in the Northern Chou Dynasty, Wen-ti seized the crown. His important legacies included a reunited country (as a result of his campaigns of 587-589) and a legal code.

YANG-TI **605-spring 618** assassinated.

T'ang Dynasty

LI YÜAN **summer 618-626** when forced to abdicate; fate uncertain.

T'AI-TSUNG (personal name LI SHIH-MIN) **626-650,** second son of Li Yüan, b 600.

KAO-TSUNG 650-683, son of T'ai-tsung. His reign saw the zenith of T'ang power - an empire stretching west to the Aral Sea.

CHUNG-TSUNG 684 deposed.

JUI-TSUNG 684-690 deposed.

Chou Dynasty

WU (Empress) **690-705** forced to abdicate, widow of T'ai-tsung and of Kao-tsung her stepson, b 625, d 16 Dec 705. In turn concubine then Empress to two Emperors, and once a nun, Wu deposed her sons to become sovereign herself. A dynamic reformist, who shocked the Court by her amorous intrigues, she fostered the Buddhist faith declaring herself to be an incarnation of the Buddha.

T'ang Dynasty

CHUNG-TSUNG **705-710,** son of Wu; probably poisoned by his Empress (Wei).

(Empress WEI, widow of Chung-tsung, attempted to seize the throne in 710 but cannot be said to have reigned.)

JUI-TSUNG **710-713** abdicated, son of Wu, b 662; d 716.

HSÜAN-TSUNG (personal name LI LUNG-CHI; also called MING HUANG) **713-late 756** abdicated, son of Jui-tsung, b 685; d 762.

SU-TSUNG 756-762.

TAI-TSUNG 762-779.

TE-TSUNG 780-805.

SHUN-TSUNG 805-806.

HSIEN-TSUNG **806-820** murdered. After the reign of this dynamic autocrat the Emperors became the prisoners of the Court eunuchs and palace intrigues. None of the succeeding 'puppet Emperors' can be said to have reigned in more than a ceremonial sense.

820-907 The age of 'puppet' T'ang Emperors.

The Northern Five Dynasties
(907-960)

In 907 China again subdivided into smaller states: LATER LIANG (907-923). LATER T'ANG (923-936). LATER TSIN (936-947). LATER HAN (947-950): Emperor LIU CHIH-YUAN (947-950 assassinated). LATER CHOU (950-960): Emperor KUO WEI (950-954); Emperor CHOU SHIH-

TSUNG (954-959); Emperor CHOU KUNG-TI (959-960 deposed), d 973.

The Southern Ten Kingdoms

From 907 to the 970s southern China was subdivided into several Kingdoms: WU KINGDOM (907-937). SOUTHERN T'ANG KINGDOM (937-975). SOUTHERN P'ING KINGDOM (907-963). CH'U KINGDOM (927-951). EARLIER SHU KINGDOM (907-925). LATER SHU KINGDOM (934-965). MIN KINGDOM (909-944). SOUTHERN HAN KINGDOM (907-971). WU-YÜEH KINGDOM (907-978).

960 China was reunited under the Sung Dynasty.

† LATER EMPERORS

THE SUNG DYNASTY
T'AI-TSU (personal name CHAO K'UANG-YIN) **960-976,** b 927.
T'AI-TSUNG **976-997,** brother of T'ai-tsu, b 939.
TSENG-TSUNG (also called CHEN-TSUNG) **998-1022,** b 968.
JEN-TSUNG **1023-1063,** b 1010.
YING-TSUNG **1064-1067.**
SHEN-TSUNG **1068-1085,** son of Ying-tsung, b 1048.
CHE-TSUNG **1086-1100.**
HUI-TSUNG (personal name CHAO CHI) **1101-1125** abdicated, b 1082; d a captive of the Juchen 1135.
CH'IN-TSUNG **1125-1126** when the Juchen invaded, son of Hui-tsung, b 1100; d a captive of the Juchen 1160.
937-1125 Northern China was under the LIAO DYNASTY - Juchen.

THE SUNG DYNASTY IN SOUTH CHINA
KAO-TSUNG (personal name K'ANG) **1127-1162** abdicated, brother of Ch'in-tsung; d 1187. He re-established a Sung state south of the Yangtze.
HSIAO-TSUNG **1163-1189** abdicated; date of death uncertain.
KUANG-TSUNG **1190-1194,** son of Hsiao-tsung.
NING-TSUNG **1195-1224,** grandson of Hsiao-tsung, b 1168.
LI-TSUNG **1225-1264,** adopted son of Ning-tsung.
TU-TSUNG **1265-1274,** adopted son of Ning-tsung. He ruled but a small southern state as effective power had passed to the Mongols in northern China.

THE YÜAN (MONGOL) DYNASTY
This dynasty, founded by Temüjin - Genghis Khan - was proclaimed as a Chinese imperial line in 1271 by Khubilai Khan. Peking had been taken in 1215 and by 1254 most of north China was in Mongol hands. See also the Mongol Empire.

KHUBILAI **1271-1294**; see the Mongol Empire.

(From the death of Khubilai, the Great Khan's authority disappeared and no Mongol ruler after him could be said to have effective control of all China.)
1368 The last Mongol ruler left China.

THE MING DYNASTY
T'AI TSU (personal name CHU YÜAN-CHANG/ era name HUNG-WU) **early 1368-Jun 1398,** b 1328. A former beggar, he seized power, reunited China, expelled the Mongols and effected many reforms.
HUI TI (personal name CHU YÜN-WEN/era name CHIEN-WEN) **Jun 1398-1402** probably died in the palace fire started by his uncle's forces during a revolt, grandson of T'ai tsu, b 1377.
CH'ENG TSU (personal name CHU TI/era name YUNG-LO) **1402-2 Aug 1424,** son of T'ai tsu, b 2 May 1360. The reign of this brilliant monarch, who usurped his nephew's throne, saw new heights in art and the recognition of Chinese overlordship in the East Indies, Indo-China, Korea and Japan. He encouraged trade and sent Cheng Ho on his famous voyages to Africa and Arabia.
JEN TSUNG (personal name CHU KAO-CHIH/ era name HUNG-HSI) **Aug 1424-1425,** son of Ch'eng tsu, b 1378.
HSÜAN TSUNG (personal name CHU CHAN-CHI/era name HSÜAN-TE) **1425-1435,** son of Ch'eng tsu, b 1398.
YING TSUNG (personal name CHU CH'I-CHEN/ era name CH'ENG-T'UNG) **1435-1449** deposed *in absentia*, son of Hsüan tsung, b 1427. Taken captive during the war between China and the Mongols he was deposed; after being ransomed he was restored during his brother's terminal illness.
CHING TI (personal name CHU CH'I-YÜ/era name CHING-T'AI) **1449-1457,** brother of Ying tsung, b 1428.
YING TSUNG (personal name CHU CH'I-CHEN/ second era name T'IEN-SHUN) **1457-1464.**
HSIEN TSUNG (personal name CHU CHIEN-SHEN/era name CH'ENG HUA) **1464-1487,** son of Ying tsung, b 1447.
HSIAO TSUNG (personal name CHU YU-T'ANG /era name HUNG-CHIH) **1487-1505,** son of Hsien tsung, b 1470.
WU TSUNG (personal name CHU HOU-CHAO/ era name CHENG-TE) **1505-1521,** son of Hsiao tsung, b 1491.
SHIH TSUNG (personal name CHU HOU-TSUNG /era name CHIA-CHING) **1521-1566,** grandson of Hsien tsung, b 1507.
MU TSUNG (personal name CHU TSAI-KOU/era name LUNG-CH'ING) **1566-1572,** son of Shih tsung, b 1537.
SHEN TSUNG (personal name CHU I-CHÜN/era name WAN-LI) **1572-1620,** son of Mu tsung, b 1563.

KUANG TSUNG (personal name CHU CH'ANG-LO/era name T'AI-CH'ANG) **1620** - reigned for about 1 month, son of Shen tsung, b 1582.

HSI TSUNG (personal name CHU YU-CHIAO/era name T'IEN-CH'I) **1620-1627,** son of Kuang tsung, b 1605.

CHUANG-LIEH-TI (also called SSU TSUNG, HUAI TSUNG and I TSUNG; personal name CHU YU-CHIEN/era name CH'UNG-CHEN) **1627-24 Apr 1644** hanged himself when the rebels of Li Tzu-ch'eng invaded Peking, son of Kuang tsung, b 1611.

SHUN DYNASTY

LI TZU-CH'ENG **Apr-6 Jun 1644**; killed late 1644 or early 1645. A rebel leader whose forces seized Peking but who used his power to loot rather than to secure his position as monarch.

CH'ING (MANCHU) DYNASTY

Manchu Emperors Outside China

NURHACHU **1616-1626** died of wounds received in battle.

T'AI TSUNG (personal name ABAHAI) **1626-1643.** He invaded north China and established a strong state threatening the Ming.

SHUN-CHIH **1643-Jun 1644** when he became Emperor of China.

MANCHU OR CH'ING DYNASTY IN CHINA

The Emperors of this line are best known by their era names, which are placed first in the following list: these names are not and cannot be used as the name of a person, they signify only the reign as a period of time; the personal name was never referred to in China, thus the safest name by which an Emperor could be designated was his temple name rather than his posthumous name. All four names will be found in most cases below.

SHUN-CHIH (personal name FU-LIN/temple name SHIH TSU/posthumous name CHANG HUANG TI) Ruler of the Manchus from 1643; Emperor of China **Jun 1644-5 Feb 1661,** ninth son of T'ai tsung, b 15 Mar 1638. At first influenced by the able Regent (his uncle Dorgon) who completed the Manchu conquest of China and later by the German Jesuit von Schall, Shih tsu sinicised the Manchus and provided a fairer and more efficient government for the Chinese thus in part reconciling them to Manchu rule.

K'ANG HSI (personal name HSÜAN-YEH/temple name SHENG-TSU/posthumous name JEN HUANG-TI) **Feb 1661-20 Dec 1722,** son of Shih-tsu, b 4 May 1654.

YUNG-CHENG (personal name YIN-CHEN/temple name SHIH TSUNG/posthumous name HSIEN HUAN TI) **Dec 1722-8 Oct 1735** probably murdered, fourth son of Sheng-tsu, b 13 Dec 1678.

CH'IEN-LUNG (personal name HUNG-LI/temple name KAO TSUNG/posthumous name CH'UN HUANG-TI) **Oct 1735-1796** abdicated, son of Shih tsung, b 25 Sep 1711; d 7 Feb 1799. He removed the Turkish and Mongol threats to his vast empire which included Burma, Nepal and much of Indo-China; he strenghtened the army, but the huge military budget meant heavy taxes. Great damage was done to the finances by the Minister Ho-Shen who milked 10 years' revenue into his pocket.

CHIA-CH'ING (personal name YUNG-YEN/temple name JEN TSUNG/posthumous name CH'ENG HUANG TI) **1796-2 Sep 1820,** son of Kao tsung, b 13 Nov 1760.

TAO-KUANG (personal name MIN-NING/temple name HSÜAN TSUNG/posthumous name CH'ENG HUANG TI) **1821-25 Feb 1850,** son of Jen tsung, b 16 Sep 1782. He tried to end anarchy and corruption in a country shocked by defeat by Britain in the Opium War.

HSIEN-FENG (temple name WEN TSUNG) **1851-1861,** son of Hsüan tsung, b 1831.

T'UNG CHIH (personal name TSAI-CH'UN/temple name MU TSUNG/posthumous name I HUANG-TI) **1862-12 Jan 1875,** son of Wen tsung, b 27 Apr 1856. The serious Taiping rising (1853-64), led by Hung Hsiu-Ch'uan who established a revolutionary state in central China, was ended but the country was much weakened by corruption and grossly unequal trade treaties imposed by European nations. Mu-tsung attempted reform by austerity but power remained in the hands of his fiery mother Tz'u-Hsi.

KUANG-HSÜ (personal name TSAI T'IEN/temple name TE TSUNG/posthumous name CHING HUANG TI) **Jan 1875-14 Nov 1908** murdered by order of the dying Tz'u-Hsi; cousin of Mu tsung, b 14 Aug 1871. After an unsuccessful attempt to break free of Tz'u-Hsi and to reform China (the Hundred Days' Reform) he was kept captive by the Dowager Empress Tz'u-Hsi. Her fierce resistance to changes she did not understand, and her support for the xenophobic Boxer Rising (1900) by a declaration of war against the western powers (whose strength she could not comprehend), reduced China to a virtual colony of eight trading nations. As dissent grew the Manchu Dynasty became increasingly irrelevant to the future of China.

HSÜAN-TUNG (personal name P'U-I/name after the revolution HENRY PU YI/name while Emperor of Manchoukuo K'ANG-TE) **Nov 1908-12 Feb 1912** abdicated; later Emperor of Manchoukuo (Manchuria), nephew of Te tsung, b 7 Feb 1906; d 17 Oct 1967. The child Emperor, a victim of circumstances, 'reigned' twice; from 1934 to 1945 he was Emperor of the Japanese 'puppet state' of Manchoukuo; after a spell in gaol as a war criminal (1950-59) he ended his days as handyman in a botanical garden in Communist Peking.

THE REPUBLIC OF CHINA

PRESIDENTS

SUN YAT-SEN provsional President **Feb 1912.**

Gen **YÜAN SHIH-K'AI** provisional President **Feb-Oct 1912**; President **Oct 1912-Jun 1916,** b 20 Sep 1859; d in office. This general, who was planning to install himself as Emperor in 1916, has been greatly maligned, but at least was relatively honest and able to maintain order.
LI YÜAN-HUNG   Jun 1916-1 Jul 1917, b ? 1864; d 3 Jun 1928.

THE CHINESE EMPIRE

EMPEROR
HSÜAN-TUNG   1-8 Jul 1917 deposed; was later Emperor of Manchoukou (Manchuria).

THE REPUBLIC OF CHINA
Northern Regime

PRESIDENTS
FENG KUO-CHANG   Jul 1917-Sep 1918, b ?1859; d 6 Jan 1920.
HSÜ SHIH CH'ANG   Sep 1918-Jun 1922, b ?1858; d 6 Jun 1939.
LI YÜAN-HUNG   12 Jun 1922-Oct 1923.
TS'AO K'UN   4 Oct 1923-Nov 1924, b 1862; d 1938.
Marshal **TUAN CHI-JUI   Nov 1924-Apr 1926,** b 6 Mar 1865; d 2 Nov 1936. By the term of this President the southern regime had become the more powerful Government.

DE FACTO RULER
CHANG TSO-LIN   Apr 1926-Jun 1928, b 1873; d 'in office' from injuries received when his train was blown up. A former leader of bandits, this warlord controlled much of northern China but was obliged to withdraw as Chiang Kai-shek's forces swept into the north.

THE REPUBLIC OF CHINA
Southern Regime

PRESIDENTS
SUN YAT-SEN self-proclaimed President **31 Aug 1917-12 Mar 1925,** b 12 Nov 1866; d in office. Sun Yat-sen, the 'Father of the Republic', played a major role in the overthrow of the monarchy. Falling out with Yüan Shih-k'ai, whom he suspected of betraying the Republic, Sun went into exile. He returned to found a separate 'purified' regime (the Kuomintang) in Canton.
HU HAN-MIN   Mar 1925-1927 though he ceased to be effective before that date, b 9 Dec 1879; d 12 May 1936.

THE REPUBLIC OF CHINA
Nanking Kuomintang Regime

HEAD OF GOVERNMENT
CHIANG KAI-SHEK   Apr 1927-10 Oct 1928 when he gained control of all China.

THE REPUBLIC OF CHINA
(reunited)

PRESIDENTS
CHIANG KAI-SHEK   Oct 1928-Dec 1931.
LIN SEN provisional President **15-26 Dec 1931**; President **26 Dec 1931-May 1943,** b 11 Feb 1867; d 1 Aug 1943.
CHIANG KAI-SHEK provisional President **30 May-Sep 1943**; President **13 Sep 1943-Jan 1949,** b (Chiang Chung-cheng) 31 Oct 1887; d 5 Apr 1975. The effective leader of Kuomintang from 1926, Chiang fought the northern warlords, initially with Communist help. Having founded his own government in Nanking he reunited China in Oct 1928 but quickly lost large tracts of the north to Japanese forces. Virtual dictator of China he led his country's war effort but he failed to win the civil war against the Communists in 1949 owing to the unpopularity of a regime that had not improved the lot of the masses and to the inefficiency of many corrupt Ministers. Exiled to the island of Taiwan he continued the Nationalist Government in Taipei, unrealistically planning the return to the mainland but also creating one of the most prosperous communities in Asia.
Gen **LI TSUNG-JEN** acting President **20 Jan-Dec 1949** when he withdrew to Taiwan; see Taiwan - the Nationalist Government of China.

PRIME MINISTERS
Officially styled Presidents of the Executive Yuan.

T'AN YEN-K'AI   Oct 1928-22 Sep 1930, b 1879; d in office.
Dr **SOONG TZU-WEN   Sep-Nov 1930.**
CHIANG KAI-SHEK   Dec 1930-Dec 1931.
Dr **SUN FO   Dec 1931-Jan 1932.**
CHONG MING-SHU acting PM **Jan 1932.**
Dr **WANG CHING-WEI   28 Jan 1932-Dec 1935,** b 4 May 1883; d 10 Nov 1944.
CHIANG KAI-SHEK   6 Dec 1935-Jan 1938.
Dr **KUNG HSIANG-HSI** (H.H. Kung) **1 Jan 1938-Nov 1939,** b 1891; d 15 Aug 1967.
CHIANG KAI-SHEK   20 Nov 1939-May 1945.
Dr **SOONG TZU-WEN   31 May 1945-Mar 1947,** b 4 Dec 1894; d 24 Apr 1971 in exile. The brother-in-law of Chiang Kai-shek and Sun Yat-sen and the brother of Madame Soong Ching-ling, this leading financier and industrialist (said, in the 1930s, to be the richest man in the world) reformed the Chinese economy and ended his days as an American banker.
CHIANG KAI-SHEK   1 Mar-17 Apr 1947.
Gen **CHANG CHUN   17 Apr 1947-May 1948,** b 1889.
Dr **WONG WEN-HAO   24 May-Nov 1948,** b 1889.
Dr **SUN FO   26 Nov 1948-Mar 1949,** b 1895. The son of Sun Yat-sen.
Gen **HO YING-CHIN   12 Mar-2 Jun 1949,** b 1890.
Marshal **YEN HSI-SHAN   2 Jun-Dec 1949** when he retired to Taiwan; see Taiwan - the Nationalist Government of China.

THE PEOPLE'S REPUBLIC OF CHINA

Heads of State

CHAIRMEN OF THE REPUBLIC
MAO TSE-TUNG 1 Oct 1949-Dec 1958; see Chairman Mao.
Marshal **CHU TEH** acting Chairman **Dec 1958-Apr 1959.**
LIU SHAO-CHI 27 Apr 1959-Oct 1968, b 1898; d 1972.
TUNG PI-WU acting Chairman **31 Oct 1968-Jan 1975,** b 1885; d 2 Apr 1975.

CHAIRMEN OF THE STANDING COMMITTEE
OF THE NATIONAL PEOPLE'S CONGRESS
Marshal **CHU TEH 17 Jan 1975-6 Jul 1976,** b 1886; d in office. His military skill played an important role in deciding the outcome of the Chinese Civil War (1946-9).
Madame **SOONG CHING-LING** acting Head of State **6 Jul 1976-Mar 1978,** b 1892. Widow of Sun Yat-sen, sister of Soong Tzu-wen and sister-in-law of Chiang Kai-shek.
Marshal **YEH CHIEN-YING since 4 Mar 1978.**

Prime Ministers

CHOU EN-LAI 1 Oct 1949-8 Jan 1976, b 1898; d in office. A leading member of the Communist Party since the 1920s Chou was an able statesman with great flexibility of mind. He was a force for stability during the wilder excesses of the Cultural Revolution.
HUA KUO-FENG acting PM **Jan-Apr 1976;** PM **since 7 Apr 1976.**

Chairmen of the Communist Party of China

MAO TSE-TUNG 1 Oct 1949-9 Sep 1976, b 26 Dec 1893; d in office. A former headmaster and the son of a prosperous farmer, Mao was one of the founders of the Chinese Communist Party some of whose members he led in the 'Long March' across China after fighting the forces of Chiang Kai-shek's Kuomintang. He established the Chinese People's Republic in Oct 1949 after a three year civil war against the Nationalists. The country was modernised and the economic lot of the peasants improved but this progress (for which Chou En-lai must take much of the credit) was achieved at terrible human cost: the people were regimented and lost even basic freedoms; Christians were persecuted; thousands were eliminated; and the extraordinary and totally unnecessary Cultural Revolution brought a destructive reign of terror. A prolific poet and Marxist theorist (his views were rejected by the Soviet leaders with whom he quarrelled bitterly), Mao stands as one of the most influential figures of the 20th century.
HUA KUO-FENG since 7 Oct 1976.

The young Mao Tse Tung. Between 1966 and 1971 800 million copies of his 'Quotations' were distributed (Radio Times Hulton Picture Library)

Manchuria

The Japanese invaders set up the northern Chinese province of Manchuria as an 'independent' state. Crushed by Soviet troops in Aug 1945 the 'Empire of Manchoukuo' was returned to Chinese rule in Feb 1946.

PROVISIONAL GOVERNMENT

Head

Gen **YUAN CHIN-KAI 10 Nov 1931-Feb 1932.**

Administrator

PU YI (formerly Emperor of China) **20 Feb-9 Mar 1932;** see Emperor K'ang te.

Chief Executive

PU YI 9 Mar 1932-Feb 1934 when he became Emperor K'ang te.

Simon Bolivar, the Liberator of Colombia, who became authoritarian in his unrealistic attempts to impose unity on Latin America (Radio Times Hulton Picture Library)

THE EMPIRE OF MANCHOUKUO

† Emperor

K'ANG-TE 28 Feb 1934-22 Aug 1945 when taken prisoner by Soviet forces; see also the Hsuantung Emperor of China.

Taiwan - The Nationalist Government of China

After the Communist takeover of China the legal Nationalist Government was confined to the island of Taiwan.

Presidents

Gen **LI TSUNG-JEN** President of China from 20 Jan 1949; President in Taiwan **8 Dec 1949-Mar 1950.**
CHIANG KAI-SHEK 1 Mar 1950-5 Apr 1975; was also President Chiang Kai-shek of the Republic of China

Dr **YEN CHIA-KAN 6 Apr 1975-May 1978,** b 23 Oct 1905.
CHIANG CHING-KUO since 20 May 1978, son of Chiang Kai-shek, b 18 Mar 1910.

Prime Ministers

Marshal **YEN HSI-SHAN** PM of China from 2 Jun 1949; PM in Taiwan **Dec 1949-7 Mar 1950.**
Gen **CHEN CHENG 7 Mar 1950-May 1954.**
O.K. YUI 25 May 1954-Jun 1958, b 1897; d Jun 1960.
Gen **CHEN CHENG 24 Jun 1958-Dec 1963,** b 1897; d 5 Mar 1965.
Dr **YEN CHIA-KAN 16 Dec 1963-May 1972.**
CHIANG CHING-KUO since 18 May 1972.

Choson, Kingdom of *see* Korea

Cola Kingdom *see* India

Colombia

The Spanish Captain-Generality of New Granada was settled in the 1530s and remained subject to the crown of Spain until 17 Dec 1819 when independence was achieved. From 1819 to 1830 the country formed part of Greater Colombia - a union of New Granada, Venezuela, Panama and Ecuador. Upon the secession of Venezuela and Ecuador in 1830 the state was renamed New Granada. In 1858, three years after the first secession of Panama, the nomenclature was changed to the Granadine Confederation and in 1863, upon the readherence of Panama, to Colombia. Panama finally withdrew in 1903.

THE REPUBLIC OF GREATER COLOMBIA

Presidents

SIMÓN BOLIVAR 17 Dec 1819-1823 *de facto*; Sep 1827-Jan 1830 *de jure*; President **Dec 1819-Jan 1830,** b 24 Jul 1783; d 17 Dec 1830. The architect of the independence of Latin America, Bolivar personally liberated Colombia and Venezuela and co-ordinated the efforts of others in Peru, Ecuador and Bolivia.
FRANCISCO de PAULA SANTANDER acting President (in the absence of Bolivar) **1823-1827,** b 2 Apr 1792; d 6 May 1840. Bolivar's able lieutenant, he played a major role in winning the Battle of Boyacá. He was recalled from exile after he had been banished for allegedly plotting to assassinate Bolivar whose rule he found increasingly dictatorial. He became the first

President of New Granada after the secession of Venezuela and Ecuador.

Marshal **ANDRÉS SANTA CRUZ** nominal President *in absentia* **Jan-4 Jun 1830**; was also President of Bolivia.

THE REPUBLIC OF NEW GRANADA

Presidents

JOAQUIN MOSQUERA Head of provisional government **Jun 1830-Oct 1832,** b 1787; d 1877.

FRANCISCO de PAULA SANTANDER Oct **1832-Mar 1837.**

JOSÉ IGNACIO de MARQUEZ Mar 1837-May 1841.

PEDRO ALCANTARA HERRAN May 1841-Mar 1844, b 1800; d 1872. A major civil war (1840-1842) virtually destroyed the power of the central government.

Gen **TOMÁS CIPRIANO de MOSQUERA** acting President **Mar 1844-Apr 1845**; President **Apr 1845-Mar 1849** deposed in coup, b 20 Sep 1798; d 7 Oct 1878. A successful general and a powerful personality, he achieved some economic progress in several dictatorships during which he ruled impetuously busily settling grudges, in particular against the Church.

JOSÉ HILARIO LÓPEZ Mar 1849-Apr 1853, b c 1800; d 1869.

Gen **JOSÉ MARIA OBANDO Apr 1853-Apr 1855** deposed in coup, b 1795; d 1861.

MANUEL MARIA MALLARINO Apr 1855-Apr 1857, b 1808; d 1872.

MARIANO OSPINA RODRIGUEZ Apr 1857-May 1858 when he became President of the Granadine Confederation.

THE GRANADINE CONFEDERATION

Presidents

MARIANO OSPINA RODRIGUEZ May 1858-Mar 1861, b 1806; d 1875.

JULIO ARBOLEDA Mar 1861-Nov 1862, b 1817; d in office.

Gen **TOMÁS CIPRIANO de MOSQUERA** Nov **1862-Feb 1863.**

THE REPUBLIC OF COLOMBIA
(1863-1885 styled the United States of Colombia)

Presidents

FROILÁN LARGARCHA acting President **Feb-Jun 1863.**

Gen **TOMÁS CIPRIANO de MOSQUERA** Jun **1863-Apr 1864.**

JUAN AGUSTIN URICOECHEA acting President **Apr 1864.**

MANUEL MURILLO TORO Apr 1864-Mar 1866, b 1816; d 1880.

JOSÉ MARÍA ROJAS GARRIDO acting President **Mar 1866.**

Gen **TOMÁS CIPRIANO de MOSQUERA Mar 1866-May 1867** deposed in coup.

Gen **SANTOS ACOSTA May 1867-Apr 1868.**

Gen **SANTIAGO GUTIÉRREZ Apr 1868-Apr 1870,** b 1820; d 1872.

Gen **EUSTORJIO SALGAR Apr 1870-Apr 1872,** b 1831; d 1885.

MANUEL MURILLO TORO Apr 1872-Apr 1874.

SANTIAGO PÉREZ Apr 1874-Apr 1876, b 1830; d 1900.

AQUILEO PARRA Apr 1876-Apr 1878, b 1825; d 1900.

JULIÁN TRUJILLO Apr 1878-Apr 1880, b 1829; d 1884.

Gen **RAFAEL NUÑEZ Apr 1880-Apr 1882.**

FRANCISCO JAVIER ZALDUA Apr-Dec 1882, b?1811; d in office.

CLIMACHO CALDERÓN acting President **Dec 1882-Apr 1883.**

JOSÉ EUSEBIO OTALORA Apr 1883-Apr 1884, b 1828; d 1884.

EZEQUIEL HURTADO acting President **Apr-Aug 1884.**

Gen **RAFAEL NUÑEZ Aug 1884-1886** deposed in coup, b 28 Sep 1825; d 12 Sep 1894. Poet and author.

JOSÉ MARÍA CAMPO SERRANO acting President **1886-1887.**

ELISEO PAYÁN 1887.

Gen **RAFAEL NUÑEZ 1887-1888.**

CARLOS HOLGUIN 1888-Aug 1892, b 1832; d Oct 1894.

Gen **RAFAEL NUÑEZ** acting President **Aug 1892-12 Sep 1894.**

MIGUEL ANTONIO CARO Sep 1894-1896, b 1843; d 5 Aug 1909.

GUILLERMO QUINTERO CALDERÓN 1896.

MIGUEL ANTONIO CARO 1896-Aug 1898.

JOSÉ MANUEL MARROQUÍN acting President **Aug 1898.**

MANUEL ANTONIO SANCLEMENTE Aug 1898-Jul 1900.

JOSÉ MANUEL MARROQUÍN Jul 1900-Aug 1904, b 1827; d 1908. The refusal of his government to grant permission for a canal through Panama led to the eventual secession of that country from Colombia.

PRIETO RAFAEL REYES Aug 1904-Jul 1908.

EUCLIDES de ANGULO Jul-Aug 1908.

PRIETO RAFAEL REYES Aug 1908-Aug 1909 forced to withdraw, b 1850; d 19 Feb 1921. As a youth he spent ten years in the Amazon jungle where his brother was eaten by cannibals; as President he brought firm realistic government, but was forced to resign for accepting the loss of Panama.

Gen **JORGE HOLGUIN** acting President **Aug-Jul 1909.**

RAMÓN GONZALEZ VALENCIA Aug 1909-Aug 1910, b 1854; d 1928.

CARLOS E. RESTREPO Aug 1910-Aug 1914, b 1867; d 1937.
JOSÉ VICENTE CONCHA Aug 1914-Aug 1918, b 1867; d 1937.
MARCO FIDEL SUÁREZ 7 Aug 1918-Nov 1921, b 1855; d 1927.
Gen JORGE HOLGUIN acting President 11 Nov 1921-Aug 1922.
Gen PEDRO NEL OSPINA 7 Aug 1922-Aug 1926, b 1867; d 1 Jul 1927.
Dr MIGUEL ABADÍA MÉNDEZ 7 Aug 1926-Aug 1930, b 1867; d 15 May 1947.
Dr ENRIQUE OLAYA HERRERA 7 Aug 1930-Aug 1934, b 1881; d 20 Feb 1937.
Dr ALFONSO LÓPEZ PUMAREJO 7 Aug 1934-Aug 1938, b 1886; d 20 Nov 1950.
Dr EDUARDO SANTOS 7 Aug 1938-Aug 1942, b 1888.
Dr ALFONSO LÓPEZ PUMAREJO 7 Aug 1942-Jul 1945.
Dr ALBERTO LLERAS CAMARGO acting President Jul-Aug 1945; President 7 Aug 1945-Aug 1946.
Dr MARIANO OSPINA PÉREZ 7 Aug 1946-Aug 1950, b 24 Nov 1891, d 14 Apr 1976.
Dr LAUREANO ELEUTERIO GÓMEZ CASTRO 7 Aug 1950-13 Jun 1953 deposed in coup, b 20 Feb 1889; d 13 Jul 1965.
Gen GUSTAVO ROJAS PINILLA 13 Jun 1953-10 May 1957 deposed in coup, b 12 Mar 1900; d 17 Jan 1975. He replaced the dictatorship of Gómez with a particularly corrupt one of his own. In response the rival Liberal and Conservative parties united in their efforts to save Colombian democracy and formulated the remarkable power sharing arrangement that governed the state once military involvement was ended.
Gen GABRIEL PARÍS acting President and Head of military junta 10 May 1957-13 Feb 1958.
13 Feb-7 Aug 1958 Gen GABRIEL PARÍS, Brig RAFAEL NAVAS PARDO, Maj-Gen DEOGRACIAS FONSECA, Rear-Admiral RUBEN PIEDRAHITA and Brig LUIS E. ORDOÑEZ (the five members of the junta, co-equal Heads of State, by judgement of the Supreme Court).
Aug 1958 Civilian rule was restored, since when Colombia has been one of the three Latin American states to have a free democratic system based upon the West European model.
Dr ALBERTO LLERAS CAMARGO 7 Aug 1958-Aug 1962, b 3 Jul 1906.
Dr GUILLERMO-LÉON VALENCIA 7 Aug 1962-Aug 1966, b 27 Apr 1909; d 5 Nov 1971
Dr CARLOS LLERAS RESTREPO 7 Aug 1966-Aug 1970, cousin of Dr Lleras Camargo, b 12 Apr 1908.
Dr MISAEL PASTRANA BORRERO 7 Aug 1970-Aug 1974, b 14 Nov 1923.
Dr ALFONSO LOPEZ MICHELSEN 7 Aug 1974-6 Aug 1978, b 30 Jun 1913.
Dr JULIO CESAR TURBAY since 7 Aug 1978.

The Comoros

Mayotte became French in 1841 and a protectorate was established over the other three islands in 1886. A unilateral declaration of independence (6 Jul 1975) in Anjouan, Grande-Comore and Mohéli set up the Republic which was recognised as sovereign by France from 31 Dec 1975. Mayotte remains French.

Presidents

AHMED ABDALLAH 7 Jul-3 Aug 1975 deposed in coup.
Prince SAID MOHAMMED JAFFAR 10 Aug 1975-2 Jan 1976.
ALI SOILIH 2 Jan 1976-12 May 1978 deposed in coup; killed attempting to escape prison 28 May 1978.
AHMED ABDALLAH since May 1978.

Prime Ministers

AHMED ABDALLAH Premier per interim 24 Jul-3 Aug 1975 deposed in a coup.
ALI SOILIH Head of the Provisional Executive 4-10 Aug 1975.
Prince SAID MOHAMMED JAFFAR 10 Aug 1975-2 Jan 1976.
ABDALLAH MOHAMMED 6 Jan 1976-12 May 1978 deposed in coup.
SAID ATTHOUMANI since 12 May 1978.

Confederate States of America see United States of America

Congo

Most of the territory of Congo (usually known as Congo-Brazzaville) became French in the period 1876-1888; the northern part of the country was included in the German colony of Kamerun until World War I when it was reincorporated into the French colony of the Middle Congo. Independence, as a Republic, was achieved on 15 Aug 1960.

Presidents

Abbot FULBERT YOULOU 15 Aug 1960-15 Aug 1963 when he was deposed in a coup, b 9 Jun 1917; d 5 May 1972. (President Youlou continued to use the clerical title Abbot although he had been suspended by the Church for entering politics.)

16 Aug-19 Dec 1963 Presidency suspended.

ALPHONSE MASSEMBA-DÉBAT 19 Dec 1963-2 Aug 1968 when he was deposed; restored **4 Aug-4 Sep 1968,** b 1921; executed Mar 1977.

Major **ALFRED RAOUL 5 Sep 1968-1 Jan 1969.**

Major **MARIEN NGOUABI** President of Congo **1 Jan 1969-3 Jan 1970**; President of the People's Republic of Congo, deemed to be a 'new state', **3 Jan 1970-18 Mar 1977** when he was assassinated, b 1938.

18 Mar-3 Apr 1977 Presidency suspended.

Col **JOACHIM YHOMBI-OPANGO** President of the Military Committee **since 3 Apr 1977.**

Prime Ministers

Abbot **FULBERT YOULOU 15 Aug 1960-15 Aug 1963.**

ALPHONSE MASSEMBA-DÉBAT 16 Aug 1963-19 Dec 1963.

PASCAL LISSOUBA 24 Dec 1963-15 Apr 1966, b 10 Nov 1931.

AMBROISE NOUMAZALAY 19 Apr 1966-Jan 1968, b 23 Sep 1933.

ALPHONSE MASSEMBA-DÉBAT 12 Jan-2 Aug 1968; 4-22 Aug 1968.

Major **ALFRED RAOUL 22 Aug 1968-3 Jan 1970.**

Jan 1970-Aug 1974 Premiership in abeyance.

HENRI LOPES 25 Aug 1974-Dec 1975, b 1937.

Major **LOUIS SYLVAIN GOMA 18 Dec 1975-Mar 1977.**

Mar-Apr 1977 Rule by a Military Committee.

Col **JOACHIM YHOMBI-OPANGO** President of the Military Committee; Head of Government **since 3 Apr 1977.**

Congolese Republic or Congo-Kinshasa *see* Zaire

Cordoba, Emirate of *see* Spain

Costa Rica

Spanish from the 1520s Costa Rica became independent in 1821. The state formed part of Mexico (1822-3) and then of the United Provinces of Central America (1823-39). After the dissolution of the latter federation Costa Rica became an independent nation but was not able to establish an effective governmental system until 1847. Today, with Colombia and Venezuela, Costa Rica is one of the few Latin American states to enjoy a West European style free democratic society.

Presidents

BRAULIO CARILLO Jun 1838-Apr 1842; acting President **Apr-Jun 1842.**

FRANCISCO MORAZAN acting President **Jun-Jul 1842**; President **Jul-Sep 1842** deposed, b 1792; d 1842.

JOSÉ MARIA ALFARO Sep 1842-Nov 1844.

FRANCISCO MARIA OREAMUNO Nov-Dec 1844, b 1800; d 1856.

RAFAEL MOYA Dec 1844-May 1845; d in office.

JOSÉ RAFAEL de GALLEGOS May 1845-Jun 1846.

JOSÉ MARIA ALFARO Jun 1846-May 1847.

JOSÉ MARIA CASTRO May 1847-Jan 1849, b 1 Sep 1816; d 1892. He is regarded as the founder of the Republic.

JUAN RAFAEL MORA Jan 1849-Aug 1859 deposed in coup, b 8 Feb 1814; d 30 Sep 1860. He aided the Nicaraguans in the campaign that ousted the American adventurer Walker.

JOSÉ MARIA MONTEALEGRA acting President **Aug 1859-Feb 1860**; President **Feb 1860-Apr 1863.**

JÉSUS JIMÉNES Apr 1863-May 1866, b 1823; d 1897.

JOSÉ MARIA CASTRO May 1866-Sep 1868.

JÉSUS JIMÉNES acting President **Sep-Nov 1868**; President **Nov 1868-Apr 1870.**

BRUNO CARRANZA Apr-Aug 1870.

Gen **TOMÁS GUARDIA Aug 1870-1871.**

VICENTE QUADRA 1871.

Gen **TOMÁS GUARDIA** acting President **1871-May 1872**; President **May 1872-Nov 1873,** b 1832; d 7 Jul 1882.

SALVADOR GONZALEZ Nov-Dec 1873.

RAFAEL BARROETA Dec 1873-Feb 1874.

Gen **TOMÁS GUARDIA Feb 1874-May 1876.**

ANICETO ESQUIVEL May-Jul 1876.

VICENTE HERRERA Jul-Sep 1876.

Gen **TOMÁS GUARDIA Sep 1876-May 1877.**

SERGIO CAMARGO May 1877.

Gen **TOMÁS GUARDIA May 1877-7 Jul 1882** when he died in office.

PROSPERO FERNÁNDEZ Jul 1882-Mar 1885, b 18 Jul 1834; d 12 Mar 1885.

Gen **BERNARDO SOTO Mar 1885-May 1890,** b 12 Feb 1854; d 1931.

JOSÉ JOAQUIN RODRIGUEZ 8 May 1890-May 1894, b 1838; d 1917. The first democratically elected President in Central America, Rodriguez was the first of an almost unbroken line of freely elected Costa Rican rulers.

RAFAEL IGLESIAS May 1894-May 1902, b 1861; d 1924.

ASCENSIÓN ESQUIVEL 8 May 1902-May 1906, b 1848; d 1927.

CLETO GONZÁLEZ VIQUEZ 8 May 1906-May 1910, b 1858; d 1937.

RICARDO JIMÉNEZ OREAMUNO 8 May 1910-May 1914, b 1859; d 1945.

ALFREDO JIMÉNEZ FLORES 8 May 1914-Jan 1917 when deposed in the last coup in Costa Rica.

Gen **FEDERICO TINOCO GRANADOS Jan 1917-May 1919,** b 1870; d 1931.

JULIO ACOSTA GARCÍA May-Aug 1919.

FRANCISCO AGUILAR BARQUERO acting President **Aug 1919.**

JUAN BAUTISTA QUIRÓS Aug 1919-May 1920.

JULIO ACOSTA GARCÍA 8 May 1920-May 1924, b 1872; d 6 Jul 1954. His term saw a border war with Panama.

RICARDO JIMÉNEZ OREAMUNO 8 May 1924-May 1928.

CLETO GONZÁLEZ VIQUEZ 8 May 1928-May 1932.

RICARDO JIMÉNEZ OREAMUNO 8 May 1932-May 1936.

LÉON CORTÉS CASTRO 8 May 1936-May 1940, b 1882; d 1946.

Dr **RAFAEL ANGEL CALDERÓN GUARDIA 8 May 1940-May 1944,** b 10 Mar 1900; d 9 Jun 1970.

TEODORO PICADO MICHALSKI 8 May 1944-Mar 1948, b 1900; d 1 Jun 1960.

LEON HERRERA acting President **Apr-May 1948.**

JOSÉ FIGUERES FERRER May 1948-Jan 1949.

OTILIO ULARTE 19 Jan 1949-Sep 1952, b 1895.

ALBERTO OREAMUNO FLORES Sep 1952-May **1953.**

JOSÉ FIGUERES FERRER 8 May 1953-May 1958.

MARIO ECHANDI JIMÉNEZ 8 May 1958-May 1962, son of Ricardo Jiménez Oreamuno, b 17 Jun 1915.

JOSÉ FRANCISCO ORLICH BOLMARICH 8 May 1962-May 1966, b 10 Mar 1907; d 29 Oct 1969.

Dr **JOSÉ JOAQUIN TREJOS FERNÁNDEZ 8 May 1966-May 1970,** b 18 Apr 1916.

JOSÉ FIGUERES FERRER 8 May 1970-May 1974, b 25 Sep 1906.

DANIEL ODUBER QUIRÓS 9 May 1974-May 1978, b 25 Aug 1925.

RODRIGO CARAZO since 8 May 1978.

Croatia *see* Yugoslavia

The Crusader States

As an outcome of the First Crusade the Kingdom of Jerusalem, the Principality of Antioch and the Counties of Tripoli and Edessa were founded by the Franks.

ANTIOCH

Perhaps the wealthiest of the Crusader states, Antioch (modern SE Turkey) lasted until 1268.

† Princes

BOHEMOND I 1098-1111, b Bohemond Guiscard *c* 1050; d in exile. Defeated, he left Antioch for Europe (1103) but never returned with the promised reinforcements.

TANCRED 1111-12 Dec 1112, nephew of Bohemond I. Arrogant and perhaps the ablest of the Crusaders, Tancred played a major role in securing Antioch and Jerusalem.

ROGER Dec 1112-28 Jun 1119 died in battle, nephew of Tancred.

BOHEMOND II Jun 1119-Feb 1130 died in battle, he did not succeed *de facto* until Oct 1126 when he came from Europe to claim his inheritance, son of Bohemond I, b *c* 1106.

CONSTANCE (Princess) co-ruler **Feb 1130-late 1162** when she was deposed, daughter of Bohemond II, b 1128; d 1163.

RAIMOND de Poitiers co-ruler **Apr 1136-29 Jun 1149** died in battle, first husband of Constance, b 1099.

REYNAUD de Châtillon co-ruler **1153-late 1162,** second husband of Constance; personally executed by Saladin 4 Jul 1187.

BOHEMOND III co-ruler **Jun 1149-late 1162**; sole ruler **1162-Apr 1201,** son of Constance, b 1144.

BOHEMOND IV Apr 1201-1216 deposed; was also Bohemond I of Tripoli.

RAIMOND-ROUPEN 1216-1221, grandson of Bohemond III, b *c* 1195.

BOHEMOND IV 1221-Mar 1233; was also Bohemond I of Tripoli.

BOHEMOND V Mar 1233-Jan 1252; was also Bohemond II of Tripoli.

BOHEMOND VI Jan 1252-18/19 May 1268 when Antioch was taken by the Egyptians; Bohemond and subsequent Counts of Tripoli used the title Prince of Antioch; was also Bohemond III of Tripoli.

TRIPOLI

The state of Tripoli (northern Lebanon) is dated from late 1103 although the city of Tripoli did not fall to the Crusaders until 12 Jul 1109.

The County of Tripoli

† Counts

RAIMOND I late 1103-28 Feb 1105, Count of Toulouse.

ALPHONSE-JOURDAIN Mar 1105-1108 *de facto*; **1108-Jun 1109** *de jure,* son of Raimond I, b late 1104; d 1148.

GUILLAUME-JOURDAIN 1108-Jun 1109, distant cousin of Raimond I; usurper.

BERTRAND Jul 1109-Jan/Feb 1112, illegitimate son of Raimond I; formerly Count of Toulouse, he exchanged inheritances with Alphonse-Jourdain.

PONS Jan/Feb 1112-early 1137 assassinated, son of Bertrand.

RAIMOND II early 1137-early 1152 assassinated, son of Pons, b 1115.

RAIMOND III early 1152-late 1187, son of Raimond II, b 140.

BOHEMOND I and IV **late 1187-Mar 1233,** younger son of Bohemond III of Antioch. Inheriting Tripoli from his godfather Raimond III, Bohemond united his two states except for the period of the Antiochene War of Succession.

BOHEMOND II and V **Mar 1233-Jan 1252,** son of Bohemond I.

BOHEMOND III and VI **Jan 1252-1275,** son of Bohemond II, b 1237. He continued to use the princely title of Antioch after the fall of the Principality, 18/19 May 1268.

BOHEMOND IV and VII **1275-19 Oct 1287,** son of Bohemond III, b c 1261.

SIBYLLE (Princess) **Oct 1287,** widow of Bohemond III.

The Commune of Tripoli

Nov 1287-1288 A Republic was established.

The County of Tripoli

† COUNT

LUCIE (Princess) recognised as Princess of Antioch and Countess of Tripoli **early 1288,** sister of Bohemond IV. Tripoli fell to the Moslems on 26 Apr 1289.

EDESSA

The shortest-lived of the Crusader states, Edessa lasted for half a century as an independent Frankish state in northern inland Syria.

† COUNTS

BAUDOUIN I **1100**; was also Baudouin I of Jerusalem.

BAUDOUIN II **1100-1118,** relative by marriage to Baudouin I.

JOSCELIN I **1119-Sep 1131,** cousin of Baudouin II.

JOSCELIN II **Sep 1131-Apr 1150,** son of Joscelin I, b c 1113; d a prisoner of the Moslems 1159. Having lost his capital in Dec 1144, Joscelin was captured by the Moslems in Apr 1150.

summer 1150 Joscelin's wife Beatrice sold the rights of what remained of the County to Byzantium.

JERUSALEM

The Kingdom of Jerusalem, founded 1099, was the principal Crusader state established by the French in the· Levant. The state lasted beyond the final capture of the city of Jerusalem (1244) by Moslems until the fall of Acre (1291). The Kings of Cyprus continued to be titular Kings of Jerusalem after the loss of the last outposts in the Holy Land.

† Advocate of the Holy Sepulchre

GODEFROI de Bouillon **summer 1099-1100,** b c 1061; d 1100. Leader of the First Crusade, Godefroi de Bouillon captured Jerusalem and established the Kingdom, but would not accept the title 'King' as he envisaged the foundation of an enlightened theocracy.

† Kings

BAUDOUIN I **1100-2 Apr 1118,** brother of Godefroi de Bouillon, b c 1059.

BAUDOUIN II **14 Apr 1118-21 Aug 1131,** cousin of Baudouin I.

MELISENDE (Queen) co-ruler **Aug 1131-1152** when she was deposed by her son Baudouin III; d Sep 1161.

FOULQUES co-ruler **Aug 1131-10 Nov 1143** when he was killed accidentally, husband of Queen Melisende, b 1090.

BAUDOUIN III co-ruler **Nov 1143-1152**; sole ruler **1152-10 Feb 1162,** son of Foulques and Melisende, b 1130.

AMAURY I **18 Feb 1162-11 Jul 1174,** brother of Baudouin III, b 1135. Amaury was an able ruler and general - the decline of the Kingdom after his death was due as much to the incompetence of the Crusaders as to the skill of their opponents.

BAUDOUIN IV sole ruler **15 Jul 1174-20 Nov 1183**; co-ruler **20 Nov 1183-Mar 1185,** son of Amaury I, b 1161. He was unable to rule normally owing to his leprosy.

BAUDOUIN V co-ruler **20 Nov 1183-Mar 1185**; sole ruler **Mar 1185-Aug 1186,** nephew of Baudouin IV and son of Sibylle, b summer 1177.

SIBYLLE (Queen) co-ruler **Aug 1186-1190,** mother of Baudouin V and daughter of Amaury I.

GUI de Lusignan co-ruler **Sep 1186-1190**; sole ruler **1190-Apr 1192** when he was deposed, husband of Sibylle, b 1140; d 1194. His defeat at Hattin (4 Jul 1187), followed by Saladin's capture of the city of Jerusalem, was a blow from which the Kingdom never recovered.

ISABELLE I (Queen) co-ruler **Apr 1192-summer 1205**; although she was not crowned Queen until Jan 1198, half-sister of Sibylle, b 1172. Reigned jointly with three of her four husbands.

CONRAD I de Montferrat co-ruler **5-28 Apr 1192** assassinated, second husband of Isabelle.

HENRI I de Champagne co-ruler **5 May 1192-10 Sep 1197** when he died accidentally falling from a window, third husband of Isabelle I. He was never formally installed as King.

AMAURY II co-ruler **Jan 1198-Apr 1205,** fourth husband of Isabelle I, b c 1144; he was King of Cyprus and the brother of Gui de Lusignan.

MARIE de Montferrat (Queen) sole ruler **summer 1205-3 Oct 1210**; co-ruler **3 Oct 1210-1212,** daughter of Isabelle I and Conrad I, b 1192.

JEAN I de Brienne co-ruler **3 Oct 1210-1212,** husband of Queen Marie, b 1148; d 1237.

ISABELLE II (Queen, sometimes called YOLANDE) sole ruler **1212-Nov 1225**; co-ruler **Nov 1225-1 May 1228,** daughter of Queen Marie, b 1211.

FRÉDÉRIC co-ruler **Nov 1225-May 1228,** husband of Isabelle II, b 1195; d 1250. He illegally recrowned himself King of Jerusalem on 18 Mar

1229; was also Emperor Friedrich II of the Holy Roman Empire.

CONRAD II May 1228-May 1254, son of Isabelle II, b 5 Apr 1228. The reign of this absentee monarch saw the Kingdom reduced to a tiny coastal strip following the final capture of Jerusalem by the Moslems in 1244; was also Emperor Konrad IV of the Holy Roman Empire.

CONRAD III (CONRADIN) May 1254-1268 when he was executed, son of Conrad II, b 1252; was also Emperor Konrad V of the Holy Roman Empire.

HUGUES 24 Sep 1269-4 Mar 1284, great-grandson of Isabelle I and Henri I de Champagne; was also King Hugues III of Cyprus.

CHARLES d'Anjou Rival King **1277-late 1282,** brother of St Louis, King of France, b 1226; d 1285. Assumed the title King of Jerusalem after buying the 'rights' of Marie of Antioch to Jerusalem; from 1277-82 his bailiff was in control of the Kingdom.

JEAN II May 1284-20 May 1285; was also King Jean I of Cyprus.

HENRI II 15 Aug 1286-18 May 1291 when Acre, the last remnant of the Kingdom, fell; was also King Henri II of Cyprus.

Cuba

Spanish from 1492 until 1762, British from 1762 to 1763, Spanish again from 1763 to 1898, Cuba was ceded to the United States of America on 10 Dec 1898 after the Spanish American war. The island became independent in 1902 but returned to American rule from 1906 to 1909. A Communist regime was gradually established after the 1959 revolution.

Presidents

TOMÁS ESTRADA PALMA 20 May 1902-28 Sep 1906, b 9 Jul 1835; d 14 Nov 1908. A superb administrator who fought against Spanish rule, he was faced with a revolution in 1906 which brought American intervention.

29 Sep 1906-Jan 1909 United States administration.

Gen **JOSÉ MIGUEL GÓMEZ 28 Jan 1909-May 1913,** b 1858; d 13 Jun 1921.

Gen **MARIO GARCIÁ MENOCAL 20 May 1913-May 1921,** b 1866; d 7 Sep 1941.

Dr **ALFREDO ZAYAS y ALFONSO 20 May 1921-May 1925,** b 1861; d 11 Apr 1934.

Gen **GERARDO MACHADO y MORALES 25 May 1925-12 Aug 1933** fled, b 29 Sep 1871; d 29 Mar 1939. A hero of the Cuban War of Independence, he became an unpopular dictatorial ruler.

Gen **ALBERTO HERRERA** *c* 10 a.m. - *c* 12.30 a.m. **12 Aug 1933.** The second shortest Presidential term on record, Gen Herrera was

sworn in as Head of State but replaced before he could enjoy his office.

CARLOS MANUEL de CÉSPEDES y QUESADA 12 Aug-5 Sep 1933, b 1871; d 1939.

5-10 Sep 1933 Military junta.

Dr **RAMÓN GRAU SAN MARTÍN 10 Sep 1933-Jan 1934,** b 1889; d 28 Jul 1969.

CARLOS HEVIA acting President **15-17 Jan 1934,** b 1900.

Col **CARLOS MENDIETA 17 Jan 1934-Dec 1935,** b 1873; d 27 Sep 1960.

Dr **JOSÉ BARNET y VINAGERAS 13 Dec 1935-May 1936,** b 1864; d 1945.

Dr **MIGUEL MARIANO GÓMEZ y ARIAS 20 May-Dec 1936** when he was impeached, son of Gen José Miguel Gómez, b 1890; d 26 Oct 1950.

Dr **FEDERICO LAREDO BRU 24 Dec 1936-Oct 1940,** b 1875; d 1946.

Col **FULGENCIO BATISTA y ZALDÍVAR 10 Oct 1940-Oct 1944.**

Dr **RAMÓN GRAU SAN MARTÍN 10 Oct 1944-Oct 1948.**

Dr **CARLOS PRÍO SOCARRÁS 10 Oct 1948-10 Mar 1952** deposed in coup; b 1904; d (committed suicide) 5 Apr 1977.

Gen **FULGENCIO BATISTA y ZALDÍVAR 11 Mar 1952-1 Jan 1959** deposed in coup, b 16 Jan 1901; d 6 Aug 1973. His first term saw efficient government; his second term was an oppressive and most corrupt dictatorship bringing the discontent that allowed Castro's takeover.

Maj-Gen **EULALIO CANTILLO** Head of junta **1 Jan 1959.**

Judge **CARLOS PIEDRA** acting President **1-2 Jan 1959.**

Dr **MANUEL URRUTIA LLEO** acting President **2 Jan-17 Jul 1959,** b 8 Dec 1901.

OSVALDO DORTICOS TORRADO 17 Jul 1959-Dec 1976, b 17 Apr 1919.

Dr **FIDEL CASTRO RUZ since 3 Dec 1976,** b 13 Aug 1926.

Prime Ministers
(Chairman of Council of Ministers)

Dr **JOSÉ MIRO CARDONA 4 Jan-13 Feb 1959,** b 1901; d 10 Aug 1974.

Dr **FIDEL CASTRO RUZ since 16 Feb 1959.**

First Secretary of the Communist Party of Cuba

Dr **FIDEL CASTRO RUZ since 3 Oct 1965.**

Cyprus

Part of the Roman and then the Byzantine Empires, Cyprus was taken by King Richard I of England in 1191, ceded to the Templars and then to Gui de Lusignan, ex-King of Jerusalem. The

Kingdom of Cyprus lasted from 1192 to 1489, Venetian rule from 1489 to 1571, Turkish rule from 1571 to 1878 *de facto*. British rule began *de facto* in 1878 when Britain occupied the island with Turkish consent but Cyprus did not become a colony until 1914. Independence as a Republic was achieved on 16 Aug 1960.

THE KINGDOM OF CYPRUS

† Kings

HOUSE OF LUSIGNAN

GUI de Lusignan **1192-1194**; was also Gui de Lusignan, King of Jerusalem.

AMAURY (or AMALRIC) **1194-Apr 1205,** brother of Gui; was also Amaury II of Jerusalem.

HUGUES I 1205-1218, son of Amaury.

HENRI I ('The Fat') **1218-1253,** son of Hugues I. In this reign Genoa was granted trading privileges that led to Cyprus' stormy relations with the Italian Republics.

HUGUES II 1253-1267, son of Henri I.

HOUSE OF LUSIGNAN-ANTIOCH

HUGUES III 1267-4 Mar 1284, grandson of Henri I; was also Hugues, King of Jerusalem.

JEAN I Mar 1284-20 May 1285, son of Hugues III; was also Jean II of Jerusalem.

HENRI II May **1285-1324,** brother of Jean I, b 1271. King of Jerusalem until 1291, Henri did little to save the mainland Kingdom and mismanaged affairs in Cyprus - which became a battleground for the rivalries of Genoa and Venice. A bitter dispute with his brother Amaury led to the King's temporary exile.

HUGUES IV 1324-1359, nephew of Henri II.

PIERRE I 1359-Jan 1369 assassinated, son of Hugues IV.

PIERRE II Jan 1369-1382, son of Pierre I, b 1355.

JACQUES I 1382-1398, uncle of Pierre I.

JANUS 1398-1432, son of Jacques I, b 1374. Fat King Janus was taken captive by the Mamelukes who raided Cyprus in 1426.

JEAN II 1432-1458, son of Janus.

CHARLOTTE (Queen) **1458-1460** deposed, daughter of Jean II; d after 1485.

JACQUES II 1460-1473, illegitimate son of Jean II. An Archbishop he seized the throne and abandoned the cloth to continue the dynasty.

JACQUES III 1473-1474, son of Jacques II, b 1472.

CATHERINE (Cornaro) **1474-1489** when forced to abdicate, widow of Jacques II; d after 1500. A Venetian, she was 'adopted' by the Republic before her marriage and ceded the island to Venice after a nominal reign.

1489-1960 Rule by various foreign powers.

THE REPUBLIC OF CYPRUS

Presidents

Archbishop **MAKARIOS III 16 Aug 1960-15 Jul 1974** deposed in coup.

NICOS SAMPSON acting President **15-23 Jul 1974,** b 1935.

GLAFKOS KLERIDES acting President **23 Jul-5 Dec 1974,** b 1919.

Archbishop **MAKARIOS III 5 Dec 1974-13 Aug 1977,** b (Michael Christedoulos Mouskos) 13 Aug 1913; d in office. Head of the Greek Orthodox Church in Cyprus he was originally a strong supporter of Enosis (union with Greece) and was suspected of links with the Eoka terrorist campaign against British rule.

SPYROS KYPRIANOU acting President **13-31 Aug 1977**; President **since 31 Aug 1977,** b 28 Oct 1932.

THE TURKISH FEDERATED STATE OF CYPRUS

Following the Turkish invasion of northern Cyprus in 1974 a Turkish 'state' totally unrecognised by the international community, was formed.

President

RAUF DENKTASH since 13 Feb 1975, b 27 Jan 1924.

Czechoslovakia

At the close of World War I the Austrian Kingdom of Bohemia and Margraviate of Moravia were merged with the Slovak lands of the Hungarian Crown to form the new nation of Czechoslovakia whose independence was proclaimed on 28 Oct 1918. The Munich agreement of Sep 1938 ceded border areas to Germany, Poland and Hungary and in Mar 1939 the whole country was occupied by German forces. Bohemia and Moravia became a German 'Protectorate'; Slovakia an 'independent' puppet state of Germany, and a Government in exile was established in 1940. The restored independent Republic of Czechoslovakia was victim to a Communist coup in Feb 1948. The country is now styled the Federal Socialist Republic of Czechoslovakia.

THE REPUBLIC OF CZECHOSLOVAKIA

Presidents

TOMÁS GARRIGUE MASARYK acting President **Nov 1918-May 1920**; President **26 May 1920-Dec**

Edvard Benes, co-founder and second President of Czechoslovakia for whose freedom he fought Imperial Austria, Nazi Germany and the Communists (Radio Times Hulton Picture Library)

1935, b 7 Mar 1850; d 14 Sep 1937. The 'Father of Czechoslovakia' Masaryk worked for the Slavic nationalist cause for forty years before he was rewarded by the creation of Czechoslovakia.

EDVARD BENES 18 Dec 1935-Oct 1938, b 28 May 1884; d 3 Sep 1948. Of peasant origin he was, with Masaryk, the co-founder of the state whose dismemberment by the Munich pact he was unable to prevent. Leader of the Government in exile during World War II he returned to be President of his restored country but was powerless against the Soviet subversion that culminated in the Communist coup of Feb 1948.

Gen **JAN SIROVY** acting President **4 Oct-20 Nov 1938.**

Dr **EMIL HACHA 20 Nov 1938-15 Mar 1939** when German forces invaded, b 1872; d 30 Jun 1945 under arrest as a war criminal.

Prime Ministers

Dr **KAREL KRAMÁR Nov 1918-Jul 1919,** b 1860; d 1937.

VLASTIMIL TUSAR 8 Jul 1919-Sep 1920, b 1880; d 1924.

Dr **JAN CERNY 15 Sep 1920-Sep 1921,** b 1874; d 1959.

EDVARD BENES 26 Sep 1921-Oct 1922; see President Benes.

Dr **ANTONÍN SVELHA 7 Oct 1922-Mar 1926,** b 1873; d 1933.

Dr **JAN CERNY 19 Mar-Oct 1926.**

Dr **ANTONÍN SVELHA 12 Oct 1926-Oct 1927.**

Msgr **JAN SRÁMEK 13 Oct 1927-Feb 1929,** b 1870; d 1956.

FRANTISEK UDRZAL 1 Feb 1929-Oct 1932, b 1866; d 1938.

MILAN J. MALYPETR 29 Oct 1932-Nov 1935, b 1873; d 1947.

Dr **MILAN HODZA 8 Nov 1935-Sep 1938,** b 1878; d 27 Jun 1944. He resigned when his country was dismembered by the Munich agreement.

Gen **JAN SIROVY 22 Sep-20 Nov 1938**; see acting President Sirovy.

RUDOLF BERAN 20 Nov 1938-15 Mar 1939 when German forces invaded, b 1887; d 1957.

THE REPUBLIC OF SLOVAKIA

A puppet state of Nazi Germany, Slovakia was established on 14 Mar 1939 and lasted until May 1945.

President

Dr **JOSEF TISO 16 Mar 1939-May 1945,** b 1887; d 16 Apr 1947 when he was executed as a war criminal.

Prime Ministers

Dr **JOSEF TISO 14 Mar-28 Oct 1939.**

Dr **BELA TUKA 28 Oct 1939-Sep 1944**; b 1880; d 20 Aug 1946 when he was executed as a war criminal.

STEFAN TISO 5 Sep 1944-May 1945, nephew of President Tiso.

THE PROTECTORATE OF BOHEMIA AND MORAVIA

President

Dr **EMIL HACHA 17 Mar 1939-May 1945**; see President Hacha of Czechoslovakia.

THE CZECHOSLOVAK NATIONAL LIBERATION COMMITTEE

Chairman
(later President)

EDVARD BENES Nov 1939-Dec 1942 when he became recognised as President in exile; see President Benes.

THE PROVISIONAL CZECHOSLOVAK GOVERNMENT IN EXILE

President

EDVARD BENES President **from 23 Jul 1940**; President with international recognition **18 Dec 1942-Feb 1945** when he returned to Czechoslovakia.

Prime Minister

Msgr **JAN SRAMEK** **Dec 1942-Feb 1945** when he returned to Czechoslovakia.

THE REPUBLIC OF CZECHOSLOVAKIA

President

EDVARD BENES President in exile **from Dec** 1942; in Czechoslovakia **Feb 1945-7 Jun 1948.**

Prime Ministers

Msgr **JAN SRAMEK** PM **from 1942**; in Czechoslovakia **Feb-Apr 1945.**
ZDENEK FIERLINGER **7 Apr 1945-May 1946,** b 11 Jul 1891; d 2 May 1976.
KLEMENS GOTTWALD **May 1946-Jun 1948.**

THE SOCIALIST REPUBLIC OF CZECHOSLOVAKIA

(since 1 Jan 1969 the Federal Socialist Republic of Czechoslovakia)

Presidents

EDVARD BENES until **7 Jun 1948.**
KLEMENS GOTTWALD **7 Jun 1948-14 Mar 1953,** b 23 Nov 1896; d in office. A hard line Stalinist, he carried out the Communist coup of Feb 1948 destroying Parliamentary democracy and individual freedoms.
ANTONÍN ZAPOTOCKY **21 Mar 1953-13 Nov 1957,** b 19 Dec 1884; d in office.
ANTONÍN NOVOTNY **19 Nov 1957-22 Mar 1968,** b 10 Dec 1904; d 28 Jan 1975. He was replaced during Alexander Dubcek's attempts to liberalise the regime - a movement which ended with the Soviet invasion (Aug 1968).
Gen **LUDVIK SVOBODA** **30 Mar 1968-May 1975,** b 25 Nov 1895.
Dr **GUSTÁV HUSÁK** **since 29 May 1975,** b 13 Jan 1913.

Prime Ministers

KLEMENS GOTTWALD PM **from May 1946; Feb-Jun 1948;** see President Gottwald.
ANTONÍN ZAPOTOCKY **7 Jun 1948-Mar 1953;** see President Zapotocky.
VILIAM SIROKY **21 Mar 1953-Sep 1963,** b 31 May 1902; d 6 Oct 1971.
JOSEF LENÁRT **22 Sep 1963-Apr 1968,** b 3 Apr 1923.
OLDRICH CERNIK **4 Apr 1968-Jan 1970,** b 27 Oct 1921.
LUBOMIR STROUGAL **since 28 Jan 1970,** b 9 Oct 1924.

General Secretaries of the Czechoslovak Communist Party

KLEMENS GOTTWALD **Feb 1948-14 Mar 1953.**
ANTONÍN NOVOTNY **21 Mar 1953-Jan 1968.**
ALEXANDER DUBCEK **5 Jan 1968-17 Apr 1969,** b 27 Nov 1921.
Dr **GUSTÁV HUSÁK** **since 17 Apr 1969.**

Bohemia

A Principality from the 9th century and a Kingdom from the 12th, Bohemia became one of the leading states of medieval Europe. The Habsburgs ruled the country from 1526 slowly absorbing it into the Austrian Empire. After World War I and the collapse of the Habsburg monarchy Bohemia became part of the new country of Czechoslovakia.

† Princes of the Moravians

Moravia had a brief existence as an independent state in the 9th century and from the 11th century formed part of Bohemia.

MOJMÍR I **c815-?**
ROSTISLAV **c845-?** During Rostislav's reign Christianity was introduced by Frankish priests and the Byzantine Saints Methodius and Constantine.
SVATOPLUK **before c870.**
MOJMÍR II **c892-905 or 908.** Mojmír ceased to reign when the Moravians were conquered by the Hungarians.

BOHEMIA

† Princes

VÁCLAV (in English Wenceslas) **921-929** murdered by his brother Boleslav I; canonised and known as 'Good King Wenceslas'.
BOLESLAV I **929-967,** brother of Václav.
BOLESLAV II **967-999,** son of Boleslav I.
BOLESLAV III **999-1003** deposed by Vladivoj; son of Boleslav II; d c 1035.
VLADIVOJ **1003-1034.**
BRETISLAV I **1034-1055,** grandson of Boleslav II. He united Moravia and Bohemia.
SPITHNJEV **1055-1061,** son of Bretislav I.
VRATISLAV II **1061-1085** when he became King.

† King

VRATISLAV I Prince from 1061; King **1085-1092,** brother of Spithnjev; named King *ad personam* by the Emperor.

† Princes

BRETISLAV II 1092-1100.
BORIVOJ II 1100-1107.
SVARTOPLUK 1107-1109.
VLADISLAV I (in English Ladislas) 1109-1114 when he became Elector.

† Electors

VLADISLAV I Prince from 1109; Elector 1114-1125. Made Elector by the Emperor despite the anarchy reigning in Bohemia.
SOBJISLAV 1125-1140.
VLADISLAV II 1140-1158 when he became King.

† King

VLADISLAV I (II as Elector) Elector from 1140; King 1158-1173; named King *ad personam* by the Emperor Frederick Barbarossa against whom he had fought in Italy.
1173-1198 A period of anarchy during which no single ruler can be recognised.

† Kings

HOUSE OF PREMYSL
The House of Premysl had provided virtually all of the Princes and Electors of Bohemia.

PREMYSL OTAKAR 1198-15 Dec 1230, b *c* 1155. Gained from the Emperor the royal title for himself and his descendants.
VÁCLAV I Dec 1230-1253, son of Premysl Otakar I, b 1205.
PREMYSL OTAKAR II 1253-26 Aug 1278, son of Václav I, b 1230. Winning Austria through marriage and other lands through conquest, Premysl Otakar built a short-lived empire stretching from Silesia to the Adriatic. Rivalry with Rudolph of Habsburg for Austria led to war in which the Bohemian was killed.
VÁCLAV II Aug 1278-1305, only son of Premysl Otakar II, b 1271; was also King of Poland from 1296.
VÁCLAV III 1305-1306 assassinated, son of Václav II, b 1289; was also King of Poland from 1305.
1306-1310 Interregnum.

HOUSE OF LUXEMBOURG
JÁN (John the Blind) 1310-26 Aug 1346 killed at the Battle of Crécy, son-in-law of Václav II, b 10 Aug 1296. Elected King by the nobility, this chivalrous knight became the hero of legend but was disliked by the people for his heavy taxes to pay for his pro-French wars.
KAREL Aug 1346-29 Nov 1378, son of Ján, b 14 May 1316. From 1347 as Emperor he made Bohemia one of Europe's leading states and Prague, where he founded the university and the palace, a great city.

VÁCLAV IV Nov 1378-16 Aug 1419, son of Karel, b 26 Feb 1361.
SIGISMUND Aug 1419-1437, son of Karel; was also Sigismund of Hungary.

HOUSE OF HABSBURG
ALBREKT 1437-1439; was also Albert of Hungary.
1439-1443 Interregnum.
VLADISLAV II 1443-Nov 1457; was also Ladislaus of Austria.
Nov 1457-Mar 1458 Interregnum.

HOUSE OF PODEBRADY
JIRÍ Z PODEBRAD Mar 1458-22 Mar 1471, b 23 Apr 1420. Jirí (George) was a noble and the leader of the conservative Protestant Hussites. In an attempt to settle the vexed religious questions, Jirí asked Rome to sanction the Compacts (a religious compromise). The Pope refused and in the Catholic revolt that followed Jirí's excommunication Mátyás of Hungary made himself King of Bohemia in Brno.

HOUSE OF HUNYADI
MATEJ 3 May 1469-May 1471; was also Mátyás I of Hungary.

HOUSE OF JAGELLION
VLADISLAV III (sometimes referred to as II.) May 1471-13 Mar 1516; was also Ulászló II of Hungary.
LUDVIK Mar 1516-29 Aug 1526; was also Lajos II of Hungary.
Aug-Oct 1526 Interregnum.

HOUSE OF HABSBURG
Until the time of Ferdinand II the reigns of the Austrian rulers as Kings of Bohemia did not necessarily coincide. The Emperor's heir could become King of Bohemia during the Emperor's lifetime.

FERDINAND I 23 Oct 1526-25 Jul 1564; was also Ferdinand I of Austria.
MAXIMILIAN Jul 1564-12 Oct 1576; was also Maximilian II of Austria.
RUDOLF Oct 1576-May 1611; was also Rudolf II of Austria.
MATEJ II May 1611-1617; was also Matthias of Austria.
FERDINAND II 1617-Aug 1619 deposed; was also Ferdinand II of Austria.

HOUSE OF THE PALATINATE
FREDERIK 26 Aug 1619-Nov 1620 when he fled, elector of the Palatinate of the Rhine, b 26 Aug 1596; d 29 Nov 1632. The Protestant Bohemians rebelled against Austria and elected this Rhenish prince King. Crowned in Nov 1619 he reigned briefly (The Winter King) being finally deserted by his allies and defeated at the Battle of the White Mountain (Nov 1620).

HOUSE OF HABSBURG
FERDINAND II Nov 1620-15 Feb 1637; was also Ferdinand II of Austria.
(The ruler of Austria reigned as King of Bohemia until 28 Oct 1918 when the Austro-Hungarian Empire collapsed.)

Dahomey *see* Benin

Dambadeniya, Kingdom of *see* Sri Lanka

Danzig

Danzig was established as a Free City under the League of Nations in Jun 1919, and was incorporated into Germany on 1 Sep 1939. The city is now the Polish port Gdansk.

Presidents of the Senate

Dr **HEINRICH SAHM Jun 1919-Jan 1931.**
Dr **E. ZIEHM 9 Jan 1931-Jun 1933.**
Dr **HERMAN RAUSCHNING 20 Jun 1933-Nov 1934.**
Dr **ARTHUR CARL GREISER 28 Nov 1934-Aug 1939**; d 21 Jul 1946 when executed as a war criminal. The infamous Nazi Gauleiter of Poland.
Dr **ALBERT FORSTER 24 Aug-1 Sep 1939**; d 20 Aug 1948 when executed as a war criminal.

Deheubarth *see* Wales, United Kingdom

Deira *see* Anglo-Saxon Kingdoms, United Kingdom

Delhi, Sultanate of *see* India

Denmark

Europe's oldest Kingdom, Denmark achieved unity *c*960 and has maintained its independence almost continuously.

† Kings

EARLY KINGS
GUDFRED ?-810. King of the Danes.
HEMMING ?-812. King of the Danes.
HARTHAKNUD c824-855. King of the Danes.

HOUSE OF GORM
GORM c883-c940. Danish King in Jutland.
HARALD II (called Blatånd meaning 'bluetooth') **c940-c986,** son of Gorm. Harald united the Danes into one Kingdom and briefly conquered Norway.
SVEN I c986-1014, son of Gorm or of Harald; was also Swegn, King of England.
HARALD III 1014-c1018, son of Sven I.
KNUD II c1018-12 Nov 1035; was also Cnut, King of England.
KNUD III (or HARTHAKNUD II) **Nov 1035-8 Jun 1042**; was also Harthacnut, King of England.

HOUSE OF NORWAY
MAGNUS summer 1042-1047; was also Magnus I of Norway.

HOUSE OF ESTRITH
SVEN II Estrithsson **1047-28 Apr 1074,** nephew of Knud II, b *c*1020. Sven reunited Denmark and resisted an attempted Norwegian invasion.
HARALD IV c1074-1080, son of Sven II.
KNUD IV (St Canute) **1080-Jul 1086,** son of Sven II, b *c*1043. A generous patron of the clergy, Knud was murdered in Odense Cathedral by nobles who resented his imposition of tithes. Canonised, he became the patron saint of Denmark.
OLAF I Jul 1086-1095, son of Sven II.
ERIK I (called Ejegod meaning 'evergood') **1095-1103,** son of Sven II, b *c*1056.
ERIK II (called Emune meaning 'memorable') **1103-1104,** son (possibly illegitimate) of Erik I.
NIELS 1104-1134, son of Sven II, b 1063. Fought a long civil war with Erik II for the throne and was eventually killed in battle.
ERIK II (called Emune meaning 'memorable') **1134-1137.**
ERIK III 1137-1147, possibly the son of Erik II. Became a monk and left a country divided by civil war.
SVEN III 1147-1157 killed by Valdemar I; illegitimate son of Erik III.
KNUD V 1147-1157 killed by Sven III with whom he fought a civil war for the throne, grandson of Niels.
VALDEMAR I (the Great) sole ruler **1157-1170**; co-ruler **1170-12 May 1182,** grandson of Erik I, b 14 Jan 1131. Allied to Frederick Barbarossa, Valdemar defeated the Wends and gained for Denmark her first Baltic possessions.
KNUD VI co-ruler **1170-May 1182**; sole ruler **1182-12 Nov 1202,** son of Valdemar I, b 1163.
VALDEMAR II Nov 1202-28 Mar 1241, brother of Knud VI, b 1170. Valdemar greatly extended the Danish Baltic empire from the Elbe to Estonia but lost most of it to secure his release after falling prisoner in Germany.
VALDEMAR III co-ruler **?-1231,** son of, and co-ruler with, Valdemar II.
ERIK IV co-ruler **1232-Mar 1241**; sole ruler **1241-1250** killed by his brother Abel; son of Valdemar III, b 1216.

Christian IV who was slightly larger than life and spent as much effort and money on enjoyment as in governing (Radio Times Hulton Picture Library)

ABEL   1250-1252 killed in battle, brother of Erik IV whom he deposed; b c 1218.
CHRISTOPHER I   1252-1259 deposed, son of Valdemar III, b 1219.
ERIK V   1259-22 Nov 1286 murdered by rebellious nobles, son of Christopher I, b c 1249.
ERIK VI   Nov 1286-13 Nov 1319, son of Erik V, b 1274. His attempts to regain the empire of Valdemar II left Denmark bankrupt and in a state of civil war.
1319-1320 Interregnum. Civil war.
CHRISTOPHER II   1320-1326 deposed, son of Erik V, b 1276; d 1333. Christopher gained the crown by accepting the supremacy of the nobles. When he revoked the agreement a twenty year civil war between King and nobility resulted.
1326-1330 Interregnum. Rule by Duke Valdemar of Slesvig who did not assume the kingship.
CHRISTOPHER II   1330-1332 deposed.
1332-1340 Interregnum. Anarchy and civil war.
VALDEMAR IV Atterdag **1340-24 Oct 1375,** son of Christopher II, b 1320. An able aggressive ruler who ended the civil wars, broke the power of the avaricious barons, reformed the army and the shaky finances of the Kingdom and, taking advantage of the weakness of Sweden, made Denmark the leading Scandinavian state.

OLAF II   1375-1387, son of Valdemar's IV daughter Margrethe I, b 1370; was also Olav IV of Norway.
MARGRETHE I (Queen) **1387-28 Oct 1412,** mother of Olaf II and daughter of Valdemar IV, b 1352. Margrethe ruled with great skill as Regent, Queen sovereign and co-monarch in all three Scandinavian states. Her forceful, despotic manner enabled her to impose her authority on Norway and Denmark; her strength allowed her to overthrow Albrecht of Sweden when called upon by rebellious nobles. Her ambition to unite the Nordic countries was frustrated partly by existing nationalism and partly by her own pro-Danish sympathies, but her efforts united Norway and Denmark for 400 years and brought temporary union with Sweden by the Kalmar Agreement (Jun 1397) - the union was not legally binding and the existing document is thought to be a rejected proposal.

HOUSE OF POMERANIA
ERIK VII co-ruler **1397-Oct 1412;** sole ruler **1412-1438** deposed, great-nephew of Margrethe, b c 1381; d c Jun 1459.
1438-1440 Interregnum.

HOUSE OF BAVARIA
CHRISTOPHER III   1440-5 Jan 1448, nephew of Erik VII, b 26 Feb 1418.

HOUSE OF OLDENBURG
CHRISTIAN I   1448-21 May 1481, son of Count Dietrich of Oldenburg, b 1426. Elected King of Denmark, Christian I was a brave, rather glamorous figure gifted with the enquiring mind of the Renaissance and the manners of chivalry. He gained Slesvig and Holstein for Denmark, and with them endless international problems.
HANS   May 1481-20 Feb 1513, elder son of Christian I, b 5 Jun 1455.
CHRISTIAN II   Feb 1513-1523 deposed, son of Hans, b 1 Jul 1481; d 25 Jan 1559 (imprisoned).
FREDERIK I   1523-10 Apr 1533, younger son of Christian I, b 7 Oct 1471.
CHRISTIAN III   Apr 1533-1 Jan 1559, elder son of Frederik I, b 12 Aug 1503. Christian, excluded from the succession because of his Protestant zeal, had to fight his younger brother Hans for the throne. Firmly established, he founded the state Lutheran Church (1536) and arrested the Catholic bishops who had all favoured his brother.
FREDERIK II   Jan 1559-4 Apr 1588, son of Christian III, b 1 Jul 1534.
CHRISTIAN IV   Apr 1588-28 Feb 1648, son of Frederik II, b 12 Apr 1577.
FREDERIK III   Apr 1648-9 Feb 1670, son of Christian IV, b 18 Mar 1609.
CHRISTIAN V   Feb 1670-25 Aug 1699 died in a hunting accident, son of Frederik III, b 15 Apr 1646.
FREDERIK IV.   Aug 1699-12 Oct 1730, son of Christian V, b 11 Oct 1671.

CHRISTIAN VI Oct 1730-6 Aug 1746, son of Frederik IV, b 30 Nov 1699.

FREDERIK V Aug 1746-14 Jan 1766, son of Christian VI, b 31 Mar 1723.

CHRISTIAN VII Jan 1766-13 Mar 1808, elder son of Frederik V, b 29 Jan 1749. Unpleasantly and alarmingly insane, Christian VII was unfit to rule, power remaining mostly in the hands of others - at first the brilliant, unscrupulous minister Struensee, who became the Queen's lover and was eventually executed, then the Crown Prince.

FREDERIK VI Mar 1808-3 Dec 1839, son of Christian VII, b 28 Jan 1768. His ill-judged alliance with Napoleon lost Denmark most of her possessions, including Norway.

CHRISTIAN VIII Dec 1839-20 Jan 1848, grandson of Frederik V, b 18 Sep 1786.

FREDERIK VII Jan 1848-15 Nov 1863, son of Christian VIII, b 6 Oct 1808. Although he renounced the autocracy of his ancestors, Frederik VII retained enough power to take two decisions that were to prove disastrous to his heirs: he rashly rejected a plan to divide Slesvig with Prussia and more unwisely approved a new constitution which provocatively included Slesvig and Holstein in Denmark. Dying two days later he left the resulting war, in which Denmark lost the Duchies to Prussia and Austria, for his successor.

HOUSE OF OLDENBURG
(Schleswig-Holstein-Sonderburg-Glücksburg Branch)

CHRISTIAN IX Nov 1863-29 Jan 1906, great-grandson of Frederik V, b 8 Apr 1818.

FREDERIK VIII Jan 1906-14 May 1912, eldest son of Christian IX, b 3 Jun 1843.

CHRISTIAN X May 1912-20 Apr 1947, eldest son of Frederik VIII, b 26 Sep 1870. Christian X's great dignity and courage were a constant encouragement to the Danish people during the Nazi occupation, but the stress and his imprisonment broke the King's health.

FREDERIK IX Apr 1947-14 Jan 1972, elder son of Christian X, b 11 Mar 1899.

MARGRETHE II (Queen) since 14 Jan 1972, eldest daughter of Frederik IX, b 16 Apr 1940.

Prime Ministers

CARL THEODOR ZAHLE 21 Jun 1913-Mar 1920, b 1866; d 1946.

OTTO LIEBE 30 Mar-4 Apr 1920, b 1860; d 1929.

MICHAEL PETERSEN FRIIS 5 Apr-4 May 1920, b 1857; d 1944.

NIELS NEERGAARD 5 May 1920-Apr 1924, b 1854; d 1936.

THORVALD STAUNING 23 Apr 1924-Dec 1926, b 26 Oct 1873; d 3 May 1942.

THOMAS MADSEN-MYGDAL 10 Dec 1926-Apr 1929, b 1876; d 1943.

THORVALD STAUNING 30 Apr 1929-3 May 1942.

VILHELM BUHL 4 May-Nov 1942, b 16 Oct 1881; d 18 Dec 1954.

ERIK SCAVENIUS 9 Nov 1942-28 Aug 1943 when the occupying Germans suspended the civilian government after Hr Scavenius refused to implement martial law when Danish patriots committed acts of sabotage against the Germans.

Aug 1943-May 1945 No Government.

VILHELM BUHL 5 May-Oct 1945.

KNUD KRISTENSEN 31 Oct 1945-Nov 1947, b 26 Oct 1880; d 29 Sep 1962.

HANS CHRISTIAN HEDTOFT HANSEN 13 Nov 1947-Oct 1950.

ERIK ERIKSEN 26 Oct 1950-Apr 1953; acting PM 25 Apr-3 May 1953; PM 3 May-Sep 1953, b 1902; d 1972.

HANS CHRISTIAN HEDTOFT HANSEN 27 Sep 1953-29 Jan 1955, b 1903; d in office.

HANS CHRISTIAN SVANE HANSEN 1 Feb 1955-19 Feb 1960, b 8 Nov 1906; d in office.

VIGGO KAMPMANN acting PM 19-21 Feb 1960; PM 21 Feb 1960-Sep 1962, b 1910; d 1976.

JENS OTTO KRAG 3 Sep 1962-Feb 1968, b 15 Sep 1914; d 22 Jun 1978.

HILMAR TORMOD INGOLF BAUNSGAARD 1 Feb 1968-Oct 1971, b 26 Feb 1920.

JENS OTTO KRAG 6 Oct 1971-Oct 1972.

ANKER JØRGENSEN 5 Oct 1972-Dec 1973.

POUL HARTLING 17 Dec 1973-Jan 1975; acting PM 25 Jan-13 Feb 1975, b 14 Aug 1914.

ANKER JØRGENSEN since 13 Feb 1975, b 13 Jul 1922.

Djibouti

The former French Somaliland, later known as the Territory of the Afars and the Issas, Djibouti became an independent Republic on 27 Jun 1977 having been French since 1884.

President

HASSAN GOULED APTIDON since 27 Jun 1977.

Prime Ministers

HASSAN GOULED APTIDON 27 Jun-12 Jul 1977.

AHMED DINI AHMED 12 Jul-Dec 1977.

HASSAN GOULED APTIDON acting PM Dec 1977-Feb 1978.

ABDALLAH MOHAMED KAMIL since 5 Feb 1978.

The Dominican Republic

Spanish from 1492 to 1795, French from 1795 to 1801, part of Haiti from 1801 to 1808, Spanish again from 1808 to 1821 and then part of Haiti again from 1821 to 1844, the Dominican Republic was not formed as an independent state until Apr 1844. From 1861 to 1865 the country was restored to Spanish rule and from 1916 to 1924 was under American rule.

Presidents

PEDRO SANTANA Apr 1844-1848, b 1801; d 1864.
MANUEL JIMÉNEZ 1848-1849.
BUENAVENTURA BAEZ 1849-Mar 1853, b 1810; d 1884. One of the leaders of the revolt against Haiti - at one time he advocated the annexation of his country by the United States.
PEDRO SANTANA Mar 1853-Jun 1856.
MANUEL de REGLA-MOTTA Jun-Oct 1856.
BUENAVENTURA BAEZ Oct 1856-Jun 1858 deposed.
JOSÉ DESIDERIO VALVERDE Jun 1858-Feb 1859.
PEDRO SANTANA Feb 1859-18 Mar 1861 when the Republic returned to Spanish rule.
Mar 1861-5 May 1865 Spanish rule restored.
PEDRO PIMENTEL acting President May-Nov 1865.
JOSÉ MARIA CABRAL Nov 1865.
BUENAVENTURA BAEZ Nov 1865-Oct 1866.
JOSÉ MARIA CABRAL Oct 1866-May 1868.
BUENAVENTURA BAEZ May 1868-Jan 1874 deposed in coup.
Gen GANIER d'ABIN acting President Jan 1874.
IGNACIO MARIA GONZALEZ Jan 1874-Feb 1876.
ULISES FRANCISCO ESPAILLAT acting President Feb-Jun 1876; President Jun-Nov 1876, b 1823; d 1878.
IGNACIO MARIA GONZALEZ Nov-Dec 1876.
BUENAVENTURA BAEZ Dec 1876-Feb 1878.
Gen CAESARIO GUILLERMO Apr 1878-Dec 1879.
GREGORIO LUPÉRON Dec 1879-Sep 1880.
FERNANDO ARTURO de MERINO Sep 1880-Sep 1884, b 1833; d 1906.
Gen ULISES HEUREAUX Sep 1884-Sep 1885, b 1845; d 1899.
FRANCISCO G. BELLINI Sep 1885-Sep 1887, b 1838; d 1898.
Gen ULISES HEUREAUX Sep 1887-Aug 1899.
JUAN WENCESLAO FIGUEREO 1-31 Aug 1899.
HORACIO VASQUEZ Aug-Nov 1899.
JUAN ISIDRO JIMÉNEZ Nov 1899-May 1902.
HORACIO VASQUEZ May 1902-Apr 1903.
ALEJANDRO WOSS y GIL Apr-Nov 1903.
JUAN ISIDRO JIMÉNEZ Dec 1903-Jun 1904.

CARLOS MORALES LAUGUASCO Jun 1904-Jan 1906, b 1867; d 1914.
RAMÓN CÁCERES Jan 1906-19 Nov 1911, b 1868; d in office.
ALFREDO VICTORIA Dec 1911-Dec 1912.
Archbishop ADOLFO NOUEL Dec 1912-Apr 1913, b 1862; d 1937.
JOSÉ BORDAS VALDES Apr 1913-Apr 1914; acting President Apr-Aug 1914.
RAMÓN BAEZ Aug-Dec 1914.
JUAN ISIDRO JIMÉNEZ Dec 1914-May 1916.
FRANCISCO HENRIQUEZ y CARVAJAL President under American supervision May 1916-Oct 1922, b 1848; d 1922. As the nation was bankrupt, he was forced to give way to an American administration which serviced the Republic's debts.
JUAN BAUTISTA VICINI BURGOS Oct 1922-Jul 1924 when the American administration ended.
HORACIO VASQUEZ Jul 1924-Feb 1930.
RAFAEL ESTRELLA URENA Mar-Aug 1930.
Generalissimo RAFAEL LEONIDAS TRUJILLO MOLINA 18 Aug 1930-Jun 1938.
JACINTO B. PEYNADO Jun 1938-8 Mar 1940, b 1878; d in office.
MANUEL JESÚS TRONCOSO de la CONCHA Mar 1940-May 1942, b 1878; d 1955.
Generalissimo RAFAEL LEONIDAS TRUJILLO MOLINA May 1942-May 1952, b 24 Oct 1891; assassinated 30 May 1961. Called 'el Jefe' (the Chief), Trujillo, a vainglorious dictator who denied basic human rights and who renamed the capital city after himself, was absolute ruler from 1930 to 1961 although not President for all that time.
Gen HÉCTOR BIENVENIDO TRUJILLO MOLINA May 1952-Aug 1960, brother of Generalissimo Trujillo, b 1908.
Dr JOAQUIN BALAGUER 3 Aug 1960-Jan 1962.
Dr RAFAEL F. BONNELLY 18 Jan 1962-Feb 1963, b 1904.
Prof JUAN BOSCH 27 Feb-25 Sep 1963 deposed in coup, b 1909.
Dr EMILIO de los SANTOS Head of military junta Sep 1963.
Dr DONALD J. REID CABRAL Sep 1963-26 Apr 1965 deposed in coup, b 9 Jun 1923.
Apr-Sep 1965 Civil war was fought between two juntas.
Col PEDRO BENOIT Head of one military junta 28 Apr-8 May 1965.
Gen ANTONIO IMBERT Successor to Col Benoit 8 May-4 Sep 1965.
Col FRANCISCO CAAMAÑO Head of rival junta 4 May-4 Sep 1965.
Dr HÉCTOR GARCIA-GODOY Provisional President 4 Sep 1965-Jul 1966, b 1921; d 20 Apr 1970.
Dr JOAQUIN BALAGUER since 1 Jul 1966, b 1909.

Dubai *see* United Arab Emirates

East Anglia *see* Anglo-Saxon Kingdoms, United Kingdom

East Germany *see* German Democratic Republic

East Saxons or Essex *see* Anglo-Saxon Kingdoms, United Kingdom

Ecuador

Spanish from 1534, Ecuador (formerly Quito province of the Vice-Royalty of Peru) gained independence from Spain on 15 Jun 1822 but did form a state at that time. The territory joined Greater Colombia from which it seceded on 11 May 1830. The Republic of Ecuador was declared on 13 May 1830.

PRESIDENTS OF ECUADOR

Gen JUAN JOSÉ FLORES May 1830-Aug 1835 deposed in coup, b 19 Jul 1800; d 1 Oct 1864.
VICENTE ROCAFUERTE Aug 1835-Jan 1839, b 1783; d 1847.
Gen JUAN JOSÉ FLORES Jan 1839-Dec 1845.
VICENTE RAMÓN ROCA Dec 1845-Dec 1850, b c 1790; d in office.
DIEGO NOBOA Dec 1850-Sep 1851 deposed, b 1789; d 1870.
JOSÉ MARIA URBINA Sep 1851-Oct 1856, b 1808; d 1891.
Gen FRANCISCO ROBLES Oct 1856-Aug 1859, b 1811; d 1 Oct 1893.

PROVISIONAL GOVERNMENT IN QUITO

Head

GABRIEL GARCÍA MORENA Aug 1859-Apr 1861.

PROVISIONAL GOVERNMENT IN GUAYAQUIL

Head

Gen GUILLERMO FRANCO Aug 1859-Apr 1861.

PRESIDENTS OF ECUADOR

GABRIEL GARCÍA MORENA Apr 1861-Aug 1865.

GERÓNIMO CARRION Aug 1865-Dec 1867, b 1812; d 1873.
JAVIER ESPINOSA Jan 1868-Aug 1869, b ?1815; d 1870.
GABRIEL GARCÍA MORENA Aug 1869-14 Aug 1875, b 24 Dec 1821; d in office - assassinated. His extreme measures ended the anarchy which plagued Ecuador, but after his death the state collapsed into chaos again.
ANTONIO BORRERO Aug 1875-Jan 1877, b 1827; d 1912.
IGNACIO de VEINTEMILLA acting President Jan-May 1877; President May 1877-Feb 1884, b 1830; d 21 Jul 1908.
JOSÉ MARÍA PLÁCIDO CAAMAÑO Feb 1884-Jul 1888, b 1838; d 1901.
ANTONIO FLORES Aug 1888-Jul 1892, b 1833; d 1912.
LUIS CORDERO Aug 1892-Dec 1896.
ELOY ALFARO Jan 1897-Sep 1901.
LEONIDAS PLAZA GUTIÉRREZ Sep 1901-Aug 1905, b 1866; d 1932.
LIZARDO GARCÍA Sep 1905-Dec 1906, b 1842; d 1937.
ELOY ALFARO Jan 1907-Aug 1911, b 1846; d 28 Jan 1912 assassinated by the mob who dragged him from gaol.
EMILIO ESTRADA Aug-Dec 1911; d in office.
LEONIDAS PLAZA GUTIÉRREZ Dec 1911-Aug 1916.
ALFREDO BAQUERIZO MORENA Sep 1916-Aug 1920, b 1859; d 1951.
JOSÉ LUIS TAMAYO Sep 1920-Aug 1924.
GONZALO CÓRDOBA Sep 1924-11 Jul 1925 deposed in coup; d 1938.
1925-1926 Military junta.
ISIDRO AYORA Apr 1926-Aug 1931.
Col LUIS A. LARREA ALBA 24 Aug-15 Oct 1931 deposed in coup, b 1895.
ALFREDO BAQUERIZO MORENA 15 Oct 1931-Jul 1932.
Col LUIS A. LARREA ALBA Jul 1932 - briefly ruled during an unsuccessful coup.
ALFREDO BAQUERIZO MORENA Jul-28 Aug 1932 fled.
NAFTALIO BONIFAZ acting President Aug-Sep 1932.
JUAN de DIOS MARTÍNEZ MERA Sep 1932-Oct 1933, b 1875; d 1955.
ABELARDO MONTALVO acting President Oct 1933-Aug 1934, b 1876; d 1950.
JOSÉ MARIA VELASCO IBARRA 1 Sep 1934-21 Aug 1935 deposed in coup, b 19 Mar 1893.
ANTONIO PONS acting President Aug-Sep 1935.
FEDERICO PÁEZ Sep 1935-24 Oct 1937 deposed in coup, b 10 Nov 1897.
Gen ALBERTO ENRÍQUEZ 24 Oct 1937-Aug 1938, b 1896; d 1962.
Dr MANUEL MARIA BORRERO Aug-Sep 1938, b 1883.
AURELIO MOSQUERA NARVAEZ Sep 1938-17 Nov 1939, b 1884; d in office.
Dr CARLOS ALBERTO ARROYO del RIO acting President Nov 1939-Jan 1940.

ANDRÉS CORDOVA Jan-Aug 1940.
JULIO MORENO acting President **Aug-Sep 1940.**
Dr **CARLOS ALBERTO ARROYO del RIO 8 Sep 1940-29 May 1944** deposed in coup, b 1893; d 31 Oct 1969.
Dr **JOSÉ MARIA VELASCO IBARRA** acting President **May-Aug 1944**; President **Aug 1944-24 Aug 1947** deposed in coup.
Col **CARLOS MANCHENO** acting President **24 Aug-3 Sep 1947** deposed in coup.
MARIANO SUÁREZ VEINTIMILIA acting President **3-15 Sep 1947.**
CARLOS JULIO AROSEMENA TOLA 15 Sep 1947-31 Aug 1948, b 1894; d 1952.
GALO PLAZA LASSO 1 Sep 1948-31 Aug 1952, b 1906.
Dr **JOSÉ MARIA VELASCO IBARRA 1 Sep 1952-31 Aug 1956.**
Dr **CAMILO PONCE ENRÍQUEZ 1 Sep 1956-31 Aug 1960,** b 1912.
Dr **JOSÉ MARIA VELASCO IBARRA 1 Sep 1960-8 Nov 1961.**
Dr **CARLOS JULIO AROSEMENA MONROY 8 Nov 1961-11 Jul 1963** deposed, son of Carlos Julio Arosemena.
Cpt **RAMÓN CASTRO JIJON** (later Rear-Admiral) Head of military junta **11 Jul 1963-29 Mar 1966** deposed, b 1915.
29-31 Mar 1966 Military junta.
CLEMENTE YEROVI INDABURU acting President **31 Mar-Nov 1966,** b 1904.
Dr **OTTO AROSEMENA GÓMEZ 17 Nov 1966-Sep 1968,** b 1922.
Dr **JOSÉ MARIA VELASCO IBARRA 1 Sep 1968-15 Feb 1972** deposed in coup.
Brig-Gen **GUILLERMO RODRÍGUEZ LARA 17 Feb 1972-11 Jan 1976** deposed in coup, b 4 Nov 1923.
Vice-Admiral **ALFREDO POVEDA BURBANO** Chairman of Supreme Council of Government and acting Head of State **since 11 Jan 1976.**

Edessa *see* Crusader States

Egypt

Ancient Egypt

Originally divided into Lower Egypt (North) and Upper Egypt (South), a united country was achieved *c* 3100 BC - the dates quoted are approximate at least up to Dynasty XX, but recent research, upon which the following time scales are based, suggests that the earlier Dynasties flourished at least 400 years nearer the present day than was previously suspected. There are very considerable divergences in the king lists: the order

and spellings given below are usually those adopted by the Cambridge Ancient History with such alterations that modern findings indicate. Some alternative spellings are given: the Hellenised names favoured by Manetho, the 3rd century historian who compiled the earliest king lists dividing Egypt's rulers into dynasties, are to be found bracketed (or in the case of two terms within brackets it will be the latter double bracketed term). It used to be maintained that succession was by matrilineal descent: the throne was often obtained by marriage to the Queen-heiress (referred to as God's Wife) but this appears to have been a device adopted by outsiders seeking to validate their claim to the throne. Marriage to the Queen-heiress does not seem to have become a regular feature until Dynasty XVIII at which time unions in a degree of consanguinity were normal. A few heiresses ruled in their own right, particularly in the Ptolemaic period. Some of the later dates given reveal interregna: succession was not automatic on the death of the Pharoah and the following reign was not deemed to have begun until the solemn entombment of the previous sovereign. From Dynasty XII in Ancient Egypt it was common to have co-rulers. Owing to the complex nature of the Ptolemaic reigns in particular, the co-ruling and sole ruling periods have not always been identified.

† KINGS OR PHARAOHS OF EGYPT

PREDYNASTIC KINGS
(before c3100 BC)
TIU, King of Lower Egypt.
THESH, King of Lower Egypt.
HSEKIU, King of Lower Egypt.
RO, King of Upper Egypt.
UAZNAR, King of Lower Egypt.

DYNASTY I
(c3100-c2890 BC)
NARMER (or NARMERZA (MENES)). Traditionally the founder of Dynasty I and unifier of Egypt.
AHA. Excluded from some lists: it used to be thought Aha was another name for Narmer.
DJER (or ZER ATOTI (ATHOTHIS)).
ZA (or ZET (KENKENES)).
DEN (DEN SEMTI or UDY-MU (OUSAPHAIS)).
MERPEBA (or ENEZIB MERPEBA (MIEBIS)).
SEMERKHET NEKHT (SEMEMPSES).
QA (or KA SEN (BIENEKHES)).

DYNASTY II
(c2890-c2686 BC)
HOTEPSEKHEMUI (BOETHOS).
RENEB (or RA-NEB (KAIEKHOS)).
NENETER (or NETERI-MU (BINOTHRIS)).
PERIBSEN (OTLAS). Probably a usurper, his reign was a time of civil war.
(SENEDI (SETHENES), NEFERKERE (NEPHERKERES), NEFERKESOKARI (SESOKH-

RIS) and HUZEFA (KHENERES) are traditionally included in Dynasty II but their place is uncertain.)
KHASEKHEM (NECHEROPHES). Sometimes included in Dynasty III, Khasekhem was probably the contemporary and rival of Peribsen.
(KHASEKHEMUI. Included in some lists: Probably a second regnal name taken by Khasekhem following his final conquest of Peribsen.)

DYNASTY III
(c2686-c2613 BC)
This marks the start of the period usually referred to as the Old Kingdom.

SANAKHT (TYREIS, MESOCHRIS or SOYPHIS). Once placed in the middle of Dynasty III but now usually held to be its founder.
KA-RA. Excluded from many lists: his place is uncertain.
DJOSER (or ZOSER (TOSORTHROS)). A great builder, aided by an extraordinarily able 'Vizier' (Imhotep), Djoser's reign seems to have been one of progress and prosperity.
(The order of the next Pharaohs is uncertain though Huni is known to have been the last of Dynasty III.)
ZOSERTETI (or ZOSER-NETERKHET (TOSERTASIS)).
SEKHEMKHET.
SEZES (ACHES).
KHABA (possibly Ka-Ra ?).
NEFERKA (KERPHERES).
HUNI.

DYNASTY IV
(c2613-c2494 BC)
SNEFRU (or SNEFERU (SNEPHOURIS)). Formerly included in Dynasty III, Snefru, builder of the first pyramid, is now held to be the founder of Dynasty IV.
(SHARU (SORIS) is included at this point on some lists.)
KHUFU (SOUPHIS or CHEOPS), son of Snefru. A particularly active King, he centralised the government and reduced the excessive power of the priests. His reign began one of the most splendid eras of Ancient Egypt whose wealth can be gauged from his tomb - the Great Pyramid of Giza.
REDJEDEF (or DADEF-RE (RATOISES)). Possibly a usurper.
KHAFRE (SOUPHIS or CHABRYES), a younger son of Khufu.
MENKAURE (MENCHERES or MYKERINOS).
SHEPSESKAF (SEBERCHERES).
SEBEK-KA-RE (THAMPHTHIS).

DYNASTY V
(c2494-c2345 BC)
The order of Pharaohs in the middle of this dynasty is uncertain.

USERKAF (OUSERCHERES).
SAHURE (SEPHRES). A warrior King famed for his campaigns in Syria and Libya.
NEFERIRIKERE KAKAU (NEPHERCHERES).
NEFEREFRE SHEPSESKERE (SISIRES).
KHANEFERRE (CHERES).
NEUSERRE (RATHOURES).
MENKAUHOR (MENCHERES).
DEDKERE ISESI (TANCHERES).
UNAS (or WENIS (ONNOS)).

DYNASTY VI
(c2345-c2160 BC)
TETI (OTHOES).
(USERKERE. Not included in all lists: probably another name for Teti.)
PEPI I (PHIOS).
MERENRE (or MERENRE MEHTIMSAF I (METHESOUPHIS)), son of Pepi I.
PEPI II (PHIOPS). Coming to the throne aged 6 (c2294 BC) and living to be a centenarian, Pepi II is believed to have reigned 94 years making him the world's longest reigning monarch. His weak rule saw an increase in unrest leading to the anarchy of the First Intermediate Period.
MERENRE MEHTIMSAF II (MENTHESOUPHIS).
NETERKERE (NITOKRIS).
NEITH-AQERT (Queen) seems to have reigned in her own right towards the end of Dynasty VI.

DYNASTY VII
(from c2160)
This marks the start of the era known as the First Intermediate Period.

(Manetho believed there to be 70 Kings in this dynasty; it is probable that they were Princes ruling only a small part of Egypt each.)

DYNASTY VIII
(from c2160)
Probably a local dynasty contemporary with Dynasty VII. Manetho claimed 27 Pharoahs for this dynasty.

DYNASTY IX
(c2160-c2130 BC)
AKHTOY (or MERIEBRE EKHTAI (ACHTHOES)). Nomach (Governor) of Upper Egypt, Akhtoy declared himself King.
EKHTAI II.
(Manetho states that 29 Kings ruled in the period of Dynasties IX and X.)

DYNASTY X
(from c2130 BC)
UAZKERE.
MERIKARE.

DYNASTY XI
(c2130-c1991 BC)
This dynasty marks the beginning of the Middle Kingdom.

(MENTUHOTEP I. Established the dynasty but probably did not assume the regality himself.)
INTEF I or SEHERTOWY INTEF.
INTEF II.
MENTUHOTEP II *c2060 BC.* A successful, warlike King who reunited Egypt.
SANKHARE MENTUHOTEP III.
MENTUHOTEP IV, deposed *c*1991 BC by his 'Vizier', Amenemhet I.

DYNASTY XII
(c1991-c1786 BC)
AMENEMHET I (or SEHETEPIBRE AMONEM-HAT (AMMENEMES)) *c1991-c1961 BC* when he was assassinated.
SESOSTRIS I (or SENUSRET I (SESONKHO-SIS)) co-ruler *c1971-c1961 BC*; sole ruler *c1961-c1929 BC* ; co-ruler to *c1926 BC,* son of Amenemhet I.
AMENEMHET II (AMMENEMES) co-ruler *c1929-c1926 BC* ; sole ruler *c1926-c1894 BC,* son of Sesostris I.
SESOSTRIS II or SENUSRET II *c1894-c1878 BC.*
SESOSTRIS III (or KHAKAURE SENUSRET III (LAKHARES)) *c1878-c1840 BC.* An outstanding King, Sesostris III reformed government, began major public works and skillfully fought the Nubians.
AMENEMHET III (or NEMAATRE AMONEM-HAT (LAMARIS)) *c1840-c1795 BC,* son of Sesostris III.
AMENEMHET IV (AMMENEMES) *c1795-c1786 BC.*
SEBEK-NEFRU (SKEMIOPHRIS) (Queen) *c1786 BC*; probably co-ruler before that date.

DYNASTY XIII
(c1786-c1686 BC)
This dynasty marks the beginning of the Second Intermediate Period. After Queen Sebek-Nefru central government collapsed. Dynasty XIII was probably a local one in Thebes. It is unlikely to have contained the 60 Kings claimed by Manetho and it is even less likely they were elected as some historians have suggested.

DYNASTY XIV
(c1686-? BC)
This shadowy dynasty ruled only in the western Delta.

DYNASTY XV
(c1674-c1567 BC)
A dynasty founded by the Hyksos in the Delta to which its authority may have been confined. It is likely that a successor to Dynasty XIII ruled in Thebes.

DYNASTY XVI
(date uncertain)
A minor dynasty in the Delta, probably contemporary with Dynasty XV.

DYNASTY XVII
(c1650-c1570 BC)
SEQENENRE I. Probably descended from Dynasty XIII.
SEQENENRE II. Probably killed in battle with the Hyksos.
(SEQENENRE III Possibly the same person as Seqenenre II.)
KAMOSE, son of Seqenenre II.

DYNASTY XVIII
(c1570-1200 BC)
AHMOSE (AMOSIS) *c1570-1546 BC,* elder brother of Kamose. Expelling the Hyksos from the Delta, Ahmose reunited Egypt. Ahmose married his sister, promoting the marriages within a degree of consanguinity once thought to be normal practice in royal Egypt - from this time the King often validated his claim to the throne by wedding the heiress.
AMENHOTEP I (AMENOPHIS) 1546-1526 BC, son of Ahmose.
THUTMOSE I (or THOTHMES I (TETHMOSIS)) **1526-c1512** BC. A usurper, he married Ahmose's heiress; a brilliant general, he extended Egyptian rule deep into Palestine.
THUTMOSE II (or THOTHMES II (KHEBRON)) *c1512-1504 BC,* son of Thutmose I.
HATSHEPSUT (Queen AMENSIS) 1505-1482 BC, widow of Thutmose II. At first Regent for, then co ruler with, her stepson, Hatshepsut was a major patroness of the arts and religion and a powerful, fascinating woman.
THUTMOSE III (or THOTHMES III (MEPHRES)) co-ruler **1504-1482 BC**; sole ruler **1482-1452 BC**; co-ruler **1452-1450 BC,** stepson of Hatshepsut. Perhaps the greatest of the Pharaohs, he created in the Middle East an Egyptian empire, the result of many campaigns.
AMENHOTEP II (AMENOPHIS) co-ruler **1452-1450 BC**; sole ruler **1450-1425 BC,** son of Thutmose III, b 1470 BC.
THUTMOSE IV (or THOTHMES IV (TOUTHMOSIS)) **1425-1417 BC,** son of Amenhotep II.
AMENHOTEP III (HOROS) **1417-1379 BC,** son of Thutmose IV, b *c* 1429 BC.
AKHENATON (before 1374 BC known as AMENHOTEP IV) sole ruler **1379-1364 BC**; co-ruler **1364-1362 BC,** son of Amenhotep III. A Pharoah whose actions have been foolishly romanticised. Disputing with the priests of Amon, he promoted (but did not create) the cult of Aton. He was not a monotheist as is often claimed.
SMENKHARE (AKENKHERES) co-ruler **1364-1362 BC**; sole ruler **1362-1361 BC,** son of Akhenaton.
TUTANHKAMEN (originally TUTANKHATON (KHEBRES)) **1361-1352 BC,** brother of Smenk-

hare. His extraordinarily lavish burial (which has made him one of the best known of the Pharoahs) was probably a reward from the priests of Amon to the King who restored the old religion.

AY (AKHERRE) 1352-1348 BC. A priest who usurped the throne.

HOREMHEB (or HAREMHAB (HARMAIS)) **1348-1320 BC.** A gifted ruler who restored law and order; he established his claim by marrying Akhenaton's sister-in-law.

DYNASTY XIX
(1320-1200 BC)

RAMSES I (MENOPHRES) co-ruler **1320-1318 BC.** 'Vizier' to Horemheb who adopted him.

SETI I (or SETEKHY I (SETHOS)) co-ruler **1320-1318 BC**; sole ruler **1318-1304 BC**, son of Ramses I.

RAMSES II (RAMESSES) 1304-1237 BC, son of Seti I. Called 'the Great' on account of his many buildings, a prosperous reign and a great victory over the Hittites. However, modern research shows that he had many buildings of earlier Pharaoh's reworked to his glory and that his Kadesh campaign was really a Hittite victory.

MERNEPTAH (AMENOPHATH) 1236-1223 BC, thirteenth son of Ramses II. Traditionally, and without evidence, said to be the Pharaoh of the Exodus.

AMENMOSE (or AMENMESSE (AMON-MESES)) **1222-1217 BC.** A usurper.

SETI II (or SETEKHY II (SETHOS)) **1216-1210 BC,** son of Merneptah.

SIPTAH (or RAMSES-SIPTAH (THOUORIS)) **1209-1203 BC.** A Syrian usurper who married Seti II's widow.

TAUSERT (Queen) **1202-1200 BC,** widow of Seti II and Siptah.

DYNASTY XX
(1200-1085 BC)

SETNAKHT 1200-1198 BC.

RAMSES III HIKON 1198-1166 BC, son of Setnakht. The last great Pharaoh.

RAMSES IV 1166-1160 BC, son of Ramses III.

RAMSES V 1160-1156 BC.

RAMSES VI 1156-1148 BC, probably a son of Ramses III. A weak ruler who lost the Asian provinces.

RAMSES VII sometime between **1148-1140 BC.** The order of the reigns of Ramses VII and Ramses VIII is uncertain.

RAMSES VIII sometime between **1148-1140 BC.** The order of the reigns of Ramses VII and Ramses VIII is uncertain.

RAMSES IX 1140-1121 BC.

RAMSES X 1121-1113 BC.

RAMSES XI (once referred to as RAMSES XII) **1113-1085 BC.**

DYNASTY XXI
(1085-945 BC)

Throughout this dynasty the high priest at Thebes assumed 'kingship': once listed as Kings the

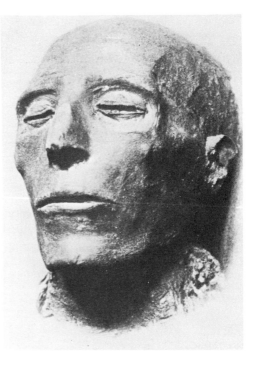

The mummified head of Ramses II who fooled posterity by having his name superimposed on monuments to earlier Pharoahs (Radio Times Hulton Picture Library)

Theban priest-Kings are now recognised as subordinate to the Tanite Kings of Dynasty XXI.

SMENDES or NESUBANEBDED **1085-c1075 BC.**

PSIBKHENNO I (or PSUSENNES I) *c*1075-*c*1055 BC.

AMENEMOPE *c*1055-*c*1005 BC.

PSIBKHENNO II (or PSUSENNES II) *c*1005-? BC.

SIAMON ?-945 BC.

DYNASTY XXII
(945-c730 BC)

SHESHONK I. Leader of the Libyan Meshwesh who quickly adopted Egyptian ways.

OSORKON I, son of Sheshonk.

TAKELOTH I.

SHESHONK II.

TAKELOTH II.

SHESHONK III.

PAMAY.

SHESHONK IV.

PEDUBAST.

OSORKON III was forced to retire to the Delta when Ethiopians invaded.

TAKELOTH III.
PIANKHY (possibly the same person as KASH-TA). An Ethiopian usurper.

DYNASTY XXIII
(date uncertain)
A minor dynasty at Thebes probably contemporary with Dynasty XXII.

DYNASTY XXIV
(720-714 BC)
BOCCHORIS 720-714 BC. A mysterious figure who broke the Ethiopian power. He was burned alive by Shabaka.

DYNASTY XXV
(716-667 BC)
SHABAKA 716-686 BC. Re-established Ethiopian rule in Egypt.
(PIANKHY II is included in some lists.)
SHEBITKU or SHABATAKA, elder son of Shabaka.
TAHARKA, brother of Shebitku. Fled before an Assyrian invasion.
TANUTAMON. Fled when the Assyrians sacked Thebes.

DYNASTY XXVI
(664-525 BC)
PSAMTIK I 664-? BC. The Assyrians were obliged to rule through local nobles one of whom, Psamtik, declared himself Pharoah. A conciliatory King, he reunited the country and promoted trade with the Greeks.
NECHO, son of Psamtik I.
PSAMTIK II.
PSAMTIK III.
APRIES or HOPHRA. Disastrous military campaigns led to his deposition.
AHMOSE (Amasis). The officer who deposed Apries became a successful King who maintained peace and contained the growing influence of the Greeks.
PSAMTIK IV 526-525 BC committed suicide when the Persians invaded, son of Ahmose.

DYNASTY XXVII
(525-404 BC)
The Iranians who conquered Egypt assumed the kingship and were in most cases Rulers of Persia (Iran).

CAMBYSES 525-521 BC.
DARIUS I 521-486 BC.
XERXES 486-465 BC.
INAROS 465-454 BC when he was crucified by the Persians. A Libyan usurper.
DARIUS II 454-404 BC.

DYNASTY XXVIII
(404-399 BC)
AMYRTAEUS 404-399 BC. A Libyan who reigned in Upper Egypt.

DYNASTY XXIX
(399-380 BC)
ACHORIS 399-380 BC. Founded a Delta state based on Mendes.
NEPHERITES 380 BC deposed, son of Achoris.

DYNASTY XXX
(380-343 BC)
NECTANEBO I or NEKHTNEBEF **380-360 BC.** A general who usurped the throne.
TACHOS 360-359 BC deposed, son of Nectanebo I.
NECTANEBO II or NEKHTHAREHBE **359-343 BC** he fled to Ethiopia when the Persians returned, nephew of Tachos. The last native Pharoah: he usurped the throne in a popular rising against Tachos' heavy taxes.

DYNASTY XXXI
ARTAXERXES (III of the Iranians) **343-338 BC**; was also Artakhshathra III, King of the Iranians.
KHABABASHA 338-335 BC. A Nubian who founded a short-lived Egyptian state.
DARIUS III 335-333 BC; was also Darayavaush III, King of the Iranians.
(333 BC Alexander the Great conquered Egypt adding it to his empire. Following his death Egypt was ruled by a Satrap (Governor) who eventually declared himself King.)

PTOLEMAIC DYNASTY
There is more than one numbering system of the Ptolemaic Kings.

PTOLEMY I SOTER 305-282 BC, b c 360 BC. After the death of Alexander (323 BC), Ptolemy defeated Antigonos to become Satrap of Egypt. Self-proclaimed King, he was an astute ruler who embellished the new capital, Alexandria, where he founded the famous library.
PTOLEMY II PHILADELPHUS 284-246 BC, son of Ptolemy I, b c 309 BC.
ARSINOE (Queen) **282?-270 BC**, wife and sister of Ptolemy II, b c 316 BC.
PTOLEMY III EUERGETES I 246-221 BC, son of Ptolemy II, b c 280 BC.
PTOLEMY IV PHILOPATOR 222-205 BC, eldest son of Ptolemy III, b 245 BC.
PTOLEMY V EPIPHANES 205-180 BC, son of Ptolemy IV, b c 210 BC.
PTOLEMY VI PHILOMETOR 180-145 BC, elder son of Ptolemy V, b c 186 BC.
CLEOPATRA I (Queen) **180-176 BC**, widow of Ptolemy V. It is uncertain if she ruled as Regent or Sovereign in her own right.
CLEOPATRA II (Queen) **c 175-c 118 BC**; c 130-118 BC Sovereign in Upper Egypt, daughter of Ptolemy V and wife of Ptolemies VI and VII; d 116 BC.
PTOLEMY NEOS PHILOPATOR 145 BC, son of Ptolemy VI. Included in some lists as Ptolemy VII.
PTOLEMY VII EUERGETES II 145-116 BC, brother of Ptolemy VI, b c 190 BC.

Cleopatra VII of Egypt emerging from the carpet in which she was smuggled to Caesar - a groundless legend (Radio Times Hulton Picture Library)

PTOLEMY VIII EUPATOR   145 BC, son of Ptolemy VI.

PTOLEMY IX APION King in Cyrenaica **117-90 BC,** half-brother of Ptolemies VI and VII or son of Ptolemy VII. Excluded from some lists.

CLEOPATRA III (Queen) **116-101 BC,** daughter of Ptolemy VI and widow of Ptolemy VII.

PTOLEMY X SOTER II   116-110 BC deposed, elder son of Cleopatra III and Ptolemy VII. Contested the throne with his brother.

PTOLEMY XI ALEXANDER I   110-109 BC deposed, brother of Ptolemy X. Deposed for desecrating the tomb of Alexander the Great.

PTOLEMY X SOTER II 109-107 BC deposed.

PTOLEMY XI ALEXANDER I   107-88 BC deposed.

CLEOPATRA IV BERENICE (Queen) **101-88 BC,** sister of Ptolemies X and XI, and wife of Ptolemy X (her brother).

PTOLEMY X SOTER II 88-81 BC.

PTOLEMY XII ALEXANDER II 80 BC assassinated, son of Ptolemy XI, b *c* 105 BC.

PTOLEMY XIII NEOS DIONYSOS (Auletes) **80-58 BC** deposed, son of Ptolemy X. Obliged to become a 'puppet' of Rome.

CLEOPATRA VI TRYPHAENA (Queen) ruled alternately with her sister **58-55 BC.**

BERENICE (Queen) ruled alternately with her sister **58-55 BC**; Both probably daughters of Ptolemy X.

PTOLEMY XIII NEOS DIONYSOS (Auletes) **55-51 BC.**

PTOLEMY XIV   52-47 BC, elder son of Ptolemy XIII, b *c* 61 BC.

PTOLEMY XV 47-44 BC, younger son of Ptolemy XIII, b *c* 59 BC.

CLEOPATRA VII 52-30 BC, daughter of Ptolemy XIII, b *c* 69 BC. Cleopatra was both remarkably beautiful and determined - both to survive and to be on the victorious side in Rome's civil war - but many of the 'facts' about her are probably myths. Her famous affairs with Julius Caesar, whom she accompanied to Rome, and Antony may have been politic - both offered her security on her throne. After Antony's defeat at Actium, in which battle the actions of the Egyptian fleet are inexplicable, she killed herself though there is no historical evidence for the asp.

PTOLEMY XVI CAESAR (Caesarion) **44-30 BC,** son of Cleopatra VII and Julius Caesar, b 47 BC; executed by Octavius.

Roman Egypt

Egypt formed a province of the Roman Empire from 30 BC to AD 395. Egypt was under the Eastern or Byzantine Roman Empire from 395 to 616, and from 628 to 639, though the last Byzantine troops did not leave Alexandria until 642.

Islamic Egypt (Early Period)

616-628 Persian Rule.
639 Islamic invasion.
(For nearly 900 years Egypt was ruled by Governors (some of whom were able to establish dynasties) who were in theory appointed by the Caliph but often exercised almost complete independence from him.)
639-868 Individual Governors. Under these early Governors the change to Arab ways and language and to Islam was very slow, the Coptic and Greek Christians being accorded a toleration never matched by the later Christian Crusaders.
868-905 Tulunid Dynasty of Governors.
905-935 Individual Governors
935-969 Ikhshidid Dynasty of Governors
969-973 Individual Governors
973-1171 Fatimid Dynasty of Caliphs. Originally from Yemen, the Fatimides established in Egypt an independent Caliphate and an empire that included not only most of North Africa but also Sicily, Yemen and Palestine.
1171-1250 Ayyubid Dynasty of Sultans. Egypt was returned to the Sunni Caliphate by Salah-ed-Din (Saladin) who founded this dynasty.
1250-1517 Mamluk Dynasty of Sultans. The Mamluks (mercenaries) overthrew the Ayyubids to establish their own 'dynasty' - this very confused period of Egyptian history contains 45 rulers.
1517-1914 Ottoman Egypt. The Mamluks were defeated by the Ottomans (1516-7) who incorporated the country in their empire. The decline begun under the Mamluks accelerated and Egypt remained in relative isolation until the French occupation (1798-1805). Ottoman rule,

which from 1805 became increasingly nominal, ended when Britain established a protectorate in Dec 1914. The story of modern Egypt begins with the remarkable Muhammad Ali who fought his way to the vice-regality in 1805.

Modern Royal Rulers of Egypt (1805-1953)

† Hereditary Vice-Roys

MUHAMMAD ALI summer 1805-Jul 1848, b 1769; d 1849. Muhammad Ali, an Albanian soldier, forced the Ottoman Turks to recognise him as Vice-Roy. Ambitious, he reformed Egypt; avaricious, he made himself the only landowner in the country; able, his military campaigns in Arabia, Greece and the Sudan made Egypt respected but most of the gains were lost before he was deposed in his senility.
IBRAHIM Jul-Nov 1848, eldest son of Muhammad Ali.
ABBAS HILMI I Nov 1848-1854 possibly murdered, nephew of Muhammad Ali.
SA'ID 1854-1863, second son of Muhammad Ali.
ISMA'IL 1863-1867 when he became Khedive.

† Khedives

ISMA'IL 1867-Jun 1879 when he was deposed, son of Ibrahim.
TAWFIQ Jun 1879-1892, son of Isma'il.
ABBAS HILMI II 1892-Dec 1914, son of Tawfiq, b 1875. He was deposed by the British when a protectorate was established over Egypt in 1914.

† Sultans of the British Protectorate

HUSAYN KAMIL Dec 1914-Oct 1917, second son of Isma'il. Husayn Kamil was granted the style of Sultan by Britain.
AHMAD FUAD Oct 1917-15 Mar 1922 when he became King.

† Kings of the Independent Kingdom

Britain granted independence to Egypt as a constitutional monarchy on 28 Feb 1922. Briefly the monarch retained the title Sultan but on 15 Mar 1922 assumed the title of King.

FUAD I (formerly Sultan Ahmad Fuad) **15 Mar 1922-28 Apr 1936,** third son of Isma'il, b 26 Mar 1868. An unpopular autocrat, Fuad I faced crippling difficulties from the Wafd party and a British policy which made Egypt's independence an illusion.
FARUQ (better known as FAROUK) **Apr 1936-23 Jul 1952** when he abdicated following a coup, son of Fuad I, b 11 Feb 1920; d 18 Mar 1965. In an unstable political situation Faruq's interventions

into affairs of state and the corruption of his Court led to revolution.

FUAD II (Ahmad Fuad) **23 Jul 1952-Jun 1953** when a Republic was proclaimed, son of Faruq, b 16 Jan 1952.

Prime Ministers of the Kingdom

ABDUL SARWAT PASHA 15 Mar-Nov 1922; d 1938.

MOHAMMED TEWFIK NESSIM PASHA 30 Nov 1922-Mar 1923.

ABDEL FATTAH YEHIA PASHA Mar 1923-Jan 1924.

SAAD ZAGHLUL PASHA 27 Jan-Nov 1924, b 1852; d 23 Aug 1927 from wounds inflicted in an assassination attempt in Nov 1924.

AHMED ZIWER PASHA 24 Nov 1924-Jun 1926; d 1945.

ADLY PASHA 8 Jun 1926-Apr 1927; d 1933.

ABDUL SARWAT PASHA 26 Apr 1927-Mar 1928.

MUSTAFA NAHAS PASHA 17 Mar-25 Jun 1928.

MOHAMMED MAHMUD PASHA 25 Jun 1928-Oct 1929; d Feb 1941.

ADLY PASHA 5 Oct 1929-Jan 1930.

MUSTAFA NAHAS PASHA 1 Jan-Jun 1930.

ISMAIL SIDKY PASHA 20 Jun 1930-Sep 1933; d Jul 1950.

ABDEL FATTAH YEHIA PASHA 25 Sep 1933-Nov 1934, b 1876; d 1951.

MOHAMMED TEWFIK NESSIM PASHA Nov 1934-Jan 1936.

ALY PASHA MAHER 30 Jan-May 1936, b 1884; d 1960.

MUSTAFA NAHAS PASHA 9 May 1936-Dec 1937, b 15 Jun 1876; d 23 Aug 1965. Leader of the Wafd Party he dominated Egypt for a generation. His relations with the Kings, whose powers he wanted strictly limited, were stormy and he supported the Allied cause in World War II from 1939.

MOHAMMED MAHMUD PASHA 30 Dec 1937-Aug 1939.

ALY PASHA MAHER 18 Aug 1939-Jun 1940.

HASSAN PASHA SABRY 28 Jun-Nov 1940; d in office.

HUSSEIN SIRRY PASHA 15 Nov 1940-Feb 1942.

MUSTAFA NAHAS PASHA 2 Feb 1942-Oct 1944.

Dr **AHMED MAHER PASHA 9 Oct 1944-24 Feb 1945,** b 1893; assassinated 24 Feb 1945.

MAHMOUD FAHMY NOKRASHY PASHA 24 Feb 1945-Feb 1946.

ISMAIL SIDKY PASHA 17 Feb-Dec 1946.

MAHMOUD FAHMY NOKRASHY PASHA 9 Dec 1946-28 Dec 1948, b 1888; assassinated 28 Dec 1948.

IBRAHIM ABDUL HADI PASHA 28 Dec 1948-Jul 1949.

HUSSEIN SIRRY PASHA 25 Jul 1949-Jan 1950.

MUSTAFA NAHAS PASHA 12 Jan 1950-Jan 1952.

ALY PASHA MAHER 27 Jan-1 Mar 1952.

AHMED NAGUIB HILALY PASHA 1 Mar-Jul 1952, b 1891; d 1958.

HUSSEIN SIRRY PASHA 2-22 Jul 1952, b ?1892; d 15 Dec 1960.

AHMED NAGUIB HILALY PASHA 22-23 Jul 1952 deposed in coup.

ALY MAHER (formerly ALY PASHA MAHER) **24 Jul-7 Sep 1952** deposed.

Gen **MOHAMED NEGUIB 7 Sep 1952-Jun 1953** when he became PM of the Republic.

THE REPUBLIC OF EGYPT

Presidents

Gen **MOHAMED NEGUIB 18 Jun 1953-22 Feb 1954** deposed; restored **27 Feb-14 Nov 1954** deposed, b 20 Feb 1901.

Col **GAMAL ABDEL NASSER** acting President **14 Nov 1954-26 Jun 1956**; President **26 Jun 1956-1 Feb 1958** when he became President of the United Arab Republic.

Prime Ministers

Gen **MOHAMED NEGUIB 18 Jun 1953-Feb 1954.**

Col **GAMAL ABDEL NASSER 22 Feb-1 Mar 1954.**

Gen **MOHAMED NEGUIB 1 Mar-17 Apr 1954.**

Col **GAMAL ABDEL NASSER 17 Apr 1954-1 Feb 1958** when the post of Premier was abolished.

THE UNITED ARAB REPUBLIC

President

Col **GAMAL ABDEL NASSER 2 Feb 1958-28 Sep 1961** when Syria seceded from the federation; continued as President of Egypt.

THE EGYPTIAN ARAB REPUBLIC

Until 2 Sep 1971 it was known as the United Arab Republic despite the dissolution of that federation.

Presidents

Col **GAMAL ABDEL NASSER** President since 14 Nov 1954; **28 Sep 1961-28 Sep 1970,** b 15 Jan 1918; d in office. Strongly nationalistic and popular throughout the Arab world, Nasser nationalised the Suez Canal and turned to the Communist bloc after failing to win support for the Aswan Dam in the West. A leading 'Third World' figure he instituted an authoritarian one party state and through vast military spending ruined the economy - however the Aswan project has proved of immeasurable value.

ANWAR SADAT acting President **28 Sep-17 Oct 1970**; President **since 17 Oct 1970,** b 25 Dec 1918.

Col Gamal Abdel Nasser (centre) with Gen Mohamed Neguib (on Nasser's left) who initially led the Egyptian revolution together (Radio Times Hulton Picture Library)

Prime Ministers

The post of Premier was revived by constitutional amendment in Sep 1962.

Wing Commander **ALI SABRY 29 Sep 1962-Oct 1965,** b 30 Apr 1920.
ZAKARIA MOHIEDDIN 2 Oct 1965-Sep 1966, b 1918.
MOHAMMED SIDKI SOLAIMAN 10 Sep 1966-Jun 1967, b 1919.
Col **GAMAL ABDEL NASSER 19 Jun 1967-28 Sep 1970.**
ANWAR SADAT acting PM **28 Sep-21 Oct 1970.**
Dr **MAHMOUD FAWZI 21 Oct 1970-Jan 1972,** b 1900.
Dr **AZIZ SIDKY 16 Jan 1972-Mar 1973,** b 1 Jul 1920.
ANWAR SADAT 26 Mar 1973-Sep 1974.
Dr **ABDUL AZIZ MUHAMMED HEGAZY 25 Sep 1974-Apr 1975,** b 3 Jan 1923.
MAMDOUH MOHAMMED SALAM since 14 Apr 1975.

Eire *see* Irish Republic

El Salvador

From 1526 to 1821 part of Spanish Guatemala; independent from 1821 to 1822; part of Mexico from 1822 to 1823 and then of the United Provinces of Central America from 1823 to 1839, el Salvador was not formally declared independent until 30 Jan 1841, but over 10 years of anarchy followed until an effective governmental system evolved.

Heads of State and of Government

JUAN LINDO Jan 1841-Jan 1842.
ANTONIO CAÑAS 1842.
PEDRO ARCE 1842.
ESCOLASTICO MARIN 1842.
JUAN JOSÉ GUZMAN 1842-Feb 1844.
FRANCISCO MALESPIN Feb 1844-Feb 1845.
JUAN JOSÉ GUZMAN Feb 1845-Feb 1846.
FRANCISCO PALACIO Feb 1846.
EUGENIO AGUILAR Feb 1846-Feb 1848.
DOROTEO VASCONCELOS Feb 1848-Mar 1851.
JUAN QUIROS Mar 1851-Jan 1852.
FRANCISCO DUEÑAS acting Head of State **Jan-Mar 1852**; Head of State **Mar 1852-Feb 1854.**
JOSÉ MARIA SAN MARTIN Feb 1854-Feb 1856.
RAFAEL CAMPO Feb 1856-Jan 1858.
MIGUEL SANTIN del CASTILLO Jan 1858-Mar 1859.
GERARD BARRIOS Mar 1859-Feb 1860 when he became President.

Presidents

GERARD BARRIOS 1 Feb 1860-Nov 1863; murdered 1864.
FRANCISCO DUEÑAS acting President **Nov 1863-Feb 1864**; President **Feb 1864-Apr 1871.**
Gen **SAN JUAN GONZALES** acting President **Apr 1871-Feb 1872**; President **Feb 1872-Jan 1876.**
ANDRÉS VALLE Jan-Jul 1876.
RAFAEL ZALDÍVAR y LAZO Jul 1876-May 1885 deposed in coup, b 1834; d 1896.
Gen **FRANCISCO MENENDEZ Jun 1885-Jun 1890.**
CARLOS EZETA acting President **Jun 1890-Jun 1894.**
RAFAEL GUTIÉRREZ Jun 1894-Nov 1898; nominally President until Mar 1899.
TOMÁS REGALADO acting President **Nov 1898-Mar 1899**; President **Mar 1899-Mar 1903.**
PEDRO JOSÉ ESCALÓN 1 Mar 1903-Mar 1907, b 1847; d 1923.
FERNANDO FIGUEROA 1 Mar 1907-Mar 1911, b 1849; d 1912.
MANUEL ENRIQUE ARAÚJO 1 Mar 1911-Feb 1913; d in office.
CARLOS MELÉNDEZ acting President **Feb 1913-Aug 1914,** b 1861; d 1919.
ALFONSO QUIÑÓNEZ Aug 1914-Feb 1915, b 1876; d 1950.
CARLOS MELÉNDEZ Mar 1915-Feb 1919.
JORGE MELÉNDEZ 1 Mar 1919-Feb 1923, brother of Carlos Meléndez.
ALFONSO QUIÑÓNEZ 1 Mar 1923-Feb 1927.
PIO ROMERO BOSQUE 1 Mar 1927-Feb 1931.
ARTURO ARAÚJO Feb-Dec 1931 deposed in coup.

Gen **MAXIMILIANO HERNÁNDEZ MARTÍNEZ**
acting President **Dec 1931-Mar 1932**; President **1
Mar 1932-1934.**
Gen **ANDRES IGNACIO MENÉNDEZ** acting
President **1934-1935** - Gen Hernández Martínez
remained nominally President.
Gen **MAXIMILIANO HERNÁNDEZ MARTÍNEZ
1935-May 1944,** b 29 Oct 1882; d 17 May 1966.
Gen **ANDRES IGNACIO MENÉNDEZ 9 May-Oct
1944.**
**OSMIN AGUIRRE SALINAS 21 Oct 1944-Mar
1945** deposed, b 1889.
**SALVADOR CATANEDA CASTRO 8 Mar
1945-14 Dec 1948** deposed, b 1888; d 5 Mar 1965.
Col **MANUEL de CORDOBA** Head of military
junta **14 Dec 1948-Feb 1949.**
Major **OSCAR OSORIO** Head of military junta **19
Feb 1949-Sep 1956,** b 1910; d 6 Mar 1969.
Lieut-Col **JOSÉ MARIA LEMUS Sep 1956-26 Oct
1960** deposed in coup, b 22 Jul 1911.
Col **CESAR YANES URIAS 26 Oct 1960-25 Jan
1961** deposed in coup.
Lieut-Col **ARTURO ARMANDO MOLINA BAR-
RAZA** Head of military junta **Jan-Feb 1961.**
Col **MIGUEL CASTILLO** Head of military junta
Feb 1961-Jan 1962.
Dr **EUSEBIO RODOLFO CORDÓN CEA** acting
President **25 Jan-Jul 1962.**
Col **JULIO ADALBERTO RIVERA 1 Jul 1962-Jul
1967,** b 1921; d 29 Jul 1973.
Col **FIDEL SÁNCHEZ HERNÁNDEZ 1 Jul
1967-Jul 1972,** b 7 Jul 1917.
Col **ARTURO ARMANDO MOLINA BARRAZA 1
Jul 1972-Jul 1977,** b 6 Aug 1927.
Gen **CARLOS HUMBERTO ROMERO since 1 Jul
1977.**

England *see* United Kingdom

Epirus

A Greek Kingdom beside the Ionian Sea whose
sovereigns pretended descent from Achilles. The
country became a power under the Aeacid Dynasty
(before 310 BC) but ceased to be of importance by
235 BC.

† Kings

AEACID DYNASTY
AEACIDES c 310 BC.
PYRRHUS I 307-c 302 BC deposed; restored
297-272 BC, son of Aeacides, b 319 BC; died in
a street skirmish at Argos. He much enlarged his
realm during the power struggle between the
successors of his relative Alexander the Great. A
brilliant strategist, he won his campaigns against
Rome and Macedonia at a terrible cost - hence
the term 'Pyrrhic victory'.

NEOPTOLEMUS co-ruler **297-c 296 BC** murdered,
kinsman of Pyrrhus I.
ALEXANDROS II 272-c 240 BC, son of Pyrrhus I.
PYRRHUS II c 240-c 236 BC, son of Alexandros
II.
PTOLEMAEUS c 236-c 235 BC killed, son of
Alexandros II. The fabric of the state was
destroyed in a civil war which was won by the
'Republican party'
(DEIDAMEIA may be considered to have reigned
very briefly before her murder shortly after that
of her brother Ptolemaeus.)
235 BC Republican government was instituted.
However, the country fell apart into three units
all of which were absorbed into the Roman
Empire by *c* 167 BC.

Equatorial Guinea, Republic of

The islands of Fernando Po and Annobon (both
Spanish since 1778) were merged with the
mainland territory of Rio Muni (Spanish from
1843) to form the Republic of Equatorial Guinea
which has been independent since 12 Oct 1968.

President

MASIE NGUEMA BIYOGO NEGUE NDONG
(formerly FRANCISCO MACIAS NGUEMA)
since 12 Oct 1968, b 1 Jan 1924.

Estonia

The land of the Estonians was autonomous until
the 13th century, under the Teutonic Knights (13th
century-1561, with a period of Danish rule from
1219 to 1346), Swedish (1561-1721) and then
Russian. A Republic was proclaimed on 19 Nov
1918 but Estonia's independence was not recognised by Soviet Russia until 2 Feb 1920. The little
Republic, which was particularly unstable in the
1920s, was forcibly incorporated into the USSR
following a Russian invasion and a rigged election
in 1940.

Provisional Head of Government

KONSTANTIN PÄTS Nov 1918-May 1919.

Heads of State and of Government
(Riigivanem)

OTTO STRANDMAN May-Nov 1919, b 1875; d
1941.
JAAN TÖNISSON Nov 1919-Oct 1920, b 1868; fate
uncertain.

Haile Selassie, Emperor of Ethiopia, with his family. He claimed descent from King Solomon and the Queen of Sheba (Radio Times Hulton Picture Library)

ANTS PIIP Oct 1920-Oct 1922, b 1884; d 1 Oct 1942 after being deported.
JOHÄN KUKK Oct 1922-Aug 1923, b 1885; d 1945.
KONSTANTIN PÄTS Aug 1923-Mar 1924.
FRIEDRICH AKEL Mar-Dec 1924.
JÜRI JAAKSON Dec 1924-Dec 1925, b 1870; d ? 1943.
JAAN TEEMANT Dec 1925-Feb 1927.
JÜRI ULUOTS Feb-Dec 1927.
JAAN TÖNISSON Dec 1927-Nov 1928.
AUGUST REI Nov 1928-Jul 1929, b 1886; d 29 Mar 1963.
OTTO STRANDMAN Jul 1929-Feb 1931.
KONSTANTIN PÄTS 12 Feb 1931-Feb 1932.
JAAN TEEMANT 18 Feb-Jul 1932.
KARL EINBUND (later KAAREL EENPALU) 19 Jul-Nov 1932.
KONSTANTIN PÄTS 1 Nov 1932-Apr 1933; provisional Riigivanem Apr-May 1933.
JAAN TÖNISSON May-Oct 1933.
KONSTANTIN PÄTS provisional Riigivanem Oct 1933-Jan 1934.

President
(under new constitution)

KONSTANTIN PÄTS Provisional Head of State Jan-Dec 1934; President Dec 1934-1 Jan 1938; Guardian of the State 1 Jan-24 Apr 1938;

President Apr 1938-22 Jun 1940, b 24 Feb 1874; d? 1956 having been deported by the Russians - his fate is uncertain. Of peasant origin, Päts was in many ways 'Father of Estonia' - several times Riigivanem, and later dictator, he exercised almost unrestricted powers without a Parliament but enjoyed great popularity.

Prime Ministers
(under new constitution)

KONSTANTIN PÄTS Dec 1934-Nov 1937.
KAAREL EENPALU (formerly KARL EINBUND) Nov 1937-Oct 1939.
JÜRI ULUOTS Oct 1939-Jun 1940 when deposed by a Soviet invasion.

Provisional Head of Government

JOHANNES VARRE 22 Jun-6 Aug 1940.

Ethiopia

Aksum, the ancestor state of Ethiopia (formerly called Abyssinia), was established before the 1st century BC and its King had taken the grand title 'Negusa nagast' - King of Kings. Ruled by the Solomonic Dynasty, which claimed to be descended from King Solomon and the Queen of Sheba, the country entered a long decline from the 7th century to be reunited in the 14th century. From c 1769 to 1855 Ethiopia ceased to exist, being divided into petty local states. The country was reunited from 1855, under Italian occupation from 1936 to 1941 and became a Republic on 21 Mar 1975.

THE EMPIRE

† Emperors

AMDA SION I 1314-1344.
SAIFA AR'AD 1344-1372, son of Amda Sion I.
NEWAYA MARYAM 1372-1381, son of Saifa Ar'ad.
DAWIT I 1381-c1410, son of Saifa Ar'ad.
THEODOR I c1410-1414 assassinated, eldest son of Dawit I.
YESHAQ c1414-c1429, son of Dawit I.
1429-1434 Civil war and a period with no undisputed ruler.
ZAR'A YA'QOB 1434-1468, son of Dawit I.
BA'DA MARYAM 1468-1478, son of Zar'a Ya'qob.
ESKENDER 1478-1494, son of Ba'da Maryam.
AMDA SION II 1494 - reigned for a couple of months, son of Eskender.
NA'OD 1494-1508, brother of Eskender.

LEBNA DENGEL 1508-1540, son of Na'od. A major Muslim campaign almost destroyed Christian Ethiopia during this reign and the survival of a greatly reduced realm was in part due to Portuguese intervention.

GALAWDEWOS 1540-1559 died in battle, son of Lebna Dengel.

MINAS 1559-1563, son of Galawdewos.

SARSA DENGEL 1563-1597, son of Minas.

YA'QOB 1597-c1600.

ZA-DENGEL c1600-1607.

SUSENYOS 1607-1632. His adherence to Catholicism provoked a Coptic nationalist backlash which led to a long period of isolation and xenophobia.

FASILADAS 1632-1667, son of Susenyos.

YOHANNES I 1667-1682.

IYASU I ('The Great') 1682-1706 deposed, son of Yohannes I; assassinated after deposition. A popular ruler who temporarily reversed the decline of Ethiopia and was known for his justice, good humour and his prosecutions against avaricious tax gatherers.

TEKLA HAYMANOT after c1706, son of Iyasu I; date of death uncertain.

1706-1721 Period of anarchy.

BAKAFFA 1721-1730. In reuniting some of the semi-independent states into which the country had split he recreated a small Ethiopian Empire.

IYASU II 1730-1755, son of Bakaffa.

IYO'AS 1755-1769 assassinated by Yohannes II; son of Iyasu II.

YOHANNES II 1769-? A usurper who was unable to prevent the complete disintegration of Ethiopia into sub-states.

1769-1855 Period of anarchy during which no single Ethiopian state existed.

THEODOR (KASSA) 1855-Easter 1868 committed suicide, b 1818. A former monastic novice, then a bandit, Kassa married the heiress to Begemder and reunited by his sword the lands of the Abyssinian Highlands. A genuine reformer, he became mad and cruel and his imprisonment of the British Consul led to a war ending in heavy defeat and his suicide at Magdala.

TEKLA GIYORGIS II (GOBAZYE) 1868-1872. Ruler of Lasta.

YOHANNES IV 1872-1889 died in battle against Sudanese Mahdists. Kassa, ruler of Tigre.

MENELIK II 1889-1913. Ruler of Shoa.

LIDJ IYASU 1913-1916 deposed, grandson of Menelik II, b 1896; d 1935. Pro-Turkish, Lidj Iyasu offended Ethiopian Christians and was deposed by Dejazmatch Tafari (Haile Selassie).

ZAUDITU (Empress) 1916-Apr 1930, daughter of Menelik II, b 1876.

HAILE SELASSIE Apr 1930-12 Sep 1974 deposed, great-nephew of Menelik II, b (Dejazmatch Tafari) 23 Jul 1892; d 27 Aug 1975 in captivity. Haile Selassie, the elder statesman of Africa, returned in triumph (May 1941) after his long struggle against the Italians who deposed him and annexed Ethiopia in 1935. His reforms came too late for the army which deposed him.

King-Designate

ASFA WOSSEN nominally King in exile, though he did not recognise his position as Head of State Sep 1974-21 Mar 1975 when a Republic was declared, son of Haile Selassie, b 27 Jul 1916.

Prime Ministers

AKLILOU HABTE WOLD 29 Mar 1960-Feb 1974, b ? 1891; executed 23 Nov 1974.

LIJ ENDALKATCHEW MAKONNEN 28 Feb-Jul 1974; executed 23 Nov 1974.

LIJ MIKHAIL IMRU HAILE SELASSIE 22 Jul-12 Sep 1974 deposed in coup, b 1930.

Heads of Government after the Military Coup
(Heads of the Military Council)

Lieut-Gen AMAN MIKHAIL ANDOM 12 Sep-17 Nov 1974; executed 23 Nov 1974.

Brig-Gen TEFERI BENTI 17 Nov 1974-21 Mar 1975 when the Republic was declared.

THE REPUBLIC OF ETHIOPIA

Heads of State

Brig-Gen TEFERI BENTI 21 Mar 1975-3 Feb 1977 assassinated - allegedly in a gun battle with other members of the military council, b 1921.

Lieut-Col MENGISTU HAILE MARIAM since 11 Feb 1977.

Heads of Government

Brig-Gen TEFERI BENTI 21 Mar 1975-Dec 1976.

Lieut-Col MENGISTU HAILE MARIAM since 29 Dec 1976.

Etruria *see* Italy

Fiji

Fiji became a British colony on 10 Oct 1874; it obtained independence on 10 Oct 1970.

Governors-General

Sir ROBERT FOSTER 10 Oct 1970-1973, b 6 Jun 1915.

Ratu Sir GEORGE CAKOBAU since 1973, b 1912.

Prime Minister

Ratu Sir KAMISESE K.T. MARA since 10 Oct 1970, b 13 May 1920.

Finland

The Finns came to owe allegiance to Sweden from the end of the 13th century and were governed by a Swedish Duke (acting as 'Viceroy') until 1561 and then by a Governor, from the 17th century a Governor-General. The country passed to Russia as a Grand Duchy in 1809 from which state independence was proclaimed on 6 Dec 1917.

THE KINGDOM OF FINLAND

Regents

(Friedrich, Elector of Hesse, the brother-in-law of Kaiser Wilhelm II, was elected King on 9 Oct 1918 but withdrew his candidature in Nov 1918)
Dr **PEHR EVIND SVINHUFVUD May-Nov 1918**; see President Svinhufvud.
Marshal Baron **CARL GUSTAV EMIL MANNERHEIM Nov 1918-Jul 1919**; see President Mannerheim.

THE REPUBLIC OF FINLAND

Presidents

Dr **KAARLO JUHO STAHLBERG 25 Jul 1919-Feb 1925,** b 28 Jan 1865; d 22 Sep 1952.
LAURI KRISTIAN RELANDER 17 Feb 1925-Mar 1931, b 1883; d 1942.
Dr **PEHR EVIND SVINHUFVUD 2 Mar 1931-Feb 1937,** b 15 Dec 1861; d 29 Feb 1944.
KYÖSTI KALLIO 28 Feb 1937-29 Nov 1940, b 1873; d 19 Dec 1940.
RISTO HEIKKI RYTI acting President **29 Nov-21 Dec 1940**; President **21 Dec 1940-Aug 1944,** b 1889; d 1956. An outstanding economist who took Finland into the Axis alliance with Germany, largely out of fear of Russia. In 1948 he was tried as a war criminal.
Marshal Baron **CARL GUSTAV EMIL MANNERHEIM 1 Aug 1944-Mar 1946,** b 4 Jun 1867; d 27 Jan 1951. 'The Liberator of Finland', Mannerheim led the White Finns against the Communists after independence, the spirited Finnish defence against the Russian invasion in 1939 and the campaign against the USSR during World War II.
JUHO KUSTI PAASIKIVA 9 Mar 1946-Feb 1956, b 27 Nov 1870; d 14 Dec 1956.
Dr **URHO KALEVA KEKKONEN since 15 Feb 1956,** b 3 Sep 1900.

Prime Ministers

JUHO KUSTI PAASIKIVA May-Nov 1918; see President Paasikiva.

LAURI JOHANNES INGMAN Nov 1918-Apr 1919, b 1868; d 1934.
KAARLO CASTREN 17 Apr-Aug 1919, b 1860; d 1938.
JUHO HEIKKI VENNOLA 15 Aug 1919-Mar 1920, b 1872; d 1938.
RAFAEL ERICH 14 Mar 1920-Apr 1921, b 1879; d 1946.
JUHO HEIKKI VENNOLA 9 Apr 1921-Jun 1922.
Prof **AINO KAARLO CAJANDER 2 Jun-Nov 1922.**
KYOSTI KALLIO 14 Nov 1922-Jan 1924; see President Kallio.
Prof **AINO KAARLO CAJANDER 18 Jan-May 1924.**
LAURI JOHANNES INGMAN 31 May 1924-Mar 1925.
ANTTI AGATON TULENHEIMO 31 Mar-Dec 1925.
KYOSTI KALLIO 31 Dec 1925-Dec 1926; see President Kallio.
VAINO ALFRED TANNER Dec 1926-Dec 1927, b 12 Mar 1881; d 19 Apr 1966.
JUHO EMIL SUNILA Dec 1927-Dec 1928.
OSKARI MANTERE Dec 1928-Aug 1929, b 1874; d 1942.
KYOSTI KALLIO Aug 1929-Jul 1930; see President Kallio.
Dr **PEHR EVIND SVINHUFVUD Jul 1930-Mar 1931**; see President Svinhufvud.
JUHO EMIL SUNILA Mar 1931-Dec 1932, b 1875; d 1936.
TOIVO MIKAEL KIVIMÄKI 18 Dec 1932-Sep 1936, b 1886; d 1968.
KYOSTI KALLIO 27 Sep 1936-Mar 1937; see President Kallio.
Prof **AINO KAARLO CAJANDER 12 Mar 1937-Nov 1939,** b 1879; d 21 Jan 1943. He resigned upon the Russian invasion of Finland.
RISTO HEIKKI RYTI 30 Nov 1939-Jan 1941; see President Ryti.
JOHAN WILHELM RANGELL 4 Jan 1941-Feb 1943, b 1894.
Prof **EDWIN LINKOMIES Feb 1943-Aug 1944,** b 1894; d 1963.
ANTTI HACKZELL 8 Aug-2 Sep 1944, b 1881; d 1944. He presented Finland's surrender to the Allied Powers.
URHO CASTREN 2 Sep-11 Nov 1944, b 1886; d 1965.
JUHO KUSTI PAASIKIVI 11 Nov 1944-Mar 1946; see President Paasikiva.
MAUNO PEKKALA 24 Mar 1946-Jul 1948, b 1890; d 30 Jun 1952.
KARL-AUGUST FAGERHOLM 24 Jul 1948-Mar 1950, b 1901.
Dr **URHO KALEVA KEKKONEN 14 Mar 1950-Nov 1953**; see President Kekkonen.
Dr **SAKARI TUOMIOJA 4 Nov 1953-May 1954,** b 1911; d 1964.
RÄLF TÖRNGREN 5 May-Oct 1954, b 1900; d 1961.
Dr **URHO KALEVA KEKKONEN 14 Oct 1954-Feb 1956**; see President Kekkonen.

KARL-AUGUST FAGERHOLM **17 Feb 1956-May 1957.**
Dr **VEINO JOHANNES SUKSELAINEN 27 May-Oct 1957**; caretaker PM **18 Oct-29 Nov 1957,** b 12 Oct 1906.
Dr **RAINER von FIEANDT 29 Nov 1957-Apr 1958,** b 1890; d 1972.
Dr **REINO KUUSKOSKI 26 Apr-30 Jul 1958**; caretaker PM **30 Jul-2 Aug 1958,** b 1907; d 1965.
ONNI HILTUNEN PM **2-6 Aug 1958**; caretaker PM **6-26 Aug 1958.**
KARL-AUGUST FAGERHOLM **26 Aug-Dec 1958.**
Dr **VEINO JOHANNES SUKSELAINEN 19 Dec 1958-Jun 1961.**
MARTTI MIETTUNEN Jun **1961-Mar 1962**; acting PM **1-16 Mar 1962.**
Dr **AHTI KARJALAINEN 16 Mar 1962-Aug 1963**; caretaker PM **Aug-Dec 1963.**
Dr **REINO RAGNAR LEHTO 18 Dec 1963-Sep 1964,** b 2 May 1898.
Dr **JOHANNES VIROLAINEN 11 Sep 1964-Apr 1966**; caretaker PM **14 Apr-21 May 1966,** b 31 Jan 1914.
KUSTAA RAFAEL PAASIO **21 May 1966-Mar 1968.**
Dr **MAUNO HENRIK KOIVISTO 1 Mar 1968-Mar 1970**; caretaker PM **Mar-13 May 1970,** b 25 Nov 1923.
TEUVO ENSIO AURA **13 May-13 Jul 1970,** b 28 Dec 1912.
Dr **AHTI KARJALAINEN 13 Jul 1970-Oct 1971,** b 10 Feb 1923.
TEUVO ENSIO AURA **29 Oct 1971-Feb 1972.**
KUSTAA RAFAEL PAASIO **22 Feb-Jul 1972**; caretaker PM **19 Jul-4 Sep 1972,** b 6 Jun 1903.
TAISTO KALEVI SORSA **4 Sep 1972-Jun 1975.**
KEIJO LIINAMAA **13 Jun-Nov 1975,** b 1929.
MARTTI MIETTUNEN **30 Nov 1975-May 1977,** b 17 Apr 1907.
TAISTO KALEVI SORSA since **15 May 1977,** b 21 Dec 1930.

Flanders *see* Belgium

Florence and Florentine

Republic *see* Italy

France

From the middle of the 5th century there existed a number of Frankish Kingdoms of which three were dominant - Neustria in the north, Burgundy in the south and Austrasia in the east and the Rhinelands. A Kingdom of France, as opposed to of the Franks, dates from the Treaty of Verdun (843) which divided the Empire of Charlemagne. The consolidation of the French realm, of which the royal domain was originally only a very small part, took centuries there being many powerful rulers who were nominally vassals of the king but in reality semi-independent Princes. The monarchy was abolished in the revolution on 10 Aug 1792. The First Republic consisted of the Convention (1792-1795), the Directorate (1795-1799) and the Consulate (1799-1804). The First Empire was proclaimed in 1804 and overthrown in 1814 when the Bourbon monarchy was restored. After the brief restoration of the Empire (the 100 Days), the Kingdom lasted until 1848 when the Second Republic was established. The Second Empire was proclaimed in 1852 and overthrown in 1870 when the monarchy was finally abolished. The Third Republic lasted from 1870 to 1940; the French State (not recognised by many) from 1940 to 1944; the Provisional Government from 1944 to 1947; the Fourth Republic from 1947 to 1958. The Fifth Republic was established on 4 Oct 1958.

FRANKISH KINGS

† Kings of the Franks

MEROVINGIAN DYNASTY
PHARAMOND, sometimes stated to be the first King of the Franks, is almost certainly legendary; CHLODION, or Clodio, and MÉROVÉE, or Merovech, are known to have been tribal chiefs of the Salian Franks in present day Flanders, but cannot be considered as Kings of the Franks as once claimed.

CHILDÉRIC I King of the Salian Franks **457-481 or 482,** son of Mérovée, b *c* 436. Childéric fought the Visigoths and established a Kingdom which extended into France as far as the Somme.
CLOVIS I King of the Franks **481 or 482-511,** son of Childéric I, b *c* 466. Overthrowing Syagrius' Roman state in the Île de France, he made Paris his capital *c* 486. The true founder of the Frankish kingdom, Clovis had conquered all of northern Gaul by 494, but upon his death the Kingdom was divided between his four sons.
THIERRY I (Theudéric I) Frankish King of Reims **511-534,** son of Clovis I.
CLODOMIR Frankish King of Orléans **511-25 Jun 524** when he was killed in battle fighting the Burgundians. After his death his children were killed and his lands divided by his three brothers.
CHILDEBERT I Frankish King of Paris **511-23 Dec 558,** son of Clovis, b *c* 495. By treachery and war he greatly extended his authority, momentarily as far as Pamplona.
CLOTAIRE I Frankish King of Soissons **511-555**; King of Soissons and Metz **555-Dec 558**; sole King of the Franks **Dec 558-561,** son of Clovis, b *c* 497. Clotaire extended his rule into central Germany, but faced a serious revolt from his son Chram, whom he had burnt to death.
THIBERT I (Theudebert I) Frankish King of Metz **534-548,** son of Thierry I.

THÉODEBALD (Theudebald) Frankish King of Metz **548-555,** son of Thibert I.

† Kings of Neustria

MEROVINGIAN DYNASTY

CARIBERT (Charibert) King of Paris **561-Nov 567,** son of Clotaire I.

CHILPÉRIC I King of Soissons **561-Nov 567**; sole King of Neustria **Nov 567-Sep 584** assassination ended the cruel reign of Chilpéric who was called 'Herod' by contemporaries; illegitimate son of Clotaire I, b 539. He waged a bitter war against his half-brother Sigebert I of Austrasia.

CLOTAIRE II **Sep 584-18 Oct 629,** son of Chilpéric I, b 584.

DAGOBERT I **Oct 629-19 Jan 639,** son of Clotaire II, b c 600. Ably aided by St Eloi, Dagobert reorganised the Kingdom which he extended in wars with the Slavs, Bretons, Thuringians and Basques. Dagobert was the last Merovingian king to rule rather than reign - his successors were the 'rois fainéants', mere puppets in the hands of the mayors of the palace.

CLOVIS II **639-657,** son of Dagobert I, b c 634.

CLOTAIRE III **657-10 or 11 Mar 673,** son of Clovis II.

THIERRY III (Theudéric III) King of Neustria and Burgundy **673** when he was deposed by Childéric II of Austrasia; brother of Clotaire III. Defeated at Tertry (687) by Pépin de Herstal, mayor of the palace of Austrasia, Thierry lost executive power in all his territories to the mayor.

CHILDÉRIC II **673-675**; was also Childéric II of Austrasia.

THIERRY III (Theudéric III) **675** deposed for Clovis III.

CLOVIS III **675-676**; was also Clovis III of Austrasia.

THIERRY III (Theudéric III) **676-690 or 691.**

† Kings of Austrasia

MEROVINGIAN DYNASTY

SIGEBERT I **561-Dec 575** when he was assassinated, son of Clotaire I, b 535. Married to the intelligent, warlike Brunehaut, the real power in this reign, Sigebert conducted a long, bitter war against Chilpéric of Neustria. Eventually victorious, Sigebert was murdered before he could take Neustria.

CHILDEBERT II **Dec 575-Dec 595,** son of Sigebert I, b c 570.

THIBERT II (Theudebert II) **595 or 596-611 or 612,** deposed by Thierry II.

THIERRY II (Theudéric II) **611 or 612-613**; King of Burgundy and Orléans from **595 or 596,** son of Childebert II and brother of Thibert II whom he deposed with the aid of Queen Brunehaut.

SIGEBERT II **613** killed by Clotaire II; son of Thierry II, b 601.

CLOTAIRE II **613-623**; was also Clotaire II of Neustria.

DAGOBERT I **623-634**; was also Dagobert I of Neustria.

SIGEBERT III **634-1 Feb 659,** son of Dagobert I, b 630 or 631.

DAGOBERT II **Feb 659-660 or 661** when he was deposed by Childebert and exiled to Ireland, son of Sigebert III, b c 650.

CHILDEBERT **660 or 661-662,** adopted son of Sigebert III. (Childebert was given no regnal number being unrecognised by the Merovingians.)

CHILDÉRIC II **662-autumn 675** when he was assassinated, nephew of Sigebert III, b 649.

CLOVIS III **675-676,** possibly the son of Childéric II.

DAGOBERT II **676-23 Dec 679.**

† Kings of the Franks

From the end of the 7th century Neustria and Austrasia were usually united under one puppet king who was normally sovereign of Burgundy also.

MEROVINGIAN DYNASTY

THIERRY III (Theuderic III) **679-690 or 691**; see Thierry III of Neustria.

CLOVIS IV **691-695,** b 682.

CHILDEBERT III **695-711,** said to be descended from Chilpéric I, b c 683.

DAGOBERT III King of Neustria and Burgundy **711-715 or 716,** son of Childebert III, b 699.

CHILPÉRIC II King of Neustria and Burgundy **715 or 716-721,** claimed to be the son of Childéric II. Taken from a monastery, monk Daniel was set up as a puppet King by Charles Martel, the powerful mayor of the palaces of Neustria and Austrasia.

CLOTAIRE IV King of Neustria **718-719,** second puppet King set up by Charles Martel.

THIERRY IV **721-737,** son of Dagobert III. In one of the most significant battles of the 'Dark Ages' Charles Martel, the real ruler of the Franks, halted the Arab advance across western Europe in the Battle of Poitiers (732). After the death of Thierry, Martel and his son Pépin kept the throne vacant for seven years.

CHILDÉRIC III **743-751** deposed, son of Chilpéric II; d 754 having been deposed, then sent to a monastery, by Pépin, mayor of the palace of Neustria and Burgundy, who became King himself.

CAROLINGIAN DYNASTY

PÉPIN (le Bref-the short) **Nov 751-24 Sep 768,** son of Charles Martel, mayor of the palaces of Austrasia and Neustria, b c 715.

CHARLES I (usually called CHARLEMAGNE) King of the Franks **Sep 768-28 Jan 814,** elder son of Pépin, b 2 Apr 742. Sole King of the Franks after the death of Carloman, Charlemagne conquered nearly all the Christian peoples of western Europe. His Kingdom, over which he established an administration of counts and bishops, included France, Germany, the Low Countries, the Spanish March and much of Italy and central Europe. He came to the aid of beleaguered Pope Leo III who crowned him Emperor of the Romans (25 Dec 800) - a title which gave him few new powers but which began the Holy Roman Empire.

CARLOMAN King of the Austrasian Franks **Sep 768-771,** younger son of Pépin, b 751.

LOUIS I (le Pieux - the pious) King of the Franks **Jan 814-20 Jun 840**; co-Emperor of the Romans 813-814, sole Emperor from Jan 814, son of Charlemagne, b 778.

† KINGS OF FRANCE

CAROLINGIAN DYNASTY

CHARLES II (le Chauve - the bald) King of 'Francia occidentalis' (France) **843-6 Oct 877**; Emperor 875-877, son of Louis I's second wife, b 13 Jun 823.

LOUIS II (le Bègue - the stammerer) **Oct 877-10 Apr 879**, son of Charles II, b 846.

LOUIS III Apr 879-5 Aug 882, eldest son of Louis II, b 863. Louis III divided the Kingdom with his brother Carloman.

CARLOMAN King of Aquitaine and Burgundy but titled King of France **Apr 879-884,** second son of Louis III.

(In 884-885 Charles III (Karl III) Holy Roman Emperor, reunited the realm of his great-grand-father Charlemagne absorbing France in his empire.)

CAPETIAN DYNASTY

EUDES 888-898, b c 860. Eudes, count of Paris, was elected to the throne following the deposition of Charles the Emperor; Eudes had distinguished himself in the defence of Paris against the Vikings.

CAROLINGIAN DYNASTY

CHARLES III (le Simple - the simple) **28 Jan 893-923** deposed, half-brother of Carloman, and posthumous son of Louis II, b 17 Sep 879; d 7 Oct 929. Too young to succeed Carloman, Charles' Kingdom was placed in the care of Emperor Charles. Charles III's coronation started a civil war against King Eudes which was only ended by the latter's death. In 922-3 Charles faced a challenge from Eudes' brother Robert and although his rival was killed Charles was taken, deposed and imprisoned.

CAPETIAN DYNASTY

ROBERT I 922-15 Jun 923 when he was killed at the Battle of Soissons, brother of Eudes, b c 865. Robert I was elected King by nobles dissatisfied with the rule of Charles III.

RAOUL 923-14 or 15 Jan 936, son-in-law of Robert I. Duke of Burgundy from 921.

CAROLINGIAN DYNASTY

LOUIS IV (d'Outremer - from overseas) **19 Jun 936-10 Sep 954,** son of Charles III, b 921.

LOTHAIRE sole ruler **Sep 954-8 Jun 979**; co-ruler **8 Jun 979-986,** son of Louis IV, b 941.

LOUIS V co-ruler **8 Jun 979-986**; sole ruler **986-21 or 22 May 987** died in a hunting accident, son of Lothaire, b 967.

CAPETIAN DYNASTY

HUGUES sole ruler **3 Jul-Dec 987**; co-ruler **Dec 987-14 Oct 996,** grandson of Robert I, b c 938-941. When Louis V died without heirs, Hugues Capet was elected King by the nobles.

ROBERT II (le Pieux - the pious) co-ruler **Dec 987-Oct 996**; sole ruler **Oct 996-1026**; co-ruler **1026-20 Jul 1031,** son of Hugues, b c 970.

HENRI I co-ruler **1026-20 Jul 1031**; sole ruler **20 Jul 1031-May 1059**; co-ruler **May 1059-2 Aug 1060,** son of Robert II, b c 1008.

PHILIPPE I co-ruler **May 1059-2 Aug 1060**; sole ruler **2 Aug 1060-29 or 30 Jul 1108,** elder son of Henri I, b 1052.

LOUIS VI (le Gros - the fat) **Jul 1108-1 Aug 1137,** son of Philippe I, b 1081.

LOUIS VII (le Jeune - the young) Sole ruler **Aug 1137-1 Nov 1179**; co-ruler **1 Nov 1179-18 Sep 1180,** son of Louis VI, b c 1120. He pursued a series of wars against his rival Henry II of England.

PHILIPPE II AUGUSTE co-ruler **1 Nov 1179-18 Sep 1180**; sole ruler **18 Sep 1180-14 Jul 1223,** son of Louis VII, b 21 Aug 1165. Philippe II exploited the differences between Henry II and his rebellious sons and later the inactivity of King John to conquer the English possessions in France which had been a constant threat to him.

LOUIS VIII (le Lion - the lion) **Jul 1223-8 Nov 1226,** son of Philippe II, b 5 Sep 1187. This short reign was important for he introduced the legal means to prevent Crown lands falling into the hands of others.

LOUIS IX (St Louis) **Nov 1226-25 Aug 1270** died on Crusade at Tunis, son of Louis VIII, b 25 Apr 1214. Louis led the sixth Crusade and although defeated and captured in Egypt, he was eventually able to assist Christian settlements in Syria. St Louis was regarded as the ideal of mediaeval Kingship : he had a genuine interest in the poor and often administered justice personally.

PHILIPPE III (le Hardi - the bold) **Aug 1270-5 Oct 1285,** second son of Louis IX, b 3 Apr 1245.

PHILIPPE IV (le Bel - the fair) **Oct 1285-29 Nov 1314,** second son of Philippe III, b 1268. This aloof, handsome King did much for France: he made significant reforms in the government; he consolidated the power of the monarchy at the expense of the Pope; he temporarily subdued the nobles. His ambition was ruthless: although outwardly pious he quarrelled seriously with Rome, 'arrested' Boniface VIII and later installed the papacy at Avignon; his financial difficulties led to the persecution of Jews and

Francois I who held glittering Court with poets and painters at his beautiful chateaux of the Loire (Radio Times Hulton Picture Library)

Lombard bankers and the cruel suppression of the wealthy Templars.

LOUIS X (le Hutin - the stupid) **Nov 1314-5 Jun 1316,** eldest son of Philippe IV, b 4 Oct 1289.

Jun-13 or 14 Nov 1316 Interregnum during the pregnancy of Louis X's widow.

JEAN I (le Posthume - the posthumous) **13 or 14 Nov-19 Nov 1316,** posthumous son of Louis X. He lived only 5 or 6 days.

PHILIPPE V (le Long - the tall) **Nov 1316** when he declared himself King **or Jan 1317** when he obtained recognition by annointing **-3 Jan 1322,** second son of Philippe IV, b *c* 1293. In overriding the claims of Jeanne, daughter of Louis X, he established the principle that a woman could not reign.

CHARLES IV (le Bel - the fair) **Jan 1322-1 Feb 1328,** brother of Philippe V, b 1294.

Feb-May 1328 Interregnum during the pregnancy of Charles IV's widow.

VALOIS DYNASTY

PHILIPPE VI **May 1328-22 Aug 1350,** son of Charles de Valois who was brother of Philippe IV, b 1293. He succeeded when Charles IV's widow bore a daughter. The claim of Edward III of England, who was grandson of Philippe IV through the female line, began the Hundred Years' War. Philippe alienated Robert d'Artois who could have been a strong ally, lost the Battle of Crécy (1346) and left a country racked by war and plague.

JEAN II (le Bon - the good) **Aug 1350-8 Apr 1364,** son of Philippe VI, b 16 Apr 1319. Captured by the English at Poitiers (1356), Jean was released in 1360 to raise his ransom. Chivalrously he returned to London where he died when a hostage who had taken his place escaped.

CHARLES V (le Sage - the wise) **Apr 1364-16 Sep 1380,** son of Jean II, b 21 Jan 1338. Regent during his father's captivity, Charles, a fine soldier and patron of the arts, put down the Jacquerie revolt. As King, with his outstanding commander du Guesclin, he retook most of the provinces held by England.

CHARLES VI (le Bien-Aimé - the well beloved) **Sep 1380-21 Oct 1422,** son of Charles V, b 3 Dec 1368. The country suffered civil war, defeat at Agincourt (1415), and English occupation north of the Loire. Charles' madness (he imagined he was glass and would break if moved) left France without government for long periods. He married his daughter Catherine to Henry V, declaring the English King to be his heir.

CHARLES VII **Oct 1422-22 Jul 1461,** he was not annointed King until 1429, son of Charles VI, b 22 Feb 1403. After initial defeats at the hands of the English, the liberation of Orléans by Jeanne d'Arc stirred him and the nation to success in battle. By 1453 only Calais remained of England's French possessions. Charles VII rebuilt France and re-established an administration.

LOUIS XI **Jul 1461-30 Aug 1483,** son of Charles VII, b 3 Jul 1423.

CHARLES VIII **Aug 1483-7 Apr 1498,** son of Louis XI, b 30 Jun 1470.

VALOIS-ORLÉANS DYNASTY

LOUIS XII **Apr 1498-1 Jan 1515,** grandson of Louis d'Orléans who was the younger brother of Charles VI; Louis XII was also son-in-law of Louis XI, b 27 Jun 1462.

VALOIS-ORLÉANS-ANGOULÊME DYNASTY

FRANCOIS I **Jan 1515-31 Mar 1547,** son of Charles d'Orléans who was the brother of Louis XII, b 12 Sep 1494. The rival of the Emperor Charles V and of Henry VIII, Francois I was a great humanist Renaissance prince, an athletic chivalrous commander who set up a standing army, and a patron of poets and painters who held brilliant court at his châteaux of the Loire. His wars against the Emperor had mixed fortunes. Captured at Pavia (1625), he was forced into a disadvantageous peace, but later victories ended the Italian War and finally won Burgundy for France.

HENRI II **1 Apr 1547-10 Jul 1559** died 10 days after being wounded in a tournament, son of Francois I, b 19 Mar 1519.

FRANCOIS II **Jul 1559-5 Dec 1560,** eldest son of Henri II, b 19 Jan 1544.

CHARLES IX Dec 1560-30 May 1574, second son of Henri II, b 27 Jun 1550. Weak and mentally unstable, Charles IX was dominated by his ruthless mother Catherine de Médicis and the Guise family. Fearing Spain, Charles allied France, weakened by religious feuds, to England and the Dutch - the Protestant alliance. and the growing influence of de Coligny alarmed Catherine who persuaded her son to order the massacre of St Bartholomew's Eve (23 Aug 1572) when 3000 Protestants died and civil war recommenced.

HENRI III May 1574-2 Aug 1589 assassinated by a friar while beseiging Paris, third son of Henri II, b 19 Sep 1551. Elected King of Poland (May 1573), he fled that country when the death of Charles IX made him King of France. Although he revoked the edicts of toleration for Protestants, the Catholic League found him too conciliatory and Paris rebelled.

BOURBON DYNASTY

HENRI IV Aug 1589-14 May 1610 when he was assassinated, King of Navarre from 1562, a descendant of Robert, sixth son of Louis IX, b 13 Dec 1553. Henri, the sole legitimate heir to France, became, with de Coligny, the leader of the Protestant party in France, but was forced to become a Catholic to escape the St Bartholomew's Eve massacre. He temporarily reverted to the Huguenot faith and joined Henri III in fighting the rebellion of Paris. Ably aided by Sully and de Serres, Henri restored the unity and prosperity of the country, stimulated agriculture and industry, and encouraged France's first colonial venture in Canada.

LOUIS XIII (le Juste - the just) **May 1610-14 May 1643,** eldest son of Henri IV, b 27 Sep 1601. A moody man, Louis suffered poor health and a violent relationship with his mother Marie de Médicis, who was Regent until 1617. With Richelieu he reformed the finances and the army, greatly centralised the government, founded the Académie francaise and through successful war and diplomacy made France a great power.

LOUIS XIV (le Roi-Soleil - the Sun King) **14 May 1643-1 Sep 1715,** elder son of Louis XIII, b 5 Sep 1638. A great King who cared much for France but little for the French. Humiliated in his youth by the Fronde civil war Louis determined to be powerful. Assuming the government upon Mazarin's death (1661), he conceived the notion of his divine right to absolute dictatorship which it was sinful to oppose. He was lucky to have so many extraordinary talents at hand: Colbert to control the finances; Vauban to fortify the frontiers; Louvois to remodel the forces; Molière and Racine to raise French literature to new heights; Le Nôtre to design the gardens at Versailles where Le Vau, d'Orbay and Le Brun created the glory of the palace. With Colbert he developed roads, canals, ports, the navy and the merchant fleet, industry and a police force as part of a grand design to make France

Louis XIV. A wax effigy of 'le Roi-Soleil' wearing a wig that belonged to the Great King. (Giraudon)

self-sufficient. His culture brought a new way of life to Royal Europe; his wars dominated the continent. The Dutch wars and the wars of the League of Augsburg and of the Spanish Succession won for Louis much glory, for France the Franche-Comté and part of Flanders and for Louis' grandson Philippe the crown of Spain but they, and the extravagance of Versailles, ruined France's finances. By reducing the nobles to courtiers he brought domestic peace; by concentrating power into the King's hands he helped destroy the monarchy.

LOUIS XV (le Bien-Aimé - the well-beloved) **1 Sep 1715-10 May 1774,** great-grandson of Louis XIV, b 15 Feb 1710. His weak, uncertain rule increased unrest and brought a decline in royal authority.

LOUIS XVI 10 May 1774-21 Sep 1792 when the Republic was proclaimed; styled 'King of the French', not 'of France', after autumn 1791, third son of Louis who was the son of Louis XV, b 23 Aug 1754; executed 21 Jan 1793. Louis XVI was unable to counter vested interests which prevented necessary reform, in particular of the extortionate taxation system from which the clergy and nobility were exempt. Forced by circumstance to summon the States-General,

Louis was overwhelmed when the Third Estate declared itself the National Assembly - perhaps a greater King could have assumed leadership of the reform movement. Events moved quickly: the Bastille fell (4 Jul 1789); France collapsed in anarchy; Louis' family was taken to Paris in semi-captivity. The flight to Varennes (Jun 1791) sealed their fate: the Republic was declared (21 Sep 1792) and Louis tried, accused of conspiring with foreign powers to invade France - a charge almost certainly without substance. Louis requested there be no attempt to avenge his death but his execution united Europe against France. (LOUIS XVII, proclaimed King by the royalists in exile on 28 Jan 1793; second son of Louis XVI, b 27 Mar 1785; d a prisoner in the Temple gaol 8 Jun 1795. He cannot be said to have reigned.)

THE FIRST FRENCH REPUBLIC

The Convention

The Convention, a national revolutionary assembly, ran the country from 21 Sep 1792-26 Oct 1795. Between 6 Apr 1793 and 26 Oct 1795 everyday executive power was exercised by the Committee of Public Safety which had nine members.

The Directorate

The Directorate was a 'Cabinet' of five members and ruled the country from 26 Oct 1795-9 Nov 1799.

The Consulate

CONSULS
NAPOLÉON BONAPARTE provisional First Consul **Nov-Dec 1799**; see Napoléon I.
EMMANUEL JOSEPH SIEYÈS provisional Second Consul **Nov-Dec 1799,** b 1748; d 1836.
ROGER DUCOS provisional Third Consul **Nov-Dec 1799,** b 1747; d 1816.
NAPOLÉON BONAPARTE First Consul **Dec 1799-18 May 1804**; see Napoléon I.
JEAN-JACQUES de CAMBACÉRÈS Second Consul **Dec 1799-18 May 1804,** under the Empire titular Duke of Parma, b 1753; d 1824.
CHARLES FRANCOIS LEBRUN Third Consul **Dec 1799-18 May 1804,** under the Empire titular Duke of Piacenza, b 1739; d 1824.

THE FIRST EMPIRE

† Emperor

NAPOLÉON I 18 May 1804-6 Apr 1814 when he abdicated; restored **20 Mar-22 Jun 1815** deposed, second son of Carlo Buonaparte and Letizia Ramolino, b 15 Aug 1769; d exiled on St Helena 5 May 1821. From a large Corsican family of limited means, Napoléon showed his indepen-

dent spirit even as a precocious boy at Brienne military academy. A political pamphlet brought him early command at the seige of Toulon; in 1795 his 'whiff of grapeshot' saved the Government. His outstanding Italian campaign led to command in Egypt from which country he returned to effect the coup that established the Consulate. As First Consul he achieved a reconciliation with the papacy after the outrages of the revolution and promulgated the Code civile - still the basis of French law. Proclaimed Emperor, he owed his throne to his brilliance in battle and a coalition of European powers soon faced the new sovereign. A remarkable series of French victories - Austerlitz (1805), Jena (1806), Friedland (1807) and Eckmühl and Wagram (1809) - made him master of Europe, and although his rule was arbitrary much of the continent enjoyed better government than ever before. His relations were given client states in his visionary united Europe and to secure the succession he divorced the graceful Joséphine (1809) and wed Marie-Louise of Austria. Several factors led to his fall: the rising tide of nationalism in Europe; the actions of his grasping relatives in positions far beyond their abilities; the Continental Blocade; the disasterous Spanish and Russian campaigns. Defeated and exiled to Elba, he returned for the 'Hundred Days' which included Waterloo. He gave France order after the Revolution and left her many institutions including her legal system, the Bank of France, new universities, a local government system and the Légion d'honneur.

THE KINGDOM OF FRANCE

† King

BOURBON DYNASTY
LOUIS XVIII assumed the title King in **1795**; restored **Apr 1814-Mar 1815 deposed,** brother of Louis XVI, b 17 Nov 1755.

THE FIRST EMPIRE

† Emperors

NAPOLÉON I restored for the 'Hundred Days' **20 Mar-22 Jun 1815.**
(NAPOLÉON II, only child of Napoleon I and Marie-Louise, b 20 Mar 1811; d 22 Jul 1832 as Franz, Duke of Reichstadt. Proclaimed Emperor on 22 Jun 1815, 'l'Aiglon' cannot be said to have reigned.)

THE KINGDOM OF FRANCE

† Kings

BOURBON DYNASTY
LOUIS XVIII Jun 1815-16 Sep 1824.

Napoléon I crowning the Empress Josephine. This the official portrait of the coronation includes several people who were not present at the actual ceremony, including Napoléon's mother (Lauros-Giraudon)

Napoléon III, whom Victor Hugo called Napoléon le Petit, bore little resemblance to his renowned uncle Napoléon I (Radio Times Hulton Picture Library)

CHARLES X 16 Sep 1824-2 Aug 1830 when he abdicated, younger brother of Louis XVIII, b 9 Oct 1757; d 6 Nov 1836. Charles X was an extreme reactionary who issued repressive ordinances, restored powers to the clergy and compensated the nobility for losses in the Revolution and thus caused another revolution himself in 1830.

LOUIS XIX nominally King of France for a few hours on **2 Aug 1830** abdicated, son of Charles X, b 6 Aug 1775; d 3 Jun 1844 in exile. Legally this is the shortest reign on record.

HENRI V 2-9 Aug 1830 deposed, only son of Charles X's second son Charles, duc de Berry, b 29 Sep 1820; d 24 Aug 1883. The last legitimate male member of the Elder Bourbon Line. Nominally King for a week with Louis-Philippe as Lieutenant-General of the Realm.

† King of the French

BOURBON-ORLÉANS DYNASTY

LOUIS-PHILIPPE 9 Aug 1830-24 Feb 1848 when he abdicated, great-great-great-great-grandson of Louis XIII, b 6 Oct 1773; d 26 Aug 1850. This 'bourgeois King' became more repressive as dissent, increased by agricultural and industrial depression, grew and was overthrown by revolution in 1848.

THE SECOND FRENCH REPUBLIC

The Provisional Government

The provisional Government ruled the country from Feb-May 1848.

The Constituent Assembly

The Constituent Assembly met on 4 May 1848 and after serious rioting in Paris in late Jun 1848 delegated near dictatorial powers temporarily to a 'Chief Executive'.

CHIEF EXECUTIVE POWER
Gen **LOUIS EUGÈNE CAVAIGNAC late Jun-10 Dec 1848,** b 15 Oct 1802; d 28 Oct 1857. After crushing the Paris revolt, Cavaignac, a zealous republican, was given sweeping powers to protect the Assembly.

PRESIDENT
Prince **LOUIS-NAPOLÉON BONAPARTE 10 Dec 1848-2 Dec 1852** when he became Emperor.

THE SECOND EMPIRE

† Emperor

NAPOLÉON III 2 Dec 1852-4 Sep 1870 when a Republic was proclaimed, third but only surviving son of Louis Bonaparte (the former King of Holland), and Hortense de Beauharnais, the daughter of Joséphine, b 20 Apr 1808; d in exile 9 Jan 1873. Carried to the presidency by the magic of the Bonaparte name, Louis-Napoléon effected a coup on the anniversary of Austerlitz (2 Dec 1851) and, following a plebiscite for which opposition was safely silenced, proclaimed the Second Empire a year later. Considerable prosperity and the military glory of the campaigns in the Crimea and Lombardy made the Empire of Napoléon III popular. Unrest grew, particularly following the ill-fated Mexican expedition, and the Franco-Prussian War, entered as a diversion to public dissent, ended in crushing defeat and deposition.

THE THIRD FRENCH REPUBLIC

The Republic was proclaimed on 4 Sep 1870.

The Government of National Defence

A Government of self-proclaimed Ministers ran the country until elections could be held for a National Assembly.

Presidents

LOUIS ADOLPHE THIERS Chief executive power of the French Republic **13 Feb-31 Aug**

1871; President **31 Aug 1871-24 May 1873** when he resigned, b 18 Apr 1797; d 3 Sep 1877.

MARIE EDME PATRICE MAURICE MAC-MAHON (comte de Mac-Mahon, duc de Magenta, Marshal of France) **24 May 1873-28 Jan 1879** when he resigned, b 13 Jul 1808; d 17 Oct 1893. The soldier Mac-Mahon distinguished himself in the Crimea and in Italy where he won a great victory at Magenta (1859); the statesman Mac-Mahon was a monarchist who accepted the presidency unwillingly - his defeat by Parliament in a constitutional crisis confirmed the supremacy of the legislature over a weak President in the Third Republic.

FRANCOIS PAUL JULES GRÉVY 30 Jan 1879-Nov 1887 when he resigned, b 15 Aug 1807; d 19 Sep 1891.

MARIE-FRANCOIS SADI CARNOT 3 Dec 1887-24 Jun 1894 when he was assassinated by an Italian anarchist, b 11 Aug 1837.

JEAN PAUL PIERRE CASIMIR-PÉRIER 27 Jun 1894-Dec 1894 when he resigned, b 8 Nov 1847; d 11 Mar 1907.

FRANCOIS FÉLIX FAURE 17 Jan 1895-16 Feb 1899 when he died in office, b 30 Jan 1841.

ÉMILE FRANCOIS LOUBET 18 Feb 1899-Jan 1906, b 31 Dec 1838; d 20 Dec 1929.

CLEMENT ARMAND FALLIÈRES 18 Jan 1906-Jan 1913, b 6 Nov 1841; d 22 Jun 1931.

RAYMOND POINCARÉ 17 Jan 1913-Feb 1920, b 20 Aug 1860; d 15 Oct 1934. Poincaré never forgave Germany for the partition of his native Lorraine (1871), and was determined to regain the lost provinces and to strengthen France by rearming and by European alliances ready for the war which he believed to be inevitable. As Premier twice in the 1920s his economic policies saved the franc.

PAUL DESCHANEL 17 Feb-20 Sep 1920 when he resigned, b 13 Feb 1855; d 28 Apr 1922.

ALEXANDRE MILLERAND 20 Sep 1920-May 1924 when he resigned, b 10 Feb 1859; d 7 Apr 1943.

GASTON DOUMERGUE 13 Jun 1924-May 1931, b 1 Aug 1863; d 18 Jun 1937.

PAUL DOUMER 13 May 1931-6 May 1932 when he was assassinated, b 22 Mar 1857.

ALBERT LEBRUN 10 May 1932-Jul 1940 when he agreed to the 'Vichy' revisions of the constitution, b 29 Aug 1871; d 6 Mar 1950. A compromise candidate to the presidency, he proved an ineffective war leader. He conceded power to Pétain, was interned by the Germans (1943-4) and in 1944 recognised de Gaulle's provisional government.

Prime Ministers

RENÉ VIVIANI Jun 1914-Oct 1915, b 3 Nov 1863; d 7 Sep 1925. A great orator he resigned after serious ammunition shortages threatened the French war effort.

ARISTIDE BRIAND 29 Oct 1915-Mar 1917, b 28 Mar 1862; d 7 Mar 1932. An outstanding debater, Briand was much criticised for his conduct of the war. Later his work for the League of Nations and in the Locarno Treaty and Kellogg-Briand Pact won him the Nobel Peace Prize.

ALEXANDRE RIBOT 20 Mar-Sep 1917, b 7 Feb 1842; d 13 Jan 1923.

PAUL PAINLEVÉ 12 Sep-Nov 1917.

GEORGES CLEMENCEAU 17 Nov 1917-Jan 1920, b 28 Sep 1841; d 24 Nov 1929. The veteran radical Clemenceau was a great war leader whose fighting spirit earned him the epithet 'Tiger'. He dominated the Versailles Peace Conference but was frustrated in his ambition to become President.

ALEXANDRE MILLERAND 19 Jan-Sep 1920; became President Millerand.

GEORGES LEYGUES 24 Sep 1920-Jan 1921, b 1857; d 1933.

ARISTIDE BRIAND 16 Jan 1921-Jan 1922.

RAYMOND POINCARÉ 15 Jan 1922-Jun 1924; formerly President Poincaré.

FRÉDÉRIC FRANCOIS-MARSAL 8-15 Jun 1924, b 1874; d 1958.

ÉDOUARD HERRIOT 15 Jun 1924-Apr 1925, b 5 Jul 1872; d 26 Mar 1957. President of the Assembly (1947-54) and Mayor of Lyon for 50 years this distinguished writer was interned by the Germans during World War II.

PAUL PAINLEVÉ 17 Apr-Nov 1925, b 5 Dec 1863; d 29 Oct 1933.

ARISTIDE BRIAND 23 Nov 1925-Jul 1926.

ÉDOUARD HERRIOT 19-21 Jul 1926.

RAYMOND POINCARÉ 21 Jul 1926-Jul 1929.

ARISTIDE BRIAND 29 Jul-Oct 1929; acting PM **22 Oct-2 Nov 1929.**

ANDRÉ TARDIEU 2 Nov 1929-Feb 1930, b 22 Sep 1876; d 15 Sep 1945.

CAMILLE CHAUTEMPS 21-25 Feb 1930; acting PM **25 Feb-2 Mar 1930.**

ANDRÉ TARDIEU 2 Mar-Dec 1930.

THÉODORE STEEG 13 Dec 1930-24 Jan 1931, b 1868; d 1963.

PIERRE LAVAL 24 Jan 1931-20 Feb 1932.

ANDRÉ TARDIEU 20 Feb-May 1932; acting PM **10 May-4 Jun 1932.**

ÉDOUARD HERRIOT 4 Jun-Dec 1932.

JOSEPH PAUL-BONCOUR 14 Dec 1932-Jan 1933, b 1873; d 1972.

ÉDOUARD DALADIER 31 Jan-Oct 1933, b 18 Jun 1884; d 10 Oct 1970. The unpopularity he gained through appeasement, in particular by signing the Munich Pact, was countered by the sympathy gained through his imprisonment by the Vichy régime.

ALBERT SARRAUT 26 Oct-23 Nov 1933, b 28 Jul 1872; d 26 Nov 1962.

CAMILLE CHAUTEMPS 23 Nov 1933-Jan 1934, b 1 Feb 1885; d 1 Jul 1963.

ÉDOUARD DALADIER 30 Jan-7 Feb 1934.

GASTON DOUMERGUE 7 Feb-Nov 1934; formerly President Doumergue.

PIERRE-ÉTIENNE FLANDIN 9 Nov 1934-Jun 1935, b 1889; d 1958.

FERNAND BOUISSON 1-4 Jun 1935, b 1874; d 1959.
PIERRE LAVAL Jun 1935-Jan 1936.
ALBERT SARRAUT 24 Jan-Jun 1936.
LÉON BLUM 4 Jun 1936-Jun 1937; see Provisional Government.
CAMILLE CHAUTEMPS 22 Jun 1937-Mar 1938.
LÉON BLUM 13 Mar-8 Apr 1938.
ÉDOUARD DALADIER 8 Apr 1938-Mar 1940.
PAUL REYNAUD 21 Mar-17 Jun 1940, b 15 Oct 1878; d 21 Sep 1966. A supporter of de Gaulle's rearmament plans before the war it was natural that this opponent of appeasement be called on to lead France in war. He resigned rather than accept the surrender advocated by Pétain.
PHILIPPE PÉTAIN (Marshal of France) 17 Jun-11 Jul 1940 when he became Head of State of the French State; see Head of State of French State.

THE FRENCH STATE

Head of State

PHILIPPE PÉTAIN (Marshal of France) 11 Jul 1940-1944, b 24 Apr 1856; d in detention on Yeu island 23 Jul 1951. Pétain's unpopular defence policies delayed his promotion - he became a general at 58. His ideas were vindicated by the great victory he won at Verdun (1916). He became Premier when France was defeated in 1940 and after negotiating a settlement with the Germans became Head of the administration in unoccupied France. He was tried as a collaborator after the war.

Heads of Government

The post of Premier did not officially exist in the French State.

PHILIPPE PÉTAIN (Marshal of France) 12-14 Jul 1940.
PIERRE LAVAL 14 Jul-15 Dec 1940.
PHILIPPE PÉTAIN (Marshal of France) 15 Dec 1940-Feb 1941.
Admiral FRANCOIS DARLAN Feb 1941-Apr 1942, b 1881; assassinated 24 Dec 1942 having declared for the Allies and formed a 'Government' in Algiers.
PIERRE LAVAL 18 Apr 1942-Apr 1944 when he fled, b 28 Jun 1883; executed as a traitor 15 Oct 1945.
(The French State was not formally abolished until 10 Sep 1944 but had ceased to exist by Apr 1944.)

FREE FRANCE

A French National Committee was formed by General de Gaulle in London after the capitulation - this Committee received full diplomatic recognition from the UK, USA and USSR on 26 Aug 1943. The Committee was broadened and became the Provisional Government of the French Republic on 2 Jun 1944 in liberated Algiers - it was transferred to liberated Paris on 31 Aug 1944.

THE PROVISIONAL GOVERNMENT OF THE FRENCH REPUBLIC

Heads of State and of Government

Gen CHARLES ANDRÉ MARIE JOSEPH de GAULLE 3 Jun 1944-21 Jan 1946.
FÉLIX GOUIN 23 Jan-Jun 1946, b 1884; d 1977.
GEORGES AUGUSTIN BIDAULT 19 Jun-28 Nov 1946, b 5 Oct 1899.
LEON BLUM 12 Dec 1946-16 Jan 1947, b 9 Apr 1872; d 30 Mar 1950. The veteran Socialist leader Blum was called upon to preside over the transfer from the Provisional Government to the Fourth Republic. His outstanding Ministry (1936-7) effected many important social reforms but neglected defence.

THE FOURTH FRENCH REPUBLIC

Presidents

VINCENT AURIOL 16 Jan 1947-Jan 1954, b 25 Aug 1884; d 1 Jan 1966. His presidency was marred by political factions which often rendered the formation of a Cabinet impossible.
RENÉ COTY 17 Jan 1954-Jan 1959 under the constitution of the Fourth Republic although the Fifth Republic entered into force on 4 Oct 1958, b 20 Mar 1882; d 22 Nov 1962. The instability of the Fourth Republic came to a head in the Algerian crisis of 1958. He remained as a figurehead, having summoned de Gaulle to power with dictatorial authority for six months.

Prime Ministers

PAUL RAMADIER 17 Jan-Nov 1947, b 1888; d 1961.
ROBERT SCHUMAN 22 Nov 1947-Jul 1948, b 29 Jun 1886; d 4 Sep 1963. With Jean Monnet he was the author of the Plan that established the European Coal and Steel Community and laid the foundation for the Common Market.
ANDRÉ MARIE 21 Jul-30 Aug 1948, b 1897; d 1974.
ROBERT SCHUMAN 30 Aug-8 Sep 1948.
HENRI QUEUILLE 8 Sep 1948-Oct 1949; caretaker PM 8-23 Oct 1949, b 1884; d 1970.
GEORGES BIDAULT 23 Oct 1949-Jun 1950; see Provisional Government.
HENRI QUEUILLE 28 Jun-8 Jul 1950.
RENÉ PLEVEN 8 Jul 1950-Mar 1951, b 15 Apr 1901.
HENRI QUEUILLE 2 Mar-10 Jul 1951; caretaker PM 10 Jul-3 Aug 1951.
RENÉ PLEVEN 3 Aug 1951-Jan 1952.
EDGAR FAURE 16 Jan-Mar 1952, b 18 Aug 1908.

ANTOINE PINAY **3 Mar-25 Dec 1952**; caretaker
PM **25-31 Dec 1952,** b 1891.
RENÉ JOËL SIMON **31 Dec 1952-May 1953**;
caretaker PM **26 May-24 Jun 1953,** b 1895.
JOSEPH LANIEL **24 Jun 1953-Jun 1954,** b 1889;
d 1975.
PIERRE MENDÈS-FRANCE **12 Jun 1954-Feb
1955**; caretaker PM **6-14 Feb 1955,** b 11 Jan 1907.
CHRISTIAN PINEAU **14-19 Feb 1955,** b 14 Oct
1904.
EDGAR FAURE **20 Feb 1955-Jan 1956.**
GUY MOLLET **26 Jan 1956-May 1957**; caretaker
PM **24 May-4 Jun 1957,** b 31 Dec 1905.
MAURICE JEAN-MARIE BOURGES-
MAUNOURY **4 Jun-30 Sep 1957**; caretaker PM
30 Sep-11 Oct 1957, b 19 Aug 1914.
ANTOINE PINAY **11-18 Oct 1957.**
GUY MOLLET **18-29 Oct 1957.**
FÉLIX GAILLARD **30 Oct 1957-Apr 1958**;
caretaker PM **15 Apr-9 May 1958,** b 1919.
PIERRE PFLIMLIN **9-29 May 1958,** b 5 Feb 1907.
Gen CHARLES ANDRÉ MARIE JOSEPH de
GAULLE **29 May 1958-Jan 1959**; see President
de Gaulle.

THE FIFTH FRENCH REPUBLIC

Presidents

Gen CHARLES ANDRÉ MARIE JOSEPH de
GAULLE **8 Jan 1959-28 Apr 1969** when he
resigned, b 22 Nov 1890; d 9 Nov 1970. In World
War I de Gaulle was thrice wounded; in the
1930s, like Churchill, he warned against appeasement. After the fall of France (1940), he set up a
committee of the Free French in London and
made inspiring broadcasts to his occupied
country. After heading the Provisional Government he retired and concentrated upon his
writing. Recalled to power in the conditions of
near civil war in the Algerian crisis (1958), he
replaced the discredited Fourth Republic with the
Fifth under which the presidential authority is
greatly increased at the expense of the
premiership.
ALAIN POHER President *per interim* **Apr-20 Jun
1969,** b 1909.
GEORGES JEAN RAYMOND POMPIDOU **20
Jun 1969-2 Apr 1974** when he died in office, b 5
Jul 1911.
ALAIN POHER President *per interim* **Apr-27 May
1974,** b 1909.
VALÉRY GISCARD d'ESTAING **since 27 May
1974,** b 2 Feb 1926.

Prime Ministers

MICHEL JEAN-PIERRE DEBRÉ **8 Jan 1959-Apr
1962,** b 15 Jan 1912.
GEORGES JEAN RAYMOND POMPIDOU **14
Apr 1962-Jul 1968**; see President Pompidou.
JACQUES MAURICE COUVE de MURVILLE **11
Jul 1968-Jun 1969,** b 24 Jan 1907.

JACQUES PIERRE MICHEL CHABAN-DELMAS
20 Jun 1969-Jul 1972, b 7 Mar 1915.
PIERRE AUGUSTE JOSEPH MESSMER **5 Jul
1972-May 1974,** b 20 Mar 1916.
JACQUES RENÉ CHIRAC **27 May 1974-Aug
1976,** b 29 Nov 1932.
RAYMOND BARRE **since 25 Aug 1976,** b 12 Apr
1924.

Anjou

Corresponding roughly with the Gaulish district of
Andécaves, the County of Anjou was governed by
an energetic family whose descendants are known
in English history as the Plantagenets. Reunited to
France in 1205, Anjou did not become part of the
royal domain until 1481.

† Counts

INGELGER **late 9th century,** d *c* 900.
FOULQUES I (le Roux - the red) **c 900-942,** son of
Ingelger, b 865.
FOULQUES II (le Bon - the good) **942-961,** son of
Foulques I, b 900.
GEOFFROI I (Grisegonelle - greygown) **961-987,**
son of Foulques II.
FOULQUES III (le Noir - the black) **987-1040,** son
of Geoffroi I, b 979.
GEOFFROI II **1040-1060,** only surviving son of
Foulques III by his second wife, b 1006. An
energetic ruler who greatly extended his
dominions.
GEOFFROI III (le Barbu - the bearded) **1060-1069**
when he was deposed and imprisoned by his
brother Foulques; elder nephew of Geoffroi III,
b 1040; d 1098.
FOULQUES IV (le Rechin - the bad-tempered)
1069-1103 when he abdicated, younger brother of
Geoffroi III, b 1043; d 1109. Foulques was
excommunicated for his usurpation; he abando-
ned his first wife, Hermengarde, while his second
Countess was willingly abducted by Philippe I of
France.
GEOFFROI IV (Martel) **1103-1106** died in battle
against his father, Foulques IV; son of Foulques
IV by his first wife. He released his uncle
Geoffroi from gaol.
FOULQUES V **1106-1129** when he abdicated and
left for Palestine, eventually to become King of
Jerusalem, half-brother of Geoffroi IV, b 1090; d
1143.
GEOFFROI V (Plantagenet) **1129-1151,** third son
of Foulques V - the elder sons were heirs to
Jerusalem, b 24 Aug 1113. Married in his youth to
the fiery Matilda, heiress to England's Henry I,
he was more successful than his wife in
reclaiming her inheritance - he conquered
Normandy (1135-44).
GEOFFROI VI **1151-1158,** second son of Geoffroi
V.

GUILLAUME de Poitou **1158-1164,** third son of Geoffroi V.

HENRI 1164-1189, eldest son of Geoffroi V; was also King Henry II of England.

RICHARD 1189-1199; was also King Richard I of England.

JEAN 1199-1205 when the County was lost to France; was also King John of England.

Brittany

In the mid 5th century the Celts first arrived in Armor, which they converted over the next 200 years to Brittany; unity was achieved by Nominoé who threw off Frankish suzerainty (845); the Duchy of Brittany was at times virtually sovereign, particularly under the de Montfort Dukes (1364-1488). Brittany was not finally united to France until 1532, the last Duchess having married Francois I.

† Dukes

NOMINOÉ 826-851 named Duke by Louis I of the Franks; Duke until 845 when he adopted the style of King. A gifted man of modest origins, Nominoé was made Count of Vannes by Charlemagne then Duke of Brittany by Louis I. In 845 he rose against the Franks and established the virtual independence of Brittany.

ERISPOÉ 851-857.

SALOMON 857-?

PASQUITO *fl.*870s, Count of Vannes rather than Duke of all Brittany.

GURVAN *fl.*870s, Count of Rennes rather than Duke of all Brittany.

JUDICAEL *fl.* **end of 9th century,** Count of Rennes rather than Duke of all Brittany.

ALAIN III (le Grand - the great) **877-907.** Originally Count of Vannes, Alain reunited Brittany as a single Duchy after his victory over the Normans (888).

GURMALLION 907-*c***930.** The Norman invasion of 919 reduced Brittany to anarchy.

BÉRENGER 930-937, Count of Vannes rather than Duke of all Brittany.

ALAIN IV (Barbe-Torte - Crookbeard) **937-952.** Returning from exile in England Alain drove out the Normans and reunited the Duchy.

DROGO 952-?

GUÉROC 980-987.

CONAN I 987-992.

GEOFFROI I 992-1008.

ALAIN V 1008-1040.

CONAN II 1040-1066.

HOEL V 1066-1084.

ALAIN VI 1084-1112.

CONAN III (le Gros - the fat) **1112-1148,** b 1089.

EUDES 1148-1156. Disputed succession 1148-1156.

HOEL VI 1148-?Claimed to be Duke of Brittany.

(GEOFFROI of Anjou, father of Henry II of England, ruled part of Brittany 1148-1151.)

CONAN IV 1156-1171. A weak ruler who submitted to King Henry II of England.

CONSTANCE (Duchess) co-ruler **1171-1196,** daughter of Conan IV. Joint-ruler with her husband Geoffroi.

GEOFFROI II or III co-ruler **1171-1196,** son of Henry II of England, b 1158.

ARTHUR I 1196-Apr 1203, son of Constance and Geoffroi II, b 1187. By primogeniture, not then firmly established, Arthur had a better claim to the English crown than King John, who was responsible for Arthur's death.

1203-1213 Interregnum.

PIERRE I (Mauclerc) **1213-1237;** d 1250. A Capetian prince who was installed as Duke largely through the influence of Conan, Count of Rennes.

JEAN I 1237-1286, b 1217.

JEAN II 1286-1305, b 1239.

ARTHUR II 1305-1312, b 1262.

JEAN III 1312-1341, b 1276.

JEANNE de Penthièvre (Duchess) **1341-1365** when she was forced to cede her rights to her cousin, Jean de Montfort, daughter of Jean III, b 1319; d 1384. She fought her uncle, Jean IV de Montfort, for control of Brittany.

JEAN IV de Montfort **1341-1345,** brother of Jean III, b 1293.

JEAN V de Montfort **1365-1 Nov 1399,** cousin of Jeanne, b *c* 1340.

JEAN VI de Montfort **Nov 1399-28 Aug 1442,** b 24 Dec 1439.

FRANCOIS I Aug 1442-1450, b 1414.

PIERRE II 1450-1457.

ARTHUR III de Richemont **1457-1458,** b 1393. An outstanding strategist, de Richemont played a major role in defeating the English in the Hundred Years' War.

FRANCOIS II 1458-1488, b 1435. His participation in the wars of the League of 'Public Good' against Louis XI and the 'Guerre folle' against Anne, the mother of Charles VIII, made the continued independence of Brittany intolerable to France.

ANNE (Duchess) **1488-1514,** daughter of Francois II, b 1477. Small, thin and lame, the Duchess Anne remained sovereign of her country despite her marriages to Charles VIII of France and his successor Louis XII.

CLAUDE (Duchess) **1514-1524,** daughter of Anne and Louis XII, b 1499. By her marriage to the future Francois I, Brittany was finally attached to France.

FRANCOIS III 1524-1532 when he annexed Brittany to his Kingdom of France, widower of Claude; was also Francois I, King of France.

Burgundy

The name Burgundy has been applied to several territorial units in European history: a Kingdom of Burgundy flourished in the Dark Ages; Burgundy was one of the divisions of the Frankish Empire; two Burgundian Kingdoms existed in the 10th century and a Burgundian Duchy - situated to the West of both former Burgundian Kingdoms - became one of the great powers of Medieval Europe.

† KINGS OF THE BURGUNDIANS

The Kingdom of the Burgundians

GUNDICAR (or GUNTHER) **c413-437** killed in battle.
GUNDERIC 437-466.
CHILPÉRIC 466-491.
GONDEBAUD 491-516. He enlarged the Kingdom to include most of present day eastern France and promulgated the 'loi gombette'.
SIGISMOND (Saint Sigismund) **516-523** murdered, son of Gondebaud.
GONDEMAR 523-532 assassinated, son of Gondebaud. He lost his life and his state at the hands of the Franks.
532-534 Burgundy was conquered by the Franks and was formally incorporated into their empire in 534.
534-879 Frankish rule.
840 Burgundy formed a separate territorial division within the Frankish Empire.
879 Burgundy became an independent state.

The Kingdom of Lower Burgundy
(Regnum Provinciae)

Also called the Kingdom of Provence and the Kingdom of Arles.

BOSON 879-887, brother-in-law of Charles II of France.
LOUIS 887-924, son of Boson; d 928.
HUGUES 924-933 or 934 when deprived of his Kingdom, kinsman of Boson; d 947.

The Kingdom of Upper Burgundy
(Regnum Jurense)

Also called the Kingdom of Transjurane Burgundy.

RODOLPHE I 890-912, son of the Count of Auxerre.
RODOLPHE II 912-934 when he became King of united Burgundy

† KINGS OF BURGUNDY

A Kingdom which included present day Provence, Savoy, Dauphiné, Lyonnais, Franche-Comté and western Switzerland but not Burgundy.

RODOLPHE II King of Regnum Jurense **from 912**; King of reunited Burgundy **934-937,** son of Rodolphe I.
CONRAD I 937-993, son of Rodolphe II.
RODOLPHE III 993-1032, son of Conrad I.
CONRAD II 1033-1039, cousin of Rodolphe III; was also Konrad II, Holy Roman Emperor.
(From 1033 the Kingdom of Burgundy belonged to the Holy Roman Empire and quickly ceased to exist as a separate unit, being divided into many small feudal states owing allegiance to the Emperor - most of these territories were acquired by the French monarchy during the Middle Ages.)

THE DUCHY OF BURGUNDY

The Duchy corresponded to present day Burgundy and later included Franche-Comté and much of the Low Countries.

† Dukes of Burgundy

HOUSE OF CAPET
OTTON 956-965, brother of Hugues Capet.
HENRI I ('The Great') **965-1002,** brother of Otton. He willed the Duchy to his relative Robert II, King of France.
ROBERT I 1002-1015 when he ceded the Duchy to his son; was also Robert II of France.
HENRI II 1015-1031 when he inherited France; was also Henri I of France.
ROBERT II (sometimes called ROBERT I) **1031-1075,** son of Robert I.
HUGUES I 1075-1078, grandson of Robert II.
EUDES I 1078-1102, brother of Hugues I.
HUGUES II ('The Peaceful') **1102-1142.**
EUDES II 1142-1162.
HUGUES III 1162-1193, grandson of Hugues II, b c1150. One of the leaders of the Third Crusade.
EUDES III 1193-1218, son of Hugues III.
HUGUES IV 1218-1272, grandson of Hugues III, b 1212.
ROBERT III or II **1272-1305,** kinsman of Hugues III.
HUGUES V 1305-1315, grandson of Hugues IV.
EUDES IV 1315-1350, son of Robert III (or II).
PHILIPPE I de Rouvres **1350-1361,** kinsman of Eudes IV, b 1346. Upon the death of this Duke the possessions of the Burgundian Ducal family were divided with most of Burgundy proper going to France.
1361-1363 French rule.

HOUSE OF VALOIS
PHILIPPE II ('The Bold') **1363-1404,** son of Jean II of France, b 1342. Philippe, who married the

widow of Philippe I, was granted Burgundy by his father after his valour at the Battle of Poitiers.
JEAN ('The Fearless') **1404-10 Sep 1419** assassinated by supporters of the Dauphin; son of Philippe II, b 28 May 1371. Jean, who fought Louis d'Orléans for control of the mad King Charles VI, entered the Hundred Years' War on the English side and occupied Paris after the Battle of Agincourt.

† Dukes of Burgundy with the Personal Title 'Grand-Duc Du Ponant'
(Grand Duke of the Occident)

PHILIPPE III ('The Good') **Sep 1419-1467,** son of Jean, b 1396. Allied to England he made Burgundy a great power but was frustrated in his desire to make the state a Kingdom and had to console himself with the grandiose style Grand-Duc du Ponant and with the dramatic creation of the Order of the Golden Fleece at his marriage ceremony.
CHARLES I ('The Bold') **1467-5 Jan 1477** d in battle, son of Philippe III, b 10 Nov 1433. He made Burgundy an independent Kingdom in all but name, but its power was destroyed by France, the Swiss and the Emperor (all of whom were alarmed by his ambitions). Upon his death the war waged against him by his neighbours was taken into Burgundy itself which was annexed to France in 1477.

† Dukes of Burgundy
(in the Low Countries)

These Dukes ruled the Burgundian inheritance in the Low Countries but not the Duchy of Burgundy proper.

HOUSE OF VALOIS
MARIE (Duchess) **Jan 1477-27 Mar 1482,** daughter of Charles I, b 13 Feb 1457. She lost Burgundy proper to France but, through the influence of her husband (Maximilian of Austria) she maintained the Burgundian possessions in the Low Countries and the ducal style of Burgundy.

HOUSE OF HABSBURG
PHILIPPE IV   Mar 1482-25 Sep 1506, son of Marie; was also Felipe I of Spain.
CHARLES II   Sep 1506-1529 when the Duchy of Burgundy was renounced in the Peace of Cambrai; was also Carlos I of Spain (Emperor Charles V).
(The Habsburgs continued to use the empty style Duke of Burgundy until the final overthrow of their dynasty.)

Lorraine

The Duchy of Lorraine was founded in 895 and divided in 956 into Upper and Lower Lorraine: the

former survived, in a reduced form, as the Duchy of Lorraine; the latter, considerably diminished, became the Duchy of Brabant.

† Dukes of Lorraine

GISELBERT   916-940.
HENRI I   940-944.
BRUNO   944-959, Archbishop of Cologne. In his reign the Duchy became divided into Upper and Lower.

† Dukes of Upper Lorraine

HOUSE OF ALSACE
FRÉDÉRIC I   959-984.
THIERRY I   984-1026.
FRÉDÉRIC II   1026-1033.
GOTHELON I   1033-1043.
GOTHELON II   1043-1046.
ALBERT   1046-1048.
GÉRARD   1048-1070.
THIERRY II ('The Valiant') **1070-1115.**
SIGISMOND I   1115-1139.
MATTHIEU I   1139-1176.
SIGISMOND II   1176-1205.
FERRI I   1205-1206.
FERRI II   1206-1213.
THIBAUT I   1213-1220.
MATTHIEU II   1220-1251.
FERRI III (or FRÉDÉRIC III) **1251-1304.**
THIBAUT II   1304-1312.
FERRI IV (or FRÉDÉRIC IV) **1312-1328.**
RAOUL (also known as RODOLPHE) **1328-1346.**
JEAN I   1346-1391.
CHARLES II ('The Bold') **1391-25 Jan 1431,** son of Jean I, b 1365. Through careful diplomacy in alliance with Burgundy and by the marriage of his heiress Isabelle to the heir to Bar he made Lorraine a significant power.
ISABELLE (Duchess) co-ruler **Jan 1431-1453,** daughter of Charles II.

HOUSE OF ANJOU
RENÉ I co-ruler **Jan 1431-1453,** husband of Isabelle; was also Rinaldo, King of Naples.
JEAN II   1453-1470, son of Isabelle.
NICOLAS   1470-1473, son of Isabelle.
JOLANTHE (Duchess) co-ruler **1473-1480,** kinswoman of Jean II.
RENÉ II co-ruler **1473-1480** when he became sole Duke of Bar and of Lorraine.

† Dukes of Bar and of Lorraine

HOUSE OF ANJOU
RENÉ II Duke from 1473; Duke of Bar and Lorraine **1480-1508,** husband of Jolanthe and grandson of René I, b 1451.
ANTOINE   1508-1544, kinsman of René II.
FRANCOIS I   1544-1545, kinsman of René II.
CHARLES III (sometimes called CHARLES II) **1545-14 May 1608,** b 18 Feb 1543. He suffered a French invasion, the loss of the Three Bishoprics

to France and eight years captivity in that country. After his release he reformed the administration and judiciary of the remainder of his state.

HENRI II 1608-1624, son of Charles III.

NICOLE (Duchess) 1624-1625 deposed, daughter of Henri II; d after 1630.

FRANCOIS II 1625 abdicated, brother of Henri II; d 1632. He deposed his niece and abandoned the principle of female succession in Lorraine.

CHARLES IV (sometimes called CHARLES III) 1625-1632 abdicated, son of Francois II and husband of Nicole, b 5 Apr 1604; d 18 Sep 1675. The victim of French ambitions on the Duchy he was restored in 1641 but under French supervision and in 1662 he illegally sold Lorraine to France.

NICOLAS FRANCOIS 1632-1641 deposed, brother of Charles III. A Cardinal of the Catholic Church.

CHARLES IV 1641 deposed - nominally Duke until 1659.

NICOLAS FRANCOIS 1659-1670.

1670-1697 Lorraine was under French occupation.

CHARLES V (sometimes called CHARLES IV) nominally Duke 1675-1690, nephew of Charles IV.

LÉOPOLD nominally Duke 1690-1697; sovereign Duke 1697-27 Mar 1729, son of Charles V.

FRANCOIS III Mar 1729-11 Apr 1736 when he renounced Lorraine, son of Léopold; was also Francesco II, Grand Duke of Tuscany, and Franz I, Emperor of the Holy Roman Empire.

HOUSE OF LESZCZYNSKI

STANISLAS 1738-23 Feb 1766, Duke with the personal title King; was also Stanislaw I, King of Poland.

Normandy

A Duchy of northern France founded in 911 by Charles III of France for Rollon the Viking leader and incorporated into France in 1204.

† Dukes

HOUSE OF NORMANDY

ROBERT I (better known as ROLLON - the name he had before his conversion to Christianity) 911-?932, b c860. The Norse leader ravaged much of northern France before being 'bought off' by the grant of Normandy from the French King.

GUILLAUME I ('Longsword') co-ruler 927-932; sole ruler 932-17 Dec 942, son of Robert I, b c900; murdered by Flemings.

RICHARD I ('The Fearless') Dec 942-20 Nov 996, son of Guillaume I, b 933.

RICHARD II ('The Good') Nov 996-23 Aug 1027, elder son of Richard I.

RICHARD III Aug 1027-6 Aug 1028, eldest son of Richard II.

ROBERT II (sometimes called Robert I) Aug 1028-2 Jul 1035, second son of Richard II.

GUILLAUME II Jul 1035-9 Sep 1087; was also William I of England.

ROBERT III (sometimes called Robert II) Sep 1087-28 Sep 1106 when he was captured at the Battle of Tinchebrai, eldest son of Guillaume II, b c1054; d Feb 1134 a captive in Cardiff Castle. Duke Robert, who declined the throne of Jerusalem, lost that of England through the usurpation of his brother Henry I who eventually deposed his rival.

HENRI I Sep 1106-1 Dec 1135; was also Henry I of England.

HOUSE OF BLOIS

ÉTIENNE Dec 1135-Jan 1144 when he ceased to control the Duchy; was also King Stephen of England.

HOUSE OF NORMANDY

MATHILDE (Duchess) co-ruler 19 Jan 1144-10 Sep 1167; was also Queen Matilda of England.

HOUSE OF ANJOU

GEOFFROI co-ruler 19 Jan 1144-1149 abdicated; was also Geoffroi V of Anjou.

HENRI II co-ruler 1149-1167; sole ruler Sep 1167-6 Jul 1189; was also Henry II of England.

RICHARD IV Jul 1189-6 Apr 1190; was also Richard I of England.

JEAN Apr 1190-1204 when Normandy was taken by France; was also King John of England.

Frankfurt, Grand Duchy of *see* Germany

Fujeirah *see* United Arab Emirates

Gabon

The coast of Gabon became French in 1842; the country became independent on 17 Aug 1960.

Presidents

LÉON M'BA Head of State 17 Aug 1960-12 Feb 1961; President 12 Feb 1961-28 Nov 1967 when he died in office, b 1902.

OMAR BONGO (formerly Albert-Bernard Bongo) since 2 Dec 1967, b 1936.

Prime Minister

LÉON MÉBIAME **since 12 Apr 1975** when the office of Premier was created by a constitutional amendment.

The Gambia

Although the Gambia was discovered by the Portuguese, the first European settlement was by the British in 1810. A Crown colony from 1843, independence was granted on 18 Feb 1965. The Gambia became a Republic on 24 Apr 1970.

THE DOMINION OF THE GAMBIA

Governors-General

Sir **JOHN WARBURTON PAUL 18 Feb 1965-1966,** b 1916.
Alhaji Sir **FARIMANG SINGHATEH 1966-24 Apr 1970,** b 1912.

Prime Minister

Sir **DAVID DAUDA KAIRABA JAWARA 18 Feb 1965-24 Apr 1970,** became first President.

THE REPUBLIC OF THE GAMBIA

President

The President is also Head of the Government.

DAUDA KAIRABA JAWARA (formerly Sir David Dauda Kairaba Jawara) **since 24 Apr 1970,** b 11 May 1924.

Gampola *see* Sri Lanka

Georgia

A Kingdom of the Caucasus, Georgia first emerged as an independent power under the descendants of Pharnavas (*c* 302-*c* 237 BC). The state later subdivided in the time of the Sassanian Dynasty but was reunited by Bagrat III *c* 1008. Subdivided again in the 15th century the Kingdom of Georgia may be said to have ceased to exist but the Karthli and Kakheth Kings continued to be styled Kings of Georgia until the annexation of Georgia by Russia in 1801. A Georgian state briefly maintained independence from 1918 to 1921 before being reinvaded by Russia.

THE KINGDOM OF GEORGIA

† Kings

BAGRATID DYNASTY
The Georgian kingship was usually collegiate thus it was not uncommon to have several co-Kings.

BAGRAT III Ruler of Abasgia from 979; King of reunited Georgia *c* 1008-1014. His state stretched from the Black Sea to the Caspian.
GIORGI I 1014-1027, son of Bagrat III.
BAGRAT IV 1027-1072, son of Giorgi I.
GIORGI II sole ruler **1072-1089**; co-ruler **1089-1112,** son of Bagrat IV.
DAWITH III or II ('The Builder') co-ruler **1089-1112**; sole ruler **1112-1125**; co-ruler **1125,** son of Giorgi II. Dawith made Georgia a great power and shook off any remaining nominal allegiance to the Byzantine Emperor.
DMITRI I co-ruler **1125**; sole ruler **1125-1155**; co-ruler **1155**; sole ruler **1155-1156** when he abdicated to enter a monastery, son of Dawith III; date of death uncertain.
DAWITH IV or III co-ruler **1155** - for 6 months, son of Dmitri I.
GIORGI III sole ruler **1156-1179**; co-ruler **1179-1184,** brother of Dawith IV.
THAMAR (or TAMARA) co-ruler **1179-1184**; sole ruler **1184-*c* 1193**; co-ruler *c* **1193-1212,** daughter of Giorgi III. Under Queen Thamar, Georgia reached its zenith of power. Her Kingdom occupied all the Caucasian region; her court was known for its brilliance. Her marriage to a Russian Prince began the long, and often unhappy, relationship between Georgia and Russia.
DAWITH SOSLAN co-ruler *c* **1193-1207,** cousin of Queen Thamar.
GIORGI IV ('The Resplendent') co-ruler **1205-1212**; sole ruler **1212-1223,** son of Queen Thamar.
RUSADAN (Queen) sole ruler **1223-1234**; co-ruler **1234-1245,** sister of Giorgi IV.
DAWITH V or IV co-ruler **1234-1258** when he seceded in Abasgia, son of Queen Rusadan; date of death uncertain.
DAWITH VI or V co-ruler **1250-1258**; sole ruler **1258-1269,** son of Giorgi IV.
1269-1273 Period of Mongol domination.
DMITRI II ('The Devoted') **1273-1289** when he was executed by the Mongols after submitting himself as a victim to save his people, son of Dawith VI.
VAXTANG II sole ruler **1289-1291**; co-ruler **1291-1292,** son of Dawith V.
DAWITH VII or VI co-ruler **1291-1292**; sole ruler **1292-1299**; co-ruler **1299-1310,** son of Dmitri II.
VAXTANG III co-ruler **1301-1307,** brother of Dawith VII.

GIORGI V ('The Little') co-ruler **1307-1314,** son of Dawith VII.

GIORGI VI ('The Illustrious') co-ruler **1299-1314;** sole ruler **1314-1346,** son of Dmitri II. He recovered Abasgia reuniting Georgia.

DAWITH VIII or VII sole ruler **1346-c 1355;** co-ruler **1355-1360,** son of Giorgi VI.

BAGRAT V ('The Great') co-ruler **c 1355-1360;** sole ruler **1360-1369;** co-ruler **1369-1386** when taken captive by Timur; son of Dawith VIII; d 1395.

GIORGI VII co-ruler **1369-1386** *de facto*; sole ruler **1386-1405** - though his father, Bagrat V, might be considered to be King until his death; d in battle, son of Bagrat V.

KONSTANTIN I sole ruler **1405-c 1408**; co-ruler **c 1408-1412** d in battle, brother of Giorgi VII.

ALEKSANDR I co-ruler **c 1408-1412**; sole ruler **1412-1442** abdicated, son of Konstantin I; d 1446. Alexander made Georgia great again but his subdivision of the realm between his sons during his lifetime led to the destruction of the Kingdom.

VAXTANG IV co-ruler **before 1442**; sole ruler **1442-1446,** son of Aleksandr I.

DMITRI III **before 1446-1453** *de jure* deposed, brother of Vaxtang IV.

GIORGI VIII co-ruler **before 1446-1465,** brother of Dmitri III.

GIORGI IX (I of Kakheth) co-ruler **c 1460-1465** King of Kakheth **1465-1478,** son of Giorgi VIII. The ancestor of the later Kings of Georgia.

BAGRAT VI co-ruler **1465-1478,** nephew of Giorgi IX (or I).

(After the reign of Bagrat VI, Georgia subdivided into three main Kingdoms and five Principalities.)

† Later Kings of Georgia
Kings of Karthli and Kakheth

BAGRATID DYNASTY

TAYMURAZI II King of Karthli or Kartlia **1744-1762.**

IRAKLI II King of Kakheth **1744-1762** when he became King of Georgia.

† Kings of Georgia
(Kakheth and Karthli united)

IRAKLI II **1762-early 1798** died in the mountains having fled before a Russian invasion, son of Taymurazi II.

GIORGI XIII **early 1798-28 Dec 1800,** son of Irakli II. He may be considered to have abdicated in favour of Tsar Alexander I of Russia in Sep 1799.

1800-1801 Georgian resistance to Russia when the country was annexed to the Russian Empire.

THE GEORGIAN REPUBLIC

Independent from 26 May 1918 to 25 Feb 1921 having declared her secession from Russia after the revolution. Russian recognition of Georgian independence was secured on 7 May 1920.

Heads of State and of Government

NOE RAMISHVILI **26 May-24 Jun 1918.**

NOE JORDANIA **24 Jun 1918-Feb 1921** when Georgia was annexed to the Soviet Union following a Russian invasion.

German Democratic Republic

The German Democratic Republic was established as a Communist state in the Soviet zone of occupation in Germany in Oct 1949 and was said to be sovereign from 25 Mar 1954.

HEADS OF STATE

President

WILHELM PIECK **11 Oct 1949-7 Sep 1960,** b 3 Jan 1876; d in office.

(On 12 Sep 1960 the post of President was replaced by that of Chairman of the State Council.)

Chairmen of the State Council

WALTER ULBRICHT **12 Sep 1960-1 Aug 1973,** b 30 Jun 1893; d in office. A deserter in World War I Ulbricht, who spent the World War II in Russia, was installed as leader of the Communist regime established by the USSR in 1949. He caused the Berlin Wall to be erected to prevent the East Germans 'voting with their feet' to escape the harsh extreme Stalinist system he created.

WILLI STOPH **3 Aug 1973-29 Oct 1976,** b 9 Jul 1914.

ERICH HONECKER **since 29 Oct 1976,** b 25 Aug 1912.

Prime Ministers

WALTER ULBRICHT **5-12 Oct 1949.**

OTTO GROTEWOHL **12 Oct 1949-21 Sep 1964,** b 1912; d in office.

WILLI STOPH **24 Sep 1964-Aug 1973.**

HORST SINDERMANN **3 Aug 1973-Oct 1976,** b 5 Sep 1914.

WILLI STOPH **since 29 Oct 1976.**

General Secretary of the Socialist Unity Party
(Communist Party)

WILHELM PIECK **Oct 1949-Jul 1950.**

WALTER ULBRICHT **25 Jul 1950-3 May 1971.**

ERICH HONECKER **since 3 May 1971.**

Otto, Prince von Bismarck, who was known as the 'Iron Chancellor' but who was also a sensitive and gifted writer (Radio Times Hulton Picture Library)

Germany

German unity was not achieved until Jan 1871 when the German Empire was founded. Defeat in World War I brought the overthrow of the Empire and revolutionary governments existed until the constitution of the Weimar Republic came into force in 1919. Hitler's Reich lasted from 1934 to 1945 when Germany was partitioned and occupied by the Allies. The Federal Republic of Germany was established on 21 Sep 1949 and gained complete sovereignty on 5 May 1955.

THE GERMAN EMPIRE

† German Emperors

HOUSE OF HOHENZOLLERN

WILHELM I 8 Jan 1871-9 Mar 1888, King of Prussia, brother of Friedrich Wilhelm IV, b 22 Mar 1797. Hard working and loyal, Wilhelm I may have been deeply conservative but he was never as reactionary as Bismarck who held power for most of the reign. By a series of wars, which the Minister-President later claimed to have planned, Prussia came to dominate Germany, and following the defeat of France by the German states, Wilhelm was persuaded (with difficulty for he regarded the Imperial title as empty) to become Emperor of a united and Prussian controlled Germany.

FRIEDRICH III 9 Mar-15 Jun 1888, only son of Wilhelm I, b 31 Oct 1831. The early death from throat cancer of liberal Friedrich III, son-in-law of Queen Victoria, was a tragedy for Germany.

WILHELM II Jun 1888-28 Nov 1918 when he abdicated or 10 Nov 1918 when he was deposed, eldest son of Friedrich III, b 27 Jan 1859; d 4 Jun 1941. Wilhelm II was too moody to rule. Lacking judgement, jealous of his British relatives (of whom he was, however, deeply fond) 'the Kaiser' has often been misrepresented. He has been called a warmonger but despite his sabre rattling and obscure Imperial pronouncements, he genuinely favoured peace. However, his supposed attitude encouraged an unscrupulous clique in the military and his more warlike Ministers. Far from wanting or planning the war as has been alleged, Wilhelm II tried to prevent it and in particular attempted to stop his generals from invading Belgium. The Kaiser discovered he did not have the powers the rest of the world believed him to possess.

Chancellors
(Premiers)

OTTO, Prince von BISMARCK-SCHÖNHAUSEN (Duke of Lauenburg) **21 Mar 1871-Mar 1890,** b 1 Apr 1815; d 30 Jul 1898. A brilliant manipulator, Bismarck united Germany under his Prussian master after skillfully exploiting pan-German feelings in a series of wars against Denmark, Austria and France. His successful foreign policy balanced the powers and he acted as 'honest broker' in the 1878 Balkan crisis. Stealing the political clothes of the Social Democrats (whom he disliked as much as he hated the Catholics, the victims of his Kulturkampf), he created Europe's first social security system. He fashioned the economic, monetary and legal German union but the 'pilot' was dropped by inexperienced Wilhelm II.

GEORG LEO, Count von CAPRIVI 18 Mar 1890-Oct 1894, b 24 Feb 1831; d 6 Feb 1899.

CHLODWIG KARL VICTOR, Prince von HOHENLOHE-SCHILLINGSFÜRST Oct 1894-Oct 1900, b 1819; d 1901.

BERNHARDT HEINRICH MARTIN KARL, Prince von BÜLOW 17 Oct 1900-Jul 1909, b 3 May 1849; d 28 Oct 1929. The last effective Imperial Chancellor (the last Chancellors could not control the military clique, particularly Tirpitz) he strove to build a colonial Empire. The Moroccan crisis and naval expansion soured the intense rivalry with Britain.

THEOBALD THEODOR FRIEDRICH ALFRED von BETHMANN-HOLLWEG 14 Jul 1909-Jul 1917, b 29 Nov 1856; d 2 Jan 1921.

Dr **GEORG MICHAELIS 13 Jul 1917-Oct 1918,** b
8 Sep 1857; d 24 Jul 1936.
Prince MAXIMILIAN of Baden 31 Oct-8 Nov 1918,
cousin of the last Grand Duke of Baden, b 10 Jul
1867, d 6 Nov 1929.
FRIEDRICH EBERT 9 Nov 1918; see President
Ebert.
9 Nov 1918 The Republic was declared.

THE REPUBLIC OF GERMANY

Federal Presidents

FRIEDRICH EBERT 6 Feb 1919-28 Feb 1925, b 4
Feb 1871; d in office.
Marshal **PAUL von BENECKENDORFF und von
HINDENBURG 26 Apr 1925-2 Aug 1934,** b 2 Oct
1847; d in office. Chief of the General Staff in
1916 and architect of the 'Siegfried Line', this
devoted monarchist was a war hero despite
Germany's defeat.

Federal Chancellors
(Premiers)

Nov 1918-Feb 1919 Six-man ruling council.
PHILIPP SCHEIDEMANN 13 Feb-Jun 1919, b 26
Jul 1865; d 29 Nov 1939 in exile. He declared the
Republic of his own initiative on 9 Nov 1918.
GUSTAV ADOLF BAUER 21 Jun 1919-Mar 1920,
b 6 Jan 1870; d 16 Sep 1944.
HERMANN MÜLLER 27 Mar-25 Jun 1920.
**KONSTANTIN FEHRENBACH 25 Jun 1920-May
1921,** b 11 Jan 1852; d 26 May 1926.
KARL JOSEPH WIRTH May 1921-Nov 1922, b 6
Sep 1879; d 3 Jan 1956.
**WILHELM CARL JOSEF CUNO 22 Nov
1922-Aug 1923,** b 2 Jul 1876; d 3 Jan 1933.
Dr **GUSTAV STRESEMANN 13 Aug-Nov 1923,** b
10 May 1878; d 3 Oct 1929.
WILHELM MARX 30 Nov 1923-Jan 1925, b 15 Jan
1863; d 5 Aug 1946.
Dr **HANS LUTHER 15 Jan 1925-May 1926,** b 10
Mar 1879; d 11 May 1962.
WILHELM MARX 17 May 1926-Jun 1928.
HERMANN MÜLLER 28 Jun 1928-Apr 1930, b 18
May 1876; d 20 Mar 1931.
Dr **HEINRICH BRÜNING 1 Apr 1930-Jun 1932,** b
26 Nov 1885; d 30 Mar 1970.
FRANZ von PAPEN 2 Jun 1932-21 Nov 1932;
acting PM **21-23 Nov 1932;** PM **23 Nov-4 Dec 1932,**
b 29 Oct 1879; d 2 May 1969.
Gen **CURT von SCHLEIDER 4 Dec 1932-30 Jan
1933,** b 7 Apr 1882; d Jun 1934.
ADOLF HITLER 30 Jan 1933-Aug 1934 when he
became Führer.

THE THIRD GERMAN REICH

Leaders of the Reich

The holder of this position held the title of 'Führer'
and the powers of Federal President and Federal
Chancellor.

ADOLF HITLER Chancellor from 30 Jan 1933;
Führer **2 Aug 1934-30 Apr 1945,** b 16 Sep 1891; d
(suicide) 30 Apr 1945. Hitler was an unsuccessful
art student who migrated from his native Austria
to Munich in 1913. The ultra-nationalistic ideas of
the Nazi Party he founded in 1921 were rejected
by the Bavarians in 1923 when his coup in
Munich proved abortive, but after the Depression had brought ruin to Germany his
'philosophy' found ready listeners. To achieve
his scheme of reuniting all the Germans he
ravaged Austria and Czechoslovakia, sent
millions of Jews to their death in concentration
camps and attacked Poland calculating that once
the latter had fallen the war would end. Far from
building the Reich that would last 1000 years he
left Germany devastated and Europe, North Africa
and the Far East racked by a terrible conflict that
cost over 40 million lives - the victims of his cruel
madness.
Admiral **KARL DÖNITZ 1-7 May 1945,** b 16 Sep
1891.
(Germany was divided into four zones of
occupation controlled by Britain, France, The
United States and the Soviet Union in 1945. The
Soviet zone became the German Democratic
Republic (see p95) while the three western zones
became the Federal Republic of Germany (see
p109).)

The Duchy of Anhalt

Founded as a County in the 11th century
(becoming a Principality in the 13th century),
Anhalt was several times divided between
branches of the ruling family. The line of
Anhalt-Dessau, which assumed the title of Duke in
1807, reunited the country in 1863 when the line of
Anhalt-Bernburg became extinct. The Duchy of
Anhalt is now included within the Halle and
Magdeburg Districts of the German Democratic
Republic.

† Dukes

LEOPOLD III Prince from 16 Dec 1751; Duke **18
Apr 1807-9 Aug 1817,** b 10 Aug 1740.
LEOPOLD IV Aug 1817-22 May 1871, grandson of
Leopold III, b 1 Oct 1794.
FRIEDRICH I May 1871-24 Jan 1904, son of
Leopold IV, b 29 Apr 1831.
FRIEDRICH II Jan 1904-21 Apr 1918, eldest
surviving son of Friedrich I, b 19 Aug 1856.

EDUARD Apr-13 Sep 1918, brother of Friedrich II, b 18 Apr 1861.

JOACHIM ERNST Sep-12 Nov 1918 when the Regent abdicated in his name, son of Eduard, b 11 Jan 1901; d 18 Feb 1948 a Russian prisoner-of-war.

The Grand Duchy of Baden

The Dukes of Zahringen become Margraves (1362), Electors (1803) and then Grand Dukes (1806) of Baden. The state was greatly strengthened by the merger of Baden-Baden and Baden-Durlach in 1771 upon the extinction of the former line and by large grants of territory from the alliance made with Napoleon I. The Grand Duchy of Baden is now part of Baden-Wurttemberg Land in Germany.

† Grand Dukes

KARL FRIEDRICH Margrave of Baden-Durlach from **1738**; Grand Duke of Baden from **12 Jul 1806-10 Jun 1811,** b 22 Nov 1728. In the longest reign in European history, Karl Friedrich became ruler of all Baden and then had his territory quadrupled in size through an alliance with Napoleon.

KARL Jun 1811-8 Dec 1818, grandson of Karl Friedrich, b 8 Jun 1786.

LUDWIG I Dec 1818-30 Mar 1830, second son of Karl Friedrich, b 9 Feb 1763.

LEOPOLD Mar 1830-24 Apr 1852, eldest son of Karl Friedrich by his second (morganatic) marriage - made a full Prince of Baden when it became clear the elder line would become extinct; b 29 Aug 1790.

LUDWIG II Apr 1852-5 Sep 1856 when he was formally deposed by his family as medically unfit to reign, eldest son of Leopold, b 15 Aug 1824; d 22 Jan 1858.

FRIEDRICH I Sep 1856-28 Sep 1907, second son of Leopold, b 9 Sep 1826.

FRIEDRICH II Sep 1907-14 Nov 1918 when he abdicated, son of Friedrich I, b 9 Jul 1857; d 9 Aug 1928.

The Kingdom of Bavaria

The Duchy of Bavaria gained independence from the Carolingian Emperors in 911. The state was ruled by the Welfs from 1061 to 1180 when the Wittelsbachs, who reigned until 1918, gained control. The Duchy became an Electorate in 1623 and was raised to a Kingdom in 1805.

† Dukes

ARNULF sole ruler **911-938**; co-ruler **938-947.** Arnulf refused to admit the overlordship of the Emperor and established the independence of Bavaria.

BERCHTOLD co-ruler **938-947** when he was deposed, brother of Arnulf; d 955.

HEINRICH I 947-955.

HEINRICH II 955-978 deposed, son of Heinrich I, b 915.

HEINRICH III 982-985, brother of Heinrich II.

HEINRICH II 985-995.

HEINRICH IV 995-1002 when he became Emperor, son of Heinrich II; see Holy Roman Emperor Heinrich II.

HEINRICH V 1002-1026.

HEINRICH VI 1026-1042; was also Holy Roman Emperor Heinrich III.

HEINRICH VII 1042-1047.

KONRAD I 1049-1053.

HEINRICH VIII 1053-1056; was also Holy Roman Emperor Heinrich IV.

KONRAD II 1056.

AGNES (Duchess) **1056-1061.**

House of Welf

OTTO von Nordheim **1061-1070** deposed; d ?1083.

WELF I 1070-1101, son-in-law of Heinrich VIII.

WELF II 1101-1120, son of Welf I.

HEINRICH IX 1120-1126, brother of Welf II.

HEINRICH X 1126-1139, son of Heinrich IX, b c 1110.

House of Babenberg

LEOPOLD 1139-1141; was also Leopold IV of Austria.

HEINRICH XI 1143-1156, brother of Leopold.

House of Welf

HEINRICH XII (the Lion) **1156-1180** when he was deposed, son of Henry X, b 1129; d 1195.

House of Wittelsbach

OTTO I 1180-1183, b c 1120.

LUDWIG I 1183-15 Sep 1231 murdered, son of Otto I, b 23 Dec 1174.

OTTO II Sep 1231-1253, son of Ludwig I.

LUDWIG II 1253-1294, son of Otto II, b 1229.

RUDOLPH sole ruler **1294-1314**; co-ruler **1314-1347**? son of Ludwig II, b 1274.

LUDWIG III co-ruler **1314-1347,** brother of Rudolph; was also Holy Roman Emperor Ludwig IV.

1347-1375 Upon the death of Ludwig III, Bavaria and the Rhenish Palatinate were divided upon several occasions between various branches of the Wittelsbach family. Not until 1375 could a Bavarian state be recognised again although reunification was not completed until 1505.

† Dukes of Bavaria-Munich

House of Wittelsbach

JOHAN 1375-1397 when he abdicated, grandson of Ludwig III; d c 1415.

ERNST 1397-1438, son of Johan.

ALBRECHT III 1438-1460, son of Ernst.

SIGISMUND co-ruler **1460-1467** when he abdicated, son of Albrecht III; d 1501.
ALBRECHT IV co-ruler **1460-1467**; sole ruler **1467-1505** when he became Duke of all Bavaria.

† Dukes of Bavaria

HOUSE OF WITTELSBACH
ALBRECHT IV Duke of Bavaria-Munich from 1460; Duke of Bavaria **1505-1508,** brother of Sigismund, b 1447.
WILHELM IV 1508-1550, son of Albrecht IV.
ALBRECHT V 1550-1579, son of Wilhelm IV.
WILHELM V 1579-1597 when he abdicated, son of Albrecht V.
MAXIMILIAN I 1597-1623 when he became Elector.

† Electors of Bavaria

HOUSE OF WITTELSBACH
MAXIMILIAN I Duke from 1597; Elector **25 Feb 1623-27 Sep 1651,** son of Wilhelm V, b 17 Apr 1573. Inheriting a bankrupt state from his father, he transformed the economy and reformed the army and the administration. A major figure of the Counter-Reformation, Maximilian founded the Catholic League, remained leader of the Catholic forces despite Wallenstein and suffered temporary defeat and deposition at the hands of the Swedes. A grateful Emperor rewarded him with an electorship.
FERDINAND MARIA Sep 1651-26 May 1679, son of Maximilian I, b 31 Oct 1636.
MAXIMILIAN II EMANUEL May 1679-1706 deposed; restored **1713-26 Feb 1726,** son of Ferdinand Maria, b 11 Jul 1662. A brave and able soldier, Maximilian II displayed his prowess early by his daring capture of Belgrade from the Turks (1688). Later he fell victim to overweening ambition: his scheming for the Spanish, Polish and Imperial crowns led to an alliance with France and he was deposed after Blenheim though restored by the Treaty of Utrecht.
KARL ALBRECHT Feb 1726-20 Jan 1745, son of Maximilian II, b 6 Aug 1697. He achieved the Imperial crown his father had sought but he reigned as a puppet Emperor, powerless to prevent Austria occupying his Kingdom for two years.
MAXIMILIAN III JOSEPH Jan 1745-30 Dec 1777, son of Karl Albrecht, b 28 Mar 1727.
KARL THEODOR Dec 1777-16 Feb 1799, head of the Palatinate branch of the Wittelsbachs, b 11 Dec 1724.
MAXIMILIAN IV JOSEPH Feb 1799-26 Dec 1805 when he became King.

† Kings of Bavaria

HOUSE OF WITTELSBACH
MAXIMILIAN I Elector from Feb 1799; King **26 Dec 1805-13 Oct 1825,** head of the Zweibrücken branch of the Wittelsbachs, b 27 May 1756. With his talented Minister Montgelas, Maximilian shaped a united, prosperous Kingdom with perhaps the most liberal constitution in Germany. His alliance with Napoleon, necessary because of his justified distrust of Austria, gained him new lands and a kingly crown.
LUDWIG I Oct 1825-20 Mar 1848 when he abdicated, eldest son of Maximilian I, b 25 Aug 1786; d 29 Feb 1868. A great patron of the arts, Ludwig rebuilt Munich as a classical city. Alienating his subjects by his reactionary measures and by his relationship with the dancer-adventuress Lola Montez, he was obliged to abdicate in the revolution of 1848.
MAXIMILIAN II Mar 1848-10 Mar 1864, eldest son of Ludwig I, b 28 Nov 1811.
LUDWIG II Mar 1864-13 Jun 1886 drowned probably suicide, elder son of Maximilian I, b 25 Aug 1845. The patron of Wagner, Ludwig II had little taste for government and concerned himself with extravagant building projects, eg the absurd Neuschwanstein. Increasingly unstable he was declared unfit to rule in 1886.
OTTO Jun 1886-5 Nov 1913 when he was legally deposed, younger son of Maximilian II, b 27 Apr 1848; d 11 Oct 1916. Reigned but did not rule owing to his insanity.
LUDWIG III Nov 1913-8 Nov 1918 when he was deposed, cousin of Otto, b 7 Jan 1845; d 18 Oct 1921.

The Electorate of Brandenburg

The Margraviate of Brandenburg, founded by the Ascanian Albrecht in the 12th century, was raised to the dignity of an Electorate in 1351. From 1417 the state was ruled by the Hohenzollerns who strengthened the country in size and military strength to become the leading German state, the Kingdom of Prussia.

† Electors

HOUSE OF WITTELSBACH
LUDWIG 1351-1365, b 1330.
OTTO 1365-1373, b 1341; d 1379.

HOUSE OF LUXEMBOURG
KARL 1373-1378; was also, Karel, King of Bohemia.
SIGISMUND 1378-1417; was also Sigismund, King of Bohemia and Hungary.

HOUSE OF HOHENZOLLERN
FRIEDRICH I 1417-20 Sep 1440, son of Friedrich V, Burgrave of Nürnberg, b autumn 1371. Nominated to cast Brandenburg's vote in the Imperial election, Friedrich was rewarded with the electorship as an hereditary right by a grateful Emperor Sigismund.

FRIEDRICH II Sep 1440-1470 abdicated, eldest brother of Friedrich I, b 1413; d 1471.

ALBRECHT III 1470-11 Mar 1486, brother of Friedrich II, b 24 Nov 1414.

JOHANN CICERO Mar 1486-9 Jan 1499, son of Albrecht III, b 2 Aug 1455.

JOACHIM I Jan 1499-11 Jul 1535, son of Johann Cicero, b 24 Feb 1484.

JOACHIM II Jul 1535-3 Jan 1571, elder son of Joachim I, b 13 Jan 1505.

JOHANN GEORG Jan 1571-8 Jan 1598, son of Joachim II, b 11 Sep 1525.

JOACHIM FRIEDRICH Jan 1598-18 Jul 1608, son of Johann Georg, b 27 Jan 1546.

JOHANN SIGISMUND Jul 1608-2 Jan 1620, son of Joachim Friedrich, b 8 Nov 1572.

GEORG WILHELM Jan 1620-1 Dec 1640, son of Johann Sigismund, b 3 Nov 1595.

FRIEDRICH WILHELM (The Great Elector) **Dec 1640-29 Apr 1688,** son of Georg Wilhelm, b 16 Feb 1620. His inheritance had been ravaged by the Thirty Years' War thus Friedrich Wilhelm had to rebuild not only towns and the economy but also the army, which was greatly strengthened to become the guarentee of his independence. His creation of a centralised absolutism and the acquisition of Prussian territories laid the foundations of his son's Kingdom.

FRIEDRICH III Apr 1688-18 Jan 1701 when he became King in Prussia.

The Duchy of Brunswick

In 1569 Heinrich, Duke of Brunswick-Lüneburg-Dannenberg, founded the Duchy of Brunswick-Wolfenbüttel. The state was subdivided several times between branches of the Guelph family but reunited under Karl I to form a single Duchy but in eight segments. The Duchy is now part of Nieder Sachsen Land in Germany.

† Dukes of Brunswick

HOUSE OF GUELPH
Brunswick-Wolfenbüttel Branch

KARL I 3 Sep 1735-26 Mar 1780, b 1 Aug 1713.

KARL II Mar 1780-10 Nov 1806 died of wounds received in battle, eldest son of Karl I, b 9 Oct 1735.

(Brunswick was annexed by France then ceded to Westphalia in 1808, but restored in 1813.)

FRIEDRICH WILHELM de facto from 1813; de jure Nov 1806-16 Jun 1815 when he was killed at the Battle of Quatre Bras, youngest son of Karl II, b 9 Oct 1771.

KARL III Jun 1815-2 Dec 1830 deposed, elder son of Friedrich Wilhelm, b 30 Oct 1804; d 19 Aug 1873. Having fled during the revolutions of 1830, Karl was declared deposed and unfit to rule by the Diet of German Princes.

WILHELM de facto Sep 1830-Apr 1831; de jure 25 Apr 1831-18 Oct 1884, younger son of Friedrich Wilhelm, b 25 Apr 1806.

HOUSE OF GUELPH
Hannover Branch
Upon the extinction of the Senior Branch, the heir to Brunswick was Ernst August, rightful King of Hanover, who was banned from succeeding by the Imperial Government as he refused to recognise the Empire's constitution which included Hanover in Prussia.

Oct 1884-1 Nov 1913 Regencies.

ERNST AUGUST 1 Nov 1913-8 Nov 1918 when he abdicated, son of Ernst August who was prevented from succeeding in 1884, b 17 Nov 1887; d 30 Jan 1953.

The Grand Duchy of Frankfurt

One of Napoléon I's puppet states, this Grand Duchy was created for his adopted son Eugène de Beauharnais.

† Grand Duke

EUGEN 1 Mar 1810-Oct 1813 when the state fell, Eugène Rose de Beauharnais, son of Empress Josephine by her first marriage and adopted son of Napoléon I, b 3 Sep 1781; d 21 Feb 1824. Said by Napoléon to be 'a whole man', Eugène was blessed with many of the virtues the Bonapartes lacked: bravery, loyalty, charm and amiability. After the Empire he was made a Duke by his father-in-law, Maximilian I of Bavaria, and his issue was later 'adopted' as a collateral branch of the Romanovs.

The Kingdom of Hanover

The territories of the Hanoverian family were finally united under Georg I who succeeded to Hanover in 1698 and Celle in 1705. An electorate from 1692 and a Kingdom from 1815, Hanover was united with Great Britain in a personal union from 1714 until 1837 when the Salic Law of the German Kingdom prevented the accession of Queen Victoria. The Kingdom of Hanover was annexed by Prussia in 1866.

† Electors of Hanover

HOUSE OF WELF

ERNST AUGUST 1692-23 Jan 1698, b 1629.

GEORG I Jan 1698-11 Jun 1727, son of Ernst August; was also George I of England.

GEORG II Jun 1727-25 Oct 1760; was also George II of England.

GEORG III Oct 1760-12 Oct 1814 when he became King.

HOUSE OF WELF

GEORG III 12 Oct 1814-26 Jun 1830; was also George III of England.

WILHELM Jun 1830-20 Jun 1837; was also William IV of England.

ERNST AUGUST (Duke of Cumberland) **Jun 1837-18 Nov 1851,** fifth son of George III of Britain and Hanover, b 5 Jun 1771. The most notorious of Queen Victoria's 'wicked uncles', Ernst August became a 'bogeyman' and perhaps the most hated man in England. He was not helped by his frightening appearance - he received hideous battle scars, losing an eye, in the French Revolutionary Wars. The subject of ridiculous slanders, he is seldom given credit for his bravery and his administrative ability; he ruled as a near-absolute King, yet this arch-reactionary was popular with his subjects who recognised his qualities.

GEORG V 18 Nov 1851-20 Sep 1866 when his Kingdom was annexed by Prussia, only son of Ernst August, b 27 May 1819; d 12 Jun 1878. The blind King (he lost his sight in a childhood accident) fell foul of Bismarck's ambitions to join Prussia and the Prussian Rhineland; Hanover, between those two areas, was seized when Georg took Austria's side in the 1866 war.

The Grand Duchy of Hesse

Founded as a Landgraviate in 1567, Hesse-Darmstadt became a Grand Duchy in 1806 - the Grand Duchy of Hesse and by Rhine - and a Republic in 1918.

† Landgraves of Hesse-Darmstadt

GEORG I 31 Mar 1567-7 Feb 1596, b 10 Sep 1547.

LUDWIG V Feb 1596-27 Jun 1626, son of Georg I, b 24 Sep 1577.

GEORG II Jun 1626-11 Jun 1661, son of Ludwig V, b 7 Mar 1605.

LUDWIG VI Jun 1661-24 Apr 1678, b 25 Jan 1630.

LUDWIG VII 24 Apr-31 Aug 1678, b 22 Jun 1658.

ERNST LUDWIG Aug 1678-12 Sep 1739, b 15 Dec 1667.

LUDWIG VIII Sep 1739-17 Oct 1768, son of Ernst Ludwig, b 5 Apr 1691.

LUDWIG IX Oct 1768-6 Apr 1790, eldest son of Ludwig VIII, b 15 Dec 1719.

LUDEWIG X Apr 1790-13 Aug 1806 when he became Grand Duke.

† Grand Dukes of Hesse and by Rhine

LUDEWIG I (formerly X) 13 Aug 1806-6 Apr 1830, eldest son of Ludwig IX, b 14 Jun 1753.

LUDWIG II sole ruler **Apr 1830-5 Mar 1848;** co-ruler **5 Mar-16 Jun 1848,** eldest son of Ludwig I, b 26 Dec 1777.

LUDWIG III co-ruler **5 Mar-16 Jun 1848;** sole ruler **Jun 1848-13 Jun 1877,** eldest son of Ludwig II, b 9 Jun 1806.

LUDWIG IV Jun 1877-13 Mar 1892, nephew of Ludwig III, b 12 Sep 1837. Best known in Britain as a son-in-law of Queen Victoria.

ERNST LUDWIG Mar 1892-9 Nov 1918 when a Republic was proclaimed, son of Ludwig IV, b 25 Nov 1868; d 9 Oct 1937.

The Electorate of Hesse-Cassel

The Landgraviate of Hesse was founded in the 13th century but later divided into several Landgraviates. Hesse-Cassel was established by Wilhelm IV in 1567 and ceased to exist as a separate unit in 1866 when annexed by Prussia.

† Landgraves

WILHELM IV (The Wise) 31 Mar 1567-25 Aug 1592, b 24 Jun 1532.

MORITZ Aug 1592-17 Mar 1627 when he abdicated, son of Wilhelm IV, b 25 May 1572; d 15 Mar 1632.

WILHELM V Mar 1627-21 Sep 1637, son of Moritz, b 13 Feb 1602.

WILHELM VI Sep 1637-16 Jul 1663, son of Wilhelm V, b 23 May 1629.

WILHELM VII Jul 1663-21 Sep 1670, son of Wilhelm VI, b 21 Jun 1651.

KARL Sep 1670-23 Mar 1730, brother of Wilhelm VII, b 3 Aug 1654.

FRIEDRICH I Mar 1730-Apr 1751, son of Karl; was also King of Sweden.

WILHELM VIII 5 Apr 1751-1 Feb 1760, brother of Friedrich I, b 10 Mar 1682.

FRIEDRICH II Feb 1760-31 Oct 1785, son of Wilhelm VIII, b 14 Aug 1720.

WILHELM IX Nov 1785-27 Apr 1803 when he became Elector.

† Electors

WILHELM I (formerly IX) 27 Apr 1803-Jul 1807 when he was deposed, eldest surviving son of Friedrich II, b 3 Jun 1743.

Jul 1807-Nov 1813 Hesse-Cassel was annexed to the Kingdom of Westphalia.

WILHELM I 21 Nov 1813-27 Feb 1821.

WILHELM II Feb 1821-20 Nov 1847, son of Wilhelm I, b 28 Jul 1777. In the revolutionary year of 1830 the Hessian peasants, grossly overtaxed to support the extravagant Elector, revolted. Forced to grant a liberal constitution, Wilhelm II withdrew, appointing his son Regent.

FRIEDRICH WILHELM   Nov 1847-20 Sep 1866
when the Electorate was annexed by Prussia, son
of Wilhelm II, b 20 Aug 1802; d 6 Jan 1875.

The Landgraviate of Hesse-Homburg

Although the Landgraviate was founded in 1622 it
did not become independent until 1768. The state
ceased to exist, being absorbed first by Hesse then
by Prussia, when the ruling family died out in 1866.

† Landgraves

FRIEDRICH V LUDWIG   Landgrave from Feb
1751; Sovereign **Sep 1768-1806,** b 30 Jan 1748.
1806-1816   Hesse-Homburg was included in the
Grand Duchy of Hesse.
FRIEDRICH V LUDWIG   1816-20 Jan 1820.
FRIEDRICH VI   Jan 1820-2 Apr 1829, eldest son
of Friedrich V Ludwig, b 30 Jul 1769.
LUDWIG   Apr 1829-19 Jan 1839, second son of
Friedrich V Ludwig, b 29 Aug 1770.
PHILIPP   Jan 1839-15 Dec 1846, fifth son of
Friedrich V Ludwig, b 11 Mar 1779.
GUSTAV   Dec 1846-8 Sep 1848, sixth son of
Friedrich V Ludwig, b 17 Feb 1781.
FERDINAND   Sep 1848-24 Mar 1866, seventh son
of Friedrich V Ludwig, b 26 Apr 1783. The last
male member of the Royal Family of Hesse-
Homburg.

The Principality of Lippe

The Seigniory of Lippe, dating from the 12th
century, was raised to a County in 1529. The
territory was twice subdivided in the 17th century
but most of it was reunited by the House of
Detmold which became Princely in 1789. The
Principality is now part of Nordrhein-Westfalen
Land in Germany.

† Princes

HOUSE OF LIPPE-DETMOLD
LEOPOLD I   Count from 1782; Prince **16 Dec
1789-4 Apr 1802,** b 2 Dec 1767.
LEOPOLD II   Apr 1802-1 Jan 1851, son of Leopold
I, b 6 Nov 1796.
LEOPOLD III   Jan 1851-8 Dec 1875, eldest son of
Leopold II, b 1 Sep 1821.
WOLDEMAR   Dec 1875-20 Mar 1895, second son
of Leopold II, b 18 Apr 1824.
ALEXANDER   Mar 1895-25 Oct 1905, fifth son of
Leopold II, b 16 Jan 1831. The last male member
of the Lippe-Detmold family.

HOUSE OF LIPPE-BIESTERFELD
LEOPOLD IV   Oct 1905-12 Nov 1918 when he
abdicated, distant kinsman of Alexander, b 30
May 1871; d 30 Dec 1949.

The Grand Duchy of Mecklenburg-Schwerin

A Principality from the 12th century and a Duchy
from the 14th, Mecklenburg did not finally divide
into two Duchies until the start of the 18th century.
In 1815 Mecklenburg-Schwerin was raised to a
Grand Duchy - it is now part of the German
Democratic Republic.

† Dukes
(before 1713 of Mecklenburg-Grabow)

KARL LEOPOLD   1713-Nov 1747, b c 1680.
CHRISTIAN LUDWIG II   Nov 1747-30 May 1756,
brother of Karl Leopold, b 15 May 1683.
FRIEDRICH   May 1756-24 Apr 1785, son of
Christian Ludwig II, b 9 Nov 1717.
FRIEDRICH FRANZ I   Apr 1785-14 Jun 1815
when he became Grand Duke.

† Grand Dukes

FRIEDRICH FRANZ I   Duke from Apr 1785;
Grand Duke **14 Jun 1815-1 Feb 1837,** nephew of
Friedrich, b 10 Dec 1756.
PAUL FRIEDRICH   Feb 1837-7 Mar 1842,
grandson of Friedrich Franz I, b 15 Sep 1800.
FRIEDRICH FRANZ II   Mar 1842-15 Apr 1883,
eldest son of Paul Friedrich, b 28 Feb 1823.
FRIEDRICH FRANZ III   Apr 1883-10 Apr 1897,
eldest son of Friedrich Franz II, b 19 Mar 1851.
FRIEDRICH FRANZ IV   Apr 1897-14 Nov 1918
when he abdicated, son of Friedrich Franz III, b
9 Apr 1882; d 17 Nov 1945.

The Grand Duchy of Mecklenburg-Strelitz

This Duchy, raised to a Grand Duchy in 1815, was
founded by a junior branch of the House of
Mecklenburg-Schwerin in 1701. It is now part of
the German Democratic Republic.

† Dukes

ADOLF FRIEDRICH II   8 Mar 1701-12 May 1708,
b 19 Oct 1658.
ADOLF FRIEDRICH III   May 1708-11 Dec 1752,
elder son of Adolf Friedrich II, b 7 Jun 1686.
ADOLF FRIEDRICH IV   Dec 1752-2 Jun 1794,
nephew of Adolf Friedrich III, b 5 May 1738.

KARL   Jun 1794-28 Jun 1815 when he became
Grand Duke.

† Grand Dukes

KARL   Duke from Jun 1794; Grand Duke **28 Jun
1815-6 Nov 1816,** brother of Adolf Friedrich IV,
b 10 Oct 1741.
GEORG Nov 1816-6 Sep 1860, eldest surviving son
of Karl, b 12 Aug 1779.
FRIEDRICH WILHELM Sep 1860-30 May 1904,
elder son of Georg, b 17 Oct 1819.
ADOLF FRIEDRICH V May 1904-11 Jun 1914,
son of Friedrich Wilhelm, b 22 Jul 1848.
ADOLF FRIEDRICH VI Jun 1914-24 Feb 1918
when he committed suicide, elder son of Adolf
Friedrich V, b 17 Jun 1882. Upon his death the
throne became vacant as the only heir had
renounced the succession and become a Russian
citizen.

The Duchy of Nassau

The County, later the Principality, of Nassau-
Weilburg was established in the 12th century.
Several times divided (one junior branch became
the Royal Family of the Netherlands) Nassau was
not reunited as a single state until 1816, but was
annexed by Prussia 50 years later. The Duchy is
now part of the Land of Hessen in Germany.

† Dukes

WILHELM   Prince of Nassau-Weilburg from Jan
1816; Duke of Nassau **24 Mar 1816-20 Aug 1839,**
b 14 Jun 1792.
ADOLF Aug 1839-20 Sep 1866 when Nassau was
annexed by Prussia, son of Wilhelm; became
Grand Duke of Luxembourg in 1890.

The Grand Duchy of
Oldenburg

The ancient County of Oldenburg became a Duchy
in 1774 and a Grand Duchy in 1829. From the
beginning of the 19th century Oldenburg was
united with the Principality of Lübeck and the
Principality of Birkenfeld. It is now part of Nieder
Sachsen Land in Germany.

† Duke of Oldenburg, Prince of Lübeck and
of Birkenfeld

PETER I   Prince of Lübeck **from Feb 1803**; Prince
of Birkenfeld **from Apr 1817**; Duke of Oldenburg
2 Jul 1823-21 May 1829, b 17 Jan 1755.

† Grand Dukes of Oldenburg, Princes of
Lübeck and of Birkenfeld

AUGUST   Duke from 21-28 May 1829; Grand Duke
from **28 May 1829-27 Feb 1853,** eldest son of
Peter I, b 13 Jul 1783.
PETER II Feb 1853-13 Jun 1900, eldest son of
August, b 8 Jul 1827.
FRIEDRICH AUGUST   Jun 1900-11 Nov 1918
when he abdicated, elder son of Peter II, b 16
Nov 1852; d 24 Feb 1931.

The Palatinate of the Rhine

A leading German state of the Middle Ages the
Palatinate occupied the region of the confluence of
the Rivers Rhine and Neckar. There were
independent Counts from 1294 in which year the
Rhenish Palatinate separated from Bavaria.

† Counts

RUDOLF I ('The Stammerer') **1294-1319.**
ADOLF ('The Simple') **1319-1327,** son of Rudolf I,
b 1300.
RUDOLF II ('The Blind') **1327-1353,** son of Rudolf
I, b 1306.
RUPPRECHT I ('The Red') **1353-1356** when he
became Elector.

† Electors

RUPPRECHT I   Count from 1353; Elector
1356-1390, son of Rudolf I, b 1309.
RUPPRECHT II ('The Little') **1390-1398,** grandson
of Rudolf I, b 1335.
RUPPRECHT III KLEM **1398-18 May 1410,** son of
Rupprecht II; was also Rupprecht Klem, Holy
Roman Emperor.
LUDWIG III May 1410-1436, son of Rupprecht
III.
LUDWIG IV 1436-1449, son of Ludwig III, b 1424.
FRIEDRICH I ('The Victorious') **1449-1476,** son of
Ludwig III, b 1425.
PHILIPP ('The Sincere') **1476-1508,** grandson of
Ludwig III, b 1448.
LUDWIG V ('The Pacific') **1508-1544,** son of
Philipp, b 1478.
FRIEDRICH II ('The Wise') **1544-1556,** son of
Philipp, b 1482.
OTTO HEINRICH 1556-1559, grandson of Phi-
lipp, b 1502.
FRIEDRICH III ('The Pious') **1559-1576,** kinsman
of Otto Heinrich, b 1515.
LUDWIG VI ('The Easy') **1576-1583,** son of
Friedrich III, b 1539.
FRIEDRICH IV ('The Upright') **1583-1610,** son of
Ludwig VI, b 1574.
FRIEDRICH V ('The Winter King') **1610-1623**
deposed, son of Friedrich IV; was also Frederik,
King of Bohemia.
1623-1648 Bavarian rule.

Friedrich II of Prussia (Frederick the Great) who, despite being a military genius, always appeared uncomfortable and untidy in uniform (Radio Times Hulton Picture Library)

KARL LUDWIG 1648-1680, son of Friedrich V, b 1617. He had most of the Palatinate restored to him by the Peace of Westphalia.

KARL II 1680-1685, son of Karl Ludwig, b 1651.

PHILIPP WILHELM 1685-1690, cousin of Karl II, b 1615.

JOHANN WILHELM 1690-1716, son of Philipp Wilhelm, b 1658.

KARL PHILIPP 1716-1743, son of Philipp Wilhelm, b 1661.

KARL THEODOR 1743-30 Dec 1777 when he became Duke of Bavaria thus uniting the Palatinate to that country; see the Kingdom of Bavaria.

The Kingdom of Prussia

The union of the Electorate of Brandenburg with the Prussian territories to the east created a strong state which was to become the Kingdom of Prussia around which the German Empire was united by the sword in 1871.

† Kings in Prussia
(Kings of Prussia after 1742)

HOUSE OF HOHENZOLLERN

FRIEDRICH I Elector of Brandenburg from Apr 1688; King **18 Jan 1701-25 Feb 1713,** son of Elector Friedrich Wilhelm, b 11 Jul 1657. His pretensions fathered an extravagant court, an excessively large army and three grandiose palaces which his Treasury could not support. In return for joining the Grand Alliance against France in the War of Spanish Succession, the Emperor rewarded Friedrich with the title King.

FRIEDRICH WILHELM I Feb 1713-31 May 1740, son of Friedrich I, b 14 Aug 1688. The spendthrift policies of his father led Friedrich Wilhelm to make many economies (pruning the luxurious court, levying additional taxes, etc). Prussia was modernised: industry flourished; compulsory universal primary education was introduced; and, with the aid of Leopold of Anhalt-Dessau, the famous Prussian fighting machine, which Friedrich II was to make the strongest power in Europe, was created. Overshadowed by his son, Friedrich Wilhelm's legacies - army reform and efficient finance - made the achievements of Friedrich the Great possible.

FRIEDRICH II (The Great) **May 1740-17 Aug 1786,** eldest surviving son of Friedrich Wilhelm I, b 24 Jan 1712. This talented translator and gifted musician became an astonishing military leader. In some ways enlightened he relaxed censorship, granted religious liberties and enjoyed the friendship of Voltaire - he was nevertheless basically despotic. Although his military skill was undoubted he owed much to luck: the weakness of Austria allowed him to seize Silesia and if Peter III of Russia had not been treasonably pro-Prussian, Friedrich's Kingdom might have been destroyed in the Seven Years' War.

FRIEDRICH WILHELM II Aug 1786-16 Dec 1797, nephew of Friedrich II, b 25 Sep 1744.

FRIEDRICH WILHELM III Dec 1797-7 Jun 1840, eldest son of Friedrich Wilhelm II, b 3 Aug 1770. The talents of Stein, Scharnhorst and Hardenburg saw this nervous King through the Napoleonic Wars.

FRIEDRICH WILHELM IV Jun 1840-2 Jan 1861, eldest son of Friedrich Wilhelm III, b 15 Oct 1795.

WILHELM I Jan 1861-9 Mar 1888; was also Emperor Wilhelm I of Germany.

FRIEDRICH III Mar-15 Jun 1888; was also Emperor Friedrich III of Germany.

WILHELM II Jun 1888-28 Nov 1918 when he abdicated or 10 Nov 1918 when he was deposed; was also Emperor Wilhelm II of Germany.

The Principality of Reuss zu Greiz

The ancient County of Reuss zu Obergreiz was raised to the status of a Principality in 1778. All male members of the ruling family were named Heinrich and numbered in a sequence which began in 1693. These numbers must be regarded as purely personal numbers and are in no way regnal numbers - the Princes of Reuss zu Greiz and Reuss zu Schleiz are often wrongly accorded the record for the highest post-regnal numbers. The Principality is now part of the Gera and Karl-Marx-Stadt Districts of the German Democratic Republic.

† Princes

HEINRICH XI Count from 1723; Prince **12 May 1778-28 Jun 1800,** b 18 Mar 1722.

HEINRICH XIII **Jun 1800-29 Jan 1817,** son of Heinrich XI, b 16 Feb 1747.

HEINRICH XIX **Jan 1817-31 Oct 1836,** second son of Heinrich XIII, b 1 Mar 1790.

HEINRICH XX **Oct 1836-8 Nov 1859,** brother of Heinrich XIX, b 29 Jun 1794.

HEINRICH XXII **Nov 1859-19 Apr 1902,** eldest surviving son of Heinrich XX, b 28 Mar 1846.

HEINRICH XXIV **Apr 1902-11 Nov 1918** when he abdicated, son of Heinrich XXII, b 20 Mar 1878; d 13 Oct 1927. The last member of the Royal Family of Reuss zu Greiz.

The Principality of Reuss zu Schleiz

The ancient County of Reuss zu Schleiz was raised to a Principality in 1806, ie later than its namesake of Greiz. Like Greiz, Reuss zu Schleiz knew the curious arrangement by which all members of the ruling family were named Heinrich and, like Greiz, Schleiz is often wrongly accorded the record for the highest post-regnal numbers. In a complicated system the 'Heinrichs of Schleiz' were numbered in three sequences: one began in 1695 (ending with Heinrich LXXV), another began in 1803 (ending with Heinrich XLVII) and the third began in 1910. As with Reuss zu Greiz these must be regarded as purely personal numbers and it is wrong to consider them as regnal. The Principality is now part of Gera District in the German Democratic Republic.

† Princes

HEINRICH XLII Count from 1784; Prince **9 Apr 1806-17 Apr 1818,** b 27 Feb 1752.

HEINRICH LXII **Apr 1818-19 Jun 1854,** eldest surviving son of Heinrich XLII, b 31 May 1785.

HEINRICH LXVII **Jun 1854-11 Jul 1867,** brother of Heinrich LXII, b 20 Oct 1789.

HEINRICH XIV **Jul 1867-29 Mar 1913,** son of Heinrich LXVII, b 28 May 1832.

HEINRICH XXVII **Mar 1913-11 Nov 1918** when he abdicated, son of Heinrich XIV, b 10 Nov 1858; d 21 Nov 1928.

The Duchy of Saxe-Altenburg

Upon the extinction of the Royal House of Saxe-Gotha-Altenburg, the Duke of Saxe-Hildburghausen received Altenburg in exchange for Hildburghausen. His new territories when added to a segment of his old Duchy formed a tiny Duchy in two parts. It is now part of the Gera and Leipzig Districts of the German Democratic Republic.

† Dukes

FRIEDRICH Duke of Saxe-Hildburghausen from Sep 1780; Duke of Saxe-Altenburg **12 Nov 1826-29 Sep 1834,** b 29 Apr 1763.

JOSEPH **Sep 1834-30 Nov 1848** when he abdicated, eldest surviving son of Friedrich, b 27 Aug 1789; d 25 Nov 1868. Duke Joseph was one of the casualties of the revolutionary movements of 1848.

GEORG **Dec 1848-3 Aug 1853,** brother of Joseph, b 24 Jul 1796.

ERNST I **Aug 1853-7 Feb 1908,** eldest son of Georg, b 16 Sep 1826.

ERNST II **Feb 1908-13 Nov 1918** when he abdicated, nephew of Ernst I, b 31 Aug 1871; d 22 Mar 1955.

The Duchy of Saxe-Coburg and Gotha

The small Duchies of Saxe-Coburg and Saxe-Saalfeld were united in 1699. In 1826 their Duke gained Gotha from the extinct House of Saxe-Gotha-Altenburg (but had to relinquish Saalfeld to Saxe-Meiningen) to form a small state in two segments. The Duchy is now partly in Bavaria Land, Germany and partly in Erfurt District of the German Democratic Republic.

† Dukes

ERNST I Duke of Saxe-Coburg-Saalfeld from Dec 1806; Duke of Saxe-Coburg and Gotha **1826-29 Jan 1844,** b 2 Jan 1784. The father of Albert, the Prince Consort.

ERNST II **Jan 1844-22 Aug 1893,** elder son of Ernst I, b 21 Jun 1818.

ALFRED (Duke of Edinburgh) **Aug 1893-30 Jul 1900,** second son of Prince Albert and Queen Victoria (their eldest son, later Edward VII, renounced any rights to Saxe-Coburg), b 6 Aug 1844.

KARL EDUARD (Duke of Albany) **Jul 1900-Nov 1918** when he was deposed, only son of Leopold, Duke of Albany, and nephew of Alfred, Duke of Edinburgh (Arthur, Duke of Connaught having renounced any rights to Saxe-Coburg), b 19 Jul 1884; d 6 Mar 1954. Like his predecessor Alfred, Karl Eduard was born a Prince of Great Britain (his sister is Princess Alice, Countess of Athlone - the longest lived member of the British Royal House). As a result of his participation in World War I in the German interest, the Duke was deprived of his British orders and rank as Duke of Albany.

The Duchy of Saxe-Meiningen

This Duchy, founded in 1681, was extended by territory received upon the extinction of the Royal House of Saxe-Gotha-Altenburg to form a small state in one major and several minor segments. It is now part of Suhl District in the German Democratic Republic.

† Dukes

CARL co-ruler **Jan 1763-21 Jul 1782.**

GEORG I co-ruler **Jan 1763-21 Jul 1782;** sole ruler **21 Jul 1782-24 Dec 1803,** brother of Carl, b 4 Feb 1761.

BERNHARD II Dec 1803-20 Sep 1866 when he abdicated, son of Georg I, b 17 Dec 1800; d 3 Dec 1882. The abdication of anti-Prussian Bernhard II was a condition of the peace after the Austro-Prussian War.

GEORG II Sep 1866-25 Jun 1914, son of Bernhard II, b 21 Jun 1831.

BERNHARD III Jun 1914-10 Nov 1918 when he abdicated, eldest son of Georg II, b 1 Apr 1851; d 16 Jan 1928.

The Grand Duchy of Saxe-Weimar-Eisenach

The descendants of Johann, Duke of Saxe-Weimar, divided their inheritance over a couple of generations creating a crazy jigsaw of mini-states in Thuringia. The Duchy, later Grand Duchy, of Saxe-Weimar-Eisenach can be said to date from 1741 when three such states reunited to form a small country in three segments. It is now a part of Erfurt and the adjoining Districts of the German Democratic Republic.

† Dukes

ERNST AUGUST I Ruler of a reunited Duchy **1741-Jan 1748.**

ERNST AUGUST II Jan 1748-28 May 1758, son of Ernst August I, b 2 Jun 1737. His cultured Duchess became patroness of writers and artists to establish an artistic centre that reached its peak in the following reign.

CARL AUGUST May 1758-21 Apr 1815 when he became Grand Duke.

† Grand Dukes

CARL AUGUST Duke from May 1758; Grand Duke **21 Apr 1815-14 Jun 1828,** elder son of Ernst August II, b 3 Sep 1757. Continuing the interests of his mother, Carl August made Weimar the intellectual and artistic capital of Germany. Goethe, Schiller and others attended his court; Jena University was patronised, and the theatre and fine arts were encouraged.

CARL FRIEDRICH Jun 1828-8 Jul 1853, eldest son of Carl August, b 2 Feb 1783.

CARL ALEXANDER Jul 1853-5 Jan 1901, son of Carl Friedrich, b 24 Jun 1818. An intellectual he re-established Weimar as the German cultural capital.

WILHELM ERNST Jan 1901-9 Nov 1918 when he was deposed, grandson of Carl Alexander, b 10 Jun 1876; d 24 Apr 1923.

The Kingdom of Saxony

The ancient Duchy of Saxony became an Electorate in 1423, was divided between Albertine and Ernestine branches of the Wettin family in 1485, was reunited in the 16th century and raised to a Kingdom in 1806.

† Electors

HOUSE OF WETTIN

FRIEDRICH I (the Warlike) Duke from 1381; Elector **1423-4 Jan 1428,** b 11 Apr 1370. Allied to Emperor Sigismund against the Bohemian Hussites, Friedrich was rewarded for his services with an electorship when the Ascanian electoral family became extinct.

FRIEDRICH II Jan 1428-7 Sep 1464, eldest son of Friedrich I, b 22 Aug 1411.

ERNST co-ruler **Sep 1464-1485;** sole ruler **1485-1486,** son of Friedrich II, b 1441. In 1485 Ernst divided the electorate with his brother.

ALBRECHT III co-ruler **Sep 1464-1485.**

FRIEDRICH III 1486-5 May 1525, son of Ernst, b 17 Jan 1463. Friedrich, the patron of Durer, was known for his ability and religious sincerity. Though a Catholic, he gave sanctuary at Wartburg to Martin Luther whom he appointed to his new university at Wittenberg, thereby earning an Imperial Ban.

JOHANN   May 1525-1532, younger brother of
Friedrich III, b 1469.
JOHANN FRIEDRICH 1532-1547 when he lost the
electorship to the Albertine Wettins, b 1503; d
1554.

† Dukes

Albertine rulers of the Meissen district of Saxony.

HOUSE OF WETTIN
ALBRECHT III 1485-12 Sep 1500, brother of
Ernst, b Jul 1443.
GEORG Sep 1500-17 Apr 1539, eldest son of
Albrecht III, b 27 Aug 1471.
HEINRICH Apr 1539-18 Aug 1541, brother of
Georg, b 17 Mar 1473.
MORITZ Aug 1541-19 May 1547 when he became
Elector.

† Electors

HOUSE OF WETTIN
MORITZ 19 May 1547-9 Jul 1553 killed in battle,
son of Heinrich, Duke of Saxony-Meissen, b 21
Mar 1521. Through the cunning use of alliance
and counter alliance, Moritz gained the electoral
dignity from the Ernestine Wettins.
AUGUST I Jul 1553-12 Feb 1586, brother of
Moritz, b 31 Jul 1526. Saxony owed to August I
her position as the leading German state of the
late 16th century: he revitalised the economy
encouraging trade, and reformed the judiciary
and the administration. One of the Protestant
leaders, he used his considerable influence to end
the Reformation wars and bring peace to
Germany.
CHRISTIAN I Feb 1586-25 Sep 1591, son of
August I, b 25 Oct 1560.
CHRISTIAN II Sep 1591-26 Jun 1611, son of
Christian I, b 23 Sep 1583.
JOHANN GEORG I Jun 1611-8 Oct 1656, younger
brother of Christian II, b 5 Mar 1585. Saxony lost
her position as the leading German state largely
owing to the drunken misrule of Johann Georg I.
JOHANN GEORG II Oct 1656-22 Aug 1680, son of
Johann Georg I, b 31 Mar 1613.
JOHANN GEORG III Aug 1680-12 Sep 1691, son
of Johann Georg II, b 20 Jun 1647.
JOHANN GEORG IV Sep 1691-27 Apr 1694,
eldest son of Johann Georg III, b 18 Oct 1668.
FRIEDRICH AUGUST I Apr 1694-1 Feb 1733,
brother of Johann Georg IV, b 12 or 22 May 1670.
A spendthrift ruler of little ability but much
cunning, he secured the throne of Poland by
becoming Catholic. With designs upon Livonia,
he formed a league against Sweden in the Great
Northern War which temporarily cost him his
Polish crown. He left over 350 illegitimate
children - which is thought to be a record.
FRIEDRICH AUGUST II Feb 1733-5 Oct 1763, son
of Friedrich August I, b 17 Oct 1696.

*Friedrich August I, Elector of Saxony (and King of
Poland as August II), who recognised over 350
illegitimate children* (Radio Times Hulton Picture
Library)

FRIEDRICH CHRISTIAN 5 Oct-17 Dec 1763,
eldest surviving son of Friedrich August II, b 5
Sep 1722.
FRIEDRICH AUGUST III Dec 1763-11 Dec 1806
when he became King.

† Kings

HOUSE OF WETTIN
FRIEDRICH AUGUST I (the Just) Elector from
Dec 1763; King 11 Dec 1806-5 May 1827, eldest
son of Friedrich Christian, b 23 Dec 1750.
Inheriting a near bankrupt state he gradually
repaired the Treasury but became involved in the
Napoleonic Wars when it was no longer possible
to remain neutral. The most loyal of Napoleon's
German allies, he gained the Grand Duchy of
Warsaw and a kingly crown but lost half his
Kingdom when the Emperor was defeated.
ANTON May 1827-6 Jun 1836, brother of
Friedrich August I, b 27 Dec 1755.
FRIEDRICH AUGUST II Jun 1836-9 Aug 1854
died accidentally - falling from a carriage,
nephew of Anton, b 18 May 1797.
JOHANN Aug 1854-29 Oct 1873, brother of
Friedrich August II, b 12 Dec 1801.

ALBRECHT Oct 1873-19 Jun 1902, son of Johann, b 23 Apr 1828. This able general played a major role in securing a German victory at Sedan in the Franco-Prussian War.

GEORG Jun 1902-15 Oct 1904, brother of Albrecht, b 8 Aug 1832.

FRIEDRICH AUGUST III Oct 1904-13 Nov 1918 when he abdicated, eldest son of Georg, b 25 May 1865; d 18 Feb 1932.

The Principality of Schaumberg-Lippe

The small County of Schaumberg-Lippe became a Principality in 1807, having been founded as a County in the middle of the 17th century. It is now part of Nieder Sachsen Land in Germany.

† Princes

GEORG I Count from 1806; Prince **18 Apr 1807-21 Nov 1860.**

ADOLF I Nov 1860-8 May 1893, eldest son of Georg I, b 1 Aug 1817.

GEORG II May 1893-29 Apr 1911, eldest son of Adolf I, b 10 Oct 1846.

ADOLF II Apr 1911-16 Nov 1918 when he abdicated, eldest son of Georg II, b 23 Feb 1883; d 26 Mar 1936 in an air crash.

The Principalities of Schwarzburg

The Principalities of Schwarzburg-Rudolstadt and Schwarzburg-Sondershausen became sovereign in 1807. Both could trace their ancestry to a Count Sizzo of Schwarzburg in the 12th century. In 1909, when the ruling family of Schwarzburg-Sondershausen died out the two states merged to form a small single Principality in five parts. It is now part of the Erfurt, Gera and Halle Districts of the German Democratic Republic.

† Princes of Schwarzburg-Rudolstadt

FRIEDRICH GUNTHER 1807-28 Jun 1867, b 6 Nov 1793.

ALBRECHT Jun 1867-26 Nov 1869, brother of Friedrich Gunther, b 30 Apr 1798.

GEORG Nov 1869-19 Jan 1890, son of Albrecht, b 23 Nov 1838.

GUNTHER Jan 1890-28 Mar 1909 when he became Prince of Schwarzburg.

† Princes of Schwarzburg-Sondershausen

GUNTHER FRIEDRICH KARL I Prince from 1794; sovereign Prince **1807-19 Aug 1835** when he abdicated, b 5 Dec 1760; d 22 Apr 1837.

GUNTHER FRIEDRICH KARL II Aug 1835-17 Jul 1880 when he abdicated upon losing his sight, son of Gunther Friedrich Karl I, b 24 Sep 1801; d 15 Sep 1889.

KARL Jul 1880-28 Mar 1909 when the Royal House of Schwarzburg-Sondershausen became extinct, son of Gunther Friedrich Karl II, b 7 Aug 1830.

† Prince of Schwarzburg

GUNTHER Prince of Schwarzburg-Rudolstadt from 1890; Prince of all Schwarzburg **28 Mar 1909-22 Nov 1918** when he abdicated, cousin of Georg of Schwarzburg-Rudolstadt, b 21 Aug 1852; d 16 Apr 1925.

The Principality of Waldeck and Pyrmont

The rulers of Waldeck, Counts since the 14th century, gained the lands of Pyrmont (some 50 miles to the north) two centuries later. A Principality from 1712, the dual state gained sovereignty in 1807. Waldeck is now in Hessen Land, Germany; Pyrmont is in Nieder Sachsen Land, Germany.

† Princes

GEORG I 1807-9 Sep 1813.

GEORG II Sep 1813-15 May 1845, son of Georg I, b 20 Sep 1789.

GEORG VIKTOR May 1845-12 May 1893, eldest surviving son of Georg II, b 14 Jan 1831.

FRIEDRICH May 1893-13 Nov 1918 when he abdicated, elder son of Georg Viktor, b 20 Jan 1865; d 26 May 1946.

The Kingdom of Westphalia

A short-lived puppet state created by Napoleon I for his youngest brother Jerome.

† King

HIERONYMUS NAPOLEON 8 Jul 1807-26 Oct 1813 when he fled, b (Jerome Buonaparte) 15 Nov 1784; d 24 Jun 1860. The most dissolute of Napoleon's brothers is remembered for his marital adventures (the first an illegal union with Elizabeth Patterson; the second to long-suffering Catherine of Wurttemberg; the third to the fortune of Giustina Pecori), his frivolous extravagance, his elegance, and his total unreliability - Napoleon, who called him 'mauvais sujet', foolishly gave him command of a wing of the Grande Armée with predictable disastrous results.

The Kingdom of Wurttemberg

Ruled by the same family since 1083, Wurttemberg became a County in 1135, a Duchy in 1495, an Electorate in 1802 and a Kingdom in 1806.

† Dukes

EBERHARD I Count from 1480; Duke **Dec 1495-24 Feb 1496,** b 11 Dec 1445.
EBERHARD II Feb 1496-11 Jun 1498 deposed, nephew of Eberhard I, b 1 Feb 1447; d Feb 1504.
ULRICH VI Jun 1498-1519 deposed; restored **1534-6 Nov 1559,** nephew of Eberhard II, b 8 Feb 1487.
CHRISTOPH Nov 1559-26 Dec 1568, son of Ulrich VI, b 12 May 1515.
LUDWIG III Dec 1568-18 Aug 1593, son of Christoph, b 1 Jan 1554.
FRIEDRICH I Aug 1593-29 Jan 1608, distant kinsman of Ludwig III, b 19 Aug 1557.
JOHANN FRIEDRICH Jan 1608-18 Jul 1628, son of Friedrich I, b 5 May 1582.
EBERHARD III Jul 1628-2 Jul 1674, son of Johann Friedrich, b 16 Aug 1614.
WILHELM LUDWIG Jul 1674-23 Jun 1677, son of Eberhard III, b 7 Jan 1647.
EBERHARD LUDWIG Jun 1677-31 Oct 1733, son of Wilhelm Ludwig, b 18 Sep 1676. He rebuilt the state that had lain devasted since the Thirty Years' War: schools were founded, defences organised and Protestant refugees with industrial skills were encouraged to settle.
KARL ALEXANDER Oct 1733-12 Mar 1737, cousin of Eberhard Ludwig, b 24 Jan 1684.
KARL EUGEN Mar 1737-24 Oct 1793, son of Karl Alexander, b 11 Feb 1728.
LUDWIG EUGEN Oct 1793-20 May 1795, brother of Karl Eugen, b 6 Jan 1731.
FRIEDRICH EUGEN May 1795-23 Dec 1797, brother of Ludwig Eugen, b 21 Jan 1732.
FRIEDRICH II Dec 1797-25 Feb 1803 when he became Elector.

† Elector

FRIEDRICH I Duke from Dec 1797; Elector **25 Feb 1803-26 Dec 1805** when he became King.

† Kings

FRIEDRICH Duke from 1797; Elector from 1803; King **26 Dec 1805-30 Oct 1816,** eldest son of Friedrich Eugen, b 6 Nov 1754. Through alliance with Napoleon, Friedrich gained much extra territory and improved his personal status.

WILHELM I Oct 1816-25 Jun 1864, elder son of Friedrich, b 27 Sep 1781.
KARL Jun 1864-6 Oct 1891, only son of Wilhelm I, b 6 Mar 1823.
WILHELM II Oct 1891-29 Nov 1918 when he abdicated; the last reigning monarch in the German Empire, nephew of Karl, b 25 Feb 1848; d 2 Oct 1921.

Germany, Federal Republic of

The Federal Republic was established on 21 Sep 1949; the occupation by Allied forces came to an end on 26 May 1952 and the state became a fully independent sovereign country on 5 May 1955.

Federal Presidents

Prof **THEODOR HEUSS 21 Sep 1949-Sep 1959,** b 31 Jan 1884; d 12 Dec 1963.
Dr **HEINRICH LÜBKE 15 Sep 1959-Jul 1969,** b 14 Oct 1894; d 6 Apr 1972.
Dr **GUSTAV HEINEMANN 1 Jul 1969-Jul 1974,** b 23 Jul 1899; d 7 Jul 1976.
WALTER SCHEEL since 1 Jul 1974, b 8 Jul 1919.

Federal Chancellors
(Premiers)

KONRAD ADENAUER 21 Sep 1949-Oct 1963, b 5 Jan 1876; d 19 Apr 1967. The Lord Mayor of Cologne, Adenaur was imprisoned by the Nazis whom he despised. His legacy was the re-establishment of Germany as a respected member of the international community - in particular he supported NATO and worked for reconciliation with France.
Prof **LUDWIG ERHARD 16 Oct 1963-Nov 1966,** b 4 Feb 1897; d 5 May 1977. A brilliant economist he was responsible for Germany's economic miracle - the restoration of the economy to a position of pre-eminence in Europe.
Dr **KURT GEORG KIESINGER 10 Nov 1966-Oct 1969,** b 6 Apr 1904.
Dr **WILLY BRANDT 21 Oct 1969-May 1974,** b (Herbert Ernst Frahm) 18 Dec 1913.
WALTER SCHEEL acting Chancellor **6-16 May 1974;** see President Scheel.
HELMUT SCHMIDT since 16 May 1974, b 23 Dec 1918.

Ghana

The British colony of the Gold Coast, established in 1874, was granted independence on 6 Mar 1957 and became a Republic on 1 Jul 1960. It took the name Ghana from a powerful state which flourished from the 4th to the 13th century in the modern state of Mali.

THE DOMINION OF GHANA

Governors-General

Sir **CHARLES ARDEN-CLARKE 6 Mar-Jun 1957.**
WILLIAM FRANCIS HARE, 5th Earl of LIS-TOWEL 13 Nov 1957-1 Jul 1960, b 1906.

Prime Minister

Dr **KWAME NKRUMAH 6 Mar 1957-1 Jul 1960** when he became first President - the office of Premier was abolished until 1969; see President Nkrumah.

THE REPUBLIC OF GHANA

Presidents

Dr **KWAME NKRUMAH 1 Jul 1960-24 Feb 1966** when he was deposed *in absentia*,b Sep 1909; d in exile 27 Apr 1972. Beginning his campaign for independence in 1947 with his book 'Towards Colonial Freedom', Nkrumah directed the affairs of Ghana from independence with an increasingly dictatorial manner. Aspects of the regime were corrupt and some development plans extravagant, although the Volta project has been of great value. Deposed, he took refuge in Guinea where he was made titular Head of State.
Maj-Gen **JOSEPH A. ANKRAH** Chairman of National Council of Liberation **24 Feb 1966-2 Apr 1969,** b 1917.
Brig **AKWASI AMANKWA AFRIFA** (later Gen) Chairman of National Council of Liberation **2 Apr 1969-28 Aug 1970**; relinquished duties as Head of Government 3 Sep 1969 when the office of Premier was restored, b 1936.
EDWARD AKUFO-ADDO 28 Aug 1970-13 Jan 1972 when he was deposed in a coup,b 1906.
Lieut-Gen **IGNATIUS KUTU ACHEAMPONG** (later General Acheampong) Chairman of the Council of National Redemption **13 Jan 1972-9 Oct 1975**; President of the Supreme Military Council **9 Oct 1975-5 Jul 1978,** b 1931.
Lieut-Gen **FRED AKUFFO** President of the Supreme Military Council **since 5 Jul 1978.**

Prime Minister

Dr **KOFI ABREFA BUSIA 3 Sep 1969-13 Jan 1972** when he was deposed in a coup and the office of Premier suspended, b 1933.

Golkonda *see* India

Granadine Confederation *see* Colombia

Great Britain *see* United Kingdom

Greece

Early Greece, a land of 'tribes' (genos), was transformed in the 12th century BC by the Dorian invasion into a land of what is inadequately described as city states (polis) of which two, Athens and Sparta, became dominant. However, at no time in ancient Greece could a Greek state be said to have existed. Centuries of foreign rule began in 338 BC when the Macedonians conquered the country; Roman rule began in 146 BC to be replaced by that of Byzantium in AD 395. In the Middle Ages several Latin states flourished in the peninsula (eg the Principality of Achaea) while the islands passed into the control of the Italian states, Venice and Genoa. Over-running Greece between 1354 and 1461, the Ottoman Turks placed a heavy yoke upon the Greeks who were not able regain their liberties until the conclusion of a bloody struggle in the 1820s. The heroism of the Greeks against overwhelming odds (eg Missolonghi) encouraged the Western Powers to intervene to establish the independence of a small Greek state.

THE REPUBLIC OF GREECE

Presidents

IOANNIS ANTONIOS CAPODISTRIAS 1828-9 Oct 1831 when he was assassinated, b 11 Feb 1776. Count Capodistrias, from Corfu, was a seasoned member of the Russian diplomatic staff. His autocratic ways brought Greece to the verge of civil war.
AGOSTINOS CAPODISTRIAS Oct 1831-Apr 1832, brother of Ioannis Capodistrias, b 1778; d 1857.

THE KINGDOM OF GREECE

† King of Greece

HOUSE OF WITTELSBACH
OTHON 5 Oct 1832-24 Oct 1862 when he fled, b (Prince Otto Friedrich Ludwig of Bavaria) 1 Jun 1815; d 26 Jul 1867. Totally German in outlook and unwisely surrounded by Bavarian troops and advisers, eccentric King Otto was never really accepted by the Greeks who deposed him in Oct 1862.

† Kings of the Hellenes

HOUSE OF OLDENBURG
Also known as the House of Schleswig-Holstein-Sonderburg-Glucksbürg.

GIORGIOS I 6 Jun 1863-18 Mar 1913 when he was assassinated, b (Prince Wilhelm of Denmark) 12 Sep 1845. Chosen because of his links with Britain's Royal Family, Giorgios I had a successful if stormy reign and saw the enlargement of Greece.

KONSTANTINOS I Mar 1913-11 Jul 1917 abdicated, eldest son of Giorgios I, b 2 Aug 1866; d 11 Jan 1923. Twice the victim of Venizelos: Konstantinos lost his throne after Venizelos (unfairly) convinced the Allies the King was pro-German and again when Greece was defeated by Turkey in a war begun by that politician.

ALEXANDROS I Jun 1917-25 Oct 1920, second son of Konstantinos I, b 1 Aug 1893.

KONSTANTINOS I 19 Dec 1920-27 Sep 1922 abdicated.

GIORGIOS II Sep 1922-1 Apr 1924 deposed.

THE HELLENIC REPUBLIC

Presidents

Admiral **PAVLOS KONDORIOTIS 14 Apr 1924-13 Apr 1926.**

Gen **THEODOROS PANGALOS 13 Apr-22 Aug 1926** when his dictatorship was overthrown, b 1878; d 1952.

Admiral **PAVLOS KONDORIOTIS Aug 1926-Dec 1929,** b 1857; d 22 Aug 1935.

ALEXANDROS ZAIMIS 14 Dec 1929-11 Oct 1935 when he was overthrown in a monarchist coup, b 28 Oct 1855; d 13 Sep 1936.

Prime Ministers

ELEUTHERIOS VENIZELOS 5 Jun-Nov 1932, b 23 Aug 1864; d 18 Mar 1936. Five times Premier of Greece, Venizelos took his country into World War I on the Allied side, acquired much extra territory by skilful diplomacy and worked for the establishment of a Republic - his conduct towards King Konstantinos I verged upon the treasonable.

PANAGIOTES E. TSALDARIS 3 Nov 1932-Jan 1933, b 1868; d 17 May 1936.

ELEUTHERIOS VENIZELOS 13 Jan-6 Mar 1933 deposed in coup.

Gen **NIKOLAOS PLASTIRAS 6 Mar 1933.**

Gen **ALEXANDROS OTHONAIOS 6 Mar 1933-Oct 1934,** b 1880; d 20 Sep 1970.

PANAGIOTES E. TSALDARIS Oct 1934-9 Oct 1935 deposed in coup.

Gen **GIORGIOS KONDILIS 9 Oct-25 Nov 1935,** b 1879; d 31 Jan 1956. Called 'Thunderbolt' this authoritarian leader was largely responsible for the restoration of the monarchy in 1935.

THE KINGDOM OF GREECE

† Kings of the Hellenes

HOUSE OF OLDENBURG
GIORGIOS II 3 Nov 1935-1 Apr 1947, eldest son of Konstantinos I, b 19 Jul 1890. Giorgios II was deposed in the anarchy of 1924 but was recalled and served his country well showing great bravery in his defence of Greece in World War II.

PAVLOS I Apr 1947-6 Mar 1964, brother of Giorgios II, b 14 Dec 1901.

KONSTANTINOS II Mar 1964-1 Jun 1973 when Greece became a Republic, son of Pavlos, b 2 Jun 1940.

Prime Ministers

KONSTANTINOS DEMERDJIS 25 Nov 1935-13 Apr 1936, b 1876; d in office.

Gen **IOANNIS METAXAS 13 Apr 1936-29 Jan 1941,** b 12 Apr 1871; d in office. His dictatorship allowed few personal freedoms but achieved great economic reforms.

ALEXANDROS KORIZIS 29 Jan-18 Apr 1941, b 1885; d in office (suicide).

Dr **EMMANUEL TSOUDEROS 20-23 Apr 1941;** from **23 Apr-20 May 1941** in Crete - the mainland being under German occupation; **May 1941-Apr 1944** PM in exile, b 1882; d 1956.

SOPHOCLES VENIZELOS 13-26 Apr 1944.

GIORGIOS PAPANDREOU 27 Apr-18 Oct 1944 in exile; **18 Oct 1944-Jan 1945** PM in Greece, b 13 Feb 1888; d 1 Nov 1968.

Gen **NIKOLAOS PLASTIRAS 3 Jan-8 Apr 1945,** b 1883; d 1953.

Admiral **PETROS VOULGARIS 8 Apr-Oct 1945,** b 1883; d 1957.

Archbishop **DAMASKINOS 17 Oct-1 Nov 1945,** b 3 Mar 1891; d 20 May 1949. Regent for the absent King George II the Archbishop played a major role in the affairs of state after the war, being one of the few figures respected by all Greeks.

PANAYOTIS KANELLOPOULOS 1-20 Nov 1945, b 13 Dec 1902.

THEMISTOCLES SOFOULIS 20 Nov 1945-Apr 1946.

PANAYOTIS POULITSAS 4-17 Apr 1946.

KONSTANTINOS TSALDARIS 17 Apr 1946-Jan 1947.

DEMETRIOS MAXIMOS 23 Jan-Aug 1947, b 1873; d 1955.

KONSTANTINOS TSALDARIS 24 Aug-7 Sep 1947.

THEMISTOCLES SOFOULIS 7 Sep 1947-24 Jun 1949, b 20 Nov 1860; d in office. In his youth he led a revolt against Turkish rule in his native Samos; as Premier he led his country in a long civil war against an attempted Communist takeover in the north.

KONSTANTINOS TSALDARIS 24-30 Jun 1949, b 1884; d 15 Nov 1970.

ALEXANDROS DIOMEDES 30 Jun 1949-Jan 1950, b 1875; d 12 Nov 1950.

IOANNIS THEOTOKIS 6 Jan-Mar 1950, b 1880; d 1963.

SOPHOCLES VENIZELOS 22 Mar-14 Apr 1950, son of Eleutherios Venizelos, b 17 Nov 1894; d 7 Feb 1964.

Gen NIKOLAOS PLASTIRAS 15 Apr-Aug 1950.

SOPHOCLES VENIZELOS 18 Aug-9 Sep 1950.

KONSTANTINOS TSALDARIS 9-11 Sep 1950.

SOPHOCLES VENIZELOS 11 Sep 1950-Oct 1951.

Gen NIKOLAOS PLASTIRAS 27 Oct 1951-Nov 1952.

DEMETRIOS KIOUSSOPOULOS 16-23 Nov 1952, b 1892.

Marshal ALEXANDROS PAPAGOS 23 Nov 1952-4 Oct 1955, b 9 Dec 1883; d in office.

STEPHANOS STEPHANOPOULOS 4 Oct 1955.

KONSTANTINOS KARAMANLIS 4 Oct 1955-Mar 1958.

KONSTANTINOS GIORGAKOPOULOS 2 Mar-17 May 1958, b 1890.

KONSTANTINOS KARAMANLIS 17 May 1958-Sep 1961.

Gen KONSTANTINOS DOVAS 10 Sep-4 Nov 1961, b 1898.

KONSTANTINOS KARAMANLIS 4 Nov 1961-Jun 1963.

PANAYOTIS PIPINELIS 17 Jun-27 Sep 1963, b 1899; d 19 Jul 1970.

STYLOS MAVROMIHALIS 27 Sep-8 Nov 1963, b 1900.

GIORGIOS PAPANDREOU 8 Nov-30 Dec 1963.

IOANNIS PARASKEVOPOULOS 30 Dec 1963-18 Feb 1964, b 25 Dec 1900.

GIORGIOS PAPANDREOU 18 Feb 1964-Jul 1965.

GIORGIOS ATHANASIADIS-NOVAS 15 Jul-20 Aug 1965.

ELIAS TSIRIMOKOS 20 Aug-17 Sep 1965, b 2 Aug 1907; d 13 Jul 1968.

STEPHANOS STEPHANOPOULOS 17 Sep 1965-Dec 1966, b 1898.

IOANNIS PARASKEVOPOULOS 21 Dec 1966-Apr 1967.

PANAYOTIS KANELLOPOULOS 3-21 Apr 1967 deposed in the 'Colonels Coup', b 1902.

KONSTANTINOS V. KOLLIAS 21 Apr-Dec 1967, b 1901.

GIORGIOS PAPADOPOULOS 13 Dec 1967-1 Jun 1973 when he became Premier of the Republic.

THE HELLENIC REPUBLIC

Presidents

GIORGIOS PAPADOPOULOS 1 Jun-25 Nov 1973, b 5 May 1919.

Gen PHAEDON GIZIKIS 25 Nov 1973-Dec 1974, b 16 Jun 1917.

MIKAEL STASSINOPOULOS 18 Dec 1974-Jun 1975, b 27 Jul 1905.

KONSTANTINOS TSATSOS since 19 Jun 1975, b 1899.

Premiers

GIORGIOS PAPADOPOULOS Premier since 13 Dec 1967; 1 Jun-Oct 1973 - also President, b 5 May 1919.

SPYROS MARKEZINIS 1 Oct-25 Nov 1973, b 1909.

ADAMANTIOS ANDROUTSOPOULOS 25 Nov 1973-Jul 1974, b 1919.

KONSTANTINOS KARAMANLIS since 24 Jul 1974, b 23 Feb 1907.

Macedonia

A leading Kingdom of the ancient world Macedonia briefly ruled the vast empire founded by Alexander the Great and dominated the Greek world. The state fell to Rome in 168 BC.

† Kings of the Macedonians

DYNASTY OF PERDICCAS

AMYNTAS I c 500-c 498 BC.

ALEXANDROS I c 498-c 450 BC.

PERDICCAS II c 450-413 BC, son of Alexandros I.

ARCHELAUS 413-399 BC assassinated, son of Perdiccas II.

399-c 393 BC Period of anarchy and civil war.

AMYNTAS III c 393-370 or 369 BC, nephew of Perdiccas II.

ALEXANDROS II 369-367 BC assassinated, son of Amyntas III.

PERDICCAS III 367-359 BC probably murdered, son of Amyntas III.

AMYNTAS IV 359 BC deposed, son of Perdiccas III; executed 336 BC.

PHILIPPOS II 359-336 BC assassinated, son of Amyntas III, b 382 BC. He deposed his nephew, reunited a realm racked by civil war, made Macedonia the leading Greek state and united the Hellenes in the League of Corinth to oppose Persia.

ALEXANDROS III (Alexander 'The Great') 336-13 Jun 323 BC, son of Philippos II, b 356 BC. One of the most able military strategists and romantic figures in the ancient world, Alexander the Great, whose philosophy tutor was Aristotle, quelled early revolts and assumed leadership of the Greeks at 20. Moving into Asia to counter the Persian threat to the Hellenes he took Syria and Palestine after his greatest victory (Tyre 332 BC). Adding Egypt (332-331 BC), Mesopotamia (331 BC) and Persia (330-327 BC), he next passed into Central Asia before reaching the Indus (spring 326 BC). This vast empire, too large to be administered by those who had not Alexander's amazing energy, fell apart as his generals (the 'successors') argued over the spoils when Alexander died of over indulgence at a feast.

PHILIPPOS III (Arrhidaeus) co-ruler **323-Mid-317 BC** murdered, illegitimate son of Philippos II.

ALEXANDROS IV co-ruler **late 323-mid 317 BC**; sole ruler **317-316 BC** deposed, posthumous son of Alexander III the Great; murdered by Cassander 310 or 309 BC.

Dynasty of Antipater

CASSANDER Ruler 316-305 BC when he assumed kingship; King **305-297 BC**, son of Antipater (one of Alexander's generals), b 358 BC. A usurper who seized Macedonia and most of Greece during the disputes of the diadochoi (the Successors).

PHILIPPOS IV co-ruler **297 BC** - reigned four months, first son of Cassander.

ANTIPATER I co-ruler **297-296 BC** deposed, second son of Cassander; murdered in 285 BC.

ALEXANDROS V co-ruler **297-296 BC**; sole ruler **296-294 BC** assassinated, third son of Cassander.

Antigonid Dynasty

The descendants of Antigonus I, King of Asia - one of the diadochoi.

DEMETRIOS I (Poliorcetes) **294-Sep 288 BC** fled, son of Antigonus I of Asia, b 336 BC; d in captivity 285 BC. A fine soldier he took Greece and Macedonia, but his early promise gave way to a frightening despotism and his overthrow by Epirus and Thrace was welcomed.

288-285 BC Macedonia was partitioned between Thrace and Epirus.

Thracian Dynasty

LYSIMACHUS 285-281 BC; was also Lysimachus of Thrace.

Seleucid Dynasty

SELEUCUS 281-Sep 280 BC; was also Seleucus I of The Seleucid Empire.

Ptolemaic Dynasty

The descent of the Egyptian diadochoi.

PTOLEMAIOS (Keraunos) **Sep 280-early 279 BC** killed by Gauls.

MELEAGER early 279 BC deposed as unfit to rule, brother of Ptolemaios; fate unknown.

Dynasty of Antipater

ANTIPATER II 279 BC - reigned 42 days; deposed, nephew of Cassander; fate uncertain.

279-277 BC Interregnum.

Antigonid Dynasty

ANTIGONUS II (Gonatas) Ruler from 277 BC; King **early 276-spring 239 BC**, grandson of Antigonus I of Asia, b c 320 BC.

DEMETRIOS II 239-spring 229 BC, son of Antigonus II, b c 276 BC.

PHILIPPOS V spring 229 BC deposed; restored **autumn 221-179 BC**, son of Demetrios II, b 238 BC. A man of alternating charm and vile temper he underestimated the resources of Rome when he intervened in Illyria and in the resulting war his power was confined to Macedonia proper.

PERSEUS 179-168 BC when Macedonia was annexed by Rome, son of Philippos V, b c 212 BC; d a captive in Rome c 165 BC.

Sparta

The extraordinary military state of Sparta, always the rival of democratic republican Athens, had a strict social structure: at the head were two co-equal Kings (most of whom were drawn from the Agidae and Eurypontidae families), and the Spartiatai (the governing class). The lower classes - Perioikoi (freemen) and Helots (slaves) - had no rights.

† Co-Kings

ANAXANDRIDES c 560-c 520 BC. His victories over Argos made the Spartan military machine supreme in Peloponnesus.

ARISTON c 560-c 520? BC.

DEMARATUS c 519-491 BC deposed; fate uncertain.

CLEOMENES I c 519-487 BC committed suicide, son of Anaxandrides.

LEOTYCHIDES 491-476 BC.

LEONIDAS I 487-480 BC died in battle bravely attempting to hold the Pass of Thermopolyae against Persia; son of Anaxandrides.

PLEISTARCHUS 480-458? BC, son of Leonidas I.

ARCHIDAMUS II 476-427 BC. The serious revolt of the Helots in 466 BC occurred in this reign.

PLEISTOANAX 458-c 400 BC. Through a series of petty quarrels Sparta, the greatest military power in Europe, began her long war with Athens (431 BC) - a clash that, despite later claims, had nothing to do with ideologies. The supremacy in Greece that Sparta won on the battlefield was lost by her arrogant conduct, and Pleistoanax was blamed for the misfortunes that the war brought Sparta.

AGIS I c 427-c 401 BC, son of Archidamus II.

AGESILAUS II c 401-c 361 BC, half-brother of Agis I, b c 445 BC. Though short and lame he was a superb general who beat the Persians and held Sparta's enemies at bay when his country's hegemony was ended in c 371 BC.

AGESIPOLIS I c 400-380 BC.

CLEOMBROTUS II 380-371 BC died in battle.

AGESIPOLIS II 371-370 BC.

CLEOMENES II 370-309 BC, son of Cleombrotus II.

ARCHIDAMUS III c 361-338 BC. He conducted successful campaigns in Italy and Sicily but defeat by the Macedonians temporarily made Sparta a vassal state.

AGIS II   338-331 BC died in battle, son of Archidamus III.
EUDAMIDAS I   330-309? BC.
AREUS I   309-265 BC.
ARCHIDAMUS IV   309-265? BC.
ACROTATUS   265-263 BC, son of Areus I.
EUDAMIDAS II   265-245 BC.
AREUS II   ?263-256? BC.
AGIS IV   245-241 BC murdered, son of Eudamidas II, b *c* 264 BC. A reformer who had his avaricious co-ruler Leonidas II impeached and deposed.
LEONIDAS II   256-242 BC deposed; restored **241-235 BC.**
EURYDAMIDAS   ?241-237? BC.
CLEOMBROTUS III   242-241 BC deposed and exiled, son-in-law of Leonidas II; fate uncertain.
CLEOMENES III   ?237-222 BC fled when Sparta fell to Macedonia, son of Leonidas II; d by suicide 220 BC.
ARCHIDAMUS V   ?235-221 BC.
221-219 BC Sparta was under Macedonian rule.
AGESIPOLIS III   219-210? BC.
LYCURGUS   219-210? BC.
(The revived kingship of Sparta was effectively ended by the dictatorships of Machanidas and Nabis and by Sparta's forced adhesion to the Achaean League.)
146 BC Sparta fell to Rome.

Thrace

Thrace was briefly an independent Kingdom during the power struggle between the diadochoi (Successors) to Alexander the Great.

† Kings

LYSIMACHUS Governor from 323 BC; ruler from 311 BC; King **305-281 BC** died in battle, one of Alexander the Great's bodyguards.
281-spring 280 BC Thrace was ruled by the Seleucids.
PTOLEMAEUS nominally King **spring-summer 280 BC** deposed, son of Lysimachus; date of death uncertain.
280 BC Thrace fell to Macedonia through the treachery of Queen Arsinoe.

Grenada

French from 1650, Grenada became British in 1763 and remained a possession of the Crown (except for a spell of French rule from 1779 to 1783) until autonomy was granted in 1967. Independence was achieved on 1 Feb 1974.

Governor-General

Sir **LEO de GALE since 1974,** b 1921.

Prime Minister

Sir **ERIC MATTHEW GAIRY since Feb 1974,** b 18 Feb 1922.

Guastalla *see* Italy

Guatemala

Spanish from 1519 to 1821, Guatemala joined the Mexican Empire almost immediately after gaining independence. Guatemala formed part of the United Provinces of Central America from Jul 1823 until that state broke up in 1839. The independent Republic of Guatemala was not finally proclaimed until 21 Mar 1847.

PROVISIONAL GOVERNMENT

Heads

MARIANO RIVERA PAZ   Apr 1839-Dec 1841.
VENANCIO LOPEZ   Dec 1841-May 1842.
MARIANO RIVERA PAZ   May 1842-Dec 1844.
RAFAEL CARRERA   Dec 1844-Mar 1847 when he became President.

THE REPUBLIC

Presidents

RAFAEL CARRERA   Mar 1847-Oct 1848.
JUAN MARTINÉZ   Oct-Nov 1848.
BERNARDO ESCOBAR   Nov-Dec 1848.
MARIANO PAREDES   Jan 1849-Oct 1851, b 1800; d 1856.
RAFAEL CARRERA   Oct 1851-4 Apr 1865, b 24 Oct 1814; d in office. A half Indian illiterate, Carrera founded the Guatemalan Republic which he ruled harshly but which he rescued from anarchy.
PEDRO AYCINENA   Apr-May 1865.
Gen **VICENTE CERNA   May 1865-2 Jun 1871** deposed in coup.
MIGUEL GARCIA GRANADOS   Jun 1871-May 1873.
JUSTO RUFINO BARRIOS   May 1873-Jul 1882.
JOSÉ MARIA ORANTES acting President **Jul 1882-Jan 1883.**
JUSTO RUFINO BARRIOS   Jan 1883-2 Apr 1885, b 17 Jul 1835; d in office - killed in battle. Called 'The Reformer' he became obsessed with the

idea of recreating the Central American federation and died while trying to conquer el Salvador.
ALEJANDRO SINIBALDI 2-7 Apr 1885.
MANUEL LISNADRO BARILLAS acting President **Apr 1885-Mar 1886**; President **Mar 1886-Mar 1892,** b 1864; d 1907.
JOSÉ MARIA REINA-BARRIOS Mar 1892-8 Feb 1898, b 1853; d in office - assassinated. The nephew of Justo Rufino Barrios.
MANUEL ESTRADA CABRERA Feb 1898-8 Apr 1920 deposed, b 21 Nov 1857; d 24 Sep 1924 in gaol. This dictator was deposed by Parliament as insane and was imprisoned for his gross corruption.
CARLOS HERRERA Apr 1920-Dec 1921, b 1856; d 1930.
Gen **JOSÉ MARIA ORELLANA Dec 1921-Sep 1926,** b 1872; d in office.
LÁZARO CHACÓN Sep 1926-Dec 1930, b 1873; d 1931.
BAUDILLO PALMA 13-17 Dec 1930.
Gen **MANUEL ORELLANA 17 Dec 1930-Jan 1931.**
JOSÉ MARIA REINA-ANDRADE Jan-Feb 1931, b 1860; d 1947.
Gen **JORGE UBICO CASTAÑEDA Feb 1931-1 Jul 1944** deposed in coup, b 10 Nov 1878; d 14 Jun 1946. Called 'Tata' (Father), Ubico instituted a harsh dictatorship with forced labour and conscripted teachers. His regime did, however, make outstanding progress in public health.
1-4 Jul 1944 Military junta.
Gen **FEDERICO PONCE-VAIDES 4 Jul-Oct 1944,** b 1878; d 1946.
Oct-Dec 1944 Military triumvirate.
Lieut-Col **JACOBO ARBENZ-GUZMAN Dec 1944-Mar 1945.**
Dr **JUAN JOSÉ AREVALO 15 Mar 1945-Mar 1951,** b 10 Sep 1904.
Lieut-Col **JACOBO ARBENZ-GUZMAN 15 Mar 1951-27 Jun 1954** deposed in coup, b 14 Sep 1913; d 27 Jan 1971.
Col **CARLOS ENRIQUE DIAS 27-29 Jun 1954** Head of military junta.
Col **ELFEGO MONZON 29 Jun-8 Jul 1954** Head of military junta.
Col **CARLOS CASTILLO-ARMAS 8 Jul 1954-26 Jul 1957,** b 1914; d in office - assassinated by the Palace Guard.
LUIS ARTURO GONZÁLEZ-LÓPEZ acting President **27 Jul-24 Oct 1957,** b 1900; d 11 Dec 1965.
Col **OSCAR MENDOZA AZURDIA** Head of military junta **24-27 Oct 1957.**
GUILLERMO FLORES-AVENDAÑO acting President **27 Oct 1957-Mar 1958,** b 1898.
Gen **MIGUEL YDIGORAS-FUENTES 2 Mar 1958-30 Mar 1963** deposed in coup, b 17 Oct 1895.
Col **CARLOS ENRIQUE PERALTA-AZURDIA 30 Mar 1963-Jul 1966,** b 11 Jun 1908.
Dr **JULIO CÉSAR MÉNDEZ-MONTENEGRO 1 Jul 1966-Jul 1970,** b 23 Nov 1915.
Col **CARLOS MANUEL ARAÑA-OSORIO 1 Jul 1970-Jul 1974,** b 17 Jul 1918.
Gen **KJELL EUGENIO LAUGERUD-GARCIA 1 Jul 1974-Jul 1978,** b 24 Jan 1930.

Gen **FERNANDO ROMEO LUCAS GARCIA since 1 Jul 1978,** b 1925.

Guinea

A French territory from 1895, Guinea became an independent Republic on 2 Oct 1958.

Heads of State

AHMED SÉKOU TOURÉ Head of State **2 Oct 1958-Jan 1961**; President **since Jan 1961,** b 9 Jan 1922.
KWAME NKRUMAH titular Head of State **2 Mar 1966-27 Apr 1972** when he died, the former President of Ghana, b 1909.

Prime Ministers

AHMED SÉKOU TOURÉ 2 Oct 1958-Jan 1961; see President Touré.
1961-1972 Premiership in abeyance.
Dr **LOUIS LANSANA BEAVOGUI since 26 Apr 1972.**

Guinea-Bissau

Portuguese from 1480 the former colony of Portuguese Guinea became an independent Republic known as Guinea-Bissau on 10 Sep 1974.

President

LUIS CABRAL since 10 Sep 1974, b 1931.

Prime Ministers

FRANCISCO MENDES Sep 1974-7 Jul 1978; d in office - in a car crash.
LUIS CABRAL acting PM **since 7 Jul 1978.**

Gupta Empire *see* India

Guyana

A Dutch settlement from c 1620 to 1796, this territory became the colony of British Guiana in 1814. Independence was achieved on 26 May 1966 and a Republic was declared on 23 Feb 1970.

THE DOMINION OF GUYANA

Governors-General

Sir **RICHARD LUYT 26 May-31 Oct 1966,** b 1915.
Sir **DAVID JAMES GARDINER ROSE 31 Oct 1966-10 Nov 1969** when he died in an accident, b 1923; d in office.
Sir **EDWARD LUCKHOO Jan-Feb 1970.**

Prime Minister

LINDEN FORBES SAMPSON BURNHAM 26 May 1966-22 Feb 1970.

THE CO-OPERATIVE REPUBLIC OF GUYANA

President

RAYMOND ARTHUR CHUNG since 17 Mar 1970, b 10 Jan 1918.

Prime Minister

LINDEN FORBES SAMPSON BURNHAM since 22 Feb 1970, b 20 Feb 1923.

Gwynedd *see* Wales, United Kingdom

Haiti

Spanish from 1492 to 1630, Haiti fell to French adventurers in 1630 and was annexed by the French crown in 1697. After an unsuccessful attempt to gain independence in 1801 sovereignty was achieved on 1 Jan 1804. On three occasions a monarchy has been established and once the state divided into two separate countries. From 1915 to 1934, after a period of total anarchy, the Republic came under American administration.

PROVISIONAL GOVERNMENT

Governors

FRANCOIS DOMINIQUE TOUSSAINT L'OUVERTURE 9 May 1801-7 May 1802 when taken prisoner by the French, b *c* 1743; d (in France) 7 Apr 1803. From 1791 he led a guerrilla group against French rule.
May 1802-Nov 1803 French rule restored.
JEAN JACQUES DESSALINES Nov 1803-Jan 1804.

Governor of Independent Haiti

JEAN JACQUES DESSALINES 1 Jan-8 Oct 1804.

THE EMPIRE OF HAITI

† Emperor

JACQUES I (formerly Jean Jacques Dessalines) **8 Oct 1804-17 Oct 1806** assassinated, b (in West Africa) *c* 1758. A former slave and field hand he became a guerrilla leader and established Haiti's independence. The self-proclaimed Emperor fostered racial hatred and indulged in a massacre of whites.
Oct 1806 to Feb 1807 A period of anarchy when no central authority existed.
Feb 1807 The country broke into two states.

HAYTI
(The northern part of Haiti)

Provisional Ruler

HENRI CHRISTOPHE Feb 1807-1811 when he became King.

† King

HENRI I (formerly Henri Christophe) **1811-8 Oct 1820** committed suicide, b 6 Oct 1767. His Kingdom was overthrown by Pétion.

SAINT-DOMINGUES
(The southern part of Haiti)

Presidents

ALEXANDRE SABÈS PÉTION 1807-Mar 1818, b 1770; d in office. His campaign against Hayti reduced that Kingdom to a tiny mountainous district.
JEAN-PIERRE BOYER 1818-Oct 1820 when he reunited Haiti.

THE REPUBLIC OF HAITI

Presidents

JEAN-PIERRE BOYER Oct 1820-1843 deposed, b 1776; d 1850. He crushed the northern Kingdom, annexed the Dominican Republic and inflicted a harsh corrupt regime upon all Hispaniola.
1843 A period of anarchy.
CHARLES HÉRARD 1843-May 1844.
PHILIPPE GUERRIER May 1844-Apr 1845.
LOUIS PIERROT Apr 1845-Feb 1846.
JEAN-BAPTISTE RICHE Feb 1846-Feb 1847, b 1780; d in office.

FAUSTIN-ÉLIE SOULOUQUE   Mar   1847-Aug 1849.

THE EMPIRE OF HAITI

† Emperor

FAUSTIN I (formerly President Soulouque) **26 Aug 1849-Dec 1858** deposed, b 1782; d 6 Aug 1867 in exile. A former slave he became leader of the black majority against the mulatto ruling class.

THE REPUBLIC OF HAITI

Presidents

Gen **NICOLAS FABRE GEFFRARD** acting President **Dec 1858-Feb 1859**; President **Feb 1859-Mar 1867**; nominally ruler after 1866, b 1806; d 1879.
Gen **SYLVAIN SALNAVE May 1867-Dec 1869** when he was assassinated.
Gen **NISSAGE SAGET** acting President **Dec 1869-Mar 1870**; President **May 1870-May 1874.**
Gen **MICHEL DOMINGUE Jun 1874-May 1876.**
Gen **BOISROND CANAL May 1876-Oct 1879.**
Gen **LOUIS ÉTIENNE FÉLICITÉ SALOMON** Nov **1879-Aug 1888,** b 1820; d in office.
FRANCOIS DENIS LÉGITIME Sep 1888-Aug 1889, b 1833; d 1905.
LOUIS FLORÉAL HIPPOLYTE acting President **Aug-Oct 1889**; President **Oct 1889-24 Mar 1896,** b 1827; d in office.
TIRESIAS SIMON SAM Mar 1896-May 1902.
Gen **BOISROND CANAL May-Dec 1902.**
ALEXIS NORD Dec 1902-Dec 1908, b 1822; d 1910.
ANTOINE SIMON Dec 1908-Aug 1911.
SIMON MICHEL CINCINNATUS LECONTE Aug 1911-Aug 1912; d in office.
TANCRÈDE AUGUSTE Aug 1912-2 May 1913; d in office.
MICHEL ORESTE May 1913-Feb 1914.
ORESTE ZAMOR Feb-Oct 1914.
DAVILMARE THÉODORE Nov 1914-Mar 1915.
JOSEPH VILBRUN-GUILLAUME Mar-28 Jul 1915 when he was murdered by the mob.
1915-1934 United States administration.

THE REPUBLIC OF HAITI

Presidents

STÉNIO JOSEPH VINCENT President under American supervision **from 1930**; President of a sovereign state **Aug 1934-Apr 1941,** b 1874; d 1959.
ÉLIE LESCOT acting President **Apr-Aug 1941**; President **15 Aug 1941-11 Jan 1946** deposed in coup, b 1883; d 22 Oct 1974.
Col **FRANK LEVAUD 12 Jan-Aug 1946** Head of military junta.

DUMARSAIS ESTIMÉ 15 Aug 1946-10 May 1950 deposed in coup, b 1900; d 1953.
Col **FRANK LEVAUD 10 May-Oct 1950** Head of military junta.
Gen **PAUL E. MAGLOIRE Oct 1950-12 Dec 1956** b 1907.
JOSEPH PIERRE-LOUIS acting President **12 Dec 1956-Feb 1957.**
FRANCK SYLVAIN acting President **7 Feb-12 Apr 1957.**
12 Apr-20 May 1957 Executive Council.
Gen **LEON CANTAVE** acting President **20-26 May 1957.**
Prof **DANIEL FIGNOLE** acting President **26 May-14 Jun 1957.**
ANTOINE KEBREAU Head of military junta **Jun-Oct 1957.**
Dr **FRANCOIS DUVALIER 22 Oct 1957-21 Apr 1971,** b 14 Apr 1907; d in office.
JEAN-CLAUDE DUVALIER since 22 Apr 1971, son of Francois Duvalier, b 3 Jul 1951.

Hanover   *see* Germany

Hasmonean State   *see* Israel

Hatti   *see* The Hittites

Hawaii   *see* United States of America

Hayti, Kingdom of   *see* Haiti

Hejaz   *see* Saudi Arabia

Hellenic Republic   *see* Greece

Helvetic Confederation   *see* Switzerland

Herodian Kingdom   *see* Israel

Hesse (Darmstadt)   *see* Germany

Hesse-Cassel   *see* Germany

Hesse-Homburg   *see* Germany

The Hittites

The history of this mysterious people whose Kingdom flourished in Asia Minor for 500 years has been rediscovered through 20th century archaeology. The dates of the Hittite (or, more correctly, Hatti) period are a matter of considerable controversy, as is the practice of dividing Hittite history into two periods, but it is safe to assume a break c 1460 BC, possibly brought about by a new dynasty, but the change was not great enough to distinguish a Kingdom before that time and an Empire after.

† Kings

TUDHALIYAS I c 1740-c 1710 BC
PU-SARRUMAS c 1710-c 1680 BC.
(These first two 'Kings' are known to have existed but it has not yet been established that they were Kings of Hatti.)
LABARNAS I c 1680-c 1650 BC, son of Pu-Sarrumas.
HATTUSILIS I (originally called LABARNAS II) c 1650-c 1620 BC, son of Labarnas I.
MURSILIS I c 1620-c 1590 BC when he was assassinated by Hantilis; adopted son of Hattusilis I. He conquered northern Syria and Babylon.
HANTILIS I c 1590-c 1560 BC, brother-in-law of Mursilis I.
ZIDANTAS I c 1560-c 1550 BC, thought to be the son-in-law of Hantilis I.
AMMUNAS I c 1550-c 1530 BC, son of Zidantas I.
HUZZIYAS I c 1530-c 1525 BC when he was deposed by Telipinus; probably son of Ammunas I.
TELIPINUS c 1525-c 1500 BC, brother-in-law of Huzziyas I.
(Then an obscure period in which the names and dates are still uncertain.)
ALLUWAMNAS (?) c 1500-c 1490 BC ?, said to be the son-in-law of Telipinus.
HANTILIS II (?) c 1490-c 1480 BC ?
ZIDANTAS II (?) c 1480-c 1460 BC ?
(The above are sometimes referred to as the Kings of the Old Kingdom; those following are known as the Kings of the Empire.)
TUDHALIYAS II c 1460-c 1440 BC.
ARNUWANDAS I c 1440-c 1420 BC, son of Tudhaliyas II.
HATTUSILIS II c 1420-c 1400 BC, brother of Arnuwandas I.
TUDHALIYAS III c 1400-1380 BC, son of Hattusilis II.
SUPPILULIUMAS I c 1380-c 1346 BC, son of Tudhaliyas III. Suppiluliumas was a brilliant general whose campaigns in Syria created an Empire.
ARNUWANDAS II c 1346-c 1345 BC, eldest son of Suppiluliumas I.

MURSILIS II c 1345-c 1315 BC, younger son of Suppiluliumas I.
MUWATALLIS c 1315-c 1296 BC, son of Mursilis II.
MURSILIS III (thought to be the regnal name of URHI-TESHUB) c 1296-c 1289 BC when he was deposed by Hattusilis III; son of Muwatallis.
HATTUSILIS III c 1289-c 1265 BC, uncle of Mursilis III, b c 1320 BC.
TUDHALIYAS IV c 1265-c 1235 BC, son of Hattusilis III.
ARUNWANDAS III c 1235-c 1215 BC, son of Tudhaliyas IV.
SUPPILULIUMAS II c 1215-? BC, said to be the brother of Arnuwandas III.
c 1200 BC The Hittite Kingdom collapsed under attack from the Phrygians.

Holland *see* The Netherlands

The Holy Roman Empire

A European sovereignty, never a country, which is traditionally said to have started on 25 Dec 800 when the Pope crowned Charlemagne 'Emperor of the Romans' - although the style Holy Roman Emperor was not formally assumed until 962. The Emperor was styled King of the Germans before his coronation in Rome but in practice the reigns of the Emperors are dated from their accession to power, and after 1493 the imperial title was assumed without journeying to Rome. The Emperor was chosen by Electors of whom there were at first seven; the Prince-Archbishops of Cologne, Mainz and Trier and the Dukes of the Franks, Saxons, Bavarians and Swabians. Later the Electors were the three Archbishops plus the secular rulers of Prussia Bohemia (the Austrian ruler), Bavaria, Saxony and Hanover. Just before the empty imperial title was discarded by the last Emperor (Franz II) the rulers of Baden, Wurttemberg, Salzburg and Hesse-Cassel gained the electoral dignity.

† Emperors of the Romans

HOUSE OF THE CAROLINGIANS
KARL I (Charlemagne) sole ruler **25 Dec 800-813**; co-ruler **813-28 Jan 814**; was also Charles I of France.
LUDWIG I co-ruler **813-Jan 814**; sole ruler **Jan 814-20 Jun 840**; was also Louis I of France.
LOTHAR I sole ruler **840-850**; co-ruler **850-29 Sep 855**; crowned 843, son of Ludwig I, b 795. Lothar wished to maintain the unity of Charlemagne's empire but he was forced to partition by his brothers at Verdun (843) and was left with direct sovereignty over a long, narrow territory stretching from the Low Countries to Italy.

LUDWIG II co-ruler **850-Sep 855** ; sole ruler **Sep 855-12 Aug 875,** son of Lothar I, b c 822.

KARL II 875-6 Oct 877; was also Charles II of France.

KARL III ('The Fat') **877-887** deposed; crowned 881, great-grand-son of Karl I (Charlemagne), b 839; d 888. Karl III almost succeeded in his ambition to reunite the empire of Charlemagne, briefly ruling both France and Germany before he was deposed because of his inability to deal with the Norman menace.

ARNULF 887-8 Dec 898; crowned 896, illegitimate grandson of Ludwig II, b c 850.

LUDWIG III ('The Child') **899-911;** never crowned thus technically Emperor-elect, son of Arnulf, b 893.

House of Lahngau or Franconia

KONRAD I Nov 911-23 Dec 918; never crowned thus technically Emperor-elect, Duke of Franconia.

House of Saxony

HEINRICH I ('The Fowler') **919-2 Jul 936;** never crowned thus technically Emperor-elect, Duke of Saxony, b c 876.

† Holy Roman Emperors
(the style adopted in 962)

House of Saxony

OTTO I ('The Great') **936-7 May 973;** crowned Feb 962, son of Heinrich I, b 23 Nov 912. Otto the Great, regarded by the Papacy as a champion of the Church, inaugurated a reformed and more consolidated Empire, adopted a new imperial style, crushed revolts and won a major victory over the Magyars.

OTTO II May 973-7 Dec 983, son of Otto I, b c 955.

OTTO III Dec 983-23 Jan 1002; crowned 996, son of Otto II, b Jul 980.

HEINRICH II (St Henry) **1002-Jul 1024;** crowned Feb 1014, great-grandson of Heinrich I, b 6 May 973.

House of Speyer or Franconia

KONRAD II 1024-4 Jun 1039; crowned 1027, descendant of Otto I, b c 990.

HEINRICH III 1039-5 Oct 1056; crowned 1046, son of Konrad II, b 28 Oct 1017. In Henry III's reign the Empire was at its most powerful: he added Hungary, Bohemia and southern Italy to his feudal lands; he intervened in the scandal of the anti-Popes deposing the pretenders and securing the election of Clement II.

HEINRICH IV Oct 1056-1105 when forced to abdicate; crowned 1084, son of Heinrich III, b 11 Nov 1050; d 7 Aug 1106. He conducted a bitter struggle over investiture, which the Pope saw as an abuse, against that sternest advocate of the Church's temporal powers Gregory VII, whose campaign the Emperor saw as an attempted attack upon his rights. The quarrel reached its head when Henry defiantly, and illegally,

declared the Pope deposed. Forced to concede, the Emperor stood as a penitent in the snows of Canossa (Jan 1077) before the Pope, but soon revived his rebellion beseiging Gregory at Rome and erecting an anti-Pope. After a later contest with Rome he was deposed by his son, having achieved nothing by his famous challenge but having made important advances in promoting a German identity and in suppressing overmighty Princes of the Empire.

HEINRICH V 1105 de facto; **1106-23 May 1125** de jure, son of Heinrich IV, b 8 Nov 1086. Husband of the future Queen Matilda of England, Henry V made peace with the Papacy by the concordat of Worms.

House of Saxony-Supplinburg

LOTHAR II 1125-3 or 4 Dec 1137; crowned 1133, b Jun 1075.

House of Hohenstaufen

KONRAD III Mar 1138-15 Feb 1152; never crowned thus technically Emperor-elect, Duke of Franconia, b 1093.

FRIEDRICH I ('Barbarossa' - red beard) **Feb 1152-10 Jun 1190;** crowned 1155; drowned while on Crusade, nephew of Konrad III, b c 1123. He reduced the rebellious German Princes by diplomatic skill and the judicious grant of flattering titles; he achieved peace in Italy, after devastating campaigns and defeat at Legnano, by conciliation. Able as a fighter and an administrator, the handsome and popular Barbarossa is said by legend to sleep beneath a German mountain to return at the hour of Germany's greatest need.

HEINRICH VI ('The Cruel') **Jun 1190-28 Sep 1197;** crowned 1191; was also Enrico, King of Sicily.

PHILIPP Mar 1198-Jun 1208 assassinated; never crowned thus technically Emperor-elect, youngest son of Friedrich Barbarossa, b c 1177. Rival to Otto IV, Philipp was not able to assert his position as Emperor.

House of Saxony

OTTO IV 1198 deposed; **Nov 1208-1215** deposed; crowned Oct 1209, son of Henry the Lion of Saxony, b between 1175 and 1182; d 19 May 1218. The Empire was racked by civil war as Otto disputed the throne with Philipp.

House of Hohenstaufen

FRIEDRICH II 1215-13 Dec 1250; was also Federigo I, king of Sicily.

KONRAD IV Dec 1250-21 May 1254; never crowned thus technically Emperor-elect; was also Corrado I, King of Sicily.

KONRAD V 1254 - cannot be considered to have reigned as Emperor either de facto or de jure; was also Corrado II, King of Sicily.

HOUSE OF ANJOU
RICHARD elected **May 1257** but cannot be considered to have reigned, second son of King John of England, b 6 Jan 1209; d 2 Apr 1272.

HOUSE OF BURGUNDY
ALFONS elected **1267** but cannot be considered to have reigned; was also Alfonso X, King of Castile and Leon, Spain.

HOUSE OF HABSBURG
RUDOLF I 1273-15 Jul 1291; never crowned thus technically Emperor-elect; was also Rudolf I, Duke of Austria.

HOUSE OF NASSAU
ADOLF May 1292-23 Jun 1298 deposed; never crowned thus technically Emperor-elect, son of Walram II of Nassau, b c 1250; murdered by Albrecht I 2 Jul 1298.

HOUSE OF HABSBURG
ALBRECHT I 1298-1308; was also Albrecht I, Duke of Austria.

HOUSE OF LUXEMBOURG
HEINRICH VII Nov 1308-24 Aug 1313; crowned 1312, son of the Count of Luxembourg, b c 1275.

HOUSE OF WITTELSBACH
LUDWIG IV (Ludwig III of Bavaria) **1314-11 Oct 1347**; crowned 1328, b c 1283; Ludwig became Emperor overcoming the rivalry of Friedrich the Fair and secured the independence of imperial elections from the Papacy.

HOUSE OF HABSBURG
FRIEDRICH (the Fair), claimed but never secured the imperial title; was also Friedrich I, Duke of Austria.

HOUSE OF LUXEMBOURG
KARL IV 1347-29 Nov 1378; was also Karel, King of Bohemia.
WENZEL Nov 1378-21 Aug 1400 deposed; was also Vacláv IV of Bohemia.

HOUSE OF THE PALATINATE
RUPPRECHT KLEM 22 Aug 1400-18 May 1410; never crowned thus technically Emperor-elect, Elector of the Palatinate, b 5 May 1352.

HOUSE OF LUXEMBOURG
SIGISMUND 1410-1437; crowned 1433; was also Sigismund of Bohemia and Hungary.

HOUSE OF HABSBURG
ALBRECHT II 1438-27 Oct 1439; never crowned thus technically Emperor-elect; was also Albrecht V, Duke of Austria.
FRIEDRICH III 1440-19 Aug 1493; crowned 1452 - the last Emperor to go to Rome for coronation; all succeeding Emperors assumed the imperial title upon election; was also Friedrich III, Duke

of Austria.
MAXIMILIAN I 1493-12 Jan 1519; was also Maximilian I, Archduke of Austria.
KARL V 1519-25 Oct 1555 abdicated; was also Carlos I of Spain.
FERDINAND I 1556-25 Jul 1564; was also Ferdinand I, Archduke of Austria.
MAXIMILIAN II 1564-12 Oct 1576; was also Maximilian II, Archduke of Austria.
RODOLF II 1576-20 Jan 1612; was also Rudolf II, Archduke of Austria.
MATTHIAS 1612-20 Mar 1619; was also Matthias, Archduke of Austria.
FERDINAND II 1619-15 Feb 1637; was also Ferdinand II, Archduke of Austria.
FERDINAND III 1637-2 Apr 1657; was also Ferdinand III, Archduke of Austria.
LEOPOLD I 1658-5 May 1705; was also Leopold I, Archduke of Austria.
JOSEPH I 1705-17 Apr 1711; was also Joseph I, Archduke of Austria.
KARL VI 1711-20 Oct 1740; was also Karl II Archduke of Austria.

HOUSE OF WITTELSBACH
KARL VII 1742-20 Jan 1745; was also Karl Albrecht, Elector of Bavaria.

HOUSE OF LORRAINE
FRANZ I STEPHAN Sep 1745-18 Aug 1765; was also Francesco II of Tuscany.

HOUSE OF HABSBURG-LORRAINE
JOSEPH II Aug 1765-20 Feb 1790; was also Joseph II, Archduke of Austria.
LEOPOLD II Feb 1790-1 Mar 1792; was also Leopold II, Archduke of Austria.
FRANZ II Jun 1792-6 Aug 1806 when he abdicated and abolished the Holy Roman Empire; was also Franz II and I, Archduke and Emperor of Austria.

Holy See, The *see* The Papal State

Honduras

Spanish from 1526 to 1821; independent from 1821 to 1822; part of Mexico from 1822 to 1823 and of Central America from 1823 to 1838, Honduras was declared independent again on 5 Nov 1838. An effective central government was not formed until 1841.

Presidents

FRANCISCO FERRERA Jan 1841-Jan 1845.
CORONADO CHAVEZ Jan 1845-Jan 1847.
JUAN LINDO Jan 1847-Mar 1852 - although unable to exercise full control.

Gen **TRINIDAD CABAÑAS Mar 1852-Oct 1855.**
FRANCISCO AGUILAR Oct 1855-Feb 1856.
Gen **SANTOS GUARDIOLA Feb 1856-Jan 1862**
when he was assassinated.
VITTORIANO CASTELLANOS Jan-Oct 1862; d
in office.
JOSÉ FRANCISCO MONTES acting President
Oct 1862-Jun 1863.
Gen **JOSÉ MARIA MEDINA Jun 1863-Jul 1872.**
CELIO ARIAS Aug 1872-Feb 1874.
PARIANO LEIVA Feb 1874-Aug 1876.
MARCO AURELIO SOTO Aug 1876-Nov 1883, b
1846; d 1908.
Gen **LUIS BOGRAN Nov 1883-Nov 1891.**
PARIANO LEIVA Nov 1891-Apr 1893.
DOMINGO VÁSQUEZ Apr 1893-Feb 1894.
POLICARPO BONILLA Feb 1894-Feb 1899, b
1859; d 1926.
TERENCIO SIERRA Feb 1899-Feb 1903; d 1907.
MANUEL BONILLA Feb 1903-Aug 1907.
MIGUEL DAVILA Aug 1907-Mar 1911; d 1927.
FRANCISCO BERTRAND acting President **Mar
1911-Feb 1912;** d 1927.
MANUEL BONILLA Feb 1912-21 Mar 1913, b
1849; d in office.
FRANCISCO BERTRAND Mar 1913-Nov 1919.
**RAFAEL LÓPEZ GUTIÉRREZ Nov 1919-10 Mar
1924;** d in office.
FAUSTO DAVILA acting President **27-31 Mar
1924.**
VICENTE TOSTA 1 Apr 1924-Feb 1925; d 1928.
His dictatorship ended the short civil war
following the revolution which overthrew López
Gutiérrez.
MIGUEL PAZ BARAONA Feb 1925-Feb 1929.
**VICENTE MEJÍA COLINDRES Feb 1929-Feb
1933.**
Gen **TIBURCIO CARÍAS ANDINO 1 Feb 1933-Oct
1948,** b 15 Mar 1876; d 24 Aug 1969. His stern
dictatorship brought an end to a long period of
anarchy and much material progress was made.
Dr **JUAN MANUEL GÁLVEZ 1 Oct 1948-Oct
1954,** b 1887.
Dr **JULIO LOZANO DÍAZ** acting President
Oct-Dec 1954; President **Dec 1954-21 Oct 1956**
deposed in coup, b 1895; d 20 Aug 1957.
Col **HECTOR CARACCIOLI** and **ROQUE ROD-
RIGUEZ** Heads of military junta **21 Oct
1956-Dec 1957.**
**JOSÉ RAMÓN VILLEDA MORALES 21 Dec
1957-3 Oct 1963** deposed in coup, b 1908; d 8 Oct
1971.
Col **OSWALDO LOPEZ ARELLANO 4 Oct
1963-Jun 1971.**
**RAMÓN ERNESTO CRUZ UCLÉS Jun 1971-4
Dec 1972** deposed in coup, b 4 Jan 1903.
Col **OSWALDO LOPEZ ARELLANO 4 Dec
1972-22 Apr 1975** deposed in coup, b 30 Jun 1921.
Col **JUAN ALBERTO MELGAR CASTRO 22 Apr
1975-7 Aug 1978** deposed in coup, b 1931.
Since **7 Aug 1978** Military junta consisting of Gen
POLICARPO PAZ GARCIA, Gen **DOMINGO
ALVAREZ CRUZ** and Lieut-Gen **AMILCAR
CELAYA.**

Hungary

The Magyars entered the Pannonian Basin from
the Ukraine c 896 and by the end of the 10th
century were organised in a state which became
the Kingdom of Hungary in 1000. With a few brief
intervals the Kingdom lasted, not always as an
independent state, until 1 Feb 1946. The
constitution of the Communist People's Republic
dates from 1949.

† Princes of the Magyars

GÉZA c972-997.
ISTVÁN 997-Dec 1000 when he became King.

THE KINGDOM OF HUNGARY

† Kings of Hungary

HOUSE OF ÁRPÁD
ISTVÁN I (St Stephen) **25 Dec 1000-15 Aug 1038,**
son of Géza, b 977. St Stephen, patron of
Hungary, converted the Magyars to Christianity,
founded bishoprics and monasteries, established
an administration and gained a kingly crown from
the Pope.

HOUSE OF ORSEOLO
PETER Aug 1038-1041 deposed, nephew of István
I, b c 1012.

HOUSE OF ABA
SAMUEL 1041-1044 executed, brother-in-law of
István I.

HOUSE OF ORSEOLO
PETER 1044-1046 assassinated.
1046-1047 Interregnum.

HOUSE OF ÁRPÁD
ANDRÁS I 1047-1060 murdered, grandson of
Prince Géza's brother, b c 1014.
BÉLA I 1060-1063, brother of András I.
SALAMON 1063-1074 deposed, son of András I,
b 1052; d 1087.
GÉZA I 1074-1077, eldest son of Béla I.
LÁSZLÓ I 1077-29 Jun 1095, son of Béla I, b 27
Jun 1040. St László reunited Hungary after the
anarchic reigns of Salamon and Géza I and
enlarged the state gaining Croatia
KÁLMÁN Jun 1095-3 Feb 1116, son of Géza I, b
c 1070.
ISTVÁN II Feb 1116-1131, son of Kálmán, b 1101.
BÉLA II (the Blind) **1131-1141,** nephew of Kálmán,
b c 1108.
GÉZA II 1141-1161, son of Béla II, b 1131.
ISTVÁN III 1161-1162 deposed, son of Géza II, b
1148. Twice deposed by uncles.
LÁSZLÓ II 1162-1163, uncle of Istvan III.

István I (St Stephen). His crown, which came to symbolise Hungary's sovereignty, was returned to Budapest in 1978 by America (Radio Times Hulton Picture Library)

Deposed his nephew with the aid of the Byzantine Emperor.

ISTVÁN III 1163 deposed.

ISTVÁN IV 1163-1165, uncle of István III. Deposed his nephew with the aid of the Byzantine Emperor.

ISTVÁN III 1165-1173.

BÉLA III 1173-1196, son of Géza II, b 1150. Greatly extended Hungary to become the most powerful King in Europe.

IMRE 1196-1204, son of Béla III, b 1174.

LÁSZLÓ III 1204-1205 probably murdered, son of Imre, b 1199.

ANDRÁS II 1205-1235, brother of Imre, b 1175. Gained the throne by removing his nephew. András ruined the Treasury by weak and extravagant government and was eventually forced by the nobility to sign the Golden Bull - a document, presented to all succeeding Magyar Kings, giving the lords the right to reject by force any royal act

BÉLA IV sole ruler **1235-1254**; co-ruler **1254-3 May 1270,** son of András II, b 1206. Expelled by the Mongols' invasion (1241) when half the population of Hungary was killed, Béla returned to rebuild the country.

ISTVÁN V co-ruler **1254-May 1270**; sole ruler **1270-1272,** son of Béla IV, b 1239.

LÁSZLÓ IV 1272-10 Jul 1290 assassinated, son of István V, b 1262.

ANDRÁS III Jul 1290-1301, grandson of András II, b 1264. When he died the Arpád dynasty died with him.

House of Premysl
LÁSZLÓ 1301-1305; was also Vacláv II, King of Bohemia. Not considered to have reigned.

House of Wittelsbach
OTTO 1305-1307 or 1308. Not considered to have reigned.

House of Anjou
KAROLY I 1308-16 Jul 1342, great-grandson of István V, b 1288. Karoly I (Charles Robert of Naples) was elected King as a child. He became devoted to Hungary, restoring order and the economy.

LAJOS I Jul 1342-10 Sep 1382, son of Karoly I, b 5 Mar 1326. Called 'the Great', Lajos (Louis) made Hungary a major power surrounding her with puppet states and gaining the Polish throne for himself.

MARIA (Queen) **Sep 1382-1385** deposed, elder daughter of Lajos I, b 1370.

KAROLY II 1385-17 Feb 1386 assassinated, descendant of István V, b 1345; was also Carlo III of Naples.

MARIA (Queen) sole ruler **Feb 1386-1387**; co ruler **Feb 1386-1395.**

House of Luxembourg
SIGISMUND co-ruler **1387-1395**; sole ruler **1395-1437,** husband of Maria, b 1368. Although he sponsored the arts and the merchant classes Sigismund was unpopular as an extravagant absentee despot.

House of Habsburg
ALBRECHT 1 Jan 1438-27 Oct 1439; was also Albrecht, Duke V of Austria.

House of Jagiellion
ULÁSZLÓ I Oct 1439-10 Nov 1444; was also Wladyslaw III, King of Poland.

House of Habsburg
LÁSZLÓ V 15 May 1444-23 Nov 1457, son of Albrecht, b 22 Feb 1440. The reign of Albrecht's posthumous son, László was dominated by the patriot János Hunyadi who fought to keep the Turks at bay despite the interference of jealous nobles, the Czechs and the Emperor.

House of Hunyadi
MÁTYÁS I Corvinus **24 Jan 1458-9 May 1490,** son of the patriot János Hunyadi, b 24 Feb 1443. Mátyás, who in many ways was responsible for

the introduction of the ideas of the Renaissance to central Europe, was an enormously gifted administrator, an able general, a talented linguist and a cultured and learned collector and patron of the arts. His justice, his talents and victories are remembered though the despotism and crippling taxes of this national hero are usually forgotten.

House of Jagiellon
ULÁSZLÓ II sole ruler **1490-4 Jun 1508**; co-ruler **4 Jun 1508-13 Mar 1516,** son of Kazimierz IV of Poland, b 1456. Called 'Dobre' (meaning 'I agree') Ulászló was elected by the self-interested nobles because of his weakness.

LAJOS II co-ruler **4 Jun 1508-Mar 1516**; sole ruler **Mar 1516-29 Aug 1526** drowned fleeing from the Battle of Mohács at which Turkey crushed the Magyars; son of Ulászló II, b 1 Jul 1506.

House of Zápolya
JÁNOS 1526-1540, b 1487. Installed as a puppet by the Turks who annexed most of the country on his death.

House of Habsburg
FERDINAND I   1526-25 Jul 1564; was also Ferdinand I of Austria.

MAXIMILIAN Jul 1564-12 Oct 1576; was also Maximilian II of Austria.

RUDOLPH Oct 1576-1608; was also Rudolph II of Austria.

MÁTYÁS II   1608-1618; was also Matthias of Austria.

FERDINAND II   1618-15 Feb 1637; was also Ferdinand II of Austria.

FERDINAND III sole ruler **Feb 1637-1647**; co-ruler **1647-2 Apr 1657**; was also Ferdinand III of Austria.

FERDINAND IV co-ruler **1647-1654,** son of Ferdinand III, b 1633.

LEOPOLD I   Apr 1657-5 May 1705; was also Leopold I of Austria.

JÓSZEF I May 1705-17 Apr 1711; was also Joseph I of Austria.

KAROLY III Apr 1711-20 Oct 1740; was also Karl of Austria.

MARIA THERESIA (Queen) **Oct 1740-29 Nov 1780**; was also Maria Theresia of Austria.

JÓSZEF II Nov 1780-20 Feb 1790; was also Joseph II of Austria.

LEOPOLD II Feb 1790-1 Mar 1792; was also Leopold II of Austria.

FERENC I Mar 1792-2 Mar 1835; was also Franz I of Austria.

FERDINAND V 2 Mar 1835-2 Dec 1848; was also Emperor Ferdinand I of Austria.

THE REPUBLIC OF HUNGARY

Governors

In the revolutionary disturbances of 1848-9 the Magyars revolted in an attempt to recover their independence and to obtain various democratic freedoms. The Habsburgs were deposed on 14 Apr 1849 but the Republic can said to have ceased to exist by mid-Aug in the same year.

LAJOS KOSSUTH 14 Apr-12 Aug 1849, b 1802; d 20 Mar 1894. Kossuth, a noted journalist, led the fight in the Diet for democratic freedoms and the abolition of serfdom. His inflammatory speeches contributed to the 1848 revolt and when Austria abolished Hungary's constitution he persuaded the Diet to depose the Habsburgs. As Governor he could not resist the armies of Russia and Austria and fled when the revolution was crushed. Lionised by European liberals, he worked in exile for Hungarian liberty and refused to recognise the Dual Monarchy which restored his country's independence in 1867.

ARTÚR GÖRGEY 12-13 Aug 1849, b 1818; d 1916. The military leader of the Hungarian revolution, his jealousy of Kossuth aided his country's enemies.

THE KINGDOM OF HUNGARY

† Kings

House of Habsburg
FERENC JÓSZEF I Dec 1848-21 Nov 1916; deposed Apr-Aug 1849. Obliged to concede the re-establishment of Hungary as an independent state in the Dual Monarchy 29 May 1867; was also Franz Joseph of Austria.

KAROLY IV Nov 1916-13 Nov 1918 when he temporarily gave up his position in Hungary; officially deposed in Hungary 5 Nov 1921; was also Karl I of Austria.

PROVISIONAL GOVERNMENT
(originally termed the National Council)

Prime Minister

Count **MIHÁLY KAROLYI 25 Oct-16 Nov 1918.**

THE REPUBLIC OF HUNGARY

President

Count **MIHÁLY KAROLYI 13 Jan-21 Mar 1919** deposed, b 4 Mar 1875; d 20 Mar 1955 in exile.

Prime Ministers

Count **MIHÁLY KAROLYI 16 Nov 1918-Jan 1919.**

KAROLY HUSZAR Jan-Mar 1919 deposed.

THE HUNGARIAN SOVIET REPUBLIC

Head of Government

BÉLA KUN 21 Mar-1 Aug 1919 deposed, b 20 Feb 1886; d in Stalin's purges probably in 1939. A naive man, totally unsuited to rule, his regime collapsed amid chronic food shortages and a Roumanian invasion.
Aug-Nov 1919 Hungary under Roumanian rule.

PROVISIONAL GOVERNMENT

Head

Admiral MIKLÓS HORTHY de NAGYBÁNYA 15 Nov 1919-28 Feb 1920.

THE KINGDOM OF HUNGARY

Regents

Admiral MIKLÓS HORTHY de NAGYBÁNYA 1 Mar 1920-Oct 1944 when arrested by the Germans, b 18 Jun 1868; d in exile 9 Feb 1957. Leader of the White Hungarians against Béla Kun, Regent Horthy was obliged to prevent the return of ex-King Karoly IV (Habsburg rule being forbidden by the peace treaty). Circumstances obliged him to ally Hungary with the Axis bloc but when he tried to extricate his country from the War the Germans engineered a Fascist coup.
16 Oct 1944-Apr 1945 Regency Council consisting of Col-Gen KAROLY BEREGFAY, Dr FERENC RAJNISS and Dr SANDOR CSIA.

Prime Ministers

Count PÁL TELEKI 1 Mar 1920-Apr 1921.
Count ISTVÁN BETHLEN Apr 1921-Aug 1931, b 8 Oct 1874; d (in Communist hands) probably in 1947. A dictatorial ruler he tried to undo the Treaty of the Trianon which had dismembered Hungary after World War I.
Count MIHÁLY KAROLYI 22 Aug 1931-Oct 1932.
Gen GYULA von GÖMBÖS 4 Oct 1932-6 Oct 1936, b 26 Dec 1886; d in office.
Dr KÁLMÁN von DARANYI 12 Oct 1936-May 1938, b 22 Mar 1886; d 1 Nov 1939.
Dr BÉLA IMRÉDY 13 May 1938-Feb 1939, b 29 Dec 1891; d 28 Feb 1946 executed as a war criminal.
Count PÁL TELEKI 16 Feb 1939-3 Apr 1941, b 1 Nov 1879; d in office - committed suicide rather than ally Hungary to Germany.
LASZLO BARDOSSY 3 Apr 1941-Mar 1942, b 1890; d 10 Jan 1946 executed as a war criminal.

MIKLÓS de KALLAY 9 Mar 1942-21 Mar 1944 deposed, b 23 Jan 1887; d 14 Jan 1967 in exile. When he tried to withdraw Hungary from the Axis pact he was deposed in a Fascist coup.
Maj-Gen DOEME SZTOJAY 23 Mar-31 Aug 1944; d in office.
Col-Gen K. LAKATOS Aug-Oct 1944.
Maj FERENC SZALASI 16 Oct 1944-4 Apr 1945 fled, b 6 Jan 1897; d 12 Mar 1946 executed as a war criminal.

PROVISIONAL GOVERNMENT

Prime Minister

Col-Gen BÉLA MIKLÓS 24 Dec 1944-Nov 1945, b 1890; d 1948.

THE KINGDOM OF HUNGARY

Acting Regent

Prof BÉLA ZSEDENYI Nov 1945-Feb 1946.

Prime Minister

ZOLTAN TILDY 15 Nov 1945-Feb 1946.

THE REPUBLIC OF HUNGARY

Presidents

ZOLTAN TILDY 1 Feb 1946-Jul 1948, b 18 Nov 1889; d 3 Aug 1961. A former cleric he was forced out of office by Communist pressure.
ARPAD SZAKASITS 3 Aug 1948-18 Aug 1949, b 8 Dec 1888; d 3 May 1965.

Prime Ministers

ZOLTAN TILDY 1-4 Feb 1946.
FERENC NAGY 4 Feb 1946-30 May 1947, b 8 Oct 1903.
LAJOS DINNYÉS 31 May 1947-Dec 1948, b 16 Apr 1901; d 4 May 1961.
ISTVAN DOBI 10 Dec 1948-18 Aug 1949 when he became PM of the Hungarian People's Republic.

THE PEOPLE'S REPUBLIC OF HUNGARY

Presidents
(styled Chairman of the Presidium of the National Assembly)

ARPAD SZAKASITS 18 Aug 1949-Apr 1950.
SÁNDOR RÓNAI 26 Apr 1950-Aug 1952, b 6 Oct 1892; d 28 Sep 1965.
ISTVAN DOBI 14 Aug 1952-Apr 1967, b 31 Dec 1898; d 24 Nov 1968.

PÁL LOSONCZI since 14 Apr 1967, b 18 Sep 1919.

Prime Ministers

ISTVAN DOBI 18 Aug 1949-Aug 1952.
MÁTYÁS RÁKOSI 14 Aug 1952-Jul 1953, b 14 Mar 1892; d 31 Aug 1963.
IMRE NAGY 4 Jul 1953-Apr 1955.
ANDRAS HEGEDUS 18 Apr 1955-24 Oct 1956, b 1922.
IMRE NAGY 24 Oct-4 Nov 1956 deposed by Soviet invasion, b 7 Jun 1896; d 16 Jun 1958 executed. Nagy formed a coalition Government and asked the Soviet forces to leave, but a further Soviet invasion crushed the attempted revolution and he was kidnapped and taken to Romania. His efforts to regain national independence for Hungary cost Nagy his life.
JANOS KADAR 4 Nov 1956-Jan 1958, b 22 May 1912.
Dr FERENC MÜNNICH 27 Jan 1958-Sep 1961, b 1886; d 29 Nov 1967.
JANOS KADAR 13 Sep 1961-Jun 1965.
GYULA KALLAI 28 Jun 1965-Apr 1967, b 1 Jun 1910.
JENÖ FOCK 14 Apr 1967-May 1975, b 17 May 1916.
GYÖRGY LÁZÁR since 15 May 1975, b 15 Sep 1924.

First Secretary (previously Secretary General) of the United Workers' (Communist) Party of Hungary

MÁTYÁS RÁKOSI 18 Aug 1949-Jun 1953.
Gen MIHALY FARKAS Jun-Aug 1953.
MÁTYÁS RÁKOSI Aug 1953-Jul 1956.
ERNÖ GERÖ 18 Jul-25 Oct 1956, b (Ernö Singer) 8 Jul 1898.
JANOS KADAR since 25 Oct 1956.

Iceland

Scandinavians first settled in Iceland in 874 and from 930 to 1264 the island was an independent Republic. Norwegian from 1264, Iceland passed with Norway to the Danish crown in 1381. The country achieved independence on 1 Dec 1918 as a Kingdom under the Danish sovereign. A Republic was declared on 17 Jun 1944.

THE KINGDOM OF ICELAND

Prime Ministers

JON MAGNUSSON Dec 1918-Mar 1922.
SIGURDUR EGGERZ Mar 1922-Mar 1924, b 1875; d 1945.

JON MAGNUSSON Mar 1924-23 Jun 1926, b 1859; d in office.
JON THORLAKSSON Jun 1926-Aug 1927, b 1877; d 1935.
VIGFUS THORHALLSSON Aug 1927-Jun 1932, b 1889; d 1935.
ASGEIR ASGEIRSSON Jun 1932-1934.
HERMANN JONASSON 1934-May 1942, b 1896.
OLAFUR THORS 16 May-Dec 1942.
BJORN THORDARSON Dec 1942-17 Jul 1944 when he became PM of the Republic.

THE REPUBLIC OF ICELAND

Presidents

SVEINN BJÖRNSSON 17 Jun 1944-24 Jan 1952, b 27 Feb 1881; d in office.
ASGEIR ASGEIRSSON Jul 1952-Aug 1968, b 13 May 1894; d 15 Sep 1972.
Dr KRISTJAN ELDJARN since 1 Aug 1968, b 6 Dec 1916.

Prime Ministers

BJÖRN THORDARSON 17 Jul-Sep 1944; acting PM 16 Sep-21 Oct 1944, b 1879; d 1963.
OLAFUR THORS 21 Oct 1944-Oct 1946; acting PM 10 Oct 1946-Feb 1947, b 19 Jan 1892; d 31 Dec 1964. A former trawlerman, Thors became the leading statesman of modern Iceland and was largely responsible for the state's independent post-war foreign policy.
STEFAN JOHANN STEFANSSON 4 Feb 1947-Dec 1949, b 20 Jul 1894.
OLAFUR THORS 7 Dec 1949-Mar 1950.
STEINGRIMUR STEINTHORSSON 13 Mar 1950-Sep 1953, b 12 Feb 1893; d 14 Nov 1966.
OLAFUR THORS 13 Sep 1953-Jul 1956.
HERMANN JONASSON 24 Jul 1956-Dec 1958.
EMIL JÓNSSON 20 Dec 1958-Nov 1959, b 27 Oct 1902.
OLAFUR THORS 19 Nov 1959-Nov 1963.
Dr BJARNI BENEDIKTSSON 14 Nov 1963-10 Jul 1970, b 30 Apr 1909; d in office in a fire at the Premier's official country residence.
JOHANN HAFSTEIN acting PM 11 Jul-Oct 1970; PM 10 Oct 1970-Jul 1971, b 19 Sep 1915.
OLAFUR JOHANNESSON 14 Jul 1971-Jul 1974; acting PM 2 Jul-29 Aug 1974, b 1 Mar 1913.
GEIR HALLGRÍMSSON 29 Aug 1974-Jul 1978 ; Acting PM since Jul 1978, b 16 Dec 1925.

Il-Khan Empire see Iran

Ataw Wallpa 'Inka (Atahuallpa) - the Emperor who was held to ransom by Pizarro for a room filled with gold (Radio Times Hulton Picture Library)

Illyria

Illyria, the modern Yugoslavian coast, was united *c* 250 BC. Briefly a great power, the Kingdom fell to Rome in 219 BC, although it was not formally included in the empire until 35 BC.

† Kings

AGRON before 245-winter 231 BC. He made the united Illyrians feared as pirates throughout Greece.

PINNES winter 231-219 BC when the first Romano-Illyrian war ended, son of Agron; date of death uncertain.

The Inca Empire or Tahuantinsuyu

Tahuantinsuyu ('The Kingdom of the Four Quarters') originated in the Cuzco Valley and spread until the Inca state - an extraordinarily rigid communistic society with no concept of personal freedom and little intellectual development - covered Peru, Ecuador, Bolivia and neighbouring areas. The Spanish invasion of the 1530s did not kill the Inca Empire immediately - it lasted in eastern Peru until 1572. In the list below the accepted phonetic version of the Quechua language Inca name is given first; the more common Spanish version follows.

† Sapa Incas
(Inca Emperors)

MANQO QHAPAQ (Manco Capac) *fl.* **12th century.** The founder of the Inca state.

ZINCHI ROQ'A (Sinchi Roca) *fl.* **12th/13th century,** son of Manqo Qhapaq.

LLOQ'E YUPANKI (Lloque Yupanqui) *fl.* **13th century,** son of Zinchi Roq'a.

MAYTA QHAPAQ (Mayta Capac) *fl.* **13th century,** son of Lloq'e Yupanki.

QHAPAQ YUPANKI (Capac Yupanqui) *fl.* **13th/14 th century,** son of Mayta Qhapaq.

'INKA ROQ'A 'INKA (Inche Roca) *fl.* **14th century,** son of Qhapaq Yupanqui.

YAWAR WAQAQ (Yahuar Huacac; original name Cusi Huallpa) *fl.* **14th century,** son of 'Inka Roq'a 'Inka; probably assassinated by one of his wives.

WIRAQOCHA 'INKA (Viracocha; original name Hatun Tupac) **?-1438** in Cuzco; **1438-*c* 1440** in Calca, son of Yawar Waqaq. Deposed in the capital Cuzco, he fought a civil war against his son Pachakuti.

'INKA 'URQON (Urco) ***c* 1440-*c* 1441** rival Emperor in Calca, son of Wiraqocha 'Inka; d in battle in the civil war against his brother.

PACHAKUTI 'INKA YUPANKI (Pachacuti Inca Yupanqui; original name Cusi Yupanqui,) **1438-1441?** disputed Emperor; sole ruler ***c* 1441-1471** abdicated, son of Wiraqocha 'Inka; d *c* 1475. The real creator of the Inca Empire he greatly extended the boundaries of his realm, rebuilt Cuzco, put down revolts, ruled wisely if harshly (even executing his brother for exceeding orders) and initiated important agricultural works and reforms.

THUPA 'INKA YUPANKI (Topa Inca Yupanqui) **1471-1493,** son of Pachakuti 'Inka Yupanki, b *c* 1408. He seized modern Ecuador and conquered the major state of Chimu (the 'Athens' to Cuzco's 'Rome').

WAYNA QHAPAQ (Huayna Capac; original name Tito Cusi Hualpa) **1493-1525** died in smallpox epidemic, son of Thupa 'Inka Yupanki, b *c* 1480-1485.

NINAN CUYUCHI 1525 - for a very brief period; died in the same smallpox epidemic as his father; son of Wayna Qhapaq.

WASHKAR 'INKA (Huascar; original name Tupac Cusi Huallpa) **1525-Apr 1532** when he was captured during the civil war against his brother; son of Wayna Qhapaq, b after 1500; murdered (poisoned) by order of Ataw Wallpa late 1532.

ATAW WALLPA 'INKA (Atahuallpa) **Apr-16 Nov 1532** when kidnapped by Pizarro or 29 Aug 1533 when he died, b c 1500; garrotted by the Spanish. The haughty illegitimate son of Wayna Qhapaq, Ataw Wallpa fought his half-brother for the throne, winning through the efforts of an able general Quizquiz who savagely removed rivals and opposition. The victorious Ataw Wallpa was immediately threatened by the Spaniards under Pizarro who kidnapped, held to ransom and finally 'legally' murdered him on trumped up charges of treason (ie trying to defend himself).

THUPA WALLPA (Topa Huallpa) **Sep-?Dec 1533** murdered by poison, son of Wayna Qhapaq.

PAWLLU THUPA 'INKA (Paullu Topa Inca) **c 1535?**, son of Wayna Qhapaq.

MANQO 'INKA YUPANKI (Manco Inca Yupanqui) **1533-1535** puppet Emperor under Spanish rule; **1535-1545** independent ruler in eastern Peru, assassinated; son of Wayna Qhapaq. After trying to regain independence he retreated to the east where he ruled a greatly reduced but sovereign Kingdom.

THUPA 'AMARU (Topa Amaru) **1545-1572**, son of Manqo 'Inka Yupanki. Upon his death the small remnant Inca state in the east ceased to exist.

(It is often stated that there are no descendants of the Sapa Incas: in fact the Spanish Marquesses de la Conquista and their family are traced to the union of Pizarro and Ataw Wallpa's sister.)

India

Although the Mughal Empire at its height united most of present day India, an Indian nation cannot be said to have existed until the sub-continent was united under British rule - much of India was British by 1805; all was British by 1858. India became independent in Aug 1947 and a Republic on 26 Jan 1950.

THE MAGADHAN KINGDOM

This was an important state in the Ganges Valley.

† Kings

BIMBISARA c 543-c 491 BC.

AJATASATRU c 491-c 459 BC, son of Bimbisara. Upon his death the Kingdom fell to pieces.

THE MAURYAN EMPIRE OR ASOKA EMPIRE

† Kings

CANDRAGUPTA MAURYA c 325 or c 320-c 297 BC abdicated; d 397 BC of self-imposed starvation as a Jain. He conquered most of north India.

BINDUSARA (known by the Greeks as AMITROCHATES) c 297-c 272 or c 268 BC, son of Candragupta Maurya.

ASOKA c 272 or c 268-c 235 or c 231 BC, son of Bindusara. The famous edicts of this Buddhist King and the many records of his reign have assured the memory of a not very successful monarch.

KUNALA after c 231 BC, son of Asoka. Ruled in the Punjab.

DASARATHA after c 231 BC, grandson of Asoka. Ruled in Orissa.

(The Empire collapsed in the reigns of Kunala and Dasaratha who may have partitioned the realm between them.)

THE GUPTA EMPIRE

† Kings of Kings (Maharajadhiraja) of the Gupta State

CANDRA GUPTA I Ruler before c AD 320: independent c AD 320-c 330. He created an independent state occupying most of the Ganges Valley.

SAMUDRA GUPTA c 330-c 380, son of Candra Gupta I. A savage warrior who won most of northern India; he was also a poet and musician.

CANDRA GUPTA II c 380-c 415, son of Samudra Gupta.

KUMARA GUPTA c 415-c 455, son of Candra Gupta II.

SKANDA GUPTA c 455-c 467, son? of Kumara Gupta. After his death the succession disputes destroyed the unity of an empire weakened by a Hun invasion.

THE RASTRAKUTA KINGDOM

A major state in the west and central Deccan.

† Kings
(at the Kingdom's zenith)

DHRUVA c 780-c 793.

GOVINDA III c 793-c 814.

AMOGHAVARSA c 814-c 878.

KRSNA II c 878-c 914.

INDRA III c 914-c 927. After his death the Rastrakuta state was greatly weakened by struggles against the Pala and Pratihara Kingdoms.

THE COLA KINGDOM

The main state in southern India for a period of 200 years.

† Kings

PARANTAKA I 907-953.
953-985 A confused period of co-rulers and rival
Kings when the Cola Kingdom was, in practice,
subdivided.
RAJARAJA sole ruler **985-1012;** co-ruler
1012-1014. The King who reunited the state and
established an empire stretching from Ceylon and
the Maldives to the Krishna River.
RAJENDRA co-ruler **1012-1014;** sole ruler
1014-1044, son of Rajaraja. The Cola Empire
dissolved in the succession disputes after the
death of Rajendra.

THE SULTANATE OF DELHI

The principal Islamic state of India following the
Muslim conquest of the northern part of the
sub-continent.

† Sultans of the Mu'izzi Dynasty

QUTB-ud-DIN AYBAK *c*1208-1210 died in a polo
accident. A former slave, he conquered the
Upper Ganges Valley and the Punjab.
ILTUTMISH *c*1211-1236, son-in-law of Qutb-ud-
Din. He moved the seat of the Sultanate from
Lahore to Delhi.
1236-1246 Sultanate divided.
NASIR-ud-DIN MAHMUD 1246-1266.
GHIYAS-ud-DIN BALBAN 1266-1287.
1287-1290 Interregnum and civil war.

† Sultans of the Khaljis Dynasty

JALAL-ud-DIN FIRUZ KHALJI 1290-1296 assassinated by his successor.
'ALA-ud-DIN KHALJI 1296-1316, nephew of
Jalal-ud-Din whom he murdered. A very able
reformer who used gold taken from the south and
his own military prowess to make the Sultanate
the leading state in India.
QUTB-ud-DIN MUBARAK SHAH 1316-1320
assassinated, son of 'Ala-ud-Din.

† Sultans of the Tughluq Dynasty

GHIYAS-ud-DIN TUGHLUQ 1320-1325 died
when a roof collapsed on him.
MUHAMMAD ibn TUGHLUQ 1325-1351, son of
Ghiyas-ud-Din. A well-meaning but not very able
ruler who inherited most of the sub-continent but
lost the south by 1350 and died in the midst of
rebellions in the north.
FIRUZ SHAH ibn RAJAH 1351-1388, cousin of
Muhammad ibn Tughluq. A saintly ruler whose
realm was diminished by revolts.
1388 A disputed succession and further revolts
destroyed the Sultanate as a power.

THE LODI KINGDOM IN THE PUNJAB

The leading state of north India in the 15th century.

† Sultans

BAHLUL LODI 1451-1489. He conquered much
of the former Delhi Sultanate.
SIKANDER 1489-1517.
IBRAHIM 1517-1526 died in battle. Ibrahim's
uncle called in the Mughals from Kabul to depose
him - having done so they stayed to found an
empire.

THE BAHMANI SULTANATE OF THE DECCAN

An Islamic state in the Deccan, the Bahmani
Kingdom dominated central India from the mid
14th century until the 16th century.

† Sultans of the Bahmani Dynasty

**'ALA-ud-DIN HASAN BAHMANI SHAH
1347-1358.** Also called Zafar Khan and Hasan
Gangu. He was a local governor who revolted
against the Delhi Sultan and founded his own
Kingdom.
MUHAMMAD I (or MUHAMMAD SHAH I)
1358-1373, son of 'Ala-ud-Din.
'ALA-ud-DIN MUJAHID 1373-1378 murdered by
Da'ud; son of Muhammad I.
DA'UD 1378 murdered, cousin of 'Ala-ud-Din
Mujahid, whom he murdered.
MUHAMMAD II 1378-1397, brother of Da'ud. He
lost much land in the west to Vijayanagar.
GHIYAS-ud-DIN 1397 - reigned for two months
until he was assassinated, son of Muhammad II.
SHAMS-ud-DIN 1397 deposed, brother of Ghiya-
s-ud-Din; date of death unknown.
TAJ-ud-DIN FIRUZ 1397-1422 abdicated, brother
of Shams-ud-Din; d in same year as abdication?
He made Bahmani Deccan the strongest state in
India but lost his third war against Vijayanagar.
SHIBAB-ud-DIN AHMAD I 1422-1435, brother of
Taj-ud-Din Firuz.
'ALA-ud-DIN AHMAD II (or 'ALA-ud-DIN II or
AHMAD II) **1435-1457,** son of Shibab-ud-Din
Ahmad I.
HUMAYUN 1457-1461 assassinated?, son of
'Ala-ud-Din Ahmad II.
NIZAM-ud-DIN AHMAD III (or NIZAM)
1461-1463, son of Humayun.
MUHAMMAD III 1463-1482 died of drink, brother
of Nizam.
SHIHAB-ud-DIN MAHMUD (or MAHMUD)
1482-1518, son of Muhammad III. The last of the
Dynasty - the extensive Kingdom was subdivided
by provincial governors upon his death.

THE KINGDOM OF VIJAYANAGAR

The main Hindu state of India during the Middle Ages, Vijayanagar occupied most of southern India.

† Kings (Rajas) of Vijayanagar

FIRST DYNASTY OR HOUSE OF SANGAMA

HARIHARA I sole ruler **1336-1346**; co-ruler **1346-1354**. A governor who revolted against Delhi and established his independence.

BUKKA I co ruler **1346-1354**; sole ruler **1354-1377**, brother of Harihara I.

(Three other brothers disputed the throne but they cannot be said to have reigned.)

HARIHARA II 1377-c1404, son of Bukka I.

BUKKA II c**1404-1406**, son of Harihara II. He fought Virupaksa for the throne.

VIRUPAKSA 1404-1406 deposed, brother of Bukka II, whom he fought for the throne; date of death uncertain.

DEVARAYA I 1406-1422, brother of Bukka II.

RAMCHANDRA 1422?, son of Devaraya I. He fought his brother Vira Vijaya for the crown.

VIRA VIJAYA 1422-1425, son of Devaraya I. He beat Ramchandra in the struggle for power.

DEVARAYA II (or **IMMADI**) co-ruler before 1425; sole ruler **1425-1447**, son of Vira Vijaya. He extended the realm to include all south India and Ceylon.

MALLIKARJUNA 1447-1465, son of Devaraya II.

VIRUPAKSHA 1465-1485 assassinated by his son Praudhadevaraya; cousin of Mallikarjuna.

PRAUDHADEVARAYA 1485-1486 murdered?, son of Virupaksha.

SECOND DYNASTY OR HOUSE OF SALUVA

SALUVA NARASIMHA 1486-c1491. An able military leader who seized power.

IMMADI NARASIMHA c**1491-1505** assassinated, son of Saluva. He was but a puppet for the Regent Narasa Nayaka (1491-1503) and his son Vira Narasimha (1503-1505).

THIRD DYNASTY OR HOUSE OF TULUVA

VIRA NARASIMHA 1505-1509, the former Regent.

KRSNADEVARAYA 1509-1529, brother of Vira Narasimha. Under him Vijayanagar reached its zenith but his manner alienated his neighbours who united to oppose him. He established good relations with the Portuguese who opened trading posts.

ACHYUTA (DEVA RAYA) **1529-1542**, son of Vira Narasimha.

VENKATA I 1542 murdered, son of Vira Narasimha.

SADASIVA sole ruler **1542-c1550**; co-ruler c**1550-1576**, nephew of Venkata I. A puppet of Rama Raya who made himself co-ruler c1550.

FOURTH DYNASTY OR HOUSE OF KARNATA

RAMA RAYA co-ruler c**1550-1565** died in battle. This powerful Minister made himself sovereign.

TIRUMALA c**1570-1572** abdicated, brother of Rama Raya. He made himself sovereign as his brother had done.

SRIRANGA (or RANGA I) c**1572-1585**, son of Tirumala.

VENKATA II 1585-1614?, brother of Sriranga.

RANGA II 1614? - reigned for four months before he was assassinated, nephew of Venkata II.

1614-1618 Civil war.

RAMA DEVA RAYA 1618-1630?, kinsman of Venkata II. He ruled unchallenged for perhaps only the last year of his reign.

1630-c1642 Civil war during which time the Empire rapidly dissolved.

RANGA III c**1642-1645 or 1646** when he lost most of the Kingdom or after 1684 when he died, kinsman of Rama Deva Raya.

(The Kingdom and Dynasty both disappeared at the end of the 17th century.)

THE SULTANATE OF BIJAPUR

A Kingdom of the southern Deccan, Bijapur, though not large, was for a time one of the leading Indian states.

† Sultans of the Adil Shahi Dynasty of Bijapur

Sometimes referred to as Kings.

YUSUF ADIL SHAH (also called YUSUF ADIL KHAN) **1489-1510**. A slave at the Bahmani court who rose to be Governor of Bijapur, he claimed to be (and probably was) a son of Murad II of Turkey.

ISMAIL SHAH 1510-1534, son of Yusuf Adil Shah.

MALLU SHAH 1534-1535 deposed and blinded, son of Ismail Shah; date of death uncertain.

IBRAHIM ADIL SHAH I 1535-1557, brother of Mallu Shah.

ALI ADIL SHAH I 1557-1579 assassinated, son of Ibrahim Adil Shah I. In his reign Bijapur briefly became the leading power in south India upon the defeat of Vijayanagar in 1565.

1579-1580 Interregnum.

IBRAHIM ADIL SHAH II 1580-1626, nephew of Ali Adil Shah.

MUHAMMAD SHAH 1626-1656, son of Ibrahim Adil Shah II.

ALI II (or ALI ADIL SHAH II) **1656-1673**, son of Muhammad Shah.

SIKANDER SHAH 1673-1686 when taken captive by Aurangzeb and Bijapur's independence was ended; son of Ali II; date of death uncertain.

*Aurangzeb (meaning 'Ornament of the Throne')
murdered his way to the crown, then lived in fear of
similar treachery* (Radio Times Hulton Picture
Library)

THE SULTANATE OF GOLKONDA

A powerful state of the east and central Deccan.

† Sultans

QULI QUTB SHAH 1518-1543 assassinated by his
son Jamshid, b 1453. A former Turkish officer
and Bahmani official he declared himself
independent.
JAMSHID 1543-1550, son of Quli Qutb Shah
whom he murdered.
IBRAHIM 1550-1580, son of Quli Qutb Shah.
MUHAMMAD QULI 1580-1611, kinsman of
Ibrahim. After his death Golkonda ceased to be
a significant Kingdom - it was annexed by the
Mughals in 1687.

THE MUGHAL EMPIRE

The Mughal Empire at its height controlled most of
the sub-continent but was in a period of decline
when British involvement in north India became
pronounced in the 18th century.

† The Mughal Emperors

BABUR Apr 1526-1530, a descendant of Timur
and Genghis Khan, b 1483. Invited to India to
intervene in a Lodi dynastic dispute (see the Lodi
Kingdom), he founded an Empire based on
Delhi.
HUMAYAN 1530-1539 when he fled.

† Usurping Emperors

SHER SHAH 1539-22 May 1545. A noble who
seized the throne.
ISLAM SHAH May 1545-1553, son of Sher Shah.
FIRUZ 1553 murdered by Muhammad Adil Shah;
kinsman of Sher Shah, b 1541.
MUHAMMAD 'ADIL SHAH 1553-Jul 1555
deposed; d in battle 1557.

† Mughal Emperors

HUMAYAN Jul 1555-Jan 1556 died accidentally,
son of Babur.
AKBAR ('The Great') **Jan 1556-25 or 26 Oct 1605,**
son of Humayan, b 10 Apr 1542. After a difficult
succession Akbar greatly extended the Empire
taking Rajasthan, Bengal, Orissa, Sind, Bihar,
Baluchistah, Afghanistan, the Deccan, Kashmir
and Gujerat (the latter in an amazing campaign -
his army covering nearly 500 miles in 11 days).
JAHANGIR Oct 1605-7 Nov 1627, eldest son of
Akbar, b (Salim) 31 Aug 1569.
DAWAR BAKHSH Nov 1627-Feb 1628, grandson
of Jahangir; probably assassinated but may have
escaped to Iran.
SHAH JAHAN Feb 1628-31 Jul 1658 deposed,
third son of Jahangir, b 5 Jan 1592; d a captive 1
Feb 1666. This extravagant, pleasure-loving
Emperor, who built the magnificent Taj Mahal as
a mausoleum for his favourite wife, was deposed
when his sons' quarrel over the succession led to
civil war.
AURANZEB ALAMGIR I 31 Jul 1658-3 Mar 1707,
son of Shah Jahan, b (Muhi-ud-Din Muhammad)
24 Oct 1618. A cultured Prince, Aurangzeb was
a fanatical Muslim whose persecution of the
Hindus was in part responsible for the decline of
the Empire.
Mu'azzam **BAHADUR SHAH I** (or SHAH ALAM
I) **Mar 1707-27 Feb 1712,** second son of
Aurangzeb, b 14 Oct 1643.
JAHANDAR SHAH 1712-11 Feb 1713 assassinated
by the Sayyid brothers; eldest son of Bahadur
Shah I.
FARRUKHSIYAR Feb 1713-Feb 1719 assassinated
by the Sayyid brothers who had placed him on
the throne; nephew of Jahandar Shah.
RAFI-ud-DAULAT Feb-Jun 1719 deposed, neph-
ew of Jahandar Shah; probably assassinated after
deposition.

SHAHJAHAN II (or RAFI-ud-DARAJAT) Jun-Aug 1719 deposed, brother of Rafi-ud-Daulat; assassinated after deposition.

NIKUSIYAR Aug-Sep 1719 deposed, grandson of Aurangzeb; assassinated after deposition.

MUHAMMAD SHAH 28 Sep 1719-1 Oct 1720 deposed, nephew of Jahandar Shah. Puppet Emperor for the Sayyid brothers, under his weak rule the Mughal state entered its long decline.

MUHAMMAD IBRAHIM 1 Oct-8 Nov 1720, brother of Shahjahan II; a usurper who was probably assassinated.

MUHAMMAD SHAH 8 Nov 1720-Apr 1748.

AHMAD SHAH Apr 1748-2 Jun 1754 abdicated, son of Muhammad Shah, b 1727; d after 1754.

'ALAMGIR II Jun 1754-29 Nov 1759 assassinated, son of Jahandar Shah.

SHAHJAHAN III Nov 1759-Sep? 1760, kinsman of 'Alamgir II; date of death uncertain. A usurper.

SHAH 'ALAM II *de jure* Nov 1759-10 Nov 1806; ruler *in absentia* until 1771; from Sep 1802 usually termed King of Delhi, son of 'Alamgir II, b (Ali Gauhar) 15 Jun 1728. The last sovereign Mughal Emperor, his state was reduced by wars to the region around Delhi and from Sep 1802 this blind monarch (who had been blinded by the Afghan invaders in 1788) was the British protected King of Delhi.

† 'KINGS OF DELHI'
(successors to the Mughal Emperors)

SHAH 'ALAM II 'King of Delhi' Sep 1802-10 Nov 1806.

AKBAR SHAH II Nov 1806-1837, son of Shah 'Alam II.

BAHADUR SHAH II 1837-Sep 1857 deposed by the British, son of Akbar Shah II, b 24 Oct 1775; d 7 Nov 1862. The last Mughal, he became involved in the Indian Mutiny against his will and after his surrender was exiled to Burma.

THE MARATHA STATE OF THE DECCAN

The Maratha state was the major power of the Deccan in the 17th and 18th centuries.

† Emperors of the Maratha State
(using the style Chhatrapati)

SIVAJI Ruler from *c* 1653; Emperor 6 Jun 1674-4 Apr 1680, b 1627. A scion of the gentry Sivaji, perhaps the most attractive of all Indian rulers, built his state between *c* 1653 and 1660. After imprisonment by Aurangzeb - he made his famous escape in a fruit basket - he established himself as sovereign in 1674. This pious, just, kindly sage founded a major state in Maharashtra and Karnataka and an efficient army and administration.

SAMBHAJI Apr 1680-Oct 1687 hacked to death by Mughals; son of Sivaji.

RAJA RAM late 1687-1700, brother of Sambhaji.

TARA BAI (Empress) 1700-1707, widow of Raja Ram.

SHAHU 1707-1727; nominal ruler only 1727-1749, son of Sambhaji. Dominated by able Ministers (Balaji Visvanath and his son Baji Rao) he retired from all administrative and ceremonial duties in 1727 leaving his Peshwa as ruler.

† Peshwas of the Marathas

BALAJI VISVANATH 1707-1720.

BAJI RAO I 1720-Apr 1740; from 1727 effective ruler of the state, son of Balaji Visvanath, b 1700. A most able administrator, Baji Rao - *de facto* Head of State and Government from 1727 - made the Maratha state the strongest in India.

BALAJI RAO Apr 1740-1761, son of Baji Rao I, b 1721.

MADHAV RAO I 1761-1772.

MADHAV RAO II 1772-Sep 1795 died in suspicious circumstances.

BAJI RAO II Sep 1795-1802 fled; restored as British vassal Dec 1802-1817 deposed; d 1853. He foolishly raised the Marathas, weakened by wars against Britain, in revolt and was defeated and exiled.

(After Plassey (1757) British rule was firmly established in Bengal and Bihar; by 1818 most of the sub-continent was in the hands of the British East India Company or formed British protected states under native rulers. In 1858 government was transferred from the Company to the Crown and in 1877 the Indian Empire was proclaimed - the Queen adopting the style Kaiser-I-Hind. British India consisted of the British Crown Territories and over 300 protected Native States - the latter occupying some 40 per cent of the total area.)

THE DOMINION OF INDIA

Governors-General

LOUIS, 1st Earl MOUNTBATTEN of Burma Aug 1947-Jun 1948, b (a Prince of Battenberg) 25 Jun 1900.

CHAKRAVARTI RAJAGOPALACHARI 21 Jun 1948-26 Jan 1949, b 1879; d 25 Dec 1972.

Prime Minister

JAWAHARLAL NEHRU 16 Aug 1947-26 Jan 1949 when he became PM of the Republic.

THE REPUBLIC OF INDIA

Presidents

Dr RAJENDRA PRASAD 26 Jan 1949-May 1962, b 3 Dec 1884; d 26 Feb 1963.

Dr **SARVAPALLI RADHAKRISHNAN   13 May 1962-May 1967,** b 5 Sep 1888; d 17 Apr 1975.

Dr **ZAHIR HUSSAIN   13 May 1967-3 May 1969,** b 8 Feb 1897; d in office.

VARAHGIRI VENKATA GIRI acting President **3 May-24 Aug 1969;** President **24 Aug 1969-Aug 1974,** b 10 Aug 1894.

FAKHRUDDIN ALI AHMED   20 Aug 1974-11 Feb 1977, b 13 May 1905; d in office.

BASAPPA DANAPPA JATTI acting President **Feb-Jul 1977,** b 10 Sep 1912.

NEELAM SANJIVA REDDY   since 25 Jul 1977, b 1913.

Prime Ministers

JAWAHARLAL NEHRU   26 Jan 1949-27 May 1964, b 14 Nov 1889; d in office. Associated with Gandhi in the Congress Movement from 1919 - and like Gandhi frequently gaoled for civil disobedience - Nehru was one of the leaders of the Indian independence campaign. He played a major role in framing the constitution and tried, but not too successfully, to keep India neutral ('non-aligned') in world affairs.

GULZARILAL NANDA acting PM **27 May-2 Jun 1964,** b 4 Jul 1898.

LAL BAHADUR SHASTRI   2 Jun 1964-11 Jan 1966, b 20 Oct 1904; d in office. He died in Tashkent after concluding peace talks to end the war with Pakistan.

GULZARILAL NANDA acting PM **11-24 Jan 1966.**

Mrs **INDIRA GANDHI   24 Jan 1966-Mar 1977,** b 19 Nov 1917. The daughter of Jawaharlal Nehru.

SHRI MORARJI RANCHODJI DESAI since **24 Mar 1977,** b 29 Feb 1896.

Indonesia

The Dutch East Indies, the major part of the Netherlands' colonial empire, was effectively founded in 1619 with establishment of the settlement of Batavia (now Djakarta). Large areas of the East Indies remained, however, outside Dutch control until the close of the 19th century. Seized by the Japanese in 1942 the East Indies was the scene of a bitter colonial war (1945-49) as the Dutch, initially with British help, attempted to retake the archipelago in the face of opposition from the self-proclaimed Republic of Indonesia.

THE PROVISIONAL GOVERNMENT

A unilateral declaration of independence occurred on 17 Aug 1945.

Head of Government
(controlling parts of Java and Sumatra)

Dr **MOHAMMAD ACHMAD SUKARNO** Nov **1945-27 Dec 1949.**

THE REPUBLIC OF INDONESIA

Officially independent from 27 Dec 1949. Initially the United States of Indonesia.

Presidents

Dr **MOHAMMED ACHMAD SUKARNO   27 Dec 1949-22 Feb 1967;** 'honorary President' **22 Feb-12 Mar 1967,** b 6 Jun 1901; d 21 Jun 1970. The leader of the Javanese nationalists, he created Indonesia by the unilateral declaration of independence and the war against the Dutch. However, in power he became dictatorial, indulged in an unrealistic foreign policy to take public attention off the economy he had ruined and was eventually gradually retired after the attempted Communist coup (Oct 1965) with which he sympathised.

Gen **RADEN SUHARTO** acting President **12 Mar 1967-27 Mar 1968;** President **since 27 Mar 1968,** b 8 Jun 1921.

Prime Ministers

Dr **MOHAMMED HATTA   27 Dec 1949-Aug 1950,** b 12 Aug 1902.

Dr **MOHAMMED NATSIR   22 Aug 1950-Mar 1951.**

Dr **SARTONO   20 Mar-18 Apr 1951.**

Dr **SUKIMAN   18 Apr 1951-Mar 1952.**

Dr **WILOPO   18 Mar 1952-Jun 1953;** acting PM **5 Jun-20 Jul 1953.**

Dr **WONGSONEGORO   20-30 Jul 1953.**

Dr **ALI SASTROAMIDJOJO   30 Jul 1953-Jul 1954.**

Dr **MOHAMMED HATTA** acting PM **24 Jul-11 Aug 1954.**

BURHANUDDIN HARAHAP   11 Aug 1954-Mar 1956.

Dr **ALI SASTROAMIDJOJO   3 Mar 1956-Mar 1957,** b 1903; d 13 Mar 1975.

Dr **SUWIRJO** acting PM **15 Mar-4 Apr 1957.**

Dr **DJUANDA KARTAWIDJAJA   4 Apr 1957-6 Nov 1963;** d in office.

Dr **MOHAMMED ACHMAD SUKARNO   6 Nov 1963-Jul 1966;** nominally PM until 11 Oct 1967.

Gen **RADEN SUHARTO** acting PM **25 Jul 1966-Oct 1967;** PM **since 11 Oct 1967.**

Iran

In the second millenium BC the Iranians entered Iran: one branch, the Medes, settled in the west; the other, the Persians, in the south. Media and Persia united under Cyrus the Great c 550 BC. Iran (formerly Persia) was taken by Alexander the Great between 336 and 330 BC and passed to the Seleucid state (c312 BC) before reasserting independence as Parthia under the Arsacid Dynasty (c250 BC-AD 22). After rule by the Sasanid Dynasty (226-651), the country was ruled by the Caliphate of the East (651-1040), the Seljuq Turks (1040-1157) and then a number of small states (1157-c1220), the Atbeg Principalities. Mongol rule began c1220 but by the 1290s the Il-Khans, the vassals of the Great Khan, had become independent rulers and by 1335 the Il-Khan Empire had subdivided into smaller units. Iran passed to the Timurid Empire (1393-c1447) and then in part to the Koyunlu Turkmen (c1447-1490) before being split into small Emirates. The country was reunited in 1501 by the Safavid Dynasty - subsequent Imperial Houses have been the Ashfar (1736-1796), the Qajar (1796-1925) and the Pahlavi (since 1925).

THE KINGDOM OF MEDIA
(central and west Iran)

† Kings of the Medes

(DEIOCES, sometimes listed as first King of Media, was mythical.)
PHRAORTES *c*675-*c*653 BC.
*c*653-*c*625 BC Period of Scythian rule.
UVAKHSHATRA (or CYAXARES) *c*625-*c*585 BC. The ally of Babylon in the destruction of Assyria.
ASTYAGES *c*585-*c*550 BC.
*c*550 BC Media merged with Persia on the death of Astyages whose heir was his son-in-law Cyrus the Great of Persia.

THE KINGDOM OF PERSIA
southern Iran

† Kings of the Persians

(HAXAMANISH or ACHAEMENES, sometimes listed as first King of Persia, was mythical.)
TEISPES *fl.*7th century BC.
KURASH I (or CYRUS I) *fl.*late 7th Century BC, son of Teispes. Ruled part of Persia.
ARIARAMNES *fl.*late 7th century BC, son of Teispes. Ruled part of Persia.
KAMBUJIA I (or CAMBYSES I) ?-559 BC, son of Kurash I.
KURASH II (or CYRUS II) 559-*c*550 BC when he became King of Kings of the Iranians.

† Kings of Kings (Shahanshah) of the Iranians

KURASH II (or CYRUS II) King of Persia from 559 BC; Shahanshah of Iran **559-529 BC** died in battle, son of Kambuyia I, b *c*600 BC. Heir to Astyages of Media, Cyrus united both Iranian realms and taking Babylonia and much of Asia Minor he created the Persian Empire. He was known as 'The Great'.
KAMBUJIA II (or CAMBYSES II) **529-522 BC** died from gangrene not suicide as often claimed, eldest son of Kurash II. The subject of a now totally discredited Greek history he added Egypt to the realm.
BARIYA Mar-Autumn 522 BC killed. Once thought to be an imposter named Gaumata it is likely this usurper was Kambujia II's brother.

ACHAEMENID DYNASTY
DARAYAVAUSH I (or DARIUS I) **autumn 522-Nov 486 BC,** great-grandson of Ariaramnes, b *c*550 BC. A brilliant general and administrative innovator, Darius extended the empire east to the Indus and west into Greece where he was defeated at Marathon (Aug 490 BC).
XERXES I Nov 486-465 BC assassinated, son of Darayavaush I, b *c*520. His hopes of adding Greece to the empire, upon which he placed a heavy yoke, were boosted by the victory at Thermopylae but ended by defeat at Salamis (480 BC).
ARTAKHSHATHRA I (or ARTAXERXES I) **465-late 425 BC,** son of Xerxes I.
XERXES II 425-424 BC - reigned 45 days when he was murdered by a drunken half-brother; son of Artakhshahthra I.
DARAYAVAUSH II (or DARIUS II) **early 424-404 BC,** son of Artakhshathra I.
ARTAKHSHATHRA II (or ARTAXERXES II) **404-359 or 358 BC,** son of Darayavaush II.
ARTAKHSHATHRA III (or ARTAXERXES III) **359 or 358-Nov 338 BC** poisoned, son of Artakhshathra II.
ARSES Nov 338-Jun 336 BC poisoned, son of Artakhshathra III.
DARAYAVAUSH III (or DARIUS III) **Jun 336-Apr 330 BC** when Persepolis fell to Alexander the Great; great-nephew of Artakhshathra II, b *c*381 BC; murdered summer 330 BC.
330-323 BC Iran was part of Alexander the Great's empire.
323-312 BC The Macedonian generals disputed Alexander's inheritance.
312-*c*250 BC Iran was included in the Seleucid Empire.

THE PARTHIAN KINGDOM IN IRAN

†The Arshakuni or Arsacid Dynasty of Parthian Rulers

At one time some writers accorded the name Arsaces to all rulers of this family ignoring their true names and the problems thus created with regard to regnal numbers for usurpers.

ARSACES I *c*250-*c*248 BC. He gained independence for his state from the Seleucids.

TIRIDATES I *c*248-*c*230 BC when he became King.

† Arsacid Kings of Parthia

TIRIDATES I (or TRDAT I) Ruler from *c*248 BC; King *c*230-*c*211 BC, brother of Arsaces I. Self-proclaimed King.

ARTABANUS I (or ARSACES II) *c*211-*c*191 BC, son of Tiridates I.

PRIAPATIUS *c*191-*c*176 BC, kinsman of Artabanus I.

PHRAATES I (or FARHAD I) *c*176-*c*171 BC, son of Priapatius.

MITHRADATES I *c*171-*c*138 BC, son of Priapatius. In taking Media and Babylonia from the crumbling Seleucid state he recreated the Persian realm but his Kingdom was more Hellenistic than Iranian.

PHRAATES II (or FARHAD II) *c*138-*c*128 BC assassinated, son of Mithradates I.

ARTABANUS II *c*128-*c*123 BC murdered, uncle of Phraates II.

MITHRADATES II *c*123-*c*90 BC when he became King of Kings.

† Kings of Kings (Shahanshah) of the Parthian State in Iran

MITHRADATES II King from *c*123 BC; Shahanshah *c*90-88 BC, son of Artabanus II. His reign was the zenith of the Parthian Empire whose western limits he agreed with Rome and whose eastern frontier he pushed into central Asia.

GOTARZES I (or GODARZ I) 91-87 or 80 BC deposed; date of death uncertain. Rival to Mithradates II.

ORODES I (or WYRWY I) 87 or 80-76? BC, son of Gotarzes I.

SANATRUCES (or ARSHAKAN) 76-70 BC murdered by Phraates III; descendant of Mithradates I.

PHRAATES III (or FARHAD III) 70-58 or 57 BC murdered by his sons; son of Sanatruces.

MITHRADATES III 58 or 57-55 BC murdered by Orodes II; son of Phraates III.

ORODES II (or WYRWY II) *c*57-37 BC murdered by Phraates IV; son of Phraates III.

PHRAATES IV (or FARHAD IV) 37-2 BC murdered by PhraatesV; son of Orodes II.

TIRIDATES II (or TRDAT II) *c*32 BC - briefly usurped the throne with Roman help; fate uncertain.

PHRAATES V (or FARHAD V) 2 BC-AD 4 assassinated, son of Phraates IV. A pro-Roman who married his own mother.

ORODONES III AD 4-6 or 7.

VONONES I AD 7-11 deposed, son of Phraates V; killed *c*AD 16.

ARTABANUS III 11 or 12-38, an Arsacid on his mother's side.

TIRIDATES III (or TRDAT III) *c*35-36 deposed, grandson of Phraates IV; fate unknown. Briefly usurped the throne.

CINNAMUS 37. A short-lived usurper of unknown ancestry.

VARDANES 38-47 assassinated.

GOTARZES II (or GODARZ II) 38-51 murdered?, brother of Artabanus III.

VONONES II 51 murdered?

VOLOGASES I (or WLGS I) 51-77 or 78.

PACORUS 78 deposed.

ARTABANUS IV 79-80 or 81.

PACORUS 80 or 81-109 or 110

OSROES 109 or 110-128 or 129, brother-in-law of Pacorus.

VOLOGASES II (or WLGS II) 105 or 106-*c*147. A rival to Pacorus and Osroes - civil war resulted from the dynastic dispute.

VOLOGASES III (or WLGS III) 148-192, son of Vologases II. Weakened Parthia was no match for the Romans who destroyed his capital, Ctesiphon.

VOLOGASES IV (or WLGS IV) 192-208, son of Vologases III.

VOLOGASES V (or WLGS V) 208-222 King in Babylonia, son of Vologases IV.

ARTABANUS V 213-224 deposed, brother of Vologases V; d 226 killed in battle by Ardashir I. Ruler of only Media, Artabanus was killed by his powerful vassal the King of Fars who ended the Parthian monarchy.

(ARTAVASDES, son of Artabanus V, attempted resistance to Ardashir between 224 and *c*228.)

THE IRANIAN EMPIRE

† Kings of Kings of the Iranians

SASANID DYNASTY

ARDASHIR I (or ARTAKHSHATHRA V) 226-241 abdicated, 'King' of Fars - a vassal state in Iran; d soon after abdication. Totally unscrupulous he built up a state around his west Persian power base. Overthrowing the Arsacids, he established his own Empire and made Zoroastrianism the national religion.

SHAPUR I 241-Sep 272, son of Ardashir I. The Manichaeist Shapur defeated Rome to build a vast Iranian realm stretching from the Indus to the Euphrates, from Oman to Armenia.

HORMIZD I *c*Sep 272-Sep 273, son of Shapur I.

VAHARAN I (or BAHRAM I) Sep 273-Sep 276, son of Shapur I. He destroyed Manichaeism in Iran executing its founder Mani.

VAHARAN II (or BAHRAM II) Sep 276-293, son of Vaharan I.

VAHARAN III (or BAHRAM III) late 293 deposed, son of Vaharan II.

NARSEH late 293-302, youngest son of Shapur I.

HORMIZD II 302-309, son of Narseh.

ADHUR-NARSEH 309 - reigned about a week when he was assassinated, son of Hormizd II.

SHAPUR II 309-379, posthumous son of Hormizd II (succeeded at birth). An egocentric genius - he styled himself 'Partner of the Stars' - Shapur ruled firmly but fairly though Christians were persecuted. The Sasanid Empire reached its peak when he conquered Armenia and five Roman provinces.

ARDASHIR II 379-383 deposed, brother of Shapur II; d same year as deposition - probably violently.

SHAPUR III 383, son of Shapur II.

VAHARAN IV (or BAHRAM IV CHUBIN) **383-399,** probably son of Shapur II.

YAZDEGERD I (or YZDKRT I) **399-420** assassinated, grandson of Shapur II. A sagacious Shah whose religious toleration, particularly to Christians, led to his murder by Zoroastrians.

VAHARAN V (or BAHRAM V) **420-438,** son of Yazdegerd I; known as 'The Wild Ass'.

YAZDEGERD II (or YZDKRT II) **438-457,** son of Vaharan V.

HORMIZD III 457-459, son of Yazdegerd II.

FIRUZ I 459-484 died in battle, son of Yazdegerd II.

VALAKHSH 484-488 deposed and blinded, son of Yazdegerd II; fate uncertain.

KAVADH I (or QOBAD I) **488-496** deposed, son of Firuz I.

JAMASP 496-499, brother of Kavadh I; fate uncertain.

KAVADH I (or QOBAD I) **499-531.**

KHOSROW I 531-579, son of Kavadh I.

HORMIZD IV 579-590 deposed, son of Khosrow I; executed after deposition.

KHOSROW II PARVIZ ('The Victorious') **590** deposed, son of Hormizd IV; murdered by his son Kavadh II in 628.

MIHRAN DYNASTY
VAHARAN VI (or BAHRAM VI CHUBIN) **590-591** when he fled; killed by Turks c 592. A general who usurped the throne.

SASANID DYNASTY
KHOSROW II PARVIZ ('The Victorious') **591-628.**

KAVADH II SHIRUYE 628, son of Khosrow II.

ARDASHIR III 628-630 assassinated, grandson of Khosrow II.

SHAHRBARAZ 630.

PURANDOKHT 629-631. Rival to Shahrbaraz.

HORMIZD V 631-632.

KHOSROW III 632.

YAZDEGERD III (or YZDKRT III) **632-642** when most of Iran was lost to the Arabs or 651 when he was assassinated; grandson of Khosrow II.

(FIRUZ II, son of Yazdegerd III, breifly attempted resistance against the invading Arabs; he fled to China and his fate is unknown.)

651-1040 Iran was ruled by the Caliphate of the East.

1040-1157 Iran was ruled by the Seljuq Empire.

1157-c 1220 Iran was divided into small states - the Atbeg Principalities.

c 1220-c 1290 Iran was ruled by the Mongol Great Khans.

THE IL-KHAN EMPIRE IN IRAN

† Il-Khan Rulers in Iran
(nominally subject to the Great Khan)

GAYKHATU 1291-1295.
BAYDU 1295.

† Il-Khan Emperors in Iran
(self-styled 'Emperors of Islam')

MAHMUD GHAZAN 1295-1304. A convert to Islam, he claimed to be sovereign of all Muslims and built a realm including Iran, Mesopotamia, Georgia and part of central Asia.

OLJEITU 1304-1316.

ABU SA'ID 1317-1335. Upon his death the Il-Khan Empire collapsed.

1335-1393 Iran subdivided into many local states.

1393-c 1447 Iran was subject to the Timurid Empire.

KOYUNLU TURKMEN RULERS OF IRAN

Ruled the greater part of Iran.

† Kara Koyunlu Sultan in Iran

JAHAN SHAH c 1447-1467 deposed, leader of the 'Black Sheep' Turkmen; d 1468.

† Ak Koyunlu Sultans in Iran

UZUN HASAN 1453-1478, leader of the 'White Sheep' Turkmen. He virtually re-established an Iranian state.

YA'QUB 1478-1490, son of Uzun Hasan.

c 1490-c 1501 Iran split into small states.

THE IRANIAN EMPIRE

† Kings of Kings (Shahanshah) of Iran

SAFAVID DYNASTY
ESMA'IL I Ruler from 1499; Shahanshah **1501-1524,** b 17 Jul 1487. Esma'il reunited Iran by 1510 and converted the state from Sunni to Shia Islam.

TAHMASP I 1524-1576, son of Esma'il I, b 3 Mar 1514.

ESMA'IL II 1576-1577, son of Tahmasp I, b 1551.

MOHAMMAD 1577-1586, son of Tahmasp I.

SHAH ABBAS I ('The Great') **1587-19 Jan 1629,** son of Mohammad, b 27 Jan 1571. Shah Abbas reformed the army with the aid of Robert Sherley, encouraged trade with Europe, reformed government and sponsored the arts making Isfahan a glittering capital. He also

Mohammad Reza Shah Pahlavi, Shah of Iran, with his third Empress, Farah, who provided Iran with a long-awaited heir (Popperfoto)

ruthlessly eliminated rivals and kept relatives in near solitary captivity thus none was capable of succeeding.

SHAH SAFI I   Jan 1629-1642, grandson of Shah Abbas I.

SHAH ABBAS II   1642-1667, son of Shah Safi I, b 1632.

SHAH SAFI II SULEYMAN   1668-1694, grandson of Shah Safi I.

SHAH SOLTAN HOSEYN   1694-1726 murdered, son of Shah Safi II, b 1668. A weak ruler who gave his time to religion and his purse to mullahs.

TAHMASP II   1726-1732 deposed, son of Shah Soltan Hoseyn; d 1739. A puppet for the dictator Nader Qoli Beg.

SHAH ABBAS III   1732-1736 deposed, son of Tahmasp II; d 1736? A puppet for the dictator Nader Qoli Beg.

DYNASTY OF THE AFSHARS

NADER SHAH   1736-Jun 1747 assassinated, b (Nader Qoli Beg) 22 Oct 1688. Making himself Shah after ruling through two puppets this former bandit chief strengthened the army, founded the Iranian navy and conducted a war against the Indian Moghul whose confiscated wealth restored the economy. Harsh, he blinded his son and became mad.

SHAH ROKH   Jun 1747-1796 killed by Agha Mohammad Khan; grandson of Nader Shah. Legally sovereign of Iran he was confined to the Mashad area by the Zand dictators - Karim Khan Zand (Dictator 1747-Mar 1779), Ali Murad, Ja'afer and Loft 'Ali Khan (Dictator 1789-1794) who declared themselves to be Regents.

SAFAVID DYNASTY

ESMA'IL III   1757-1760, grandson of Shah Soltan Hoseyn. Raised to the throne as a puppet by the Zands in an attempt to legitimate their dictatorship.

QAJAR DYNASTY

AGHA MOHAMMAD KHAN   Ruler from 1794; Shahanshah 1796-1797 assassinated. Eunuch-chief of the Qajars he reunited Iran after the Zand period, suppressed rebellious provinces and ended the rule of the shadow Emperor Shah Rokh - all with great cruelty.

FATH 'ALI SHAH   1797-1834, nephew of Agha Mohammad Khan, b 1771.

MOHAMMAD SHAH   1834-1848, grandson of Fath 'Ali Shah.

NASER od-DIN SHAH   1848-May 1896 assassinated, son of Mohammad Shah, b 1831.

MOZAFFAR od-DIN SHAH   May 1896-9 Jan 1907, son of Naser od-Din Shah, b 1852.

MOHAMMAD 'ALI SHAH   Jan 1907-1909 when he fled, son of Mozaffar od-Din Shah, b 1872; d in exile 1930. Civil war broke out when he suppressed the constitution which his predecessor had been forced to grant in 1906.

AHMED MIRZA SHAH   1909-31   Oct   1925 deposed, son of Mohammad 'Ali Shah, b 1898; d in exile 1930. An absentee Shah formally deposed by Parliament.

PAHLAVI DYNASTY

REZA SHAH PAHLAVI   Head of State 1 Nov-13 Dec 1925; Shahanshah 13 Dec 1925-16 Sep 1941 abdicated, b 16 Mar 1878; d 26 Jul 1944. A gifted officer, he gained power by a coup in 1921. Premier when the absentee Qajar sovereign was deposed he was elected Emperor (Shahanshah) by Parliament. Reza Shah, who did much to create modern Iran, was obliged to abdicate when he was slow to break trading pacts with Germany during World War II.

MOHAMMAD REZA SHAH PAHLAVI   since 16 Sep 1941, son of Reza Shah Pahlavi, b 26 Oct 1919.

Prime Ministers

ALI FURANGHI   27 Aug 1941-Mar 1942, b c 1880; d Dec 1942.

ALI SOLHEILY   9 Mar-Aug 1942.

QAVAM es-SULTANEH   3 Aug 1942-Feb 1943.

ALI SOLHEILY   16 Feb 1943-Mar 1944, b 1897; d 1958.

MOHAMMED SAED   19 Mar-Nov 1944.

NURTEZA QUALIKHAN BAYATT   9 Nov 1944-May 1945.

Dr IBRAHIM HAKIMI   11 May-7 Jun 1945.

MUHSIN SADR   7 Jun-24 Oct 1945.

Dr IBRAHIM HAKIMI   24 Oct 1945-Jan 1946, b c 1870; d 1959.

QAVAM es-SULTANEH   26 Jan 1946-Dec 1947.

SARDAR FAKHER HEKMAT   10-21 Dec 1947.

Dr IBRAHIM HAKIMI   21 Dec 1947-Jun 1948.

ABDUL HUSSEIN HAJIR   13 Jun-4 Nov 1948 ; d in office - assassinated.

MOHAMMED SAED   8 Nov 1948-Mar 1950.

ALI MANSUR 19 Mar-26 Jun 1950, b 1895.

Gen ALI RAZMARA 26 Jun 1950-7 Mar 1951, b *c* 1900; d 1951 assassinated.

HUSSEIN ALA 11 Mar-28 Apr 1951.

Dr MOHAMMED MUSSADEQ 28 Apr 1951-Jul 1952.

QAVAM es-SULTANEH 17-22 Jul 1952, b 1876; d 1955.

Dr MOHAMMED MOSSADEQ 22 Jul 1952-19 Aug 1953 removed from office by a royal coup and later found guilty of treason, b 1883; d 5 Mar 1967.

Gen FAZULLA ZAHEDA 16 Aug *de jure*; 19 Aug *de facto* 1953-Apr 1955, b 1897, d 2 Sep 1963.

HUSSEIN ALA 7 Apr 1955-Apr 1957, b 1883; d 13 Jul 1964.

Dr MANOUCHEHR EGHBAL 3 Apr 1957-Aug 1960, b 1909.

Dr JAFAR SHARIF EMAMI 29 Aug 1960-May 1961, b 1910.

Dr ALI AMINI 7 May 1961-Jul 1962, b 1905.

ASSADOLLAH ALAM 19 Jul 1962-Mar 1964, b 1919.

HASSAN ALI MANSUR 7 Mar 1964-21 Jan 1965, b 18 Feb 1919; d in office - assassinated.

AMIR ABBAS HOVEIDA acting Premier 21-27 Jan 1965; Premier 27 Jan 1965-Aug 1977.

Dr JAMSHID AMOUZEGAR since 6 Aug 1977, b 25 Jun 1923.

Iraq

Incorporated into the Ottoman Empire in the 16th century the territories that became Iraq were occupied by the British from 1916 to 1920 and granted to Britain as a League of Nations mandate in the latter year. Three diverse provinces (Basra, Mosul and Baghdad) were united to form a Kingdom in 1921 which was granted independence in 1932. A Republic was declared following the revolution in 1958.

THE KINGDOM OF IRAQ

† Kings

HASHEMITE DYNASTY

FAYSAL I King under British protection 11 Jul 1921-Oct 1932; sovereign 3 Oct 1932-8 Sep 1933, son of King Husayn of the Hejaz, b 20 May 1885. Briefly King of Syria, this Hashemite Prince who played a leading part in liberating the Middle East from Ottoman rule was installed by Britain as King of Iraq in an attempt to still very considerable opposition to British rule.

GHAZI Sep 1933-4 Apr 1939 died in a car accident, son of Faysal I, b 21 Mar 1912.

FAYSAL II Apr 1939-14 Jul 1958 when he was murdered in the revolt that overthrew the monarchy, son of Ghazi, b 2 May 1935.

Prime Ministers

The title Pasha was not used after 1952.

Gen NURI PASHA es-SAID 3 Oct 1932-Mar 1933.

SAYID RASHID ALI el GAILANI 20 Mar-Nov 1933.

JAMIL MIDFAI 9 Nov 1933-Sep 1934.

ALI JAUDAT BEY Sep 1934-Mar 1935.

JAMIL MIDFAI 5-16 Mar 1935.

Gen YASIN PASHA el HASHIMI 16 Mar 1935-30 Oct 1936 deposed.

SEYYID HIKMAT SULAIMAN 30 Oct 1936-Aug 1937.

JAMIL MIDFAI 16 Aug 1937-Dec 1938.

Gen NURI PASHA es-SAID 26 Dec 1938-Mar 1940.

SAYID RASHID ALI el GAILANI 31 Mar 1940-30 May 1941 when he fled, b 1893; d 28 Aug 1965. An Axis sympathiser he was deposed with British assistance.

JAMIL MIDFAI May-Oct 1941.

Gen NURI PASHA es-SAID Oct 1941-Jun 1944.

HAMDI el-PACHACHI Jun 1944-Feb 1946, b 1891; d 1948.

TEWFIQ SUWAIDI Feb-Jun 1946.

ARSHAD el-UMARI Jun-Nov 1946.

Gen NURI PASHA es-SAID Nov 1946-Mar 1947.

SALEH JABR 30 Mar 1947-Jan 1948, b 1892; d 1957.

MOHAMMED el-SADR 29 Jan-Jun 1948.

MUZAHIM el-PACHICHI 26 Jun 1948-Jan 1949, cousin of Hamdi el-Pachachi.

Gen NURI PASHA es-SAID 6 Jan-Dec 1949.

SAYED ALI JAWDAT AYUBI 10 Dec 1949-Feb 1950.

TEWFIQ el-SUWEIDI 5 Feb-Sep 1950.

Gen NURI PASHA es-SAID 16 Sep 1950-Jul 1952.

SAYED MUSTAFA el-UMARI 9 Jul-Nov 1952.

Gen NUREDDIN MOHAMMED 23 Nov 1952-Jan 1953.

JAMIL MIDFAI 26 Jan-Sep 1953.

Dr MOHAMMED FADIL JAMALI Sep 1953-1954.

Gen NURI PASHA es-SAID 1954-Jun 1957.

SAYED ALI JAWDAT AYUBI Jun-Dec 1957.

ABDUL WAHAB MIRJAN 15 Dec 1957-Mar 1958.

Gen NURI PASHA es-SAID 3 Mar-19 May 1958, b 1888; murdered 14 or 15 Jul 1958 during the savage Iraqi revolution. This outstanding diplomat who did much to found the Arab League was Premier eight times. His friendship towards the West (particularly Britain) and his devotion to the monarchy alienated radical Arab nationalists.

AHMED MUKHTAR BABAN 19 May-14 Jul 1958 when the Republic was formed during the revolution.

THE REPUBLIC OF IRAQ

Presidents

Gen **MUHAMMAD NAJIB RUBAI** Chairman of the Council of Sovereignty **Jul 1958-8 Feb 1963** deposed in coup.

Col **ABDUL SALAM MOHAMMED AREF** (later Marshal) **8 Feb 1963-13 Apr 1966** when he died in an air accident, b 21 Mar 1921.

Maj-Gen **ABDUL RAHMAN AREF   17 Apr 1966-17 Jul 1968** deposed in coup, brother of Marshal Abdul Salam Mohammed Aref, b 1916.

Maj-Gen **AHMED HASSAN BAKR   since 17 Jul 1968,** b 1914.

Prime Ministers

Brig **ABDUL KARIM KASSEM   14 Jul 1958-8 Feb 1863** when he was assassinated, b 1914. The leader of the ugly coup that ended the monarchy.

Brig **AHMED HASSAN BAKR   8 Feb-20 Nov 1963**; see President Bakr.

Lieut-Gen **TAHER YAHYA   20 Nov 1963-Sep 1965.**

Brig **AREF ABDUL RAZZAK   3-16 Sep 1965** fled after an attempted coup.

Dr **ABDUL RAHMAN al BAZZAZ   21 Sep 1965-Aug 1966.**

Maj-Gen **NAJI TALEB   6 Aug 1966-May 1967.**

Maj-Gen **ABDUL RAHMAN AREF   10 May-10 Jul 1967**; see President Aref.

Lieut-Gen **TAHER YAHYA   10 Jul 1967-17 Jul 1968** deposed in coup.

Col **ABDUL RAZZAK al NAYEF   19 Jul-12 Aug 1968** banished; d 10 Jul 1978 of wounds received in an assassination attempt in London 9 Jul 1978.

Maj-Gen **AHMED HASSAN BAKR   12 Aug 1968-9 Nov 1969** when the post of Prime Minister was abolished by constitutional amendment; see President Bakr.

Irish Republic

The ancient High Kingship of Ireland can never be said to have united the island which was divided into five Kingdoms: Connaught, Leinster, Meath, Munster and Ulster. The Anglo-Norman conquest of Ireland in the 12th century established control over but little of Ireland and until Tudor days English writ was effective only in the area around Dublin ('The Pale') and in a few coastal districts. From 1556 to 1610 the conquest of Ireland was undertaken in earnest but revolts were frequent. Union with Britain occurred in 1801 but was always uneasy. British rule over most of Ireland was effectively ended by the climate of opinion created by the rejection of Gladstone's Home Rule Bills and the Easter Rising of 1916. A Republic was declared by Sinn Fein in Jan 1919 but the 26 county Irish Free State did not achieve independence until Jan 1922 under the terms of the Treaty of London. The counties of Northern Ireland chose to remain part of the United Kingdom. The sovereignty of the Free State was confirmed by the Statue of Westminster in 1931. In Dec 1937 a republican constitution came into force and in Apr 1949 the Republic of Ireland ceased to be a member of the Commonwealth.

THE IRISH FREE STATE

Governors-General

TIMOTHY MICHAEL HEALY   Dec 1922-Dec 1927, b 17 May 1855; d 26 Mar 1931.

JAMES McNEILL   Dec 1927-Oct 1932, b 27 Mar 1869; d 12 Dec 1938.

DONAL BUCKLEY   Nov 1932-14 Dec 1936 when the post of Governor-General was abolished.

Presidents of the Executive Council

'Prime Ministers' of the Irish Free State

ARTHUR GRIFFITH   Jan-13 Aug 1922, b 31 Mar 1872; d in office. One of the founders of the Sinn Fein movement, he negotiated the Treaty of London which established the Free State.

MICHAEL COLLINS Head of Provisional Government **Aug-Sep 1922,** b 1890; d in office - assassinated. Collins fought in the Easter Rising and in later guerrilla movements against British rule, but took part in the talks in London that led to the establishment of the Free State. He was killed by republicans in the civil war that racked the newly formed state for a year.

WILLIAM THOMAS COSGRAVE   9 Sep 1922-9 Mar 1932, b 6 Jun 1880; d 16 Nov 1965. He pursued a policy of moderation trying to reconcile the warring factions and religions.

EAMON de VALERA   9 Mar 1932-29 Dec 1937 when he became PM of the Republic.

THE REPUBLIC OF IRELAND

Presidents

29 Dec 1937-Jun 1938 Presidential Commission consisting of Chief Justice O'Sullivan, Attorney-General Maguire and Chairman of the Dail F. Fahy.

Dr **DOUGLAS HYDE   25 Jun 1938-Jun 1945,** b 17 Jan 1860; d 12 Jul 1949.

SEAN THOMAS O'KELLY   25 Jun 1945-Jun 1959, b 25 Aug 1882; d 23 Nov 1966.

EAMON de VALERA   25 Jun 1959-Jun 1973, b 14 Oct 1882; d 29 Aug 1975. The last commander of the Easter Rising to surrender, de Valera, who was half-Irish and half-Spanish, led the republican opposition to the Free State in the civil war of 1922.

ERSKINE CHILDERS 24 Jun 1973-17 Nov 1974, b
1905; d in office.
CEARBHALL O'DALAIGH 3 Dec 1974-22 Oct
1976, b 12 Feb 1911; d 20 Mar 1978.
Dr PATRICK JOHN HILLERY since 3 Dec 1976,
b 2 May 1923.

Prime Ministers

EAMON de VALERA 29 Dec 1937-Feb 1948.
JOHN ALOYSIUS COSTELLO 18 Feb 1948-Jun
1951, b 20 Jun 1891.
EAMON de VALERA 13 Jun 1951-Jun 1954.
JOHN ALOYSIUS COSTELLO 2 Jun 1954-Mar
1957.
EAMON de VALERA 20 Mar 1957-Jun 1959.
SEAN LEMASS 23 Jun 1959-Nov 1966, b 15 Jul
1899; d 11 May 1971.
JOHN MARY LYNCH (more commonly known as
JACK LYNCH) 9 Nov 1966-Mar 1973.
LIAM COSGRAVE 14 Mar 1973-Jul 1977, son of
William Thomas Cosgrave, b 30 Apr 1920.
JOHN MARY LYNCH (more commonly known as
JACK LYNCH) since 5 Jul 1977, b 15 Aug 1917.

*Eamon de Valera who served the Irish Free State
(later Republic) as President, Premier, Foreign
Minister and international representative* (Radio
Times Hulton Picture Library)

Israel

The Hebrews entered Israel c 14th century BC but
a Kingdom of Israel was not established until
c 1021 BC - there had been religious objections that
the institution of kingship was inconsistent with
the Covenant. The state was divided c 922 BC into
Israel in the north (which eventually fell to
Assyria) and Judah in the south (it fell to
Babylonia). After the Exile (587-539 BC) came
Persian rule (539-332 BC), inclusion in Alexander
the Great's empire, the Antigonid state and from
305 BC the Seleucid Kingdom. The Maccabean
revolt gained independence for the Hasmonean
Kingdom (141-63 BC). In 63 BC Palestine became
a Roman province which formed the puppet
Herodian Kingdom from 37 BC-AD 44. The revolt
of AD 66-70 led to the dispersion (Diaspora) of the
Jews although some remained in Palestine
throughout the succeeding centuries. With the
division of the Roman Empire Palestine passed to
Byzantium (AD 395) and in 634 came under the
Arab Caliphate of the East. The Crusader states of
Outremer formed an interlude to Arab rule from
the 12th to the 13th centuries. In 1516 the area
came under Ottoman rule which, with the brief
intervals of French intervention in 1799 and the
Egyptian period of 1831-41, lasted until the Holy
Land was taken by British and Arab forces in 1917.
The British League of Nations mandate was ended
by the establishment of the State of Israel on 14
May 1948.

THE KINGDOM OF ISRAEL

† Kings of United Israel

HOUSE OF SAUL
SHAUL (Biblical Saul) c 1021-c 1000 BC died in
battle against the Philistines. Shaul faced great
opposition from those who regarded kingship as
blasphemous, particularly when he neglected his
religious obligations. Falling out with his son
Jonathan, his son-in-law Dawid (of whose
popularity he was jealous) and Samuel (whose
support had won him the throne), he became
unbalanced.
ISHBAAL (Biblical Ishboseth) c 1000 BC defeated,
and killed? by Dawid. Son of Shaul. Briefly
reigned in north Israel.

HOUSE OF DAVID
DAWID (Biblical DAVID) c 1000-c 962 BC, son-in-
law of Shaul. Dawid, the Biblical ideal King, beat
Ishbaal for the throne and the Philistines to
secure his Kingdom to which he added modern
Jordan and a new capital, Jerusalem, which he
took from the Canaanites. His eventful reign,
marred by the revolt of his son Absolam, was a
fruitful time for Jewish literature and Dawid may
have written some of the Psalms traditionally
said to be his.
SHELOMOH (Biblical SOLOMON) c 962-c 922
BC, son of Dawid. He reorganised government,
built the Temple in Jerusalem, worked for peace
and encouraged trade - in this context the Queen
of Saba (Sheba) in Yemen visited his court.

Although able and a remarkable judge of men, the wisdom of Solomon was an illusion for his extravagance, paid for in forced labour and exorbitant taxes, it led to the revolt that divided and destroyed the Kingdom.

REHOBOAM *c*922 BC when he became King of Judah.

† Kings of Israel
(The Northern Kingdom)

HOUSE OF JEROBOAM

YEROBOAM I *c*922-*c*901 BC. Yeroboam was the general who led the revolt against the House of David in northern Israel thus dividing the state into two - Israel and Judah.

NADAB *c*901-*c*900? BC assassinated, son of Yeroboam.

BAASHA *c*900-*c*877 BC. The probable murderer of Nadab.

ELAH *c*887? BC assassinated, son of Baasha.

ZIMRI *c*877? BC.

TIBINI *c*876? BC.

OMRI *c*876-869 BC. Hardly mentioned in the Bible, this King was probably the greatest of his dynasty - records from Assyria tell of his wars, alliances with the Phoenicians and his new Samarian capital.

ACHAB *c*869-*c*853 BC killed at the siege of Ramoth, son of Omri. The King who married Jezebel.

AHAZIYAH *c*853-*c*849 BC, son of Achab.

YEHORAM *c*849-*c*842 BC murdered by Yehu, son of Achab.

HOUSE OF JEHU

YEHU ben-NIMSHI *c*842-*c*815 BC. Yehu, who is remembered for his reckless chariot driving, warred against Judah and killed most of the Royal House of that state where Baal worship had become entrenched.

AHAZ (Biblical JEHOAHAZ) *c*815-*c*798 BC, son of Yehu.

YOASH *c*798-*c*782, son of Ahaz.

YEROBOAM II *c*782-*c*753 BC, son of Yoash. The last powerful King of Israel, he owed his peaceful reign to Assyria's temporary decline.

ZEKARIYAH *c*753-*c*746 BC assassinated, son of Yeroboam II.

HOUSE OF JABESH

SHALLUM *c*746 - reigned for one month when he was killed.

LAST HOUSE OF ISRAEL

MENOCHEM *c*746-*c*736 BC. He seized power and maintained his throne by cruelty.

PEKAHIYAH *c*736-*c*734 BC murdered, son of Menochem.

PEKAH 734-*c*732 BC murdered.

HOSHEA *c*732-724 BC deposed; d in Assyrian captivity after 723 BC. Hoshea revolted against his Assyrian overlords but was taken prisoner and his capital Samaria was destroyed by Sargon II who deported many Jews to other parts of his empire.

† Kings of Judah
(The Southern Kingdom)

HOUSE OF DAVID

REHOBOAM *c*922-*c*915 BC, son of Shelomoh.

ABBIYAH *c*915-*c*913 or *c*908 BC, son of Rehoboam.

ASA *c*908-*c*867 BC, son of Abbiyah.

YEHOSHAPHAT *c*867-*c*849 BC, son of Asa.

YEHORAM *c*849-*c*842 BC killed, son of Yehoshaphat.

AHAZIYAH *c*842 BC killed by Yehu of Israel; son of Yehoram.

ATHALIYAH (Queen) *c*842-*c*835 BC died in a coup, widow of Jehoram.

YOASH *c*835-*c*800 BC killed by his servants, son of Ahaziyah.

AMAZIYAH *c*800-*c*791 BC assassinated, son of Yoash.

AHAZARIYAH (or UZZIYAH) *c*791-*c*739 BC, son of Amaziyah.

YOTHAM *c*739-*c*732 BC, son of Ahazariyah.

AHAZ *c*732-*c*715 BC, son of Yotham.

HIZQIYYA *c*715-*c*686 BC, son of Ahaz.

MENASSEH *c*686-*c*642 BC, son of Hizqiyya.

AMON *c*642-*c*640 BC assassinated, son of Menasseh.

YOSHIYAH *c*640-*c*609 BC, son of Amon, b *c*648.

AHAZ (Biblical JEHOAHAZ) *c*609 BC, son of Yoshiyah. Taken a prisoner by Egypt his fate is unknown.

YEHOIAKIM *c*609-autumn 598 deposed, son of Yoshiyah; d *c*Dec 598. A tyrant, he oppressed the people and restored alien cults. His revolt against Nebuchadnezzar brought the Babylonians down on Jerusalem and his deposition.

YEHOIACHIN autumn 598-Mar 597 BC deposed, son of Yehoiakim, b *c*615; d after 560 BC having been taken with 8000 prisoners into exile in Babylonia.

TSIDQIYAH (Biblical ZEDEKIAH) **Mar 597-Jul 587** deposed, blinded and taken into exile, son of Yoshiyah; fate uncertain.

587 BC Jerusalem was totally wrecked by the Babylonians who took most Jews remaining there into exile to Babylon.

587-*c*539 BC The Exile - many Jews were detained in Babylon which power ruled their homeland.

539-332 BC Persian rule - in the former year Cyrus allowed a return from the Exile.

332-305 BC Macedonian rule, by Alexander the Great and then his successors.

305-141 BC Seleucid rule.

THE HASMONEAN STATE IN PALESTINE

† Heads of State
(de facto Kings)

SHIMON 141-135 BC murdered, brother of Judas Maccabaeus who between 165 and 160 BC led the revolt against the Seleucid Kings.
YEHOKHANAN HYRCANUS I 135-104 BC, son of Shimon. Both Head of State (not King) and High Priest like his father.

† Kings of Judaea

HASMONEAN DYNASTY
YEHUDAH ARISTOBULUS I 104-103 BC, son of Yehokhanan Hyrcanus I, b c 140 BC. Proclaimed himself King.
ALEXANDER YANNAI 103-76 BC, son of Yehokhanan Hyrcanus I.
SHALOM ALEXANDRA (Queen) 76-67 BC, widow of Alexander.
YEHOKHANAN HYRCANUS II 67-63 BC, son of Queen Alexandra; d 40 BC. High Priest from 76 to 40 BC.
ARISTOBULUS II 67-63 BC deposed by the Romans who made Palestine part of their empire; d 48 BC from poison while a Roman captive. He fought a civil war against his rival Hyrcanus II.
63-37 BC Palestine was a Roman province.

THE HERODIAN KINGDOM OF JUDAEA
(A client state of The Roman Empire)

† Kings of the Jews of the Herodian Dynasty

HEROD ('The Great') 37-4 BC; the latter date is explainable - Christ was born in 6 or 5 BC; son of Hyrcanus II's Minister, b 73 BC. Named King by the Romans who established him in Jerusalem this Hellenist, who lived beyond Judaea's means, became insane, eg the massacre of the Innocents of Bethlehem after the birth of Christ.
HEROD ARCHELAUS King in Judaea and Samaria 4 BC-AD 6 deposed by the Romans, son of Herod, b 22 BC; d c AD 18.
HEROD ANTIPAS King in Galilee 4 BC-AD 39 deposed by Rome, son of Herod, b 21 BC; d in the year of his deposition. He is remembered for his wife's vendetta, using Salome, against John the Baptist and for his weakness in returning the arrested Jesus to Pilate.
PHILIPPUS King in Coele-Syria 4 BC-AD 34, son of Herod.
HEROD AGRIPPA I King in Coele-Syria from AD 37; in Galilee from 39 BC; in Judaea AD 41-44, grandson of Herod, b c 10 BC.
AD 44 Palestine reverted to being a province.
HEROD AGRIPPA II King in Chalcis from AD 50; in Galilee AD 53-93, son of Herod Agrippa I, b

AD 27. He kept his throne in part of Palestine despite the revolt (AD 66-70) after which Jerusalem was destroyed and the Jews dispersed.
70 The Diaspora.
44-395 Roman rule.
395-634 Byzantine rule.
634-1516 Caliphate 'rule' with intervals under the Crusader states in the 12th and 13th centuries.
1516-1917 Ottoman rule with short interruptions - see introduction to Israel.
1918-1948 British rule under a League of Nations mandate.

THE STATE OF ISRAEL

Presidents

Dr CHAIM AZRIEL WEIZMANN acting President 17 May 1948-17 Feb 1949; President 17 Feb 1949-9 Nov 1952, b 27 Nov 1874; d in office. Of Polish origin he was the leader of the World Zionist Organisation before World War II.
Dr JOSEPH SPRINGZAK acting President 9 Nov-10 Dec 1952.
ISHVAK BEN-ZVI 10 Dec 1952-23 Apr 1963, b (Isaac Shimshelevich) 24 Nov 1884; d in office.
ZALMAN SHAZAR 22 May 1963-May 1973, b (Schneor Zalman Rubashou) 6 Oct 1889.
Prof EPHRAIM KATZIR 25 May 1973-May 1978, b (Ephraim Katchalski) 16 May 1916.
YGZHAK NAVOM since 29 May 1978, b Apr 1921.

Prime Ministers

DAVID BEN GURION 15 May 1948-Oct 1950; acting PM 18-25 Oct 1950; PM 25 Oct 1950-Dec 1953, b (David Gruen) 16 Oct 1886; d 1 Dec 1973. An ardent supporter of the creation of the State of Israel from his youth he went to Palestine when it was still under Ottoman rule. He proclaimed Israel's independence and is, with Weizmann, regarded as the founder of the state.
MOSHE SHARETT 7 Dec 1953-Nov 1955, b Oct 1894; d 7 Jul 1965.
DAVID BEN GURION 2 Nov 1955-Jun 1963.
LEVI ESHKOL 24 Jun 1963-26 Feb 1969, b (Levi Shkolnik) 25 Oct 1895; d in office.
Gen YIGAL ALLON acting PM 26 Feb-11 Mar 1969, b 10 Oct 1918.
Mrs GOLDA MEIR 11 Mar 1969-Apr 1974; acting PM 10 Apr-3 Jun 1974, b 3 May 1898.
Gen ITZHAK RABIN 3 Jun 1974-Jun 1977, b 1 Mar 1922.
MENAHEM BEGIN since 9 Jun 1977, b 16 Aug 1913.

Italy

Upon the fall of the Roman Empire a Scirian Kingdom was set up in Rome in the middle of the 5th century. An Ostrogoth Kingdom lasted from *c*493 to 553 after which Italy briefly passed to the Byzantine Empire. The Lombard Kingdom, based in north Italy, flourished from *c*568 to 774 when Italy was taken by the Carolingian Franks who were the first to use the style King of Italy. In the late 9th and early 10th centuries the kingship was assumed by many individuals most of whom controlled only part of the peninsula. From 951 the title King of Italy was used by the Holy Roman Emperor who was the leading ruler in Italy, but from the middle of the 13th century Italy divided into many small states and the word Italy had only a geographical meaning until the Napoleonic Kingdom was created in 1805. In 1814 Italy was again divided into a number of countries which were eventually united by the House of Savoy in 1859-1860 to form the Kingdom of Italy. The Kingdom was ended by a referendum following World War II and the last King (Umberto II) left the country on 13 Jun 1946, since when Italy has been a Republic.

† King of the Scirians

ODOACER 476-15 Mar 493 assassinated, King of the Scyri, Heruli and Rugii, b *c*433. He became ruler of all Italy after deposing the last Roman Emperor.

† Kings of the Ostrogoths

THEODORIC Mar 493-526, b *c*455. Encouraged to invade Italy by a jealous Byzantine Emperor Theodoric took Rome and personally murdered Odoacer.
ATHALARIC 526-534, grandson of Theodoric, b *c*515.
THEODAHAD co-ruler **534-535;** sole ruler **535-536** assassinated, husband of Queen Amalasuntha.
AMALASUNTHA (Queen) co-ruler **534-535** assassinated, daughter of Theodoric.
WITIGIS 536-540, brother-in-law? of Athalaric.
THEODEBALD 540 assassinated.
ERARIC c541.
TOTILA c541-552 killed, nephew of Theodebald.
TEIA 552-553.
(From 553 to 568 Italy was under Byzantine rule, parts of the peninsula remaining under the control of the Eastern Empire until the 8th century - Ravenna did not fall to the Lombards until 752.)

† Kings of the Lombards

ALBOIN King outside Italy from 565; inside Italy **568-28 Jun 572**. The Germanic Lombards, of whom Alboin was the very able military leader, invaded Italy in 568 taking control of most inland areas. Unlike the Ostrogoths they destroyed much of the existing culture.
CLEPH Jun 572-574.
574-584 Interregnum during which Lombard territory was divided into about 35 'Duchies'.
AUTHARI 584-590, son of Cleph. The Lombard Kingdom was reformed when a Frankish invasion threatened.
ROMANUS 590-591.
THEODELINDA (Queen) co-ruler **591-628,** widow of Authari.
AGILULF co-ruler **591-616,** second husband of Queen Theodelinda.
ADALOALD co-ruler **616-c626** poisoned, son of Agilulf and Theodelinda, b *c*602. An insane ruler who wished to kill all the Lombard 'Dukes'.
ROTHARI co-ruler *c*626-628; sole ruler **628-652,** son-in-law of Agilulf.
RODOALD 652-653.
ARIBERT I 653-661.
BERTHARITUS 661-662?, possible co-ruler with Gondibert.
GONDIBERT 661-662, possible co-ruler with Bertharitus.
GRIMOALD 662-671, son-in-law? of Aribert.
GARIBALD 671-674, son of Grimoald.
BERTHARITUS 674-c687.
CUNIBERT c687-c700, son of Bertharitus.
LUITBERT 700-701.
RAGIMBERTUS 701.
ARIBERT II 701-712 deposed; date of death uncertain.
LUIDPRAND 712-744, b *c*690. Perhaps the most able Lombard King, a noted law-giver, this patron of the Church was so pious that he would not take up arms against Ravenna for fear of offending the Pope.
HILDEBRAND 744.
RACHIS 744-749.
AISTULF 749-757 killed in a hunting accident. His expansion in central Italy alarmed the Pope who called upon the Carolingians to aid him.
DESIDERIUS 757-Apr 774 deposed by his son-in-law Carolus; date of death uncertain.

Carolingian King of the Lombards

CAROLUS Apr 774-781; was also Charles I of France.

THE KINGDOM OF ITALY

† Kings of Italy

In practice rulers of northern and part of central Italy.

Carolingian Kings

Until 843 not sovereign Kings but tributary to the Carolingian Empire.

PEPIN   781-810, son of Carolus, b 777.
BERNARDUS 813-817 deposed, illegitimate son of Pepin, b *c* 797; d 818.
LOTHARIO 817-29 Sep 855; see Emperor Lothair I, The Holy Roman Empire.
LUDOVICUS (Emperor Ludwig II) **Sep 855-12 Aug 875,** son of Lotherio, b *c* 822.
CAROLUS Aug 875-6 Oct 877; was also Charles II of France.
CARLOMAN Oct 877-880, son of Ludovicus, b 828.
CAROLUS ('The Fat') **880-887** deposed, brother of Carloman, b 839; d 13 Jan 888.

Non-Carolingian Kings

A period of anarchy existed in Italy from 888 to 951 during which the largely empty royal title was often claimed by several individuals.

GUIDO (Guy of Spoleto) **889-894.** Never exercised full kingly authority.
BERENGARIUS I (Berengar of Friuli) **888-923,** great-grandson of Carolus; murdered 7 Apr 924. Exercised authority effectively *c* 905-922.
LAMBERTUS co-ruler with Guido **892-894**; sole ruler **894-898,** son of Guido. Never recognised as undisputed ruler.
LUDOVICUS (Louis III of Burgundy and Provence) **899-905,** grandson of Ludovicus.
RODULFUS (Rodolphe II of Burgundy) **922-926** abdicated.
HUGO (of Ivrea) **933-947.**
LOTHARIO II 947-950, son of Hugo.
BERENGARIUS II (Berengar of Ivrea) **950-951/2,** grandson of Berengarius I, b *c* 900; d 966. Deposed when Adelaide, widow of Lothario II, called upon Otto I to redress the ills of Italy.
OTTO (Otto I the Great) **951-973**; see Holy Roman Empire.
(From the time of Otto, the title King of Italy was used by the Holy Roman Emperors as a subsidiary style. Italy broke up into a considerable number of small states from the 13th century and a Kingdom of Italy did not reappear until the 19th century - firstly the Napoleonic Kingdom, preceded by the puppet Italian Republic; secondly, the Kingdom of Italy founded on 17 Mar 1861.)

THE ITALIAN REPUBLIC

Formerly the Cisalpine Republic consisting of Lombardy, Emilia and the Marches and initially founded 29 Jun 1797.

President

NAPOLEONE BUONAPARTE President of the Cisalpine Republic from Jun 1800; President of the Italian Republic **Jan 1802-17 Mar 1805**; see Napoléon I of France.

Vice-President

FRANCESCO MELZI d'ERIL Jan 1802-17 Mar 1805.

THE KINGDOM OF ITALY

The Italian Republic renamed and extended into Venetia.

† King

NAPOLEONE 17 Mar 1805-11 Apr 1814; was also Emperor Napoleon I, France.

Viceroy

Prince **EUGENE de BEAUHARNAIS   7 Jun 1805-Apr 1814**; was also Eugen, Grand Duke of Frankfurt.

THE KINGDOM OF ITALY

† Kings

HOUSE OF SAVOY
Carignano Branch
VITTORIO EMANUELE II King of Sardinia from 23 Mar 1849; King of Italy **17 Mar 1861-9 Jan 1878,** eldest son of Carlo Alberto of Sardinia, b 14 Mar 1820. Vittorio Emanuele (the honest King) was the idol and hope of Italian nationalists. A democrat by temperament rather than conviction, he left government largely to his Premier Cavour whose skill and diplomacy in the French alliance and the war in Habsburg Lombardy against Austria made the King master of north Italy. After secretly encouraging Garibaldi in his efforts to depose the Bourbons of the Two Sicilies and openly encouraging the Central Duchies to revolt against their sovereigns he was proclaimed King of a united Italy which did not include Rome until he invaded that city wresting it from the Papacy (with whom relations were subsequently bitter) in Sep 1870.
UMBERTO I Jan 1878-29 Jul 1900 assassinated, eldest son of Vittorio Emanuele II, b 14 Mar 1844.
VITTORIO EMANUELE III Jul 1900-9 May 1946 abdicated, son of Umberto I, b 11 Nov 1869; d in exile 28 Dec 1947. He failed to prevent Mussolini's Fascists from taking absolute powers, and failed to use the initiative gained by his dismissal and arrest of Mussolini when the Allies invaded Sicily. He also failed to abdicate soon

Benito Mussolini, Duce (dictator) of Italy, who seized power in 1922 by his 'March on Rome' - by train (Popperfoto)

enough to give his dynasty - tarnished through its association with Fascism - the chance to survive.

UMBERTO II 9 May-13 Jun 1946, son of Vittorio Emanuele III, b 15 Sep 1904. He left Italy after a national referendum showed a majority for a Republic.

Prime Ministers

FRANCESCO NITTI 23 Jun 1919-Jun 1920, b 19 Jul 1868; d 20 Feb 1953.

GIOVANNI GIOLITTI 17 Jun 1920-Jun 1921, b 22 Oct 1842; d 17 Jul 1928. Five times Premier he dominated Italy for a generation. Giolitti was against Italian participation in World War I for he knew the country to be unprepared for a campaign. He allowed the Fascists to gather strength when he could easily have crushed the movement at birth.

IVANOE BONOMI Jun 1921-Feb 1922.

LUIGI FACTA 27 Feb-Oct 1922, b 16 Nov 1861; d 5 Nov 1930.

BENITO AMILCARE ANDREA MUSSOLINI 29 Oct 1922-26 Jul 1943, b 29 Jul 1883; d when shot by partisans 28 Apr 1945. The founder of the Fascist party in 1919 his movement quickly gained strength and in Oct 1922 he marched on Rome to seize power. His dictatorship achieved amazing economic progress at a terrible human cost and all the gains were lost in the war. He allied Italy to Nazi Germany and attempted to create an Italian Empire annexing Albania and Ethiopia. The defeat of the Italian forces in North Africa and the subsequent invasion of Sicily led to his dismissal and arrest. Rescued by German paratroopers in a daring raid, he was finally taken by partisans near the Swiss border.

Marshal **PIETRO BADOGLIO 26 Jul 1943-Jun 1944,** b 28 Sep 1871; d 1 Nov 1956. The loser of the World War I battle of Caporetto, Badoglio abolished the Fascist party, surrendered to the Allies and declared war on Germany.

IVANOE BONOMI 9 Jun 1944-Jun 1945, b 18 Oct 1873; d 20 Apr 1951.

FERRUCCIO PARRI 17 Jun-Nov 1945; acting PM **24 Nov-4 Dec 1945,** b 19 Jun 1890.

ALCIDE de GASPERI 4 Dec 1945-18 Jun 1946 when he became PM of the Republic.

THE REPUBLIC OF ITALY

Presidents

ALCIDE de GASPERI acting Head of State **from 18 to 28 Jun 1946.**

ENRICO de NICOLA provisional President **28 Jun 1946-May 1948,** b 9 Nov 1877; d 1 Oct 1959.

LUIGI EINAUDI 12 May 1948-May 1955, b 24 Mar 1874; d 30 Oct 1961.

GIOVANNI GRONCHI 11 May 1955-May 1962, b 10 Sep 1887.

ANTONIO SEGNI 11 May 1962-Dec 1964, b 2 Feb 1891; d 1 Dec 1972.

GIUSEPPE SARAGAT 29 Dec 1964-Dec 1971, b 19 Sep 1898.

GIOVANNI LEONE 2 Dec 1971-15 Jun 1978, b 3 Nov 1908.

AMINTORE FANFANI acting President **15 Jun-Jul 1978.**

ALESSANDRO PERTINI since 9 Jul 1978, b 1898.

Prime Ministers

ALCIDE de GASPERI 18 Jun 1946-Aug 1953, b 3 Apr 1881; d 19 Aug 1954. As a young man he fought against Austrian rule in his native South Tirol; later as a newspaper editor he fought the Fascists and was gaoled. His legacy was the reestablishment of the democratic system in Italy.

GIUSEPPE PELLA 13 Aug 1953-Jan 1954, b 18 Apr 1902.

AMINTORE FANFANI 5-12 Jan 1954; acting PM **12 Jan-8 Feb 1954.**

MARIO SCELBA 8 Feb 1954-Jun 1955, b 5 Sep 1901.

ANTONIO SEGNI 26 Jun 1955-May 1957.

ADONE ZOLI 15 May-18 Jun 1957; acting PM **18-22 Jun 1957;** PM **22 Jun 1957-Jun 1958,** b 16

Dec 1887; d 20 Feb 1960.

AMINTORE FANFANI 25 Jun 1958-Jan 1959; acting PM **26 Jan-9 Feb 1959**, b 6 Feb 1908.

ANTONIO SEGNI 9 Feb 1959-Feb 1960; acting PM **24 Feb-25 Mar 1960**.

FERNANDO TAMBRONI 25 Mar-Jul 1960, b 25 Nov 1901; d 18 Feb 1963.

AMINTORE FANFANI 22 Jul 1960-May 1963; acting PM **16 May-20 Jun 1963**.

GIOVANNI LEONE 20 Jun-Nov 1963; acting PM **5 Nov-5 Dec 1963**.

ALDO MORO 5 Dec 1963-Jun 1968, b 23 Sep 1916; d 8/9 May 1978 having been kidnapped by terrorists.

GIOVANNI LEONE 19 Jun-Nov 1968.

MARIANO RUMOR 26 Nov 1968-Feb 1970; acting PM **7-13 Feb 1970**; PM **13 Feb-3 Mar 1970**; acting PM **3-27 Mar 1970**; PM **27 Mar-Jul 1970**; acting PM **6-25 Jul 1970**, b 6 Jun 1915.

EMILIO COLOMBO 25 Jul 1970-Jan 1972; acting PM **15 Jan-17 Feb 1972**, b 11 Apr 1920.

GIULIO ANDREOTTI 17 Feb 1972-Jun 1973, b 14 Jan 1919.

MARIANO RUMOR 20 Jun 1973-Oct 1974; acting PM **3 Oct-20 Nov 1974**; PM **20 Nov 1974-Feb 1978**; acting PM **Feb-Mar 1978**; PM **since Mar 1978**.

The Kingdom of Etruria

A short-lived puppet state established in Tuscany by the French Emperor Napoleon I.

† Kings

HOUSE OF BOURBON
LODOVICO I Jul 1801-1803, son of Ferdinando, Duke of Parma, b 5 Jul 1773.

LODOVICO II 1803-10 Dec 1807, son of Lodovico I; was also Carlo II, Duchy of Parma and Piacenza.

Florence

The Republic of Florence, established in 1208, came to be dominated by the de 'Medici family who though originally merchants acquired dictatorial powers, a Ducal title and then the Grand Ducal dignity in 1569 when the country became known as Tuscany.

Leaders of the Florentine Republic

COSIMO de 'MEDICI (Cosimo the Elder) **1434-1464**, b 1389; d 1464. Elected Leader of Florence after being proved right in his doubts over the war against Lucca, Cosimo the Elder governed wisely restoring peace and order and patronising the arts.

PIERO I de 'MEDICI 1464-1469, son of Cosimo, b 1414; d 1469.

GIULIANO I de 'MEDICI co-ruler **1469-1478**, brother of Lorenzo I; d in office - assassinated in Florence Cathedral.

LORENZO I de 'MEDICI ('The Magnificent') co-ruler **1469-1478**, sole ruler **1478-1492**, son of Piero I, b 1449; d 1492. In his marriage to a Roman noblewoman he took the de 'Medicis' first step to princely status, indeed, although he remained a commoner, he has been called the ideal Renaissance Prince for his learning, his poetry and his patronage of the arts.

PIERO II de 'MEDICI 1492-Nov 1494 deposed, son of Lorenzo I, b 1471; d 1503.

GIROLAMO SAVONAROLA Nov 1494-1498, b 21 Sep 1452; executed by strangulation 23 May 1498. A passionate orator and the first Vicar-General of the Dominicans, Savonarola tried to set up a Christian commonwealth in Florence but the extravagance of his ascetism alienated some of the Florentines and the vehemence of his criticism of Pope Alexander VI, plus his unorthodox interpretation of the Apocalypse, alienated Church authorities, and he was tried, on charges of heresy, and executed.

PIERO SODERINI 1502-1512, b 1448; d 1552.

GIULIANO II de 'MEDICI 1512-1514, b 1479; d 1516.

LORENZO II de 'MEDICI 1514-1519, son of Piero II de 'Medici, b 1492; d 1519.

GIULIO de 'MEDICI 1519-1523; later Pope Clemens VII.

IPPOLITO de 'MEDICI 1523-1527, grandson of Piero II de 'Medici, b 1511; d 1535.

† Dukes of Florence

ALESSANDRO de 'MEDICI 1531-1537 assassinated, b 1510. The corrupt leader of the de 'Medici, who faced much opposition from the republican opposition, was made Duke by the de 'Medici Pope Clemens VII.

COSIMO de 'MEDICI 1537-1569 when he became Grand Duke of Tuscany; see Cosimo I, Tuscany.

The Principality of Guastalla

A County from 1406, a Duchy from 1621, the tiny (six square miles) state of Guastalla belonged for much of its history to the Gonzaga rulers of Mantua, later passing to Austria and the Spanish Bourbons. Revived as an 'independent' principality in 1806 it had one notorious ruler.

† Princess and Duchess

PAULINE 30 Mar-24 May 1806 abdicated, second surviving sister of Napoleon I, b 20 Oct 1780; d 9 Jun 1825. Obsessed with her own looks, extravagant, beautiful Pauline Bonaparte, famed for her lusts and immortalised in stone by Canova, was amused to become a sovereign but abdicated rather than quit the luxury of Paris.

The Duchy of Lucca

A Roman colony from 177 BC, a Lombard state from the Dark Ages, Lucca was an independent Republic from 1369 to 1797 when it fell to the French. Erected as a sovereign Duchy for Napoleon's sister Elisa, Lucca was the subject of complicated arrangements at the Vienna Settlement, being finally ceded to Tuscany in 1847 by Carlo Lodovico before he regained Parma for his family.

† Dukes

HOUSE OF BACCIOCHI
ELISA sole-ruler **19 Mar-25 Jun 1805**; co-ruler **25 Jun 1805-Mar 1814** deposed, eldest surviving sister of Napoleon I, b 3 Jan 1777; d 7 Aug 1820. Plain, artistic, sarcastic and unusually sparing for a Bonaparte, Elisa ruled her state well, encouraging trade, industry and reforms. She added Tuscany to Lucca and Piombino in 1809 but lost all her thrones in treacherously abandoning Napoleon in 1814.
FELICE co-ruler **25 Jun 1805-Mar 1814** deposed, husband of Elisa, b (Félix Pascal Bacciochi) 18 May 1762; d 27 Apr 1841.

HOUSE OF BOURBON
MARIA LUISA (Duchess) **Nov 1817-13 Mar 1824**, b (a Princess of Spain) 6 Jul 1782. The ugly former Queen of Etruria was awarded Lucca as compensation by the Vienna Settlement.
CARLO LODOVICO Mar 1824-15 Oct 1847 abdicated after a revolt; was also Carlo II of The Duchy of Parma and Piacenza.

The Duchy of Milan

The republican form of government in Milan was replaced by an hereditary Seigniory in 1317 and a Duchy in 1395. Losing its independence in 1535 Milan passed to Spain (1535-1714), Austria (1714-1797), the French dominated Cisalpine Republic (1797-1790 and 1800-1805) and Kingdom of Italy (1805-1814), Austria (1814-1859) and finally to Italy in 1859.

Captains-General of Milan of the Visconti Family

OTTONE 1277-1287, Archbishop of Milan, b 1207; d 1295.
MATTEO I 1287-1302 deposed; restored **1310-1317** when he became hereditary Captain-General and Seignior.

† Hereditary Captains-General and Seigniors of Milan

HOUSE OF VISCONTI
MATTEO I 1317-May 1322 abdicated, great nephew of Ottone, b 1250; d 24 Jun 1322. Having defeated the rival Della Torre family, Matteo I gained the hereditary Seigniory of Milan.
GALEAZZO I May 1322-1328, son of Matteo I, b c 1277.
AZZO 1328-1339, son of Galeazzo I, b 1302.
LUCCHINO co-ruler **1339-1349** assassinated, son of Matteo I, b 1292.
GIOVANNI co-ruler **1339-1354,** son of Matteo I, b 1290. The Archbishop of Milan, Giovanni reunited the Seigniory and added much of Liguria and Emilia.
MATTEO II co-ruler **1354-1355** assassinated, nephew of Giovanni, b c1319.
GALEAZZO II co-ruler **1354-1378,** brother of Matteo II, b c1321. Ruled the SW of the Seigniory from Pavia.
BERNABO co-ruler **1354-1385** assassinated, brother of Matteo II and Galeazzo II, b 1323. Ruled the NE of the Seigniory from Milan.
GIAN GALEAZZO I co-ruler **1378-1385**; sole ruler **1385-1395** when he became duke.

† Dukes of Milan

HOUSE OF VISCONTI
GIAN GALEAZZO I Seignior from 1378; Duke **1395-3 Sep 1402,** son of Galeazzo II, b 1351. He established the Visconti dynasty as 'Royal' by buying the Ducal title from the Emperor and marrying a French Princess. Milan reached its zenith under this ruler who founded the cathedral and extended his sway over Lombardy, Liguria and Emilia.
GIOVANNI MARIA Sep 1402-1412 assassinated, son of Gian Galeazzo I, b 1388. Cruel and insane he undid most of the work of his great father.
FILIPPO MARIA 1412-1447, brother of Giovanni Maria, b 1392. On his death the male line of the Visconti became extinct.
1447-1450 The Ambrosian Republic, named for Milan's patron saint.

HOUSE OF SFORZA
FRANCESCO 26 Feb 1450-8 Mar 1466, son-in-law of Filippo Maria, b 23 Jul 1401. Leader of the Condottiere (mercenaries) of the Ambrosian Republic, Sforza gained high office through his military skill. Overthrowing the Republic he proclaimed himself Duke.
GALEAZZO MARIA Mar 1466-1476 assassinated, son of Francesco, b 1444. Although a cruel despot he was perhaps the most able administrator the Sforzas produced.
GIAN GALEAZZO II 1476-Oct 1494 possibly poisoned, son of Galeazzo Maria, b 1469.
LODOVICO (il Moro) **Oct 1494-1499** deposed, son of Francesco, b 27 Jul 1452; d 27 May 1508. He deposed his sister-in-law as Regent and probably

murdered her son (Gian Galeazzo II) to secure the throne. He was deposed and imprisoned by the French.

1499-1512 French occupation.

MASSIMILIANO   1512-1515 deposed, son of Lodovico, b 1491; d 1530. Restored with Swiss help he reigned briefly before Milan again fell to the French.

1515-1525 French occupation.

FRANCESCO II 1525-1535, brother of Massimiliano, b 1492. Restored after the Battle of Pavia, Francesco was the last Sforza on whose death the Duchy passed to the Emperor Charles V.

The Duchy of Modena

The ancient and illustrious family of Este divided into two branches in the 11th century: one line became the German Welfs, ancestors of Britain's House of Hanover; the other stayed in Italy to rule various territories including the Seigniory of Modena acquired in 1288. Modena was elevated to a Duchy for Borso in 1452 and ceased to exist in 1859 when annexed to Sardinia.

† Dukes

HOUSE OF ESTE

BORSO   1452-1471, b 1413.

ERCOLE I 1471-1505, b 1431.

ALFONSO I 1505-1535, son of Ercole I, b 1486. Remembered as the husband of Lucrezia Borgia, Alfonso's gifts as a soldier, statesman and poet are often ignored.

ERCOLE II 1535-1559, son of Alfonso I, b 1508.

ALFONSO II 1559-1597, son of Ercole II, b 1533.

CESARE   1597-1628, grandson of Alfonso II.

ALFONSO III   1628-1629 abdicated, son of Cesare; d 1644.

FRANCESCO I 1629-1658, brother of Alfonso III, b 1610.

ALFONSO IV 1658-1662, son of Francesco I, b 1634.

FRANCESCO II 1662-Sep 1694, son of Alfonso IV, b 1660.

RINALDO   Sep 1694-26 Oct 1737, uncle of Francesco II, b 25 Apr 1655.

FRANCESCO III Oct 1737-22 Feb 1780, eldest son of Rinaldo, b 2 Jul 1698.

ERCOLE III   Feb 1780-Feb 1797 when Modena was absorbed into the Cispadane Republic; eldest surviving son of Rinaldo, b 22 Nov 1727; d 14 Oct 1823 (having surrendered his rights to his son-in-law, Archduke Ferdinand).

1797-1814 Modena was under French occupation.

1803-1806 Archduke Ferdinand, son-in-law of Ercole III claimed to be sovereign Duke Ferdinando of Modena.

HOUSE OF HABSBURG-LORRAINE OR AUSTRIA-ESTE

FRANCESCO IV   Apr 1814-21 Jan 1846, eldest surviving son of Archduke Ferdinand, b 6 Oct 1779, an Archduke of Austria.

FRANCESCO V Jan 1846-Mar 1860 when Modena was annexed to the Kingdom of Sardinia, son of Francesco IV, b 1 Jun 1819; d 20 Nov 1875 when the Ducal House of Modena became extinct.

The Kingdom of Naples

Part of Roger II's Sicilian realm, the Kingdom of Naples was that part of peninsular Italy retained by the House of Anjou after their expulsion from the island of Sicily. From the start of the 16th century Naples and Sicily usually shared the same sovereign and from Dec 1816 both states were merged in the Kingdom of the Two Sicilies (see The Kingdom of Sicily). The Kings of Naples styled themselves of Sicily.

† Kings

HOUSE OF ANJOU

CARLO I 1265 *de jure*; **1266-1285**; was also Carlo I of the Kingdom of Sicily.

CARLO II 1285-5 May 1309, son of Carlo I, b *c* 1245.

ROBERTO ('The Good') **May 1309-1343,** son of Carlo II.

GIOVANNA I (Queen) **1343-22 May 1382** murdered by suffocation, granddaughter of Roberto, b 1326. The anarchic reign of Queen Giovanna, who may have murdered one of her four husbands, was ended by her deposition and murder by Carlo III.

HOUSE OF ANJOU
Durazzo Branch

CARLO III May 1382-17 Feb 1386, great-grandson of Carlo II; was also Karoly I of Hungary.

LASLO   Feb 1386-6 Aug 1414, son of Carlo III, b 11 Feb 1377.

GIOVANNA II (Queen) **Aug 1414-2 Feb 1435,** daughter of Carlo III, b 1371.

HOUSE OF ANJOU
Lorraine Branch

RINALDO (or RENÉ) Titular King only **Feb 1435-10 Jul 1480,** son of Louis of Anjou to whom Giovanna willed her crown in one of her testaments, b 16 Jan 1409. René, in whose name Naples was governed until 1442, continued his pretensions to the Kingdom in exile.

HOUSE OF TRASTAMARA

ALFONSO I 1442-27 Jun 1458, to whom Giovanna II had willed Naples in an earlier testament; was also Alfonso I of Aragon.

FERRANTE I (or FERDINANDO I) **Jun 1458-25 Jan 1494,** illegitimate son of Alfonso I, b 1423. A

Joachim Murat whose good looks won him the hand of Caroline, sister of Napoléon who gave him the Neapolitan Kingdom (Radio Times Hulton Picture Library)

troubled reign, René tried to regain the throne and a barons' revolt was suppressed with great severity.

ALFONSO II Jan 1494-23 Jan 1495 when forced to abdicate by a French invasion, son of Ferrante I, b 1448; d 1495.

FERRANTE II (or **FERDINANDO II**) **Jan 1495; Jul 1495-5 Oct 1496,** son of Alfonso I, b 26 Jul 1467.

FEDERIGO Oct 1496-1501, uncle of Ferrante II, b 1452; d 1504. Deposed by an invasion of French and Aragonese forces.

1501-1504 Interregnum. Naples disputed by France and Aragon.

FERDINANDO III 1504-23 Jan 1516; was also Fernando V, King of Spain.

GIOVANNA III (Queen) nominally Jan 1516-11 Apr 1555; was also Queen Juana of Spain.

HOUSE OF HABSBURG

CARLO IV Jan 1516-16 Jan 1556; was also Carlos I, King of Spain.

FILIPPO I Jan 1556-13 Sep 1598; was also Felipe II, King of Spain.

FILIPPO II Sep 1598-31 Mar 1621; was also Felipe III, King of Spain.

FILIPPO III Mar 1621-17 Sep 1665; was also Felipe IV, King of Spain.

CARLO V Sep 1665-1 Nov 1700; was also Carlos II, King of Spain.

HOUSE OF BOURBON

FILIPPO IV Nov 1700-1707 *de facto*; continued his claims until 1735; was also Felipe V, King of Spain.

HOUSE OF HABSBURG

GUISEPPE 1707-17 Apr 1711; was also Joseph I, Archduke of Austria.

CARLO VI Apr 1711-May 1735; was also Karl II, Archduke of Austria.

HOUSE OF BOURBON

CARLO VII May 1735-6 Oct 1759; was also Carlos III, King of Spain.

FERDINANDO IV Oct 1759-Mar 1806 and **May 1815-Dec 1816** when he became King of the Two Sicilies; was also Ferdinando I, King of the Two Sicilies.

HOUSE OF BONAPARTE

GIUSEPPE (Joseph Bonaparte) **30 Mar 1806-6 Jun 1808**; was also José, King of Spain.

(In theory Napoleon I was King of Naples from 6 Jun-1 Aug 1806.)

HOUSE OF MURAT

GIOACCHINO NAPOLEONE (Joachim Murat) **1 Aug 1806-19 May 1815** deposed, brother-in-law of Napoleon I, b 25 Mar 1767; executed (shot) 13 Oct 1815. Married to Caroline Bonaparte, perhaps the most ungrateful of Napoleon's grasping relatives, the handsome Murat tried to be a real King rather than the puppet Napoleon intended. His military skill and bravado were matched by his treachery and on the Emperor's downfall he abandoned the French cause in an attempt to save himself but, changing sides again in the Hundred Days, he lost his crown and life. (In 1815 Ferdinando IV was restored as Ferdinando I, King of the Two Sicilies.)

The Duchy of Parma and Piacenza

The cities of Parma and Piacenza with their environs, formerly belonging to the families of Correggio, Este and Visconti, passed into Papal hands in 1511. Pope Paul III (Alessandro Farnese) ceded the territory to his illegitimate son for whom the Emperor raised it to a sovereign Duchy. The little state has had a turbulent history with several changes of dynasty. It was annexed to the Kingdom of Sardinia in 1859.

† Dukes

HOUSE OF FARNESE
PIER-LUIGI 1545-1547 assassinated, illegitimate son of Pope Paul III, b 1503.
OTTAVIO 1547-1586, son of Pier-Luigi, b 1520.
ALESSANDRO 1586-1592, son of Ottavio, b 1545. One of the ablest generals of the 16th century, Alessandro distinguished himself at Lepanto and was appointed Regent of the Netherlands.
RANUCCIO I 1592-1622, son of Alessandro, b 1569.
ODOARDO 1622-1646, son of Ranuccio I, b 1612.
RANUCCIO II 1646-1694, son of Odoardo, b 1630.
FRANCESCO 1694-1727, eldest son of Ranuccio II, b 1678.
ANTONIO 1727-Jan 1731, brother of Francesco, b 1679. Upon his death the male line of the Farnese family became extinct.

HOUSE OF BOURBON
CARLO I Jan 1731-Oct 1735 when he lost Parma by the Third Treaty of Vienna, nephew of Antonio and son of the famed Elizabeth Farnese; was also Carlos III, King of Spain.

HOUSE OF HABSBURG
CARLO Oct 1735-Oct 1740; was also Karl II, Archduke of Austria.
MARIA TERESA (Duchess) **Oct 1740-Oct 1748**; was also Maria Theresia, Archduchess of Austria.

HOUSE OF BOURBON
FILIPPO 18 Oct 1748-18 Jul 1765, younger brother of Carlo I, b 15 Mar 1720. The scheming determination of Elizabeth (Isabella) Farnese to secure her family's Duchies for one of her sons succeeded in 1748 when Don Felippe gained Parma from the Treaty of Aix-la-Chapelle.
FERDINANDO Jul 1765-9 Oct 1802, son of Filippo, b 20 Jan 1751.
1802-1814 Upon Ferdinando's death Parma was annexed to France.

HOUSE OF HABSBURG
MARIA LUISA (Duchess) **Apr 1814-17 Dec 1847,** second wife of Napoléon I, b (a daughter of Franz I of Austria) 7 Dec 1791. Married to the French Emperor as a robust but timid girl, she wished to retire after the First Empire, only accepting Parma to give Napoléon's son (who predeceased her) an inheritance. Ruling Parma well, she consoled herself with two morganatic husbands.

HOUSE OF BOURBON
CARLO II (II rather than III - the 'reign' of Karl II being ignored) **Dec 1847-14 Mar 1849** abdicated, grandson of Ferdinando, b 22 Dec 1799; d 16 Apr 1883. A sovereign who wore and lost three crowns: Etruria was annexed by Napoléon, while he abdicated both Lucca and Parma after deposition in revolts.

CARLO III Mar 1849-27 Mar 1854 assassinated, son of Carlo II, b 14 Jan 1823.
ROBERTO Mar 1854-Jun 1859 when Parma was annexed by the Kingdom of Sardinia, elder son of Carlo III, b 9 Jul 1848; d 16 Nov 1907.

Kingdom of Sardinia

The House of Savoy's efforts against Louis XIV were rewarded in the Treaty of Utrecht by a kingly style - that of Sicily, which was exchanged by the Quadruple Alliance of 1718 for the island of Sardinia. The Kingdom consisted of the island plus Nice, Savoy and Piedmont; after the Napoleonic Wars Liguria was added. The addition of the Central Duchies, Lombardy, the Papal Legations and the Two Sicilies (1859-60) created the Kingdom of Italy.

† Kings

HOUSE OF SAVOY
VITTORIO AMEDEO II Duke of Savoy from Jun 1675; King of Sicily Sep 1713-Aug 1718; King of Sardinia **2 Aug 1718-3 Sep 1730** abdicated, son of Carlo Emanuele II, Duke of Savoy, b 14 May 1661; d 31 Oct 1732 confined by his son after regretting his abdication and attempting to regain the throne. Through diplomacy - subtly changing sides in the wars with Louis XIV to keep with the victors - he enhanced the status of his House and gained the kingly title long coveted by the Dukes of Savoy.
CARLO EMANUELE III Sep 1730-20 Feb 1773, son of Vittorio Amedeo II, b 27 Apr 1701.
VITTORIO AMEDEO III Feb 1773-16 Oct 1796, eldest surviving son of Carlo Emanuele III, b 26 Jun 1726.
CARLO EMANUELE IV Oct 1796-4 Jun 1802 abdicated, eldest son of Vittorio Amedeo III, b 24 May 1751; d 6 Oct 1819. A pious, cautious ruler not capable of confronting the revolutionary French who annexed Piedmont (1798). Retiring to the island of Sardinia, he abdicated to become a Jesuit.
VITTORIO EMANUELE I Jun 1802-13 Mar 1821 abdicated, brother of Carlo Emanuele IV, b 24 Jul 1759; d 10 Jan 1824.
CARLO FELICE Mar 1821-27 Apr 1831, brother of Vittorio Emanuele I, b 6 Apr 1765.

HOUSE OF SAVOY
Carignano Branch
CARLO ALBERTO Apr 1831-23 Mar 1849 abdicated, great-great-great-great-great-grandson of Carlo Emanuele I (see Savoy), b 29 Oct 1798; d in exile 28 Jul 1849. He abdicated after being defeated in his attempt to take Austrian Lombardy.
VITTORIO EMANUELE II Mar 1849-Mar 1861 when he became King of Italy; see Italy.

Savoy

The House of Savoy (originally of Salmourenc) gradually acquired territories in Savoy, Switzerland and Piedmont through marriage and diplomacy. The state became a Duchy in 1417 and having gained the island of Sardinia in 1718 became known as the Kingdom of Sardinia. (See Sardinia.)

† Counts of Maurienne

UMBERTO I Count of Salmourenc from 1003; Count of Maurienne *c* **1034-*c* 1049.** Umberto gained Nyon, Val d'Aosta, Tarentaise, Maurienne and parts of Savoy from the Emperor.

AMEDEO I *c* **1049-*c* 1056,** son of Umberto I.

ODDONE *c* **1056-*c* 1057,** brother of Amedeo I.

PIETRO I *c* **1057-*c* 1078,** son of Oddone.

AMEDEO II *c* **1078-1080,** brother of Pietro I.

UMBERTO II **1080-1103,** son of Amedeo II.

† Counts of Savoy and Margraves of Turin

AMEDEO III **1103-1148 or 1149,** son of Umberto II, b 1095.

UMBERTO III **1148 or 1149-1188 or 1189,** son of Amedeo III, b *c* 1135.

TOMMASO **1188 or 1189-1233,** son of Umberto III, b 1178. Tommaso greatly increased the power of the County gaining Geneva, Vaud and Carignano but he divided the lands between his sons.

AMEDEO IV **1233-1253,** son of Tommaso, b *c* 1197.

BONIFACIO **1253-1263,** son of Amedeo IV, b *c* 1244.

PIETRO II **1263-1268,** son of Tommaso, b *c* 1215. Residing in England after his niece wed Henry III he built the palace later called the Savoy, received an English Earldom and saw his brother become Archbishop of Canterbury.

FILIPPO I **1268-1285,** son of Tommaso, b *c* 1207.

AMEDEO V ('The Great') **1285-1323,** son of Amedeo IV, b *c* 1252.

EDUARDO **1323-1329,** son of Amedeo V, b *c* 1285.

AIMONE **1329-1343,** son of Amedeo V, b 1291.

AMEDEO VI ('The Green Count') **1343-1 Mar 1383,** son of Aimone, b 1334. The Green Count, so called from his green silk clothing, extended Savoy as far north as Neuchâtel, before dying of plague.

AMEDEO VII ('The Red Count') **Mar 1383-1 Nov 1391,** son of Amedeo VI, b 1360. The scarlet cloaked Count captured Nice to give Savoy a coastline.

AMEDEO VIII **Nov 1391-19 Feb 1417** when he became Duke.

† Dukes of Savoy and Piedmont

AMEDEO VIII Count from Nov 1391; Duke **19 Feb 1417-1434** abdicated, son of Amedeo VII, b 1383; d 1451. Having abdicated to become a monk, Amedeo was elected 'Pope' by the illegal Council of Basle. The last anti-Pope from 1439 to 1449 ('Felix V') he was made a Cardinal after resigning his 'office'.

LODOVICO **1434-1465,** son of Amedeo VIII, b 1413.

AMEDEO IX **1465-1472,** son of Lodovico, b 1435.

FILIBERTO I **1472-1482,** second son of Amedeo IX, b 1464 or 1465.

CARLO I **1482-1490,** fourth son of Amedeo IX, b 1468.

CARLO II **1490-1496,** son of Carlo I, b 1489.

FILIPPO II **1496-1497,** son of Lodovico, b 1443.

FILIBERTO II **1497-1504,** son of Filippo II, b 1480.

CARLO III **1504-Aug 1553,** brother of Filiberto II, b 1486.

EMANUELE FILIBERTO **Aug 1553-30 Aug 1580,** son of Carlo III, b 8 Jul 1528. A celebrated soldier and diplomat who freed his state from French control, he transferred his capital from Chambéry to Turin emphasising the growing Italian character of Savoy.

CARLO EMANUELE I ('The Great') **Aug 1580-26 Jul 1630,** son of Emanuele Filiberto, b 12 Jan 1562.

VITTORIO AMEDEO I **Jul 1630-7 Oct 1637,** son of Carlo Emanuele I, b 8 May 1587.

FRANCESCO GIACINTO **Oct 1637-4 Oct 1638,** son of Vittorio Amedeo I, b 14 Sep 1632.

CARLO EMANUELE II **Oct 1638-12 Jun 1675,** brother of Francesco Giacinto, b 20 Jun 1634.

VITTORIO AMEDEO II **Jun 1675-3 Sep 1730;** King of Sicily 22 Sep 1713-2 Aug 1718; King of Sardinia from 2 Aug 1718; see Sardinia.

The Kingdom of Sicily

The Guiscard rulers of Sicily gained the title King in 1130 from anti-Pope Anacletus II. The country passed to German, French and Spanish dynasties, was occupied by several powers and was finally annexed to the lands of the House of Savoy in 1860 (see Italy). For part of its history Sicily has been united with the Kingdom of Naples as the Two Sicilies.

† Counts

HOUSE OF GUISCARD

RUGGIERO I (or ROGER I) **1072-22 Jun 1101,** Roger Guiscard, brother of the Duke of Apulia, b 1031. Taking Sicily from the Arabs, the 'Great Count' established a strong Norman state.

SIMONE (or SIMON) **Jun 1101-1105,** son of Ruggiero I.

RUGGIERO II (or ROGER II) 1105-1130 when he became King.

† Kings

HOUSE OF GUISCARD

RUGGIERO II (or ROGER II) Count from 1105; King 1130-24 Feb 1154, son of Ruggiero I, b 22 Dec 1095. One of the most distinguished monarchs of the Middle Ages, Ruggiero II ruled with cunning, energy and skill to create a united state in Sicily and south Italy whose efficient administration and powerful navy were the envy of Europe. He treated Arab, Greek, Italian and Norman with equal tolerance and his Arab 'civil service' was a wonder of the age.

GUGLIELMO I (or GUILLAUME I) Feb 1154-7 May 1166, son of Ruggiero II, b 1120. Known as 'The Bad'.

GUGLIELMO II (or GUILLAUME II) May 1166-18 Nov 1189, son of Guglielmo I, b 1154. Known as 'The Good'.

TANCREDE Nov 1189-20 Feb 1194, illegitimate grandson of Ruggiero II.

GUGLIELMO III (or GUILLAUME III) Feb-Dec 1194 probably murdered by order of Emperor Heinrich VI 1195; son of Tancrede.

COSTANZA (or CONSTANCE) de jure from Nov 1189; Queen and co-ruler 25 Dec 1194-27 Nov 1198, daughter of Ruggiero II and wife of Emperor Heinrich VI, b 1154.

HOUSE OF HOHENSTAUFEN

ENRICO (or HEINRICH) co-ruler 25 Dec 1194-28 Sep 1197, husband of and co-ruler with Queen Constanza, b autumn 1165. Henry easily conquered his wife's inheritance of Sicily which gave the Hohenstaufen family a valuable power base. This Emperor, who tried to make the imperial dignity hereditary, had a bitter struggle with Henry the Lion of Saxony. He was also Emperor Heinrich VI of the Holy Roman Empire.

FEDERIGO I RUGGIERO or FRIEDRICH Apr 1198-13 Dec 1250, son of Enrico and Queen Costanza, b 26 Dec 1194.

CORRADO I (or KONRAD I) Dec 1250-21 May 1254, son of Federigo I Ruggiero, b 25 Apr 1228; was also Conrad II, King of Jerusalem, and Emperor Konrad IV of The Holy Roman Empire.

CORRADO II (or KONRAD II) May 1254-1258 deposed; 1266-1268 disputed, son of Corrado I, b 25 Mar 1252, beheaded 29 Oct 1268. Natural leader of the anti-Papal Ghibellines, Conrad, the last male member of the Hohenstaufen family, was deposed by his uncle then had to fight for his throne and life against Charles of Anjou whom the Pope had recognised as King. Was also Conrad III, King of Jerusalem and Emperor Konrad V of The Holy Roman Empire.

MANFRED 1258-1266 killed, illegitmate son of Federigo I, b 1232. Usurped the throne but was defeated by Charles of Anjou.

HOUSE OF ANJOU

CARLO I de jure from 1265; de facto 1268-1282 deposed, son of Louis VIII of France, b Mar 1226; d 7 Jan 1285. Granted Naples and Sicily by the Pope, Carlo lost the island after a popular revolt known as the Sicilian Vespers.

HOUSE OF BARCELONA

PIETRO I 1282-1285, son-in-law of Manfred; was also Pedro III of Aragon.

GIACOMO 1285-1295; was also Jaime II of Aragon.

FEDERIGO III 1295-25 Jun 1337, brother of Giacomo, b 1272. Elected King by the Sicilian Parliament, Federigo styled himself III counting Federigo I (the Emperor) as II after his Imperial regnal number.

PIETRO II Jun 1337-1342, son of Federigo III.

LODOVICO 1342-1355, son of Pietro II.

FEDERIGO IV ('The Simple') 1355-1377, descendant of Federigo III, b 1342.

MARIA (Queen) sole ruler 1377-1391; co-ruler 1391-1402, daughter of Federigo IV.

MARTINO I co-ruler 1391-1402; sole ruler 1402-1409, huband of Queen Maria.

MARTINO II 1409-1410, father of Martino I; was also Martin I of Aragon.

1410-1412 Interregnum (see Aragon).

HOUSE OF TRASTAMARA

FERDINANDO I 1412-2 Apr 1416; was also Fernando I of Aragon.

ALFONSO I Apr 1416-27 Jun 1458; was also Alfonso I of Aragon.

GIOVANNI Jun 1458-1460 when he ceded Sicily to his son; was also Juan II of Aragon.

FERDINANDO II (III of Naples) 1460-23 Jan 1516; was also Fernando V, King of Spain.

GIOVANNA (III of Naples) Nominally Queen Jan 1516-11 Apr 1555; was also Queen Juana of Spain.

HOUSE OF HABSBURG

CARLO I (IV of Naples) Jan 1516-16 Jan 1556; was also Carlos I of Spain, and Emperor Karl V of the Holy Roman Empire.

FILIPPO I Jan 1556-13 Sep 1598; was also Felipe II, King of Spain.

FILIPPO II Sep 1598-31 Mar 1621; was also Felipe III, King of Spain.

FILIPPO III Mar 1621-17 Sep 1665; was also Felipe IV, King of Spain.

CARLO II (V of Naples) Sep 1665-1 Nov 1700; was also Carlos II, King of Spain.

HOUSE OF BOURBON

FILIPPO IV Nov 1700-1707 de facto; continued in his claims until 1735; was also Felipe V, King of Spain.

HOUSE OF HABSBURG

GIUSEPPE 1707-17 Apr 1711; was also Joseph I, Archduke of Austria.

CARLO III (VI of Naples) **Apr 1711-Sep 1713**; was also Karl II of Austria.

HOUSE OF SAVOY
VITTORIO AMEDEO Sep 1713-Aug 1718; was also Vittorio Amedeo II, King of Sardinia.

HOUSE OF HABSBURG
CARLO III (VI of Naples) **Aug 1718-May 1735.**

HOUSE OF BOURBON
CARLO IV (VII of Naples) **May 1735-6 Oct 1759**; was also Carlos III, King of Spain.
FERDINANDO III (IV of Naples) **Oct 1759-Dec 1816** when he became King of the Two Sicilies.

† Kings of the Two Sicilies

HOUSE OF BOURBON
FERDINANDO I (formerly IV of Naples and III of Sicily) King of Naples Oct 1759-Mar 1806 and May 1815-Dec 1816; of Sicily Oct 1759-Dec 1816; of the Two Sicilies **8 Dec 1816-4 Jan 1825,** son of Carlo IV (VII), b 12? Jan 1751.
FRANCESCO I Jan 1825-8 Nov 1830, son of Ferdinando I, b 19 Aug 1777.
FERDINANDO II Nov 1830-22 May 1859, eldest surviving son of Francesco I, b 12 Jan 1810. Although Ferdinando II was a despot he was in no way vicious, debauched or uncaring as is still often claimed. His outspoken contempt for radicals made him a bête noir of liberal historians and the gross misrepresentation of his character and actions by Gladstone - who called him a 'negation of God' - was politically motivated. It is true that his troops used bombs in suppressing the 1848 revolt - hence his epithet 'Bomba' - but he was clement - he granted generous pardons and fair trials for the rebels (less than 100 of whom were detained; less than 10 executed).
FRANCESCO II d'ASSISI May 1859-17 Dec 1860 when his Kingdom was annexed by Sardinia, eldest son of Ferdinando II, b 16 Jan 1836; d in exile 27 Dec 1894. When Garibaldi and the Thousand invaded the Two Sicilies, gentle Francesco and his spirited Queen bravely held out at Gaeta until Feb 1861 although the Kingdom was lost.

Tuscany

The Grand Duchy of Tuscany erected for Cosimo I, Duke of Florence, by Pope Paul V in 1569 remained in de 'Medici hands until the extinction of that family in 1737 when it passed to the Duke of Lorraine, the husband of Maria Theresa of Austria. Absorbed into the Kingdom of Etruria in 1801, Tuscany became a Grand Duchy again in 1809 and was annexed to the Kingdom of Sardinia in 1860. (For the earlier rulers of Tuscany see Florence.)

† Grand Dukes

HOUSE OF DE 'MEDICI
COSIMO I 1569-1574, formerly Duke of Florence, b 1519. Cosimo greatly reformed the Florentine state developing the armed forces and the economy and annexing Siena.
FRANCESCO I 1574-1587, son of Cosimo I, b 1541.
FERRANTE I (or FERDINANDO I) **1587-1609,** son of Francesco I, b 1549.
COSIMO II 1609-1621, son of Ferrante I, b 1590.
FERRANTE II (or FERDINANDO II) **1621-24 May 1670,** son of Cosimo II, b 14 Jul 1610. An important scientist he invented a new thermometer and the condensation hygrometer.
COSIMO III May 1670-1723, son of Ferrante II, b 1642.
GIAN GASTONE 1723-9 Jul 1737, son of Cosimo III, b 1671.

HOUSE OF LORRAINE
FRANCESCO II Jul 1737-18 Aug 1765, formerly Francois III of Lorraine, b 8 Dec 1708. The husband of Maria Theresa of Austria.

HOUSE OF HABSBURG-LORRAINE
LEOPOLDO I Aug 1765-21 Jul 1790; was also Leopold II, Archduke of Austria.
FERDINANDO III Jul 1790-9 Feb 1801 deprived of Tuscany; Prince-Elector of Salzburg 26 Dec 1802-25 Dec 1805; Grand Duke of Wurzburg Dec 1805-30 May 1814; restored to Tuscany **May 1814-18 Jun 1824,** second son of Leopoldo I, b 6 May 1769.
1801-1809 Tuscany absorbed into Etruria.

HOUSE OF BONAPARTE
ELISA (Elisa Bonaparte) **3 Mar 1809-1 Feb 1814,** Grand Duchess; was also Elisa, Duchess of Lucca.

HOUSE OF HABSBURG-LORRAINE
FERDINANDO III May 1814-Jun 1824.
LEOPOLDO II 18 Jun 1824-21 Jul 1859 abdicated, son of Ferdinando III, b 3 Oct 1797; d 29 Jan 1870. The popular, liberal Grand Duke was obliged to flee when Tuscany was invaded by Sardinia (1859).
FERDINANDO IV ruler *in absentia* **Jul 1859-22 Mar 1860** when Tuscany was annexed to Sardinia, eldest son of Leopoldo II, b 10 Jul 1835; d 17 Jan 1908.

Venice

The Most Serene Republic of Venice was one of the leading states of the Middle Ages and of the Renaissance. From the 10th century, Venice was the centre of an aristocratic Republic ruled by an absolute but elected sovereign - the Doge. At its height the state included not only Venetia but also much of Lombardy, Dalmatia, Albania, Macedonia and many of the Greek islands. Its independence was ended in 1797 by Bonaparte.

† Doges

GIOVANNI MOCENIGO   1478-1485. From a family which produced five doges, he invited Charles VIII of France to intervene in the wars raging in Italy thus contributing greatly to the disturbances that racked the peninsula in the 15th and 16th centuries.

MARCO BARBARIGO   1485-1486.

AGOSTINO BARBARIGO   1486-1501. He formed the League of Venice to try to expel the French from Italy.

LEONARDO LOREDANO   1501-1521.

ANTONIO GRIMANI   1521-1523.

ANDREA GRITTI   1523-1539.

PIETRO LANDO   1539-1545.

FRANCESCO DONATO   1545-1553.

MARCANTONIO TREVISANO   1553-1554.

FRANCESO VENIER   1554-1556.

LORENZO PRIULI   1556-1559.

GIROLAMO PRIULI   1559-1567.

PIETRO LOREDANO   1567-1570.

ALVISO MOCENIGO I   1570-1577.

SEBASTIANO VENIER   1577-1578. The commander of the Venetian fleet at the Battle of Lepanto in 1571, Venier should get most of the credit for turning the tide of Turkish victory in the Mediterranean.

NICOLO da PONTE   1578-1585.

PASQUALE CICOGNA   1585-1595.

MARINO GRIMANI   1595-1606.

LEONARDO DONATO   1607-1612.

MARCANTONIO MEMO   1612-1615.

GIOVANNI BEMBO   1615-1618.

NICOLO DONA   1618.

ANTONIO PRIULI   1618-1623.

FRANCESCO CENTURIONI   1623-1625.

GIOVANNI CORNARI I   1625-1630.

NICOLO CENTURIONI   1630-1631.

FRANCESCO ERIZZO   1631-1646.

FRANCESCO MOLIN   1646-1655.

CARLO CONTARINI   1655-1656.

BERTUCCIO VALIER   1656-1658.

GIOVANNI PESARO   1658-1659.

DOMENICO CONTARINI   1659-1675. During his term, major losses in the Greek islands, particularly Crete, were sustained.

NICOLO SAGREDO   1675-1676.

ALVISO CONTARINI   1676-1683.

MARCANTONIO GIUSTINIANI   1683-1688.

FRANCESCO MOROSINI   1688-1694.

SILVESTRO VALIER   1694-1700. He played a major role in the defeat of the Turks at Vienna and also took the Peloponnese - these were the last days of glory of Venice, which then entered its final period of decline.

ALVISO MOCENIGO II   1700-1709.

GIOVANNI CORNARI II   1709-1722.

ALVISO MOCENIGO III   1722-1732.

CARLO RUZZINI   1733-1734.

ALVISO PISANI   1734-1741.

PIETRO GRIMANI   1741-1752.

FRANCESCO LOREDANO   1752-1762.

MARCO FOSCARINI   1762-1763.

ALVISO MOCENIGO IV   1763-1779.

PAOLO RENIER   1779-1789.

LODOVICO MANIN   1789-1797, d 1802. The Venetian Republic was overrun by Napoléon Bonaparte during his Italian campaign of 1797 and although Manin and the Senate offered reparation to France the 120th and last Doge was deposed and the Republic 'lent' to Austria.

Ivory Coast

The coast became French in 1842, but a colony was not organised until 1882. Independence as a Republic was granted on 7 Aug 1960.

President

FÉLIX HOUPHOUËT-BOIGNY Head of State and Head of Government **7 Aug-27 Nov 1960;** President and Head of Government **since 27 Nov 1960,** b 18 Oct 1905.

Jamaica

Jamaica was Spanish from 1509 to 1655 when it was taken by the English in whose hands it was confirmed by the Treaty of Madrid (1670). Independence was achieved on 6 Aug 1960.

THE DOMINION OF JAMAICA

Governors-General

Sir **KENNETH BLACKBURNE   6 Aug 1960-19 Oct 1962.**

Sir **CLIFFORD CLARENCE CAMPBELL   19 Oct 1962-1972,** b 1892.

FLORIZEL AUGUSTUS GLASSPOLE   since 1972, b 25 Sep 1909.

Prime Ministers

Sir **ALEXANDER BUSTAMENTE** (born William Alexander Clarke) **6 Aug 1960-22 Feb 1967,** b 24 Feb 1884; d 6 Aug 1977.

Sir **DONALD BURNS SANGSTER   22 Feb 1967-11 Apr 1967,** b 26 Oct 1911; d in office.

HUGH LAWSON SHEARER   11 Apr 1967-2 Mar 1972, b 18 May 1923.

MICHAEL N. MANLEY since 2 Mar 1972, a cousin of Sir Alexander Bustamente, b 10 Dec 1923.

Japan

Traditionally the first Emperor of Japan was Jimmu Tenno, said to be a descendant of the Sun Goddess, but the existence of imperial personalities can only be verified from the time of the Emperor Sujin. Few Emperors have ruled: a military dictatorship (the Shogunate) has held power for much of the country's history. The Tokugawa Shogunate was abolished in 1868 when the Emperor regained ascendancy, but since World War II the monarch has been deprived of all legislative authority. In Japan the Emperor is referred to as 'Tenno Heika' (Heavenly Monarch) and never by his personal name. After death the Emperor is known by his 'nengo', or title, which he selects upon accession - thus the present monarch is never called by his personal name (Hirohito) and his reign will be referred to as Showa (Radiant Harmony).

Emperor Hirohito, who is an eminent marine biologist seen here with Empress Nagako (Popperfoto)

† Emperors

SUJIN ?-30 BC; said to have been crowned in 97 BC.

SUININ AD?-70; said to have been crowned in 29 BC.

KEIKO ?-130; said to have been crowned in AD 71.

SEIMU ?-190; said to have been crowned in 131.

CHUAI ?-200; said to have been crowned in 192. (Interregnum which included the Regency of Jingu Kogo.)

OJIN ?-310; said to have been crowned in 270.

NINTOKU ?-399; said to have been crowned in 313.

RICHU ?-405; crowned 400.

HANZEI ?-410; crowned 406.

INGYO ?-453; crowned 412.

ANKO 453-456.

YURYAKU 456-479.

SEINEI ?-484; crowned 480.

KENZO ?-487; crowned 485.

NINKEN ?-498; crowned 488.

BURETSU 498-506.

KEITAI ?-531; crowned 507.

ANKAN 531-535.

SENKA 535-539.

KIMMEI 539-571.

BIDATSU ?-585; crowned 572.

YOMEI 585-587.

SUSHUN 587-592.

SUIKO (Empress) **592-628.** The power behind the throne in this reign was Prince Shotoku Taishi who did much to introduce Buddhism and many aspects of the Chinese civilisation to Japan.

JOMEI ?-641; crowned 629.

KOGYUKU (Empress) ?-645; crowned 642.

KOTOKU 645-654.

SAIMEI (Empress) ?-661; crowned 655.

TENJI ?-671; crowned 668.

KOBUN 671-672.

TEMMU ?-686; crowned 673. A strong ruler who copied the administrative system of China, used his ritual position in religion to strengthen his authority and codified the civil and criminal laws of Japan.

JITO (Empress) ?-697; crowned 690.

MOMMU 697-707.

GEMMEI (Empress) **707-715.**

GENSHO (Empress) **715-724.**

SHOMU 724-749.

KOKEN/SHOTOKU (Empress) Under the 'nendo' Koken **749-758** when she abdicated; restored under the 'nendo' Shotoku **764-770.**

JUNNIN 758-764.

KONIN 770-781.

KAMMU 781-806. Kammu was the last powerful Emperor before the 'clans' of nobles, particularly the Fujiwara, gained ascendancy, eventually to found the Shogunate and confine the monarch to a splendid isolation at Kyoto. Kammu greatly increased the influence of the central authorities, established a militia and improved the finances.

HEIZEI 806-809.
SAGA 809-823.
JUNNA 823-833.
NIMMYO 833-850.
MONTOKU 850-858.
SEIWA 858-876.
YOZEI 876-884.
KOKO 884-887.
UDA 887-897.
DAIGO 897-930.
SUZAKU 930-946.
MURAKAMI 946-967.
REIZEI 967-969.
EN-YU 969-984.
KAZAN 984-986.
ICHIJO 986-1011.
SANJO 1011-1016.
GO-ICHIJO 1016-1036.
GOSUZAKU 1036-1045.
GOREIZEI 1045-1068.
GOSANJO 1068-1072.
SHIRAKAWA 1072-1086.
HORIKAWA 1086-1107.
TOBA 1107-1123.
SUTOKU 1123-1141.
KONOE 1141-1155.
GOSHIRAKAWA 1155-1158.
NIJO 1158-1165.
ROKUJO 1165-1168.
TAKAKURA 1168-1180.
ANTOKU 1180-1183.
GOTOBA 1183-1198. Following a split in the Fujiwara 'clan', a struggle for power rent the nobility: this reign saw the climax of that contest. Eventually Minamoto Yoritomo set up a military dictatorship (the Shogunate), restored order and reformed the judiciary.
TSUCHIMIKADO 1198-1210.
JUNTOKU 1210-1221.
CHUKYO 1221.
GONORIKAWA 1221-1232.
SHIJO 1232-1242.
GOSAGA 1242-1246.
GOFUKAKUSA 1246-1259.
KAMEYAMA 1259-1274.
GO-UDA 1274-1287.
FUSHIMI ?-1298; crowned in 1288.
GOFUSHIMI 1298-1301.
GONIJO 1301-1308.
HANAZONO 1308-1318.
GODAIGO 1318-1339.
GOMURAKAMI ?-1368; crowned in 1339? The accession of Gomurakami saw the start of 60 years anarchy and civil war stemming from a complicated succession dispute: the northern line of the Imperial family was supported by the Shogun but the junior southern line possessed the authentic Imperial regalia (mirror, jewel and sword).
CHOKEI 1368-1383.
GOKAMEYAMA 1383-1392. Despite the anarchy in the country, the arts flourished in this and the following reign as the culture of the Chinese Ming dynasty began to be experienced in Japan,

largely owing to the influence of the Shogun Ashikaga Yoshimitsu.
GOKOMATSU 1392-1412.
SHOKO 1412-1428.
GOHANAZONO ?-1464; crowned 1429. Despite his long reign, this Emperor, like later generations until Meiji, isolated in an aesthetic court and circumscribed by ceremony, had no influence on the continuous violence or the commercial progress of the period.
GOTSUCHAMIKADO 1465-1500.
GOKASHIWABARA 1500-1526.
GONARA 1526-1557, son of Gokashiwabara, b c 1498. In this reign St Francis Xavier made the first Japanese converts to Christianity and trade with the West began.
OGIMACHI 1557-1586 abdicated, son of Gonara, b 1517; d c 1593.
GOYOZEI 1586-1611 abdicated, grandson of Ogimachi, b 1571; d c 1617.
GOMIZUNO-O 1611-1629 abdicated, son of Goyozei, b 1596; d after 1670. In this reign the Emperor ceased to have any influence and all power passed to the Tokugawa Shogunate.
MEISHO (Empress) 1629-1643 abdicated, daughter of Gomizuno-o, b 1623; d 1696.
GOKOMYO 1643-1654, brother of Meisho, b 1633.
GOSAI 1654-1663 abdicated, brother of Meisho, b 1637; d 1685.
REIGEN 1663-1687 abdicated, brother of Meisho, b 1654; d 1732.
HIGASHIYAMA 1687-1709, son of Reigen, b 1675.
NAKAMIKADO 1709-1735 abdicated, son of Higashiyama, b 1702; d 1737.
SAKURAMACHI 1735-1747 abdicated, son of Nakamikado, b 1720; d 1750?
MOMOZONO 1747-1762, son of Sakuramachi, b 1741.
1762-1763 Interregnum.
GOSAKURAMACHI 1763-1771 abdicated, brother-in-law of Momozono, b 1740; d 1813.
GOMOMOZONO 1771-1779, cousin of Momozono, b c 1758.
KOKAKU 1779-1817 abdicated, cousin of Momozono, b 1771; d 1840.
NINKO 1817-1846, son of Kokaku, b 1800.
KOMEI (personal name OSAHITO) 1846-1866, son of Ninko, b 1831.
MEIJI (personal name MUTSUHITO) Feb 1867-29 Jul 1912, son of Komei, b 3 Nov 1852. In the most momentous reign in Japanese history Meiji ended the Shogunate whose deadening influence had retarded progress. The Emperor turned Japan into a modern state but this intelligent, energetic monarch did not, as is often maintained, assume supreme power himself - the government was placed in the hands of Ministers.
TAISHO (personal name YOSHIHITO) Jul 1912-25 Dec 1926, third but eldest surviving son of Meiji, b 31 Aug 1879.
SHOWA (better known abroad by his personal name HIROHITO) since 25 Dec 1926, son of

Taisho, b 29 Apr 1901. The Emperor is never referred to by his personal name in Japan - after death he will be known by his 'nendo'.

† Tokugawa Shoguns

The *de facto* rulers of Japan from the early 17th century until 1867.

IEYASU TOKUGAWA 1603-1605.
HIDETADA TOKUGAWA 1605-1623. This strong ruler restored order and maintained it by obliging the war lords to leave hostages at his court. Xenophobic, he closed the ports and expelled most of the Europeans.
IEMITSU TOKUGAWA 1623-1651.
IETSUNA TOKUGAWA 1651-1680.
TSUNAYOSHI TOKUGAWA 1680-1709.
IENOBU TOKUGAWA 1709-1713.
IETSUGU TOKUGAWA 1713-1716.
YOSHIMUNE TOKUGAWA 1716-1745.
IESHIGE TOKUGAWA 1745-1761.
IEHARU TOKUGAWA 1761-1787.
IENARI TOKUGAWA 1787-1838.
IEYOSHI TOKUGAWA 1838-1853.
IESADA TOKUGAWA 1853-1858.
IEMOCHI TOKUGAWA 1858-1866.
KEIKI TOKUGAWA 1866-Nov 1867 when the Emperor Meiji abolished the post of Shogun, b 1827; d 1913.

Prime Ministers

TAKASHI HARA Sep 1918-4 Nov 1921, b 1865; d in office.
Count **YASUYA UCHIDA 4-13 Nov 1921.**
Count **KOREKIYO TAKAHASHI Nov 1921-Jun 1922,** b 1854; d 1936.
Baron **TOMO SABURO KATO Jun 1922-24 Aug 1923,** b 1859; d in office.
Admiral Count **GOMBEI YAMAMOTO Aug 1923-Jan 1924,** b 1852; d 8 Dec 1933.
Viscount **KEIGO KYOURA Jan-Jun 1924,** b 1850; d 1942.
Viscount **TAKAAKIRA KATO Jun 1924-Aug 1925,** b 1860; d Jan 1926.
Baron **REIJIRO WAKATSUKI Aug 1925-Apr 1927,** b 1866; d Nov 1949.
GIICHI TANAKA Apr 1927-Jul 1929, b 1863; d 30 Sep 1929.
OSACHI HAMAGUCHI Jul 1929-Apr 1931, b 1870; d 26 Aug 1931 of wounds received in an assassination attempt in Nov 1930.
Baron **REIJIRO WAKATSUKI Apr-Dec 1931.**
TSUYOSHI INUKAI 13 Dec 1931-16 May 1932 when assassinated, b 1855.
Admiral Viscount **MAKOTO SAITO 26 May 1932-Jul 1934,** b 1858; assassinated 26 Feb 1936.
Admiral **KEISUKE OKADO 3 Jul 1934-Feb 1936,** b 1862; d 1952.
Count **FUMIO GOTO 26-29 Feb 1936.**
Admiral **KEISUKE OKADO 29 Feb-9 Mar 1936.**
KOKI HIROTA 9 Mar 1936-Jan 1937, b 1878; d Dec 1948.

Gen **SENJURO HAYASHI Feb-Jun 1937,** b 1870; d 1943.
Prince **FUMINARO KONOYE 6 Jun 1937-Jan 1939,** b 1891; committed suicide following his arrest as a war criminal 16 Dec 1945. He continued the war against China and during his second Ministry he established a totalitarian pro-Axis state.
Count **KIICHIRO HIRANUMA 4 Jan-Aug 1939,** b 1867; d Aug 1952.
Gen **NOBUYUKI ABE 28 Aug 1939-Jan 1940,** b 1875; d 7 Sep 1953.
Admiral **MITSUMASA YONAI 14 Jan-Jul 1940,** b 1880; d 1948.
Prince **FUMINARO KONOYE 18 Jul 1940-Oct 1941.**
Lieut-Gen **HIDEKI TOJO 17 Oct 1941-Jul 1944,** b 1884; executed as a war criminal 24 Dec 1948. Tojo ruthlessly planned war to gain Japan a large zone of occupation in the Pacific and Far East ('Greater East Asia Co-Prosperity Sphere'). The treacherous attack on Pearl Harbour (7 Dec 1940) gave Japan temporary advantages in the Pacific but it was a major political error to unite the Americans against the Axis powers in this way. He resigned after Japanese reverses in New Guinea and the Carolines.
Gen **KUNIAKI KOISO 18 Jul 1944-Apr 1945,** b 1879; d 1950.
Admiral Baron **KANTARO SUZUKI 5 Apr-15 Aug 1945,** b 1867; d 1948. Suzuki resigned the day following Japan's surrender.
Aug 1945-28 Apr 1952. Japanese Governments functioned under the authority of the Allied Commander-in-Chief of the Forces of Occupation. From 1952 Japan regained her sovereignty.
Prince **NARUHIKO HIGASHIKUNI Aug 16-Oct 1945,** b 1887. The son-in-law of Emperor Meiji, the Prince was the only member of the Imperial Family to be Premier.
Baron **KIJURO SHIDEHARA 6 Oct 1945-May 1946,** b 17 Aug 1872; d 10 Mar 1951. A democrat and diplomat who had taken no part in public life during the war, Shidehara was an important moderating influence who sought to replace the 'old order'.
ICHIRO HATOYAMA 2 May 1946 - his appointment was not allowed by Gen MacArthur, the Allied Commander-in-Chief.
TETSU KATAYAMA 2-15 May 1946; unable to form a Government.
SHIGERU YOSHIDA 15 May 1946-May 1947, b 22 Sep 1878; d 20 Oct 1967.
TETSU KATAYAMA 23 May 1947-Feb 1948, b 1887.
HITOSHI ASHIDA 21 Feb 1948-Oct 1948 when he resigned, and was later arrested because of a financial scandal, b 1887; d 20 Jun 1959.
SHIGERU YOSHIDA Oct 1948-Dec 1955.
ICHIRO HATOYAMA 9 Dec 1955-Dec 1956.
TANZAN ISHIBASHI 20 Dec 1956-Feb 1957, b 25 Sep 1884; d 24 Apr 1973.
NOBUSUKE KISHI 24 Feb 1957-Jul 1960, b 23 Nov 1896.

HAYATO IKEDA   Jul 1960-Nov 1964, b 3 Dec 1899; d 13 Aug 1965.
EISAKU SATO   9 Nov 1964-Jul 1972, the brother of Nobusuke Kishi (each adopted the family name of his wife), b 27 Mar 1901; d 2 Jun 1975.
KAKEUI TANAKA   5 Jul 1972-Dec 1974, b 4 May 1918.
TAKEO MIKI   9 Dec 1974-Dec 1976, b 17 Mar 1907.
TAKEO FUKUDA   since 24 Dec 1976, b 14 Jan 1905.

Jerusalem, Kingdom of *see*
Crusader States

Jordan

The lands east of the Jordan belonging to the Ottoman Empire from 1516 were occupied by British forces during World War I. Transjordan was occupied by the British from 1918 to 1923 when it became a protectorate under Emir Abdullah ibn Hussein. Independence was gained on 22 Mar 1946 and the name of the state was changed to Jordan on 2 Jun 1949.

† Kings

HASHEMITE DYNASTY
ABDULLAH ibn HUSSEIN   Emir from 1923; sovereign Emir 22 Mar-25 May 1946; King **25 May 1946-20 Jul 1951** assassinated, son of King Hussein of the Hejaz, b 1881. The creator of Jordan, he incurred the wrath of some Palestinians - one of whom murdered him - by his moderate policies and his annexation of the West Bank.
TALAL ibn ABDULLAH   Jul 1951-11 Aug 1952 when deposed as medically unfit to reign, b 1911; d 9 Jul 1972.
HUSSEIN ibn TALAL   since 11 Aug 1952, son of Talal, b 14 Nov 1935.

Prime Ministers

The title Pasha was not used after 1952.

SAYED PASHA el-MUFTI   13 Apr-Dec 1950.
SAMIR PASHA RIFAI   3 Dec 1950-Jul 1951.
TEWFIK PASHA ABULHUDA   25 Jul 1951-May 1953.
Dr **FAWZI el-MULKI   5 May 1953-May 1954.**
TEWFIK ABULHUDA   2 May 1954-May 1955.
SAYED el-MUFTI   30 May-Dec 1955.
HAZZA el-MAJALI   14-19 Dec 1955.
IBRAHIM HASHIM   19 Dec 1955-8 Jan 1956.
SAMIR RIFAI   8 Jan-May 1956, b 1898.
SAYED el-MUFTI   22 May-2 Jul 1956, b 1898.
IBRAHIM HASHIM   2 Jul-Oct 1956.

King Abdullah (seated) who created a Kingdom from the ruins of Turkish power in Transjordan after World War I (Radio Times Hulton Picture Library)

SULIMAN NABULSI   29 Oct 1956-Apr 1957, b 1910; d 14 Oct 1976.
Dr **HUSSEIN KHALIDI   11-13 Apr 1957.**
Dr **NIMR   13-15 Apr 1957.**
Dr **HUSSEIN KHALIDI   15-24 Apr 1957,** b 1895; d 1962.
IBRAHIM HASHIM   24 Apr-19 May 1957, b 1888; d 14 Jul 1958 murdered in Baghdad during the Iraqi revolution.
SAMIR RIFAI   19 May 1957-May 1959.
HAZZA el-MAJALI   5 May 1959-29 Aug 1960, b 1917; d in office - assassinated.
BAHJAT TALHOUNI   29 Aug 1960-Jan 1962.
WASFI al-TELL   27 Jan 1962-Mar 1963.
SAMIR RIFAI   28 Mar-21 Apr 1963, b 1901; d 1965.
Sherif **HUSSEIN bin NASSER   21 Apr 1963-Jul 1964,** great-uncle of King Hussein.
BAHJAT TALHOUNI   6 Jul 1964-Feb 1965.
WASFI al-TELL   13 Feb 1965-Mar 1967.
Sherif **HUSSEIN bin NASSER   5 Mar-24 Apr 1967.**
SAAD JUMAA   24 Apr-Oct 1967, b 21 Mar 1916.
BAHJAT TALHOUNI   7 Oct 1967-Mar 1969.
ABDUL MONEIM RIFAI   21 Mar-Aug 1969, brother of Samir Rifai, b 1917.
BAHJAT TALHOUNI   12 Aug 1969-Jun 1970, b 1913.
ABDUL MONEIM RIFAI   28 Jun-16 Sep 1970.

Brig **MOHAMMED DAOUD   16-26 Sep 1970**; d
1972.
AHMED TOUKAN   26 Sep-28 Oct 1970, b 1903.
WASFI al-TELL   28 Oct 1970-28 Nov 1971, b 1918;
d in office - murdered by Palestinians.
AHMED LOUZI   29 Nov 1971-May 1973.
ZAID RIFAI   26 May 1973-Jul 1976, son of Samir
Rifai, b 27 Nov 1936.
MUDAR BADRAN   since 13 Jul 1976, b 1934.

Judah and Judaea *see* Israel

Jugoslavia *see* Yugoslavia

Kakheth *see* Georgia

Karthli *see* Georgia

Kent *see* Anglo-Saxon Kingdoms, United Kingdom

Kenya

Once known as the British East African Protectorate, Kenya was not annexed to the Crown until
1920. Independence was granted on 12 Dec 1963
and a Republic was declared on 12 Dec 1964.

THE DOMINION OF KENYA

Governor-General

**MALCOLM MacDONALD   12 Dec 1963-12 Dec
1964, b** 1901.

Prime Minister

JOMO KENYATTA   12 Dec 1963-12 Dec 1964
when he became the first President.

THE REPUBLIC OF KENYA

President

JOMO KENYATTA   since 12 Dec 1964, b 1889?
d. 22 August 1978.

Vice-Presidents

OGINGA ODINGA   12 Dec 1964-14 Apr 1966.
JOSEPH MURUMBI   3 May 1966-Jan 1967.
DANIEL T. ARAP MOI   since Jan 1967.

Khans, The Great *see* Mongol Empire

Khmer Republic *see* Cambodia

Kish *see* Babylonia

Knights of Malta *see* Malta

Korea

The three Kingdoms of Koguryo, Paekche and
Silla were united to form a single Korean Kingdom
in AD 676 but soon fell apart again. Reunited in 936
as the Koryo Kingdom the country was ruled by
the Koryo Dynasty until 1392 and then by the Yi
Dynasty until 1910. However, the state seldom
enjoyed sovereignty being subject to the Chinese
Emperors. Independent again from 1894 the
Korean Kingdom of Choson was transformed into
the Empire of Taehan in Oct 1894, became a
Japanese protectorate in Dec 1905 and was
annexed by Japan on 22 Aug 1910. Following
Japanese rule the country was divided along the
line of the 38th parallel in 1945: north of the line
Soviet forces set up the Korean People's
Democratic Republic; south of the parallel the
Republic of Korea was established with American
support.

THE KINGDOM OF CHOSON

† King of Choson

Yı Dynasty
KOJONG (YI T'AE WANG) King from 1864;
sovereign King **1876-Oct 1894** when he became
Emperor of Taehan.

THE EMPIRE OF TA'EHAN

† Emperors of Taehan

19|7|07

Yı Dynasty
KOJONG (YI T'AE WANG) King from 1864;
Emperor **Oct 1894-1907** abdicated; under Japane-
se protection from Dec 1905, b 1852; d late 1907.
He attempted to open Korea to western
influences but, despite the nationalist fervour
after the establishment of the Taehan Empire, he
failed to prevent the country coming under
Japanese control.
SUJONG   1907-Aug 1910, son of Kojong.
Aug 1910-May 1945 Japanese rule.

May 1945 Korea partitioned between Soviet and American forces.

THE REPUBLIC OF KOREA
(South Korea)

Presidents

Dr SYNGMAN RHEE 20 Jul 1948-Apr 1960, b (Lee Sung Man) 26 Mar 1875; d 19 Jul 1965. A descendant of the Yis, he fought Japanese rule and can be said to have virtually founded the Korean Republic; an authoritarian ruler he quarrelled with his American allies as he wished to continue the Korean War which began when the North Koreans invaded in 1950.
HUH CHUNG acting President 27 Apr-12 Aug 1960; see Prime Minister Huh Chung.
YOON BO SUN 12 Aug 1960-Mar 1962, b c 1899.
Gen PARK CHUNG HI since 22 Mar 1962, b 17 Nov 1917.

Prime Ministers

Gen LEE BUM SUK 4 Aug 1948-Mar 1950.
Dr JOHN MYUN CHANG 23 Mar 1950-Apr 1952, b 1899; d 1966.
CHANG PAIK SONG Apr-Oct 1952.
PAIK TOO CHIN Oct 1952-Jun 1954, b 1909.
PYUN YUNG TAI Jun-Oct 1954.
(The post of Premier was abolished in 1954 but recreated by constitutional amendment in Apr 1960.)
HUH CHUNG 27 Apr-19 Aug 1960, b ?1900.
Dr JOHN MYUN CHANG 19 Aug 1960-16 May 1961 deposed in coup.
16-21 May 1961 Supreme Council for National Reconstruction.
Lieut-Gen CHANG DO YUNG 21 May-3 Jul 1961.
Maj-Gen SONG YO CHAN 3 Jul 1961-Jun 1962.
Gen PARK CHUNG HI 18 Jun-10 Jul 1962; see President Park.
KIM HYUN CHUL 10 Jul 1962-Dec 1963.
Dr CHOI DOO SUN 12 Dec 1963-May 1964, b 1904.
Gen CHUNG IL KWON 11 May 1964-Dec 1970, b 21 Nov 1917.
PAIK TOO CHIN 19 Dec 1970-Jun 1971.
KIM CHONG PIL 3 Jun 1971-Dec 1975, b 7 Jan 1926.
CHOI KYU HAH since 19 Dec 1975, b 16 Jul 1919.

Korean People's Democratic Republic (North Korea)

The Korean People's Democratic Republic was proclaimed on 9 Sep 1948 in the Soviet occupied zone of Korea.

Presidents

KIM DU BON Sep 1948-1957, b 1889.
CHOI YONG KUN 1957-Dec 1972, b 1900.
Marshal KIM IL SUNG since Dec 1972, b (Kim Sing Ju) 15 Apr 1912.

Prime Ministers

Marshal KIM IL SUNG 11 Sep 1948-Dec 1972; see President Kim Il Sung.
KIM IL Dec 1972-Apr 1976.
PARK SUNG CHUL Apr 1976-Dec 1977
LI JONG OK since 17 Dec 1977.

General Secretary of the Korean Workers' Party
(Communist Party)

Marshal KIM IL SUNG since Sep 1948; see President Kim Il Sung.

Kotte, Kingdom of see Sri Lanka

Koyunlu Sultans, The see Iran

Krakow, Grand Duchy of see Poland

Kurunegala, Kingdom of see Sri Lanka

Kuwait

The Gulf State of Kuwait, under Ottoman protection until World War I and then under British protection, was recognised as a sovereign state on 19 Jun 1961.

† Emirs

SABAH DYNASTY
ABDULLAH es-SALEM es-SABAH 19 Jun 1961-24 Nov 1965, b 1892.
SABAH al-SALEM al-SABAH Nov 1965-31 Dec 1977, b 1913.
JABIR al-AHMED al-JABIR es-SABAH since 31 Dec 1977, b 1928.

Prime Ministers

ABDULLAH es-SALEM es-SABAH 17 Jan 1962-Jan 1963; see Emir Abdullah.
Shaikh SABAH al-SALEM al-SABAH 27 Jan 1963-Dec 1965; see Emir Sabah.

Shaikh **JABIR al-AHMED al-JABIR es-SABAH Dec 1965-Feb 1978**; see Emir Jabir.

Shaikh **SAAD al-AHMED es-SABAH since 7 Feb 1978,** Crown Prince of Kuwait.

Lagash *see* Babylonia

Laos

A Laotian state (Lan Xang) flourished from the 14th to the 17th centuries but was then partitioned into three: Luang Prabang, Vientiane and Champassak. These territories became French protectorates in 1893 and were formally annexed in 1904 and 1907. In 1946 the King of Luang Prabang became King of an autonomous Kingdom of Laos which became independent from France on 22 Oct 1953. In May 1975 there was a Communist coup and in Nov 1975 the Communist People's Democratic Republic of Laos was established.

THE KINGDOM OF LAOS

† Kings

SISAVANG VONG King of Luang Prabang from 1905; of an autonomous Laos from 1946; of a sovereign state **22 Oct 1953-29 Oct 1959,** b 14 Jul 1885.

SAVANG VATTHANA Oct 1959-29 Nov 1975 abdicated, son of Sisavang Vong, b 13 Nov 1907.

Prime Ministers

Prince **SOUVANNA PHOUMA 22 Oct 1953-Nov 1954.**

KATHAY DON SASORITH 25 Nov 1954-Mar 1956.

Prince **SOUVANNA PHOUMA 21 Mar 1956-Jun 1957.**

KATHAY DON SASORITH 3 Jun-2 Jul 1957.

BONG SOUVANNAVONG 2-6 Jul 1957; acting PM **6 Jul-9 Aug 1957.**

Prince **SOUVANNA PHOUMA 9 Aug 1957-Aug 1958.**

PHOUI SANANIKONG Aug 1958-31 Dec 1959.

Gen **PHOUMI NOSAVAN** acting PM **1-7 Jan 1960.**

KOU ABHAY 7 Jan-30 May 1960; acting PM **30 May-2 Jun 1960.**

Prince **TIAO SOMSANITH 2 Jun-9 Aug 1960** deposed in coup.

Prince **SOUVANNA PHOUMA Aug-Dec 1960** fled in civil war.

Prince **BOUN OUM NA CHAMPASSAK Dec 1960-Jun 1962,** b 11 Dec 1911.

Prince **SOUVANNA PHOUMA 23 Jun 1962-19 Apr 1964** deposed in coup.

Gen **KHOUPRASITH ABHAY** *de facto* Head of Government **19-24 Apr 1964.**

Prince **SOUVANNA PHOUMA 24 Apr 1964-2 Dec 1975** deposed by Communists, half-brother of Souphanouvong, b 7 Oct 1901.

THE PEOPLE'S DEMOCRATIC REPUBLIC OF LAOS

President

SOUPHANOUVONG since 2 Dec 1975, half-brother of Prince Souvanna Phouma, b (Prince Souphanouvong) 1902.

Prime Minister

KAYSONE PHOMVIHAN since 2 Dec 1975, b 1920.

La Plata, United Provinces of
see Argentina

Latin Empire, The *see* Byzantine Empire

Latvia

The Land of the Letts, corresponding to the ancient states of Kurland and Livonia, passed to the Teutonic Knights in the 13th century and to Poland-lithuania in 1561. Kurland remained Polish while Livonia became Swedish in 1629. Both territories subsequently passed to Russia - Livonia in 1710, Kurland in 1795. The Letts achieved their freedom during the Russian Revolution although independence was not formally declared until 18 Nov 1918 and was not recognised by Soviet Russia until 11 Aug 1920. The Republic was forcibly incorporated into the USSR after a rigged election 5 Aug 1940.

Provisional Heads of State

VOLDEMARS ZAMUELS Nov 1917-Nov 1918.

KARLIS ULMANIS 18 Nov 1918-Apr 1919.

ANDRIEVS NIEDRA Apr-Jul 1919.

KARLIS ULMANIS Jul 1919-Jun 1921.

ZIGFRIDS MEIEROVICS Jun-Nov 1921.

JAN CHAKSTE Nov 1921-Sep 1922.

Presidents

JAN CHAKSTE Sep 1922-14 Mar 1927, b 1859; d in office.

GUSTAVS ZEMGALS Mar 1927-Apr 1930, b 1871; d 1939.

ALBERT KVIESIS 9 Apr 1930-Apr 1936, b 1881; d 1944.

KARLIS ULMANIS 9 Apr 1936-Jun 1940, b Sep 1877; deported to the USSR he is assumed to have been murdered at a place and date unknown. In the increasing tension of eastern Europe Latvia became unstable until Ulmanis established a strict but effective nationalist dictatorship. He was forced to resign when the invading Russians took Latvia.

Provisional Head of State

Prof **AUGUSTUS KIRCHENSTEINS 22 Jun-5 Aug 1940.**

Prime Ministers

HUGO CELMINS Dec 1928-Mar 1931, b 1877; fate unknown - he was deported after the Soviet takeover.

KARLIS ULMANIS Mar-Nov 1931.

MARGERS SKUJENIEKS Nov 1931-Feb 1933, b 1886; fate uncertain - he was said to have been deported after the Soviet invasion.

ADOLFS BLODNIEKS Feb 1933-Mar 1934, b 1890; d 1962 in exile.

KARLIS ULMANIS Mar 1934-Jun 1940.

Prof **AUGUSTUS KIRCHENSTEINS Jun-Aug 1940.**

Lebanon

A French mandated territory from 1920, and formerly part of the Ottoman Empire, the Lebanon became an independent Republic on 1 Jan 1944.

Presidents

BISHARA al-KHURI 1 Jan 1944-Sep 1952, b 1891; d 11 Jan 1964.

CAMILLE CHAMOUN 23 Sep 1952-Sep 1958, b 3 Apr 1900.

Gen **FUAD CHEHAB 23 Sep 1958-Sep 1964,** b 9 Mar 1902; d 25 Apr 1973. Perhaps the most successful Lebanese President, he promoted good relations between the various religious groups, quelled revolts and provided good, honest and stable government.

CHARLES HÉLOU 23 Sep 1964-Aug 1970, b 24 Sep 1912.

SULEIMAN FRANJIEH 17 Jun 1970-Sep 1976, b 14 Jun 1910.

ELIAS SARKIS since 13 Sep 1976.

Prime Ministers

RIAD SOHL 1 Jan 1944-Dec 1944.

ABDUL HAMED KARAMI Jan-Aug 1945.

SAMI SOHL Aug 1945-May 1946, b 1888; d 1968.

SAADI MOUNLA 22 May-Dec 1946.

RIAD SOHL 15 Dec 1946-Feb 1951, b 1894; assassinated 16 Jul 1951.

HUSSEIN OUENI 14 Feb-Jun 1951.

Dr **ABDULLAH AREF al-YAFI 5 Jun 1951-Feb 1952,** b 1901.

SAMI SOHL 2 Feb-Sep 1952, brother of Riad Sohl.

NAZIM AKKARI 9-15 Sep 1952; caretaker PM 15-18 Sep 1952.

Gen **FAUD CHEHAB 18-24 Sep 1952;** caretaker PM 24 Sep-1 Oct 1952.

KHELAB CHEBAB 1 Oct 1952-Apr 1953.

SAEB SALAM 29 Apr-16 Aug 1953.

Dr **ABDULLAH AREF al-YAFI 16 Aug 1953-Sep 1954.**

SAMI SOHL 17 Sep 1954-Sep 1955.

RASHID ABDUL HAMID KARAMI 19 Sep 1955-Mar 1956, b 1921.

Dr **ABDULLAH AREF al-YAFI 20 Mar-Nov 1956.**

SAMI SOHL 16 Nov 1956-Sep 1958.

RASHID ABDUL HAMID KARAMI 23 Sep 1958-May 1960.

AHMED DAOUK 14 May-Oct 1960.

SAEB SALAM Oct 1960-Oct 1961, b 1905.

RASHID ABDUL HAMID KARAMI 31 Oct 1961-Feb 1964.

HUSSEIN OUENI 20 Feb 1964-Jul 1965, b 1900; d 1971.

RASHID ABDUL HAMID KARAMI 20 Jul 1965-Apr 1966.

Dr **ABDULLAH AREF al-YAFI 5 Apr-Dec 1966.**

RASHID ABDUL HAMID KARAMI 7 Dec 1966-Feb 1968.

Dr **ABDULLAH AREF al-YAFI 5 Feb 1968-Jan 1969.**

RASHID ABDUL HAMID KARAMI 8 Jan 1969-Oct 1970.

SAEB SALAM 7 Oct 1970-Apr 1973.

Dr **AMIN HAFEZ 18 Apr-14 Jun 1973,** b 1911.

TAKIEDDINE SOHL 14 Jun 1973-Oct 1974, b 1909.

RASHID SOHL 24 Oct 1974-May 1975, b 1926.

Brig **NOUREDDIN RIFAI 23-26 May 1975.**

RASHID ABDUL HAMID KARAMI 26 May 1975-Dec 1976.

Dr **SELIM al-HOSS since 9 Dec 1976,** b 1930.

Leon *see* Spain

Lesotho

Lesotho, the former British protectorate of Basutoland - established on 12 Mar 1868 at the request of Paramount Chief Moshoeshoe I (who is regarded as the founder of the Sotho Nation), gained independence as a sovereign Kingdom on 4 Oct 1966.

† King

Constantine Bereng Seeiso **MOTLOTLEHI MOS-HOESHOE II** Paramount Chief since 1940; Sovereign King **since 4 Oct 1966,** b 2 May 1938.

Prime Minister

Chief **JOSEPH LEBUA JONATHAN since 4 Oct 1966,** b 30 Oct 1914.

Liberia

Founded as a home for freed American slaves wishing to return to Africa, Liberia was granted independence on 26 Jul 1847.

Presidents

JOSEPH JENKINS ROBERTS Jul 1847-1856, b 1809; d 1876. Called 'The Father of Liberia' he is regarded as the founder of the independent nation.
STEPHEN ALLEN BENSON 1856-1864.
DANIEL WARNER 1864-1868.
JAMES SPRIGG PAYNE 1868-1870.
EDWARD JAMES ROYE 1870-1871 when he was removed from office by impeachment, b 1815; d 1872.
JAMES SMITH 1871-1872.
JOSEPH JENKINS ROBERTS 1872-1876.
JAMES SPRIGG PAYNE 1876-1878.
ANTHONY GARDINER 1878-1883.
ALFRED RUSSELL 1883-1884.
HILLARY JOHNSON 1884-1892.
JOSEPH CHEESEMAN 1892-1896.
WILLIAM COLEMAN 1896-1900, b 1842; d 1900.
GARRETT GIBSON 1900-1904.
ARTHUR BARCLAY 1904-1912.
DANIEL HOWARD 1912-1920.
CHARLES KING 1920-1930, b 1875; d 1961.
EDWIN BARCLAY 1930-6 May 1944, b 1882; d in office.
WILLIAM VACANARARAT SHADRACH TUBMAN 6 May 1944-23 Jul 1971 14, b 1895; d in office. President Tubman introduced many reforms and in particular improved the lot of the native peoples of the interior who form the majority of the population.
WILLIAM RICHARD TOLBERT acting President **23 Jul 1971-Jan 1972;** President **since 3 Jan 1972,** b 13 May 1913.

Libya

Italian involvement in Libya began in 1888 but Cyrenaica, Fezzan and Tripolitania were not ceded to Italy by the Ottoman Empire until 1912. Libya became a United Nations mandated territory after World War II and an independent Kingdom on 24 Dec 1951. In 1969 Libya became a Republic styled the Libyan Arab Republic from 1 Sep 1969; the Libyan Arab People's Republic from 22 Nov 1976 and the Popular Socialist Libyan Arab State of the Masses from 2 Mar 1977.

THE KINGDOM OF LIBYA

† King

IDRIS I 24 Dec 1951-1 Sep 1969 deposed in coup, formerly Emir of Cyrenaica, b 13 Mar 1890.

Prime Ministers

MAHMUD MUNTASSER 24 Dec 1951-Feb 1954.
MOHAMMED SAQIZLY 15 Feb-8 Apr 1954.
MUSTAFA HALIM 8 Apr 1954-May 1957.
ABDUL MAJID COOBAR 26 May 1957-Oct 1960.
MOHAMMED bin-OTHMAN al SAID Oct 1960-Mar 1963.
Dr **MOHIEDDINE FEKINI 20 Mar 1963-Jan 1964.**
MAHMUD MUNTASSER 22 Jan 1964-Mar 1965.
HUSAIN MAZIQ 21 Mar 1965-Jul 1967.
ABDEL KADER al BADRI Jul-Oct 1967.
ABDEL HAMID BAKKOUCHE Oct 1967-Sep 1968.
WANIS al GEDDAFI Sep 1968-1 Sep 1969 deposed in coup.

THE LIBYAN ARAB REPUBLIC

Now the Popular Socialist Libyan Arab State of the Masses.

President

Col **MU'AMMAR MUHAMMAD al-GADDAFI** Chairman of Revolutionary Council **Sep 1969-2 Mar 1977;** President **since 2 Mar 1977,** b 1941.

Prime Ministers

Dr **MAHMOUD SULAIMAN al MAGHRABI 8 Sep 1969-Jan 1970,** b 1935.
Col **MU'AMMAR MUHAMMAD al-GADDAFI 16 Jan 1970-Jul 1972.**
Maj **ABDUL SALAM AHMED JALLUD 10 Jul 1972-Mar 1977,** b 15 Dec 1944.
ABDULLAH OBEIDI since 22 Mar 1977.

The Principality of Liechtenstein

The Liechtensteins, one of the leading families of the Holy Roman Empire, acquired their Princely titles nearly a century before they gained their present Principality. Prince Johann Adam obtained Schellenberg (northern Liechtenstein) in 1699 and Vaduz (southern Liechtenstein) in 1712, but they were not united as a single state until 1719. Today Liechtenstein remains as the last of over a hundred German-speaking monarchies that once flourished in central Europe.

† Princes

JOHANN ADAM Head of the Princely Family of Liechtenstein from 1689; Ruler of all of present day Liechtenstein **Feb-16 Jun 1712,** b 16 Aug 1662. Founder of the Principality.

JOSEPH WENZEL Ruler of Liechtenstein **Jun 1712-1718** when he ceded its territory to Anton Florian; a cousin of Johann Adam, b 9 Aug 1696. A distinguished soldier, he fought the Turks beside Eugene of Savoy; a connoisseur he laid the foundations of what is probably the finest private art collection in the world.

ANTON FLORIAN Ruler of Liechtenstein **1718-23 Jan 1719;** Sovereign Prince **23 Jan 1719-11 Oct 1721,** uncle of Joseph Wenzel, b 28 May 1656.

JOSEPH JOHANN Oct **1721-17 Dec 1732,** son of Anton Florian, b 27 May 1690.

JOHANN KARL Dec **1732-22 Dec 1748,** son of Joseph Johann, b 8 Jul 1724.

JOSEPH WENZEL Dec **1748-10 Feb 1772.**

FRANZ JOSEPH I Feb **1772-18 Aug 1781,** nephew of Joseph Wenzel, b 19 Nov 1726.

ALOYS I Aug **1781-24 Mar 1805,** eldest surviving son of Franz Joseph I, b 14 May 1759.

JOHANN I Mar **1805-20 Apr 1836,** brother of Aloys I, b 27 Jun 1760. A soldier-Prince Johann I played an important role in the Austrian armies fighting Napoleon I. He is remembered for his gallantry at Wagram and for the part he played framing the Treaty of Pressburg.

ALOYS II Apr **1836-15 Nov 1858,** eldest son of Johann I, b 26 May 1796.

JOHANN II Nov **1858-11 Feb 1929** - the longest reign in a European dynasty still sovereign, elder son of Aloys II, b 5 Oct 1840. Johann, called the Good, greatly developed the Principality using his private wealth liberally although he lost most of the family estates in Bohemia in 1918.

FRANZ Feb **1929-25 Jul 1938,** brother of Johann II, b 28 Aug 1853.

FRANZ JOSEPH II since **25 Jul 1938,** great-nephew of Franz, b 16 Aug 1906.

Prime Ministers

Dr **ALEXANDER FRICK** **1945-Jul 1962.**
Dr **GERARD BATLINER** **16 Jul 1962-Feb 1970,** b 9 Dec 1928.
Dr **ALFRED HILBE** Feb **1970-Mar 1974,** b 22 Jul 1928.
Dr **WALTER KIEBER** **27 Mar 1974-Feb 1978,** b 9 Dec 1931.
HANS BRUNHART since **4 Feb 1978,** b 1946.

Lippe *see* Germany

Lithuania

The Lithuanian state was united during the 13th century and through the marriage of Jogaila with Queen Jadwiga of Poland entered a personal union with that country with which it was eventually merged in 1569. Lithuania fell to Russia in the partition of Poland and did not regain its independence until 11 Nov 1918. Like the other two Baltic Republics Lithuania was forcibly incorporated into the Soviet Union in 1940.

THE GREAT DUCHY OF LITHUANIA

† Supreme Dukes of the Lithuanians

MINDAUGAS **1236-1263;** from 1253 King; murdered with his family by the Samogitians. Mindaugas united the Lithuanians within one state.

1263-1290 Period of anarchy - the country subdivided again.

VYTENIS **1290-1316.** Reunited Lithuania.

GEDIMINAS **1316-1341,** brother of Vytenis, b c 1275. He greatly extended Lithuania incorporating much of the Ukraine to make the state one of the largest in Europe.

JAUNUTIS **1341-1345** deposed, son of Gediminas; subsequent fate unknown.

ALGIRDAS **1345-1377,** son of Gediminas.

JOGAILA **1377-1381** deposed, son of Algirdas; became Wladyslaw II, King of Poland.

KESTUTIS **1381-1382** probably killed by Jogaila whom he had deposed in 1381; son of Gediminas, b c 1300.

JOGAILA **1382-1387** when he ceded Lithuania as a fief to Vytautas.

† Supreme Dukes of the Lithuanians
(de facto Viceroys)

VYTAUTAS **1387-1430,** kinsman of Jogaila (Wladyslaw II), b 1350.

WLADYSLAW III of Poland *c* **1430-1440,** was also Wladyslaw III, King of Poland.

KAZIMIERZ IV of Poland **1440-1492**; was also Kazimierz IV, King of Poland.
1492-1569 The reigns of the Kings of Poland coincide with their reigns as Supreme Dukes of Lithuania.
1569 The two Countries were formally united.
1569-1795 Polish rule.
1795-1918 Russian rule.

PROVISIONAL GOVERNMENT

(Prince Wilhelm of Urach, a junior member of the Royal House of Wurttemberg, was declared King *in absentia* in Jul 1918. Proclaimed as MINDAUGAS II his accession was annulled in Nov 1918 and he cannot be said to have reigned.)

Heads of Government

AUGUSTINAS VOLDEMARAS Nov-Dec 1918, b 16 Apr 1883; d Dec 1942. The most controversial modern Lithuanian leader, Voldemaras played a major role in the fight for independence and the war against Poland for the city of Vilnius. After involvement in a coup he was dictator under Smetona (1926-9), was later tried for treason and following acquittal was detained for attempting a further coup.
MYKOLAS SLEZEVICIUS Dec 1918-Mar 1919, b 1882; d 1939.
PRANAS DOVYDAITIS Mar-Apr 1919, b 1886; d 1942.

Presidents

ANTONAS SMETONA Apr 1919-Dec 1922.
ALEKSANDRAS STULGINSKIS Dec 1922-Jun 1926, b 1885; d 1969.
Dr **KAZYS GRINIUS 8 Jun-17 Dec 1926** deposed in coup, b 1866; d 1950.
ANTONAS SMETONA Dec 1926-Jun 1940, b 10 Aug 1874; d 9 Jan 1944. Smetona removed the controversial dictator Voldemaras from office in 1929 and established a corporate dictatorship with himself as leader. He was obliged to flee when the Russians invaded in 1940.

Prime Ministers

AUGUSTINAS VOLDEMARAS Dec 1926-Sep 1929.
Dr **JUOZAS TUBELIS Sep 1929-Mar 1938,** b 1882; d 1939.
Fr **VLADAS MIRONAS Mar 1938-Mar 1939,** b 1880; d 1954? - a prisoner in a Russian gaol. An army chaplain.
Gen **JONAS CERNIUS 28 Mar-Oct 1939,** b 1898.
Dr **URBSYS** acting PM **Oct-Nov 1939.**
Dr **ANTONAS MERKYS Nov 1939-15 Jun 1940,** b 1887; d 1955?
Gen **RASHTIKIS** acting PM **15-17 Jun 1940.**

Dr **PALECKIS** acting PM. **17 Jun-3 Aug 1940** when Lithuania was forcibly incorporated into the USSR.

Lodi Kingdom *see* India

Lombard Kingdom *see* Italy

Lorraine *see* France

Lubeck *see* Oldenburg, Germany

Lucca *see* Italy

Luxembourg

Luxembourg was founded on 12 or 17 Apr 963 when lands around the present City were granted by the Abbey of St-Maximin to Sigefroi, son of the Count of the Ardennes. The County of Luxembourg, a Duchy from 1354, passed to a Limburg family traditionally known as the House of Luxembourg who achieved a kingly crown in Bohemia and the imperial style. In 1443 the Duchy passed to Burgundy and ceased to exist as a separate country. Ruled by Spain (1506-1684), France (1684-1697), Spain again (1697-1714), Austria (1714-1795) and France again (1795-1814 during which time Luxembourg was known as the 'Département des Forêts'), the country was re-established in 1814 as a Grand Duchy to be ruled by, but independent from, the Netherlands. In 1839 the western part of the state was lost to Belgium; in 1890 an independent dynasty was established in the country as the Dutch Queen Wilhelmina was unable to succeed under the Luxembourgeois Constitution.

THE COUNTY OF LUXEMBOURG
(originally Lützelburg)

† Counts

HOUSE OF THE ARDENNES
SIGEFROI Apr 963-998. Sigefroi, whom legend says was wed to a mermaid, built the first castle at Luxembourg and is regarded as the country's founder.
HENRI I 998-1026.
HENRI II 1026-1047.
GISELBERT 1047-1059.
CONRAD I 1059-1086.
HENRI III 1086-1096.
GUILLAUME 1096-1129.

CONRAD II 1129-1136.

HOUSE OF NAMUR
HENRI IV 1136-1196.
ERMESINDE (Countess) 1196-1247. A remarkably able ruler who added territories to the County and revived the state after the misrule of a succession of absentee Counts who bankrupted it.

HOUSE OF LUXEMBOURG
Sometimes called the House of Limburg.

HENRI V 1247-1281, b 1217.
HENRI VI 1281-1288.
HENRI VII 1288-24 Aug 1313, son of Henri VI; was also Emperor Heinrich VII of The Holy Roman Empire.
JEAN I Aug 1313-26 Aug 1346, son of Henri VII; was also Ján, King of Bohemia.
CHARLES Aug 1346-1353, son of Jean I; was also Karel, King of Bohemia.
VENCESLAS I 1353-1354 when he became Duke.

THE DUCHY OF LUXEMBOURG

† Dukes

HOUSE OF LUXEMBOURG
VENCESLAS I Count from 1353; Duke 1354-1383, son of Jean I, b 1337.
VENCESLAS II 1383-1388; 1411-1412, son of Charles; was also Václav IV, King of Bohemia.

Rulers of Various Houses

JOBST ('The Moravian') 1388-1411 deposed, nephew of Charles, b 1351; d 17 Jan 1411.
ANTON co-ruler 1412-1415.
ELISABETH (Duchess) co-ruler 1412-1415; sole ruler 1415-1419.
JEAN II (John of Bavaria) 1419-1425.
ELISABETH (Duchess) 1425-1443 when the Duchy passed to Burgundy.
1443-1506 Burgundian rule.
1506-1684 Spanish rule.
1684-1697 French rule.
1697-1714 Spanish rule.
1714-1795 Austrian rule.
1795-1814 French rule.
(It would not be correct to regard a list of the rulers of the above countries as a list of Dukes of Luxembourg for the period 1443 to 1814 as some of those rulers adopted the title while others granted the title to various dignities as a title of nobility: neither group used a separate regnal number for Luxembourg.)

THE GRAND DUCHY OF LUXEMBOURG

† Grand Dukes

HOUSE OF ORANGE
GUILLAUME I 9 Jun 1815-7 Oct 1840 when he abdicated; was also Willem I, King of the Netherlands.
GUILLAUME II 7 Oct 1840-17 Mar 1849; was also Willem II, King of the Netherlands.
GUILLAUME III 17 Mar 1849-23 Nov 1890; was also Willem III, King of the Netherlands.

HOUSE OF NASSAU-WEILBURG
ADOLPHE I 23 Nov 1890-17 Nov 1905, Sovereign Duke of Nassau (1839-66), great-grandson of Carolina, the daughter of Willem IV Friso, Prince of Orange; b 24 Jul 1817 as Prince Adolf of Nassau. Having sided with Austria in the Austro-Prussian War, he lost his Duchy which was annexed to Prussia (1866); he became sovereign again at the age of 73 and served his adopted country with great devotion becoming a Luxembourger 'from the bottom of my heart'.
GUILLAUME IV 17 Nov 1905-25 Feb 1912, only son of Adolphe, b 22 Apr 1852.
MARIE-ADÉLAÏDE (Grand Duchess) 25 Feb 1912-5 Jan 1919 when she abdicated, eldest daughter of Guillaume IV, b 14 Jun 1894; d 24 Jan 1924. Having ended the personal union with the Netherlands in 1890 by adhering to Salic Law, Luxembourg abandoned that system of inheritance to allow Marie-Adélaïde to succeed; she abdicated following criticism of her war leadership, and became a nun.
CHARLOTTE (Grand Duchess) 5 Jan 1919-12 Nov 1964 when she abdicated, second daughter of Guillaume IV, b 23 Jan 1896.
JEAN I since 12 Nov 1964, elder son of Grand Duchess Charlotte, b 5 Jan 1921.

Prime Ministers

JOSEPH BECH Jul 1926-Jun 1937.
PIERRE DUPONG Jun 1937-May 1940 in Luxembourg; 10 May 1940-Sep 1944 in exile; 23 Sep 1944-22 Dec 1954 in Luxembourg, b 1885; d in office.
JOSEPH BECH acting Premier 22-29 Dec 1954; Premier 29 Dec 1954-Mar 1958, b 12 Feb 1887; d 8 Mar 1975. A much respected international figure, Dr Bech was Foreign Secretary for an eventful 33 years.
PIERRE FRIEDEN 29 Mar 1958-10 Dec 1968; caretaker Premier 10 Dec 1968-Feb 1969, b 1892; d in office - 23 Feb 1969.
PIERRE WERNER 25 Feb 1969-Jun 1974, b 29 Dec 1913.
GASTON THORN since 1 Jun 1974, b 3 Sep 1928.

Joseph Bech, the Luxembourgeois statesman, who was a popular and influential colleague of the Allied leaders in World War II (Radio Times Hulton Picture Library)

Lydia

A Kingdom of ancient Asia Minor said to have been ruled by three dynasties: the first was mythical; the second is now known to represent a period of Hittite rule; the third created a powerful independent state.

† Kings

MERMNAD DYNASTY
GYGES *c* 690 BC.
SADYATTES ?-*c* 619 BC, son of Gyges?
ALYATTES *c* 619-*c* 560 BC, son of Sadyattes.
CROESUS *c* 560-*c* 546 BC deposed, son of Alyattes: probably d after 546 BC in exile in Persia. He gained his proverbial wealth by conquering much of western Anatolia; he lost his empire, and tried to commit suicide on a funeral pyre, on the Persian invasion of 546 BC.

Macedonia *see* Greece

Madagascar

The Imérina monarchy unified the island *c* 1810 but was abolished by the French colonial authorities who established a protectorate in 1895. Independence, as the Malagasy Republic, was achieved on 26 Jun 1960 and the country was renamed the Democratic Republic of Madagascar on 30 Dec 1975.

THE KINGDOM

† Kings

RADAMA I 1810-1828. With his father Andrianimpoinimerina, Radama threw off the yoke of the warlike Sakalavas and unified the island. He encouraged British missionaries and abolished the slave trade.
RANAVALONA I (Queen) **1828-1861.** She persecuted the Christians and established a reign of terror.
RADAMA II 1861-1863 when he was assassinated, son of Ranavalona I.
RASOAHERINA (Queen) **1863-1868,** widow of Radama II.
RANAVALONA II (Queen) **1868-1883.** She encouraged the conversion of her people to Christianity.
RANAVALONA III (Queen) **1883-1896** when the monarchy was abolished, b 1862; d in exile 1917. The French completed their conquest of Madagascar on 30 Sep 1895, but a serious revolt in the following year caused them to remove the Queen who was the focus of nationalist feelings.

THE REPUBLIC

Presidents

PHILIBERT TSIRANA 26 Jun 1960-11 Oct 1972, b 12 Oct 1912; d 16 Apr 1978.
Maj-Gen **GABRIEL RAMANANTSOA 11 Oct 1972-5 Feb 1975,** b 13 Apr 1906.
Col **RICHARD RATSIMANDRAVA 5-11 Feb 1975,** b 21 Mar 1931; d in office - assassinated.
Brig-Gen **GILLES ANDRIAMAHAZO 12 Feb-15 Jun 1975** President of the National Military Directorate, b 5 May 1919.
Lieut-Commander **DIDIER RATSIRAKA** President of the Supreme Council of the Revolution **15 Jun-30 Dec 1975**; President *per interim* of the Democratic Republic of Madagascar **30 Dec 1975-4 Jan 1976**; President **Since 4 Jan 1976**, b 4 Nov 1936.

Prime Ministers

PHILIBERT TSIRANA 26 Jun 1960-18 May 1972.
Maj-Gen **GABRIEL RAMANANTSOA 18 May 1972-5 Feb 1975.**
Col **RICHARD RATSIMANDRAVA 5-11 Feb 1975** when he was assassinated.
Brig-Gen **GILLES ANDRIAMAHAZO 12 Feb-15 Jun 1975**; President of the National Military Directorate.

Lieut-Commander **DIDIER RATSIRAKA** Premier
per interim **15 Jun 1975-Jan 1976.**
Col **JOËL RAKOTOMALALA 11 Jan-30 Jul 1976**
when he was killed in a helicopter accident.
JUSTIN RAKOTONIAINA since 12 Aug 1976.

Magadhan Kingdom *see* India

Magyars, Princes of the *see*
Hungary

Malagasy Republic *see* Madagascar

Malawi

The British Central Africa Protectorate was
established in 1891; renamed Nyasaland in 1907 the
territory was joined in federation with Rhodesia
from 1953 to 1963. Independence was granted on 6
Jul 1964 and a Republic declared on 6 Jul 1966.

THE DOMINION OF MALAWI

Governor-General

Sir **GLYN SMALLWOOD JONES 6 Jul 1964-5 Jul
1966,** b 1908.

Prime Minister

Dr **HASTINGS KAMUZU BANDA 6 Jul 1964-6 Jul
1966** when he became President.

MALAWI

President

Dr **HASTINGS KAMUZU BANDA since 6 Jul
1966,** b 1906.

Malaysia

British sovereignty in the Malay peninsula began in
1786 when Penang was acquired. Malacca became
a colony in 1824 and by 1874 the Sultanates of the
peninsula had become protectorates. On 31 Aug
1957 the Malay states became an independent
member of the Commonwealth. On 16 Sep 1963
Malaya was joined in federation by Sabah (North
Borneo), Sarawak and Singapore (which seceded
in 1965) to form Malaysia.

MALAYA

Heads of State

The Yang di Pertuan Agong - Supreme Head of the
Federation - is an elected Sovereign with the style
of 'Majesty'. The 'elected King' of Malaya and
now of Malaysia serves as Head of State for five
years.

ABDUL RAHMAN (Besar of Negri Sembilan) **31
Aug 1957-1 Apr 1960,** b 1895; d in office.
HISAMUDDIN ALAM SHAH (Sultan of Selangor)
acting Sovereign **4-14 Apr 1960**; Sovereign **14
Apr-1 Sep 1960**; d in office.
SYED PUTRA ibni Almarhum Syed Hassan
Jamalullail (Raja of Perlis) **Sep 1960-16 Sep 1963**
when he became Sovereign of Malaysia.

Prime Ministers

Tuanku **ABDUL RAHMAN 31 Aug 1957-Apr 1959.**
Dato **ABDUL RAZAK** bin Dato Hussein **16 Apr-21
Aug 1959.**
Tuanku **ABDUL RAHMAN 21 Aug 1959-16 Sep
1963** when he became PM of Malaysia.

MALAYSIA

Heads of State

SYED PUTRA ibni Almarhum Syed Hassan
Jamalullail (Raja of Perlis) **16 Sep 1963-Sep 1965,**
b 16 Oct 1920.
ISMAIL NASIRUDDIN SHAH ibni Al-Marhum
Sultan Zainal Abidin (Sultan of Trengganu) **21
Sep 1965-Sep 1970,** b 24 Mar 1907.
ABDUL HALIM MU'AZZAM SHAH ibni Al-
Marhum Sultan Badishah (Sultan of Kedah) **21
Sep 1970-Sep 1975,** b 28 Nov 1927.
YAHYA PUTRA ibni Al Marhum Sultan Ibrahim
(Sultan of Kelantan) **since 21 Sep 1975,** b 10 Dec
1917.

Prime Ministers

Tuanku **ABDUL RAHMAN 16 Sep 1963-Sep 1970,**
b (a member of the Royal House of Kedah) 8 Feb
1903.
Tuanku **ABDUL RAZAK** bin Dato Hussein **22 Sep
1970-14 Jan 1976,** b 1922; d in office.
Datuk **HUSSEIN bin ONN since 15 Jan 1976,**
brother-in-law of Abdul Razak, b 12 Feb 1922.

The Maldive Islands

A former British-protected Sultanate, the Maldives
became an independent Republic on 26 Jul 1965.

President

Amir **IBRAHIM NASIR   since 26 Jul 1965,** b 2 Sep 1926.

Mali

The French colony of Soudan, opened up between 1880 and 1895, joined Senegal in the Mali Federation (1959) which achieved independence on 20 Jun 1960. Senegal withdrew from Mali on 20 Aug 1960 leaving Soudan to assert its independence and adopt the name of the federation on 22 Sep 1960.

Presidents

MODIBO KEITA   22 Sep 1960-19 Nov 1968 when he was deposed in a coup, b 4 Jun 1915; d 17 May 1977.
Lieut **MOUSSA TRAORE** (later Col) Chairman of the National Liberation Committee **20 Nov 1968-19 Sep 1969**; President and Head of Government **since 19 Sep 1969,** b 25 Sep 1936.

Prime Ministers

MODIBO KEITA   Premier of the Mali Federation and Soudan 20 Jun-22 Sep 1960; Premier of Mali **22 Sep 1960-19 Nov 1968** when he was deposed in a coup.
Captain **YORO DIAKITÉ   21 Nov 1968-19 Sep 1969.**
Lieut **MOUSSA TRAORE** (later Col) Premier **since 19 Sep 1969**; concurrently President.

Malta

Before being taken by the Arabs (870), Malta was held by the Phoenicians, Greeks, Carthaginians and Romans. After being held by Sicily (1090-1530), the islands were given by Charles V to the Knights of St John who had been expelled from Rhodes by the Turks. The French took Malta in 1798 but lost it when the Maltese revolted, aided by the British. A British Crown colony from 1814, independence was achieved on 21 Sep 1964 and a Republic declared on 13 Dec 1974.

† Grand Masters of the Sovereign Order of the Knights of St John of Malta

PIETRO da PONTE 1534-1535.
DESIDERIUS de SAINT-JAILE 1535-1536.
JEAN d'HOMEDES 1536-1553.
JEAN PARISOT de la VALETTE 1557-28 Aug

Grand Master la Valette whose spirited defence of Malta saved the island from the Turks (Radio Times Hulton Picture Library)

1568, b 1494. The capital of Malta is named after the most famous Grand Master la Valette who held the fortifications heroically during the celebrated Seige of Malta (1565). Outnumbered four to one by the Turks he maintained his position until the seige was lifted by the Neapolitans.
PIETRO da MONTÉ 1568-1572.
JEAN LEVESQUE de la CASSIÈRE 1572-1586.
HUGO VERDALE de LOUBENS 1586-1595.
MARTIN de GARZEZ 1595-1601.
ALOF de WIGNACOURT 1601-1622.
LUIZ MENDEZ de VASCONCELLOS 1622-1623.
ANTONIO de PAULE 1623-1636.
PAUL LASCARIS CASTELLARD 1636-1657.
MARTIN de REDIN 1657-1660.
ANNET de CLERMONT 1660.
RAPHAEL COTONER 1660-1663.
NICOLAS COTONER 1663-1680.
GREGORIO CARAFFA 1680-1690.
ADRIEN de WIGNACOURT 1690-1697.
RAIMON PERELLOS y ROCCAFOL 1697-1720.
MICHELE ANTONIO ZONDONARI 1720-1722.
ANTONIO MANUEL de VILHENA 1722-1736.
RAIMON   DESPUIZ   de   MONTENEGRE 1736-1741.

MANUEL PINTO de FONSECA 1741-1773.
FRANCISCO XIMENES de TEXADA 1773-1775.
EMMANUEL de ROHAN 1775-1797.
FERDINAND von HOMPESCH 1797-1798.
(The Knights of Malta continue as a Sovereign
Order in Rome but without that necessary territory
to be regarded as a state.)

DOMINION OF MALTA GC

Governors-General

Sir **MAURICE HENRY DORMAN 21 Sep 1964-21
Jun 1971,** b 1912.
Sir **ANTONY J. MAMO 5 Jul 1971-13 Dec 1974,**
became the first President of the Maltese
Republic.

Prime Ministers

**GEORGE BORG OLIVIER 21 Sep 1964-21 Jun
1971,** b 5 Jul 1911.
DOMINIC MINTOFF 21 Jun 1971-13 Dec 1974
continued in office as first Premier of the
Republic, b 6 Aug 1916.

THE REPUBLIC OF MALTA

Presidents

ANTONY J. MAMO 13 Dec 1974-27 Dec 1976, b 9
Jun 1909.
Dr **ANTON BUTTIGIEG since 27 Dec 1976,** b
1908.

Prime Minister

DOMINIC MINTOFF since 13 Dec 1974.

Manchuria *see* China

Maratha State *see* India

Maurienne *see* Savoy, Italy

Mauritania

Mauritania became a French protectorate in 1903
and an independent Republic on 28 Nov 1960.

Presidents and Premiers

MOKHTAR OULD DADDAH Head of State and
Premier **28 Nov 1960-20 Aug 1961**; President and

Premier **20 Aug 1961-10 Jul 1978** deposed in coup,
b 25 Dec 1924.
Col **MUSTAFA OULD SALEK** Head of Government and acting Head of State **since 11 Jul 1978.**

Mauritius

Known to the Arabs in the 10th century and the
Malays in the 15th century, it was not visited by
Europeans until the Portuguese landed in the early
1500s. Mauritius was settled by the Dutch in 1598
but abandoned by them in 1710. The French
occupied the island from 1715 to 1810 when it
became British. Mauritius became independent on
12 Mar 1968.

Governors-General

Sir **JOHN SHAW RENNIE 12 Mar 1968-Dec 1968.**
Sir **ARTHUR LEONARD WILLIAMS Dec 1968-27
Dec 1972**; d in office.
Sir **RAMAN OSMAN since Dec 1972,** first
Mauritian Governor-General, b 1902.

Prime Minister

Sir **SEEWOOSAGUR RAMGOOLAM since 12
Mar 1968,** b 18 Sep 1900.

Mauryan Empire *see* India

Mecklenburg-Schwerin *see* Germany

Mecklenburg-Strelitz *see* Germany

Media *see* Iran

Mercia *see* Anglo-Saxon Kingdoms, United Kingdom

Mexico

The empire of the people of the Mexica (since the
18th century universally referred to as the Aztecs)
began in 1345 and lasted until the Spanish
expedition of Cortes overthrew the society in 1520.
Spanish Mexico achieved independence on 24 Aug
1821 by the Treaty of Cordoba. Mexico was an
Empire from 1822 to 1823 and again from 1864 to

1867 - for the rest of its independent history the nation has been a Republic with varying forms of governmental system.

THE AZTECS
(The People of the Mexica)

The Mexica entered the valley of Mexico c 1168 but their chief city, Tenochtitlan, was not founded until 1345. The Aztec Empire was a 'federal' phenomenon - the combined tributary territories of Tenochtitlan, Tlatelolco and Texcoco - under the sovereignty of the Tlatoani, or Emperor, of Tenochtitlan.

† Rulers of Texcoco

IXTLILXÓCHITL 1409-1418; d in battle.
NEZAHUALCÓYOTL 1418 de jure; 1431-1472 de facto, son of Ixtlilxóchitl.
NEZAHUALPILLI 1472-1515, son of Nezahual-cóyotl, b 1465.
CACAMA 1515-1520 d in battle.

† Rulers of the Tepanecs

An Aztec people who were briefly the supreme city state of the Mexico Valley in the early 15th century.

TEZOZÓMOC 1418-1426; supreme ruler from 1418 but succeeded earlier.
MAXTLA 1426-1431 killed by Nezahualcóyotl, son of Tezozómoc.

Tlatoani (Rulers) of Tenochtitlan

† Emperors

TENOCH 1345-c 1372. Preist-King of the Mexica.
ACAMAPICHTLI c 1372-1391. A Toltec Prince adopted by the Mexica.
HUITZILHUITL 1391-1415, son of Acamapichtli.
CHIMALPOPOCA 1415-1426 when taken prisoner by Maxtla; son of Huitzihuitl; executed 1428.
ITZCÓATL 1426-1440, son of Acamapichtli, b c 1380. By defeating the Tepanecs he made the Mexica supreme in the Valley of Mexico and effectively began the Aztec Empire.
MOCTEZUMA I ILHUICAMINA 1440-1486, son of Huitzilhuitl, b c 1410. This ruler extended the empire as far as the Gulf Coast.
AXAYÁCATL 1468-1481, grandson of Itzcóatl, b c 1449.
TIZOC 1481-1486 probably murdered, elder brother of Axayácatl, b before c 1449.
AHUITZOTL 1486-1502, younger brother of Axayácatl, b after 1450. A heroic warrior he extended the empire to cover nearly all modern Mexico.
MOCTEZUMA II XOCOYOTZIN 1502-Jun 1520 deposed by Cortes; son of Axayácatl, b c 1480; d at the hands of his people in a skirmish 27 Jun

1520. He was totally at a loss to know how to deal with Cortes' invasion despite the small size of the Spanish force - he saw the impossibility of beating an alarmingly superior technology. There is no truth in the story that Moctezuma believed Cortes to be the god Quetzacoatl.
CUITLÁHUAC Jun-Sep 1520, brother of Moctezuma II.
CUAUHTÉMOC Sep 1520-13 Aug 1521 when captured by the Spaniards, son of Ahuitzotl, b 1495; hanged by the Spanish 1525. He tried to resist the Spanish invasion.

† Puppet Emperor Installed by the Spanish

(There are direct descendants of the Aztec Emperors still; the Spanish Ducal family of Moctezuma who trace their ancestry to Moctezuma II.)
TLACTOZIN (Don Diego Velasquez) 1525-1526, great-great-grandson of Huitzilhuitl.
1520-24 Aug 1821 Mexico under Spanish rule.

INDEPENDENT MEXICO

Head of Government

Generalissimo AUGUSTÍN de ITURBIDE Aug 1821-May 1822.

THE EMPIRE OF MEXICO

† Emperor

AUGUSTÍN (formerly Augustín de Iturbide) 19 May 1822-Mar 1823 abdicated, b 27 Sep 1783; shot while attempting to reclaim his throne 19 Jul 1824. Arbitrary and extravagant, Augustín wanted to change little in Mexico beyond renouncing allegiance to Spain. His very real contribution to Mexican independence is usually ignored.

THE PROVISIONAL GOVERNMENT OF MEXICO

Heads of Government

Gen VICENTE GUERRERO 1823.
Gen NICOLÁS BRAVO 1823-1824.
Gen NEGRETI 1824.

THE REPUBLIC OF THE UNITED STATES OF MEXICO

Presidents

Gen MANUEL GUADALUPE VICTORIA Oct 1824-Jan 1828, b (Felix Fernandez)) 1789; d 1843.
Gen MANUEL GÓMEZ PEDRAZA Jan-Dec 1828.

Gen **VICENTE GUERRERO Dec 1828-Jun 1829,** b
1783; betrayed, 'tried' and shot 1831. One of the
heroes of the War of Independence, he was as
poor an administrator as he was a fine soldier.
JOSÉ MARÍA de BOCANEGRA acting President
Jun-Dec 1829.
Gen **ANASTASIO BUSTAMENTE Jan 1830-Aug
1832,** b 1780; d 1853.
MELCHOR MÚZQUIZ acting President **Aug-Dec
1832.**
Gen **MANUEL GÓMEZ PEDRAZA Dec 1832-Apr
1833,** b c 1788; d 1851.
Gen **ANTONIO LÓPEZ de SANTA ANNA** acting
President **Apr 1883-Apr 1834**; President **Apr
1834-Jan 1835,** b 21 Feb 1794; d 21 Jun 1876. The
'enfant terrible' of early Mexico, Santa Anna was
a hero of the War of Independence and the Texan
revolt, a soldier of great panache and the
originator of most of the intrigues that beset the
infant Republic. Several times President, he died
blind and poverty stricken.
Gen **MIGUEL BARRAGÁN Jan 1835-Feb 1836,** b
1789; d 1836.
JOSÉ JUSTO CORRO Feb 1836-Apr 1837.
Gen **ANASTASIO BUSTAMENTE Apr 1837-Mar
1839.**
Gen **ANTONIO LÓPEZ de SANTA ANNA** acting
President **Mar-Jul 1939.**
Gen **ANASTASIO BUSTAMENTE Jul 1839-Jul
1840.**
Gen **NICOLÁS BRAVO** acting President **Jul
1840-Sep 1841,** b 1786? d 1854. One of the
founders of independent Mexico, he escalated
the 1811 peasant revolt into a national movement.
JAVIER ECHEVERRIA acting President **Sep
1841.**
Gen **VALENTÍN GÓMEZ FARIAS** acting Pre-
sident **Sep-Oct 1841,** b 14 Feb 1781; d 5 Jul 1858.
Gen **ANTONIO LÓPEZ de SANTA ANNA Oct
1841-Mar 1844** exiled.
Gen **JOSÉ JOAQUÍN HERRERA** acting President
Mar 1844-Sep 1845; President **Sep 1845-Jan 1846,**
b 1792; d 10 Feb 1854.
Gen **MARIANO PAREDES y ARRILLAGA** acting
President **Jan 1846.**
JOSÉ MARIANO SALAS Jan-Jul 1846.
Gen **ANTONIO LÓPEZ de SANTA ANNA Aug
1846.**
Gen **VALENTÍN GÓMEZ FARIAS** acting Pre-
sident **Aug 1846.**
Gen **ANTONIO LÓPEZ de SANTA ANNA Aug
1846-Sep 1847.**
PEDRO MARIA ANAYA acting President **Sep
1847-Jan 1848,** b 1795; d 1854.
MANUEL de la PEÑA y PEÑA acting President
Jan-Jun 1848.
Gen **JOSÉ JOAQUÍN HERRERA Jun 1848-Jun
1851.**
Gen **MARIANO ARISTA Jun 1851-Jan 1853,** b
c 1803; d 1855.
JUAN BAUTISTA CEBELLOS acting President
Jan-Feb 1853.
MANUEL LOMBARDINI acting President **Feb-
Mar 1853.**

*The implacable Benito Juarez who overthrew the
Mexican Empire of Maximilian whom he executed
in defiance of world opinion* (Radio Times Hulton
Picture Library)

Gen **ANTONIO LÓPEZ de SANTA ANNA** acting
President **Mar-Apr 1853**; President **Apr 1853-Aug
1855.**
MARTIN CARRERA Aug-Sep 1855.
RÓMULO DIAZ de la VEGA Sep-Oct 1855.
Gen **JUAN ÁLVAREZ Oct-Dec 1855,** b 1790; d 21
Aug 1867.
Gen **IGNACIO COMONFORT Dec 1855-Dec 1857**
fled, b 1812; d 1863.
Gen **BENITO PABLO JUÁREZ** acting President
Dec 1857-Jan 1858 ousted in civil war.
Gen **FÉLIX ZULOAGO Jan 1858-Feb 1859** *de
facto.* He asked France to consider sending
troops to help restore order in Mexico - from this
seed grew the French-sponsored Mexican
Empire.
Gen **MIGUEL MIRAMÓN Feb-Dec 1859** *de facto,*
b Sep 1832; executed 19 Jun 1867. He lost the
civil war to Juárez and then became leader of the
Imperial movement but he advised Maximilian
poorly.
Gen **BENITO PABLO JUÁREZ** undisputed
President **Dec 1859-Jan 1861**; President fighting
civil war **Jan 1861-Apr 1864,** b 21 Mar 1806; d (in
office in 2nd term) 18 Jul 1872. The incorruptible
Indian Juárez, who is Mexico's national hero,
faced foreign intervention to service the debts of
his bankrupt nation. Second Empire France,
encouraged by conservative émigrés, determined
to erect an Empire and against French and
conservative Mexican forces Juárez fought and

lost a civil war. Later, with American aid, he toppled Maximilian but having gained power failed to transfer power to the people or to abolish feudalism as he had dreamed. This man, who knew no mercy for his opponents, finally established Mexico as liberal, republican and above all Mexican.

THE EMPIRE OF MEXICO

† Emperor

HOUSE OF HABSBURG

MAXIMILIAN I 10 Apr 1864-15 May 1867, brother of Emperor Franz Joseph of Austria, b (Archduke Ferdinand Maximilian Joseph) 6 Jul 1832; executed by Mexican republicans 19 Jun 1867. Maximilian was far from the cynical adventurer sometimes depicted: honest but ill-advised, blinded by a misplaced sense of duty, and too liberal for his ultra-conservative supporters, Maximilian undertook with great diligence a hopeless task.

THE REPUBLIC OF THE UNITED STATES OF MEXICO

Presidents

Gen **BENITO PABLO JUÁREZ May 1867-18 Jul 1872.**
SEBASTIÁN LERDO de TEJADA acting President **Jul-Sep 1872;** President **Sep 1872-Nov 1876.**
JUAN MENDEZ acting President **Nov 1876-May 1877.**
Gen **PORFIRIO DIÁZ May 1877-Nov 1880.**
Gen **MANUEL GONZÁLEZ 1 Dec 1880-30 Nov 1884,** b 1833; d 1893.
Gen **PORFIRIO DIÁZ 1 Dec 1884-25 May 1911** deposed in coup, b 15 Sep 1830; d 2 Jul 1915. A half Indian dictator who deprived the Indians of their land and who maintained peace by bribing the generals with valuable sinecures. His oppressive regime made great economic progress without which the achievements of the revolution could not have been financed. The revolution, which began in Nov 1910 and came to be dominated by a peon, Pancho Villa (b Doroteo Arango), and a tenant farmer, Emiliano Zapata, was initially a rural movement demanding land reform - a direct response to Diáz's confiscations.
FRANCISCO LEÓN de la BARRA acting President **May-Oct 1911,** b 1863; d 1939.
FRANCISCO INDALECIO MADERNO Oct 1911-18 Feb 1913, b 1873; murdered by Huerta 18 Feb 1913. A moderate reformer ousted by the counter-revolution.
PEDRO LASCURAIN 18 Feb 1913 - for one hour. The shortest term as Head of State on record, Lascurain, the legal successor to Maderno (the Vice-President being disqualified by arrest), was sworn in, appointed Huerta as his successor and then resigned.
Gen **VICTORIANO HUERTA 18 Feb 1913-15 Jul 1914** deposed, b 1854; d 1916. The cruel, and frequently intoxicated, leader of the counter revolution.
FRANCISCO CARBAJAL acting President **Jul 1914.**
VENUSTIANO CARRANZA acting President **Jul-Oct 1914;** President in the provinces **Oct 1914-Apr 1915.**
Gen **EULALIO MARTÍN GUTIÉRREZ Oct 1914-Apr 1915.** He headed the extreme regime set up in Mexico City by the impatient Villa and Zapata.
(**ROQUE GONZÁLEZ GARZA** and **FRANCISCO LAGOS CHÁZARO** both headed rival extremist 'Governments' in the provinces after the return of Carranza. Neither can be considered to have been legally President.)
VENUSTIANO CARRANZA Apr 1915-20 May 1920, b 5 Feb 1917; d in office - murdered by the forces of Obregon. A leader of the second revolution, against Huerta, he reformed cautiously as the dire economic conditions permitted.
ADOLFO de la HUERTA acting President **May-Dec 1920;** d 1955.
Gen **ÁLVARO OBREGÓN 1 Dec 1920-30 Nov 1924,** b 1880; assassinated 17 Jul 1928.
Gen **PLUTARCO ELÍAS CALLES 1 Dec 1924-30 Nov 1928,** b 25 Sep 1877; d 19 Oct 1945. One of the leading figures of the revolution he advanced far along the road to creating a land-owning peasant class and founded the governing party, now called the PRI. However, the changes were achieved at a terrible cost: the dictatorship of this austere former teacher was corrupt and more brutal than that of Diáz, and the Church suffered a vicious persecution.
EMILIO PORTES GIL acting President **1 Dec 1928-4 Feb 1930.**
PASCUAL ORTIZ RUBIO 5 Feb 1930-Sep 1932.
Gen **ABELARDO RODRÍGUEZ** acting President **4 Sep 1932-Nov 1934.**
Gen **LÁZARO CÁRDENAS Dec 1934-30 Nov 1940,** b 1895; d 1970. A left wing President he nationalised oil and completed the constitutional changes of the revolution.
Gen **MANUEL ÁVILA CAMACHO 1 Dec 1940-30 Nov 1946,** b 24 Apr 1897; d 13 Oct 1955. He stabilised the nation and made post-revolutionary Mexico respectable in international eyes by joining the Allied powers, friendship with the USA, moderate policies and a conciliatory attitude to the Church.
MIGUEL ALEMAN VALDÉS 1 Dec 1946-30 Nov 1952, b 1905.
ADOLFO RUIZ CORTINES 1 Dec 1952-30 Nov 1958.
ADOLFO LÓPEZ MATEOS 1 Dec 1958-30 Nov 1964, b 26 May 1910.
Dr **GUSTAVO DIAZ ORDAZ 1 Dec 1964-30 Nov 1970,** b 12 Mar 1911.

LUÍS ECHEVERRÍA ALVAREZ 1 Dec 1970-30
Nov 1976, b 17 Jan 1922.
JOSÉ LÓPEZ PORTILLO since 1 Dec 1976, b
1920.

Milan *see* Italy

Mitanni

An ancient Kingdom on the upper Euphrates
which was a great power from about 1500 BC. Its
citizens were Hurrians but its Kings and ruling
class were Aryans from the Steppes.

† Kings

SHUTTARA I after *c* 1500 BC. Using his people's
new weapon, the war chariot, he established a
powerful Kingdom around Haran.
SAUSTATAR *c* 1450 and probably to *c* 1425 BC.
He created an empire stretching from the
Mediterranean to the Tigris.
ARTATAMA *c* 1425-*c* 1420 BC.
SHUTTARNA II *c* 1420-*c* 1390 BC.
TUSHRATTA *c* 1390-1365 BC murdered, son of
Shuttarna II. In his reign the rise of the Hittites
reduced Mitanni to a tiny state beside the
Euphrates.
SHATTUARA (?).
WASASHATTA (?).
MATTIWAZA after *c* 1340 BC, son of Tushratta.
A vassal of the Hittites who eventually annexed
the Kingdom.

Modena *see* Italy

Mogul Empire *see* Mughal Empire, India

The Principality of Monaco

Monaco passed into the hands of the Grimaldi
family, who are still the reigning dynasty, on 8 Jan
1297 when Francois (Francesco) Grimaldi used the
ploy of disguising himself in a friar's habit to enter
this Genoese citadel to be followed by his men who
took possession of the place. The tiny state was a
Seigniory, sometimes occupied by foreign forces,
until 1612 when Honoré II became the first Prince
of Monaco.

† Seigneurs

HOUSE OF GRIMALDI
RAINIER I 1297-1314, b *c* 1267.
CHARLES I 1314-1357, son of Rainier I. Although
Genoa retook Monaco, Charles I, like Rainier II
after him, styled himself Seigneur of Monaco.
RAINIER II 1357-1407, son of Charles I, b 1350.
1407-1419 Interregnum.
AMBROISE co-ruler 1419-1427, son of Rainier II.
ANTOINE co-ruler 1419-1427, son of Rainier II.
JEAN I co-ruler 1419-1427; sole ruler 1427-1454,
son of Rainier II, b 1382. Jean I finally regained
Monaco from the Genoese.
CATALAN 1454-1457, son of Jean I.
CLAUDINE (Dame of Monaco) 1457-1458 ab-
dicated, daughter of Catalan, b 1451; d 1515.
LAMBERT 1458-1493, cousin and husband of
Claudine (they married in 1465), b 1420.
JEAN II 1494-1505 murdered by Lucien; eldest
son of Lambert and Claudine.
LUCIEN 1505-1523 assassinated, brother of Jean
II. In Lucien's reign Monaco withstood a siege of
three months (1506-1507) by the Genoese.
AUGUSTIN 1523-1532, brother of Lucien. Bishop
of Grasse, he placed Monaco under the
protection of the mighty Charles V.
HONORÉ I 1532-1581, son of Lucien, b 1522.
CHARLES II 1581-1589, elder son of Honoré I, b
1555.
HERCULE 1589-1604 killed when thrown off the
cliffs by his rebellious subjects, younger son of
Honoré I, b 1562.
HONORÉ II Nov 1604-1612 when he became
Prince.

† Princes of Monaco

HOUSE OF GRIMALDI
HONORÉ II Seigneur from Nov 1604; Prince
1612-10 Jan 1662, son of Hercule, b 24 Dec 1597.
Placing his little state under French protection,
Honoré secured his position having recaptured
Monaco from the Spanish who had occupied the
rock (1605-1641).
LOUIS I Jan 1662-3 Jan 1701, grandson of Honoré
II, b 25 Jul 1642.
ANTOINE Jan 1701-21 Feb 1731, elder son of
Louis I, b 25? Jan 1661. Termed Antoine I despite
the previous reign of Co-Seigneur Antoine.
LOUISE-HIPPOLYTE (Princess) Feb-29 Dec 1731,
eldest daughter of Antoine, b 10 Nov 1697.
JACQUES Dec 1731-8 Nov 1733 when he
abdicated, husband of Louise-Hippolyte, b
(Jacques Francois Léonor Goyon de Matignon,
later Duc de Valentinois) 21 Nov 1689; d 23 Apr
1751.
HONORÉ III Nov 1733-4 Mar 1793 when he was
deposed; *de jure* Prince to 12 Mar 1795, eldest son
of Jacques, b 10 Sep 1720. Honoré III was
deprived of Monaco when it was annexed by
revolutionary France.
HONORÉ IV from Mar 1795 *de jure*; 30 May
1814-16 Feb 1819 *de facto*, son of Honoré III, b

17 May 1758. Restored by the Treaty of Paris, Monaco was placed under the protection of Sardinia three years later.

HONORÉ V Feb 1819-2 Oct 1841, elder son of Honoré IV, b 13 May 1778.

FLORESTAN Oct 1841-20 Jun 1856, younger son of Honoré IV, b 10 Oct 1785.

CHARLES III Jun 1856-10 Sep 1889, son of Florestan, b 8 Dec 1818. In 1861 Monaco was reduced to its present size when France bought Menton and Roquebrune which had renounced allegiance in 1848; Charles III greatly encouraged tourism and founded a new town in the Principality (1862) naming it after himself - Monte Carlo.

ALBERT I Sep 1889-26 Jun 1922, son of Charles III, b 13 Nov 1848. A pioneer of marine research, Prince Albert founded the famous Oceanographic Museum and personally discovered several species of marine life.

LOUIS II Jun 1922-9 May 1949, son of Albert I, b 12 Jul 1870.

RAINIER III since 9 May 1949, grandson of Louis II, b 31 May 1923.

Ministers of State

The Heads of Government of the Principality.

ÉMILE PELLETIER Jan 1959-Jan 1962.

Jan 1962-Aug 1963 After the dismissal of M. Pelletier by Prince Rainier there was no Head of Government.

JEAN REYMOND Aug 1963-May 1972.

ANDRÉ St MLEUX since 1 Jun 1972, b 25 Sep 1920.

The Mongol Empire

A loose 'confederation' of the Mongol peoples, and in no respects a state, was created by Genghis Khan in the 13th century. The various Khans owed a largely nominal allegiance to the Great Khan who was elected by an assembly of the descendants of Genghis Khan. By the end of the 13th century the system had almost broken down as various local Khans asserted their independence.

† Great Khans of all the Mongols
(plus the major local Khans of the 13th century)

GENGHIS KHAN (personal name TEMÜJIN) *c* 1206-1227, b *c* 1162. A very able military leader with a magnetic personality, Temüjin achieved a vast following among the Mongols cutting across tribal divisions as never before. A tribal leader at 13 he built up a personal 'empire' which included Mongolia, north China and much of central Asia.

(JOCHI, eldest son of Genghis Khan, was vassal Khan in central Asia before *c* 1223; d *c* 1223.)

(CHAGATAI, second son of Genghis Khan, was vassal Khan in Kashgaria 1227-1242.)

ÖGÖDEI Khan in Tarbagatai from *c* 1227; Great Khan **1229-1242,** third son of Genghis Khan.

(TOLUI, fourth son of Genghis Khan, was vassal Khan in Mongolia *c* 1227-1232.)

1242-1246 Interregnum in the Great Khanate - Töregene, widow of Ögödei, attempted to assume the dignities of the role.

GÜYÜK 1246-1248, son of Ögödei.

(BATU KHAN, son of Jochi, was vassal Khan of the Golden Horde *c* 1235-1256. He expected, and attempted to assume, but never received the dignity of the Great Khanate.)

MÖNGKE 1251-1259, son of Tolui, b *c* 1207. He added Persia and Mesopotamia to the lands that knew him as overlord.

KHUBILAI KHAN 1260-1294, brother of Möngke, b 1216. He ruled his vast empire (Mongolia, China, most of Russia, central Asia, Iran and Mesopotamia) from Kaanbaligh (Peking) using China as his power base. Remarkably tolerant of many religions and cosmopolitan he formed a 'civil service' of several nationalities which included Marco Polo.

(After the death of Khubilai Khan the Mongol Empire dissolved into a number of minor Khanates.)

Mongolia

Mongolia, which owed allegiance to the Manchu Chinese Emperors, was declared independent after the Chinese revolution of 1911 but was not established as a sovereign state until Jul 1921. International recognition of Mongolian independence was not forthcoming until 1946.

'Living Buddha'
(Mongolian Head of State)

JEBTSUNDAMBA KHUTUKHTU 1911-1918; d 1924. He declared Mongolia independent of China and placed the state under Russian protection.

1918 Chinese rule restored.

Usurping Ruler

Baron **UNGERN STERNBERG 1918-1921;** executed 1921. A White Russian leader known as the 'Mad Baron', he seized control of Mongolia but was defeated by the Bolsheviks.

THE MONGOLIAN PEOPLE'S REPUBLIC

Heads of State
(Chairmen of the Presidium of the Khural)

JEBTSUNDAMBA KHUTUKHTU Jul 1921-1924.
Marshal KHORLOGIN CHOYBOLSAN 1924-28 Jan 1952; d in office.
ZHAMSARANGIN SAMBUU acting Chairman Jan 1952-1954; Chairman 1954-20 May 1972; d in office.
SONOMYN LUVSAN acting Chairman May 1972-Jun 1974.
Marshal YUMZHAGIYN TSEDENBAL since 10 Jun 1974, b 17 Sep 1917.

Prime Ministers

SUKHE BAATOR Jul 1921-1923; d in office. The hero of the Communist regime in Mongolia, the capital was renamed Ulan Baator in his honour.
Marshal KHORLOGIN CHOYBOLSAN 1923-28 Jan 1952; see President Choybolsan.
Marshal YUMZHAGIYN TSEDENBAL acting PM Jan-May 1952; PM 28 May 1952-Jun 1974; see President Tsedenbal.
JAMBYN BATMOUNKH since 10 Jun 1974.

Head of the People's Revolutionary (Communist) Party of Mongolia

The Head was described at various times as Chairman, Secretary-General or 1st Secretary.

Marshal YUMZHAGIYN TSEDENBAL 1940-1954.
DASHIN DAMBA 1954-Nov 1958.
Marshal YUMZHAGIYN TSEDENBAL since 22 Nov 1958.

Montenegro *see* Yugoslavia

Moravia *see* Czechoslovakia

Morocco

Having been part of the Roman province of Tingatana, Morocco was taken by the Vandals in 429 and by the Arabs at the beginning of the 8th century. Until the country was divided into French and Spanish protectorates (Mar 1912) it was ruled by a series of Arab and Berber dynasties but was seldom united. On 2 Mar 1956 French Morocco became an independent Sultanate and was raised to a Kingdom on 12 Aug 1957. Spanish Morocco (Apr 1956), Tangier (Oct 1956), Ifni (Jun 1969) and part of the Western Sahara (Apr 1976) have been added to the country.

† Sultans

Mulay ABD ar-RAHMAN Nov 1822-Aug 1859.
SIDI MUHAMMAD Aug 1859-Sep 1873, son of Mulay Abd ar-Rahman.
Mulay al-HASSAN Sep-7 Jun 1894, son of Sidi Muhammad.
Mulay ABD al-AZIZ Jun 1894-Dec 1907 when he was deposed, eldest son of Mulay al-Hassan, b 1878; d 1943. Although the Algeciras conference (1906) confirmed his independence and status, his adoption of Western ways alienated his subjects and he was dethroned by his brother Mulay Abd al-Hafid.
Mulay ABD al-HAFID 1909 when he was recognised as Sultan -12 Aug 1912 when he abdicated, brother of Mulay Abd al-Aziz; b 1880; d 1937. After deposing his brother he was unable to control the country. Besieged, he requested French help and was obliged to accept a protectorate.
Mulay YUSUF Aug 1912-27 Nov 1927, brother of Mulay Abd al-Hafid, b 1882.
SIDI MUHAMMAD ben YUSUF Nov 1927-Aug 1953 when he was deposed by the French; Sovereign from 2 Mar 1956; see King Muhammad V.
SIDI MOHAMMAD ibn ARAFA Aug 1953-Nov 1955, uncle of Sidi Muhammad ben Yusuf, b 1890; d 18 Jul 1976. A puppet sultan installed by the French after Sidi Muhammad ben Yusuf had backed the Moroccan nationalist movement.
SIDI MUHAMMAD ben YUSUF Nov 1955-12 Aug 1957 when he became King.

† Kings

MUHAMMAD V 12 Aug 1957-26 Feb 1961; previously Sultan Oct 1927-Aug 1953 and Nov 1955-12 Aug 1957; Sovereign from 2 Mar 1956, son of Sultan Mulay Yusuf, b 10 Aug 1909. Picked as Sultan by the French authorities who thought he would prove docile, he became the leader of the Moroccan nationalist movement and was exiled (Aug 1953). A popular revolt demanded his recall and he returned in triumph (Nov 1955) to lead the country to independence and to become King.
HASSAN II since 26 Feb 1961, son of Muhammad V, b 9 Jul 1929.

Prime Ministers

Si M'BAREK MOSTAPHA el BEKKI 2 Mar 1956-16 Apr 1958, former Pasha of Sefrou, b 1907; d 1961.
AHMED BALAFREJ 8 May 1958-22 Nov 1959, b 1908.
MOULAY ABDALLAH IBRAHIM 16 Dec 1959-20 May 1960, b 1921.

King **MUHAMMAD V** assumed the Premiership **22 May 1960-26 Feb 1961** when he died;see King Muhammad V.

King **HASSAN II** assumed the Premiership **26 Feb 1961-13 Nov 1964**; see King Hassan II.

Hadj **AHMED BAHNINI 13 Nov 1964-8 Jun 1965**, b 1909.

King **HASSAN II** assumed the Premiership **8 Jun 1965-Jul 1967**; see King Hassan II.

Dr **MOHAMMAD BENHIMA Jul 1967-6 Oct 1969**, b 25 Jun 1924.

Dr **AHMED LARAKI 6 Oct 1969-4 Aug 1971**, b 15 Oct 1931.

KARIM LAMRANI 6 Aug 1971-Nov 1972, b 1920.

AHMED OSMAN since Nov 1972, brother-in-law of King Hassan II, b 3 Jan 1930.

Moscow, Grand Duchy of *see*
Union of Soviet Socialist Republics

Mozambique

The Mozambican coast was discovered by Vasco da Gama in 1498; the first Portuguese settlements were made at Sofala (1505) and Mocambique (1507). The interior did not come under Portuguese control until the end of the 19th century. Independence was achieved on 25 Jun 1975.

President

SAMORA MOÏSES MACHEL since 25 Jun 1975, b 1934.

Mughal Empire *see* India

Muscat and Oman *see* Oman

Muscovy *see* Union of Soviet Socialist Republics

Naples, Kingdom of *see* Italy

Nassau *see* Germany

Nauru

This small Pacific island was annexed by Germany in Oct 1888. Taken by Australian forces in 1914, it became a Trust Territory jointly adminstered by Britain, New Zealand and Australia but governed by the latter. Independence as a Republic was achieved on 31 Jan 1968.

Head of State and Government

HAMER de ROBURT 31 Jan-May 1968, b 1922; see President Hamer de Roburt.

Presidents

HAMER de ROBURT 18 May 1968-Dec 1976.

BERNARD DOWIYOGO 22 Dec 1976-19 Apr 1978, b 1946.

LAGUMOT HARRIS 19 Apr-11 May 1978.

HAMER de ROBURT since 11 May 1978.

Navarre *see* Spain

Nejd *see* Saudi Arabia

Nepal

The lands now forming Nepal were united under the Shah Dynasty *c* 1770 into a single Kingdom.

† Kings

SHAH DYNASTY

PRITHVI NARAYAN SHAH ruler since 1742; united Nepal *c* 1770-1775.

RANA PRATAP SINGH 1775-1778, son of Prithvi Narayan Shah.

RANA BAHADUR 1778-1800 abdicated; assassinated 1807.

GIRVAN JUDDHA VIKRAM 1800-1832, son of Rana Bahadur; d after 1860.

RAJENDRA VIKRAM 1832-1850 abdicated.

SURENDRA 1850-Dec 1881, son of Rajendra Vikram, b 1829. In this reign power passed into the hands of the Rana family who became hereditary Premiers.

PRITHVI BIR VIKRAM 1 Dec 1881-11 Dec 1911, grandson of Surendra, b 1875.

TRIBHUVANA BIR VIKRAM SHAH Dec 1911-13 Mar 1955; briefly deposed 7 Nov 1950-8 Jan 1951, son of Prithvi bir Vikram, b 30 Jun 1906.

(GYANENDRA, infant grandson of King Tribhuvana, was proclaimed King in the revolt of Nov 1950-Jan 1951 but he is not considered to have reigned.)

MAHENDRA BIR BIKRAM SHAH DEVA Mar 1955-31 Jan 1972, son of Tribhuvana, b 11 Jun 1920. King Mahendra modernised Nepal and made attempts to introduce Parliamentary government.

BIRENDRA BIR BIKRAM SHAH DEVA since 31 Jan 1972, son of Mahendra, b 28 Dec 1945.

Prime Ministers

HEREDITARY PREMIERS
The Premiership was hereditary in the Rana family for over a century.

Maharaja **JOODHA SHUMSHERE JUNG BAHA-DUR RANA 1932-Nov 1945.**
Maharaja **PADMA SHUMSHERE JUNG BAHA-DUR RANA Nov 1945-May 1946.**
Gen **MOHAN SHUMSHERE JUNG BAHADUR RANA May 1946-12 Nov 1951.**

PREMIERS SINCE THE RANA ERA
MATRIKA PRASAD KOIRALA 14 Nov 1951-Aug 1952, b 1 Jan 1912.
King **TRIBHUVANA 14 Aug 1952-Jun 1953.**
MATRIKA PRASAD KOIRALA 15 Jun 1953-Mar 1955.
Prince **MAHENDRA 2-13 Mar 1955** when he became King.
King **MAHENDRA 13 Mar 1955-Jan 1956.**
TANKA PRASAD ACHARYA 27 Jan 1956-Jul 1957.
Dr **K.I. SINGH 14 Jul-Nov 1957.**
King **MAHENDRA 14 Nov 1957-May 1958.**
Gen **SUBARNA SHUMSHERE May 1958-May 1959.**
BISWESWAR PRASAD KOIRALA 4 May 1959-Dec 1960, half-brother of Matrika Prasad Koirala, b 1915.
King **MAHENDRA 15 Dec 1960-Apr 1963.**
Dr **TULSI GIRI 2 Apr-Dec 1963.**
SURYA BAHADUR THAPA 23 Dec 1963-Mar 1964.
Dr **TULSI GIRI Mar 1964-Jan 1965.**
SURYA BAHADUR THAPA 26 Jan 1965-Apr 1969.
KIRTINIDHI BISTA 7 Apr 1969-Apr 1970.
King **MAHENDRA 13 Apr 1970-31 Jan 1972.**
KIRTINIDHI BISTA Feb 1972-Jul 1973.
NAGENDRA PRASAD RAIJAL 16 Jul 1973-Dec 1975.
Dr **TULSI GIRI 1 Dec 1975-Sep 1977,** b Sep 1926.
KIRTINIDI BISTA since 12 Sep 1977, b 1927.

The Netherlands

In medieval feudal times the modern Kingdom of the Netherlands was divided between several states: the County of Holland (the most important - which explains why its name is often, but wrongly, used to describe the entire country); the Counties of Friesland and Gelderland; the Prince-Bishopric of Utrecht; the Barony of Breda and the Duchy of Brabant (the major part of which is in modern Belgium). In the later Middle Ages these fiefs passed to Burgundy and then to the Austro-Spanish empire of Charles V against whose son, Philip II, the Dutch revolted to found the independent United Provinces in 1579. The republican United Provinces, whose independence was recognised by the Peace of Westphalia in 1648, was usually ruled by an hereditary 'Chief Magistrate' or Stadhouder belonging to the House of Orange. In 1795 a French invasion established the Batavian Republic which became the Kingdom of Holland for Napoleon I's brother Louis in 1806. In 1810 the whole country was annexed by France but was restored as an independent Kingdom under the House of Orange after the Napoleonic wars.

UNITED PROVINCES OF THE NETHERLANDS

† Stadhouders

The Stadhouder was 'chief executive' of the Dutch Republic.

WILLEM I, Prince of Orange **Jan 1579-10 Jul 1584** when he was assassinated; the United Provinces did not renounce allegiance to Spain until Jul 1581, b 24 Apr 1553. Four times married, William the Silent may have been taciturn but was not as staid as is sometimes imagined. Having been a member of the Council of State of Philip II of Spain, he became the leader of Dutch resistance to Spanish rule in the Netherlands. He took up arms to achieve religious freedom and, perhaps uppermost in his mind, to gain political advantages for those nobles, like himself, who were denied participation in the government of the Low Countries.

MAURITS, Prince of Orange **1584-23 Apr 1625,** only son of Willem I's second wife, b 13 Nov 1567. A considerable strategist, Maurits re-formed the army and swept the Spaniards from the northern Netherlands but could not expel them from the south. Coming into conflict with the 'peace party', who favoured a truce to foster trade, he sanctioned the execution of their leader van Oldenbarnevelt.

FREDERIK HENDRIK, Prince of Orange **1625-14 Mar 1647,** only son of Willem I's fourth wife, b 29 Jan 1584. He greatly increased the powers of the Stadhouder in domestic affairs assuming semi-monarchical status.

WILLEM II Prince of Orange **1647-6 Nov 1650,** only son of Frederik Hendrik, b 27 May 1626. During his period of office Spain finally recognised Dutch independence by the Treaty of Westphalia (1648).

WILLEM III, Prince of Orange **1672-19 Mar 1702,** only child of Willem II, b 14 Nov 1650; was also King William III of England.

WILLEM IV FRISO, Prince of Orange **1747-1751,** great-grandson of Willem II's youngest sister Albertina Agnes, b 1711.

WILLEM V, Prince of Orange **1751-23 Feb 1795** when he was dismissed, son of Willem IV Friso, b 8 Mar 1748; d as Prince of Fulda and Corvei 9

King Willem I, whose anti-Belgian policies lost the southern Netherlands for the Dutch, ironically married a Belgian after his abdication (Radio Times Hulton Picture Library)

Apr 1806. An unpopular Stadhouder: his pro-English policies antagonised the Patriotic Party during the Anglo-Dutch war (1780-1784) and he had to leave the Hague; provocatively conservative he made necessary reforms impossible; militarily undistinguished, he fled before the French invasion.

THE BATAVIAN REPUBLIC

1795-1806 A client state of France.

THE KINGDOM OF HOLLAND

† Kings

LOUIS BONAPARTE (LODEWIJK I) **5 Jul 1806-4 Jul 1810** when he abdicated, Napoléon I's third surviving brother, b 2 Sep 1778; d 25 Jul 1846. Married to the beautiful Hortense de Beauharnais, Josephine's daughter, he was the father of Louis-Napoléon, later Napoléon III. Intended by his brother as little more than a French governor, Louis took his duties as King very seriously and refused to apply the Continental System, which would have hurt the Dutch economy. In retaliation, Napoléon invaded Holland forcing Louis' abdication.

NAPOLÉON-LOUIS BONAPARTE (LODEWIJK II) **4-9 Jul 1810,** second but elder surviving son of Louis, b 1804; d 1831. The son in whose favour Louis abdicated lost his Kingdom when it was annexed to France on 9 Jul 1810.

UNITED PROVINCES OF THE NETHERLANDS

† Stadhouder

WILLEM VI, Prince of Orange **1813-21 Mar 1815** when he became first King of the Netherlands. Sovereign Prince of the Netherlands by election.

THE KINGDOM OF THE NETHERLANDS

† Kings

WILLEM I, Prince of Orange formerly Prince of the Netherlands, Fulda and Corvei; **21 Mar 1815-7 Oct 1840** when he abdicated, son of Willem V, Prince of Orange, b 24 Aug 1772; d 12 Dec 1843. An arch-conservative, he found even his Russian daughter-in-law Anna too liberal. His antipathy towards his Belgian subjects did much to foster the rebellion of the southern provinces (1830), and after Belgium became independent his obstinacy long delayed a settlement.

WILLEM II 7 Oct 1840-17 Mar 1849, elder son of Willem I, b 6 Dec 1792. Generous, charming and popular, this great collector of paintings granted the Netherlands a democratic constitution.

WILLEM III 17 Mar 1849-23 Nov 1890, eldest son of Willem II, b 19 Feb 1817. Willem III played an important role as an international arbiter.

WILHELMINA (Queen) **23 Nov 1890-4 Sep 1948** when she abdicated, only child of Willem III's second marriage, b 31 Aug 1880; d 28 Nov 1962. Deeply religious and greatly loved by her people, Queen Wilhelmina was known as 'Landsmoeder' - mother of the country. She left the Netherlands in 1940 and became a symbol of hope to the Dutch resistance to German occupation, but the war effort broke her health.

JULIANA (Queen) **since 4 Sep 1948,** only child of Queen Wilhelmina, b 30 Apr 1909.

Prime Ministers

Jonkheer Dr **CHARLES JOSEPH MARIE RUYS de BEERENBROUCK 9 Sep 1918-Aug 1925,** b 1874; d 17 Apr 1936.

Dr **HENDRIKUS COLIJN 4 Aug 1925-Mar 1926.**

Jonkheer Dr **DIRK JAN de GEER 8 Mar 1926-Aug 1929.**

Jonkheer Dr **CHARLES JOSEPH MARIE RUYS de BEERENBROUCK 7 Aug 1929-May 1933.**

Dr **HENDRIKUS COLIJN 24 May 1933-Aug 1939,** b 22 Jun 1869; d 16 Sep 1944 in a German concentration camp.

Jonkheer Dr **DIRK JAN de GEER 4 Aug 1939-May 1940;** PM in exile **14 May-Sep 1940,** b 14 Dec 1870; d 28 Nov 1960. He was disgraced for returning to the Netherlands to attempt an unauthorised separate peace with Germany.

Prof **PIETER SJOERD GERBRANDY** PM in exile **4 Sep 1940-May 1945;** PM in the Hague **23 May-23 Jun 1945,** b 13 Apr 1885; d 7 Sep 1961. He organised the Dutch war effort: the Resistance, the exiles and the colonial forces.

Prof **WILLEM SCHERMERHORN 23 Jun 1945-May 1946,** b 17 Dec 1894.

Dr **LOUIS JOSEPH MARIA BEEL 27 May 1946-Aug 1948,** b 1902.

Dr **WILLEM DREES 6 Aug 1948-Jan 1951;** caretaker PM **Jan-14 Mar 1951;** PM **14 Mar 1951-Aug 1952;** caretaker PM **6-21 Aug 1952;** PM **21 Aug 1952-Dec 1958,** b 5 Jul 1886.

Dr **LOUIS JOSEPH MARIA BEEL 22 Dec 1958-Mar 1959,** b 12 Apr 1902; d 11 Feb 1977.

Prof **JAN EDUARD de QUAY 28 Mar-27 Apr 1959,** b 26 Aug 1901.

Dr **LOUIS JOSEPH MARIA BEEL** caretaker PM **Apr-May 1959.**

Prof **JAN EDUARD de QUAY 14 May 1959-May 1963;** caretaker PM **May-Jul 1963.**

Dr **VICTOR GERARD MARIE MARIJNEN 23 Jul 1963-Mar 1965,** b 21 Feb 1917; d 5 Apr 1975.

Dr **JOSEPH MARIA LAURENS THEO CALS 30 Mar 1965-Oct 1966;** caretaker PM **Oct-Nov 1966,** b 18 Jul 1914.

Prof **JELLE ZIJLSTRA 16 Nov 1966-Apr 1967,** b 27 Aug 1918.

PETRUS J.S. de JONG 3 Apr 1967-Apr 1971; caretaker PM **29 Apr-22 Jun 1971,** b 3 Apr 1915.

BAREND WILLEM BIESHEUVEL 22 Jun 1971-Nov 1972; caretaker PM **29 Nov 1972-11 May 1973,** b 5 Apr 1920.

Dr **JOHANNES MARTEN den UYL** (more commonly known as Dr JOOP den UYL) **11 May 1973-May 1977;** caretaker PM **May-Dec 1977,** b 9 Aug 1919.

ANDREAS A.M. van AGT since 19 Dec 1977, b 2 Feb 1931.

Holland, County of

The County of Holland (present day Zeeland, Noord and Zuid Holland) was the main state of the Netherlands in the Middle Ages and still (inaccurately) gives its name to the country in common parlance.

† Counts

HOUSE OF FRIESLAND

DIRK III 1003-1039. Dirk III, a Friesian ruler, greatly enlarged his domain and assumed the style, Count of Holland.

DIRK IV 1039-1049.

FLORIS I 1049-1061. He united Holland, Friesland and Zeeland.

DIRK V 1061-1091.

FLORIS II 1091-1122.

DIRK VI 1122-1157.

FLORIS III 1157-1190.

DIRK VII 1190-1203.

WILLEM I 1203-1223.

FLORIS IV 1223-1234.

WILLEM II 1234-1256 drowned. This Count brought his House to a position of great power and he nearly acquired the imperial title.

FLORIS V 1256-1296, son of Willem II.

JAN I 1296-1299, grandson of Willem II. Upon Jan's death the County passed to the House of Hainaut whose united possessions made them the leading power in the Low Countries.

HOUSE OF HAINAUT

JAN II (Jean d'Avesnes) **1299-1304,** nephew of Willem II.

WILLEM III ('The Good') **1304-1337,** son of Jan II.

WILLEM IV 1337-1345, son of Willem III.

MARGARETHE (Countess) **1345-1356** abdicated, daughter of Willem III; d after 1356.

HOUSE OF WITTELSBACH

WILLEM V ('The Senseless') **1356-1389,** second son of Countess Margarethe. He did not govern after 1358 having become mad.

ALBERT 1389-1404, brother of Willem V.

WILLEM VI 1404-1417, son of Albert.

JACQUELINE (Countess) **1417-1436,** granddaughter of Albert. She was forced to cede Holland to Burgundy and after her death most of the Low Countries passed to that power.

New Granada *see* Colombia

New Zealand

Discovered by Tasman in 1643 the country was proclaimed British territory in 1840. New Zealand became an independent nation *de facto* on 6 Feb 1907 but did not adopt the name Dominion of New Zealand until 26 Sep 1907. The country's sovereign status was confirmed by the Statute of Westminster in Dec 1931 but this was not ratified by the New Zealand Parliament until Nov 1947.

Governors of Independent New Zealand

Although New Zealand became a Dominion in 1907 the style of the Sovereign's representative was not changed from Governor to Governor-General until Jun 1917.

William Lee Plunket, 5th Baron **PLUNKET** Governor from 1904; of an independent nation **Feb 1907-Jun 1910,** b 19 Dec 1864; d 24 Jan 1920.

Sir **ROBERT STOUT** acting Governor **Jun 1910,** b 1844; d 1930.

John Poynder Dickson-Poynder, 1st Baron **IS-LINGTON Jun 1910-Dec 1912**; d 6 Dec 1936.

Sir **ROBERT STOUT** acting Governor **Dec 1912.**

Arthur William de Brito Savile Foljambe, 2nd Earl of **LIVERPOOL Dec 1912-Jun 1917** when he became Governor-General.

Governors-General of New Zealand

Arthur William de Brito Savile Foljambe, 2nd Earl of **LIVERPOOL** Governor from 1912; Governor-General **Jun 1917-Aug 1920,** b 27 May 1870; d 15 May 1941.

Sir **ROBERT STOUT** acting Governor-General **Aug-Sep 1920.**

John Rushworth Jellicoe, 1st Viscount, later 1st Earl, **JELLICOE** of Scapa **Sep 1920-Dec 1924,** b 5 Dec 1859; d 20 Nov 1935. The Commander of the British Fleet at the Battle of Jutland in 1916.

Sir **ROBERT STOUT** acting Governor-General **Dec 1924.**

Sir **CHARLES FERGUSSON Dec 1924-Dec 1929,** b 1865; d 1951. Member of a distinguished New Zealand political family he is remembered for his pioneering work in the industrial sector.

Sir **MICHAEL MYERS** acting Governor-General **Dec 1929-Jan 1930.**

Sir Charles Bathurst, 1st Viscount **BLEDISLOE Jan 1930-Mar 1935,** b 21 Sep 1867; d 3 Jul 1958.

George Vere Arundell Monckton-Arundell, 8th Viscount **GALWAY Mar 1935-Feb 1941,** b 24 Mar 1882; d 27 Mar 1943.

Air Chief Marshal Sir Cyril Louis Norton Newall, 1st Baron **NEWALL Feb 1941-Feb 1946,** b 15 Feb 1886; d 30 Nov 1963.

Lieut-Gen Sir Bernard Cyril Freyberg, 1st Baron **FREYBERG Feb 1946-Dec 1952,** b 21 Mar 1890; d 4 Jul 1963.

Gen Sir Charles Willoughby Moke Norrie, 1st Baron **NORRIE Dec 1952-Nov 1957,** b 26 Sep 1893; d May 1977. A distinguished commander in both World Wars he led the Chindits in Burma.

Sir Charles John Lyttelton, 10th Viscount **COBHAM Nov 1957-Nov 1962,** b 8 Aug 1909; d 19 Mar 1977.

Brig Sir **BERNARD EDWARD FERGUSSON Nov 1962-Nov 1967,** son of Sir Charles Fergusson, b 1911.

Sir **ARTHUR PORRITT Nov 1967-Sep 1972,** b 1900.

Sir **EDWARD DENIS BLUNDELL Sep 1972-Oct 1977,** b 29 May 1907.

Sir **KEITH JACKA HOLYOAKE since 26 Oct 1977**; see Premier Holyoake.

Prime Ministers of the Dominion of New Zealand

Sir **JOSEPH GEORGE WARD** PM since 1906; PM of an independent nation **Feb 1907-Jul 1912,** b 26 Apr 1856; d 8 Jul 1930. The first Minister of Health in the world.

THOMAS MACKENZIE 10 Jul 1912-Aug 1915, b 1854; d 1930.

WILLIAM FERGUSSON MASSEY 12 Aug 1915-10 May 1925, b 26 Mar 1856; d in office. Violently opposed to the development of the Dominions as sovereign nations it is a fine irony that he should have signed the Treaty of Versailles for his country thus establishing it in the eyes of the international community as an independent power.

Sir **FRANCIS HENRY DILLON BELL 14-30 May 1925.**

JOSEPH GORDON COATES 30 May 1925-Dec 1928, b 3 Feb 1878; d 27 May 1943.

Sir **JOSEPH GEORGE WARD 10 Dec 1928-May 1930.**

GEORGE WILLIAM FORBES 28 May 1930-Aug 1935, b 1869; d 18 Mar 1947.

MICHAEL JOSEPH SAVAGE Aug 1935-26 Mar 1940, b 23 Mar 1872; d in office.

PETER FRASER acting PM **26 Mar-4 Apr 1940**; PM **4 Apr 1940-Dec 1949,** b 28 Aug 1884; d 12 Dec 1950. A former dockyard worker, Peter Fraser played an important part in the formation of the UNO. A vigorous spokesman for the rights of small countries, he opposed the hegemony of the Great Powers and made greater use of New Zealand's independence than his predecessors.

Sir **SIDNEY GEORGE HOLLAND 8 Dec 1949-Sep 1957,** b 18 Oct 1893; d 5 Aug 1961.

KEITH JACKA HOLYOAKE 30 Sep-11 Dec 1957.

Sir **WALTER NASH 11 Dec 1957-Dec 1960,** b 12 Feb 1882; d 4 Jun 1968.

KEITH JACKA HOLYOAKE (later Sir Keith) **12 Dec 1960-Feb 1972,** b 11 Feb 1904.

Sir **JOHN ROSS MARSHALL 7 Feb-8 Dec 1972,** b 5 Mar 1912.

NORMAN ERIC KIRK 8 Dec 1972-31 Aug 1974, b 1923; d in office.

HUGH WATT acting PM **31 Aug-6 Sep 1974.**

WALLACE EDWARD ROWLING (more commonly known as BILL ROWLING) **6 Sep 1974-Dec 1975,** b 15 Nov 1927.

ROBERT DAVID MULDOON since 12 Dec 1975, b 21 Sep 1921.

Nicaragua

Spanish from 1526 to 1821; briefly independent and then part of Mexico from 1822 to 1823, Nicaragua joined the United Provinces of Central America in 1823. Upon the collapse of the Federation, Nicaragua became a separate nation but a lengthy civil war prevented the establishment of a recognisable central government until 1848.

Presidents
(Heads of State and of Government)

TOMAS VALLADARES 1839-1840.
PATRICIO RIVAS 1840-1841.
PABLO BUITRAGO 1841.
JUAN de DIOS OROSCO 1841-1845.
JOSÉ LEON SANDOVAL 1845-1847.
JOSÉ GUERRERO 1847-1848.
NOBERTO RAMIREZ 1848-1851.
LAUREANO PINEDA May 1851-Apr 1853.
Gen FRUTOS CHAMORRO Apr 1853-Mar 1855, b 1806; d in office.
JOSÉ MARIA ESTRADA Mar 1855-Jul 1856 driven out; legally President until Oct 1856, b 1802; d in office.
WILLIAM WALKER Jul 1856-Jan 1857, b 1822; d 1860. An American adventurer who seized power, he is not regarded as a President.
PATRICIO RIVAS Legally President from Oct 1856; President de facto Jan-Jun 1857.
Gen TOMAS MÁRTINEZ Jun 1857-Mar 1867, b 1812; d 1873.
FERNANDO GUZMAN Mar 1867-Feb 1871.
VICENTE CUADRA Mar 1871-Feb 1875.
PEDRO JOAQUIN CAMORRA Mar 1875-Feb 1879.
JOAQUIN ZAVALA Mar 1879-Feb 1883.
ADAN CARDENAS Mar 1883-Feb 1885, b 1836; d 1916.
PEDRO JOAQUIN CAMORRA acting President Mar 1885-Feb 1887.
EVARISTO CARAZO Mar 1887-Aug 1889, b 1822; d in office.
ROBERTO SACASA Aug 1889-Jun 1893.
JOSÉ SANTOS ZELAYA acting President during civil war Jun 1893-Feb 1894; President Feb 1894-Dec 1909, b 1853; d 1919.
JOSÉ MADRIZ acting President Dec 1909-Aug 1910.
JOSÉ ESTRADA Aug 1910-Jan 1911; d in office.
JUAN ESTRADA Jan-May 1911, brother of José Estrada.
ADOLFO DIAZ May 1911-31 Dec 1916, b 15 Jul 1877; d 27 Jan 1964. The United States intervened on his behalf in a civil war.
EMILIANO CHAMORRO VARGAS 1 Jan 1917-Dec 1920.
DIEGO MANUEL CHAMORRO 1 Jan 1920-12 Oct 1923, nephew of Emiliano Chamorro Vargas; d in office.
BARTOLOMÉ MARTINEZ acting President Oct 1923-Dec 1924.
CARLOS SOLORZANO Dec 1924-Jan 1926.
EMILIANO CHAMORRO VARGAS Jan-Nov 1926.
ADOLFO DIAZ Nov 1926-30 Dec 1929.
Gen JOSÉ MARIA MONCADA 1 Jan 1929-Dec 1932, b 1867; d 1945.
JUAN BAUTISTA SACASA 1 Jan 1933-2 Jun 1936 deposed in coup, b 1874; d 1946.

Dr CARLOS BRENES JARQUIN acting President 11 Jun 1936-Jan 1937.
Gen ANASTASIO SOMOZA GARCÍA 1 Jan 1937-May 1947.
Dr LEONARDO ARGÜELLO 1-25 May 1947 deposed in coup, b 1875; d 1947.
BENJAMIN LESCAYO-SACASA May-Jul 1947 deposed, b 1885; d 1959.
Dr VICTOR M. ROMAN y REYES Jul 1947-6 May 1950, uncle of Gen Anastasio Somoza, b 1873; d in office.
Gen ANASTASIO SOMOZA GARCÍA acting President May 1950-May 1951; President 1 May 1951-29 Sep 1956, b 1 Feb 1896; d in office of wounds received in an assassination attempt on 21 Sep 1956. This dictator, who did much to develop Nicaragua's economy, founded a political dynasty - his family with their relatives the Gutierrezes have dominated the recent history of the state.
LUIS ANASTASIO SOMOZA DEBAYLE 29 Sep 1956-May 1963, elder son of Gen Anastasio Somoza, b 18 Nov 1922; d 13 Apr 1967.
RENÉ SCHICK GUTIERREZ 1 May 1963-3 Aug 1966, b 1909; d in office.
LORENZO GUERRERO GUTIERREZ 4 Aug 1966-Jun 1967, b 13 Nov 1900.
Gen ANASTASIO SOMOZA DEBAYLE 1 Jun 1967-May 1972, younger son of Gen Anastasio Somoza, b 5 Dec 1925.
May 1972-May 1973 Military triumvirate (Gen ROBERTO MARTINEZ LACLAYO, Gen ALFONSO LOBO CORDERO and EDMONDO PAPUAGA IRIAS).
Gen ANASTASIO SOMOZA DEBAYLE since 1 Dec 1974.

Niger

Niger was colonised by the French between 1891 and 1914; independence was granted on 3 Aug 1960.

Presidents
(also Head of Government)

HAMANI DIORI Head of State 3 Aug-9 Nov 1960; President 9 Nov 1960-15 Apr 1974 when he was deposed in a coup, b 1916.
Lieut-Col SEYNI KOUNTCHÉ since 17 Apr 1974, b 1933.

Nigeria

The colony and protectorate of Nigeria was formed in 1914 by the merger of territories which had come under British rule at various times: Lagos (British from 1861), Northern Nigeria (passed to the Crown in 1899 having been the property of the Royal Niger Company) and the Oil Rivers, later Niger Coast, protectorate (British from 1885). Nigeria became independent on 1 Oct 1960 and a Republic on 1 Oct 1963.

THE DOMINION OF NIGERIA

Governors-General

Sir **JAMES ROBERTSON** **1 Oct-16 Nov 1960.**
Dr **NNAMDI AZIKIWE** **16 Nov 1960-1 Oct 1963,** b 16 Nov 1904. Became first President.

Prime Minister

Alhaji Sir **ABUBAKAR TAFAWA BALEWA** **1 Oct 1960-1 Oct 1963,** b Dec 1912. Became Premier under the Republic.

THE REPUBLIC OF NIGERIA

Presidents

Dr **NNAMDI AZIKIWE** **1 Oct 1963-15 Jan 1966** when he was deposed in a coup.
Dr **NWAFOR ORIZU** acting President **15-21 Jan 1966.**
(The office of President was then suspended.)

Prime Minister

Alhaji Sir **ABUBAKAR TAFAWA BALEWA** **1 Oct 1960-15 Jan 1966** when he was killed in a coup, b 1912. The son of a peasant who took his name from his native village, Sir Abubakar had remarkable determination and played an important role at Commonwealth conferences.

Heads of State and Heads of the Federal Executive Council

Gen **JOHNSON T.U. AGUIYI-IRONSI** Head of Government **15-21 Jan 1966**; Head of State and Head of Government **21 Jan-1 Aug 1966** when he was deposed and later killed in a coup, b 3 Mar 1924; d 3 or 4 Aug 1966.
Lieut-Col **YAKUBU GOWON** (later Gen) **1 Aug 1966-29 Jul 1975** when he was deposed in a coup, b 19 Oct 1934.
Brig **MURTALA RAMAT MOHAMMED** **29 Jul 1975-13 Feb 1976** when he was killed in an attempted coup, b Jun 1937.
Lieut-Gen **OLUSEGUN OBASANJO** since **13 Feb 1976,** b 5 Mar 1937.

Normandy *see* France

North Korea *see* Korean People's Democratic Republic

Northumbria *see* Anglo-Saxon Kingdoms, United Kingdom

North Vietnam *see* Vietnam

North Yemen *see* Yemen

Norway

Norway initially achieved unity at the end of the 9th century, but was divided several times by civil wars in the early Middle Ages. At the start of the 15th century the country passed under Danish rule and did not regain her independence until 1814, briefly under a Danish Prince, then in a personal union under the Swedish crown. In 1905 an independent dynasty was established when the links with Sweden were dissolved.

† Kings

EARLY KINGS
The early Kings' sons - legitimate and illegitimate - were all considered to have an equal claim to kingship, providing they could gain the support of a local assembly or 'thing'. Thus, on several occasions Norway suffered division between co-rulers.

HARALD I (called Haarragre meaning 'fairhair') *c*872 or *c*892-*c*940 when he abdicated, b *c*860; d *c*945. By defeating the other Norwegian rulers at the Battle of Hafrsfjord (*c*872 or *c*892) Harald, King of Vestfold, united Norway. That he thought more of personal power than of a Norwegian state is shown by his eventual (disastrous) division of Norway between his sons.
EIRIK I (called Blodøks meaning 'bloodaxe' - he murdered seven of his brothers) co-ruler *c*940-*c*945 when he was deposed, son of Harald I, b *c*895; d 954.
HAAKON I co-ruler *c*940-*c*945; sole ruler *c*945-*c*960 killed in battle, half-brother of Eirik I, b *c*920.
HARALD II (called Graafell meaning 'greycloak') *c*960-*c*970 murdered, son of Eirik I, b *c*935. Harald's attempt to introduce Christianity resulted in his deposition and murder.
*c*970-995 Interregnum. A period of anarchy in which Jarl Haakon, sometimes wrongly described as a King, emerged as ruler.
OLAV I Tryggvesson **995-1000** killed, possibly drowned, in battle, great-grandson of Harald I, b

*c*964. A notable warrior (he had led Viking raids on England) Olav reunited Norway and forcibly converted some of his countrymen to Christianity.

1000-1016 Interregnum. The sons of Jarl Haakon - Eirik and Svein - divided Norway between them.

OLAV II Haraldsson (St Olav) **1016-1028** when he was expelled; **1030** killed, nephew of Olav I, b *c*995. Successful in reuniting Norway and in finally establishing Christianity, Olav was deposed by the nobles who, feeling threatened by him, called on Knut. Killed in an attempt to win back his throne, Olav came to be regarded as a martyr and became his people's patron saint.

KNUT 1028-1035; was also Cnut, King of England.

(Some lists insert SVEIN KNUTSON at this point - an illegitimate son of Knut, he ruled but never reigned in Norway.)

MAGNUS I (Olavsson) sole ruler **Nov 1035-1046**; co-ruler **1046-1047** killed in battle, illegitimate son of Olav II, b 1024.

HARALD III (called Hardraade meaning 'hardruler') co-ruler **1046-1047**; sole ruler **1047-23 Sep 1066** killed in battle at Stamford Bridge by Harold II of England, uncle of Magnus I, b 1015.

MAGNUS II (Haraldsson) co-ruler **Sep 1066-1069,** son of Harald III, b 1048; d 1069.

OLAV III (called Kyrre meaning 'peaceful') co-ruler **Sep 1066-1069**; sole ruler **1069-1093,** brother of Magnus II, b *c*1050.

MAGNUS III (called Barfot meaning 'barefoot') **1093-Aug 1103** killed in battle, son of Olav III, b *c*1073.

OLAV MAGNUSSON (rarely given the regnal number IV) co-ruler **Aug 1103-1115,** son of Magnus III, b *c*1090.

EYSTEIN I co-ruler **1103-1122,** son of Magnus III, b 1089.

SIGURD I (called Jorsalasfarer meaning 'Jerusalem farer') co-ruler **Aug 1103-1122;** sole ruler **1122-1130,** son of Magnus III, b 1090. The first Nordic King to go on Crusade, Sigurd ruled jointly with his brothers in surprising harmony.

MAGNUS IV co-ruler **1130-1134;** sole ruler **1134-1136** deposed and blinded by Harald IV; son of Sigurd I, b *c*1115; killed in battle 1139.

HARALD IV co-ruler **1130-1134;** sole ruler **1134-1136** killed, claimed (probably falsely) to be the illegitimate son of Magnus III, b 1103.

SIGURD II co-ruler **1136-1155,** son of Harald IV, b 1134.

INGI I (called Krokrygg meaning 'hunchback') co-ruler **1136-1157;** sole ruler **1157-1 Feb 1161** killed, half-brother of Sigurd II, b 1135. Ingi's reign was a time of civil war.

EYSTEIN II co-ruler **1142-1157,** b *c*1125. Probably an imposter, he claimed to be an illegitimate son of Harald IV.

HAAKON II co-ruler **Feb 1161-1162** killed, son of Sigurd II, b 1147?.

MAGNUS V (Erlingsson) co-ruler **1161-1162;** sole ruler **1162-15 Jun 1184** killed in battle by Sverrir, grandson of Sigurd I, b 1156.

SVERRIR Sigurdsson (or SVERRE) **1177-2 Mar 1202,** b *c*1152. A Faroese priest, Sverrir claimed to be a son of Sigurd II. Defeating Magnus V in a civil war, he temporarily restored unity and was so successful in curbing the bishops he was excommunicated.

HAAKON III (Sverresson) **Mar 1202-1204** traditionally said to have been poisoned by his stepmother, son of Sverrir, b *c*1177.

INGI II (Baardsson) **1204-1217,** nephew of Sverrir, b 1195.

HAAKON IV 1217-Dec 1263, b 1204. Alleged to be an illegitimate son of Haakon III, Haakon IV ended the civil wars, promoted trade and the arts, gained sovereignty over Greenland and Iceland and established Norway as the leading Nordic power.

MAGNUS VI (called Lagabøter meaning 'lawmender') **Dec 1263-9 May 1280,** son of Haakon IV, b 1238.

EIRIK II (Magnusson) **May 1280-1299,** son of Magnus VI, b 1268.

HAAKON V (Magnusson) **1299-8 May 1319,** son of Magnus VI, b 1270. His encouragement of the Hanse merchants was to have disastrous long-term effects for Norway.

MAGNUS VII (Eriksson) sole ruler **May 1319-1343**; co-ruler **1343-1355;** was also Magnus II, King of Sweden.

HAAKON VI (Magnusson) co-ruler **1343-1355;** sole ruler **1355-1380,** younger son of Magnus VII, b 1340. From 1362 also co-ruler of Sweden, Haakon had an ineffectual reign and witnessed the ravage of Norway by the Black Death. His marriage to Princess (later Queen) Margarethe of Denmark eventually united the Scandinavian powers in the Kalmar Union.

OLAV IV (Haakonsson) **1380-1387;** was also Olaf II, King of Denmark.

MARGRETE (Queen) co-ruler **1387-28 Oct 1412;** was also Margrethe I, Queen of Denmark.

EIRIK III co-ruler **1387-28 Oct 1412;** sole ruler **28 Oct 1412-1442;** was also Erik VII, King of Denmark.

KRISTOFER 1442-5 Jan 1448; was also Christopher III, King of Denmark.

KARL Feb 1448-1450; was also Carl VIII, King of Sweden.

LATER KINGS

From 1450 Norway became an integral part of Denmark, the Kings of that country being Kings of Norway without a separate regnal number (see Denmark).

† Independent Danish King

KRISTIAN FREDRIK 17 May-10 Oct 1814, later Christian VIII of Denmark (see Denmark).

Haakon VII, a Dane who was elected King of Norway with Queen Maud and Prince (now King) Olav (Radio Times Hulton Picture Library)

† Kings

HOUSE OF HOLSTEIN-GOTTORP
Norway was united in a personal union with Sweden but remained independent in most respects.

KARL I 4 Nov 1814-5 Feb 1818; was also Carl XIII, King of Sweden.

HOUSE OF BERNADOTTE
KARL II Feb 1818-8 Mar 1844; was also Carl XIV Johan, King of Sweden.
OSKAR I Mar 1844-8 Jul 1859; was also Oscar I, King of Sweden.
KARL III Jul 1859-19 Aug 1872; was also Carl XV, King of Sweden.
OSKAR II Aug 1872-7 Jun 1905 when he renounced the throne of Norway; was also Oscar II, King of Sweden.

HOUSE OF OLDENBURG
HAAKON VII 18 Nov 1905-21 Sep 1951, b (Prince Christian Frederik CARL Georg Valdemar Axel of Denmark) 3 Aug 1872. Prince Carl, son of Frederik VIII of Denmark, was elected King of Norway but wisely refused the Crown until confirmed by a plebiscite of the Norwegian people. A tall, dignified man, whose simple life style appealed to his adopted countrymen, Haakon became a much-loved sovereign whose tireless war effort in exile (1940-1945) was an inspiration to his people.
OLAV V since 21 Sep 1951, only son of Haakon VII, b (Prince Alexander of Denmark) 2 Jul 1903.

Prime Ministers

OTTO HALVORSEN Jun 1920-Jun 1921, b 1872; d 1923.
OTTO BLEHR Jun 1921-Mar 1923, b 1847; d 1927.
OTTO HALVORSEN Mar-May 1923.
ABRAHAM BERGE May-Nov 1923, b 1851; d 1936.
JOHAN LUDWIG MOWINCKEL Nov 1923-Mar 1926, b 1870; d 1 Oct 1942.
IVAR LYKKE 4 Mar 1926-Jan 1928, b 1872; d 1949.
CHRISTOPHER HAMARUD 26 Jan-10 Feb 1928.
JOHAN LUDWIG MOWINCKEL 10 Feb 1928-May 1931.
PEDER KOLSTAD May 1931-6 Mar 1932, b 1878; d in office.
JENS HUNDSEID 15 Mar 1932-Feb 1933, b 1883; d 1965.
JOHAN LUDWIG MOWINCKEL 27 Feb 1933-Mar 1935.
JOHAN NYGAARDSVOLD 16 Mar 1935-11 Jun 1940; PM in exile Jun 1940-May 1945; PM in Norway 31 May-19 Jun 1945, b 1879; d 13 May 1952. The leader of the Norwegian Government in exile during the German occupation of Norway.
EINAR HENRY GERHARDSEN 19 Jun 1945-Nov 1951, b 10 May 1897.
OSCAR TORP 13 Nov 1951-Jan 1955, b 8 Jan 1893; d 1 May 1958.
EINAR HENRY GERHARDSEN 14 Jan 1955-Aug 1963.
JOHAN LYNG 23 Aug-20 Sep 1963, b 22 Aug 1905; d Jan 1978.
EINAR HENRY GERHARDSEN 24 Sep 1963-Oct 1965.
PER BORTEN 11 Oct 1965-Mar 1971, b 3 Apr 1913.
TRYGVE BRATTELI 13 Mar 1971-Oct 1972, b 11 Jan 1910.
LARS KORVALD 12 Oct 1972-Oct 1973, b 29 Apr 1916.
TRYGVE BRATTELI 14 Oct 1973-Jan 1976.
ODVAR NORDLI since 9 Jan 1976, b 3 Nov 1927.

Novgorod, Princes of *see* Union of Soviet Socialist Republics

Nyasaland *see* Malawi

Oldenburg *see* Germany

Oman

The ancient state of Muscat, occupied by the Portuguese in the 16th century and the Persians in the 18th century, was reunited by Ahmed bin Said who founded the Al Bu Said Dynasty in 1749. The union of Muscat and Oman was not finally ratified until the Treaty of Sib in 1920 and the state's name was changed to the Sultanate of Oman in 1970.

† Sultans of Muscat and Oman

AL BU SAID DYNASTY
AHMED bin Said **1749-1783.** An ambitious former trader he seized Muscat, ousted the Persians and encouraged commerce. ·
SAID bin Ahmed **1783-1784,** eldest son of Ahmed bin Said.
HAMAD bin Said **1784-1792,** son of Said bin Ahmed.
SULTAN bin Ahmed **1792-1804** murdered by pirates, youngest? son of Ahmed bin Said.
BADAR bin Seif **1804-1806** murdered by Said bin Sultan; nephew of Sultan bin Ahmed.
SAID bin Sultan **1806-1856,** son of Sultan bin Ahmed, b after 1785. A great ruler who repelled Wahhabi attacks and who built an Indian Ocean empire with settlements along the East African coast - he resided in Zanzibar from 1840.
THWAINI bin Said **1856-1866** murdered by his son Salim; elder son of Said bin Sultan.
SALIM bin Thwaini **1866-1868** deposed, son of Thwaini bin Said; d in exile after 1870.
AZZAN bin Qais **1868-1871** died in battle against Turki bin Said; great-great-grandson of Ahmed bin Said. A usurper who was largely unrecognised.
TURKI bin Said **1871-1888,** son of Said bin Sultan.
FEISAL bin Turki **1888-1913,** younger son of Turki bin Said.
TAIMUR bin Feisal **1913-1932** abdicated, eldest son of Feisal bin Turki, b 1888; d 1965 in exile.
SAID bin Taimur **1932-23 Jul 1970** when he was deposed in a palace coup, eldest son of Taimur bin Feisal.
QABOOS bin Said (bin Taimur bin Feisal bin Turki bin Said bin Sultan bin Ahmed bin Said) **Jul 1970** when he became Sultan of Oman.

† Sultan of Oman

AL BU SAID DYNASTY
QABOOS bin Said Sultan of Muscat and Oman from 23 Jul 1970; Sultan of Oman **from Jul 1970,** son of Said bin Taimur, b 18 Nov 1940.

Orange Free State *see* South Africa

Ostrogoth Kingdom *see* Italy

Ottoman Empire *see* Turkey

Pakistan

The overwhelmingly Muslim areas of British India formed a separate Dominion - Pakistan ('noble land') - when the British withdrew from India. In 1956 the country became a Republic.

THE DOMINION OF PAKISTAN

Governors-General

MOHAMMED ALI JINNAH 16 Aug 1947-11 Sep 1948, b 25 Dec 1876; d in office. A lawyer who worked for the independence of India in the Congress Party, Jinnah broke with Nehru and Gandhi in 1934 to found the Muslim League advocating a separate nation for the Islamic populace of the sub-continent. The father of Pakistan, he was known as 'Qaid-i-Azam' - the Great Leader.
KHWAJA NAZIMUDDIN 14 Sep 1948-Oct 1951.
GHULAM MUHAMMAD 19 Oct 1951-Oct 1955, b 1895; d 1956.
Maj-Gen **ISKANDER MIRZA 6 Oct 1955-Mar 1956** when he became President.

Prime Ministers

LIAQUAT ALI KHAN 16 Aug 1947-16 Oct 1951, b 1 Oct 1895; assassinated - d in office.
KHWAJA NAZIMUDDIN 17 Oct 1951-Apr 1953, b 1894; d 22 Oct 1964.
MOHAMMED ALI 17 Apr 1953-Aug 1955, b 1909; d Jan 1963.
CHAUDHRI MOHAMMED ALI 7 Aug 1955-Mar 1956 when he became PM of the Republic.

THE ISLAMIC REPUBLIC OF PAKISTAN

Presidents

Maj-Gen **ISKANDER MIRZA 23 Mar 1956-Oct 1958,** b 13 Nov 1899; d 13 Nov 1969.
Gen **MOHAMMED AYUB KHAN 28 Oct 1958-Mar 1969,** b 14 May 1907; d 19 Apr 1974. His authoritarian rule benefited the economy of West Pakistan but not that of East Pakistan where separatist feeling grew; his system of

indirect elections (basic democracy) created unrest which led to his downfall.

Gen **AGHA MUHAMMAD YAHYA KHAN 31 Mar 1969-Dec 1971,** b 4 Feb 1917.

ZULFIQAR ALI BHUTTO 20 Dec 1971-Aug 1973, b 5 Jan 1928.

FAZAL ELAHI CHAUDHRI since 14 Aug 1973, b 1 Jan 1904.

Prime Ministers

CHAUDRI MOHAMMED ALI 23 Mar-Sep 1956, b 15 Jul 1905.

HUSSEIN SHAHEED SUHRAWARDY 10 Sep 1956-Oct 1957, b 1893; d 1963.

ISMAEL IBRAHIM CHUNDRIGAR 17 Oct-16 Dec 1957, b 1897; d 1960.

MALIK FIROZ KHAN NOON 16 Dec 1957-Oct 1958, b 1893; d 9 Dec 1970.

Gen **MOHAMMED AYUB KHAN 7 Oct 1958-Mar 1969**; see President Ayub Khan.

Gen **AGHA MUHAMMAD YAHYA KHAN 24 Mar 1969-Dec 1971**; see President Yahya Khan.

NURUL AMIN 7-20 Dec 1971, b 1894.

ZULFIQAR ALI BHUTTO 20 Dec 1971-5 Jul 1977 deposed in coup; see President Bhutto.

Gen **MOHAMMED ZIA ul-HAQ** Chief of Martial Law Administration (acting PM) **since 5 Jul 1977.**

Palatinate of the Rhine, The *see* Germany

Palestine *see* Israel

Pamplona, Kings of *see* Navarre, Spain

Panama

Spanish from 1510, Panama formed part of New Granada (later Colombia). Independent in 1821 the country was included in Greater Colombia and then New Granada. Independent from 1855 to 1863 Panama rejoined New Granada as part of the United States of Colombia from which country it finally seceded in 1903 after the Colombian Government had refused to accept the American plan for a canal through Panama.

FIRST PANAMANIAN REPUBLIC

Presidents

JUSTO AROSEMENA provisional Head of Government **Feb 1855-Oct 1856.**

Gen **BARTOLOMEO CALVO Oct 1856-Sep 1858.**

JOSÉ de OBALDIA Sep 1858-1862.

SANTIAGO de la GUARDIA 1862-Sep 1862 killed in coup.

MANUEL MARIA DIAZ Sep 1862-15 Jun 1863 when Panama joined Colombia.

15 Jun 1863-3 Nov 1903 Colombian rule until Panama seceded.

THE REPUBLIC OF PANAMA

Presidents

3 Nov 1903-1904 Provisional Government from the declaration of independence.

MANUEL AMADOR GUERRERO Feb 1904-Oct 1908, b 1833; d 1909.

JOSÉ DOMINGO de OBALDIA Oct 1908-1 Mar 1910, b 1845; d in office.

CARLOS ANTONIO MENDOZA acting President **Mar-Oct 1910.**

PABLO AROSEMENA Oct 1910-Oct 1912.

BELISARIO PORRAS Oct 1912-Oct 1916, b 1856; d 1942.

RAMÓN VÁLDEZ Oct 1916-4 Jun 1918, d in office.

CIRO LUIS URRIOLA acting President **Jun-Oct 1918.**

BELISARIO PORRAS Oct 1918-Oct 1920.

ERNESTO LEFEVRE acting President **Oct 1920.**

BELISARIO PORRAS Oct 1920-Oct 1924.

RODOLFO CHIARI Oct 1924-Oct 1928, b 1869; d 1937.

FLORENCIO HARMODIO AROSEMENA Oct 1928-2 Jan 1931 deposed, b 1873; d 1945.

HARMODIO ARIAS acting President **Jan 1931,** b 1886; d 1962.

RICARDO ALFARO Jan 1931-Jun 1932, b 1882; d Feb 1971.

HARMODIO ARIAS Jun 1932-Jun 1936.

Dr **JUAN DEMÓSTENES AROSEMENA Jun 1936-16 Dec 1939,** b 1879; d in office.

Dr **AUGUSTO SAMUEL BOYD** acting President **16 Dec 1939-Oct 1940,** b 1879; d 1957.

Dr **ARNULFO ARIAS MADRID 1 Oct 1940-9 Oct 1941** deposed in coup, b 15 Aug 1901.

JAEN GARCIA 9 Oct 1941.

RICARDO ADOLFO de la GUARDIA 9 Oct 1941-Oct 1945, b 1899; d 1969.

ENRIQUE ADOLFO JIMÉNEZ Oct 1945-Oct 1948.

Dr **DOMINGO DÍAZ AROSEMENA 1 Oct 1948-23 Aug 1949,** b 1875; d in office.

Dr **DANIEL CHANIS** acting President **23 Aug-20 Nov 1949** deposed in coup, b 1892.

Dr **ROBERTO FRANCISCO CHIARI** acting President **20-24 Nov 1949.**

Dr **ARNULFO ARIAS MADRID 24 Nov 1949-10 May 1951** deposed in coup.

ALCIBÍADES AROSEMENA 10 May 1951-Oct 1952, b 1883; d 1958.

Col **JOSÉ ANTONIO RAMON RAMON 1 Oct 1952-2 Jan 1955,** b 1908; d in office - assassinated.

JOSÉ RAMON GUIZADO 2-15 Jan 1955. Removed from office and impeached for complicity in the assassination of his predecessor.

RICARDO ARIAS ESPINOSA 15 Jan 1955-Oct 1956.

ERNESTO de la GUARDIA 1 Oct 1956-Oct 1960, b 1900; d 1964.

Dr ROBERTO FRANCISCO CHIARI 1 Oct 1960-Oct 1964, son of Roberto Chiari, b 2 Mar 1905.

MARCO AURELIO ROBLES 1 Oct 1964-24 Mar 1968 removed from office, b 8 Nov 1905.

MAX del VALLE acting President 24 Mar-Oct 1968.

Dr ARNULFO ARIAS MADRID 1-13 Oct 1968 deposed in coup.

Col JOSÉ MANUEL PINILLA FÁBREGA 13 Oct 1968-Dec 1969, b 28 Mar 1919.

DEMETRIO BASILIO LAKAS BAHAS since 18 Dec 1969, b 29 Aug 1925.

Head of Government

A new post created by constitutional amendment 13 Sep 1973.

Brig-Gen OMAR TORRIJOS HERRERA since 13 Sep 1973, b 13 Feb 1929.

Papal State

† The Popes

The title 'Pope' was not used by the Bishops of Rome until the reign of St Siricius (384-399). Tradition says that most of the early Popes, up to Eusebius, were martyred, but very little is known about them - even their dates are uncertain. As well as being Head of the Catholic Church, the Pope is also a sovereign, although that temporal sovereignty is today confined to the Vatican and various buildings in and around Rome. Modern opinion is that a papal reign begins at election not at coronation - where possible this list gives the date of election.

PETRUS (Saint Peter) c40-64 or 67. St Peter, a Galilean fisherman, was chosen as chief of the Apostles by Jesus. After the Resurrection, Peter preached in the Holy Land and in Asia Minor where he established his See at Antioch, before its translation to Rome (c42). Archaeological evidence suggests that he used the 'House of Hermes' on the Via Appia during his ministry. Peter was put to death in Rome by Nero.

LINUS (Saint) 64 or 67-76 or 79.

CLETUS (Saint) 76 or 79-88; also known as Anacletus.

CLEMENS I (Saint) 88 or 92-97 or 101.

EVARISTUS (Saint) 97 or 99-105 or 107.

ALEXANDER I (Saint) 105 or 107-115 or 116.

XYSTUS I (Saint) 115 or 116-125.

TELESPHORUS (Saint) 125-136 or 138.

HYGINUS (Saint) 136 or 138-140 or 142.

PIUS I (Saint) 140 or 142-155.

ANICETUS (Saint) 155-166.

SOTERUS (Saint) c166-174 or 175.

ELEUTHERIUS (Saint) 174 or 175-189.

VICTOR I (Saint) 189-198 or 199.

ZEPHYRINUS (Saint) 199-217.

CALLISTUS I (Saint) c217-222 or 223.

(HIPPOLYTUS, anti-pope, c217.)

URBANUS I (Saint) 222 or 223-230.

PONTIANUS (Saint) 21 Jul 230-28 Sep 235.

ANTERUS (Saint) 235-3 Jan 236.

FABIANUS I (Saint) 10 Jan 236-20 Jan 250.

CORNELIUS (Saint) Mar or Apr 251-Jun 253.

(NOVATIANUS, anti-pope, 251.)

LUCIUS I (Saint) 25 Jun 253-5 Mar 254.

STEPHANUS I (Saint) 12 May 254-2 Aug 257.

XYSTUS II (Saint) 30 or 31 Aug 257-6 Aug 258.

DIONYSIUS (Saint) 22 Jul 259-26 Dec 268.

FELIX I (Saint) 5 Jan 269-Dec 274.

EUTYCHIANUS (Saint) 4 Jan 275-Dec 283.

CAIUS (Saint) 17 Dec 283-22 Apr 296; also known as Gaius.

MARCELLINUS (Saint) 296-304.

MARCELLUS I (Saint) 27 May 308-16 Jan 309.

EUSEBIUS (Saint) c310.

MILTIADES (Saint) 2 Jul 311-11 Jan 314; also known as Melchiades.

SILVESTER I (Saint) 31 Jan 314-31 Dec 335. Silvester I built the first basilica of St Peter in Rome.

MARCUS (Saint) Jan-Oct 336.

JULIUS I (Saint) 6 Feb 337-12 Apr 352.

LIBERIUS 17 May 352-24 Sep 366. Liberius was exiled by the emperor Constantius II who set up the anti-pope Felix II.

(FELIX II, anti-pope, 355-365.)

DAMASUS (Saint) 1 Oct 366-11 Dec 384, b c305.

(URSICINUS, anti-pope, 366-367.)

SIRICIUS (Saint) Dec 384-26 Nov 399.

ANASTASIUS (Saint) 27 Nov 399-19 Dec 401.

INNOCENS I (Saint) 22 Dec 401-12 Mar 417. Innocens I played an important part in establishing the organisation of the Church and the primacy of Rome.

ZOSIMUS (Saint) 18 Mar 417-26 Dec 418.

BONIFACIUS I (Saint) 28 or 29 Dec 418-4 Sep 422.

CAELESTINUS I (Saint) 10 Sep 422-27 Jul 432.

XYSTUS III (Saint) 31 Jul 432-Mar or Aug 440.

LEO I (Saint) 29 Sep 440-10 Nov 461. The greatest administrator of the ancient Church, Leo the Great was energetic in his opposition to heresies which were rampant at that time. He showed much courage in persuading Attila the Hun to spare Rome. He is called a 'Father of the Church'.

HILARIUS (Saint) 19 Nov 461-29 Feb 468.

SIMPLICIUS (Saint) 3 Mar 468-10 Mar 483.

FELIX III or II (Saint) 13 Mar 483-Mar 492. Recently the regnal numbers of the Popes named

Felix have been altered to omit the anti-pope Felix 'II'.

GELASIUS I (Saint) **Mar 492-21 Nov 496.** An outstanding Pope whose letters and essays have had an influence on Church organisation.

SYMMACHUS (Saint) **22 Nov 498-19 Jul 514.** (LAURENTIUS, anti-pope, 498-505.)

HORMISDAS (Saint) **20 Jul 514-6 Aug 523.**

IOANNES I (Saint) **13 Aug 523-18 May 526.** Ioannes I died in prison where he had been confined by Theodoric, heretical King of Italy.

FELIX IV or **III** (Saint) **12 Jul 526-22 Sep 530.**

BONIFACIUS II 22 Sep 530-17 Oct 532. (DIOSCORUS, anti-pope, 530.)

IOANNES II 2 Jan 533-8 May 535. Mercurius, a Roman priest; Ioannes II was the first to change his name on becoming Pope.

AGAPETUS I (Saint) **13 May 535-22 Apr 536.**

SILVERIUS (Saint) **1 Jun 536-11 Nov 537.** Silverius died in exile; Vigilius had taken his place in Mar 537.

VIGILIUS 29 Mar 537-7 Jun 555.

PELAGIUS I 16 Apr 556-4 Mar 561.

IOANNES III 17 Jul 561-13 Jul 574.

BENEDICTUS I 2 Jun 575-30 Jul 579.

PELAGIUS II 26 Nov 579-7 Feb 590.

GREGORIUS I (Saint) **3 Sep 590-12 Mar 604,** b *c* 540. St Gregorius the Great gave up wealth and high civil office to become a Benedictine monk. It is said that he saw some fair-haired youths in the slave market and on being told they were Angles he observed they were angels and determined on the conversion of their people - thus, when Pope, he sent Augustinus to England. A much loved Pope, Gregorius reformed the chant (Gregorian) and wrote extensively ('Moralia' and 'Pastoral Care').

SABINIANUS (Saint) **13 Sep 604-22 Feb 606.**

BONIFACIUS III 19 Feb-12 Nov 607.

BONIFACIUS IV (Saint) **25 Aug 608-8 May 615.**

DEUSDEDIT I (Saint) **19 Oct 615-8 Nov 618**: also known as Adeodatus.

BONIFACIUS V 23 Dec 619-25 Oct 625.

HONORIUS I 27 Oct 625-12 Oct 638.

SEVERINUS Oct 638-2 Aug 640.

IOANNES IV 24 Dec 640-12 Oct 642.

THEODORUS I 24 Nov 642-14 May 649.

MARTINUS I (Saint) **Jul 649-16 Sep 655.** After a theological dispute, St Martinus was arrested and cruelly treated, then exiled by Emperor Constantinus II.

EUGENIUS I (Saint) **10 Aug 654-2 Jun 657.** St Eugenius was elected during St Martinus' captivity.

VITALIANUS (Saint) **30 Jul 657-27 Jan 672.**

DEUSDEDIT II 11 Apr 672-17 Jun 676.

DONUS 2 Nov 676-11 Apr 678.

AGATHO (Saint) **27 Jun 678-10 Jan 681.**

LEO II (Saint) **Dec 681-3 Jul 683.**

BENEDICTUS II (Saint) **683-8 May 685.**

IOANNES V 23 Jul 685-2 Aug 686.

CONON 21 Oct 686-22 Sep 687. (THEODORUS, anti-pope, 687.) (PASCHALIS, anti-pope, 687-692.)

SERGIUS I (Saint) **15 Dec 687-8 Sep 701.**

IOANNES VI 30 Oct 701-11 Jan 705.

IOANNES VII 1 Mar 705-18 Oct 707.

SISINNIUS 15 Jan-4 Feb 708.

CONSTANTINUS I 25 Mar 708-9 Apr 715.

GREGORIUS II (Saint) **19 May 715-11 Feb 731,** b *c* 669.

GREGORIUS III (Saint) **18 Mar 731-28 Nov 741.**

ZACHARIAS (Saint) **3 Dec 741-22 Mar 752.**

STEPHANUS II 23-25 Mar 752. Stephanus II died before he could be crowned and has thus been omitted from some lists of Popes.

STEPHANUS II or **III 26 Mar 752-26 Apr 757,** Pepin, King of the Franks, ceded to Stephanus III lands in Italy captured from the King of the Lombards. This marked the birth of the Papal States.

PAULUS I (Saint) **29 May 757-28 Jun 767,** brother of Stephanus III.

(CONSTANTINUS 'II', anti-pope, 767-768.)

(PHILIPPUS, anti-pope, 768.)

STEPHANUS III or **IV 1 Aug 768-24 Jan 772,** b *c* 720.

HADRIANUS I 1 Feb 772-26 Dec 795.

LEO III (Saint) **26 Dec 795-12 Jun 816.** Leo III, driven from Rome by a revolt, was restored by Charlemagne, who was crowned Emperor of the Romans by Leo (25 Dec 800), thus establishing the Holy Roman Empire.

STEPHANUS IV or **V 12 Jun 816-24 Jan 817.**

PASCHALIS I (Saint) **25 Jan 817-11 Feb 824.**

EUGENIUS II 8 May 824-Aug 827.

VALENTINUS Aug-Sep 827.

GREGORIUS IV 827-Jan 844. (IOANNES, anti-pope, *c* 844.)

SERGIUS II Jan 844-27 Jan 847. The Saracens terrorised Rome during the reign of this Pope.

LEO IV (Saint) **Jan 847-17 Jul 855.**

BENEDICTUS III Jul 855-7 Apr 858. (ANASTASIUS, anti-pope, 855.)

NICHOLAUS I (Saint) **24 Apr 858-13 Nov 867,** b *c* 820.

HADRIANUS II 14 Dec 867-14 Dec 872, b 792.

IOANNES VIII 14 Dec 872-16 Dec 882. Ioannes VIII was the first Pope to be assassinated, rather than martyred.

MARINUS I 16 Dec 882-15 May 884; also referred to as Marinus II.

HADRIANUS III (Saint) **17 May 884-*c* Sep 885.**

STEPHANUS V or **VI 885-14 Sep 891.**

FORMOSUS 19 Sep 891-4 Apr 896, b *c* 816. The reign of Formosus marks the start of 'The Dark Age of the Papacy' - a period of conflict when several Popes died violently, and others were deposed.

BONIFACIUS VI 4-19 Apr 896.

STEPHANUS VI or **VII 22 May 896-Aug 897**; strangled after holding a trial of Formosus' corpse.

ROMANUS Aug-Nov 897.

THEODORUS II Dec 897; probably died violently.

IOANNES IX Jan 898-Jan 900.

BENEDICTUS IV 900-903.

LEO V Jul-Sep 903; deposed and murdered by anti-pope Christophorus.

(CHRISTOPHORUS, anti-pope, 903-Jan 904; murdered.)

SERGIUS III 29 Jan 904-14 Apr 911.

ANASTASIUS III Apr 911-Jun 913.

LANDO Jul or Aug 913-Feb or Mar 914.

IOANNES X Mar 914-May 928; deposed and murdered by Marozia Theophylactus.

LEO VI May-Dec 928.

STEPHANUS VII or VIII Dec 928-Feb 931.

IOANNES XI Feb or Mar 931-Dec 935.

LEO VII 3 Jan 936-13 Jul 939.

STEPHANUS VIII or IX 14 Jul 939-Oct 942.

MARINUS II 30 Oct 942-May 946; also referred to as Marinus III.

AGAPETUS II 10 May 946-Dec 955.

IOANNES XII 16 Dec 955-14 May 964, b c936. Ioannes XII, a corrupt Pope, was driven from his throne and murdered upon regaining it.

LEO VIII 4 Dec 963-1 Mar 965. Leo became Pope during the lifetime of Ioannes XII. He was deposed in favour of Benedictus V, but was restored when the latter was himself deposed.

BENEDICTUS V May 964-965; d 4 Jul 966.

IOANNES XIII 1 Oct 965-6 Sep 972.

BENEDICTUS VI 19 Jan 973-Jun 974; deposed and murdered.

(DONUS II, placed on some old lists at this point, did not exist.)

(BONIFACIUS VII, anti-pope, 974.)

BENEDICTUS VII Oct 974-10 Jul 983.

IOANNES XIV Dec 983-20 Aug 984 (Pietro Campanora). Ioannes XIV's attempts at reform ended when he was placed in prison, where he died under suspicious circumstances.

(BONIFACIUS VII, anti-pope, 984-985.)

IOANNES XV Aug 985-Mar 996.

GREGORIUS V 3 May 996-18 Feb 999, b 972. Bruno, son of the Duke of Carinthia. Gregorius V, the first German Pope, strove to rid the Church of simony. There is no evidence that he was poisoned as rumour suggested.

(IOANNES XVI, anti-pope, 997-998.)

SILVESTER II 2 Apr 999-12 May 1003, b (Gerbert) c945. Silvester II, the first French Pope, was so interested in science that contemporary gossip maintained he was a magician.

IOANNES XVII Jun-Dec 1003.

IOANNES XVIII 25 Dec 1003-Jul 1009 (Phasinus).

SERGIUS IV 31 Jul 1009-12 May 1012 (Pietro Buccaporca).

(GREGORIUS VI, anti-pope, 1012.)

BENEDICTUS VIII 18 May 1012-9 Apr 1024 (Theophylactus, son of the Count of Tusculum).

IOANNES XIX Apr or May 1024-6 Dec 1032 (Romanus, brother of Benedictus VIII).

BENEDICTUS IX 1032-1044;d c1049. Benedictus IX had three separate reigns, having vacated the throne for Gregorius VI in return for money. He has been called 'the Boy Pope', but there is no evidence that he was 11 or 12 when he became

Pope as a much later legend suggested. It is likely that he was about 30 on first becoming Pope.

SILVESTER III 1045. The validity of his election is uncertain.

BENEDICTUS IX 1045.

GREGORIUS VI Apr 1045-20 Dec 1046; d c Nov 1047.

CLEMENS II 24 Dec 1046-9 Oct 1047 (Suidger).

BENEDICTUS IX 1047-1048.

DAMASUS II 17 Jul-9 Aug 1048 (Poppo).

LEO IX (Saint) Dec 1048-19 Apr 1054, b (Bruno, Count of Dagsbourg) 21 Jun 1002. With Leo IX the 'Dark Age of the Papacy' ended. An energetic Pope who travelled widely, he fought the many abuses of the day.

VICTOR II 13 Apr 1055-28 Jul 1057.(Count Gebhard of Dollenstein).

STEPHANUS IX (or X) 2 Aug 1057-29 Mar 1058,b c1000, the son of Duke Gozelo of Lorraine.

(BENEDICTUS X, anti-pope, 1058-1059.)

NICHOLAUS II 6 Dec 1058-27 Jul 1061 (Gerard). This Pope finally established the rights of the cardinals as the only electors in a papal conclave.

ALEXANDER II 30 Sep 1061-21 Apr 1073 (Anselmo of Baggio).

(HONORIUS II, anti-pope, 1061-1064.)

GREGORIUS VII (Saint) 22 Apr 1073-25 May 1085 (Hildebrand), b c1020. An outstanding Pope, Gregorius VII believed that his papal powers allowed him to override sovereigns. He quarrelled with the Emperor, Heinrich IV, about lay-investiture, and excommunicated and deposed him. As many rulers sided with the Pope, Heinrich was forced to submit, standing as a penitent in the snow at Canossa (Jan 1077).

(CLEMENS III, anti-pope, 1084.)

VICTOR III (Blessed) May 1086-16 Sep 1087 (Desiderius), b 1027.

URBANUS II (Blessed) 12 Mar 1088-29 Jul 1099 (Odo), b c1042.

PASCHALIS II 13 Aug 1099-21 Jan 1118 (Ranieri).

(THEODORICUS, anti-pope, 1100).)

(ALBERTUS, anti-pope, 1102.)

(SILVESTER IV, anti-pope, 1105-1111.)

GELASIUS II 24 Jan 1118-28 Jan 1119 (Giovanni Gaetani).

(GREGORIUS VIII, anti-pope, 1118-1121.)

CALLISTUS II 2 Feb 1119-13 Dec 1124 (Gui of Burgundy).

HONORIUS II 15 Dec 1124-13 Feb 1130 (Lamberto Scannabecchi).

(CAELESTINUS, anti-pope, 1124.)

INNOCENS II 14 Feb 1130-24 Sep 1143 (Gregorio Papareschi).

(ANACLETUS II anti-pope, 1130-1138.)

(VICTOR IV, anti-pope, 1138.)

CAELESTINUS II 26 Sep 1143-8 Mar 1144 (Guido di Castello).

LUCIUS II 12 Mar 1144-15 Feb 1145 (Gerardo Caccianemici).

EUGENIUS III (Blessed) 15 Feb 1145-8 Jul 1153 (Bernardo Paganelli).

ANASTASIUS IV 12 Jul 1153-3 Dec 1154 (Corrado).

Innocens III who despite being the most powerful of Pontiffs found time for a generous concern for the poor (Radio Times Hulton Picture Library)

HADRIANUS IV 4 Dec 1154-1 Sep 1159 (Nicholas Breakspeare), b c 1115. The only English Pope, Hadrianus IV was probably born at Abbots Langley in Hertfordshire. The Bull Laudabiliter (1155), which was subequently refuted, gave the sovereignty of Ireland to Henry II of England, but did not grant hereditary sovereignty to the English King.

ALEXANDER III 7 Sep 1159-30 Aug 1181 (Rolando Bandinelli), b c 1105. This Pope upheld papal authority against challenges from Emperor Friedrich I and Henry II of England. The Emperor set up a series of anti-popes before his submission.

(VICTOR IV, anti-pope, 1159-1164.)
(PASCHALIS III, anti-pope, 1164.)
(CALLISTUS III, anti-pope, 1168.)
(INNOCENS III, anti-pope, 1179-1180.)

LUCIUS III 1 Sep 1181-25 Sep 1185 (Ubaldo Allucingoli).

URBANUS III 25 Nov 1185-19 Oct 1187 (Uberto Crivelli).

GREGORIUS VIII 21 Oct-17 Dec 1187 (Alberto di Morra).

CLEMENS III 19 Dec 1187-Mar 1191 (Paolo Scolari).

CAELESTINUS III Mar 1191-8 Jan 1198 (Giacinto Buboni), b c 1106.

INNOCENS III 8 Jan 1198-16 Jul 1216 (Lothario dei Conti di Segni), b 1160 or 1161. Many consider Innocens III to have been the greatest of all the Popes. He was a man of extraordinary genius, adept at handling people. Under him the papacy's influence and power reached its Zenith, and he intervened in crises in several countries including Poland, Hungary, Spain and Portugal. His firm action solved the serious situation created by the Albigensian heresy in France. The Fourth Lateran Council was the summit of a reign that saw the foundation of both Franciscans and Dominicans.

HONORIUS III 18 Jul 1216-18 Mar 1227 (Cencio Savelli).

GREGORIUS IX 19 Mar 1227-22 Aug 1241 (Ugolino dei Conti di Segni), b c 1145.

CAELESTINUS IV 25 Oct-10 Nov 1241 (Goffredo Castiglione), b c 1170.

INNOCENS IV 25 Jun 1243-7 Dec 1254 (Sinibaldo Fieschi), b c 1200. Innocens IV is usually remembered for the culmination in his reign of the long struggle between the papacy and the imperial house of Hohenstaufen, and for the heavy taxation he imposed on the Church to meet expenses. He should be remembered as a brilliant exponent of Canon Law ('Commentaria').

ALEXANDER IV 12 Dec 1254-25 May 1261 (Rainaldo dei Conti di Segni), nephew of Gregorius IX.

URBANUS IV 29 Aug 1261-2 Oct 1264 (Jacques Pantaléon), b c 1200.

CLEMENS IV 5 Feb 1265-29 Nov 1268 (Gui Faucoi le Gros).

GREGORIUS X (Blessed) 1 Sep 1271-10 Jan 1276 (Theobaldo Visconti), b 1210. Gregorius X was elected after an interregnum of nearly three years, and a conclave at Viterbo that lasted so long that the people put the cardinals on a meagre diet and removed the roof over their heads to force them to make up their minds.

INNOCENS V (Blessed) 21 Jan-22 Jun 1276 (Pierre de Tarentaise), b c 1224.

HADRIANUS V 11 Jul-18 Aug 1276 (Ottobono dei Fieschi).

IOANNES XXI 8 Sep 1276-20 May 1277 (Pedro Juliani), b c 1210-1215. Ioannes XXI was a Portuguese philosopher and scientist who died when his laboratory collapsed on him.

NICHOLAUS III 25 Nov 1277-22 Aug 1280 (Giovanni Gaetano Orsini), b c 1215.

MARTINUS IV 22 Feb 1281-28 Mar 1285 (Simon de Brion).

HONORIUS IV 2 Apr 1285-3 Apr 1287 (Giacomo Savelli).

NICHOLAUS IV 22 Feb 1288-4 Apr 1292 (Girolamo Moschi), b 30 Sep 1227.

CAELESTINUS V (Saint) 5 Jul-13 Dec 1294 (Pietro del Morrone), b 1215. A most saintly hermit, Caelestinus V realised his own naiveté and his unfitness to rule. He abdicated - an action described by Dante as 'the Great Refusal' - and died in custody on 19 May 1296.

BONIFACIUS VIII 24 Dec 1294-11 Oct 1303 (Benedetto Gaetani), b c 1235. Bonifacius VIII, an autocrat of uncertain temper, probably due to painful illness, quarrelled violently with Philippe IV of France, claiming sovereignty over Kings. Followers of the French monarch captured and humiliated Bonifacius who died, it is said, of shock.

BENEDICTUS XI (Blessed) **22 Oct 1303-7 Jul 1304** (Nicola Boccasini), b 1240.

CLEMENS V 5 Jun 1305-20 Apr 1314 (Bertrand de Got), b *c* 1260. Crowned at Lyon, Clemens V was detained in France because of the difficult situation arising from Bonifacius VIII's struggle with Philippe IV. He established the Papacy at Avignon where it was to remain for 73 years ('The Babylonian Captivity').

IOANNES XXII 7 Aug 1316-4 Dec 1334 (Jacques Duèse), b *c* 1245.

(NICHOLAUS V, anti-pope, 1328-1330.)

BENEDICTUS XII 20 Dec 1334-25 Apr 1342 (Jacques Fournier).

CLEMENS VI 7 May 1342-6 Dec 1352 (Pierre Roger), b *c* 1291.

INNOCENS VI 18 Dec 1352-12 Sep 1362 (Étienne Aubert).

URBANUS V (Blessed) **28 Sep 1362-19 Dec 1370,** b (Guillaume Grimoard) *c* 1310.

GREGORIUS XI 30 Dec 1370-26 Mar 1378 (Pierre Roger), b 1329. The last French Pope, Gregorius XI was a devout man who restored the Papacy to Rome.

URBANUS VI 8 Apr 1378-15 Oct 1389 (Bartolommeo Prignano), b *c* 1318. Chosen in an election influenced by a Roman mob, Urbanus VI acted so severely that most of the cardinals withdrew their allegiance - an invalid gesture - and elected an anti-pope. The controversy degenerated into a political squabble, some rulers supported the Pope while others acknowledged the prentender at Avignon. This 'Great Schism' lasted 39 years.

(CLEMENS VII, anti-pope, 1378-1394.)

BONIFACIUS IX 2 Nov 1389-1 Oct 1404 (Pietro Tomacelli), b *c* 1355.

(BENEDICTUS XIII, anti-pope, 1394-1417.)

INNOCENS VII 17 Oct 1404-6 Nov 1406 (Cosimo dei Migliorati), b *c* 1336.

GREGORIUS XII 30 Nov 1406-4 Jul 1415 (Angelo Corrari), b *c* 1325; d 18 Sep 1417. Gregorius XII offered to abdicate if the anti-pope Benedictus would do likewise, but as he kept postponing this action his cardinals withdrew and invalidly elected Alexander V at Pisa, and, upon the latter's death, Ioannes XXIII. The tragedy of having a Pope challenged by one pretender in Pisa and another in Spain (Benedictus had left Avignon in 1408) could not be allowed to continue, and Gregorius abdicated, while both anti-popes were formally deposed by a Council at Constance.

(ALEXANDER V, anti-pope, 1409-1410.)

(IOANNES XXIII, anti-pope, 1410-1415.)

MARTINUS V 11 Nov 1417-20 Feb 1431 (Odo Colonna), b 1368.

EUGENIUS IV 3 Mar 1431-23 Feb 1447 (Gabriele Condolmieri), b *c* 1383.

(FELIX V, the last anti-pope, 1440-1449.)

NICHOLAUS V 6 Mar 1447-24 Mar 1445 (Tommaso Parentucelli), b 1397. A learned yet simple man who was a humanist and who gave great impetus to the Renaissance.

CALLISTUS III 8 Apr 1455-6 Aug 1458 (Alonso Borgia), b 31 Dec 1378.

PIUS II 19 Aug 1458-15 Aug 1464 (Aeneas Piccolomini), b 18 Oct 1405.

PAULUS II 30 Aug 1464-26 Jul 1471 (Pietro Barbo), b 23 Feb 1417.

XYSTUS IV 9 Aug 1471-12 Aug 1484 (Francesco della Rovere), b 21 Jul 1414. Xystus built the chapel named after him - the Sistine.

INNOCENS VIII 29 Aug 1484-25 Jul 1492 (Giovanni Battista Cibo), b 1432.

ALEXANDER VI 11 Aug 1492-18 Aug 1503 (Roderigo Borgia), b *c* 1431. The father of Cesare (b *c* 1475) and Lucrezia (b 1480), Alexander was an unscrupulous autocrat, of poor morals and addicted to nepotism. The way in which this Renaissance Prince for whom Michelangelo created the Pieta, neglected religion contributed to the call for a Reformation.

PIUS III 22 Sep-18 Oct 1503 (Francesco Todeschini), b *c* 1440.

JULIUS II 31 Oct 1503-21 Feb 1513 (Giuliano della Rovere), b 1443. A patron of the arts, he laid the foundation stone of the present St Peter's; a warlike ruler, Julius was a Prince first and Pope second.

LEO X 9 Mar 1513-1 Dec 1521 (Giovanni de 'Medici), b 11 Dec 1475.

HADRIANUS VI 9 Jan 1522-14 Sep 1523 (Adriaan Dedel), b 2 Mar 1459. The only Dutch Pope and the last non-Italian Pope.

CLEMENS VII 18 Nov 1523-25 Sep 1534 (Giulio de 'Medici), b 26 May 1478. Clemens VII was a weak man whose political indecision brought Italy under the control of the Habsburgs. With Rome in the hands of Catherine of Aragon's nephew, Charles V, Clemens was in no position to consider Henry VIII's divorce.

PAULUS III 13 Oct 1534-10 Nov 1549 (Alessandro Farnese), b 29 Feb 1468. Reformer, patron of the arts and the owner of a celebrated temper, Paulus III summoned the Council of Trent.

JULIUS III 7 Feb 1550-23 Mar 1555 (Giovanni Maria Ciocchi del Monte), b 10 Sep 1487.

MARCELLUS II 9 Apr-1 May 1555 (Marcello Cervini), b 1501. A fine churchman who was universally loved.

PAULUS IV 23 May 1555-18 Aug 1559 (Giovanni Pietro Carafa), b 28 Jun 1476.

PIUS IV 25 Dec 1559-9 Dec 1565 (Gianangelo de 'Medici), b 1499.

PIUS V (Saint) **7 Jan 1566-1 May 1572** (Michele Ghislieri), b 17 Jan 1504.

GREGORIUS XIII 13 May 1572-10 Apr 1585 (Ugo Buoncompagni), b 1502.

XYSTUS V 24 Apr 1585-27 Aug 1590 (Felice Perretti), b 13 Dec 1520. An able and vigorous reformer, Xystus V, one of the greatest Pontiffs, restored law and order to the Papal States and organised both the Curia and the Congregations, establishing the present Papal administrative system.

Pope Benedictus XIV, who is known as the 'scholar's Pope' was perhaps the greatest intellect ever to occupy the Papacy (Radio Times Hulton Picture Library)

URBANUS VII 15-27 Sep 1590 (Giovanni Battista Castagna), b 4 Aug 1521.

GREGORIUS XIV 5 Dec 1590-15 or 16 Oct 1591 (Nicolo Sfondrati), b 11 Feb 1535.

INNOCENS IX 29 Oct-30 Dec 1591 (Giovanni Antonio Facchinetti), b 20 Jul 1519.

CLEMENS VIII 30 Jan 1592-3 Mar 1605 (Ipollito Aldobrandini), b 24 Feb 1536.

LEO XI 1-27 Apr 1605 (Alessandro de 'Medici), b 1535.

PAULUS V 16 May 1605-28 Jan 1621 (Camillo Borghese), b 17 Sep 1552.

GREGORIUS XV 9 Feb 1621-3 Jul 1623 (Alessandro Ludovisi), b 9 Jan 1554.

URBANUS VIII 6 Aug 1623-29 Jul 1644 (Maffeo Barberini), b Apr 1568. Urbanus is remembered as the opponent of the Jansenist heresy and as the patron of Bernini.

INNOCENS X 15 Sep 1644-7 Jan 1655 (Giovanni Battista Pamfili), b 7 Mar 1572.

ALEXANDER VII 7 Apr 1655-22 May 1667 (Fabio Chigi), b 13 Feb 1599.

CLEMENS IX 20 Jun 1667-9 Dec 1669 (Giulio Rospigliosi), b 28 Jan 1600.

CLEMENS X 29 Apr 1670-22 Jul 1676 (Emilio Altieri), b 13 Jul 1590.

INNOCENS XI (Blessed) 21 Sep 1676-11 or 12 Aug 1689 (Benedetto Odescalchi), b 19 May 1611. Called the 'Father of the Poor', Innocens XI was a saintly reformer, but also a firm upholder of the authority of his office. There is no evidence to support the assertion that he sympathised with William III's campaign against James II of England (1688).

ALEXANDER VIII 6 Oct 1689-1 Feb 1691 (Pietro Ottoboni), b 22 Apr 1610.

INNOCENS XII 12 Jul 1691-27 Sep 1700 (Antonio Pignatelli), b 13 Mar 1615.

CLEMENS XI 23 Nov 1700-19 Mar 1721 (Gianfrancesco Albani), b 23 Jul 1649.

INNOCENS XIII 8 May 1721-7 Mar 1724 (Michelangelo de 'Conti), b 13 May 1655.

BENEDICTUS XIII 27 May 1724-21 Feb 1730 (Pietro Francesco Orsini-Gravina), b 2 Feb 1649.

CLEMENS XII 12 Jul 1730-6 Feb 1740 (Lorenzo Corsini), 7 Apr 1652.

BENEDICTUS XIV 17 Aug 1740-3 May 1758 (Prospero Lambertini), b 31 Mar 1675. 'The scholar's pope', Benedictus XIV is one of the outstanding intellects in the history of the Papacy. He made concordats with several states, founded academies, and had a wonderful sense of humour.

CLEMENS XIII 6 Jul 1758-2 Feb 1769 (Carlo della Torre Rezzonico), b 7 Mar 1693.

CLEMENS XIV 19 May 1769-22 Sep 1774 (Giovanni Vicenzo Antonio Ganganelli), b 31 Oct 1705. One of the weakest Popes, his appeasement achieved only discord.

PIUS VI 15 Feb 1775-29 Aug 1799 (Giovanni Angelo Braschi), b 25 Dec 1717. Pius VI's troubled reign began with threats of schism in Austria and Germany, and ended with the destruction of the Church in France by the revolutionaries, the invasion of Italy and his arrest and deportation by French troops. He died a captive at Valence.

PIUS VII 14 Mar 1800-20 Aug 1823 (Luigi Barnabo Chiaramonti), b 14 Aug 1742. Pius VII was the Pope who agreed a concordat with, and later crowned, Napoléon I (1804). For opposing the Emperor's ambitions, he was arrested and detained until Napoléon's defeat in 1814, when he returned to Rome.

LEO XII 28 Sep 1823-10 Feb 1829 (Annibale della Genga), b 22 Aug 1760. Usually only recalled as an arch-reactionary, whose stern and unimaginative government of the Papal States created enormous difficulties, his missionary zeal and practical help to the Church in Asia and Latin America are too often forgotten.

PIUS VIII 31 Mar 1829-1 Dec 1830 (Francesco Xaverio Castiglione), b 20 Nov 1761.

GREGORIUS XVI 2 Feb 1831-1 Jun 1846 (Bartolommeo Capellari), b 18 Sep 1765.

PIUS IX 16 Jun 1846-7 Feb 1878 (Count Giovanni Maria Mastai-Ferreti) b 13 May 1792. The longest Papal reign is also a controversial one. Hailed on election as sympathetic to Italian nationalism, neither he nor his unwise advisers seemed to appreciate the strength of the liberal forces at work. He temporarily fled Rome in the revolution of 1848, and saw the loss of most of the Papal States to the new Kingdom of Italy in

1861, and the occupation of Rome itself by Italy in 1870. The last decade of his reign witnessed stormy relations between Pius and the Italian government, and disagreement with Prussia over Bismarck's Kulturkampf. The Vatican Council (1869) defined the doctrine of Papal Infallibility.

LEO XIII 20 Feb 1878-20 Jul 1903 (Gioacchino Vincenzo Raffaele Luigi Pecci), b 2 Mar 1810. A wise and ascetic Pontiff, Leo XIII re-established the prestige of the Papacy through his actions and his attractive personality. Elected as a stopgap, his reign was one of the most important of recent years because of his major encyclicals on social questions (eg Rerum Novarum).

PIUS X (Saint) **4 Aug 1903-20 Aug 1914** (Giuseppe Sarto), b 2 Jun 1835. Pius X, saintly and unassuming, made an outstanding contribution to the devotional life of the Church.

BENEDICTUS XV 3 Sep 1914-22 Jan 1922 (Giacomo della Chiesa), b 21 Nov 1854. Benedictus XV gave away so much that the Vatican had no ready cash for his funeral.

PIUS XI 6 Feb 1922-10 Feb 1939 (Achille Ratti), b 31 May 1857. He achieved recognition of the sovereignty of the Vatican City by the Lateran Treaty (1929).

PIUS XII 2 Mar 1939-9 Oct 1958 (Eugenio Pacelli), b 2 Mar 1876.

IOANNES XXIII 28 Oct 1958-3 Jun 1963 (Angelo Giuseppe Roncalli), b 25 Nov 1881. Upon his election he was regarded as a stopgap but his was to be a highly significant pontificate. Ioannes XXIII called the second Vatican Council, heralding an age of reform, and opened contacts with Orthodox and Protestant leaders, promoting the cause of Christian unity. Of a peasant family, he had simplicity and great humanity, he was refreshingly informal yet cultured, an inspiring pastor he was universally loved.

PAULUS VI 21 Jun 1963-6 Aug 1978 (Giovanni Battista Montini), b 26 Sep 1897.

(At the time of going to press a new pope had not yet been elected).

Papua New Guinea

The territory of New Guinea was a German colony (1884-1914), then an Australian Trust Territory from 1921, and was placed in an administrative union with the territory of Papua, a British protectorate (1884-1902), then an Australian territory by the terms of the Papua New Guinea Act of 1949. Independence was granted on 16 Sep 1975.

Governors-General

Sir **JOHN GUISE 16 Sep 1975-Feb 1977,** b 1914.
Sir **TORE LOKOLOKO since Feb 1977.**

Prime Minister

MICHAEL SOMARE since 16 Sep 1975, b 9 Apr 1936.

Paraguay

The site of the famous Jesuit Mission State from 1607 to 1767, Paraguay passed to the Spanish Crown and achieved independence on 14 May 1811. However, independence from Argentina was not finally gained until 1814.

Dictators

JOSÉ GASPAR RODRIGUEZ de FRANCIA 1814-20 Sep 1840, b 6 Jan 1766; d in office. He oppressed Paraguay isolating it totally from the outside world in a vain attempt at self-sufficiency. His insane cruelty left a nation starving, bankrupt and without a government.

1840-1844 Rule by co-equal consuls.

CARLOS ANTONIO LOPÉZ a consul from 1842; **1844-10 Sep 1862,** nephew of José Gaspar Rodriguez de Francia, b 4 Nov 1790; d in office. He fought and saved Paraguay from attempts by Argentina to absorb the state, but he ruined the country's Treasury by treating its revenue as his own.

FRANCISCO SOLANO LOPÉZ 10 Sep 1862-1 Mar 1870, son of Carlos Antonio Lopéz, b 24 Jul 1827; d in battle. The megalomaniac dreams of this dictator, who coveted a throne and an empire upon the Napoleonic model and desired sainthood, were ended in battle at the hands of Brazil, Argentina and Uruguay against whom he had insanely waged war.

PROVISIONAL GOVERNMENT

Head

CIRILO ANTONIO RIVAROLA Mar-Jun 1870.

THE REPUBLIC OF PARAGUAY

Presidents

CIRILO ANTONIO RIVAROLA acting President **Jun 1870-Dec 1871.**
SALVADOR JOVELLANOS Dec 1871-Nov 1874.
JUAN BAUTISTA GIL Nov 1874-7 Apr 1877; d in office - murdered.
HIGINIO URIARTE Apr 1877-Nov 1878.
CANDIDO BARREIRO Nov 1878-Sep 1880; d in office.
ADOLFO SAGUIER Sep 1880-Nov 1881.

Gen **BERNARDINO CABALLERO** Nov 1881-Sep 1886.

Gen **PATRICIO ESCOBAR** Sep 1886-Sep 1890.

JUAN GONZÁLEZ Sep 1890-Jun 1894.

MARCOS MORINIGO Jun-Nov 1894.

JUAN BAUTISTA EGUSQUIZA Nov 1894-Nov 1898.

EMILIO ACEVAL Nov 1898-Jan 1902.

HECTOR CARVALLO Jan-Nov 1902.

JUAN BAUTISTA ESCURRA Nov 1902-Aug 1904.

JUAN GAONA acting President **Aug 1904-Dec 1905.**

CECILIO BAEZ Dec 1905-Nov 1906, b 1862; d 1941.

BENIGNO FERREIRA Nov 1906-Jul 1908.

EMILIANO GONZÁLEZ NAVARO Jul 1908-Nov 1910, b 1861; d 1938.

MANUEL GONDRA Nov 1910-Jan 1911.

ALBINO JARA acting President Jan-Jul 1911.

LIBERATO MARCIAL ROJAS Jul 1911-Jan 1912.

PEDRO PEÑA Jan-Mar 1912, b 1867; d 1943.

EMILIANO GONZÁLEZ NAVERO Mar-Aug 1912.

EDUARDO SCHAERER Aug 1912-Aug 1916, b 1873; d 1943.

MANUEL FRANCO Aug 1916-5 Jun 1919; d in office.

JOSÉ MONTERO acting President **Jun 1919-Aug 1920.**

MANUEL GONDRA Aug 1920-Oct 1921.

FÉLIX PAIVA acting President **Oct-Nov 1921.**

Dr **EUSEBIO AYALA** acting President **Nov 1921-Apr 1923.**

ELIGIO AYALA acting President **Apr 1923-Apr 1924.**

LUIS RIART Apr-Aug 1924.

ELIGIO AYALA Aug 1924-Aug 1928.

JOSÉ PATRICIO GUGGIARI Aug 1928-Oct 1931, b 1884; d Oct 1957.

EMILIANO GONZÁLEZ NAVERO acting President **Oct 1931-Jan 1932.**

Dr **EUSEBIO AYALA** 18 Jan 1932-18 Feb 1936 deposed in coup, b 1875; d 4 Jun 1942. He led Paraguay in the Chaco War against Bolivia.

Col **RAFAEL FRANCO** 18 Feb 1936-15 Aug 1937 deposed in coup.

Dr **FELIX PAIVA** 15 Aug 1937-Aug 1939.

Gen **JOSÉ F. ESTIGARRIBA** 15 Aug 1939-8 Sep 1940, b 21 Feb 1888; d in office in an air accident.

Gen **HIGINIO MORÍNIGO** Sep 1940-3 Jun 1948 deposed in coup, b 1897.

Dr **MANUEL FRUTOS** acting President **4 Jun-15 Aug 1948.**

Dr **J. NATALICIO GONZÁLEZ** 15 Aug 1948-30 Jan 1949 deposed in coup, b 1897; d 1966.

Gen **RAIMUNDO ROLÓN** 30 Jan-26 Feb 1949 deposed in coup, b 1903.

Dr **FELIPE MOLAS LOPÉZ** 27 Feb 1949-Jul 1950, b 1901; d 1954.

Dr **FEDERICO CHAVES** acting President **16 Jul-15 Aug 1950**; President **15 Aug 1950-May 1954.**

5-8 May 1954 Military junta.

TOMAS ROMERO PEREIRA 8 May-11 Jul 1954.

· Gen **ALFREDO STROESSNER** since 11 Jul 1954, b 3 Nov 1912.

Parma *see* Italy

Parthia *see* Iran

Pergamum

A Kingdom of Asia Minor which gained independence from the Seleucid state in 263 BC and was annexed by Rome in 133 BC.

ATTALID DYNASTY

† Heads of State

EUMENES I 263-241 BC.

ATTALUS I SOTER 241-230 BC when he became King.

† Kings

ATTALUS I SOTER Head of State from 241 BC; King **230-197 BC,** nephew of Eumenes I, b c 270 BC.

EUMENES II 197-160 or 159 BC, elder son of Attalus I, b before 220 BC.

ATTALUS II PHILADELPHUS 160 or 159-138 BC, second son of Attalus I, b 220 BC.

ATTALUS III PHILOMETOR EUERGETES 138-133 BC, son of Eumenes II, b c 170 BC. He willed his Kingdom to Rome.

Persia *see* Iran

Peru

Pizarro conquered the Inca Empire in 1533 but the Spanish Vice-Royalty of Peru was not organised until 1544. The country was liberated from Spain in Jul 1821.

Heads of State

JOSÉ de SAN MARTIN 28 Jul 1821-Sep 1822, b 25 Feb 1778; d 17 Aug 1850. The Argentinian general who was influential in freeing Chile from Spanish rule, San Martin came to Peru in Jul 1821 and declared it independent. As Protector of Peru he achieved little and he selflessly retired to Europe after meeting Bolivar who completed the liberation of Peru.

Gen **ANTONIO JOSÉ de SUCRE** Head of Provisional Government **Sep 1822-Feb 1823**; see Bolivia.
JOSÉ de la RIVA AGÜERO 1823, b 1783; d 1858.
JOSÉ BERNARDO TAGLE 1823-Feb 1824.
SIMÓN BOLIVAR Feb-Nov 1824; although effectively ruler until Dec 1826; see Colombia.

Presidents

MARIANO PRADO Nov 1824-1826.
ANDRÉS SANTA CRUZ 1826 - briefly seized power.
MARIANO PRADO 1826-Aug 1827.
Gen **JOSÉ de la MAR Aug 1827-Aug 1829.**
Gen **AGUSTIN GAMARRA Aug 1829-Dec 1833,** b 1785; killed 1841.
LUIS JOSÉ de ORBEGOSO acting President **Dec 1833-1834.**
MANUEL SALAZAR y BAQUÍJANO 1834-1835.
FELIPE SANTIAGO SALAVERRY 1835-1836, b 1806; d in office - assassinated.
Marshal **ANDRÉS SANTA CRUZ 1836-1839** President of the Confederation of Peru and Bolivia; see Bolivia.
Gen **AGUSTIN GAMARRA 1839-1841.**
MANUEL MENÉNDEZ acting President **1841-Apr 1845,** b 1790; d 1845.
Gen **RAMÓN CASTILLA Apr 1845-Apr 1851.**
Gen **JOSÉ RUFINO ECHINEQUE Apr 1851-Jan 1855** deposed, b 1808; d 1887.
Gen **RAMÓN CASTILLA Jan 1855-May 1862,** b 27 Aug 1797; d 25 May 1867. A dictator who made the valuable guano trade a state monopoly and who wisely used the revenue in constructing roads, schools and hospitals.
Marshal **MIGUEL de SAN RAMON May 1862-Apr 1863**; d in office.
Gen **JUAN ANTONIO PEZET** acting President **Apr 1863-Feb 1865,** b 1810; d 1879.
Gen **JOSÉ RUFINO ECHINEQUE Feb-Nov 1865.**
PEDRO DÍEZ CANSECO Nov 1865.
Gen **MARIANO IGNACIO PRADO** *de facto* ruler **Nov 1865-Feb 1867**; acting President **Feb-Aug 1867**; President **Aug-Oct 1867.**
LUIS la PUERTA acting President **Oct 1867-Aug 1868.**
Col **JOSÉ BALTA Aug 1868-22 Jul 1872,** b 1816; d in office - assassinated. In a display of staggering ineptitude he squandered the Treasury on grandiose public works.
SILVESTRO GUTIERREZ Jul 1872; d in office.
MANUEL PARDO Aug 1872-Aug 1876, b 1834; assassinated 1878. The first Peruvian President to be chosen by the civilian rather than by the military population, he made a sound economic recovery and founded the National Guard to balance the armed forces.
Gen **MARIANO IGNACIO PRADO Aug 1876-Dec 1879** fled, b 1826; d 1901. Prado withdrew after the Bolivano-Peruvian forces suffered heavy defeats in the War of the Pacific against Chile.

José de San Martin, Protector of Peru, who dramatically retired from South America after a mysterious meeting with Bolivar (Radio Times Hulton Picture Library)

NICOLÁS de PIÉROLA de facto Head of State **Dec 1879-Mar 1881** when the Peruvian regime collapsed, b 1839; d 1913.
Jan 1881-1884 Lima and much of southern Peru were under Chilean occupation.
FRANCISCO GARCIA CALDERON Head of provisional government **Mar-Jul 1881.**
LIZARDO MONTERO Head of provisional government **Jul 1881**; President **Jul 1881-Oct 1883,** b 1832; d 1905.
Gen **MIGUEL IGLESIAS** acting President **Oct 1883-Apr 1885,** b 1822; d 1901. He recovered the capital but was forced to cede the coast south of Tacna to the victorious Chileans.
ANTONIO ARENAS Apr 1885-Apr 1886.
Gen **ANDRÉS AVELINO CÁCERES** acting President **Apr 1886**; President **Apr 1886-Aug 1890,** b 10 Nov 1836; d 10 Oct 1923.
Col **REMIGIO MORALES BERMÚDEZ Aug 1890-May 1894** deposed in coup, b 1836; d 1894.
JUSTINIANO BORGOÑO May-Aug 1894.
Gen **ANDRÉS AVELINO CÁCERES Aug 1894-Mar 1895.**
MANUEL CANDAMO Mar-Sep 1895.
NICOLÁS de PIÉROLA Sep 1895-Sep 1899.
EDUARDO LÓPEZ de ROMAÑA Sep 1899-Sep 1903.

MANUEL CANDAMO Sep 1903-7 May 1904, b 1842; d in office.

SERAPIO CALDERÓN May-Sep 1904.

JOSÉ PARDO y BARREJA Sep 1904-Sep 1908, son of Manuel Pardo, b 24 Feb 1864; d 4 Aug 1947.

AUGUSTO BERNADINO LEGUÍA y SALCEDO Sep 1908-Sep 1912, b 19 Feb 1863; d 7 Feb 1932. A dictator, later gaoled for corruption, he brought considerable prosperity and economic progress to Peru.

GUILLERMO ENRIQUE BILLINGHURST Sep 1912-Feb 1914 deposed in coup, b 1851; d 1915.

Gen ÓSCAR RAIMUNDO BENAVIDES acting President 15 May 1914-Aug 1915.

JOSÉ PARDO y BARREJA Aug 1915-Jul 1919.

AUGUSTO BERNADINO LEGUÍA y SALCEDO 20 Jul 1919-24 Aug 1930 deposed in coup.

Gen MANUEL PONCE acting President 24-28 Aug 1930.

Col LUIS M. SÁNCHEZ CERRO acting President 28 Aug 1930-Mar 1931.

RICARDO LEONICIO ELIAS acting President 1-5 Mar 1931.

Col GUSTAVO JIMINÉZ acting President 5-10 Mar 1931.

DAVID SAMAMEZ OCAMPO acting President 10 Mar-Dec 1931.

Col LUIS M. SÁNCHEZ CERRO 8 Dec 1931-30 Apr 1933, b 1889; assassinated. He ruled ruthlessly, shamelessly rigged elections and put down a revolt by the left wing APRA party with ferocity.

Marshal ÓSCAR RAIMUNDO BENAVIDES (formerly Gen) 30 Apr 1933-Dec 1939, b 1876; d 2 Jul 1946.

Dr MANUEL PRADO y UGARTECHE 8 Dec 1939-Jul 1945, son of Mariano Prado, b 21 Apr 1889; d 14 Aug 1967.

Dr JOSÉ LUIS BUSTAMENTE RIVERO 28 Jul 1945-27 Oct 1948 deposed in coup, b 15 Jan 1894.

Gen MANUEL ODRÍA acting President 27 Oct 1948-Jun 1950.

Gen ZENÓN NORIEGA acting President 1 Jun-28 Jul 1950.

Gen MANUEL ODRÍA 28 Jul 1950-18 Jul 1956 deposed in coup, b 26 Nov 1897; d 18 Feb 1974.

18-24 Jul 1962 Military junta.

Gen RICARDO PÉREZ GODOY acting President and Head of junta 24 Jul 1962-3 Mar 1963 deposed in coup, b 1904.

Gen NICOLÁS LINDLEY LOPEZ acting President and Head of junta 3 Mar-28 Jul 1963.

FERNANDO BELAUNDE TERRY 28 Jul 1963-3 Oct 1968 deposed in coup, b 7 Oct 1913.

Gen JUAN VELASCO ALVARADO 3 Oct 1968-29 Aug 1975 deposed in coup, b 16 Jun 1909; d Dec 1977.

Gen FRANCISCO MORALES BERMÚDEZ since 30 Aug 1975, b 4 Oct 1921.

Prime Ministers

Peru is the only Latin American state to retain a Premier.

Gen RICARDO PÉREZ GODOY 18-24 Jul 1962.

Gen NICOLÁS LINDLEY LOPEZ 24 Jul 1962-Jul 1963.

Dr ÓSCAR TRELLES MONTES 28 Jul-31 Dec 1963.

Dr FERNANDO SCHWALE 1 Jan 1964-Sep 1965.

Dr DANIEL BECERRA de la FLOR 15 Sep 1965-Sep 1967.

EDGARDO SEOANE CORRALES 8 Sep-17 Nov 1967.

RÁUL FERRERO REBAGLIATI 17 Nov 1967-May 1968.

Dr OSVALDO HERCELLES 31 May-Oct 1968.

MIGUEL MUJICA GALLO 2-3 Oct 1968.

Gen ERNESTO MONTAGNE SÁNCHEZ 4 Oct 1968-Oct 1973, b 18 Aug 1916.

Gen EDGARDO MERCADO JARRÍN Oct 1973-Feb 1975.

Gen FRANCISCO MORALES BERMÚDEZ 1 Feb-Sep 1975.

Gen ÓSCAR VARGAS PRIETO 1 Sep 1975-Feb 1976.

Gen JORGE FERNÁNDEZ MALDONADO 1 Feb-16 Jul 1976.

Gen GUILLERMO ARBULÚ GALLIANI 16 Jul 1976-Jan 1978.

Gen ÓSCAR MOLINA PALLOCHIA since 30 Jan 1978.

The Philippines

Spanish from 1565 the Philippines were ceded to the United States on 10 Dec 1898 after the Spanish-American War. Following Japanese occupation in World War II independence was attained on 4 Jul 1946.

Presidents

Brig-Gen MANUEL ROXAS y ACUNA 4 Jul 1946-15 Apr 1948, b 1 Jan 1892.

ELPIDIO QUIRINO 17 Apr 1948-Nov 1953, b 16 Nov 1890; d 28 Feb 1956.

RÁMON MAGSAYSAY 10 Nov 1953-17 Mar 1957, b 31 Aug 1907; d in office, in an air accident. A hero of the resistance to Japanese occupation in World War II, he proved a strong and democratic President - he beat the Huk insurgents and took a major part in founding SEATO.

CARLOS POLESTICO GARCIA 18 Mar 1957-Dec 1961, b 4 Nov 1896; d 14 Jun 1971.

DIOSDADO MACAPAGAL 30 Dec 1961-Dec 1965, b 28 Sep 1910.

FERDINAND EDRALIN MARCOS since 30 Dec 1965, b 11 Sep 1917.

Piacenza *see* Parma, Italy

Poland

The Polish tribes (Polonie) settled in the Warta Basin in the 5th or 6th century and had formed small 'Principalities' by the 9th century. The Piast family of Great Poland (the area around Poznan) built up a Duchy and eventually a Kingdom of Poland, which became an elective monarchy termed a Royal Republic - the elective element seriously weakened the state and led to its destruction when it was partitioned by its neighbours at the close of the 18th century. The country reappeared on the map of Europe in 1918 when the Second Polish Republic was formed in the wake of World War I. The fourth partition of Poland in 1939 between Communist Russia and Nazi Germany ended the independence of the country. A Communist Republic was established after World War II.

EARLY POLISH SOVEREIGNS

† Dukes of Great Poland

HOUSE OF PIAST
(PIAST, said to be the founder of the dynasty, was probably legendary.)
ZIEMOWIT fl.9th century. The likely founder of the Piast family.
LESZEK (or LESTKO) fl.10th century.
ZIEMOMYSL before c963.
MIECZYSLAW I c963-992, probably son of Ziemomysl, b c930. In many ways the founder of Poland - his conversion to Christianity (966) is often given as the year of Poland's birth - he gained Silesia, Little Poland and access to the sea via Szczecin on the Oder where the long and often unhappy relationship between Poles and Germans began.
BOLESLAW I 992-1024 when he became King.

† Kings of Poland

HOUSE OF PIAST
BOLESLAW I ('The Brave') Duke from 992; King 1024-17 Jun 1025, eldest son of Mieczyslaw I, b 966 or 967.
MIECZYSLAW II 1025-1034, brother of Boleslaw I, b c990.

† Dukes of Great Poland

HOUSE OF PIAST
KAZIMIERZ I Karol Odnowiciel ('The Restorer') 1034-1037 deposed; 1039-28 Nov 1058, son of

Mieczyslaw II, b 25 Jul 1016. A former monk, Kazimierz I lost the throne in the anarchy before 1039. Regaining power he rebuilt Poland with the help of Emperor Heinrich III.
BOLESLAW II Nov 1058-1076 when he became King.

† King of Poland

HOUSE OF PIAST
BOLESLAW II ('The Bold' or 'The Generous') Duke from 1058; King 1076-1079 when he was exiled, son of Kazimierz I, b 1039; d 1081. Deprived of the throne by the nobles after he had executed a Bishop.

† Dukes of Great Poland

HOUSE OF PIAST
WLADYSLAW I Herman 1079-1102 abdicated, son of Kazimierz I, b 1043; d same year as his abdication.
BOLESLAW III ('The Wry Mouthed') 1102-28 Oct 1138, younger son of Wladyslaw I, b 20 Aug 1085. After re-establishing the Empire of Mieczyslaw I, he undid his life's work by dividing Poland between his sons and establishing the Seniorate.

THE SENIORATE OF POLAND

† Dukes of Krakow and Supreme Duke of Poland

HOUSE OF PIAST
Poland was divided into several Duchies, each ruled by a branch of the Piast family. The senior, or Supreme, Duke reigned in Krakow and was acknowledged by the other Dukes as overlord.

WLADYSLAW II ('The Exile') Oct 1138-1146 deposed by his brothers, son of Boleslaw III, b 1104; d in exile 1159.
BOLESLAW IV ('The Curly') 1146-1173 deposed, son of Boleslaw III, b 1127; d same year as deposition.
MIECZYSLAW III ('The Old') 1173-1177 deposed, son of Boleslaw III, b c1126.
KAZIMIERZ II ('The Just') 1177-1194, son of Boleslaw III, b 1138.
LESZEK I ('The White') 1194-1198 deposed, son of Kazimierz II, b c1185.
MIECZYSLAW III ('The Old') 1198-1202.
LESZEK I ('The White') 1202-1227 assassinated.
(After the death of Leszek I no Duke was able to gain recognition as Supreme Duke. From 1227-1290 there was no senior Duke but the Dukes of Little Poland occupied a position of superiority.)

† Dukes of Little Poland
(de facto Supreme Dukes)

HOUSE OF PIAST
BOLESLAW V ('The Chaste') **1227-1279,** son of Leszek I, b 1221.

HOUSE OF SIERADZ
LESZEK II ('The Black') **1279-1289,** Duke of Sieradz; willed the succession to Little Poland by Boleslaw V.

HOUSE OF PIAST
WLADYSLAW I 1289-1290 deposed.

† Duke of Poznan
(de facto Supreme Duke)

HOUSE OF POZNAN
PRZEMYSL 1290-1295 when he became King.

THE KINGDOM OF POLAND

† Kings

HOUSE OF POZNAN
PRZEMYSL Duke from 1290; King **1295-1296** assassinated, Duke of Poznan. A usurper who fought King Vaclav of Bohemia for possession of Poland.

HOUSE OF PREMYSL
WACLAW I 1296-1305; was also Vaclav II, King of Bohemia.
WACLAW II 1305-1306; was also Vaclav III, King of Bohemia.

THE SENIORATE OF POLAND

† Duke of Little Poland
(de facto Supreme Duke)

HOUSE OF PIAST
WLADYSLAW I 1305-Jan 1320 when he became King.

THE KINGDOM OF POLAND

† Kings

HOUSE OF PIAST
WLADYSLAW I Duke 1289-1290; 1305-1320; King **20 Jan 1320-1333,** son of Kazimierz II, b 1260. Finally established on the Polish throne, Wladyslaw rebuilt the country, encouraged trade and settlement by Germans and Flemings and, in alliance with Hungary and Lithuania, repelled Bohemian pretensions over Poland.
KAZIMIERZ III Wielki ('The Great') **1333-5 Nov 1370,** son of Wladyslaw I, b 30 Apr 1310.

HOUSE OF ANJOU
LAJOS I (King of Hungary) **Nov 1370-10 Sep 1382,** nephew of Kazimierz III. See Hungary.
Sep 1382-1384 Interregnum.
JADWIGA (Queen) **1384-1399,** daughter of Lajos I, King of Hungary, b 1373 or 1374. The election of the Hungarian King's younger daughter as Queen was the first step towards the elective monarchy.

HOUSE OF JAGIELLO
WLADYSLAW II Jagiello co-ruler **1386-1399**; sole ruler **1399-1 Jun 1434,** Supreme Duke of Lithuania and husband of Queen Jadwiga, b 1351. Wladyslaw brought Lithuania into union with Poland producing a vast realm stretching from the Baltic to the Ukrainian steppes. The gains brought the Poles into conflict with Russia, the Mongols and the Teutonic Order (the latter being destroyed by the Poles at Tannenberg in 1410), but gave Poland the status of a great power.
WLADYSLAW III Jagiello **Jun 1434-10 Nov 1444** died in battle against the Turks in Bulgaria, son of Wladyslaw II, b 31 Oct 1424.
1444-1447 Interregnum.
KAZIMIERZ IV Jagiellonczyk **1447-7 Jun 1492,** brother of Wladyslaw III, b 30 Nov 1427. Kazimierz IV presided over great advances in trade and acquired Bohemia, Silesia and Hungary for his son Wladyslaw III and appeared to be the dominant sovereign of Europe. However, his power was an illusion for the nobles had gained rights such as the veto and the privilege to elect the King which made the position of the sovereign weak and were in time to ruin Poland through their self-interest.
JAN I OLBRACHT Jun 1492-17 Jun 1501, second son of Kazimierz IV, b 27 Dec 1459.
ALEKSANDER Jagiellonczyk **Jun 1501-1506,** third son of Kazimierz IV, b 1461.
ZYGMUNT I ('The Old') sole ruler **1506-1530**; co-ruler **1530-1 Apr 1548,** fourth son of Kazimierz IV, b 1 Jan 1467.
ZYGMUNT II AUGUST co-ruler **1530-Apr 1548**; sole ruler **1548-7 Jul 1572,** son of Zygmunt I, b 1 Aug 1520. His reign was the 'Golden Age of Poland' with flourishing trade, a strong alliance with Emperor Charles V, important advances in learning and the founding of what was for a long time Europe's finest public education system, a remarkable tolerance during the Reformation and scientific achievement (eg the work of Copernicus). It also saw the Constitution of the Royal Republic that made Poland increasingly weak and ungovernable. The male Jagiellons died out with this King.

† Elected Kings

In each interregnum the noble electors usurped additional powers and thus reduced the status of the King.

Jul 1572-May 1573 Interregnum.

HENRYK May 1573-May 1574; was also Henri III, King of France.

May 1574-1576 Interregnum.

STEFAN I Batory **1576-1586,** son-in-law of Zygmunt II August, b 1533.

1586-Aug 1587 Interregnum.

ZYGMUNT III Wasa **Aug 1587-30 Apr 1632**; was also Sigismund, King of Sweden.

WLADYSLAW IV Wasa **May 1632-20 May 1648,** son of Zygmunt III, b 9 Jun 1595. His campaigns to defend Poland against the attacks of Sweden, Turkey and Russia were a brilliant success despite the lack of co-operation from the ruling nobility.

JAN II KAZIMIERZ Wasa **May 1648-Aug 1668** when he abdicated, son of Zygmunt III, b 22 Mar 1609, d in exile 16 Dec 1672. In a gloomy reign ended by abdication Poland suffered agonies similar to those inflicted on her nearly 300 years later: plague and religious torments racked the nation and invasions by Sweden and Russia destroyed towns and crops and killed fifty per cent of the population.

Aug 1668-1669 Interregnum.

MIKOLA Korybut Wisniowiecki **1669-1673,** b 1638. In this reign the Ukraine was finally lost.

1673-May 1674 Interregnum.

JAN III Sobieski **May 1674-17 Jun 1696,** b 17 Aug 1629. Perhaps Poland's greatest King, he won the throne by his reputation as a general, and his brave campaign against the Turks when he liberated Vienna (1683) was a turning point in Europe's history.

Jun 1696-Sep 1697 Interregnum.

AUGUST II (Zygmunt II August being reckoned as August I) **Sep 1697-1704** deposed; was also Friedrich August I, Elector of Saxony.

STANISLAW I Leszczynski **1704-1709** deposed, b 20 Oct 1677; d 23 Feb 1766. Stanislaw I was deposed by the interference of Austria and Russia (both of whom feared a strong pro-French Poland) and he received Lorraine, where he ruled wisely, as compensation.

AUGUST II 1709-Feb 1733.

STANISLAW I Leszczynski Feb-Oct 1733.

AUGUST III Oct **1733-5 Oct 1763**; was also Friedrich August II, Elector of Saxony.

Oct 1763-Sep 1764 Interregnum.

STANISLAW II AUGUST Poniatowski **7 Sep 1764-25 Nov 1795** abdicated, b 17 Jan 1732; d in semi-captivity in Russia 12 Feb 1798. One of Catherine the Great's ex-lovers, he won the throne through her influence and lost his country by her treachery. The Empress interfered in Polish religious affairs provoking a Catholic revolt which was used by Russia, Prussia and Austria as an excuse to invade and seize part of Poland (First Partition 1772). Poland, sobered by the experience, reformed instituting a fine democratic constitution (1791) which broke the nobles' power - declaring the constitution dangerous Catherine invaded Poland again and

Jan Sobieski, famed for his swift manoeuvres, became so corpulent that his slowness almost lost him victory at Vienna (Radio Times Hulton Picture Library)

with Prussia imposed the Second Partition (1793), which in turn led to a Polish revolt, led by Kosciuszko, which Russia, Prussia and Austria used to justify their Third Partition (1795) when Poland was totally annexed by her avaricious neighbours.

1795 Poland disappeared from the map of Europe absorbed by Prussia, Russia and Austria.

GRAND DUCHY OF WARSAW

A puppet state of the Napoleonic Empire established in 1807.

† Grand Duke

AUGUST 1807-1813; was also Friedrich August I, King of Saxony.

1815-1914 The bulk of Poland was ruled by Russia as the 'Kingdom of Poland' which was reduced to a Governorship-General following the revolt of 1863.

1918 Poland reconstituted as an independent state.

THE REPUBLIC OF POLAND

Presidents

Marshal **JÓZEF PILSUDSKI 11 Nov 1918-9 Dec 1922,** b 6 Dec 1867; d 12 May 1935. The creator of modern Poland, he established a Polish force to oppose the Russians in World War I. Seizing power in a coup in 1926 he was virtually dictator of Poland until his death.

GABRIEL NARUTOWICZ 9-16 Dec 1922, b 3 Mar 1865; assassinated - d in office.

STANISLAW WOJCIECHOWSKI 21 Dec 1922-May 1926, b 15 Mar 1869; d 9 Apr 1953.

Prof **IGNACY MÓSCICKI 1 Jun 1926-28 Sep 1939** *de facto*, b 1 Dec 1867; d 2 Oct 1946 in exile. An eminent scientist he had over 600 patents to his name.

Prime Ministers

M.L. KOZLOWSKI 13 May 1934-Mar 1935, b 1892; d 1944.

Col **VALERIAN SLAWEK 28 Mar-Oct 1935,** b 2 Nov 1879; d 2 Apr 1939.

MARIAN ZYNDRAM-KOSCIALKOWSKI 13 Oct 1935-May 1936, b 1892; d 1946.

Gen **FELICJAN SLAWOJ-SKLADKOWSKI 15 May 1936-28 Sep 1939** *de facto*, b 9 Jun 1885; d 31 Aug 1962 in exile.

THE POLISH GOVERNMENT IN EXILE

Presidents

Prof **IGNACY MÓSCICKI 28-30 Sep 1939.**

WLADYSLAW RACZKIEWICZ 30 Sep 1939-Jun 1945 when the Soviet sponsored Government in Poland was accorded international recognition, but continued in office after that date, b 1885; d 6 Jun 1947.

Prime Ministers

Gen **WLADYSLAW SIKORSKI 30 Sep 1939-4 Jul 1943,** b 1881; d (killed in an air accident) in office. A great patriot, he worked underground against Tsarist rule; he opposed Pilsudski's dictatorship; he co-ordinated the Polish forces in exile in the fight to free the country from German occupation.

STANISLAW MIKOLAJCZYK 5 Jul 1943-Nov 1944, b 18 Jul 1901; d 13 Dec 1966. He took part in the 1945 Government of National Unity but after his outspoken advocacy of a free Poland he had to flee after the Communist takeover.

TOMASZ ARCISZEWSKI 29 Nov 1944-Jun 1945 when the Soviet sponsored Government in Poland was accorded international recognition, but continued in office after that date, b 1877; d 1955 in exile.

POLISH COMMITTEE OF NATIONAL LIBERATION

Established under Soviet control in Moscow in 1944.

Chairman

EDWARD BOLESLAW OSOBKA-MORAWSKI 21 Jul-Dec 1944.

PROVISIONAL GOVERNMENT OF POLAND

From Jun 1945 the Government of National Unity.

Head of State

BOLESLAW BIERUT Apr 1945-Feb 1947.

Prime Minister

EDWARD BOLESLAW OSOBKA-MORAWSKI Dec 1944-Feb 1947, b 5 Oct 1909.

THE PEOPLE'S REPUBLIC OF POLAND

This style was not officially adopted until the new constitution of 1952 came into effect.

President

From 20 Nov 1952 styled Chairman of the Council of State.

BOLESLAW BIERUT acting Head of State from Apr 1945; President **5 Feb 1947-20 Nov 1952,** b 18 Apr 1892; d 12 Mar 1956. A hard line Stalinist, he was frequently gaoled for subversion before the war, Bierut played a major role in the Communist takeover of Poland.

ALEKSANDER ZAWADSKI 20 Nov 1952-7 Aug 1964, b 16 Dec 1899; d in office.

EDWARD OCHAB 12 Aug 1964-Apr 1968, b 16 Aug 1906.

Marshal **MARIAN SPYCHALSKI 10 Apr 1968-Dec 1970,** b 6 Dec 1906.

JÓZEF CYRANKIEWICZ 23 Dec 1970-Mar 1972, b 23 Apr 1911.

Prof **HENRYK JABLONSKI since 28 Mar 1972,** b 27 Dec 1909.

Prime Ministers
(Chairmen of the Council of Ministers)

JÓZEF CYRANKIEWICZ 7 Feb 1949-Nov 1952; see President Cyrankiewicz.

BOLESLAW BIERUT 20 Nov 1952-Mar 1954; see President Bierut.

JÓZEF CYRANKIEWICZ 19 Mar 1954-Dec 1970; see President Cyrankiewicz.

PIOTR JAROSZEWICZ since 23 Dec 1970, b 8 Oct 1909.

First Secretary of the Polish United Worker's (Communist) Party

First Secretary was formerly termed Secretary General.

BOLESLAW BIERUT Dec 1948-12 Mar 1956; see President Bierut.

EDWARD OCHAB 21 Mar 1956-Oct 1956; see President Ochab.

WLADYSLAW GOMULKA 19 Oct 1956-Dec 1970, b 6 Feb 1905.

EDWARD GIEREK since 20 Dec 1970, b 6 Jan 1913.

Pontus

A Kingdom of the ancient world, Pontus occupied most of the NE of modern Turkey. After the fall of Pontus proper to the Romans the Pontine possessions in the Crimea and beside the Sea of Azov continued as the Kingdom of Bosporus.

† Rulers
(not independent)

MITHRADATES c400-c363 BC.

ARIOBARZANES c363-337 or 336 BC. A Persian noble who threw off the overlordship of the King of Kings.

† Kings

MITHRIDATID DYNASTY

MITHRADATES I 337 or 336-302 or 301 BC.

MITHRADATES II 302 or 301-266 or 265 BC.

ARIOBARZANES 266 or 265-c250 BC, son of Mithradates II.

MITHRADATES III c250-c185 BC.

PHARNACES I c185-c170 BC, son of Mithradates III. An able King who established Pontus as a power and tried to overthrow the Seleucid Empire.

MITHRADATES IV PHILOPATOR PHILADELPHUS c170-157 BC - and possibly co-ruler before c170 BC, brother of Pharnaces I.

MITHRADATES V EUERGETES 157-123 BC assassinated, son of Pharnaces I.

MITHRADATES VI EUPATOR ('The Great') co-ruler **123-115 BC**; sole ruler **115-72 BC** when he fled; afterwards King of Bosporus, son of Mithradates V, b c132 BC; d AD 63 when he ordered a guard to kill him. He dominated Asia Minor, interfering in the affairs of most of his neighbours. After failing in his spirited efforts to save Pontus from Rome he retreated to Bosporus

to reign until the revolt of his son when he had himself killed.

MITHRADATES VII CHRESTOS co-ruler **123-after 115 BC** deposed, brother of Mithradates VI; fate uncertain.

† Kings of Bosporus
(the Pontine state in the Crimea)

MITHRADATES VI EUPATOR 72-63 BC.

63 BC Pontus proper was absorbed into the Roman Empire.

PHARNACES II 63-47 BC died in battle, son of Mithradates VI. He was defeated in a five day war by Julius Caesar whose description of the campaign was 'veni, vidi, vici' - I came, I saw, I conquered.

MITHRADATES VIII 47 BC died in battle. A usurper from Pergamum.

ASANDER 47-39?BC. A usurping Greek general.

DARIUS ?39-37 BC deposed; subsequent fate uncertain.

Popes, The *see* The Papal State

Portugal

The Roman province of Lusitania was taken by the Suevi, then by the Visigoths before falling to the Arabs in 711. The County of Portugal, independent from the 9th to the 11th century, was taken by Castile but re-established as a separate County in 1097. A Kingdom from 1139 to Oct 1910, Portugal remained independent except for a period of Spanish rule (1580-1640). Since the overthrow of the monarchy the country has experienced various forms of republican government.

THE COUNTY OF PORTUGAL

† Counts

HOUSE OF BURGUNDY

HENRIQUE 1097-1112, b (brother of Eudes, Duke of Burgundy) 1057. The County, that part of Portugal north of Coimbra, was given to Henrique by his father-in-law, Alfonso VI of Castile.

AFONSO 1112-Jul 1139 when he became King.

THE KINGDOM OF PORTUGAL

† Kings

HOUSE OF BURGUNDY

AFONSO I Count from 1112; King **25 Jul 1139-6 Dec 1185,** son of Count Henrique, b c1094.

Afonso took all Portugal north of the Tagus, including Lisbon, from the Arabs and declared it an independent Kingdom.

SANCHO I Dec 1185-1211, son of Afonso I, b 1154.

AFONSO II ('The Fat') 1211-25 Mar 1223, son of Sancho I, b c 1185.

SANCHO II Mar 1223-Jan 1248, elder son of Afonso II, b c 1209. Such was the anarchy under Sancho that the Pope granted his brother a commission to depose him. After civil war Sancho went into exile (Jan or Feb 1246) leaving Afonso as Regent.

AFONSO III Jan 1248-16 Feb 1279, brother of Sancho II, b 5 May 1210. King in all but name 1246-1248 after expelling his brother.

DINIS Feb 1279-1325, son of Afonso III, b 1261.

AFONSO IV 1325-28 May 1357, son of Dinis, b 1291.

PEDRO I May 1357-1367, son of Afonso IV, b 1320.

FERNANDO I 1367-1383, son of Pedro I, b 1345.

BEATRIZ (Queen) **1383-1385** *de jure* only, daughter of Fernando I; date of death uncertain. The 'reign' of Queen Beatriz, wife of Juan I of Castile, was a period of war between the Castilian armies backing the Queen and the nationalist Portuguese forces who supported John of Aviz.

HOUSE OF AVIZ

JOÃO I Defender of the Realm 1383-1385; King **Apr 1385-14 Aug 1433,** illegitimate son of Pedro I, b 11 Apr 1357. Soundly defeating the Castilian supporters of Beatriz at Aljubarrota, he secured Portugal's independence. João established a permanent alliance with England and encouraged his son Henry the Navigator (who never sailed himself) in the organisation of voyages of discovery that laid the foundations of the Portuguese empire.

DUARTE Aug 1433-9 Sep 1438, son of João I, b 30 Oct 1391.

AFONSO V Sep 1438-28 Aug 1481, son of Duarte, b 15 Jan 1432.

JOÃO II Aug 1481-Oct 1495, son of Afonso V, b 1455. Called the 'Perfect Prince', Afonso was one of Portugal's greatest rulers. Strong, ruthless and prudent, he had the overmighty Duke of Braganca judicially murdered and showed no scruples in ridding himself of other dangerous nobles. He encouraged the expansion of trade and saw Diaz reach the Cape of Good Hope and colonies established on the Guinea Coast.

MANOEL I Oct 1495-Dec 1521, grandson of Alfonso V, b 31 May 1469. Manoel ambitiously expanded colonial enterprise: Brazil was claimed; the Portuguese dominated trade in India through Goa, in the Spice Islands through Malacca and the Persian Gulf through Hormuz, and a puppet Congolese Kingdom was established.

JOÃO III Dec 1521-11 Jun 1557, son of Manoel I, b 6 Jun 1502.

SEBASTÃO Jun 1557-4 Aug 1578 killed while on a Crusade in Morocco, grandson of João III, b 20 Jan 1554. (Fake Sebastians appeared with regularity in Portugal during the Spanish occupation.)

HENRIQUE Aug 1578-31 Jan 1580, great-uncle of Sebastão, b 1512. A Catholic Cardinal.

Feb-Jun 1580 Interregnum. Regency Council.

ANTONIO Jun-Aug 1580 deposed, illegitimate nephew of Henrique, b 31 Jan 1531; d 26 Aug 1595. Denied the throne by the Regency Council, Antonio, Prior of Crato, tried to organise resistance to Philip II of Spain who claimed the crown upon the death of Henrique who was the last legitimate male member of the Aviz family.

HOUSE OF HABSBURG

FELIPPE I Aug 1580-13 Sep 1598; was also Felipe II, King of Spain.

FELIPPE II Sep 1598-1 Mar 1621; was also Felipe III, King of Spain.

FELIPPE III Mar 1621-1 Dec 1640; was also Felipe IV, King of Spain.

HOUSE OF BRAGANCA

JOÃO IV ('The Fortunate') **1 Dec 1640-6 Nov 1656,** Duke of Braganca, great-grandson of Manoel I (through the female line), b 18 Mar 1604. The leading Portuguese noble, the ambitious Duke of Braganca led the almost bloodless coup against the Spanish who had increasingly treated Portugal as a Castilian colony.

AFONSO VI Nov 1656-12 Sep 1683, eldest surviving son of João IV, b 21 Aug 1643. The achievements of the reign - such as the successful conclusion of the war of independence - were largely won despite Afonso who had to be confined through insanity.

PEDRO II Sep 1683-9 Dec 1706, brother of Afonso VI, b 26 Apr 1648.

JOÃO V Dec 1706-31 Jul 1750, eldest surviving son of Pedro II, b 22 Oct 1689. Although Brazil's silver had made him a financially independent autocrat, the extravagance of this florid King in artistic patronage and towards women ruined Portugal.

JOSÉ Jul 1750-24 Feb 1777, eldest son of João V, b 6 Jun 1714. An idle timid creature he left government to the enlightened despot Pombal.

MARIA I (Queen) co-ruler **Feb 1777-5 Mar 1786;** sole ruler **5 Mar 1786-20 Mar 1816,** eldest daughter of José, b 17 Dec 1734. Maria, insane for much of her reign, had little say in government. At the French invasion (1807) she was taken to Brazil leaving a British force under Wellington and British diplomats virtually in charge of Portugal.

PEDRO III co-ruler **Feb 1777-5 Mar 1786,** uncle and husband of Maria I, b 5 Jul 1717.

JOÃO VI Mar 1816-10 Mar 1826, son of Maria I and Pedro III, b 13 May 1767. Returning from Brazil in 1821 to end the power vacuum in Portugal João was troubled by the liberal constitution established in his absence, by his shrewish wife and by his son Miguel who temporarily imprisoned him.

PEDRO IV 10 Mar-29 Apr 1826, elder son of João VI; was also Pedro I, Emperor of Brazil.

MARIA II da GLORIA (Queen) **Apr 1826-11 Aug 1828** deposed, eldest daughter of Pedro IV, b 4 Apr 1819. Deposed by her uncle Miguel she was restored after a civil war by her father, the ex-Emperor of Brazil.

MIGUEL Aug 1828-26 May 1834, younger son of João VI, b 26 Oct 1802; d 14 Nov 1866. Dashing, ambitious and popular, Miguel led the ultra-conservatives, deposed his niece (for whom he was Regent) but was exiled after a bloody war against his brother, the former Pedro IV.

MARIA II da GLORIA 26 May 1834-15 Nov 1853.

House of Saxe-Coburg and Gotha

FERNANDO II nominal co-ruler **16 Sep 1837-15 Nov 1853,** husband of Maria II da Gloria, b (Prince Ferdinand August Franz Anton of Saxe-Coburg) 29 Oct 1816; d 15 Dec 1885.

House of Braganca and Saxe-Coburg-Gotha

PEDRO V Nov 1853-11 Nov 1861, eldest son of Maria II da Gloria and Fernando II, b 16 Sep 1837.

LUIS Nov 1861-19 Oct 1889, second son of Maria II, b 31 Oct 1838.

CARLOS Oct 1889-1 Feb 1908 assassinated, elder son of Luis, b 28 Sep 1863. Although this libertine King was initially popular, the monarchy was gravely damaged by his extravagance, a colonial conflict with Britain (1890) and the repressive government by decree and the financial irregularities of the Premier Franco.

MANOEL II Feb 1908-5 Oct 1910 when he fled in a revolution, son of Carlos, b 15 Nov 1889; d 2 Jul 1932 in exile.

THE REPUBLIC OF PORTUGAL

Presidents

Dr **JOAQUIM TÉOFILO FERNANDES BRAGA** provisional President **Oct 1910-24 Aug 1911,** b 24 Feb 1843; d 28 Jan 1924. One of Portugal's most outstanding poets and critics.

Dr **MANUEL JOSÉ de ARRIAGA 24 Aug 1911-May 1915,** b 1842; d 1917.

Dr **JOAQUIM TÉOFILO FERNANDES BRAGA May-5 Oct 1915.**

Dr **BERNARDINO LUÍS MACHADO GUIMA-RÃES 5 Oct 1915-8 Dec 1917** deposed by revolution, b 28 Mar 1851; d 29 Apr 1944.

Major **SIDÓNIO BERNARDINO CARDOSO da SILVA PAIS 11 Dec 1917-14 Dec 1918** when he was assassinated, b 1872.

Admiral **JOÃO de CANTO e CASTRO SILVA ANTUNES** provisional President **16 Dec 1918-Oct 1919.**

King Carlos I of Portugal whose paintings were very professional and would have made him famous if a commoner (Radio Times Hulton Picture Library)

Dr **ANTONIO JOSÉ de ALMEIDA 5 Oct 1919-5 Oct 1923,** b 1866; d 1929.

MANOEL TEIXEIRA GOMES 5 Oct 1923-11 Dec 1925, b 1862; d 1941.

Dr **BERNARDINO LUÍS MACHADO GUIMA-RÃES 11 Dec 1925-28 May 1926** deposed in a coup.

Commander **JOSÉ MENDES CABECADAS** Head of State and of the Provisional Government **1 Jun-late Jun 1926.**

Gen **MANOEL de OLIVEIRA GOMES de COSTA** Head of State and of the Provisional Government **Jun-9 Jul 1926.**

Gen **ANTONIO OSCAR de FRAGOSA CARMONA** (later Marshal) Head of State and of the Provisional Government **9 Jul-29 Nov 1926;** President **29 Nov 1926-18 Apr 1951,** b 24 Nov 1869; d in office.

Dr **ANTONIO de OLIVEIRA SALAZAR** provisional President **18 Apr-22 Jul 1951.** See entry under Prime Ministers of Portugal.

Marshal **FRANCISCO HIGINO CRAVEIRO LO-PES 22 Jul 1951-9 Aug 1958,** b 1894; d 3 Sep 1964.

Rear-Admiral **AMÉRICO DEUS RODRIGUES TOMÁS 9 Aug 1958-25 Apr 1974** when deposed by revolution, b 1894.

Gen **ANTONIO SEBASTIÃO RIBEIRO de SPINO-LA** provisional President **Apr-15 May 1974;** President **15 May-30 Sep 1974,** b 11 Apr 1910.

Gen **FRANCISCO da COSTA GOMES Oct 1974-Jul 1976,** b 30 Jun 1914.

Gen **ANTONIO RAMALHO EANES since 13 Jul 1976,** b 1935.

Prime Ministers

Dr **ANTONIO de OLIVEIRA SALAZAR 5 Jul 1932-Sep 1968,** b 28 Apr 1889; d 27 Jul 1970. A brilliant economist he restored the weak economy but later burdened it with a large defence budget in the effort to maintain Portugal's African colonies. His authoritarian 'New State' made much progress in the development of the nation but denied many basic freedoms.

Prof **MARCELO JOSÉ das NEVES CAETANO 26 Sep 1968-25 Apr 1974** deposed in coup, b 17 Aug 1906.

Gen **ANTÔNIO SEBASTIÃO RIBEIRO de SPINO-LA** acting PM **25 Apr-15 May 1974,** b 11 Apr 1910.

Prof **ADELINO da PALMA CARLOS 15 May-Jul 1974,** b 1906.

Lieut-Col **VASCO dos SANTOS GONCALVES 17 Jul 1974-Aug 1975,** b 3 May 1921.

Admiral **JOSÉ BAPTISTA PINHEIRO de AZEVE-DO 29 Aug 1975-Jun 1976,** b 1917.

Commander **VASCO ALMEIDA e COSTA** acting PM **23 Jun-16 Jul 1976.**

Dr **MARIO ALBERTO NOBRE LOPES SOARES 16 Jul 1976-Jul 1978;** acting PM **Jul-Aug 1978,** b 7 Dec 1924.

ALFREDO NOBRE da COSTA since 9 Aug 1978, b 1923.

Powys *see* Wales, United Kingdom

Prussia *see* Germany

Pyrmont *see* Waldeck, Germany

Qandahar, Khans in *see* Afghanistan

Qatar

The small peninsula of Qatar beside the Persian Gulf ceased to be under Ottoman rule in 1916 and became a British protected state. On 1 Sep 1971 the complete independence of Qatar was recognised internationally.

† Emirs

AL THANI DYNASTY

AHMAD bin ALI al THANI Ruler from 24 Oct 1960; sovereign Emir **1 Sep 1971-22 Feb 1972** deposed by family agreement.

KHALIFA bin HAMAD al THANI since 22 Feb 1972, cousin of Ahmad, b 1934.

Prime Minister

Shaikh **KHALIFA bin HAMAD al THANI** 29 May-1 Sep 1971 Premier of protected state; Premier of sovereign state **1 Sep 1971-22 Feb 1972;** see Emir Khalifa.

KHALIFA bin HAMAD al THANI since 22 Feb 1972; see Emir Khalifa.

Ras Al Khaimah *see* United Arab Emirates

Rastrakuta Kingdom *see* India

Reuss zu Greiz *see* Germany

Reuss zu Schleiz *see* Germany

Rhodesia

Claimed by the British South Africa Company in 1889, the colony of Southern Rhodesia was annexed to the Crown in 1923. A unilateral declaration of independence was made on 11 Nov 1965 and on 2 Mar 1970 a republican constitution adopted. Rhodesia is scheduled to become the independent black run Republic of Zimbabwe in Dec 1978.

Presidents

CLIFFORD DUPONT acting President **2 Mar-16 Apr 1970;** President **16 Apr 1970-Jan 1976,** b 1905.

JOHN J. WRATHALL since 14 Jan 1976.

Prime Minister

IAN DOUGLAS SMITH since 11 Nov 1965, b 8 Apr 1919.

Roman Empire

Archaeological evidence suggests Rome was founded by 750 BC. Writing centuries later, Livy chronicles its early history and, mixing fact and fiction, described the reigns of seven Kings: Romulus, Numa Pompilius, Tullus Hostilius, Ancus Martius, Tarquinius Priscus, Servius Tullius and Tarquinius Superbus - it is likely that several of these Kings did not exist. The Roman Republic, traditionally dated from 509 BC, cannot have been founded until after 474 BC when the Etruscans withdrew. By the 1st century the Republic, governed by a Senate and two Consuls, had become unstable; the triumvirates briefly filled the political vacuum.

THE ROMAN REPUBLIC

Rule by a Senate and two Consuls elected annually (c 474 BC-27 BC).

First Triumvirate
(60 BC)

GAIUS JULIUS CAESAR , b 12 or 13 Jul 100 BC; assassinated 15 Mar 44 BC. A military genius, Caesar conquered Gaul (58-50 BC) and landed in Britain - both exploits are described in his commentaries. Fearing his power the Senate outlawed him (49 BC) but he invaded Italy and pursued his enemies to Egypt where he sided with Queen Cleopatra in a dynastic war. Named dictator for life in 45 BC, he reformed the calendar but was unable to reform the corrupt Republic. Believing Caesar aimed at kingship, Brutus, Cassius and 60 accomplices assassinated him in the Senate.

GNAEUS POMPEIUS MAGNUS (better known as POMPEY), b 29 Sep 106 BC; d 28 Sep 48 BC - murdered. One of Rome's greatest generals, he was an associate and later an enemy of Caesar who defeated him in the Civil War, forcing him to flee to Egypt.

MARCUS LICINIUS CRASSUS , b c 115 BC; d 53 BC.

Second Triumvirate
(42-28 BC)

MARCUS ANTONIUS (better known as MARK ANTONY), b c 82 BC; committed suicide Aug 30 BC. Ruler of the eastern provinces, Antony went to Egypt (41 BC) and became Cleopatra's lover. The triumvirs quarrelled and in the resulting Civil War Antony's fleet was defeated at Actium (31 BC).

MARCUS AEMILIUS LEPIDUS , d 12 or 13 BC.

GAIUS JULIUS CAESAR OCTAVIANUS (better known as OCTAVIAN); see Emperor Augustus.

THE ROMAN EMPIRE

† Roman Emperors

Two or more Emperors could share the imperium and owing to the complexities of these reigns, the co-ruling periods have not always been identified: some Emperors reigned with their heirs; a few were forced to share the throne with usurpers.

Gaius Julius Caesar who hesitated to assume kingship - ironically his name 'Caesar' became the royal titles 'Kaiser' and 'Tsar' (Radio Times Hulton Picture Library)

CLAUDIAN EMPERORS

AUGUSTUS (OCTAVIANUS) 16 Jan 27 BC-19 Aug AD14, b 23 Sep 63 BC Octavian, Julius Caesar's great-nephew and adopted son, was appointed triumvir in 43 BC. He defeated Antony in a civil war which left him in supreme power (30 BC). Proclaimed Emperor - 'Augustus' - by the Senate (27 BC), he restored law and order, ruling firmly and wisely and always paying lip service to Rome's republican traditions. He hoped to provide 'the best civilian rule possible' - he probably did.

TIBERIUS (Claudius Nero Caesar Augustus) **AD 14 Aug-AD 16 Mar 37,** stepson of Augustus, b 16 Nov 42 BC. Unpopular Tiberius, who strengthened the imperial powers, retired to Capri for the last decade of his reign.

GAIUS CAESAR (better known by his nickname CALIGULA, meaning 'little boots') **Mar 37-24 Jan 41** assassinated, great-nephew of Tiberius, b AD 31 Aug 12. An inept ruler who squandered the Treasury, deified himself, murdered his opponents and really did raise his favourite horse to the consulship.

CLAUDIUS I (Tiberius Claudius Drusus Nero Germanicus) **Jan 41-13 Oct 54** possibly poisoned, nephew of Tiberius. b 1 Aug 10 BC.

NERO (Lucius Domitius Ahenobarbus) **Oct 54-11 Jun 68** committed suicide, step-son of Claudius,

Nero: an artist's impression of the unstable Emperor after the fire of Rome. It seems certain he was not the incendiary (Rädio Times Hulton Picture Library)

b 15 Dec 37. Nero murdered his mother, wives, tutor (Seneca) and half-brother Britannicus. He blamed, and persecuted, the Christians for the great fire of Rome (64) but there is no evidence to support the later assertion that he was the incendiary. His cruelty, bizarre behaviour and heavy taxation led to revolts and the Senate renounced allegiance to him (Jun 68).

LATER CLAUDIAN EMPERORS
(unrelated to the former)

GALBA (Servius Sulpicius Galba) **Jun 68-15 Jan 69,** b AD 24 Dec 3; murdered by Otho.

OTHO (Marcus Salvius Otho) **Jan-Apr 69** committed suicide, b AD 32.

VITELLIUS Apr-Dec? 69 murdered, b AD 15.

FLAVIAN EMPERORS

VESPASIANUS (Titus Flavius Vespasianus) **Dec? 69-24 Jun 79,** b AD 9. Of humble origin he restored order and was a popular unpretentious ruler.

TITUS (Flavius Vespasianus) **Jun 79-13 Sep 81,** son of Vespasianus, b 30 Dec 39.

DOMITIANUS (Titus Flavius Domitianus) **Sep 81-18 Sep 96** assassinated, son of Vespasianus, b 24 Oct 51.

ANTONINE EMPERORS

NERVA (Marcus Cocceius Nerva) **Sep 96-Jan 98,** b *c* 30.

TRAJANUS (Marcus Ulpius Trajanus) **Jan 98-8 or 9 Aug 117,** adopted son of Nerva, b Sep 53. An outstanding Emperor he was a fine soldier and sound administrator who extended the empire and improved social conditions. A modest man, Trajanus and his two immediate successors gave Rome 50 years peace.

HADRIANUS (Publius Aelius Hadrianus) **Aug 117-10 Jul 138,** nephew of Trajanus, b 24 Jan 76. A cultured Hellenist who spent half his reign travelling the empire for which he sought secure boundaries - after his visit to Britain Hadrian's Wall was built from the Solway Firth to Wallsend to repulse the Picts.

ANTONINUS PIUS (Titus Aurelius Fulvius Boinonius Arrius Antoninus) **Jul 138-7 Mar 161,** adopted son of Hadrianus, b 19 Sep 86.

LUCIUS VERUS (Lucius Aurelius Verus) **Mar 161-Mar 169,** adopted son of Antoninus Pius, b 15 Dec 130.

MARCUS AURELIUS co-ruler **from Mar 161**; **Mar 169-17 Mar 180,** son-in-law of Antoninus Pius, b 26 Apr 121. A Stoic philosopher and the author of 'Meditations'.

COMMODUS (Marcus Aurelius Commodus Antoninus) co-ruler **from 177; Mar 180-31 Dec 192** strangled to death by a wrestler; son of Marcus Aurelius, b 31 Aug 161. Addicted to pleasure, conceited and deranged (he believed himself to be Hercules), Commodus abandoned his father's campaign against the Germans who later ravaged the empire.

EMPERORS OF AFRICAN, ASIAN AND SYRIAN ORIGIN

A period of anarchy when many military commanders attempted to obtain the throne.

PERTINAX (Publius Helvius Pertinax) **Jan-Mar 193** murdered, b 1 Aug 126.

DIDIUS JULIANUS Mar-1 Jun 193 murdered, b *c* 135.

(**PESCENNIUS NIGER** and **ALBINUS** both declared themselves Emperor during the civil wars of 193-197, but neither can be considered to have reigned.)

SEPTIMUS SEVERUS (Lucius Septimus Severus) **Apr 193-Feb 211,** b 146. Under Severus, commander of the Danubian legions, the monarchy became a military despotism - the road to power lay through the relatively classless army rather than through the aristocratic Senate.

MARCUS AURELIUS ANTONINUS I (better known by his nickname CARACALLA, meaning 'hooded cloak') co-ruler **from 198; Feb 211-8 Apr 217** murdered by Macrinus; son of Severus, b 4 Apr 188.

GETA (Publius Septimus Geta) co-ruler **from 209-Feb 212** murdered by Caracalla; son of Severus, b 189.

MACRINUS (Marcus Opellius Macrinus) **Apr 217-Jun 218** executed, b *c* 164.

MARCUS AURELIUS ANTONINUS II (better known as ELAGABALUS, meaning 'sun-god Baal') **Jun 218-222** assassinated, cousin of Caracalla, b (Varius Avitus Bassianus) 204. An eccentric whose orgies shocked even the Romans, he tried to introduce the worship of Baal.

SEVERUS ALEXANDER (Marcus Aurelius Severus Alexander) **222-235** assassinated, descended from a brother of Septimus Severus, b 208.

MAXIMINUS (Gaius Julius Verus Maximinus) **Mar 235-Mar 238** murdered.

GORDIANUS I (Marcus Antonius Gordianus) **Mar-Apr 238** committed suicide, b *c* 157.

GORDIANUS II (Marcus Antonius Gordianus) co-ruler **Mar-Apr 238** died in battle, son of Gordianus I, b 192.

PUPIENUS MAXIMUS 238 murdered.

BALBINUS (Decimus Caelius Antonius Balbinus) **238** murdered.

GORDIANUS III (Marcus Antonius Gordianus) **238-244** murdered, grandson of Gordianus I, b 225.

PHILIPPUS 244-249 died in battle - killed by Decius.

DECIUS (Gaius Messius Trajanus Decius) **249-Jun 251** died in battle, b *c* 201.

GALLUS (Gaius Vibius Trebonianus Gallus) **Jun 251-253** murdered.

HOSTILIANUS (Gaius Valens Hostilianus Messius Quintus) co-ruler in **251,** son of Decius; fate uncertain.

AEMILIANUS (Marcus Aemilius Aemilianus) **253** murdered.

VALERIANUS (Publius Licinius Valerianus) **253-Jun 260**; taken prisoner by Persians - date of death unknown.

GALLIENUS (Publius Licinius Egnatius Gallienus) co-ruler **253-260**; **Jun 260-268** killed by Claudius II. Son of Valerianus.

ILLYRIAN EMPERORS

CLAUDIUS II (Marcus Aurelius Claudius) **268-270,** b May 214.

QUINTILLUS (Marcus Aurelius Claudius Quintillus) **270** presumed murdered, brother of Claudius II.

AURELIANUS (Lucius Domitius Aurelianus) **May 270-early 275** murdered, b *c* 215.

ULPIA SEVERINA (Empress) **early 275-Sep 275,** widow of Aurelianus.

TACITUS (Marcus Claudius Tacitus) **Sep 275-276** murdered, b *c* 200.

FLORIANUS 276 murdered, half-brother of Tacitus.

PROBUS (Marcus Aurelius Probus) **276-282** murdered. Probus took a great interest in farming but by admitting large numbers of Franks and Goths into the empire to settle depopulated areas he let the enemy into the camp.

CARUS (Marcus Aurelius Carus) **282-283** allegedly killed by lightning.

CARINUS (Marcus Aurelius Carinus) **283-285** killed by Diocletianus; son of Carus.

NUMERIANUS co-ruler **283-Nov 284** murdered, son of Carus.

'COLLEGIATE' EMPERORS

DIOCLETIANUS (Gaius Aurelius Valerius Diocletianus) **284-1 May 305** when he abdicated, b 245; d 313. Diocletianus reorganised the empire and the army, reformed the administration, recodified the legal system and instituted the Tetrachy - a college of Emperors (with the title of Augustus) who were to abdicate at fixed intervals in favour of two heirs (Caesars). Intended to promote continuity and stability, and a recognition that the empire had become too big to be ruled by one man, the collegiate imperium foundered on the ambition of others and led to anarchy. Diocletianus began one of the fiercest persecutions of the Christians (303).

MAXIMIANUS (Marcus Aurelius Valerius Maximianus) **286-1 May 305** forced to abdicate; murdered or committed suicide 310.

CONSTANTIUS I (Aurelius Valerius Constantius; better known by his nickname CHLORUS, meaning 'pale man') **1 May 305-summer 306,** b 250.

GALERIUS (Gaius Galerius Valerius Maximianus) **1 May 305-311.**

SEVERUS (Flavius Valerius Severus) **25 Jun 306-307** executed by order of Maximianus.

MAXIMIANUS (Marcus Aurelius Valerius Maximianus) **307-308** abdicated.

MAXIMINUS DAIA (Maximinus Gaius Galerius Valerius) **308-313,** nephew of Galerius.

CONSTANTINUS I (Constantine the Great) Proclaimed 307; ruled **312-22 May 337,** son of Constantius I, b late 280s. He achieved power after a series of civil wars and ascribed his victory to his conversion to Christianity. He enlarged and rebuilt Byzantium, renaming it Constantinopolis and making it capital in place of Rome. His Edict of Milan (313) accorded toleration to the Christians and marked the start of the change of the empire into a Christian state.

(LUCIUS DOMITIUS ALEXANDER proclaimed himself Emperor in 308 but cannot be said to have reigned.)

MAXENTIUS (Marcus Aurelius Valerius Maxentius) **28 Oct 306-312** killed - probably drowned by order of ConstantinusI; son of Maximianus.

LICINIUS (Valerius Licinianus Licinius) **11 Nov 308-324,** adopted son of Galerius; executed in 325 after being exiled by Constantinus I.

CONSTANTINUS II co-ruler **337-340** died in battle, son of Constantinus I, b Feb 317.

CONSTANS I (Flavius Julius Constans) co-ruler **337-350** killed by Magnus Magnentius; son of Constantinus I, b c323.

CONSTANTIUS II (Flavius Julius Constantius) **337-361,** son of Constantinus I, b 7 Aug 317.

MAGNUS MAGNENTIUS (Flavius Magnus Magnentius) co-ruler **Jan 350-11 Aug 353** committed suicide.

(VETRANIO and NEPOTIANUS both declared themselves to be Emperor c350 but neither can be said to have reigned.)

JULIANUS (Flavius Claudius Julianus) **Nov 361-Jun 363** died in battle, cousin of Constantius II, b 331/2.

JOVIANUS (Flavius Jovianus) **363-17 Feb 364** died accidentally, b c331.

'COLLEGIATE' EMPERORS RULING PART OF THE ROMAN EMPIRE

VALENTINIANUS I (Flavius Valentinianus) **26 Feb 364-17 Nov 375,** b 325. Emperor in West

GRATIANUS **24 Aug 367-383** assassinated, son of Valentinianus I, b 359. Emperor in West.

VALENS **28 Mar 364-9 Aug 378** died in battle, brother of Valentinianus I, b c328. Emperor in East.

PROCOPIUS **Sep 365-366.** Emperor in East.

VALENTINIANUS II (Flavius Valentinianus) **22 Nov 375-385** deposed, half-brother of Gratianus, b 371; d in suspicious circumstances. Emperor in West.

MAGNUS MAXIMUS **383-388** deposed; executed after deposition. Emperor in West.

FLAVIUS VICTOR **c386-388,** son of Magnus Maximus; fate uncertain. Emperor in West.

THEODOSIUS I **19 Jan 379-17 Jan 395**; from 388 Emperor of all the Roman Empire, b 11 Jan 347. Emperor in East; later in West. The last ruler of the entire empire.

VALENTINIANUS II (Flavius Valentinianus) **388-392.** Emperor in West.

EUGENIUS **392-394** died in battle. Emperor in West.

HONORIUS **23 Jan 393-395** when he became Emperor of the Western division of the Roman Empire.

WESTERN ROMAN EMPIRE

Upon the death of Theodosius I the empire was divided between the sons of that Emperor: the Western Roman Empire initially consisted of Italia, Africa, Hispania, Illyricum, Gallia and Britannia; for the Eastern Roman Empire see the Byzantine Empire.

† Western Roman Emperors

HONORIUS **Jan 395-15 Aug 423,** son of Theodosius I, b 8 Sep 384. A weak ruler, he lost much of the west to the Visigoths and Vandals and was unable to prevent the sack of Rome (410).

CONSTANTIUS III co-ruler **421,** brother-in-law of Honorius.

VALENTINIANUS III (Flavius Valentinianus) **425-16 Mar 455** murdered, son of Constantius III, b 2 Jul 419.

PETRONIUS MAXIMUS **17 Mar-31 May 455.** married the widow of Valentinianus III, b 396. He attempted to flee when Rome was threatened by Vandals but was caught and torn to pieces by the mob.

AVITUS (Eparchius Avitus) **Jun 455-17 Oct 456** when forced to abdicate. He became Bishop of Placentia and may have died in the same year.

MAJORIANUS (Julius Majorianus) **457-2 Aug 461** when he abdicated; executed 7 Aug 461. The last worthy Roman Emperor, Majorianus was a fine soldier but his humiliating peace treaty with the Vandals caused him to abdicate.

LIBIUS SEVERUS **461-465.**

ANTHEMIUS **12 Apr 467-11 Jul 472** executed, son-in-law of Byzantine Emperor Marcianus.

OLYBRIUS **Jul-2 Nov 472,** son-in-law of Valentinianus III.

GLYCERIUS **5 Mar 473-Jun 474** when forced to abdicate. He became Bishop of Salona and died after 480.

JULIUS NEPOS Jun 474-Aug 475 fled; murdered May 480.

ROMULUS AUGUSTUS 31 Oct 475-Aug 476; fate unknown. The last Roman Emperor, ironically called Augustus after the first, was expelled by Odoacer.

Romania

The former Kingdom used the spelling Roumania; the present Communist Republic uses the spelling Romania. Roman Dacia was overrun by the Visigoths and later by the Slavs, in particular the Vlachs. Two Principalities, Moldavia and Wallachia (land of the Vlachs) maintained a precarious independence for a short period in the Middle Ages before falling to the Turks. By the 18th century the Danubian Principalities were governed for the Sultan by Greek 'Princes' or Hospodars. After a rebellion, the two states gained autonomy within the Ottoman Empire in 1829 and in 1859 both elected Alexandru Ioan Cuza as their Prince thus (illegally) creating a united Principality of Roumania.

THE PRINCIPALITY OF ROUMANIA

In 1861 the union of Roumania was recognised by Turkey, to which power the Principality nominally belonged until Jun 1878 when independence was granted under the terms of the Treaty of Berlin.

† Princes

HOUSE OF CUZA

ALEXANDRU IOAN I Prince of Moldavia from Jan 1859, of Wallachia from Feb 1859; Prince of Roumania **9 Nov 1859-23 Feb 1866** when he was obliged to abdicate, b 20 Mar 1820; d 15 May 1873. Prince Cuza's 'abdication' is usually ascribed to public disgust at his (appalling) morals - in truth, Bratianu, the leading politician, ousted him jealous of the Prince's growing power.

Feb-Apr 1866 Interregnum.

HOUSE OF HOHENZOLLERN

CAROL I 20 Apr 1866-Mar 1881 when he became King.

THE KINGDOM OF ROUMANIA

† Kings

HOUSE OF HOHENZOLLERN

CAROL I Prince from Apr 1866; King **26 Mar 1881-10 Oct 1914,** b (Prince Karl of Hohenzollern-Sigmaringen) 20 Apr 1839. Carol I, who helped secure the independence of Roumania by leading her forces at Plevna (1877), did much to create modern Roumania and greatly developed the economy.

FERDINAND I Oct 1914-20 Jul 1927, nephew of Carol I, b (a Prince of Hohenzollern-Sigmaringen) 24 Aug 1865.

MIHAI I Jul 1927-8 Jun 1930.

CAROL II Jun 1930-6 Sep 1940 when he abdicated, eldest son of Ferdinand I, b 15 Oct 1893; d 4 Apr 1955. Unconventional Carol, remembered for his gaudy uniforms and his liason with Mme Lupescu, renounced the throne but returned to replace his son in the political chaos of 1930. The humiliating territorial concessions Roumania made to Hungary and Bulgaria (Aug 1940) cost him the crown.

MIHAI I Sep 1940-30 Dec 1947 when he was forced to abdicate by the Communists, son of Carol II, b 25 Oct 1921.

Prime Ministers

IONEL BRATIANU Dec 1918-Sep 1919, b 20 Aug 1864; d 24 Nov 1927.

Marshal **ALEXANDRU AVERESCU Sep 1919-Jan 1922,** b 22 Apr 1859; d 2 Oct 1938. An outstanding patriot, he served in the Romanian War of Independence and commanded the Danube Front in World War I and when defeated by German and Austrian forces refused to sign a peace treaty.

IONEL BRATIANU Jan 1922-Mar 1926.

Marshal **ALEXANDRU AVERESCU Mar 1926-Jun 1927.**

IONEL BRATIANU Jun-24 Nov 1927.

Dr **IULIU MANIU Nov 1927-Oct 1930,** b 8 Jan 1873; d (gaoled for 'treason') Jun 1953.

Prof **JORGA Oct 1930-Jun 1932.**

Dr **ALEXANDRU VAIDA VOEVOD 6 Jun-Oct 1932.**

Dr **IULIU MANIU 19 Oct 1932-Jan 1933.**

Dr **ALEXANDRU VAIDA VOEVOD 14 Jan-Nov 1933.**

ION G. DUCA 14 Nov-29 Dec 1933, b 1879; d in office - assassinated.

GHEORGHE ANGELESCU 29 Dec 1933-3 Jan 1934, b 1871; d 1948.

GHEORGHE TATARESCU 3 Jan 1934-Dec 1937, b 1892; d 1957.

Dr **OCTAVIAN GOGA 28 Dec 1937-Feb 1938,** b 1881; d 7 May 1938.

Dr **MIRON CRISTEA 11 Feb 1938-6 Mar 1939,** b 1858; d in office. The Patriach of the Roumanian Orthodox Church.

ARMAND CALINESCU Mar-21 Sep 1939, b 22 May 1893; d in office - assassinated.

Gen **ARTESEANU 21-28 Sep 1939.**

CONSTANTIN ARGETOIANU 28 Sep-23 Nov 1939.

GHEORGHE TATARESCU 23 Nov 1939-Jul 1940.

ION GIGURTU 4 Jul-3 Sep 1940.

Gen **ION ANTONESCU 4 Sep 1940-23 Aug 1944,** b 15 Jun 1882; d 1 Jun 1946 when executed as a war criminal. Leader of the Fascist Iron Guard he involved Roumania in the war as an ally of Germany. This dictator, who showed much independence of Hitler, was dismissed by King Michael after Roumania had sustained terrible losses in the war.

Gen **CONSTANTIN SANATESCU 23 Aug-Dec 1944,** b 30 Mar 1874; d 16 May 1953 in exile.
Gen **NICOLAE RADESCU 2 Dec 1944-3 Mar 1945,** b 1874; d 1953 in exile.
Prince **STIRBEY 3-6 Mar 1945.**
Dr **PETRU GROZA 6 Mar 1945-30 Dec 1947** when he became PM of the Communist Republic.

THE SOCIALIST REPUBLIC OF ROMANIA

Before 1965 termed the People's Republic of Romania

Presidents

1948-1961 Chairman of the State Presidium; 1961-1974 President of the Council of State; since 1974 President.

Prof **CONSTANTIN PARHON 9 Jan 1948-Jun 1952.**
Dr **PETRU GROZA Jun 1952-7 Jan 1958,** b 1884; d in office.
ION GHEORGHE MAURER 11 Jan 1958-Mar 1961, b 23 Sep 1902.
GHEORGHE GHEORGHIU-DEJ 21 Mar 1961-19 Mar 1965, b 8 Nov 1901; d in office.
CHIVU STOICA 22 Mar 1965-Dec 1967, b 8 Aug 1908; d 18 Feb 1975.
NICOLAE CEAUSESCU since 9 Dec 1967, b 26 Jan 1918.

Prime Ministers

Dr **PETRU GROZA 30 Dec 1947-Jun 1952.**
GHEORGHE GHEORGHIU-DEJ 2 Jun 1952-2 Oct 1955.
CHIVU STOICA 2 Oct 1955-Mar 1961.
ION GHEORGHE MAURER 21 Mar 1961-28 Mar 1974.
MANEA MANESCU since 28 Mar 1974, b 9 Aug 1916.

First Secretaries of the Romanian Communist Party

Before 1965 styled the Romanian Workers' Party.

GHEORGHE GHEORGHIU-DEJ 30 Dec 1947-Apr 1954.
GHEORGHE APOSTOL 20 Apr 1954-Oct 1955.
GHEORGHE GHEORGHIU-DEJ 2 Oct 1955-19 Mar 1965.
NICOLAE CEAUSESCU since 22 Mar 1965.

Rum, Sultanate of *see* Seljuq Empire

Russia *see* Union of Soviet Socialist Republics

Rwanda

The Tutsi Kingdom of Rwanda was absorbed into the German colony of East Africa (Tanganiyka). Ceded to Belgium as a Trust Territory after World War I, Rwanda was granted independence on 1 Jul 1962.

Presidents

The two Presidents of the Republic have also held the position of Prime Minister.

GRÉGOIRE KAYIBANDA 1 Jul 1962-5 Jul 1973 when he was deposed, b 1 May 1924; d Dec 1976.
Maj-Gen **JUVENAL HABYALIMANA since 5 Jul 1973**; Prime Minister since 1 Aug 1973, b 3 Aug 1937.

Saint-Domingues, Republic of
see Haiti

Salvador, el *see* el Salvador

Samarkand, Kings in *see* Timurid Empire

Samoa *see* Western Samoa

San Marino

A tiny sovereign Republic enclaved in Italy, San Marino was founded in the 9th century, adopted a republican constitution in the 11th century and became fully independent in 1631.

Heads of State and of Government

The state is governed by two co-equal Captains-Regent who are elected for a term of office of six months and are not eligible for immediate re-election.

Sao Tomé and Principe

The small islands of São Tomé (Portuguese since 1483) and Príncipe (Portuguese since 1485) were granted independence on 12 Jul 1975.

President

Dr **MANUEL PINTO da COSTA since 12 Jul 1975,** b 1910.

Prime Ministers

LEONEL MARIO d'ALVA Premier *per interim* **12-15 Jul 1975.**
MIGUEL TROUVOADA since 15 Jul 1975.

Sarawak

An independent state ruled by the 'White Rajas' from 1841 until 1 Jul 1946 when the country was ceded to Britain. Since 1963 Sarawak has formed part of Malaysia.

† Rajas

BROOKE DYNASTY
JAMES BROOKE 24 Sep 1841-11 Jun 1868, b 29 Apr 1803. An adventurer who came to Sarawak as a trader, he ended a civil war and gained the throne upon the abdication of the native Raja in his favour. He achieved British recognition of his independence, withstood a major Chinese revolt and suppressed piracy although his methods were criticised by those in England who knew nothing of conditions in Sarawak.
CHARLES ANTHONI JOHNSON BROOKE Jun 1868-17 May 1917, nephew of James, b 3 Jun 1829.
CHARLES VYNER de WINDT BROOKE May 1917-1 Jul 1946 when he ceded Sarawak to the British Crown, son of Charles, b 26 Sep 1874; d 9 May 1963.

Sardinia *see* Italy

Sasanid Empire, The *see* Iran

King Abdul Aziz ibn Saud who at 21 commanded but 40 men and at 40 had conquered two Kingdoms (Radio Times Hulton Picture Library)

Saudi Arabia

This modern Arab Kingdom was formed on 22 Sep 1932 by the union of the territories in a personal union under Sultan Abdul Aziz ibn Saud of Nejd - Nejd, Hejaz, Asir, al Hasa and Jabal Shammar.

† Kings

SAUDI OR WAHHABI DYNASTY
ABDUL AZIZ ibn SAUD Abdur Rahman al-Faisal **22 Sep 1932-9 Nov 1953,** b 1880. The creator of what has become a major power, ibn Saud expelled the usurping Rashidis from Riyadh and proclaimed himself Sultan of Nejd, captured Hejaz from the Hashemites, gained al Hasa and established sovereignty over Asir and Jabal Shammar and then united his lands into a new Kingdom.
SAUD ibn Abdul Aziz ibn Saud **Nov 1953-2 Nov 1964** deposed by family agreement, son of Abdul Aziz ibn Saud, b 15 Jan 1902; d 23 Feb 1969.
FAISAL ibn Abdul Aziz ibn Saud **2 Nov 1964-25 Mar 1975** assassinated by an unbalanced relative; son of Abdul Aziz ibn Saud, b 1905.
KHALED ibn Abdul Aziz ibn Saud **since 25 Mar 1975,** son of Abdul Aziz ibn Saud, b 1913.

Prime Ministers

Prince **SAUD** ibn Abdul Aziz ibn Saud   **11 Oct-9 Nov 1953**; see King Saud.

King **SAUD** ibn Abdul Aziz ibn Saud   **9 Nov 1953-Oct 1962**; see King Saud.

Prince **FAISAL** ibn Abdul Aziz ibn Saud   **17 Oct 1962-2 Nov 1964**; see King Faisal.

King **FAISAL** ibn Abdul Aziz ibn Saud   **2 Nov 1964-25 Mar 1975**; see King Faisal.

King **KHALED** ibn Abdul Aziz ibn Saud   **since 28 Mar 1975**; see King Khaled.

NEJD

† Sultan

SAUDI OR WAHHABI DYNASTY
ABDUL AZIZ ibn SAUD Abdur Rahman al-Faisal **1901-22 Sep 1932** when he merged Nejd in Saudi Arabia.

HEJAZ

† Kings

HASHEMITE DYNASTY
HUSAYN ibn Ali   **Oct 1916-5 Oct 1924** abdicated, b c 1854; d 1931. Leader of the Arab revolt against Ottoman rule in World War I, he declared himself King of the Arab Lands and although he lost his own throne he saw his sons established on the thrones of Jordan and Iraq.

ALI ibn Husayn   **Oct 1924-19 Dec 1925** when he fled before the Saudi invasion, son of Husayn, b 1871; d in exile 14 Feb 1935.

SAUDI OR WAHHABI DYNASTY
ABDUL AZIZ ibn SAUD Abdur Rahman al-Faisal **11 Jan 1926-22 Sep 1932** when he merged Hejaz in Saudi Arabia.

Savoy see Italy

Saxe-Altenburg see Germany

Saxe-Coburg and Gotha see Germany

Saxe-Hildburghausen see Saxe-Altenburg, Germany

Saxe-Meiningen see Germany

Saxe-Weimar-Eisenach see Germany

Saxony see Germany

Schaumberg-Lippe see Germany

Schwarzburg : Rudolstadt and Sondershausen see Germany

The Seleucid Empire

The greatest of the successor states to the empire of Alexander the Great, the Seleucid state was created by Seleucus Nicator in 312 BC and lasted until 64 BC when the remains of the Kingdom fell to the Romans. At its height the empire included Syria, southern Asia Minor, Mesopotamia, Iran and part of central Asia.

† Kings

SELEUCID DYNASTY
SELEUCUS I NICATOR Ruler **Oct 312-305 BC**; King from **305 BC**; sole ruler **305-Sep 292**; co-ruler **292-Sep 280 BC** assassinated, b c 256 BC. One of Alexander the Great's generals he gained Babylonia for himself after the King's death. Conquering Iran and then Syria from Antigonus he established an empire.

ANTIOCHUS I SOTER co-ruler **292-280 BC**; sole ruler **Sep 280-261 BC** assassinated, elder son of Seleucus I, b 324 BC.

ANTIOCHUS II THEOS **261-246 BC**, second son of Antiochus I, b c 287 BC. He deified himself, hence the name Theos.

SELEUCUS II CALLINICUS **246-225 BC**, eldest son of Antiochus II.

SELEUCUS III SOTER **225-223 BC** assassinated, elder son of Seleucus II.

ANTIOCHUS III ('The Great') **223-187 BC**, younger son of Seleucus II, b 242 BC. An able reformer and administrator he fought the Roman advances in Asia Minor but, defeated at Magnesia (190 BC), he lost Anatolia and the decline of the Seleucid Kingdom began.

SELEUCUS IV PHILOPATOR **187-175 BC** assassinated, son of Antiochus III, b c 217 BC.

(HELIODORUS, a non-Seleucid, briefly usurped the throne in 175 BC; fate uncertain.)

ANTIOCHUS IV EPIPHANES **175-163 BC**, son of Antiochus III, b c 215 BC. A competent and popular King, he is remembered for his sacrilege of installing a statue of Zeus in the Temple at

Jerusalem which led to the revolt of the Maccabees.

ANTIOCHUS V EUPATOR 163-162 BC assassinated, son of Antiochus IV, b 173. His short reign saw the loss of most of the eastern provinces confining the Kingdom to Syria, Palestine and Babylonia.

DEMETRIUS I SOTER 162-150 BC killed by Alexander Balas; son of Seleucus IV, b *c* 187 BC.

ALEXANDER BALAS 150-145 BC died in battle against Demetrius II; claimed to be son of Antiochus IV.

ANTIOCHUS VI EPIPHANES DIONYSIUS co-ruler **145-142 BC** killed?, son of Alexander Balas.

DEMETRIUS II NICATOR co-ruler **145-142 BC**; sole ruler **142-139 BC** when he was taken captive by the Parthians, eldest son of Demetrius I.

ANTIOCHUS VII SIDETES 139-129 BC when he died in battle against the Parthians, brother of Demetrius II.

DEMETRIUS II NICATOR 129-125 BC assassinated.

(**ALEXANDER II ZABINAS**, a usuper, claimed to be King 128-123 BC.)

SELEUCUS V 125 BC, elder son of Demetrius II.

CLEOPATRA THEA (Queen) co-ruler **125-121 BC**, widow of Demetrius II.

ANTIOCHUS VIII PHILOMETOR co-ruler **125-121 BC**; sole ruler **121-96 BC**, younger son of Demetrius II.

(**ANTIOCHUS IX CYZICENUS** Pretender 115-95 BC.)

SELEUCUS VI EPIPHANES NICATOR 96-95 BC, eldest son of Antiochus VIII.

ANTIOCHUS X EUSEBES PHILOPATOR 95-83 BC, son of Antiochus IX. In the civil wars between him and the sons of Antiochus VIII the Seleucid state was reduced to a small area of Syria.

DEMETRIUS III EUKAIROS PHILOPATOR SOTER 95-88 BC, fourth son of Antiochus VIII.

ANTIOCHUS XI EPIPHANES PHILADELPHUS 92 BC, second son of Antiochus VIII.

PHILIPPUS I EPIPHANES PHILADELPHUS 92-83 BC, third son of Antiochus VIII.

ANTIOCHUS XII DIONYSUS 87-84 BC, fifth son of Antiochus VIII.

ARMENIAN DYNASTY
TIGRANES 83-69 BC, King of Armenia.

SELEUCID DYNASTY
ANTIOCHUS XIII (Asiaticus) **69-64 BC**, son of Antiochus X.

PHILIPPUS II 65-64 BC when the Kingdom fell to Rome, son of Philippus I; d after 56 BC.

The Seljuq Empire

The Turkish nomads, the Seljuqs, established a realm in Iran, northern Mesopotamia and Anatolia in the 11th century. Their supremacy was short-lived as they had little sense of nationhood and regarded all land as personal property, thus the Seljuq Empire was partitioned several times between members of the ruling family. By the 12th century there were many small Seljuq Sultanates of which the most powerful and enduring was that of Rum in Anatolia.

† Grand Sultans of the Seljuqs

They styled themselves 'Kings of the East and West'.

TOGHRIL BEG 1038 when he proclaimed himself Sultan-**1063**. An ambitious vassal of the ruler of Ghazna he wished to create a sovereignty of his own and achieved an empire including Iran and Iraq.

Muhammad ibn Da'ud **ALP-ARSLAN 1063-1072**, kinsman of Toghril Beg, b *c* 1030.

MALIK-SHAH I 1072-1092.

BERK-YARUQ 1092-1105, eldest son of Malik-Shah I.

MUHAMMAD 1092-1118, second son of Malik-Shah I. He fought against his brother Berk-Yaruq inheriting his share of the realm (the south) to add to the Azerbaijani state he had ruled since 1092.

SANJAR 1092-1118; sole ruler **1118-1153** deposed, third son of Malik-Shah I, b 1084; d 8 May 1157. In the partition of Malik-Shah's realm he received Khorasan which for his lifetime was one of the leading states of Asia.

(Further subdivisions destroyed the Seljuq Empire.)

† Seljuq Sultans in Anatolia

They were usually called Sultans of Rum (or Roum).

SULAYMAN I ibn Qutalmish *c* **1080-1086** died in battle, brother of Toghril Beg.

MALIK-SHAH I 1086-1092; see Malik-Shah, Grand Sultan of the Seljuqs.

QILICH ARSLAN I 1092-1107 drowned, son of Sulayman I.

MALIK-SHAH II 1107-1116, son of Qilich Arslan I.

MAS'UD I 1116-1155, brother of Malik-Shah II.

QILICH ARSLAN II 1155-1192, son of Mas'ud I. A reign marred by armed conflict between his sons and the seizure of his capital (Konya) by the crusading Frederick Barbarossa.

KAY-KHUSRAW I 1192-1196 fled, son of Qilich Arslan II.

Rukn ad-Din **SULYAMAN II 1196-1204,** son of Qilich Arslan II; d in battle in 1211.
QILICH ARSLAN III 1204-1205 deposed, son of Sulayman II; fate uncertain.
KAY-KHUSRAW I 1205-1211.
KAY-KA'US I 1211-1219, son of Kay-Khusraw I.
Ala'ad-Din **KAY-QUBADH 1219-1237,** son of Kay-Khusraw I. Taking much of northern Iraq and Syria he made Rum a great power.
KAY-KHUSRAW II 1237-1245, son of Kay-Ka'us I.
'IZZ ad-DIN KAY-KAUS II 1246-1261 fled; Sultan in west Rum, son of Kay-Khusraw II; fate uncertain.
Rukn ad-Din **QILICH ARSLAN IV 1245-1265,** son of Kay-Khusraw II; executed by his Minister. Sultan of east Rum until the deposition of his brother, then Sultan of Rum.
(The last three known Sultans were puppets of the Mongols.)
KAY-KHUSRAW III 1265-c1276.
MAS'UD II c1276-c1283.
Ala'ad-Din **FARAMURZ c1283-after c1305.** The dynasty and the Seljuq state in Rum ended in the early 14th century - few details are clear.

The Seychelles

The Seychelles were claimed for France in 1756, captured by the British in 1794, ceded to Britain in 1810 and achieved independence as a Republic on 29 Jun 1976.

Presidents

JAMES MANCHAM 29 Jun 1976-5 Jun 1977 deposed in coup, b 11 Aug 1939.
FRANCE ALBERT RENÉ since 5 Jun 1977, b 16 Nov 1935.

Sharjah *see* United Arab Emirates

Siam *see* Thailand

Sicily *see* Italy

Senegal

Parts of the Senegalese coast became French in 1659; the interior was not colonised until 1854-1865. Independence was gained within the Mali Federation on 20 Jun 1960, but Senegal withdrew from the federation on 20 Aug 1960.

President

LÉOPOLD SÉDAR SENGHOR since 5 Sep 1960, b 9 Oct 1906.

Prime Ministers

MAMADOU DIA Premier of Senegal within the Mali Federation **20 Jun-20 Aug 1960;** Premier of independent Senegal **20 Aug 1960-17 Dec 1962** when he was arrested following an attempted coup, b 1910.
LÉOPOLD SÉDAR SENGHOR 17 Dec 1962-3 Mar 1963 when the premiership was abolished, b 9 Oct 1906; see President Senghor.
1970 Premiership revived.
ABDOU DIOUF since 26 Feb 1970, b 7 Sep 1935.

Serbia *see* Yugoslavia

Sierra Leone

The British colony of Sierra Leone was founded in 1787 as a home for freed African slaves; the protectorate of Sierra Leone was declared in its hinterland in 1896. Independence was granted on 27 Apr 1961; a Republic was declared on 19 Apr 1971.

THE DOMINION OF SIERRA LEONE

Governors-General

Sir **MAURICE HENRY DORMAN 27 Apr 1961-7 Apr 1962,** b 1912.
Sir **HENRY JOSIAH LIGHTFOOT-BOSTON** acting Governor-General **27 Apr-7 Jul 1962;** Governor-General **7 Jul 1962-27 Mar 1967** when he was suspended by the National Reformation Council.
(Lieut-Col ANDREW J. JUXON-SMITH Chairman of the National Reformation Council, assumed the powers of the Governor-General: 27 Mar 1967-18 Apr 1968 when he was deposed by a coup.)
Chief Justice **BANJA TEJAN-SIE** acting Governor-General **22 Apr 1968-31 Mar 1971** when he was dismissed.
Justice **CHRISTOPHER OKORO COLE** acting Governor-General **31 Mar-19 Apr 1971.**

Prime Ministers

Sir **MILTON MARGAI 27 Apr 1961-28 Apr 1964,**
b 7 Dec 1895; d in office.
Dr **ALBERT MICHAEL MARGAI 29 Apr 1964-20
Mar 1967,** brother of Sir Milton Margai, b 10 Oct
1910.
SIAKA PROBYN STEVENS 21 Mar 1967 when he
was overthrown by a coup, b 24 Aug 1903.
Brig **DAVID LANSANA** Head of Government
21-23 Mar 1967 when he was deposed in a
counter-coup.
Lieut-Col **AMBROSE PATRICK GENDA** Chairman of the National Reformation Council *in
absentia* **23-27 Mar 1967,** b 1927. Nominally
Head of Government for four days, Lieut-Col
Genda was in New York when named Chairman,
but he was replaced by Lieut-Col Juxon-Smith
before he could return home.
Lieut-Col **ANDREW J. JUXON-SMITH** Chairman
of the National Reformation Council **27 Mar
1967-18 Apr 1968** when he was deposed by a
coup, b 1933.
18-26 Apr 1968 The Anti-Corruption Revolutionary Movement held power.
**SIAKA PROBYN STEVENS 26 Apr 1968-19 Apr
1971,** became the first Premier of the Republic.

THE REPUBLIC OF SIERRE LEONE

Presidents

Justice **CHRISTOPHER OKORO COLE** acting
President **19-21 Apr 1971.**
Dr **SIAKA PROBYN STEVENS since 21 Apr 1971,**
b 24 Aug 1903.

Prime Ministers

SIAKA PROBYN STEVENS 19-21 Apr 1971.
**SORIE IBRAHIM KOROMA 21 Apr 1971-mid-Jul
1975,** b Jan 1930.
**CHRISTIAN A. KAMARA-TAYLOR since mid
Jul 1975,** b 3 Jun 1917.

Singapore

Purchased from the Sultan of Johore, Singapore
was settled by the British in 1819 but did not
become a colony until 1867. Briefly independent in
1963 before joining the Malaysian federation,
Singapore did not finally become an independent
state until 9 Aug 1965 upon secession from the
federation.

Head of State

INCHE YUSUF bin ISHAK 31 Aug-16 Sep 1963.

Prime Minister

LEE KUAN YEW 31 Aug-16 Sep 1963.
1963-1965 Singapore was part of Malaysia.

THE REPUBLIC OF SINGAPORE

Presidents

INCHE YUSUF bin ISHAK acting Head of State
9 Aug-22 Dec 1965; President **22 Dec 1965-23 Nov
1970,** b 12 Aug 1907, d in office.
Prof **BENJAMIN HENRY SHEARES since 2 Jan
1971,** b 16 Sep 1923.

Prime Minister

LEE KUAN YEW since 9 Aug 1965, b 1923.

Sinhala Kingdoms *see* Sri Lanka

Slovakia *see* Czechoslovakia

Solomon Islands

The Solomon Islands, British since 1885, became
an independent Dominion upon 7 Jul 1978.

Governor-General

B DEVESI since 7 Jul 1978.

Prime Minister

PETER KENILOREA since 7 Jul 1978, b 1943.

Somalia

The former British colony of Somaliland (independent 26 Jun 1960) and the former Italian
Trust Territory of Somalia (independent 1 Jul 1960)
merged on 1 Jul 1960 to become the Somali
Republic.

Prime Minister of Somaliland
(ex-British)

**MOHAMMED HAJI IBRAHIM EGAL 26 Jun-12
Jul 1960,** later Premier of the Somali Republic.

Prime Minister of Somalia
(ex-Italian)

ABDULLE ISSA 1-12 Jul 1960.

THE SOMALI REPUBLIC

Presidents

ADAN ABDULLE OSMAN acting President **1-6 Jul 1960**; President **6 Jul 1960-10 Jun 1967,** b 1908.

Dr **ABDELRASHID ALI SHERMAKE 10 Jun 1967-15 Oct 1969** when he was assassinated, formerly Premier, b 1919; assassinated 15 Oct 1969.

Sheikh **MUKHTAR MOHAMMED HUSSEIN** acting President **17-21 Oct 1969.**

Maj-Gen **MOHAMMED SIYAD BARREH** President of the Supreme Military Council **since 21 Oct 1969**; concurrently Head of Government, b 1919.

Prime Ministers

Dr **ABDELRASHID ALI SHERMAKE 12 Jul 1960-early Jun 1964,** became President.

ABDIRIZAK HAJI HUSSEIN 14 Jun 1964-6 Jul 1967, b 1924.

MOHAMMED HAJI IBRAHIM EGAL 6 Jul 1967-21 Oct 1969, formerly Premier of Somaliland, b 1928.

Maj-Gen **MOHAMMED SIYAD BARREH** President of the Supreme Military Council **since 21 Oct 1969.**

South Africa

A Dutch colony was founded at the Cape in 1640 and expanded to cover half the present Cape Province by 1795 when it was taken by the British. Natal was annexed by Britain in 1842 and the two former independent Afrikaans Republics (the South African Republic, usually called Transvaal, founded in 1850 and the Orange Free State founded in 1854) were added to British South Africa after the Boer War. South Africa gained *de facto* independence in 1910 as a Dominion (confirmed by the Statute of Westminster in 1931). In 1961 the country became a Republic outside the Commonwealth. It is the intention of the South African Government that South West Africa, a German possession from 1884 until the First World War and a South African mandated territory since 1920, should achieve independence as the Republic of Namibia on 31 Dec 1978.

Field Marshal Jan Christiaan Smuts who was a respected international figure and a personal friend of the British Royal Family (Radio Times Hulton Picture Library)

THE UNION OF SOUTH AFRICA

Governors-General

Herbert John Gladstone, 1st Viscount **GLADSTONE May 1910-Sep 1914,** b 7 Jan 1854; d 6 Mar 1930.

Sydney Charles Buxton, 1st Earl **BUXTON Sep 1914-Aug 1920,** b 25 Oct 1853; d 15 Oct 1934.

Prince **ARTHUR of CONNAUGHT Aug 1920-Nov 1923,** son of Prince Arthur, Duke of Connaught, b 13 Jan 1883; d 12 Sep 1938.

Alexander, 1st Earl of **ATHLONE Jan 1924-Dec 1930,** husband of Princess Alice of Albany, b (a Prince of Teck) 14 Apr 1874; d 16 Jan 1957.

George Herbert Hyde Villiers, 6th Earl of **CLARENDON Jan 1931-1937,** b 7 Jun 1877; d 13 Dec 1955.

Sir **PATRICK DUNCAN 1937-17 Jul 1943,** b 1870; d in office.

NICOLAS JACOBUS de WET acting Governor-General **Jul 1943-1946,** b 1873; d 1960.

Major **GIDEON BRAND van ZYL 1946-Dec 1950,** b 1873; d 1956.

Dr **ERNEST GEORGE JANSEN Jan 1951-28 Nov 1959,** b 1881; d in office.

Dr **LUCAS CORNELIUS STEYN** acting Governor-General **Nov 1959-Jan 1960,** b 1903.

CHARLES ROBBERTS SWART Jan 1960-31 May 1961 when he became President

Prime Ministers

Gen **LOUIS BOTHA 31 May 1910-Aug 1919,** b 27 Sep 1862; d 27 Aug 1919. The hero of the Boers he fought with great distinction against the Zulus and then against the British in the South African War. An attractive personality who did much to build national unity, he took South Africa into World War I despite Afrikaans opposition.

Field Marshal **JAN CHRISTIAAN SMUTS Aug 1919-Jun 1924.**

JAMES BARRY MUNNIK HERTZOG 1 Jun 1924-Sep 1939, b 3 Apr 1866; d 21 Nov 1942. Commander-in-Chief of the Boer armies in the South African War, Hertzog, who introduced the first elements of racial segregation in South Africa, was half-hearted in his support for the Allied cause in 1939.

Field Marshal **JAN CHRISTIAAN SMUTS 5 Sep 1939-Jun 1948,** b 24 May 1870; d 11 Sep 1950. Smuts was a fine general, a prolific writer and a respected humanist philosopher and a statesman of world stature. Dedicated to the Allied cause and to democratic ideals he strongly opposed apartheid.

DANIEL FRANCOIS MALAN 1 Jun 1948-Nov 1954, b 22 May 1874; b.7 Feb 1959. A Dutch Reformed Minister, he refounded the Nationalist Party; he appointed an entirely Afrikaans Ministry and introduced apartheid.

JOHANNES GERHARDHUS STRIJDOM 30 Nov 1954-24 Aug 1958, b 14 Jul 1873; d in office.

CHARLES ROBBERTS SWART acting PM **24 Aug-2 Sep 1958.**

HENDRIK FRENSCH VERWOERD 2 Sep 1958-31 May 1961 when he became PM of the Republic.

THE REPUBLIC OF SOUTH AFRICA

Presidents

CHARLES ROBBERTS SWART 31 May 1961-Jun 1967, b 5 Dec 1894.

JOZUA FRANCOIS T. NAUDÉ acting President **1 Jun 1967-Apr 1968.**

JACOBUS JOHANNES FOUCHÉ 10 Apr 1968-Apr 1975, b 6 Jun 1898.

Dr **NICOLAAS DIEDERICH since 19 Apr 1975,** b 17 Nov 1903.

Prime Ministers

HENDRIK FRENSCH VERWOERD PM since Sep 1958; **31 May 1961-6 Sep 1966,** b 8 Sep 1901; d in office - assassinated in Parliament. A brilliant academic, Dutch born Hendrik Verwoerd, who opposed South African participation in World War II in the Allied cause so strongly that he was interned, was largely responsible for the implementation of apartheid while Bantu Affairs Minister.

BALTHAZAR JOHN VORSTER since Sep 1966, b 13 Dec 1915.

The Boer Republics

THE SOUTH AFRICAN REPUBLIC - TRANSVAAL

Presidents

ANDRIES WILHELMUS JACOBUS PRETORIUS 17 Jan 1852-23 Jul 1853, b 27 Nov 1798; d in office. The leader of the Boers on the Great Trek out of British territory he founded Transvaal in 1850 and gained recognition of its independence in 1852.

MARTHINUS WESSELS PRETORIUS acting President **1853-1855**; President **1855-1871,** son of Andries Pretorius, b 17 Sep 1819; d 19 May 1901.

1871-1872 No President.

THOMAS FRANCOIS BURGERS Jul 1872-1877, b 15 Apr 1834; d 9 Dec 1881.

1877-1880 Transvaal annexed by the British.

1880-1883 No President.

STEPHANUS JOHANNES PAULUS KRUGER 1883-1902, b 10 Oct 1825; d 14 Jul 1904. He tried without success to involve European powers in the Boer War. The leader of the 1880 revolt against British rule 'Oom Paul' fled to exile in the Boer War.

THE ORANGE FREE STATE

Presidents

JOSIAS PHILIPPUS HOFFMAN Feb 1854-1855, b 1807; d 1879. He obtained British recognition of the independence of his Republic.

JACOBUS NICOLAAS BOSHOFF 1855-1859, b 1808; d 1881.

MARTHINUS WESSELS PRETORIUS 1859-Apr 1863; see President Pretorius of Transvaal.

Apr 1863-1864 No President.

Sir **JOHANNES HENDRICUS BRAND 1864-1888,** b 6 Dec 1823; d 14 Jul 1888.

FRANCIS WILLIAM REITZ 1888-Feb 1896, b 1844; d 1934.

MARTHINUS THEUNIS STEYN Feb 1896-May 1902, b 2 Oct 1857; d 28 Nov 1916. A leading figure of the Boer War he conducted an able guerrilla campaign after the fall of Bloemfontein.

Bophuthatswana

The second South African 'Bantustan' or African homeland to gain independence, Bophuthatswana consists of seven widely scattered enclaves and is unrecognised as a state by the international community.

President

Chief **LUCAS MANGOPE   since 6 Dec 1977** on independence.

Transkei

After becoming a self-governing territory in 1963, the Transkei became the first South African 'Bantustan' to gain independence (26 Oct 1976). It is unrecognised as a sovereign state by the international community.

President

Chief **BOTHA JONGILIZWE SIGCAU   since 26 Oct 1976,** b 1912.

Prime Minister

Chief **KAISER MATANZIMA   since 26 Oct 1976,** b 1915.

South Korea *see* Korea

South Saxons or Sussex *see* Anglo-Saxon Kingdoms, United Kingdom

South Vietnam *see* Vietnam

South Yemen or the People's Democratic Republic of Yemen

Aden passed to Britain in 1839; the hinterland - the Hadhramaut - came under British protection later in the 19th century. Aden Colony (once part of the Bombay Presidency) and the protected Shaikhdoms were merged to form the South Arabian Federation which was inaugurated in Feb 1959. However, the territory achieved independence as a unitary Republic named South Yemen on 30 Nov 1967. From 30 Nov 1970 the state has been known as the People's Democratic Republic of Yemen.

Presidents

QAHTAN as-SHAABI   30 Nov 1967-22 Jun 1969 deposed, b 1920.
22-24 Jun 1969 Presidential Council.
SALEM RUBAYYI ALI Chairman of the Presidential Council **24 Jun 1969-26 Jun 1978** deposed in coup, b 1934; executed 26 Jun 1978 - immediately after deposition.
ALI NASSER MOHAMMED HASSANIYA   since 26 Jan 1978.

Prime Ministers

QAHTAN as-SHAABI   30 Nov 1967-Apr 1969; see President as-Shaabi.
ABDUL LATIF as-SHAABI   9 Apr-22 Jun 1969 deposed.
22-24 Jun 1969 Presidential Council.
MOHAMMED ALI HAITHEM   24 Jun 1969-Aug 1971, b 1940.
ALI NASSER MOHAMMED HASSANIYA   since 2 Aug 1971.

Soviet Union *see* Union of Soviet Socialist Republics

Spain

Roman Spain was invaded by the Suevi and the Vandals before falling in the 5th century to the Visigoths who united all Iberia in a Kingdom that lasted until the Moorish invasion in 711. A separate Spanish Arab state - the Emirate, later the Caliphate, of Cordoba - was not founded until 756 and though the Arabs conquered most of Iberia a small Christian state, Asturias, remained independent in the north. The Caliphate broke into many petty 'Kingdoms' (the last of which, Granada, fell in 1492), thus the initiative passed to the Christian states - Asturias-Leon, Castile, Aragon and Navarre - which gradually retook the peninsula in a movement called the Reconquista. The dominant Kingdoms, Aragon and Castile, were united in a personal union, later to become a political union, by the marriage of Ferdinand and Isabella in the 15th century. The Spanish Kingdom was taken by Napoleon I in 1808, restored to the Bourbons in 1814 and overthrown by a revolt in 1868. A liberal monarchy under an Italian King (1870-1873) was replaced by the First Republic which was itself replaced by the restored Spanish Bourbon monarchy in 1874. The 20th century has seen the fall of the monarchy in 1931, the Second Republic (1931-1939), the terrible Civil War (1936-1939), the Spanish State (1936-1975; from 1947 officially a monarchy but without a King), and the restoration of the Kingdom on 22 Nov 1975.

THE VISIGOTH KINGDOM IN SPAIN
(an elective rather than hereditary monarchy)

† Kings

ATAULFO *c*412-415 assassinated, ruled part of northern Spain.

SIGERICO 415 - traditionally said to have reigned 7 days, assassinated.

WALLIA *c*415-419, King of Tolosa (Toulouse); ruled part of northern Spain.

TEODOREDO I *c*419-451 killed in battle, King of Tolosa.

TORISMUNDO 451-453 murdered by his brother Teodoredo II; King of Tolosa, eldest son of Teodoredo I.

TEODOREDO II 453-*c*466 murdered by his brother Eurico; King of Tolosa, brother of Torismundo.

EURICO *c*466-*c*485, King of Tolosa, brother of Teodoredo II. He established a Kingdom that included most of Spain and was perhaps the most powerful European ruler of his day.

ALARICO *c*485-507, son of Eurico.

(GEISELICO, illegitimate son of Alarico, is included in some lists at this point. He fled in 510.)

AMALARICO 507 or 510-531, son of Alarico.

TEUDIS 531-*c*548 assassinated.

TEUDISCULUS *c*548-*c*549 assassinated.

AGILA *c*549-*c*554 assassinated.

ATANAGILDO *c*554-567.

LIUVA I 567-568 or possibly 572, son of Atanagildo.

LEOVIGILDO 568 or 572-586, son of Atanagildo. Under Leovigildo the Kingdom became more Spanish, the capital being removed to Toledo and legal differences between Goths and Hispano-Romans ended.

RECAREDO I 586-601, son of Leovigildo. The Visigoth Kingdom reached its zenith in the reign of this King who abjured Arianism and brought Spain into the Catholic world.

LIUVA II 601-*c*603 assassinated.

WITERICO *c*603-610 assassinated, a usurper.

GUNDEMARO *c*610-*c*612.

SISEBUTO *c*612-621.

RECAREDO II 621, son of Sisebuto.

SUINTILA 621-631.

SISENANDO 631-636.

CHINTILA 636-639.

TULGA 639-642 deposed; date of death unknown.

CHINDAVINTO sole ruler 642-649; co-ruler 649-653.

RECESVINTO co-ruler 649-653; sole ruler 653-672, son of Chindavinto.

WAMBA 672-680 deposed; date of death unknown.

ERVIGIO 680 or 681-687.

EGICA 687-700 or 702, son-in-law of Ervigio.

WITIZA 700 or 702-710, son of Egica.

RODRIGO 710-Jul 711 killed in battle by invading Arabs; possibly descended from Chindavinto. Having obtained 'election' over the son of Witiza (who tried to establish the hereditary principle), Rodrigo was challenged by Witiza's family who called in the Arabs to depose the King - the result cannot have been anticipated.

MOORISH SPAIN

Virtually all of the Iberian Peninsula was conquered by the Arabs within three years (711-714). An Emirate nominally subject to the Caliph in Baghdad was established in Cordoba (756) - complete independence was asserted when the Emir assumed the title Caliph (929).

† Ummayad Emirs of Cordoba

ABD-ar-RAHMAN I ad Dakkil 756-788, b *c*731. A ruthless, efficient ruler, he established a strong Muslim state and repulsed Charlemagne.

HISHAM I 788-796, son of Abd-ar-Rahman I, b *c*757.

al-HAKAM I 796-822, son of Hisham I.

ABD-ar-RAHMAN II 822-852, son of al-Hakam I, b *c*788. Patron of architects, poets and musicians, this Emir governed prudently handling importunate Christians seeking martyrdom with extraordinary tact.

MUHAMMAD I 852-886, son of Abd-ar-Rahman II.

al-MUNDHIR 886-888, son of Muhammad I.

ABD ALLAH 888-912, brother of al-Mundhir.

ABD-ar-RAHMAN III 912-929 when he became Caliph.

† Ummayad Caliphs of Cordoba

an-NASIR (ABD-ar-RAHMAN III) Emir from 912; Caliph 929-961, grandson of Abd Allah, b 891. The most able of his dynasty, an-Nasir (the name he adopted upon declaring himself Caliph) quelled rebellious Arab nobility, countered the Fatimids from Morocco and reconquered many of the lands taken by Leon.

al-MUSTANSIR (al-HAKAM II) 961-976, son of an-Nasir, b *c*910-915.

al-MU'AYYAD (HISHAM II) 976-1016 or later, son of al-Mustansir; vanished without trace during the second decade of the 11th century. al-Mu'ayyad was reduced to less than a cipher by the brilliant general Abu'Amir al Ma'afiri, known as al-Mansur (the Victor). The military dictatorship of al-Mansur nearly extinguished the Christian Kingdoms, but on his death (1008) his weak sons and the shadowy Caliph could not prevent Arab Spain splitting into numerous weak, anarchic 'Kingdoms' (Ta'ifas) thus aiding the Christian reconquest (Reconquista) of Spain.

THE KINGDOM OF ASTURIAS

From whose Kings the Spanish monarchs take their regnal numbers.

† Kings

HOUSE OF PELAYO

PELAYO 718-c737. A Visigoth soldier, Pelayo was acknowledged by the Asturians as their King and leader. His victory over the Moors at Covadonga (c722) is regarded as the start of the Reconquista.

FÁVILA c737-c739 killed in a hunting accident, son of Pelayo.

ALFONSO I c739-757, son-in-law of Pelayo.

FROÍLA I 757-c768 murdered by Aurelio; son of Alfonso I. The first of the five 'reyes holgazanes' (idle Kings of whom virtually nothing is known).

AURELIO c768-c774, nephew? of Alfonso I.

SILO c774-783, brother-in-law of Aurelio.

MAUREGATO 783-788, illegitimate son of Alfonso I.

VERMUDO I ('The Deacon') **788-791** abdicated, nephew of Alfonso I; became a monk - date of death unknown.

ALFONSO II ('The Chaste') co-ruler **775-783**; sole ruler **791-842,** son of Froila I, b c759. He greatly enlarged the Kingdom, and moved the capital to Oviedo.

RAMIRO I 842-850, son of Vermudo I, b c790. Also King of Leon.

ORDOÑO I 850-866, son of Ramiro I.

ALFONSO III ('The Great') **866-20 Dec 910,** son of Ordoño I, b c840. Alfonso the Great took Galicia and northern Portugal from the Arabs.

THE KINGDOM OF LEON AND ASTURIAS

† Kings

HOUSE OF ASTURIAS

GARCÍA I 910-914, son of Alfonso III. Uniting Asturias and Leon, he moved the capital to Leon.

ORDOÑO II 914-c925, brother of García I.

FROÍLA II c925, brother of Ordoño II. Froíla II momentarily usurped the throne upon the death of his brother.

ALFONSO FROILAZ c925 deposed after a very brief reign, son of Froíla II; date of death unknown.

ALFONSO IV c925-931 deposed after a period of anarchy, son of Ordono II; d 933.

RAMIRO II 931-951 abdicated, brother of Alfonso IV, b c923; d same year as abdication.

ORDOÑO III 951-956, elder son of Ramiro II.

SANCHO I ('The Fat') **956-c958** deposed, younger son of Ramiro II.

ORDOÑO IV c958-960 deposed, cousin of Sancho I; date of death unknown.

SANCHO I ('The Fat') **960-966** poisoned.

RAMIRO III 966-984 killed by rebels, son of Sancho I, b 962.

VERMUDO II 984-999, grandson of Froíla II.

ALFONSO V ('The Noble') **999-1027** killed, son of Vermudo II, b 994.

VERMUDO III 1027-1037 killed in battle by his brother-in-law Fernando I of Castile; son of Alfonso V, b 1016.

THE KINGDOM OF CASTILE AND LEON

† Kings

HOUSE OF NAVARRE

FERNANDO I King of Castile **from 1035,** of Leon from **1037-27 Dec 1065,** son of Sancho III of Navarre, b c1017. Having founded the Kingdom of Castile from his share of his father's inheritance, Fernando seized Leon-Asturias from his brother-in-law and united the two realms. After making himself master of most of Christian Spain, he undid his work by dividing his Kingdom for his sons.

SANCHO II King of Castile **Dec 1065-7 Oct 1072** assassinated, son of Fernando I, b c1038.

ALFONSO VI ('el Bravo') King of Leon **Dec 1065-1109**; of Castile **from Oct 1072,** son of Fernando I, b spring 1040. Alfonso VI became a folk hero because of his exploits against the Moors and his struggle with too powerful nobles including Rodrigo Diaz de Vivar (el Cid) with whom he was eventually reconciled. A vigorous King, he posed as the protector of his Muslim subjects, but in reality his harshness to them brought revolt and another Arab invasion in which most of his gains were lost.

URRACA (Queen) **1109-1126,** daughter of Alfonso VI, b 1081 or 1080. A reign of almost constant civil war with her second husband (Alfonso I of Aragon) and her son by her first marriage.

HOUSE OF BURGUNDY

ALFONSO VII ('The Emperor') **1126-Aug 1157,** son of Queen Urraca by her first husband, b c1104.

SANCHO III Aug 1167-1158, King of Castile; son of Alfonso VII, b c1134.

FERNANDO II Aug 1157-1188, King of Leon; son of Alfonso VII, b c1145.

ALFONSO VIII 1158-6 Oct 1214, King of Castile; son of Sancho III, b 1155. His victory over the Arabs at Las Navas de Tolosa (1212) opened the way to the reconquest of Andalusia.

ALFONSO IX 1188-1230, King of Leon; son of Fernando II, b 1166.

ENRIQUE I 1214-1217, King of Castile; son of Alfonso VIII, b c1203.

FERNANDO III ('The Saint' - an epithet this bigot ill deserved) King of Castile **1217-1252**; King of Leon **from 1230,** son of Alfonso IX, b c1200. Marrying the daughter of Alfonso VIII he reunited Leon and Castile. He took Jaen, Murcia,

Cordoba and Seville from the Arabs, leaving only Granada in Muslim hands.

ALFONSO X ('The Wise') **1252-4 Apr 1284,** son of Fernando III, b 23 Nov 1221. Known for his astrological studies (the Alphonsine Tables), Alfonso X spent too much time and money trying to secure the Imperial Crown to which he had been elected but never wore. At home he tried to curb the power of the nobles, who were treasonably supported in rebellion by his second son Sancho, and he did achieve legal reform.

SANCHO IV   Apr 1284-1295, second son of Alfonso X, b 1257. Having usurped the throne he faced a revolt in favour of the true King, his nephew.

FERNANDO IV   1295-1312, son of Sancho IV, b 1289.

ALFONSO XI   1312-26 Mar 1350, son of Fernando IV, b 1311.

PEDRO I ('The Cruel' - an unfair epithet conferred upon him by historians writing for the Trastamara Dynasty that replaced him) **Mar 1350-1366** deposed, son of Alfonso IX, b 1334.

HOUSE OF TRASTAMARA

ENRIQUE II   1366-1367 deposed, illegitimate son of Alfonso XI, b 1333. Enrique, Count of Trastamara, seized his half-brother's throne in 1366 but was deposed by the Black Prince. With the aid of French forces and du Guesclin, Enrique recaptured the crown, murdering his rival.

HOUSE OF BURGUNDY

PEDRO I   1367-23 Mar 1369 killed by Enrique II with whom he disputed the throne.

HOUSE OF TRASTAMARA

ENRIQUE II   1369-29 May 1379.

JUAN I   May 1379-1390, son of Enrique II, b 1358.

ENRIQUE III ('The Sufferer') **1390-1406,** son of Juan I, b 4 Oct 1379.

JUAN II   1406-21 Jul 1454, son of Enrique III, b 6 Mar 1405.

ENRIQUE IV   Jul 1454-11 Dec 1474, son of Juan II, b 25 Jan 1425. Weak Enrique IV was dominated by his favourite Pacheco and the nobles who forced him to (falsely) acknowledge impotency and renounce his daughter Juana in favour of his sister Isabel whom they (incredibly) imagined to be pliable.

ISABEL (Queen); see Kings of Spain.

THE KINGDOM OF ARAGON

† Kings

HOUSE OF NAVARRE OR PAMPLONA

RAMIRO I   1035-1063, illegitimate son of Sancho III of Navarre who created the Kingdom of Aragon for his son.

SANCHO I RAMIREZ   1063-Jun 1094.

PEDRO I   Jun 1094-1104, b c 1068.

ALFONSO I   1104-1134, b c 1073. An impractical King who tried to will his state to the religious military orders. Alfonso I married, quarrelled with and fought a civil war against Queen Urraca of Castile.

RAMIRO II ('The Monk') **1134-1137** abdicated, brother of Alfonso I; d (a monk) 1154. Bishop-elect Ramiro was forced to leave the cloister to reign, marry and beget an heir. He abdicated when his daughter was born.

PETRONILLA (Queen) **1137-1162,** daughter of Ramiro II, b c 1137.

HOUSE OF BARCELONA

ALFONSO II RÁMON   1162-1196, son of Queen Petronilla and Rámon Berenguer IV, Count of Barcelona, b 1152. Alfonso inherited Aragon from his mother and Catalonia from his father to form an uneasy union ultimately to the benefit of both countries.

PEDRO II   1196-1213 killed in battle by Simon de Montfort; son of Alfonso II Rámon, b 1174.

JAIME I ('The Conqueror') **1215-27 Jul 1276,** son of Pedro II, b 2 Feb 1208. An outstanding soldier and administrator, Jaime conquered Murcia, Valencia and the Balearic Islands, laying the foundations of Aragon's Mediterranean empire. He founded the Cortes, the navy and an embryo local government.

PEDRO III ('The Great') **Jul 1276-1285,** son of Jaime I, b 1239. With a remote claim to Sicily through his Hohenstaufen wife, Pedro conquered that island after the Sicilian Vespers rising (1282).

ALFONSO III ('The Good-doer') **1285-1291,** son of Pedro III, b 1265. Alfonso III made important gains from the Arabs, had a long struggle with the Pope who refused to recognise his claim to Sicily and was forced to concede dangerous powers to the nobles.

JAIME II ('The Just') **1291-1327,** brother of Alfonso III, b 1264. He relinquished Sicily to his brother Federico, but gained Corsica and Sardinia.

ALFONSO IV ('The Debonair') **1327-Jan 1336,** son of Jaime II, b 1299.

PEDRO IV ('The Ceremonious') **Jan 1336-1387,** son of Alfonso IV, b 1319.

JUAN I   1387-1395, son of Pedro IV, b 1350.

MARTIN I ('The Humane') **1395-1410,** brother of Juan I, b c 1355. He died with neither heir nor testament causing a two year crisis and interregnum which was ended by the appointment of nine commissioners to elect a new King.

1410-1412 Interregnum.

HOUSE OF TRASTAMARA

FERNANDO I ('The Just') **1412-2 Apr 1416,** nephew of Pedro IV and a member of the Royal House of Castile, b c 1379. The accession of a Castilian King paved the way for the union of the two realms. His defection from the anti-Pope virtually ended the Great Schism.

ALFONSO V ('The Magnanimous') **Apr 1416-27 Jun 1458,** son of Fernando I, b 1396. A major early Renaissance figure, humanist and patron of the arts, Alfonso V concentrated his energies on his Italian Kingdoms of Naples and Sicily to the detriment of Aragon.

JUAN II Jun 1458-20 Jan 1479, brother of Alfonso V, b 1398. By marrying his son Fernando to Isabel of Castile he ensured the union of Spain.

FERNANDO II; see Kings of Spain.

THE KINGDOM OF NAVARRE

Originally called the Kingdom of Pamplona.

† Kings of Pamplona

HOUSE OF PAMPLONA

SANCHO I GARCÉS 905-925. Despite the ravages of the Arabs, Sancho I re-established an independent Basque-Spanish state based on Pamplona.

GARCIA I SÁNCHEZ 925-970.

SANCHO II GARCÉS (Sancho Abarca) **970-c994.**

GARCIA II c994-1000.

SANCHO III GARCÉS ('The Great') **1000-1035,** b c992. Self-proclaimed Emperor, Sancho the Great pushed back the Arabs and dominated Spain. Tragically this early chance of unity was sacrificed when he created the Kingdoms of Aragon and Castile for two of his sons.

GARCIA III 1035-1054, son of Sancho III.

SANCHO IV 1054-1076 deposed, son of Garcia III; date of death uncertain.

HOUSE OF PAMPLONA
(Aragonese Branch)

SANCHO V RAMIREZ 1076-Jun 1094; see Sancho I Ramirez of Aragon.

PEDRO I Jun 1094-1104; see Pedro I of Aragon.

ALFONSO I 1104-1134; see Alfonso I of Aragon.

HOUSE OF NAVARRE

GARCIA IV RAMIREZ (or GARCIA RAMIREZ) **1134-1150.** Chosen as King by the Navarrese nobles who refused to accept Alfonso I's will.

† Kings of Navarre

HOUSE OF NAVARRE

SANCHO VI ('The Wise') **1150-1194.** Sancho VI adopted the style King of Navarre in preference to King of Pamplona.

SANCHO VII ('The Strong') **1194-1234,** b 1154. An attractive figure, the archtype of the dashing knight of the Reconquista, Sancho VII was the last really Spanish monarch of Navarre, the later sovereigns being more French.

HOUSE OF CHAMPAGNE

From the accession of this House it is more realistic to refer to the Kings of Navarre by their French titles than the Spanish equivalent.

THIBAUT I (Teobaldo I) **1234-1253,** Count of Champagne, nephew of Sancho VII whose daughter he later married.

THIBAUT II (Teobaldo II) **1253-1270.**

HENRI I (Enrique I) **1270-1274,** b c1210.

JEANNE I (Juana I) **1274-1305,** b 1273. Queen Jeanne married Philippe IV le Bel of France with the effect that Navarre became virtually annexed to the larger Kingdom.

HOUSE OF CAPET

PHILIPPE I (Felipe I) **1284-29 Nov 1314,** husband of Jeanne I; was also Philippe IV, King of France.

LOUIS I (Luis I) **Nov 1314-5 Jun 1316**; was also Louis X, King of France.

Jun-Nov 1316 Interregnum.

JEAN I (Juan I) **13 or 14-19 Nov 1316**; was also Jean I, King of France.

PHILIPPE II (Felipe II) **Nov 1316-3 Jan 1322**; was also Philippe V, King of France.

CHARLES I (Carlos I) **Jan 1322-1 Feb 1328**; was also Charles IV, King of France.

JEANNE II (Juana II) co-ruler **Feb 1328-1349,** daughter of Louis I, b 1311. Under Jeanne II and her co-ruler husband, Navarre became an independent nation again.

HOUSE OF EVREUX

PHILIPPE III (Felipe III) co-ruler **Feb 1328-1349,** husband of Jeanne II.

CHARLES II (Carlos II) **1349-1387,** son of Jeanne II and Philippe III, b 1332. Totally unreliable as an ally, Charles II fought beside England in an attempt to expand Navarre but was defeated by du Guesclin (1364). He was known as 'The Bad'.

CHARLES III (Carlos III) **1387-1425,** son of Charles II, b 1361. He was known as 'The Noble'.

BLANCHE (Blanca) co-ruler **1425-1441,** daughter of Charles III.

HOUSE OF TRASTAMARA

JEAN II (Juan II) co-ruler **1425-1441**; sole ruler **1441-1479,** second husband of Blanche; was also Juan II of Aragon.

(CHARLES IV (or Carlos IV - Carlos de Viana), the son of Blanche and Jean II - fought a war against his father for the throne of Navarre, but can at no stage have been said to have reigned.)

ÉLÉONORE (Leonor) **1479,** daughter of Blanche and Jean II.

HOUSE OF FOIX

FRANCOIS I Phoebus (Francisco I Febo) **1479-1483,** Count of Foix, grandson of Queen Éléonore.

CATHERINE (Catalina) sole ruler **1483-1484**; co-ruler **1484-Feb 1512,** sister of Francois I.

HOUSE OF ALBRET

JEAN III (Juan III) co-ruler **1484-Feb 1512**; sole ruler **Feb 1512-1516,** husband of Queen Catherine. In this reign Upper (Spanish) Navarre was seized by Aragon leaving only a small French-Basque Kingdom north of the Pyrenees.

HENRI II 1516-1555, son of Queen Catherine and Jean III. Henri II's Queen, the poetess 'Marguerite des Marguerites', made the Court at Pau one of the intellectual centres of Europe.

JEANNE III (Queen) **1555-1572,** daughter of Henri II, b 1528. A leading Huguenot, she intervened in the religious wars in France.

HOUSE OF BOURBON

HENRI III 1572-14 May 1610, son of Jeanne III. Became King of France as Henri IV in 1589; see France.

LOUIS II May 1610-14 May 1643; was also Louis XIII, King of France. On 19/20 Oct 1620 he annexed Navarre to France, but all Bourbon French monarchs continued to use the additional style King of Navarre.

THE KINGDOM OF SPAIN

† Kings

HOUSE OF TRASTAMARA

FERNANDO V (II of Aragon) King of Aragon **Jan 1479-23 Jan 1516**; King of Castile **13 Dec 1474-Nov 1504**; Guardian of Castile with the powers but not the style of King **10 Oct 1510-23 Jan 1516**, son of Juan II of Aragon and husband of Isabel I of Castile, b 10 Mar 1452. Athletic, chivalrous and reserved, Ferdinand the Catholic was, although capable, outshone by his wife Isabel of Castile. Together they created Spain; together they secured her succession to Castile, strove to increase royal power at the expense of the nobles, encouraged Church reform, took Granada (2 Jan 1492) to end the Arab presence in Iberia, encouraged trade and colonial enterprise (they sponsored Columbus) and eased the lot of the serfs. Individually he quelled a Catalan revolt, won the Kingdom of Naples through his diplomacy and the military brilliance of Gonsalvo and fell out with his son-in-law and successor in Castile, Felipe I, though he resumed the Regency in that Kingdom upon the latter's death. He was known as 'The Catholic'.

ISABEL I ('The Catholic') **13 Dec 1474-26 Nov 1504,** daughter of Juan II of Castile and wife of Fernando II of Aragon, b 22 Apr 1451. Isabel's succession was disputed by a niece of doubtful legitimacy occasioning a four-year-war won for her by her husband and co-ruler Fernando. Handsome, noble and highly educated, she was a major patron of arts, literature, science and printing making Spain the outstanding centre of learning in Europe. Her renowned piety sometimes clouded her good sense as when she submitted to public opinion and instituted the Inquisition (1483) - a popular court with the masses, its nevertheless repugnant practices have been grossly exaggerated by north Euro-

Carlos I, better known as Emperor Charles V, abdicated 75 titles and an empire for the quiet of a monastery (Radio Times Hulton Picture Library)

pean historians. Influenced by her confessor Ximenes, Isabel worked for the spread of Catholicism (though she was not blind to the abuses of churchmen) and expelled some of Spain's Jews - two-thirds remained as converts to make a valuable contribution to Spain's culture and economy.

JUANA (La Loca - the mad) Queen of Castile **Nov 1504-Aug 1506,** then nominally Queen **Aug 1506-11 Apr 1555**; nominally Queen of Aragon **Jan 1516-11 Apr 1555**; daughter of Fernando I and Isabel I, b 6 Nov 1479.

HOUSE OF HABSBURG

FELIPE I ('The Handsome') co-ruler **Nov 1504-Aug 1506**; given complete royal powers **Aug-25 Sep 1506,** husband of Queen Juana, b (an Archduke of Austria) 22 Jul 1478.

CARLOS I (Emperor Charles V) **Jan 1516-16 Jan 1556** when he abdicated, son of Queen Juana and Felipe I, b 24 Feb 1500; d 21 Sep 1558. The most powerful King of his century, he inherited a vast empire including Spain, Burgundy, the Low Countries, Austria and the Empire, Naples and Sicily and the Spanish possessions in Africa and the New World. The last ruler to attempt to create a universal state embracing all the Christian world, Charles V was a monarch of the highest ideals and integrity whose reign may be

Felipe II, here receiving a mission, was incapable of delegating duties and wore himself out through overwork (Radio Times Hulton Picture Library)

judged to be a glorious failure. Elected Emperor (Jun 1519) his imperial pretensions cost Castile much revenue and led to revolts, while his initial preference for his Flemish subjects caused resentment, though he became more Spanish in time spending 16 years of his reign in Spain. His assumed role of universal arbitrator involved him in wars in Italy against France and in the Mediterranean against the Turks, and in the bitter Lutheran disputes in Germany. Finally confronted by an alliance of France and the German Protestants Charles' imperial concept was destroyed - tired and disillusioned he abdicated the Empire for his brother (25 Oct 1555) and Spain and her lands for his son (16 Jan 1556) before retiring to a monastery.

FELIPE II Jan 1556-13 Sep 1598, son of Carlos I, b 21 May 1527. The 'bogey-man' of English and Dutch school history books, Felipe II remains a controversial figure. Austere and extraordinarily hard working his suspicious nature and lack of judgement would not let him delegate, thus he ruled slowly and inefficiently handling all government memoranda personally. Unjustified stories persist of his relations with his strange, deformed, schizophrenic son Don Carlos (who was neither murdered nor a liberal as opera and drama insist) - in fact Felipe was a devoted father to his children. Felipe became obsessed with his imagined 'duty' as defender of the Catholic Church leading him to counter the Dutch revolt with severity and to launch the Armada against England (not as was claimed to avenge the death of Mary, Queen of Scots, but as a realisation that the Dutch rebellion could never be ended while England intervened). His grandiose schemes were too much for his resources and Spain was bankrupted.

FELIPE III Sep 1598-31 Mar 1621, son of Felipe II, b 14 Apr 1578.

FELIPE IV Mar 1621-17 Sep 1665, son of Felipe III, b 8 Apr 1605. With his Minister Olivares, Felipe IV attempted to halt the political and economic decline of Spain and to reform, but achieved little owing to vested interests. A Catalan revolt provided the chance for Portugal (Spanish since 1580) to reassert her independence.

CARLOS II Sep 1665-1 Nov 1700, son of Felipe IV, b 6 Nov 1661. His lack of an heir led Europe to fight over his inheritance in the War of Spanish Succession.

HOUSE OF BOURBON

FELIPE V Nov 1700-15 Jan 1724 abdicated, great-nephew of Carlos II, b (Philippe, Duc d'Anjou, grandson of Louis XIV) 19 Dec 1683. His accession was opposed in war by England and Austria (hostile to an extension to Louis XIV's power); his reign saw a partial recovery in Spain despite the damaging Italian wars in which his dominating Farnese wife involved him.

LUIS Jan-6 Sep 1724, eldest son of Felipe V, b 25 Aug 1707.

FELIPE V Sep 1724-9 Jul 1746.

FERNANDO VI Jul 1746-10 Aug 1759, fourth son of Felipe V, b 23 Sep 1713.

CARLOS III Aug 1759-14 Dec 1788, fifth son of Felipe V, b 20 Jan 1716. Duke of Parma and King of Naples before inheriting Spain, Charles III achieved much in Italy, developing Naples and Sicily after centuries of neglect - government and finances were reformed to the extent that taxes were cut. Interested in the arts he founded the Capodimonte pottery and built Caserta Palace, while later in Spain he constructed the Prado. As Spanish monarch he continued as an enlightened despot reviving the economy and making government more efficient and attacking Church privileges - a campaign that included the expulsion of the Jesuits.

CARLOS IV Dec 1788-19 Mar 1808 abdicated, second son of Carlos III, b 11 Nov 1748; d in exile 19 Jan 1819. The patron of Goya was accurately pictured by that master as an amiable, weak, unprepossessing individual. He was dominated by his immoral wife, Maria Luisa, and her clever, odious lover, the Minister Godoy, Prince of Peace - so named from the humiliating treaty he concluded with France in 1796. Godoy's deposition in the revolt of 1808 led to Carlos' first abdication.

FERNANDO VII 19 Mar-5 May 1808 'abdicated' then imprisoned until restoration.

CARLOS IV 5-6 May 1808 when he ceded the throne to Napoleon I.

HOUSE OF BONAPARTE

(In theory Napoléon I was King of Spain from 6 May-6 Jun 1808.)

JOSÉ (Joseph Bonaparte) **6 Jun 1808-11 Dec 1813** deposed, elder brother of Napoléon I, b 7 Jan 1768; d 28 Jul 1844. Appointed by his brother to be King of Naples, then King of Spain, Joseph Bonaparte was well-meaning but had little ability and little desire to be King of a country which became a bottomless pit into which French regiments were continuously thrown in the impossible task of ending the spirited Spanish resistance.

HOUSE OF BOURBON

FERNANDO VII 11 Dec 1813-29 Sep 1833, fifth but eldest surviving son of Carlos IV, b 13 Oct 1784. A repressive despot Fernando VII, who as a French prisoner became a symbol of Spanish resistance in the Napoleonic Wars, was faced upon his restoration with the impractically liberal 1812 Constitution which he rejected. Nearly deposed in the 1820 revolution he lost the Latin American colonies which made good use of Spain's weakness to seize their independence. With no son from four marriages he foolishly changed the succession law in favour of his daughter Isabel to the exclusion of his ultra-conservative brother Carlos - thus provoking the Carlist Wars.

ISABEL II (Queen) **Sep 1833-30 Sep 1868** when she was deposed, eldest surviving daughter of Fernando VII, b 10 Oct 1830; d 9 Apr 1904. Her disputed succession saw the bloody Carlist Wars; her marriage to an effete cousin led to an international crisis; her conduct during a reign of coups and revolts was a scandal but it was her political interference rather than her immorality that occasioned her deposition in a coup led by her ex-lover Serrano.

Regent

Gen **FRANCISCO SERRANO y DOMÍNGUEZ 30 Sep 1868-16 Nov 1870,** b 1810; d 1885. Leader of the coup against Queen Isabel II.

† King

HOUSE OF SAVOY-CARIGNANO

AMADEO 16 Nov 1870-11 Feb 1873 abdicated, b (second son of Vittorio Emanuele II of Italy) 14 Mar 1820; d 18 Jan 1890. This elected King, faced with a second Carlist War and much unrest, quit his throne as soon as was practical.

THE FIRST REPUBLIC OF SPAIN

Presidents

They were termed Chief of Executive Power.

ESTANISLAO FIGUERAS y MORAGAS Feb-Jun 1873 when he fled, b 1818; d 1882.

FRANCISCO JOSÉ PI y MARGALL Jun-Sep 1873; replaced by the Cortes.

NICOLÁS SALMERÓN Sep-Dec 1873 deposed, b 1838; d 1908.

EMILIO CASTELAR y RIPOLI Dec 1873-Jan 1874, b 7 Sep 1832; d 25 May 1899. A noted author, the tactful Castelar served as Premier after leaving the Presidency and became opposition leader upon the restoration of the monarchy.

Marshal **FRANCISCO SERRANO y DOMÍNGUEZ Jan-29 Dec 1874.**

THE KINGDOM OF SPAIN

† Kings

HOUSE OF BOURBON

ALFONSO XII 29 Dec 1874-25 Nov 1885, son of Isabel II, b 28 Nov 1857.

MARIA CRISTINA (Queen) Head of State and Regent during her pregnancy after Alfonso XII died without a son: **25 Nov 1885-17 May 1886,** b (an Archduchess of Austria) 21 Jul 1858; d 6 Feb 1929. Her tact and prudence as Regent until her son's majority created a political stability.

ALFONSO XIII 17 May 1886-14 Apr 1931 when he left Spain, posthumous son of Alfonso XIII, b (succeeded at birth) 17 May 1886; d in exile 28 Feb 1941. A courtly figure, often called 'the perfect gentleman', Alfonso XIII quit his country and throne in a noble attempt to avert civil war. The growth of Basque and Catalan nationalism and the republicanism of Lerroux, and above all the King's support for the dictatorship of Primo de Rivera perhaps made the fall of the monarchy inevitable.

Prime Ministers

Gen **MIGUEL PRIMO de RIVERO y ORBANEJA** (Marquess de ESTELLA) **15 Sep 1923-Jan 1930,** b 8 Jan 1870; d 16 Mar 1930. A dictator whose iron rule led to the build up of discontents which exploded in the declaration of the Republic and the civil war.

Gen **DAMASO BERENGUER 28 Jan 1930-Feb 1931,** b 4 Aug 1873; d 16 May 1953.

Admiral **JUAN BAUTISTA AZNAR 18 Feb-14 Apr 1931,** b 1860; d 19 Feb 1933.

THE SECOND REPUBLIC OF SPAIN

Presidents

NICETO ALCALÁ ZAMORA y TORRES provisional President **14 Apr-10 Dec 1931**; President **10 Dec 1931-7 Apr 1936** when forced to resign, b 6 Jul 1877; d 18 Feb 1949.

MANUEL AZAÑA y DIAZ 10 May 1936-Feb 1939 when he fled, b 10 Jan 1880; d 4 Nov 1940. Azaña was helpless in the face of growing Communist influence either to restore order or to prevent the Civil War during which he was largely a puppet.

Prime Ministers

NICETO ALCALA ZAMORA 14 Apr-Oct 1931; see President Alcalá Zamora.

MANUEL AZAÑA 14 Oct 1931-Sep 1933; see President Azaña.

ALEJANDRO LERROUX 19 Sep-8 Oct 1933.

DIEGO MARTINEZ BARRIO 8 Oct-18 Dec 1933, b 1883; d 1962.

ALEJANDRO LERROUX 18 Dec 1933-Apr 1934.

RICARDO SAMPER 30 Apr-Oct 1934, b 1881; d 1938.

ALEJANDRO LERROUX 4 Oct 1934-Sep 1935, b 4 Mar 1864; d 27 Jun 1949. A moderate republican who tried to effect a reconciliation with the Church, he alienated left wing opinion and withdrew from political life after a family corruption scandal. He took no part in the civil war.

JOAQUIN CHAPAPRIETA 14 Sep 1935-Dec 1935, b 1871; d 1951.

MANUEL PORTELA VALLADARES 14 Dec 1935-Feb 1936, b 1867; d 1952.

MANUEL AZAÑA 19 Feb-May 1936; see President Azaña.

AUGUSTO BARCIA 10-12 May 1936.

SANTIAGO CASARES QUIROGA 12 May-18 Jul 1936, b 1884; d 1950.

DIEGO MARTINEZ BARRIO 18 Jul 1936.

JOSÉ GIRAL 18 Jul-4 Sep 1936, b 1879; d 1962. The civil war broke out on 18 Jul 1936.

18 Jul 1936-Mar 1939 A republican government continued, controlling an increasingly smaller territory.

THE SPANISH STATE

Leader (Caudillo) of Spain and Chief of State

Generalissimo Don **FRANCISCO FRANCO y BAHAMONDE 1 Oct 1936-20 Nov 1975,** b 4 Dec 1892; d in office. The second Republic collapsed with the rise of Communist influence, anarchy and separatism. Garrison revolts in north Africa became civil war with Franco leading the Nationalist cause from Sep 1936. The terrible war, cynically exploited by European powers as a testing ground for arms and ideologies, ended with the capture of Madrid (Mar 1939). Franco's harsh rule as dictator, and his friendship with Fascist Germany and Italy, brought the international isolation of Spain. In time the influence of the Falange decreased and Franco did achieve a remarkable transformation of the Spanish economy.

Prime Ministers

Gen **FRANCISCO FRANCO y BAHAMONDE** was Head of Government from 30 Sep 1936 to Jun 1973. However, the post of Premier was in abeyance until revived by constitutional amendment in Jan 1967 and was not filled until six years later.

Admiral **LUIS CARRERO BLANCO 9 Jun-20 Dec 1973** when he was assassinated.

CARLOS ARIAS NAVARRO 29 Dec 1973-22 Nov 1975; continued as PM under the revived monarchy.

THE KINGDOM OF SPAIN

† King

HOUSE OF BOURBON
In theory the state became a Kingdom again on 31 Mar 1947 but a King was not restored until the death of Franco.

JUAN CARLOS since 22 Nov 1975, grandson of Alfonso XIII, b 5 Jan 1938.

Premiers

CARLOS ARIAS NAVARRO PM since Dec 1973; **22 Nov 1975-Jul 1976,** b 11 Dec 1908.

ADOLFO SUÁREZ GONZÁLEZ since 3 Jul 1976, b 25 Sep 1932.

Sparta *see* Greece

Sri Lanka

Singhalese Kingdoms, which seldom controlled all the island of Ceylon, flourished from the 5th century BC but the dates of the monarchs cannot be given with complete certainty until the 3rd century AD. Portuguese intervention began in 1505, lasting until 1658 when the Dutch became supreme. British control began in 1796 and became complete with the annexation of the Kingdom of Kandy in 1815. The island became independent as the Dominion of Ceylon on 4 Feb 1948 and became a Republic, under the name of Sri Lanka, on 22 May 1972.

SINHALA KINGDOM

† Kings

LAMBAKANNA DYNASTY OF MAHAVAMSA
MAHASENA 276-303. This King, who is believed to have ruled all Ceylon, was responsible for the construction of many major irrigation canals upon which the future prosperity of the people depended.
SIRIMEGHAVANNA 303-331.
JETTHATISSA II 331-340.
BUDDHADASA 340-368.
UPATISSA I 368-410.
MAHANAMA 410-432. His reign was ended by a Pandyan invasion from southern India.
432-459 Period of anarchy and Pandyan occupation.

MORIYA DYNASTY
DHATUSENA 459-477. He defeated the Pandyans and founded a new dynasty.
KASYAPA I 477-495 deposed, son of Dhatusena.
MOGGALLANA I 495-512.
KUMARA DHATUSENA 512-520.
KITTISENA 520-521.
(There follows a period of instability and anarchy when few Kings ruled all the island.)
SIVA 521-522.
UPATISSA II 522-523?.
SILAKALA 522 or 523-535.
DATHAPAHUTI 535.
MOGGALLANA II 535-555.
KITTISIRIMEGHA 555-573.
MAHANAGA 573-575.
AGGABODHI I 575-608.
AGGABODHI II 608-618.
SAMGHATISSA II 618-619?.
MOGGALLANA III 618 or 619-623.
SILAMEGHAVANNA 623-632.
AGGABODHI III 632 deposed.

JETTHATISSA III 632-633. A usurper.
AGGABODHI III 633-643.
DATHOPATISSA I 643-650.
KASSAPA II 650-659.
DAPPULA I 659.
HATTHADATHA I 659-667.
AGGABODHI IV 667-683.
DATTA 683-684.
HATTHADATHA II 684. He lost the throne in the Pallava invasion from India.

THE SECOND LAMBAKANNA DYNASTY
MANAVAMMA 684-718. Established himself on the throne with the aid of the south Indian Pallavas.
AGGABODHI V 718-724.
KASSAPA III 724-730.
MAHINDA I 730-733.
AGGABODHI VI 733-772.
AGGABODHI VII 772-777.
MAHINDA II 777-797.
UDAYA I 797-801.
MAHINDA III 801-804.
AGGABODHI VIII 804-815.
DAPPULA II 815-831.
AGGABODHI IX 831-833.
SENA I 833-853.
SENA II 853-887.
UDAYA II 887-898.
KASSAPA IV 898-914.
KASSAPA V 914-923.
DAPPULA III 923-924.
DAPPULA IV 924-935.
UDAYA III 935-938.
SENA III 938-946.
UDAYA IV 946-954.
SENA IV 954-956.
MAHINDA IV 956-972.
SENA V 972-982.
MAHINDA V 982-1029. A weak ruler whose Indian mercenaries pillaged the land and then set up their own state in the north. Forced to abandon his capital Mahinda had effectively lost his Kingdom by 1017.
1017/1029-1055 Rule by the Colas from India.

POLONNARUVA DYNASTY
VIJAYABAHU I 1055-1110. He freed most of Ceylon from the invaders and founded a new Singhalese Kingdom.
JAYABAHU I 1110-1111.
VIKRAMABAHU I 1111-1132.
GAJABAHU II 1132-1153.
PARAKRAMA BAHU I 1153-1186. Perhaps Ceylon's greatest King, he is remembered as a warrior, international statesman (he interfered in the affairs of states as far away as Burma), prolific builder (of palaces and irrigation works) and a 'character' - the subject of the epic Culavamsa.
VIJAYABAHU II 1186-1187.

KALINGA DYNASTY

NISSANKA MALLA 1186 or 1187-1196, brother-in-law of Parakrama Bahu I. A weak King who squandered the Treasury on vast statues to safeguard his memory.
VIKRAMABAHU II 1196.
CODAGANGA 1196-1197.
LILAVATI (Queen) 1197-1200 deposed.
SAHASSAMALLA 1200-1202.
KALYANAVATI (Queen) 1202-1208.
DHARMASOKA 1208-1209.
ANIKANGA 1209.
LILAVATI (Queen) 1209-1210 deposed.
LOKESVARA 1210-1211.
LILAVATI (Queen) 1211-1212 deposed. The three reigns of Queen Lilavati illustrate the anarchy of this period which allowed the terrible King Magha to seize power.
PARAKRAMA PANDU 1212-1215 deposed.

† Usurping King

MAGHA 1215-1236. A dictator who ruled with ferocious cruelty. Revolts against him destroyed the unity of Ceylon which was henceforth divided into several Kingdoms.
(The rulers of the principal Singhalese Kingdoms are listed below.)

THE SINGHALESE KINGDOM OF DAMBADENIYA

† Kings

VIJAYABAHU III 1232-1236. He ruled a small Singhalese state which is regarded as the heir to the Kingdom of Magha.
PARAKRAMA BAHU II 1236-1270. He made Dambadeniya the greatest state in Ceylon.
VIJAYABAHU IV 1270-1272.

THE SINGHALESE KINGDOM OF YAPAHUVA

† King

BHUVANIKA BAHU I 1272-1284.

THE SINGHALESE KINGDOM OF KURUNEGALA

† Kings

PARAKRAMA BAHU III 1284-1293; from 1287 principal King in Ceylon.
BHUVANAIKA BAHU II 1293-1302.
PARAKRAMA BAHU IV 1302-1326.
BHUVANAIKA BAHU III 1326-1335.
VIJAYABAHU V 1335-1341.

BHUVANAIKA BAHU IV 1341-1344 as principal King; ruled until 1351.

THE SINGHALESE KINGDOM OF GAMPOLA

† Kings

PARAKRAMA BAHU V 1344-1359.
VIKRAMABAHU III 1359-1374.
BHUVANAIKA BAHU V 1374-1408.
(Period of dispute between Gampola, Udarata, Kotte and Jaffna.)

THE KINGDOM OF KOTTE

† Kings

PARAKRAMA BAHU VI 1412-1467. He extended the Kingdom of Kotte to cover all of Ceylon but the island broke into three states upon his death.
JAYABAHU II 1467-1469.
BHUVANAIKA BAHU VI 1470-1478.
PARAKRAMA BAHU VII 1478-1484.
PARAKRAMA BAHU VIII 1484-1508. He accepted the Portuguese sovereign as his overlord and effectively ceased to be an independent King in 1505.
(From 1521, Ceylon was divided into Kingdoms of Kotte, Sitawake, Rayigama, Kandy and Jaffna - all under Portuguese control to a greater or lesser degree.)
1505-1658 Portuguese rule.
1658-1795 *de facto*; 1796 *de jure* Dutch rule.
1795/1796-1948 British rule.

THE DOMINION OF CEYLON

Governors-General

Sir HENRY MONCK-MASON MOORE Feb 1948-1949, b 1887; d 1964.
Herwald Ramsbotham, 1st Viscount SOULBURY 1949-1954, b 1887; d 1971.
Sir OLIVER ERNEST GOONETILLEKE 1954-1962, b 20 Oct 1892.
WILLIAM GOPALLAWA 1962-22 May 1974 when he became President.

Prime Ministers

DONALD STEPHEN SENANAYAKE 4 Feb 1948-22 Mar 1952, b 20 Oct 1884; d in office - falling from a bolting horse. An energetic sportsman and dedicated democrat he was known as 'Jungle John'.
DUDLEY SHELTON SENANAYAKE 26 Mar 1952-Oct 1953, son of Donald Stephen Senanayake, b 19 Jan 1911; d 13 Apr 1973.
Sir JOHN LIONEL KOTELAWALA 13 Oct 1953-11 Apr 1956, b 4 Apr 1897.

SOLOMON WEST RIDGEWAY DIAS BANDARA-NAIKE 11 Apr 1956-25 Sep 1959, b 8 Jan 1899; d in office - assassinated. His radical nationalism and neutralist stance were controversial and he was murdered by a Buddhist monk.
WIJEYANANDA DAHANAYAKE 26 Sep 1959-Mar 1960, b 22 Oct 1902.
DUDLEY SHELTON SENANAYAKE 21 Mar-21 Jul 1960.
Mrs **SIRIMAVO RATWATTE DIAS BANDARA-NAIKE 21 Jul 1960-Mar 1965,** widow of Solomon Bandaranaike, b 17 Apr 1916. The first woman Premier in the world.
DUDLEY SHELTON SENANAYAKE 25 Mar 1965-May 1970.
Mrs **SIRIMAVO RATWATTE DIAS BANDARA-NAIKE 28 May 1970-22 May 1972** when she became Premier of the Republic.

THE REPUBLIC OF SRI LANKA

Presidents

WILLIAM GOPALLAWA 22 May 1972-Feb 1978.
JUNIUS RICHARD JAYAWARDENE since 4 Feb 1978, b 17 Sep 1906.

Prime Ministers

Mrs **SIRIMAVO RATWATTE DIAS BANDARA-NAIKE 22 May 1972-Jul 1977.**
JUNIUS RICHARD JAYAWARDENE 23 Jul 1977-Feb 1978.
RANASINGHE PREMADASA since 6 Feb 1978, b 1924.

Sudan

Most of what is now called the Sudan came under Egyptian control in 1878. An Anglo-Egyptian Condominium was established in 1899; independence was granted on 1 Jan 1956.

Presidents

1 Jan 1956-17 Nov 1958 Presidential Council of State.
Gen **FERIK IBRAHIM ABBOUD 17 Nov 1958-15 Nov 1964,** b 26 Oct 1900.
3 Dec 1964-10 Jun 1965 Supreme Council of State - a collegiate presidency.
ISMAIL al AZHARI Permanent Chairman of the Supreme Council of State **10 Jun 1965-25 May 1969** when he was deposed in a coup, b 1902; d 26 Aug 1969.
Maj-Gen **JAAFER MOHAMMED al NUMERY** President and Chairman of the Revolutionary Council **since 25 May 1969,** b 1 Jan 1930.

Mrs Sirimavo Bandaranaike, the world's first woman Prime Minister, entered politics after the assassination of her husband, Solomon Bandaranaike (Popperfoto)

Prime Ministers

ISMAIL al AZHARI 1 Jan-4 Jul 1956; later became President.
ABDULLAH KHALIL 5 Jul 1956-17 Nov 1958 when he was deposed in a coup, b 1889.
Gen **FERIK IBRAHIM ABBOUD 17 Nov 1958-30 Oct 1964** when he was removed from the Premiership, but briefly retained the Presidency.
SERR al KHATIM KHALIFA 30 Oct 1964-2 Jun 1965.
MOHAMMED AHMED MAHGOUB 10 Jun 1965-25 Jul 1966, b 1908.
Dr **SAYED SADIQ al MAHDI 27 Jul 1966-15 May 1967.**
MOHAMMED AHMED MAHGOUB 18 May 1967-25 May 1969 when he was deposed in a coup.
BABIKAR AWADALLA 25 May-28 Oct 1969.
Maj-Gen **JAAFER MOHAMMED al NUMERY 28 Oct 1969-9 Aug 1976;** see President Numery.
RASHID al TAHIR BAKR 9 Aug 1976-10 Sep 1977.
Maj-Gen **JAAFER MOHAMMED al NUMERY since 10 Sep 1977.**

Sukhothai Kingdom *see* Thailand

Sumer *see* Babylon

Surinam

Dutch Guiana achieved independence as the Republic of Surinam on 25 Nov 1975.

President

Dr **JOHAN HENRI ELIZA FERRIER** since 25 Nov 1975, b 12 May 1910.

Prime Minister

HENCK ALFONSIUS EUGENE ARRON since 25 Nov 1975, b 25 Apr 1936.

Swaziland

The former British protectorate of Swaziland became an independent Kingdom on 6 Sep 1968.

† King

SOBHUZA II Paramount Chief of the Swazis since Dec 1899; sovereign King **since 6 Sep 1968,** b 4 Jul 1899.

Prime Ministers

Prince **MAKHOSINI DLAMINI 6 Sep 1968-Mar 1976,** nephew of Sobhuza II, b 1914.
Col **MAPHEVU DLAMINI since 31 Mar 1976.**

Sweden

Sweden achieved unity when the Götarike and the Svearike were combined by Olof Skötkonung c 1000. The country has maintained its independence ever since - even when joined with the other Nordic powers in the Kalmar Union at the turn of the 15th century.

† Kings

Until the accession of King Carl XVI Gustaf the title of the Swedish monarch was King of the Swedes, Goths and Wends. It is now King of the Swedes.

HOUSE OF UPPSALA
OLOF Skötkonung **995-1022.** United the Goths and the Swedes into a single Kingdom.
ANUND 1022-c 1050, son of Olof.

EMUND *c* 1050-1060, half-brother of Anund.

HOUSE OF STENKIL
STENKIL Ragnvaldssen *c* 1060-1066, son-in-law of Emund.
1066-1078 Interregnum. A period of anarchy in which HAAKON, who may not have assumed the kingship, emerged as ruler.
HALSTAN co-ruler *c* 1079-1099, son of Stenkil.
INGE I ?-1112; with a break of uncertain date for Blotsven's usurpation, son of Stenkil.

HOUSE OF BLOTSVEN
BLOTSVEN (?), brother-in-law of Inge I. Blotsven temporarily overthrew Inge in a pagan backlash.

HOUSE OF STENKIL
PHILIP *c* 1112-1118, son of Inge I.
INGE II ?-1122, brother of, and co-ruler with, Philip.

HOUSE OF BLOTSVEN
KOL (?), son of Blotsven. Referred to as King but the date and length of his reign is a mystery.
SVERKER I 1130-1150 when he was deposed, according to some accounts, or **1156** when he was assassinated, son of Kol.

HOUSE OF JEDVARDSSEN
ERIC IX (St ERIC) *c* 1150 or **1156-1160.** A pretender of unknown origin, Eric is the subject of many untrustworthy legends. It is certain that he attempted to bring Christianity to Finland and that he died violently. This misty figure, who probably never ruled more than Svearike, became Sweden's patron saint.

HOUSE OF BLOTSVEN
CARL VII Sverkerssen **1161-1167** killed by Cnud I; son of Sverker I.

HOUSE OF JEDVARDSSEN
CNUD I Ericssen **1167-1196,** son of Eric IX.

HOUSE OF BLOTSVEN
SVERKER II Carlssen **1196-***c* **1208** deposed, son of Carl VII; d *c* 1210.

HOUSE OF JEDVARDSSEN
ERIC X 1208-1216, son of Cnud I.

HOUSE OF BLOTSVEN
JOHAN I Sverkerssen **1216-1222** deposed, son of Sverker II; d 1229.

HOUSE OF JEDVARDSSEN
ERIC XI Ericssen **1222-1229** deposed, son of Eric X.

Usurping King

CNUD II 1229-1234. A usurper of uncertain origin.

† Kings

HOUSE OF JEDVARDSSEN
ERIC XI Ericssen **1234-1250.**

HOUSE OF FOLKUNG
(BIRGER Jarl, brother-in-law of Eric XI, acted as Regent for his son Valdemar from 1250 to 1266. He is often, erroneously, referred to as Birger I although he never assumed kingship.)
VALDEMAR 1250-1275 when he was deposed, nephew of Eric XI, b *c* 1238; d *c* 1302.
MAGNUS I Ladulås **1275-1290,** brother of Valdemar from whom he seized the throne, b 1240.
BIRGER (sometimes wrongly referred to as Birger II) **1290-1318** when he was deposed, son of Magnus I, b 1280; d 1321.
(ERIC and VALDEMAR, brothers of Birger, seized power 1306-1310, but are omitted from king-lists and not given regnal numbers.)
MAGNUS II Ericssen sole ruler **1319-1356;** co-ruler **1356-1364** when he was deposed, nephew of Birger, b 1316; d 1 Dec 1374. An accomplished ruler who was also King of Norway (as Magnus VII), he established a Swedish legal code. Betrayed by Valdemar IV of Denmark, he was deposed and imprisoned.
ERIC XII co-ruler **1356-1359,** son of Magnus II, b 1339. Forced his father to accept him as co-ruler.
HAAKON co-ruler **1362-1364,** son of Magnus II; was also Haakon VI, King of Norway.

HOUSE OF MECKLENBURG
ALBRECHT (of Mecklenburg) **1364-1389** deposed, nephew of Magnus II, b *c* 1340; d 1412. Installed as a puppet King by a nobles' coup, Albrecht proved to have a will of his own and was deposed by those same nobles who called on Margaret of Denmark for aid.

HOUSE OF DENMARK
MARGARETHA (Queen) sole ruler **1389-1397;** co-ruler **1397-28 Oct 1412;** was also Margrethe I, Queen of Denmark.

HOUSE OF POMERANIA
ERIC XIII (of Pomerania) co-ruler **1397-Oct 1412;** sole ruler **Oct 1412-1434;** was also Erik VII, King of Denmark.
1434-1436 Interregnum. Regency of ENGELBREKT ENGELBREKTSSEN.
1436-1440 Interregnum. Regency of CARL KNUTSSEN.

HOUSE OF BAVARIA
CHRISTOPHER 1440-5 Jan 1448; was also Christopher III, King of Denmark.

HOUSE OF KNUTSSEN
CARL VIII 1448-1457 deposed, formerly the Regent Carl Knutssen, b *c* 1408. Carl VIII's reigns were marked by near civil war between the King's nationalist and merchant faction and the

Gustaf II Adolf who, dying, replied 'I was the King of Sweden' when his identity was challenged on the battlefield (Radio Times Hulton Picture Library)

pro-Scandinavian Union faction led by Archbishop Oxenstierna and the Vasas.

HOUSE OF OLDENBURG
CHRISTIAN I 1457-1464; see Christian I, King of Denmark.

HOUSE OF KNUTSSEN
CARL VIII 1464-1465 deposed.
1465-1467 Interregnum.
CARL VIII 1467-15 May 1470.
May 1470-1497 Interregnum: Regency of STEN STURE the Elder.

HOUSE OF OLDENBURG
JOHAN II 1497-1501 deposed; was also Hans, King of Denmark.
1501-1520 Interregnum. Regency of STEN STURE the Elder 1501-1503; Regency of SVANTE STURE 1503-1512; Regency of STEN STURE the Younger 1512-1520.
CHRISTIAN II 1520-1523 deposed; was also Christian II, King of Denmark.

HOUSE OF VASA
GUSTAF I 6 Jun 1523-29 Sep 1560, b (Gustaf Ericssen) 1496?. A leading noble, elected King, Gustaf was a great ruler who secured Swedish independence from Denmark and restored the

economy by breaking the power of the Hanse League and by confiscating the Church's lands - this action led to the Reformation in Sweden though changes in worship were slow and Gustaf had few theological opinions beyond a resentment of Papal authority. A clever, harsh and avaricious ruler, he ran Sweden like a personal estate but established a strong monarchy, a standing army, the navy, and restored order. In many ways he was the founder of modern Sweden.

ERIC XIV Sep 1560-1568 deposed, eldest son of Gustaf I, b 13 Dec 1533; d 26 Feb 1577. His murder of the Sture family, his elevation of his mistress to Queen-Consort and his quarrel with his brothers led to his deposition on (groundless) charges of insanity.

JOHAN III 1568-17 Nov 1592, brother of Eric XIV, b 21 Dec 1592.

SIGISMUND Nov 1592-1599 deposed, son of Johan III, b 20 Jun 1566; d 30 Apr 1632. An absentee Catholic monarch who had gained the Polish crown through his mother. His attempts to unite Sweden and Poland brought his deposition and nearly half a century of war between the two countries.

CARL IX 1599-30 Oct 1611, brother of Johan III, b 4 Oct 1550. A coarse, unscrupulous King who maintained by terror his hold on a throne he had usurped from his unpopular nephew.

GUSTAF II ADOLF Oct 1611-6 Nov 1632 killed at the Battle of Lützen, son of Carl IX, b 9 Dec 1594. A brilliant general, his army tactics were to have a profound effect on military thinking. His intervention in the Thirty Years' War has been seen as power seeking and as the Protestant 'Lion of the North' fighting the Counter Revolution. Whatever the motive, he achieved sweeping successes in Germany and secured the future of Protestantism in north Germany. It is likely that the real reason for his campaigns was the need for a defensive war against the Imperial Habsburgs and the Catholic Polish Vasas both of whom presented a threat to his country and his throne. Gustaf's major domestic reforms, a reorganisation of local and national government carried out with his outstanding minister Oxenstierna, are often underestimated and he is chiefly remembered for making Sweden a great power and for giving her a Baltic Empire she had not the resources to maintain.

CHRISTINA (Queen) **Nov 1632-6 Jun 1654** when she abdicated, daughter of Gustaf II Adolf, b 8 Dec 1626; d 19 Apr 1689. A complex and controversial woman, her reign proved a cultural success and a financial disaster for Sweden - her extravagance, particularly in giving estates to favourites, ruined the Treasury. She found ruling burdensome and her aversion to marriage to provide an heir and her conversion to Catholicism (which was illegal in Sweden) made her abdication inevitable. In exile she achieved her lasting memorial - her patronage of Scarlatti, Corelli and Bernini, her important collection of Venetian paintings, her acts of charity and her embellishment of the cultural life of the city of Rome.

HOUSE OF ZWEIBRUCKEN
(or of the Palatinate)

CARL X GUSTAF Jun 1654-13 Feb 1660, grandson of Carl IX, b (Prince Carl of the Palatinate) 8 Nov 1622.

CARL XI Feb 1660-5 Apr 1697, son of Carl X, b 24 Nov 1655.

CARL XII Apr 1697-30 Nov 1718 killed in battle, son of Carl XI, b 17 Jun 1682. Courageous, reckless and totally devoted to Sweden, Carl XII faced an alliance of Denmark, Saxony, Russia and Poland. He defeated Poland in the Great Northern War but lost the vital Battle of Poltava (8 Jul 1709) to the Russians and was forced to flee. In five years exile in Moldavia, this remarkable man reformed the finances and government of Sweden at a distance before his dramatic journey home in disguise across a hostile Europe.

ULRIKA ELEONORA (Queen) **Dec 1718-26 Mar 1720** when she abdicated, sister of Carl XII, b 23 Jan 1688; d 24 Nov 1741.

HOUSE OF HESSE-CASSEL OR BRABANT

FREDRIK Mar 1720-25 Mar 1751, husband of Ulrika Eleonora, b (Prince Friedrich of Hesse) 17 Apr 1676.

HOUSE OF HOLSTEIN-GOTTORP

ADOLF FREDRIK 5 Apr 1751-12 Apr 1771, b (a Prince of Holstein-Gottorp) 14 May 1710. Elected King largely at the hands of the 'Hats' (a faction in favour of an aggressive foreign policy) in the hope that Sweden under a Gottorp could obtain favourable peace terms from Empress Elizabeth of Russia who fostered the Gottorps.

GUSTAF III Apr 1771-29 Mar 1792 died as a result of wounds received from an assassin at a 'bal masqué' at Stockholm Opera, elder son of Adolf Fredrik, b 24 Jan 1746. Deprived of much of his power by the 'Caps', Gustaf engineered a coup to establish an autocracy.

GUSTAF IV ADOLF Mar 1792-13 Mar 1809 deposed, son of Gustaf III, b 1 Nov 1778, d 7 Feb 1837. His stubborn anti-French stand led to an officers' coup at a time when Sweden was isolated and threatened.

Mar-Jun 1809 Interregnum.

CARL XIII 6 Jun 1809-5 Feb 1818, uncle of Gustaf IV Adolf, b 7 Oct 1748.

HOUSE OF BERNADOTTE

CARL XIV JOHAN Feb 1818-8 Mar 1844, b (Jean-Baptiste Bernadotte) 26 Jan 1763. This French Marshal was adopted by childless Carl XIII both because of his considerable abilities and because Sweden desired friendship with Napoleon. However, Carl led his adopted country against the French Empire and despite the opposition of conservative powers became

King. His realism made Sweden abandon her claims to Finland and he forcibly obtained Norway for the Swedish crown as compensation. Despite his failure to learn Swedish, the former revolutionary soldier served his country well ruling most cautiously.

OSCAR I   Mar 1844-8 Jul 1859, son of Carl XIV Johan, b 4 Jul 1799.

CARL XV   Jul 1859-19 Aug 1872, eldest son of Oscar I, b 3 May 1826.

OSCAR II   Aug 1872-8 Dec 1907, third son of Oscar I, b 21 Jan 1829. A talented writer and musician, Oscar II had little sympathy with the increasingly independent attitude adopted by the Norwegians and he cannot be said to have made the final crisis before the personal union was dissolved any easier.

GUSTAF V   Dec 1907-29 Oct 1950, eldest son of Oscar II, b 16 Jun 1858.

GUSTAF VI ADOLF   Oct 1950-15 Sep 1973, eldest son of Gustaf V, b 11 Nov 1882. The last Swedish monarch to exercise any constitutional powers, Gustaf VI Adolf was a considerable archaeologist and a world authority on Chinese porcelain.

CARL XVI GUSTAF   since 15 Sep 1973, grandson of Gustaf VI Adolf, b 30 Apr 1946.

Prime Ministers

Dr **KNUT HJALMAR HAMMARSKJÖLD   Feb 1914-Mar 1917,** b 25 Aug 1871; d 16 Jun 1945. Father of Dag Hammarskjöld (Secretary-General of the UNO), he was the first Swedish Premier appointed because he was leader of the largest party.

CARL GUSTAV JOHAN SWARTZ   Mar-Oct 1917, b 1858; d 1926. He was obliged to resign after charges that Sweden's neutrality in World War I had been compromised by the use of the Swedish cipher by the Germans.

Prof **NILS EDEN   19 Oct 1917-Mar 1920,** b 1871; d 1945.

KARL HJALMAR BRANTING   10 Mar-Oct 1920, b 23 Nov 1860; d 24 Feb 1925.

Baron **LOUIS de GEER   27 Oct 1920-Feb 1921,** b 1854; d 1935.

OSKAR FREDRIK von SYDOW   23 Feb-Sep 1921, b 1873; d 1936.

KARL HJALMAR BRANTING   Sep 1921-Apr 1923.

ERNST TRYGGER   19 Apr 1923-Oct 1924, b 1857; d 1943.

KARL HJALMAR BRANTING   18 Oct 1924-Feb 1925.

RICHARD SANDLER   27 Feb 1925-Jun 1926, b 1884; d 1965.

CARL GUSTAV EKMAN   7 Jun 1926-Oct 1928, b 1872; d 1945.

ARVID LINDMAN   2 Oct 1928-Jun 1930, b 1862; d 1936.

CARL GUSTAV EKMAN   7 Jun 1930-Aug 1932.

FELIX TEODOR HAMRIN   6 Aug-24 Sep 1932, b 1875; d 1937.

PER ALBIN HANSSON   24 Sep 1932-Jun 1936.

AXEL PEHRSSON-BRAMSTORP   19 Jun-21 Sep 1936, b 1883; d 1954.

PER ALBIN HANSSON   21 Sep 1936-5 Oct 1946, b 28 Oct 1885; d in office. A neutralist he tried to form a Scandinavian security zone but later when war threatened he rearmed, but managed to keep Sweden out of the conflict.

TAGE ERLANDER   10 Oct 1946-Oct 1969, b 13 Jun 1901. The longest serving democratically elected Premier of a sovereign state.

OLOF PALME   1 Oct 1969-Oct 1976, b 30 Jan 1927.

NILS OLOF THORBJORN FALLDIN   since 7 Oct 1976, b 24 Apr 1926.

Switzerland

Switzerland (The Helvetic Confederation) dates from the League formed on 1 Aug 1291 by Uri, Unterwalden and Schwyz (the latter giving its name to the country). The sovereignty of the Confederation was recognised internationally by the Peace of Westphalia in 1648. Each canton retained considerable powers and an effective central government was not finally formed until 1848 after a civil war.

Presidents of the Swiss Confederation

The President is Chairman of the Federal Council, or 'Cabinet', is regarded as *primus inter pares* and has few duties normally associated with a Head of State. The presidential term is one calendar year beginning on 1 January.

JONAS FURRER   1849, b 1805; d 1861.

DANIEL-HENRI DRUEY   1850, b 1799; d 1855.

MARTIN JOSEPH MUNZINGER   1851, b 1791; d 1855.

JONAS FURRER   1852.

WILHELM MATHIAS NAEFF   1853, b 1802; d 1881.

FRIEDRICH FREY-HEROSEE   1854, b 1801; d 1873.

JONAS FURRER   1855.

JAKOB STÄMPFLI   1856, b 1820; d 1879.

CHARLES-EMMANUEL-CONSTANT   FORNE-ROD   1857, b 1819; d 1899.

JONAS FURRER   1858.

JAKOB STÄMPFLI   1859.

FRIEDRICH FREY-HEROSEE   1860.

MELCHIOR JOSEPH MARTIN KNÜSEL   1861, b 1813; d 1889.

JAKOB STÄMPFLI   1862.

CHARLES-EMMANUEL-CONSTANT   FORNE-ROD   1863.

JAKOB DUBS   1864, b 1822; d 1879.

KARL SCHINK   1865, b 1823; d 1895.

MELCHIOR JOSEPH MARTIN KNÜSEL   1866.

CHARLES-EMMANUEL-CONSTANT   FORNE-ROD   1867.

JAKOB DUBS **1868.**
EMIL WELTI **1869,** b 1825; d 1899.
JAKOB DUBS **1870.**
KARL SCHINK **1871.**
EMIL WELTI **1872.**
PAUL CERESOLE **1873,** b 1832; d 1905.
KARL SCHINK **1874.**
JAKOB SCHERER **1875,** b 1825; d 1878.
EMIL WELTI **1876.**
JOACHIM HEER **1877,** b 1825; d 1879.
KARL SCHINK **1878.**
BERNHARD HAMMER **1879,** b 1822; d 1907.
EMIL WELTI **1880.**
NUMA DROZ **1881,** b 1844; d 1899.
SIMEON BAVIER **1882,** b 1825; d 1896.
LOUIS RUCHONNET **1883,** b 1834; d 1893. In his second presidential term in 1890 he had to intervene in the internal affairs of a canton (a rare event in Switzerland) when Ticino came close to revolution.
EMIL WELTI **1884.**
KARL SCHINK **1885.**
ADOLF DEUCHER **1886,** b 1831; d 1912.
NUMA DROZ **1887.**
WILHELM FRIEDRICH HERTENSTEIN Jan-Nov **1888,** b 1825; d in office.
BERNHARD HAMMER acting President **Nov-Dec 1888**; President **1889.**
LOUIS RUCHONNET **1890.**
EMIL WELTI **1891.**
WALTER HAUSER **1892,** b 1837; d 1902.
KARL SCHINK **1893.**
EMIL FREY **1894,** b 1838; d 1922.
JOSEPH ZEMP **1895,** b 1834; d 1908.
ADRIEN LACHENAL **1896,** b 1849; d 1918.
ADOLF DEUCHER **1897.**
EUGÈNE RUFFY **1898,** b 1854; d 1919.
EDUARD MÜLLER **1899,** b 1848; d 1919.
WALTER HAUSER **1900.**
ERNST BRENNER **1901,** b 1856; d 1911.
JOSEPH ZEMP **1902.**
ADOLF DEUCHER **1903.**
ROBERT COMTESSE **1904,** b 1847; d 1922.
MARC-EMILE RUCHET **1905,** b 1853; d 1912.
LUDWIG FORRER **1906,** b 1845; d 1921.
EDUARD MÜLLER **1907.**
ERNST BRENNER **1908.**
ADOLF DEUCHER **1909.**
ROBERT COMTESSE **1910.**
MARC-EMILE RUCHET **1911.**
LUDWIG FORRER **1912.**
EDUARD MÜLLER **1913.**
ARTHUR HOFFMANN **1914,** b 1857; d 1927.
GIUSEPPE MOTTA **1915,** b 1871; d Jan 1940. One of the better known Swiss Presidents, his first term was dominated by efforts to maintain neutrality in World War I; his fourth term saw industrial unrest, the Depression and violent bloody riots in Geneva which led to demands for constitutional changes that he was able to avert.
CAMILLE DECOPPET **1916,** b 1862; d 1925.
EDMUND SCHULTHESS **1917,** b 1868; d 1944.

FELIX LUDWIG CALONDER **1918,** b 1863; d 1952. He had to cope with an attempted Marxist revolution in Geneva and a general strike.
GUSTAVE ADOR **1919,** b 1845; d 1928.
GIUSEPPE MOTTA **1920.**
EDMUND SCHULTHESS **1921.**
ROBERT HAAB **1922,** b 1865; d 1959.
KARL SCHEURER **1923,** b 1872; d 1929.
ERNEST CHUARD **1924,** b 1857; d 1942.
JEAN-MARIE MUSY **1925,** b 1876; d 1952.
HEINRICH HÄBERLIN **1926,** b 1868; d 1947.
GIUSEPPE MOTTA **1927.**
EDMUND SCHULTHESS **1928.**
ROBERT HAAB **1929.**
JEAN-MARIE MUSY **1930.**
HEINRICH HÄBERLIN **1931.**
GIUSEPPE MOTTA **1932.**
EDMUND SCHULTHESS **1933.**
MARCEL PILET-GOLAZ **1934,** b 1889; d 1958. His second term (1940) was controversial as he made defence moves interpreted as appeasement.
RUDOLF MINGER **1935,** b 1881; d 1955.
ALBERT MEYER **1936,** b 1870; d 1953.
GIUSEPPE MOTTA **1937.**
JOHANNES BAUMANN **1938,** b 1874; d 1953.
PHILIPP ETTER **1939,** b 2 Dec 1891.
MARCEL PILET-GOLAZ **1940.**
ERNST WETTER **1941,** b 27 Aug 1877.
PHILIPP ETTER **1942.**
ENRICO CELIO **1943,** b 19 Jun 1889.
WALTER STÄMPFLI **1944,** b 3 Dec 1881; d 11 Oct 1965.
EDUARD von STEIGER **1945,** b 1881; d 1962.
KARL KOBELT **1946,** b 1 Aug 1891; d 5 Jan 1968.
PHILIPP ETTER **1947.**
ENRICO CELIO **1948.**
ERNST NOBS **1949,** b 1886; d 1957.
MAX PETITPIERRE **1950,** b 26 Feb 1899.
EDUARD von STEIGER **1951.**
KARL KOBELT **1952.** '
PHILIPP ETTER **1953.**
RODOLPHE RUBATTEL **1954,** b 1896; d 1961.
MAX PETITPIERRE **1955.**
MARKUS FELDMANN **1956,** b 1897; d 1958.
HANS STREULI **1957,** b 13 Jul 1892; d 23 May 1970.
THOMAS HOLENSTEIN **1958,** b 7 Feb 1896; d 31 Oct 1962.
PAUL CHAUDET **1959,** b 17 Nov 1904; d Aug 1977.
MAX PETITPIERRE **1960.**
FRIEDRICH TRAUGOTT WAHLEN **1961,** b 10 Apr 1899.
PAUL CHAUDET **1962.**
WILLY SPÜHLER **1963,** b 31 Jan 1902.
LUDWIG von MOOS **1964,** b 31 Jan 1910.
HANS-PETER TSCHUDI **1965,** b 22 Oct 1913.
HANS SCHAFFNER **1966,** b 16 Dec 1908.
ROGER BONVIN **1967,** b 12 Sep 1907.
WILLY SPÜHLER **1968.**
LUDWIG von MOOS **1969.**
HANS-PETER TSCHUDI **1970.**
RUDOLF GNÄGI **1971,** b 3 Aug 1917.

NELLO CELIO **1972,** b 12 Feb 1914.
ROGER BONVIN **1973.**
ERNST BRUGGER **1974,** b 10 Mar 1914.
PIERRE GRABER **1975,** b 6 Dec 1908.
RUDOLF GNÄGI **1976.**
KURT FURGLER **1977,** b 24 Jun 1924.
WILLI RITSCHARD **1978,** b 28 Sep 1918.

Syracuse

The main city state (an unsatisfactory translation of the Greek 'polis') of Magna Graecia - the Greek settlements of Sicily and southern Italy, Syracuse experienced several forms of government, more than once being ruled by a Tyrant possessing near monarchical powers, and twice by a monarch.

† Tyrants

GELON **485-478 BC,** b *c*540 BC. The first absolute ruler of Syracuse he seized the city and later inflicted defeat upon Carthage at Himera.
HIERON I **478-466 BC,** brother of Gelon.
THRASYBULUS **466 BC** deposed, brother of Gelon; fate uncertain.
466-406 BC Republican constitution.
DIONYSIUS I ('The Elder') **405-spring 367 BC,** b 430s BC. Judgment of Dionysius is clouded by Plato's criticism as the worst of dictators. Totally amoral, and justifiably obsessed with attempts on his life, he led Syracuse to a lucky triumph over Carthage, saved the Greek cause in Sicily and made his state supreme in the Mediterranean.
DIONYSIUS II ('The Younger') **367-357 BC** deposed, son of Dionysius I.
DION **357-356 BC** deposed, brother-in-law of Dionysius I, b *c*410 BC.
DIONYSIUS II ('The Younger') **356 BC.**
DION **356-354 BC** assassinated.
DIONYSIUS II ('The Younger') **354-343 BC.**
343 BC Republican constitution.
TIMOLEON (of Corinth) *de facto* Tyrant **343-337 BC;** d after 336 BC. One of the most attractive figures of the ancient world, Timoleon, a brilliant general whose noble life is well-known from Plutarch's account, came from Syracuse's mother city to save the Sicilian state when threatened by Carthage. His task completed (now blind) he relinquished power and founded a democracy.
337-316 BC Democratic oligarchy.
AGATHOCLES **316-304 BC** when he made himself King.

† Kings

They styled themselves 'King of Sicily'.

AGATHOCLES Tyrant from 316 BC; King **304-289 BC,** b *c*360 BC. A potter's son, he fought

an amazing campaign against Carthage having burnt his boats (thus starting a saying) on arrival in Africa.
HIKETAS **288-280 BC** deposed; fate uncertain.

† Tyrants

SOSISTRATUS co-ruler **278 BC.**
THEONON co-ruler **278 BC.**
278-270 BC Democratic oligarchy.

† Kings

HIERON II **270-215 BC,** b *c*310 BC. A patron of the arts who came to terms with Rome and ordered defence machines from his relative Archimedes.
HIERONYMUS **215-214 BC** murdered, grandson of Hieron II.
214-211 BC Republican system.
211 BC Syracuse was conquered by Rome.

Syria

Part of the Seleucid Kingdom, the Roman Empire, the Byzantine Empire, the lands of the Caliphate, and then the Ottoman Empire, Syria was granted to France as a League of Nations mandate in 1920 after a brief existence as a Kingdom after World War I. Autonomous from 1941, Syria gained complete independence on 1 Jan 1944, formed part of the United Arab Republic with Egypt from 1958 to 1961 and regained independence as the Syrian Arab Republic in Sep 1961.

THE KINGDOM OF SYRIA

† King

FAYSAL **Sep 1918-Jul 1920;** self-proclaimed King - later Faysal I, King of Iraq.
1920-Jan 1944 French rule as a League of Nations mandate.

THE REPUBLIC OF SYRIA

Presidents

SAYED SHUKRI al-KUWATLY **1 Jan 1944-30 Mar 1949** deposed in coup, b 1891; d 30 Jun 1967. The leader of the Syrian independence movement he accepted union with Egypt as a way of avoiding Communist rule.
Col **HUSNI ZAIM** (later Marshal) acting President **30 Mar-25 Jun 1949;** President **25 Jun-14 Aug 1949** deposed in coup.
Col **SAMI HINNAWI** acting Head of State **14-15 Aug 1949.**

Aug-Dec 1949 No Head of State.
HASHEM al-ATASSI 14 Dec 1949-2 Dec 1951 deposed in coup, b 1875; d 5 Dec 1960.
Col ADIB SHISHAKLI acting President **3 Dec 1951-25 Feb 1954** deposed in coup; assassinated in exile 27 Sep 1964.
Dr KASBARI acting President **26 Feb-1 Mar 1954.**
HASHEM al-ATASSI 1 Mar 1954-Sep 1955.
SAYED SHUKRI al-KUWATLY 6 Sep 1955-2 Feb 1958 when Syria joined the United Arab Republic.

Prime Ministers

SAADULLAH JABRY 1 Jan 1944-Aug 1945.
FAYEZ al-KHOURY 27 Aug-30 Sep 1945.
SAADULLAH JABRY 30 Sep 1945-Dec 1946.
JAMIL MARDAM BEY 28 Dec 1946-Dec 1948.
HASHEM al-ATASSI Dec 1948; see President al-Atassi.
Emir ABDEL ARSLAN Dec 1948.
Dr KHALED el-AZAM 16 Dec 1948-30 Mar 1949 deposed in coup.
Col HUSNI ZAIM (later Marshal) **30 Mar-25 Jun 1949.**
Dr MOHSEN BEY BARAZI 25 Jun-14 Aug 1949 deposed in coup.
Col SAMI HINNAWI acting PM **14-15 Aug 1949.**
HASHEM al-ATASSI 15 Aug-21 Dec 1949.
Dr KHALED el-AZEM 21-24 Dec 1949.
Dr NAZIM el-KUDSI 24-28 Dec 1949.
Dr KHALED el-AZEM 28 Dec 1949-May 1950, b 1903; d 1965.
Dr NAZIM el-KUDSI 29 May 1950-Mar 1951.
Dr KHALED el-AZEM 9-23 Mar 1951.
Dr NAZIM el-KUDSI 23-24 Mar 1951.
Dr KHALED el-AZEM 24 Mar-30 Jul 1951.
FARIS el-KHOURY 30 Jul-6 Aug 1951.
HASSAN BEY el-HAKIM 6 Aug-Nov 1951.
Dr MAAROUF DAWALIBI 10 Nov-1 Dec 1951 deposed in coup.
HAMID KHOJA 1-4 Dec 1951.
Col FAWZI SELO 4 Dec 1951-Feb 1954 deposed in coup.
SABRY ASSALI 1 Mar-10 Jun 1954.
SAID GHAZZI 10 Jun-Oct 1954.
FARIS el-KHOURY 14 Oct 1954-6 Feb 1955.
SABRY ASSALI 6 Feb-Sep 1955.
SAID GHAZZI 6 Sep 1955-Jun 1956.
SABRY ASSALI 15 Jun 1956-2 Feb 1958 when Syria formed the United Arab Republic with Egypt.

2 Feb 1958-28 Sep 1961 Syria formed the United Arab Republic with Egypt - see Egypt.

THE SYRIAN ARAB REPUBLIC

Presidents

Sep-Dec 1961 No Head of State.

Dr NAZIM el-KUDSI acting President **14 Dec 1961-28 Mar 1962** deposed in coup.
Maj-Gen ZAHREDDIN acting Head of State **28 Mar-13 Apr 1962.**
Dr NAZIM el-KUDSI 13 Apr 1962-8 Mar 1963 deposed in coup.
8 Mar 1963 Revolutionary Council.
Maj-Gen LOUAY ATASSI 8 Mar-27 Jul 1963 President of the National Revolutionary Council, b 1926.
Gen AMIN el HAFEZ 27 Jul 1963-23 Feb 1966 deposed in coup, b 1911.
Dr NUREDDIN ATASSI acting Head of State **23 Feb 1966-13 Nov 1970** deposed in coup, b 1929.
AHMED KHATIB 18 Nov 1970-22 Feb 1971.
Lieut-Gen HAFEZ al ASSAD acting President **22 Feb-14 Mar 1971**; President **since 14 Mar 1971,** b 1928.

Prime Ministers

Dr MAMOUN KUZBARI 29 Sep-21 Nov 1961.
Dr IZZAT el NUS 21 Nov-20 Dec 1961.
Dr MAAROUF DAWALIBI 20 Dec 1961-Apr 1962.
Dr AHMED BASHIR el AZMEH 16 Apr-Sep 1962.
Dr KHALED el-AZEM 17 Sep 1962-8 Mar 1963 deposed in coup.
SALAH ed DIN BITAR 8 Mar-11 May 1963, b 1912.
Dr JOUNDI 11-13 May 1963.
SALAH ed DIN BITAR 13 May-Nov 1963.
Gen AMIN el HAFEZ 11 Nov 1963-May 1964.
SALAH ed DIN BITAR 4 May-Oct 1964.
Gen AMIN el HAFEZ 3 Oct 1964-Sep 1965.
Dr YOUSSEF ZEAYEN 23 Sep 1965-Jan 1966.
SALAH ed DIN BITAR 2 Jan-23 Feb 1966 deposed in coup.
Dr YOUSSEF ZEAYEN 23 Feb 1966-Oct 1968.
Dr NUREDDIN ATASSI 29 Oct 1968-13 Nov 1970 deposed in coup.
Lieut-Gen HAFEZ al ASSAD 18 Nov 1970-Apr 1971.
Gen ABDEL RAHMAN KHLEIFAWI 1 Apr 1971-Dec 1972.
MAHMOUD BEN SALEH al-AYYOUBI 21 Dec 1972-1 Aug 1976, b 1932.
Gen ABDEL RAHMAN KHLEIFAWI 1 Aug 1976-Mar 1978, b 1927.
MOHAMMED ALI HALABY since 29 Mar 1978.

Taehan Empire *see* Korea

Tahuantinsuyu *see* Inca Empire

Taiwan *see* China

Tanganyika *see* Tanzania

Tanzania

The name Tanzania was adopted on 29 Oct 1964 for the union of Tanganyika and Zanzibar effected on 25 Apr 1964. Tanganyika, a German possession (1884-World War I) and then a British Trust Territory until independence (9 Dec 1961), became a Republic on 9 Dec 1962. Zanzibar, which became a Republic on 12 Jan 1964, was in turn a Portuguese trading station, an Omani possession, an independent Sultanate and from 1890 a British protectorate until independence was achieved as a Sultanate on 9 Dec 1963.

Tanganyika

THE DOMINION OF TANGANYIKA

Governor-General

Sir **RICHARD TURNBALL 9 Dec 1961-9 Dec 1962.**

Prime Ministers

Dr **JULIUS KAMBARAGE NYERERE 9 Dec 1961-22 Jan 1962,** b 1923.
RASHIDI MFAUME KAWAWA 22 Jan 1962-9 Dec 1962, b 1930.

THE REPUBLIC OF TANGANYIKA

President

Dr **JULIUS KAMBARAGE NYERERE 9 Dec 1962-26 Apr 1964** when he became President of Tanzania, b 1923.

Prime Minister

RASHIDI MFAUME KAWAWA 9 Dec 1962-26 Apr 1964 when he became second Vice-President of Tanzania, b 1930.

Zanzibar

THE SULTANATE OF ZANZIBAR

† Sultan

SEYYID JAMSHID bin-ABDULLAH bin-KHALI-FAH succeeded as Sultan 2 Jul 1963; independent Sovereign **9 Dec 1963-12 Jan 1964** when he was deposed in a coup, b 1929.

Prime Minister

Sheikh **MUHAMMED SHAMTE HAMADI 9 Dec 1963-12 Jan 1964** when he was deposed in a coup.

THE REPUBLIC OF ZANZIBAR

President

Sheikh **ABEID AMANI KARUME 12 Jan-25 Apr 1964** as President of a Sovereign state - he retained the title President of Zanzibar as first Vice-President of Tanzania; assassinated 7 Apr 1972.

Prime Minister

Sheikh **ABDULLAH KASSIM HANGA 12 Jan 1964-26 Apr 1964** as Premier of a Sovereign state - he remained Premier of Zanzibar within the federal system, b 1932.

Tanzania

President

Dr **JULIUS KAMBARAGE NYERERE since 26 Apr 1964,** b 1923.

Prime Ministers

The office of Premier was revived 17 Feb 1972.

RASHIDI MFAUME KAWAWA 17 Feb 1972-12 Feb 1977: concurrently second Vice-President, a post he still holds, b 1930.
EDWARD M. SOKOINE since 12 Feb 1977.

Tenochtitlan *see* Mexico

Tepanecs, The *see* Mexico

Texcoco *see* Mexico

Thailand

Thailand was formerly known as Siam. No Thai country existed before the late 1200s when two states were founded by the Siamese: Chiangmai and Sukhothai - the latter being an important Kingdom of 14th century SE Asia. From the 14th to 18th centuries the principal Thai state was Ayutthaya which fell to the Burmese in 1767 in which year the modern Thai Kingdom may be said to have been formed after the expulsion of the invaders from Burma.

† Thai Kings of Sukhothai

RAMKHAMHAENG c 1279-c 1317.
LOE THAI c 1317-c 1347, son of Ramkhamhaeng.
LU THAI c 1347-c 1374. Upon his death Sukhothai fell to Ayutthaya.
c 1374-1767 Period of dominance by Ayutthaya.
1767 Burmese invasion.

† Kings of Thailand

Before 24 Jun 1939 the country was known internationally as Siam.

PHRAYA TAKSIN 1767-1781 deposed. He expelled the Burmese and reunited the Thais but was deposed when he became insane.

THE CHAKKRI DYNASTY

RAMA I (Chao Phraya Chakkri) 1782-1809, b 1737. A general he expanded the Kingdom and moved the capital to Bangkok.
RAMA II (LOES LA NABHALAI) 1809-1824, son of Rama I, b 1768.
RAMA III (NANG KLAO) 1824-1851, son of Rama II, b 1788.
MONGKUT (CHOM KLOA, or RAMA IV) 1851-Oct 1868, brother of Rama III, b 18 Oct 1804. The territorial gains of the previous reign had brought the Thais into conflict with European colonial powers with whom Mongkut came to terms. To modernise Siam he invited Western advisers and teachers, including Anna Leonowens who later produced an inaccurate and fanciful account that became 'The King and I'.
CHULA CHOM KLAO (CHULALONGKORN or RAMA V) Oct 1868-23 Oct 1910, son of Mongkut, b 20 Sep 1853. He was forced to cede much land to British Malaya and French Laos and Cambodia, but he greatly reformed Siam introducing public services and education and Government Ministries.
VAJIRAVUDH (MONGKUT KLAO or RAMA VI) Oct 1910-26 Nov 1925, son of Chula Chom Klao, b 1 Jan 1881.
PRAJADHIPOK (PHRA POK KLAO or RAMA VII) Nov 1925-2 Mar 1935 abdicated, brother of Vajiravudh, b 8 Nov 1893; d 30 May 1941.
ANANDA MAHIDOL Mar 1935-9 Jun 1946 when he died in mysterious circumstances from a gunshot wound - probably murdered, nephew of Prajadhipok, b 20 Sep 1925.
BHUMIPOL ADULYADEJ since 9 Jun 1946, brother of Ananda Mahidol, b 5 Dec 1927.

Prime Ministers of Thailand

Marshal LUANG PIBUL SONGGRAM 1938-Jul 1944 deposed in coup, b 14 Jul 1897; d 12 Jun 1964. During World War II he allied Thailand, which he hoped to enlarge at the expense of Laos and Burma, to Axis Japan; during the 1950s he led his country as a member of the western alliance.
KUANG APHAIWONGSE Jul 1944-Sep 1945.
NAI THAWI BUNYAKAT 1 Sep 1945-Jan 1946.
KUANG APHAIWONGSE 31 Jan-24 Mar 1946.
NAI PRIDI PHANOMJONG 24 Mar-21 Aug 1946.
LUANG DHAMRONG NAWASASAT 23 Aug 1946-9 Nov 1947 deposed in coup.
Marshal LUANG PIBUL SONGGRAM 9-10 Nov 1947.
KUANG APHAIWONGSE 10 Nov 1947-Apr 1948.
Marshal LUANG PIBUL SONGGRAM 9 Apr 1948-17 Sep 1957 deposed in coup.
Marshal SARIT THANARAT 17-21 Sep 1957.
POTE SARASIN 21 Sep 1957-Jan 1958.
Gen THANOM KITTIKACHORN 3 Jan-Oct 1958 deposed in coup.
Marshal SARIT THANARAT 20 Oct 1958-8 Dec 1963, b 1908; d in office. His dictatorship did much to restore order and eradicate corruption.
Gen THANOM KITTIKACHORN 9 Dec 1963-Oct 1973, b 11 Aug 1911.
SANYA THAMMASAK 14 Oct 1973-Dec 1974, b 1907.
Dr SANYA DHARMASAKTI Dec 1974-Feb 1975.
SENI PRAMOJ 13 Feb-13 Mar 1975, b 26 May 1905.
KUKRIT PRAMOJ 13 Mar 1975-Apr 1976, brother of Seni Pramoj, b 20 Apr 1911.
SENI PRAMOJ 21 Apr-6 Oct 1976 deposed in coup.
THANIN KRAIVICHIEN 6 Oct 1976-Oct 1977, b 5 Apr 1927.
Gen KRIANGSAK CHANANAND Head of Revolutionary Committee since 20 Oct 1977.

Thrace *see* Greece

Tibet

Formerly owing allegiance to the Manchu Emperors - and not to China - Tibet became a sovereign nation with the overthrow of the Chinese monarchy in 1911. Tibetan independence was ended by the Chinese invasion of Oct 1950-Sep 1951.

† Dalai Lamas of Independent Tibet

The Dalai Lama was the secular and spiritual Head of State and of Government of the Tibetan people.

THUSTEN GYATSO Dalai Lama from 1875; sovereign 1911-19 Dec 1933, b 1873.
TENZING GYATSO Jul 1939-21 Sep 1951 as a sovereign ruler; ruler under Chinese occupation

21 Sep 1951-31 Mar 1959 when he went into exile, b 6 Jul 1935.

Timurid Empire

Based on Iran and central Asia the empire of Timur and his successors cannot be regarded as a state but rather as a collection of territories owing allegiance to the Timurid Dynasty. The Timurid Kings have been variously, and inaccurately, described as Kings of Samarkand or Transoxiania, but there is no recognised geographical designation in the style of the monarchs of this dynasty.

† Kings

TIMUR (LENK - 'the lame', once called TAMERLANE) c 1360-Feb 1405, a descendant of Genghis Khan, b 1336. His empire, between the Indus and Euphrates, Lake Aral and the Arabian Sea, was a brief glory; more lasting has been his superb mausoleum - one of the world's finest buildings. A savage warrior who was lame on the right side, Timur was also a fine chess player and a skilled debator.

SHAH ROKH SHAH Feb 1405-1447, son of Timur. Ruler in Iran and central Asia.

MIRANSHAH 1405-1407, son of Timur. Ruler in Iraq and Georgia.

ULUGH BEG 1447-Oct 1449 murdered by a son; son of Shah Rokh Shah, b 1394. This King, famed for his observatory in Samarkand, ruled only in central Asia - the wider empire died with his father.

ABU SA'ID 1447-1467 ruled in western central Asia.

(The descendants of these Timurids ruled a number of small states in central Asia, eastern Iran and Afghanistan while another branch of the family became the Indian Moguls.)

Togo

Before achieving independence on 27 Apr 1960 Togo was a German protectorate (1894-1914) and a French Trust Territory (1922-1960).

Presidents

SYLVANUS OLYMPIO Head of State 27 Apr 1960-9 Apr 1961; President 9 Apr 1961-13 Jan 1963 when he was killed in a coup, b 1902. An outstanding leader who by his background and education was a rare link between English- and French-speaking Africa.

EMMANUEL BODJOLLÉ Chairman of the Insurrectionary Committee 13-16 Jan 1963.

NICOLAS GRUNITZKY provisional President 16 Jan-5 May 1963; President 5 May 1963-13 Jan 1967 when he was deposed in a coup, brother-in-law of President Olympio, b 1913; d 27 Sep 1969.

Col KLÉBER DADJO President of the Committee of National Reconciliation 14 Jan-14 Apr 1967, b 1914.

Lieut-Col GNASSINGBE EYADEMA (later Gen and before May 1973 Etienne Eyadema;) since 14 Apr 1967, b 1937 or 1938.

Tonga

The Kingdom of Tonga was founded by Taufa'ahau Tupou I (1845) whose family is said to have ruled Ha'apai since the 10th century. A British protectorate from 18 May 1900, Tonga became independent again on 4 Jun 1970.

† Kings

TAUFA'AHAU TUPOU I (GEORGE TUPOU I by baptism) 1845-1893, b 1797. Known as the 'Grand Old Man of the Pacific', this astute king adapted Western ways to suit Tonga, effected an equitable land distribution for his subjects and embraced Methodism.

GEORGE TUPOU II 1893-1918, great-grandson of Taufa'ahau Tupou I.

SALOTE TUPOU III (Queen) 1918-15 Dec 1965, eldest daughter of George Tupou II, b 13 Mar 1900. Queen Salote, a practical and unassuming woman, is remembered in Britain for riding in an open carriage in the rain to Queen Elizabeth II's coronation.

TAUFA'AHAU TUPOU IV since 15 Dec 1965, elder son of Queen Salote, b 4 Jul 1918.

Prime Minister

Prince TU'IPELEHAKE since 4 Jun 1965, younger brother of King Taufa'ahau Tupou IV.

Transjordan see Jordan

Transkei see South Africa

Transvaal see South Africa

Trebizond

Upon the fall of the Byzantine Empire to the Crusaders, Prince Alexis Comnenus declared the area of which he had been governor to be an independent Empire. The Grand Comneni Emperors ruled until Trebizond fell to the Ottoman Turks in 1461.

† Emperors

GRAND COMNENI DYNASTY

ALEXIS I 1204-1222. Formerly governor in Trebizond he declared his independence as a sovereign Emperor after Byzantium fell to the Crusaders.
ANDRONICUS I 1222-1235.
IOANNES I 1235-1238.
EMMANUEL I 1238-1263.
ANDRONICUS II 1263-1266.
GEORGIUS I 1266-1280.
IOANNES II 1280-1285 deposed.
THEODORA (Empress) 1285.
IOANNES II 1285-1297.
ALEXIS II 1297-1330.
ANDRONICUS III 1330-1332.
EMMANUEL II 1332.
BASILIUS I 1332-1340.
IRENE (Empress) 1340-1341.
ANNA (Empress) 1341-1343.
IOANNES III 1343-1344.
MICHAEL 1344-1349.
ALEXIS III 1349-1390.
EMMANUEL III 1390-1417.
ALEXIS IV 1417-1446.
IOANNES IV 1446-1458.
DAVID 1458-1461 when Trebizond fell to the Ottoman Turks.

Trinidad and Tobago

Trinidad was claimed for Spain by Columbus in 1498 and ceded to Britain by the Treaty of Amiens in 1802; Tobago became Dutch in 1632, French in 1677, British in 1763, French again in 1783 and finally British in 1815. The islands were joined as a single colony in 1889 and achieved independence as a Dominion on 31 Aug 1962. A Republic was proclaimed on 1 Aug 1976.

THE DOMINION OF TRINIDAD AND TOBAGO

Governors-General

Sir **SOLOMON HOCHOY 31 Aug 1962-1973,** b 1905.
Sir **ELLIS EMMANUEL INNOCENT CLARKE 1973-1 Aug 1976,** b 28 Sep 1917. Became the first President of the Republic.

Prime Minister

Dr **ERIC EUSTACE WILLIAMS 31 Aug 1962-1 Aug 1976,** b 25 Sep 1911. Became Premier in the Republic.

THE REPUBLIC OF TRINIDAD AND TOBAGO

President

ELLIS EMMANUEL INNOCENT CLARKE since 1 Aug 1976, b 28 Sep 1917.

Prime Minister

Dr **ERIC EUSTACE WILLIAMS since 1 Aug 1976,** b 25 Sep 1911.

Tripoli *see* Crusader States

Trucial States, The *see* United Arab Emirates

Tunisia

Governed in turn by Phoenicians (9th-7th centuries BC), Carthaginians (whose Empire was based on Carthage near Tunis from the 7th century to 146 BC), Romans (to the 5th century AD), Vandals, the Byzantine Empire, Arabs (from the 7th century), Turks (from 1574) and the French (from 1881), Tunisia became independent on 20 Mar 1956. The Bey (monarch) was deposed in 1957 when a Republic was established.

TUNISIAN STATE

† Bey of Tunis

SIDI LAMINE Sovereign ruler **20 Mar 1956-25 Jul 1957,** b 1891. Deposed upon the establishment of the Republic.

Prime Ministers

TAHAR BEN AMMAR 20 Mar-9 Apr 1956.
HABIB ibn ALI BOURGUIBA 10 Apr 1956-25 Jul 1957 when he became first President of the Republic.

THE REPUBLIC OF TUNISIA

President

HABIB ibn ALI BOURGUIBA since 25 Jul 1957, b 3 Aug 1903.

Prime Ministers

The office of Premier was revived in 1969.

BAHDI LADGHAM 7 Nov 1969-1 Nov 1970, b 1913.
HEDI NOUIRA since 1 Nov 1970, b 6 Apr 1911.

Turkey

Turkey was formerly known as the Ottoman Empire. The Turks entered Asia Minor from the east at the end of the 13th century and founded several small 'Principalities'. In time those Turks owing allegiance to Osman (in Arabic Uthman hence the word Ottoman) and his descendants became paramount. Their Empire at its height included all the Middle East, northern Africa and the Balkans. The long decline of the Ottoman state ended with its defeat and partition at the close of World War I. After occupation and civil war Kemal Pasa abolished the monarchy and founded a Republic renamed Turkey.

THE OTTOMAN EMPIRE

House of Osman

† PRINCE OF THE OTTOMAN TURKS
OSMAN I (OTHMAN) c 1300-c 1326. Prince of a tribe of Turkish nomads, b c 1258. By c 1300 Osman had established a Principality in NW Turkey.

† BEYS OF THE OTTOMAN TURKS
ORHAN (ORKHAN) c 1326-c 1360, son of Osman I. Orhan took Bursa (which became the Ottoman capital) and the title Bey. He entered Europe having permission from the Byzantine Emperor Ioannes VI (whom he had helped to the throne), to sack Thrace.
MURAD I c 1360-1389 killed in battle, son of Orhan, b c 1326. Murad gained the Ottomans'

Sultan Suleyman I ('The Magnificent') brought terror to Central Europe where he was known as the 'Grand Turk' (Giraudon)

first permanent lands in Europe including Edirne (the second Ottoman capital).
BAYEZID I 1389-1396 when he became Sultan.

† OTTOMAN SULTANS
BAYEZID I ('The Thunderbolt') Bey from 1389; Sultan **1396-Jul 1402,** son of Murad I, b c 1360; died a captive of Tamerlane Mar 1403. He made major territorial advances in Anatolia and gained the style Sultan from the 'anti-Caliph' in Cairo but beaten by Timur (Tamerlane) his Empire disintegrated.
1402-1413 Interregnum. Bayezid's four sons fought the Turks' enemies and each other until Mehmed emerged triumphant.
MEHMED I 1413-26 May 1421, son of Bayezid I, b 1387.
MURAD II May 1421-Feb? 1444 abdicated, son of Mehmed I, b Jun 1404. Murad rebuilt the Empire,

fought wars against Hungary, Serbia and Venice and founded the Janissaries (a force of mercenaries formed from captive Christian youths) to counter the influence of overpowerful nobles. Abdicating to seek a religious life he returned when Edirne was threatened by Crusaders.

MEHMED II ('The Conqueror') **Feb-Nov 1444,** son of Murad II, b 30 Mar 1432. A great general and an efficient administrator, Mehmed took Constantinople (May 1453) which renamed Istanbul was developed as the cosmopolitan capital of his Empire. He added Trebizond, the Karaman state, Morea, Albania, Bosnia, Serbia and Wallachia to the Ottomans' lands but to finance his campaigns he debased the coinage causing terrifying inflation and economic distress.

MURAD II Nov 1444-3 Feb 1451.

MEHMED II ('The Conqueror') **Feb 1451-3 May 1481.**

BAYEZID II ('The Just') **May 1481-Apr 1512** when he was deposed by the Janissaries, elder son of Mehmed II, b c 1447; d May 1512.

SELIM I ('The Grim') **Apr 1512-22 Sep 1520,** brother of Bayezid II, b 1470. The Sultan who conquered Syria, Palestine and Egypt, making the Ottomans supreme in the Arab World, and wealthy as never before, murdered his brothers, nephews and all his sons except one to avoid a disputed succession.

SULEYMAN I ('The Magnificent' and 'The Lawgiver') **Sep 1520-6? Sep 1566,** only surviving son of Selim I, b c Jan 1495? Suleyman, under whom the Ottoman Empire attained its zenith, undertook a long campaign in a rather one-sided alliance with Francois I against the Habsburgs both in mainland Europe where he annexed Hungary and in the Mediterranean where his powerful fleet under Khayr ad-Din (Barbarossa) gained supremacy over that of Charles V under Doria.

SELIM II Sep 1566-Dec 1574, son of Suleyman I, b May 1524.

MURAD III Dec 1574-16 or 17 Jan 1595, son of Selim II, b 4 Jul 1546.

MEHMED III Jan 1595-22 Dec 1603, son of Murad III, b 1566.

AHMED I Dec 1603-22 Nov 1617, son of Mehmed III, b 18 Apr 1590.

MUSTAFA I Nov 1617-1618 deposed, son of Mehmed III, b 1591; d 20 Jan 1639.

OSMAN II oglu Ahmed **1618-19 May 1622** deposed, son of Ahmed I, b 15 Nov 1603; murdered by strangulation 20 May 1622.

MUSTAFA I 1622-1623 deposed.

MURAD IV 1623-8 Feb 1640, son of Ahmed I, b 27 Jul 1612.

IBRAHIM Feb 1640-8 Aug 1648 deposed, son of Ahmed I, b 4 Nov 1615; murdered 18 Aug 1648. An insane extravagant Sultan.

MEHMED IV ('The Hunter') **Aug 1648-7 Nov 1687** deposed, son of Ibrahim, b 2 Jan 1642; d 6 Jan 1693. In this reign the tide turned against Turkey in Europe with the relief of the siege of Vienna (1683) and the long decline of the Ottoman Empire set in.

SULEYMAN II Ibrahim **Nov 1687-23 Jun 1691,** son of Ibrahim, b 15 Apr 1642.

AHMED II Jun 1691-6 Feb 1695, son of Ibrahim, b 1 Aug 1642.

MUSTAFA II oglu Mehmed **Feb 1695-22 Aug 1703** deposed, son of Mehmed IV, b 5 Jun 1664; d 31 Dec 1703 in suspicious circumstances.

AHMED III Aug 1703-1730 deposed, son of Mehmed IV, b 1673; d in captivity 1736. The luxurious court life of this Sultan is termed the Tulip Period.

MAHMUD I 1730-13 Dec 1754, son of Mustafa II, b 2 Aug 1696.

OSMAN III Dec 1754-30 Oct 1757, son of Mustafa II, b 2 Jan 1699.

MUSTAFA III Oct 1757-21 Jan 1774, son of Ahmed III, b 28 Jan 1717.

ABDULHAMID I Jan 1774-7 Apr 1789, son of Ahmed III, b 20 Mar 1725.

SELIM III Apr 1789-1807 deposed, son of Mustafa III, b 24 Dec 1761; murdered by strangulation 29 Jul 1808. Selim tried to halt the decline of the Empire by instituting much needed reform, particularly in the army, but vested interests defeated him.

MUSTAFA IV 1807-28 Jul 1808 deposed, son of Abdulhamid I, b 8 Sep 1779; murdered by strangulation 17 Nov 1808. This unthinking reactionary and religious extremist reversed the reforms of Selim III and put him and those who favoured reform to death.

MAHMUD II Jul 1808-1 Jul 1839, son of Abdulhamid I, b 20 Jul 1785. Although he lost north Africa and Greece Mahmud was able to regain control over much of the Empire. The revolt of the Janissaries, the biggest obstacle to change, resulted in their suppression and massacre after which reforms began.

ABDULMECID Jul 1839-25 Jun 1861, son of Mahmud II, b 25 Apr 1823. The reforms of the respected progressive Sultan Abdulmecid started a national elementary education system, improved the judiciary and the administration and guaranteed basic human rights and liberties (but the latter largely remained on paper).

ABDULAZIZ Jun 1861-30 May 1876 deposed, son of Mahmud II, b 9 Feb 1830; d (suicide) 4 Jun 1876. He abused the powers gained through the reforms of Abdulmecid and was deposed after Balkan risings and a severe famine.

MURAD V 31 May-31 Aug 1876 deposed as insane, son of Abdulmecid, b 21 Sep 1840; d in semi-captivity 29 Aug 1904.

ABDULHAMID II Aug 1876-24 Apr 1909 deposed, son of Abdulmecid, b 21 Sep 1842; d 10 Feb 1918. Losing most of the Balkans at the Congress of Berlin (1878), he strove to preserve what was left of the Empire over which he ruled conscientiously but harshly (eg the massacre of the Armenians). The revolt of 1908 forced him to restore the Constitution and a further rising ended his reign which was not wholly negative as he encouraged trade and industry, founded colleges and railways and reformed education.

MEHMED V Resad **Apr 1909-3 Jul 1918,** son of Abdulmecid, b 2 Nov 1844. A kindly, courtly but foolish man, who wished to be a constitutional monarch - his abstention from government gave freedom to the extremists who took Turkey to war against her old enemy Russia and on the side of the Central Powers in 1914.

MEHMED VI Vahideddin **Jul 1918-1 Nov 1922** deposed, son of Abdulmecid, b 14 Jan 1861; d in exile 16 May 1926. Opposed to the ideas of Kemal Pasa's nationalists in Ankara and reduced to puppet status by the Allies occupying Istanbul, Mehmed VI represented the society that the Ankara Government wished to sweep away and was thus deposed when the Sultanate was abolished.

1-18 Nov 1922 Turkey had no Head of State.

CALIPH OF TURKEY

The Sultans were also styled Caliph. In 1922 the roles of the Sultanate and the Caliphate were separated and the religious Caliph may be said to have acted as a figurehead to the Turkish State until the Republic of Turkey was formally proclaimed.

ABDULMECID 18 Nov 1922-29 Oct 1923 when the Republic was declared; the Caliphate was abolished 3 Mar 1924, cousin of Mehmed VI, b 30 May 1868; d in exile 23 Aug 1944.

THE REPUBLIC OF TURKEY

Presidents

KEMAL ATATÜRK (also formerly known as Kemal Pasa) **29 Oct 1923-10 Nov 1938,** b (Mustafa Kemal) 1881; d in office. Of lowly origins he rose through the army to head a government in Ankara when Istanbul was occupied by the British after World War I. He resurrected Turkey, abolishing the monarchy and the Caliphate, reforming the government, the legal system and the schools, and introducing western ways in his attempt to make Turkey a modern power.

Gen **ISMET INÖNÜ 11 Nov 1938-22 May 1950,** b 24 Sep 1884; d 25 Dec 1973. The right-hand man of Atatürk in the creation of modern Turkey, he encouraged the development of Parliamentary democracy after the Menderes episode.

MAHMUD CELAL BAYER 22 May 1950-27 May 1960 deposed in coup, b 1883.

Gen **CEMAL GÜRSEL** acting President **28 May 1960-Oct 1962;** President **26 Oct 1962-Mar 1966,** b 1895; d 14 Sep 1966.

Gen **CEVDET SUNAY 28 Mar 1966-Mar 1973,** b 10 Feb 1900.

FAHRI KORUTÜRK since 6 Apr 1973, b 1903.

Prime Ministers

Gen **ISMET INÖNÜ 29 Oct 1923-Jan 1925.**

FETHI OKYAR Jan-Mar 1925.

Gen **ISMET INÖNÜ 5 Mar 1925-Sep 1937;** acting PM **27 Sep-11 Nov 1937;** see President Inonu.

MAHMUD CELAL BAYER 11 Nov 1937-Jan 1939.

Dr **REFIK SAYDAM 25 Jan 1939-8 Jul 1942,** b 1876; d in office.

SÜKRÜ SARACOGLU 9 Jul 1942-Aug 1946, b 1887; d 27 Dec 1953.

RECEP PEKER 7 Aug 1946-Sep 1947.

HASAN SAKA 9 Sep 1947-Jan 1948.

SEMSEDDIN GÜNALTAY 16 Jan 1948-May 1950, b 1883; d Oct 1962.

ADNAN MENDERES 22 May 1950-27 May 1960 deposed in coup, b 1899; executed 17 Sep 1961 after being tried for violation of the constitution.

Gen **CEMAL GÜRSEL 28 May 1960-Oct 1962.**

Gen **FAHRI ÖZDILEK** acting PM **30 Oct-10 Nov 1962.**

Gen **ISMET INÖNÜ 10 Nov 1962-10 Dec 1963;** acting PM **10-14 Dec 1963;** PM **14 Dec 1963-Feb 1965.**

SUAT HAYRI ÜRGÜPLÜ 16 Feb-Oct 1965, b 1903.

SÜLEYMAN DEMIREL 22 Oct 1965-Mar 1971.

Prof **NIHAT ERIM 19 Mar 1971-Apr 1972,** b 1912.

FERIT MELEN 17 Apr 1972-Apr 1973, b 1906.

NAIM TALU 12 Apr-Oct 1973; acting PM **23 Oct 1973-Jan 1974.**

BÜLENT ECEVIT 25 Jan-Sep 1974; acting PM **18 Sep-13 Nov 1974.**

Prof **SADI IRMAK 13 Nov 1974-Mar 1975.**

SÜLEYMAN DEMIREL 31 Mar 1975-Jun 1977.

BÜLENT ECEVIT 14 Jun-21 Jul 1977, b 28 May 1925.

SÜLEYMAN DEMIREL 21 Jul-31 Dec 1977, b 6 Oct 1924.

BÜLENT ECEVIT since 1 Jan 1978.

Tuscany *see* Italy

Tuvalu

The tiny Pacific Ocean atolls of Tuvalu (which were known as the Ellice Islands before 1975) have been British since 1892. They are scheduled to attain independence upon 1 Oct 1978.

Two Sicilies, Kings of The *see* Sicily

Uganda

The area now called Uganda became British in 1884. Independence was achieved on 9 Oct 1962; a Sovereign state (deliberately not termed a Republic) under a President was established on 9 Oct 1963 and a Republic declared on 8 Sep 1967.

THE DOMINION OF UGANDA

Governor-General

Sir **WALTER COUTTS** **9 Oct 1962-9 Oct 1963.**

Prime Minister

Dr **APOLLO MILTON OBOTE** **9 Oct 1962-9 Oct 1963,** b 1925.

THE REPUBLIC OF UGANDA

(From 1963 to 1967 the Commonwealth of Uganda)

Presidents

Sir **EDWARD MUTESA** (MUTESA II, Kabaka of Buganda) **9 Oct 1963-24 Feb 1966** when the constitution was suspended, b 19 Nov 1924; d 21 Nov 1969. The election of the Kabaka was encouraged to placate the Ganda people, but national unity was threatened by the dominance of northern tribes in the Government and by Sir Edward's insistence on Buganda's privileges. Suspended, the Kabaka fled to Britain where he died in exile.

Dr **APOLLO MILTON OBOTE** **15 Apr 1966-25 Jan 1971** when he was deposed in a coup.

Maj-Gen Al-Hajji **IDI AMIN DADA** (later Field-Marshal) **since 26 Jan 1971,** b 1925.

Prime Minister

Dr **APOLLO MILTON OBOTE** **9 Oct 1963-8 Sep 1967** when the office of Premier was abolished, b 1925.

Umma *see* Babylonia

Umm al Qaiwan *see* United Arab Emirates

Ummayad Caliphate *see* Spain

Union of Soviet Socialist Republics

Towards the end of the Dark Ages the Rus (Varangians), a group of Scandinavian origins, established a series of Principalities along the Dneipr Basin. Initially Kiev gained ascendency; then the initiative passed north to the Grand Principality of Moscow around which Russia was to be built. A Russian state can be identified from the time of Aleksandr Nevsky in the 13th century.

EARLY RUSSIAN SOVEREIGNS

† Princes of Novgorod and Grand Princes of Vladimir

RULERS OF THE 'HOUSE OF RURIK'

ALEKSANDR I (Nevsky) Ruler of Novgorod **1238-1252**; ruler of Novgorod and Vladimir **1252-1263**, son of Yaroslav II of Novgorod, b c 1220. This Prince, who established the embryo of the Russian state, remains a national hero: an Imperial Order was named for him in 1722, a Soviet military Order in 1942.

YAROSLAV III 1263-1272, son of Aleksandr I.

VASILY 1272-1276, son of Yaroslav III.

DMITRI I 1276-c 1294.

ANDREI c 1294-c 1304; sometimes referred to as Andrei III.

MIKHAIL II 1304-1319 when he was assassinated, son of Yaroslav III.

YURI 1319-1324 deposed; date of death unknown. Yuri lost his throne upon the invasion of the Golden Horde of Tatars.

DMITRI II 1324-1327.

ALEKSANDR II 1327-1328 deposed by the Tatars; date of death unknown.

† Grand Princes of Moscow

RULERS OF THE 'HOUSE OF RURIK'

IVAN I Danilovich (nicknamed Kalita - money-bags) **1328-31 Mar 1341,** grandson of Aleksandr Nevsky, b c 1304. Although obliged to pay tribute to the Tatars, Ivan I was able by 1331 to make himself supreme amongst the Russian Princes.

SIMEON Ivanovich **Mar 1341-1353,** son of Ivan I.

IVAN II Ivanovich (nicknamed Krasny - red) **1353-1359,** son of Ivan I, b 1326.

DMITRI Ivanovich Donskoy **1359-19 May 1389,** son of Ivan II, b 1350.

VASILY I Dmitriyevich **May 1389-Feb 1425,** son of Dmitri Donskoy, b 1371.

VASILY II Vasilyevich (nicknamed Temny - blind) **Feb 1425-1434** deposed, son of Vasily I, b 1415. Twice deposed, Vasily II was blinded by the usurper Dmitri Shemyaka.

YURI Vasilyevich **1434,** brother of Vasily II.
VASILY II Vasilyevich **1434-1446** deposed.
DMITRI Shemyaka **1446-1447.** A usurper.
VASILY II Vasilyevich **1447-27 Mar 1462.**
IVAN III Vasilyevich **Mar 1462-27 Oct 1505,** son of Vasily II, b 22 Jan 1440. Called 'the Great', Ivan III considerably enlarged the Russian state and threw off the Tatar yoke.
VASILY III Ivanovich **Oct 1505-3 Dec 1533,** son of Ivan III, b 1479.

† Tsars of Muscovy

'HOUSE OF RURIK'
IVAN IV Vasilyevich **Dec 1533-18 Mar 1584,** only son of Vasily III, b 25 Aug 1530. The first Tsar was either a maniac incapable of reason or a bloody tyrant whose insecurity led him to rule by terror. At his coronation (16 Jan 1541) Ivan the Terrible took the title Tsar posing as heir to the recently extinguished Byzantine Empire. His turbulent reign was marked by disastrous wars against his European neighbours and by the viciousness of his sadistic hooliganism that led to frequent mass killings. In 1564, he strangely left Moscow and founded the Oprichnina - a personal corps of delinquents who terrorised Russia half of which they ruled as a private fief. Ivan's abnormal rages saw him kill his son and heir and massacre a city, yet he kept lists of victims that they might be prayed for. His bizarre married life - seven wives, two of whom may not have legally married him - produced but two boys to survive him.
FYODOR I Ivanovich **Mar 1584-7 Jan 1598,** son of Ivan IV, b 31 May 1557.

HOUSE OF GODUNOV
IRINA (Tsarita) **7-17 Jan 1598** when she retired to a convent, b c 1560; d (a nun) 1603. The widow of Fyodor I and sister of Boris Godunov.
17 Jan-20 Feb 1598 Interregnum.
BORIS Godunov **20 Feb 1598-14 Apr 1605,** brother-in-law of Fyodor I, b c 1551. An able illiterate of Tatar stock, Godunov was elected to succeed his sister, Irina. Depicted by some as disinterested, by others as grasping, Godunov was resented as an upstart, though the revolt that would have claimed him if nature had not intervened was ignited by a severe famine.
FYODOR II Godunov **Apr-1 Jun 1605** when he was brutally murdered by the Moscow mob, son of Boris Godunov, b 1589.

USURPING IMPOSTOR
DMITRI (usually called the False Dmitri) **20 Jun 1605-17 May 1606** when he was assassinated. The leader of the revolt against Boris Godunov claimed to be Dmitri, son of Ivan IV, who had died under suspicious circumstances in 1591. His true identity has never been discovered but he may have been Yuri (Grigori) Otrepyev. Generous and progressive, (he even contemplated liberating the serfs) Dmitri was swept away

Ekaterina I, originally a Lithuanian laundry-maid who rose to be Empress of All the Russias (Radio Times Hulton Picture Library)

in a wave of Orthodox xenophobia resentful of a Catholic Tsar surrounded by Poles.

HOUSE OF SHUYSKY
VASILY IV Ivanovich Shuysky **29 May 1606-17 Jul 1610** deposed, b 1552; d 1612. Shuysky, leader of the revolt against Dmitri, was elected Tsar, was later deposed and forced to become a monk.

HOUSE OF ROMANOV
MIKHAIL Fyodorovich Romanov **7 Feb 1613-23 Jul 1645,** great-nephew of Ivan IV's first wife, b 1596.
ALEKSEY Mikhailovich **Jul 1645-8 Feb 1676,** son of Mikhail, b 20 Mar 1629.
FYODOR III Alekseyevich **Feb 1676-7 May 1682,** eldest surviving son of Aleksey, b 9 Jun 1661.
IVAN V Alekseyevich co-ruler **5 Jun 1682-8 Feb 1696,** half-brother of Fyodor III, b 6 Sep 1666. A pious, half-blind, half-witted invalid, Ivan V nominally shared the throne with his brother Peter.
PETER I Alekseyevich sole ruler **7 May-5 Jun** 1682; co-ruler **5 Jun 1682-8 Feb 1696;** sole ruler **8 Feb 1696-Nov 1721** when he became Emperor.

† Emperors and Autocrats of all the Russias

Although replaced by the title Emperor in 1721, the title Tsar continued in popular use until the end of

Nikolai II, ex-Emperor of All the Russias, imprisoned with his immediate family at Tobolsk after his abdication (Radio Times Hulton Picture Library)

the dynasty this century. Nevertheless, strictly speaking Peter I was the last Tsar.

PETER I Alekseyevich Tsar **from 7 May 1682;** Emperor **2 Nov 1721-8 Feb 1725,** son of Aleksey and brother of Ivan V, b 9 Jun 1672. Peter the Great spent 18 months in the West studying technology, visiting workshops and even working as a labourer at Zaandam shipyards. Returning to Russia he implemented his ideas: reforming the administration, founding colleges and the Russian Navy, etc, but this Westernisation affected mainly the upper classes and accentuated the dangerous gulf in Russian society. The defeat of Sweden at Poltava (1709) established Russia as a great power and on unpromising marshes taken from the Swedes he built a splendid new capital: St Petersburg. Progress was not achieved without great suffering: the Emperor ruled by terror; the peasants endured forced labour and crippling taxation; Peter's own son, the weak Aleksey, fled when threatened and was flogged to death.

EKATERINA I Alekseyevna (Empress) **Feb 1725-17 May 1727,** second wife of Peter I, b (Marta Skowronska) 1684. Having enjoyed the fruits of a rise from Lithuanian laundry-maid to Emperor's mistress then Consort, Ekaterina, a bawdy amiable woman, took advantage of the flexible law of succession to seize the throne.

PETER II Alekseyevich **May 1727-30 Jan 1730,** grandson of Peter I, b 23 Oct 1715.

ANNA Ivanovna (Empress) **Feb 1730-28 Oct 1740,** younger surviving daughter of Ivan V, b 8 Feb 1693.

IVAN VI Antonovich **Oct 1740-6 Dec 1741** when he was deposed and imprisoned, grandson of Anna's elder sister Ekaterina, b (Prince Ivan of Brunswick-Wolfenbuttel) 23 Aug 1740; murdered in gaol 16 Jul 1764.

ELISAVETA Petrovna (Empress) **Dec 1741-5 Jan 1762,** only surviving daughter of Peter I and Ekaterina I, b 29 Dec 1709. Popular, extravagant (she left 15000 dresses), plump and indolent, Elisaveta was nevertheless politically astute being one of the first to recognise the growing threat of Prussia.

PETER III Fyodorovich **Jan-9 Jul 1762** deposed, nephew of Elisaveta, b (Prince Karl Peter Ulrich of Holstein-Gottorp) 21 Feb 1728; murdered 17 Jul 1762 (there is no evidence to implicate Ekaterina II in his death as is sometimes claimed). An unpopular German Tsar, he treasonably sent Friedrich the Great Russian standing orders while Russia was at war with Prussia.

EKATERINA II Alekseyevna (Empress) **Jul 1762-17 Nov 1796,** wife of Peter III, b (Princess Sophie Auguste Friederike of Anhalt-Zerbst) 2 May 1729. Called 'the Great' - an epithet she did not deserve - Ekaterina was as devoted to power as she wished to appear to be to Russia. Posing as enlightened she ruled as a tyrant - her famous 'Instruction', heavily copied from Montesquieu, remained a dead letter and a cruel joke; her largesse to the nobility was at the expense of the peasantry who were reduced to abject slavery; her foreign policy, particularly in the partition of Poland, stored up trouble for Russia. She probably contributed more to Russia's ills and the final downfall of the dynasty than any Romanov.

PAVEL Petrovich **Nov 1796-24 Mar 1801** when he was assassinated, son of Ekaterina II, b 1 Oct 1754.

ALEKSANDR I Pavlovich **Mar 1801-19 Nov 1825,** eldest son of Pavel, b 12 Dec 1777. Aleksandr's character is difficult to fathom: utterly charming (his family worshipped him calling him 'Our Angel'), he was also devious; able, he became obsessed by religious mysticism; the proponent of liberal ideals, he was a reactionary in practice and the architect of the Holy Alliance. Splendid in uniform, he left the fighting to others and when defeated by Napoleon feigned friendship while plotting France's eventual downfall when he was hailed as the 'Liberator of Europe'.

(**KONSTANTIN** Pavlovich, second son of Pavel, was proclaimed Emperor *in absentia* 27 Nov

1825, but refused the throne he had secretly renounced in 1822.)

NIKOLAI I Pavlovich **14 Dec 1825-18 Feb 1855,** third son of Pavel, b 25 Jun 1796. The bête noire of liberal historians, Nikolai I was a short-sighted autocrat who intervened in many aspects of Russian life from determining railway routes and hospital regulations to calling for the maximum punishment for dissenters. He was also a devoted family man, usually fair and devoid of malice. It can be claimed that Nikolai's repression of opposition left revolution as the only alternative but the common picture of his Russia as one great army camp does not fit the facts: his was the Russia of Pushkin and Gogol and his the idea of liberating the serfs - a plan carried out by his son and successor.

ALEKSANDR II Nikolayevich **Feb 1855-13 Mar 1881** when he was assassinated, eldest son of Nikolai I, b 29 Apr 1818. The plump and amiable Aleksandr II emancipated the serfs, introduced trial by jury and elected local government and reformed the education system, but by relaxing the repressive regime of his father too quickly he unwittingly aided the growing terrorist movements, one of which killed him by a bomb at a time when he was about to grant a constitution.

ALEKSANDR III Aleksandrovich **Mar 1881-2 Nov 1894,** second but eldest surviving son of Aleksandr II, b 10 Mar 1845. In a reign usually dismissed as unproductive the reactionary Alcksandr III did undo many of the reforms of his father, but his strong rule and bluff manner were popular. Terrorism was reduced and prosperity increased as the industrialisation of Russia advanced. He recognised economic reform as the priority and had such strength and realism that he might eventually have been able to effect the necessary government reforms.

NIKOLAI II Aleksandrovich **Nov 1894-28 Mar 1917** when he abdicated, eldest son of Aleksandr III, b 18 May 1868; murdered by Bolsheviks 16 or 17 Jul 1918 - it now seems likely that the Empress and her daughters were not killed until perhaps a year later. Charming and inept, Nikolai II was totally unfit to rule though he considered himself to be Autocrat by the will of God. Kept almost a recluse by the security police he was dominated by his unpopular wife Alexandra who was much influenced by the evil Rasputin - a 'holy man' who afforded the haemophiliac heir some relief from suffering. Discontent grew in a repressive regime; disorders were mishandled by officialdom, eg the massacre of Fr Gapon's demonstrators; the disastrous war with Japan (1904) highlighted the inefficiency of the system; economic progress was accompanied by a political awareness that had no outlet and when a parliament (Duma) was granted it had little power. Although the Great War temporarily united the people, Russian society collapsed and the monarchy was swept away in a wave of strikes and civil unrest in Mar 1917 when the Duma illegally formed a provisional government.

THE PROVISIONAL GOVERNMENT

Prime Ministers

Prince **GEORGY YEVGENYEVICH LVOV 15 Mar-Jul 1917,** b 2 Nov 1861; d 6 Mar 1925.

ALEKSANDR FYODOROVICH KERENSKY Jul-7 Nov 1917, b 22 Apr 1881; d 11 Jun 1970. A moderate Socialist he lost the support of the right by his poor conduct of the war and the support of the left by refusing their wild schemes. He was deposed in the Bolshevik 'October' revolution.

THE RUSSIAN SOVIET SOCIALIST REPUBLIC

Presidents
(Chairmen of the Executive Committee)

YAKOV MIKHAYLOVICH SVERDLOV Nov 1917-Mar 1919, b 1885; d in office.

MIKHAIL IVANOVICH KALININ Mar 1919-Dec 1922 when he became President of the USSR.

Prime Minister

(President of the Council of People's Commissars)

VLADYMIR ILICH ULYANOV LENIN 7 Nov 1917-Dec 1922 when he became PM of the USSR, b(Vladymir Ilich Ulyanov) 22 Apr 1870; d (in office) 21 Jan 1924. The founder of the Russian Bolshevik Communist Party he was returned to wartime Russia by the Germans to create as much disorder in that country as possible. Of middle class origins he became a bitter revolutionary after the execution of his brother for terrorist activities. He led the 'October' revolution and maintained his regime through able direction and by winning the support of the peasants through the grant of land. Lenin (the name assumed when a clandestine revolutionary) was capable of inspiring great loyalty and although ruthless lacked the extreme traits of Stalin whom he did not wish to succeed him. Through his establishment of the world's first Communist society and through his writings - in particular the masterly 'Development of Capitalism in Russia' - Lenin is one of the most influential figures of our century.

Chairman of the Communist Party

JOSIF VISSARIONOVICH DJUGASHVILI STALIN Mar-Dec 1922 when he became Chairman of the Communist Party of the USSR.

THE UNION OF SOVIET SOCIALIST REPUBLICS

Established in Dec 1922.

Presidents

Presidents of the Presidium of the Supreme Soviet of the USSR - before 1938 termed Chairman of the All-Union Executive Committee.

MIKHAIL IVANOVICH KALININ Dec 1922-Mar 1946, b 2 Dec 1875; d 3 Jun 1946.
NIKOLAI SHVERNIK 19 Mar 1946-Mar 1953.
Marshal **KLIMENT EFREMOVICH VOROSHI-LOV 6 Mar 1953-May 1960,** b 4 Feb 1881; d 3 Dec 1969.
LEONID ILICH BREZHNEV 7 May 1960-Jul 1965.
ANASTAS IVANOVICH MIKOYAN 15 Jul-Dec 1965, b 25 Nov 1895.
NIKOLAI VIKTOROVICH PODGORNY 9 Dec 1965-Jun 1977, b 1903.
LEONID ILICH BREZHNEV since 16 Jun 1977, b 19 Dec 1906.

Prime Ministers

Chairmen of the Council of People's Commissars.

VLADYMIR ILICH ULYANOV LENIN Dec 1922-21 Jan 1924.
ALEKSEY IVANOVICH RYKOV 2 Feb 1924-Sep 1930, b 25 Feb 1881; d 14 Mar 1938 - executed after a show trial by Stalin whom he had helped to power.
GENRIKH GRIGORYEVICH YAGODA 29 Sep 1930-Dec 1931, b 1891; d 1938.
VYACHESLAV MIKHAYLOVICH MOLOTOV 21 Dec 1931-May 1941, b 9 Mar 1890.
Marshal **JOSIF VISSARIONOVICH DJUGASHVI-LI STALIN 6 May 1941-5 Mar 1953,** b (Josif Vissarionovich Djugashvili) 21 Dec 1879; d 5 Mar 1953. Stalin - a nom de guerre meaning 'man of steel' - was a Georgian who was expelled from an Orthodox seminary for unruly behaviour. Rising rapidly in the Communist hierachy he became head of the party and established one of the worst tyrannies ever seen - the collectivisation of agriculture and the elimination of dissidents cost countless lives. By a series of five year plans he advanced Soviet industry rapidly and made the USSR a world power. After leading the Soviet Union to victory in World War II - during the early stages of which he annexed territories from most of his western neighbours including all three Baltic Republics - Stalin imposed Communist regimes upon eastern Europe.
GEORGY MAKSIMILIANOVICH MALENKOV 6 Mar 1953-Feb 1955, b 8 Jan 1902.
Marshal **NIKOLAI ALEKSANDROVICH BULGA-NIN 8 Feb 1955-Mar 1958,** b 11 Jun 1895; d 24 Feb 1975.
NIKITA SERGEYEVICH KHRUSCHEV 27 Mar 1958-Oct 1964, b 17 Apr 1894; d 11 Sep 1971. Khruschev, son of a Ukrainian miner, denounced Stalin and his personality cult and advocated 'peaceful coexistence' with the West. The loss of prestige incurred over the Cuban missile crisis

and the failure of his agricultural development plans (the virgin lands) contributed to his downfall.
ALEXEI NIKOLAIEVICH KOSYGIN since 15 Oct 1964, b 20 Feb 1904.

First Secretaries of the Communist Party

Marshal **JOSIF VISSARIONOVICH DJUGASHVI-LI STALIN Dec 1922-5 Mar 1953.**
GEORGY MAKSIMILIANOVICH MALENKOV 6-14 Mar 1953.
NIKITA SERGEYEVICH KHRUSCHEV 14 Mar 1963-Oct 1964.
LEONID ILICH BREZHNEV since 15 Oct 1964.

United Arab Emirates

A federal state consisting of the Shaikhdoms of the former Trucial Coast (Abu Dhabi, Ajman, Dubai, Fujeirah, Ras al Khaimah, Sharjah and Umm al Qaiwain), the United Arab Emirates came into being as an independent sovereign nation on 2 Dec 1971. (Ras al Khaimah joined the federation on 23 Dec 1971, three weeks after all seven states ceased to enjoy the British protection established in 1892.)

Federal President

Shaikh **ZAYED bin SULTAN al NAHAYYAN** (Ruler of Abu Dhabi) **since 2 Dec 1971,** b 1918.

Federal Vice-President

Shaikh **RASHID bin SA'ID al MAKTOUM** (Ruler of Dubai) **since 2 Dec 1971,** b 1914.

Federal Prime Minister

Shaikh **MAKTOUM bin RASHID al MAKTOUM since 9 Dec 1971.**

United Arab Republic, The *see* Egypt

The United Kingdom of Great Britain and Northern Ireland

ENGLAND was subdivided into a number of small Kingdoms until finally united by King Athelstan (927-939) who became monarch of all England except Cumbria. WALES, originally several Kingdoms, passed under English rule in the 13th century but was not formally united with England until the reign of Henry VIII. SCOTLAND remained an independent Kingdom, despite the union of the crowns in 1603 when James VI of the Scots became James I of England, until 1 May 1707 when the Act of Union between England and Scotland came into force. IRELAND, in which English involvement began in the reign of Henry I, entered the union on 1 Jan 1801 when the United Kingdom of Great Britain and Ireland was established. The Irish Free State (later the Irish Republic) came into being in 1922, the six counties of Northern Ireland remaining British - the name of the nation then being changed to the United Kingdom of Great Britain and Northern Ireland.

England

ANGLO-SAXON KINGDOMS

The first of the Anglo-Saxon kingdoms, which were popularly known as the Heptarchy, was founded in the latter half of the 5th century. Although about a dozen such states may have existed in the 6th century, within 250 years only three remained - Wessex, Mercia and Northumbria. In Anglo-Saxon Kingdoms monarchs sometimes reigned jointly.

† Kings of Kent

Traditionally founded by Hengist and Horsa, Kent was the first Anglo-Saxon Kingdom in England. The early genealogy of the Kentish Kings is remarkably complete, but the existence of some of the later rulers is known only through the evidence of coins and charters.

HENGIST *c*455-*c*488. The founder of the Kentish Kingdom.

HORSA *c*455 killed in battle at Aylesford, brother of Hengist. He was regarded as joint ruler with his brother.

OISC (or ESC, also called Oeric) **488-*c*512**, son of Hengist.

OCTA *fl.* **early 6th century**, son of Hengist or of Oisc.

EORMENRIC, son of Octa or of Oisc; d *c* 560.

AETHELBERT I   560-24 Feb 616, son of Eormenric. Having initially confined St Augustine to Thanet, a suspicious King Aethelbert, who had a Christian Frankish wife, eventually received the missionary in Canterbury where he was allowed to build a monastery. Augustine baptised the hesitant Aethelbert as the first Christian English King.

EADBALD   Feb 616-20 Jan 640, son of Aethelbert I.

EARCONBERT   Jan 640-14 Jul 664, son of Eadbald. Earconbert restored Christianity which his pagan father had renounced.

EGBERT I (or ECGBRIHT I) **Jul 664-4 Jul 673**, son of Earconbert.

HLOTHERE (or LOTHERE) **Jul 673-6 Feb 685**, son of Earconbert.

EADRIC   Feb 685-Aug 686, son of Egbert I. In 686 Caedwalla, King of the West Saxons, overran Kent. In the resulting anarchy several kings reigned.

SUAEBHARD (or WEBHERD) *fl.*690s. Suaebhard may have been a member of the East Saxon royal house.

OSWINI *fl.* late 680s, joint ruler with Suaebhard?

WIHTRED   late 690-23 Apr 725, son of Egbert I.

EADBERT   725-748 or 762, son of Wihtred.

AETHELBERT II   725-762, brother of Eadbert, with whom he reigned.

EARDWULF   *fl.*747, probably dependent on Mercia.

SIGERED   *fl.*762, probably dependent on Mercia.

HEABERHT   *fl.*765, probably dependent on Mercia.

EGBERT II (or ECGBRIHT II) *c*765-*c*780, probably dependent on Mercia.

EALHMUND   *fl.*784, possibly the father of Egbert, King of Wessex.

EADBERT PRAEN   796-798. He was deposed and mutilated by Coenwulf, King of Mercia.

CUTHRED   *c*798-807, a member of the Mercian royal house - probably a puppet King.

EADWALD is known to have reigned briefly but it is not certain when. Either 798 or 807 seem the most likely dates.

BALDRED   ?-825. Expelled by Egbert, King of Wessex (825) Baldred was the last Kentish King.

† Kings of the South Saxons (Sussex)

There are considerable gaps in the list of the rulers of Sussex: the genealogy of the South Saxon kings has been lost and some names are known from charters only. It is possible that some of the Kings listed reigned only in the sub-kingdom of the Haestingas (Hastings) corresponding with the present county of East Sussex.

AELLE (or AELLA) *c*477-491 or later. Landing at Selsey in 477, Aelle carved out a Kingdom in West Sussex.

CISSA   *fl.*500, probably the son of Aelle who is known to have had a son called Cissa.

AETHELWALH (or AETHELWALCH) **before 674-*c*685** when he was killed in battle by Caedwalla King of Wessex. When St Wilfrid came to Sussex (*c*681), Aethelwalh encouraged him in the conversion of Sussex to Christianity.

BERTHUN   *fl.*685. With Andhun, Berthun drove Caedwalla from the Kingdom but was killed by the West Saxons.

ANDHUN   *fl.*685.

NOTHELM (or NUNNA) *fl.*700.

WATT   *fl.*700.

AETHELSTAN   *fl.*714.

AETHELBERT   *c*725-*c*750.

OSMUND   *c*758-*c*772.

OSWALD *fl.*772.

OSLAC *fl.*772.

EALDWULF *c*772-*c*791.

AELFWALD *fl.* end of 8th century. From the 770s the South Saxons were dependent on Mercia, and by the end of the century Sussex had ceased to exist as an independent Kingdom.

† Kings of the West Saxons (Wessex)

The small Kingdom of the Gewissae had by the mid-7th century become Wessex covering most of southern England. The West Saxon Royal House united England under Athelstan and are the ancestors of the present Royal Family.

CERDIC   519-534. A Saxon adventurer, but curiously with a Celtic name, Cerdic conquered parts of modern Hampshire and the Isle of Wight to found the Kingdom of the Gewissae which he ruled jointly with his grandson, Cynric.

CYNRIC   519-560 when he was expelled, grandson of Cerdic.

CEAWLIN   560-591, son of Cynric; d 593. Driving the Britons from the southern Midlands, Ceawlin greatly extended the area of the West Saxon Kingdom from which he was expelled in 591.

CEOL   591-597, grandson of Ceawlin.

CEOLWULF   597-611, brother of Ceol.

CYNEGILS   611-643, probably the son of Ceol.

CWICHELM   *c*626-636, son of Cynegils, he was joint king with his father.

CUTHRED   ?-643; d 661, son of Cwichelm, joint king with his grandfather until the latter's death in 643; he may have reigned with Cenwalh also.

CENWALH   643-645; 648-674, son of Cynegils. Cenwalh was deposed for three years when Penda of Mercia invaded the kingdom.

SEAXBURH   (Queen) 672-674, the wife of Cenwalh, Queen Seaxburh reigned jointly with her husband and then as sole ruler in her widowhood. (CENFUS, a great-grandson of Ceolwulf, may have reigned jointly with Cenwalh.)

AESCWINE   674-676, son of Cenfus.

CENTWINE   676-685, son of Cynegils. Centwine was overthrown by Caedwalla in 685, in which year he died.

CAEDWALLA   685-688 abdicated, a usurper who was probably descended from Cealwin, despite his Celtic name, b *c*659; d 20 Apr 689. After unsuccessfully attempting to take Sussex, Caedwalla seized the Kingdom of the Gewissae (which under him became known as the West Saxon Kingdom). After three turbulent years in which he devastated the South East, he abdicated (688) and went to Rome where he died ten days after his baptism.

INE   (or Ina) 688-726 abdicated, probably descended from Cealwin; d 726 in Rome where he went after his abdication. Ine, an important patron of the monasteries, greatly strengthened Wessex and drew up a legal code.

AETHELHEARD   726-*c*740.

CUTHRED   740-756, related to Aethelheard.

SIGEBERHT   756-757. Sigeberht was dethroned and possibly killed by Cynewulf in 757.

CYNEWULF   757-786. Cynewulf was assassinated at Merton by Cyneheard the brother of Sigeberht.

BEORHTRIC   786-802.

EGBERT   802-839, descended from a brother of Ine. In defeating the Mercian Beornwulf at the Battle of Ellendun (825), he was acknowledged as King in Kent, Sussex, East Anglia and Essex.

AETHELWULF   839-855, son of Egbert.

AETHELBALD   855-860, son of Aethelwulf.

AETHELBERT   860-866, brother of Aethelbald. Having succeeded to the Kingdoms of Kent, Sussex and Essex in 855, Aethelbert reunited the Kingdom of Egbert upon the death of Aethelbald.

AETHELRED   866-871, brother of Aethelbert. Aethelred fought the invading Danes in Mercia, and then in Wessex itself.

ALFRED   871-899, brother of Aethelred, b 849. A surprise attack by the Danes in mid-winter (878) forced Alfred to withdraw into Athelney from where he employed guerilla tactics against his enemy until his victory at Edington (Wiltshire). He then contained the Danish menace to Wessex by building a series of fortresses (burhs) and by creating a fleet of ships. A pious man, greatly influenced by his childhood visits to Rome, Alfred had several books produced, including his English translation of Augustine's Soliloquies, although he could neither read nor write until the age of 38.

EDWARD the Elder   899-925, son of Alfred. With the help of his sister Aethelflaed, Edward retook all of the Midlands south of the Trent from the Danes.

ATHELSTAN   925-927 as King of Wessex; then became the first King of England through his conquests; son of Edward the Elder.

† Kings of the East Saxons (Essex)

Little is known about the East Saxon Kingdom (which included Middlesex and Hertfordshire as well as Essex) before the beginning of the 7th century.

SAEBERHT   before 604-616 or 617.

SEXRED   616 or 617-617 killed in battle fighting the West Saxons. Joint king with Saeweard.

SAEWEARD   616 or 617-617 killed by the West Saxons.

SIGEBERHT I   ('Parvus') fl. before *c*653, son of Saeweard.

SIGEBERHT II   (Saint) *c*653-664. Also called St Sebbi.

SWITHELM   *c*653-664.

SIGHERE   664-675 or later, son of Sigeberht I. Sighere was the husband of St Osyth.

SEBBI   664-*c*694, grandson of Sigeberht II. Sebbi reigned jointly with Sighere and later with his own son Sigeheard in whose favour he abdicated shortly before his death.

SIGEHEARD c694-c709, son of Sebbi.

SWAEFRED c694-c709, son of Sigeheard with whom he reigned.

OFFA fl.709, son of Sighere. Offa died in or after 709 in which year he abdicated and journeyed to Rome.

SAELRED c709-746, son of St Sigeberht.

SWAEFBERHT (or Swebert); d 738 having probably reigned jointly with Saelred.

SWITHRED c746-758 or later, descended from Sebbi.

SIGERIC fl. late 8th century, son of Saelred. Sigeric may have abdicated in 798 when he went to Rome.

SIGERED c799-823 or later, son of Sigeric. In 825 Essex submitted to King Egbert of Wessex.

† Kings of East Anglia

Few details of the rulers of East Anglia are known before the accession of Redwald.

REDWALD c600-616 or 627. A pagan who was recognised by his contemporaries as the most powerful king of his time.

EARPWALD c616 or 627-627 or 628, son of Redwald.

SIGEBERHT 630 or 631-?, half-brother of Earpwald. Having abdicated, Sigeberht retired to a monastery from which he was taken by Ecgric and was killed in battle by Penda of Mercia.

ECGRIC fl. first half of 7th century, related to Sigeberht with whom he reigned and whom he succeeded.

ANNA ?-654 murdered, nephew of Redwald.

AETHELHERE 654-15 Nov 654 killed at the battle of the Winwaed with his ally Penda; brother of Anna.

AETHELWOLD late 654-664, brother of Anna.

ALDWULF 663 or 664-713, related to Aethelhere.

ALFWOLD c713-749, the son or brother of Aldwulf.

BEORNA (or BEONNA) fl. late 8th century. Beorna, who seems to be regarded as the heir of Alfwold, divided the Kingdom with Hun and Alberht (749). It is possible that he reunited the inheritance as his successor, Aethelred, seems to have been undisputed King.

HUN fl. late 8th century.

ALBERHT fl. late 8th century.

AETHELRED fl. late 8th century, is recorded as the heir of Beorna.

AETHELBERT ?-794 in which year he was beheaded upon the orders of Offa of Mercia; son of Aethelred.

ATHELSTAN fl. early 9th century.

AETHELWEARD fl. mid 9th century.

EDMUND (Saint) 855-20 Nov 870, b 841 or 842. Edmund was taken captive when his army was defeated by Danish invaders. Legend states that, having refused to share his realm with pagans, he was tied to a tree and slain by a shower of arrows. His body was later buried in an abbey which became known as Bury St. Edmunds.

OSWALD fl. late 9th century.

† Danish Kings of East Anglia

ATHELSTAN (or GUTHRUM) 880-890. Guthrum was that Danish ruler who was baptised at Wedmore, following Alfred's victory at Edington. Taking Athelstan as his Christian name, he retired to East Anglia to found a Danish Kingdom.

ERIC (Eohric) c890-902. Eric was killed in Holmesdale (Surrey) fighting a Kentish army.

† Kings of Mercia

The Kingdom of the Angles of the 'march' (border) emerged through the consolidation of earlier units in the first decades of the 7th century. Under Aethelbald and Offa, Mercia almost succeeded in uniting England, but the Kingdom was overthrown by the Danes in the latter half of the 9th century.

PENDA c626 or late 632-15 Nov 654, b c575. Sometimes misrepresented as an active persecutor of Christians, the powerful pagan Penda ended the supremacy of Christian Northumbria in a series of wars which were territorial rather than religious in origin. Having killed both Edwin (632) and Oswald (641) of the Northumbrians, Penda himself was slain in the Battle of the Winwaed by Oswiu.

EOWA ?-641 when he was killed, the brother of Penda with whom he reigned.

WULFHERE 657-674, son of Penda. After two years when Oswiu of Northumbria ruled Mercia, Wulfhere captured his father's throne and re-established the primacy of the central Kingdom. The extent of his power can be judged by his invasion of the Isle of Wight (661).

AETHELRED 674-704 abdicated to become a monk, son of Penda; d 716.

BERHTWALD c685, brother of Wulfhere; co-ruler with Aethelred.

COENRED 704-709 abdicated, son of Wulfhere; d on pilgrimage in Rome.

CEOLRED 709-716, son of Aethelred.

AETHELBALD 716-757, grandson of Eowa. Irreligious and without compassion, Aethelbald defeated the Northumbrians, harassed Wessex and contained the Welsh. The most powerful monarch of his day, he styled himself 'King of Britain'. He was murdered at Seckington, near Tamworth.

BEONRED 757; was killed by Offa.

OFFA 757-Jul 796, descended from Eowa. Offa, who claimed to be 'King of the English', became overlord of all southern and central England and had Offa's Dyke constructed as a visible boundary with the Welsh. A great King, he was treated as an equal by Charlemagne; he encouraged trade with the Continent and he patronised monasteries, but like Aethelbald he was cruel and little touched by civilisation.

EGFRITH   787-14 or 17 Dec 796, son of Offa. Egfrith reigned with his father but survived him by only five months.

COENWULF   Dec 796-821, claimed descent from Penda's father.

CEOLWULF I   821-823 when he was deposed and exiled, brother of Coenwulf.

BEORNWULF   823-825. Defeated by Egbert of Wessex in 825, he was killed by the East Angles in the same year.

LUDECAN   825-827 murdered.

WIGLAF   827-829 when he was deposed by Egbert; restored 830-840.

BEORHTWULF   840-852. Defeated by the invading Danes (852), his fate is not certain, but there is a strong tradition that he was killed.

BURGRED (or BURHRED) 852-874 when he was expelled by the Danes. He went to Rome where he died in 874 or 875.

CEOLWULF II   874-?. A puppet King set up by the Danes, Ceolwulf had ceased to reign before 883 when west Mercia acknowledged Alfred.

† Kings of Deira

Deira, between the Tees and the Humber, was eventually absorbed by its more powerful northern neighbour, Bernicia, to form the Kingdom of the Northumbrians. Curiously both names - Deira and Bernicia - are Celtic and therefore of considerable antiquity.

AELLI   559 or 560-c589. On Aelli's death Deira was ruled by Bernicia until 616.

EDWIN   616-12 Oct 632, son of Aelli, b 584. Returning from exile in East Anglia, Edwin united Deira and Bernicia to become King of Northumbria. He was killed by Penda in the Battle of Hatfield Moors (near Doncaster). He was converted to Christianity by Paulinus.

OSRIC   late 632-summer 633, nephew of Aelli. After the death of Osric, Oswald united Deira and Bernicia.

OSWINE   644-20 Aug 651 murdered, son of Osric.

AETHELWALD   summer 651-late 654 or 655, son of Oswald of Bernicia. Aethelwald was deprived of Deira after the Battle of the Winwaed, probably because of his failure to support Oswiu in that battle.

† Kings of Bernicia

At the end of the 6th century Bernicia, which stretched north as far as the Firth of Forth, took over its southern neighbour Deira to form the Kingdom of the Northumbrians.

IDA   547-559. The names of the next six Bernician Kings are known but there is no agreement about their order let alone their dates.

GLAPPA (or CLAPPA.)

ADDA.

THEODRIC (or DEORIC.)

FRIDUUALD (or FRITHEWLF.)

HUSSA.

EATHELRIC (or AEDILRIC), was probably the King who united Deira and Bernicia in 588.

AETHELFRITH   592 or 593-616 defeated and killed at the Battle of the Idle when Edwin was placed over Deira and Bernicia by Redwald of East Anglia. Son of Eathelric. Ruler of both Northumbrian Kingdoms.

EANFRITH   late 632-633, son of Aethelfrith. Eanfrith succeeded to Bernicia upon the death of Edwin.

OSWALD (Saint) 633-5 Aug 641 killed by Penda at Mirfield, near Huddersfield; son of Aethelfrith, b 604. Oswald restored Christianity to Northumbria and that Kingdom to a position of supremacy in England. Oswald came to be regarded as a martyr for Christianity.

† Kings of Northumbria

OSWIU   King of Bernicia late 641-654; King of Northumbria 654-15 Feb 670, son of Aethelfrith, b 612. In killing Penda at the Battle of the Winwaed (Nov 654), Oswiu gained revenge for the death of his sainted brother, momentarily destroyed the power of Mercia and was able finally to unite Deira and Bernicia.

EGFRITH   Feb 670-20 May 685 killed, son of Oswiu.

EALDFRITH   May 685-14 Dec 704, son (possibly illegitimate) of Oswiu.

EADWULF   late 704-early 705.

OSRED I   705-716 killed, son of Ealdfrith, b 696 or 697.

COENRED   716-718.

OSRIC   718-9 May 729 killed, son of Ealdfrith.

CEOLWULF   729-731 when he was deposed; restored 731-737 or 738 abdicated to become a monk, brother of Coenred; d 764 (or 760).

EADBERT   737-757 or 758 abdicated to become a monk; d 19 or 20 Aug 768.

OSWULF (or OSULF) 757 or 758-24 or 25 Jul 758 when he was murdered by his own servants, son of Eadbert.

AETHELWALD MULL   758 or 759-30 Oct 765 when he was was deposed and exiled. His subsequent fate is not known.

ALCHRED   765-Easter 774 deposed.

AETHELRED I   774-778 or 779 when he was deposed, son of Aethelwald Mull.

ELFWALD I   778 or 779-23 Sep 788 murdered, son of Oswulf.

OSRED II   788-790, son of Alchred; killed 14 Sep 792 on returning from exile.

AETHELRED I   790-18 Apr 796.

OSBALD   796 - a reign of 27 days; exiled, he died in 799.

EARDWULF   14 May 796-806 or 808 when he was deposed; momentarily restored 808.

ELFWALD II   806 or 808-808 or 810.

EANRED   808 or 810-840 or 841, son of Eardwulf.

AETHELRED II   840 or 841-844 when he was deposed, son of Eanred.

REDWULF   844. He usurped the throne.

AETHELRED II 844-c849.

OSBERT c849-862 or 863 when he was deposed. Osbert was recalled when Northumbria was seriously threatened by the Danes, but both he and the usurper Aelle were killed by the Danes (21 Mar 867).

AELLE 862, 863 or 867-21 Mar 867 when he was killed by the Danes.. Aelle, who was unrelated to the Northumbrian Royal House, was unable to withstand the Danes, who captured York and killed this usurping King.

OSBERT 867 killed by the Danes.

EGBERT I 867-872 or 873; d 873. A puppet King set up by the Danes.

RICSIGE 873-876. He was dependent upon the Danes.

EGBERT II 876-c873. Upon his death Northumbria was absorbed by the Scandinavian Kingdom of York.

† Scandinavian Kings of York

HALFDAN I 875 or 876-877 or 883. There is a tradition that Halfdan, the founder of the Kingdom, was killed in Ireland after his deposition.

GUTHFRITH I 883-894 or 896.

SIEFRED - dates unknown.

CNUT - dates unknown.

AETHELWALD c899; killed at the Battle of the Holme (Holmesdale) 902. The son of Edward the Elder, Aethelwald was driven from Wessex and took refuge in York where the Danes received him as King.

HALFDAN II c902-910 was killed at the Battle of Tettenhall (Wolverhampton) by a Saxon army.

EOWILS ?-910 killed at Tettenhall, brother of and co-King with Halfdan.

IVAR ?-910; Ivar perished at Tettenhall with his two co-monarchs. The brother of Eowils and Halfdan.

RAGNALD 919-921. Invading Northumbria c915, Ragnald took York in 919.

SIHTRIC CAOCH 921-927, related to Ragnald.

GUTHFRITH II 927, was deposed by Athelstan.

ANLAF GUTHFRITHSON late 939 or early 940-941, son of Guthfrith.

ANLAF SIHTRICSON 941-943 when he was exiled.

RAGNALD GUTHFRITHSON 943-944 deposed and probably killed by Edmund I of England.

ERIC (nicknamed Bloodaxe) **948.** This Norwegian prince made two attempts to establish himself in York.

ANLAF SIHTRICSON (OLAF SIHTRICSON) **949-952** deposed.

ERIC 952-954 deposed and killed. In 954 the Northumbrians submitted to King Edred.

THE KINGDOM OF ENGLAND

† Kings

Saxon Kings

ATHELSTAN 927-27 Oct 939, son of Edward the Elder, King of Wessex. Having succeeded to the throne of Wessex (925), Athelstan became the first King to be recognised as monarch of all England, except Cumbria, and was acknowledged as overlord by the rulers of Wales and southern Scotland. In 937 he won an important victory over the invading Scots and Irish-Norse at Brunanburh. Athelstan was an avid collector of books and relics.

EDMUND I 939-20 May 946, younger half-brother of Athelstan. Edmund, called the Etheling, did not gain control of all England until shortly before he was assassinated by Leofa, a robber, at Pucklechurch (now in Avon) on 20 May 946.

EDRED May 946-23 Nov 955, younger brother of Edmund I.

EDWY Nov 955-1 Oct 959, elder son of Edmund I, b c940-1.

EDGAR Oct 959-8 Jul 975, younger son of Edmund I, b c943. Rebelling against Edwy, Edgar became ruler of Mercia in 957, and succeeded his brother two years later. Called 'the Peaceful', he was a firm and capable King acknowledged as overlord by the other British Kings - the legend that they rowed him across the Dee at Chester cannot be proved. Genuinely religious, Edgar encouraged a monastic revival.

EDWARD the Martyr Jul 975-18 Mar 978 stabbed to death at Corfe Castle (Dorset) by the servants of Ethelred; elder son of Edgar, b c962.

ETHELRED Mar 978-1013 when he was deposed by Swegn; younger son of Edgar and half-brother of Edward the Martyr. Called the Unready (Un-raed meaning badly advised), he would have been better dubbed the Unlucky. A not very able leader, he faced most capable Danish opposition, was dethroned and exiled, and after Swegn's death had to contest his throne with his own son and Cnut.

Danish King

SWEGN (or SVEN) **1013-3 Feb 1014.** Swegn, nicknamed Forkbeard, invaded in 1013 either to avenge the death of a sister in England or to punish a deserting commander. The real goal, conquest, was quickly and savagely achieved, but death made his triumph brief.

Saxon Kings

ETHELRED Feb 1014-23 Apr 1016.

EDMUND II Apr 1016-16 Nov 1016, son of Ethelred. Deprived of most of the Kingdom but Wessex by the Danes, Edmund (Ironside) was defeated by Cnut at the Battle of Ashingdon, and died mysteriously afterwards.

DANISH KINGS

CNUT (CANUTE) Dec 1016-12 Nov 1035, son of Swegn, b *c* 995. A successful King, who was also ruler of Denmark (1018-1035) and Norway (1028-1035), he established order and worked to reconcile the conquerors and the conquered. Although feared, he achieved popularity, becoming the subject of legends including the improbable tale about the tide. Cnut married Ethelred's widow, despite having another 'wife': pious in other ways his Christianity did not include monogamy.

HAROLD I Nov 1035-17 Mar 1040, illegitimate son of Cnut, b *c* 1016/1017. At first styling himself regent, Harold usurped the throne left to his half-brother Harthacnut.

HARTHACNUT 1040-8 Jun 1042, son of Cnut, b *c* 1018. A vigorous ruler, whose ambiguous arrangements for the succession resulted in the Norwegian invasion in 1066, Harthacnut suffered a fatal collapse while over-indulging himself at a wedding feast.

SAXON KINGS

EDWARD the Confessor Jun 1042-5 Jan 1066, son of Ethelred and half-brother of Harthacnut, b 1002/5. Although Edward was of the old English line, he was foreign in outlook having been brought up in Normandy. In 1051 he made the Norman Duke William his heir, but this arrangement was probably repudiated later. A pious man, the Confessor became dominated by his relations by marriage, Earl Godwin and his son Harold, in whose hands the government of the Kingdom effectively rested.

HAROLD II 6 Jan-14 Oct 1066, brother-in-law of Edward the Confessor. Harold, a leader of proven ability, was chosen as King at a moment when England faced invasion on two fronts. On 25 Sep he beat the Norwegian Harald Hardrada at Stamford Bridge (now in Humberside); then, having marched his army south with amazing speed, and inexplicably not waiting for reinforcements, he faced William at Battle on 14 Oct. The Normans depicted Harold as a usurping perjurer for in 1064, while a 'guest' in Normandy, he had sworn to respect William's claim to the crown, but the oath was taken under duress.

(**EDGAR (the Aetheling) (Oct 1066),** grandson of Edmund II. Chosen as King by the Londoners after the Battle of Hastings, Edmund submitted to William the Conqueror.)

HOUSE OF NORMANDY

WILLIAM I 25 Dec 1066-9 Sep 1087, b 1027 or 1028. As Duke of Normandy - a title he inherited despite his illegitimacy - William showed military skill overcoming rebellion and French invasions. A ruthless ruler with extraordinary energy, he put down the northern revolt (1069-70) with atrocity; he confiscated Saxon lands to reward those Norman lords who had brought him victory at Hastings; he ordered the Domesday Survey (1085 onwards) and did much to create a unified England by modifying the feudal system to demand the allegiance of vassals as well as tenants thus preventing the emergence in England of those semi-independent barons who bedevilled medieval Europe. He died from injuries received falling from his horse at the seige of Mantes.

WILLIAM II 26 Sep 1087-2 Aug 1100, second surviving son of William I, b *c* 1057. Called Rufus on account of his red hair, William was an effective ruler, but as his only interest in religion seems to have been episcopal revenues, he has had a particularly 'bad press' from the chroniclers, mainly churchmen. Certainly he was a licentious and blasphemous cynic, but the most vicious charges made against him are not proven. His death from a stray arrow released by Tirrel was probably accidental, although historians have constructed conspiracy theories.

HENRY I 5 Aug 1100-1 Dec 1135, younger brother of William II, b 1068. After Rufus' death, Henry seized the throne claiming that as he had been born 'in the purple' - that is while his father reigned - his right was superior to that of his elder brother, Robert. A notoriously avaricious man, Henry II was much troubled by the succession after the death of his only surviving son, William (1120) - it is ironic that he had up to a dozen illegitimate sons. He made the barons recognise his daughter Matilda as his heir, and it seems inconceivable that he should have designated his nephew on his deathbed, as Stephen claimed, after taking such care to secure Matilda's position.

HOUSE OF BLOIS

STEPHEN 22 Dec 1135-Apr 1141 deposed, nephew of Henry I, b *c* 1100. A brave and popular man of great personal charm, Stephen usurped a crown he was totally unsuited to wear. As he was unable to control the barons the country collapsed into disorder and in 1139 Matilda landed to claim her inheritance. In the resulting civil war, he was defeated and captured at the Battle of Lincoln (2 Feb 1141). Matilda reigned briefly, but was forced to release Stephen the following November but the war continued until 1148 when she retired to Normandy. Stephen accepted her son Henry as his heir when his own son Eustace died.

HOUSE OF NORMANDY

MATILDA (Queen) Sovereign *de jure* from the death of Henry I; 'Lady of England' *de facto* **Apr-Nov 1141,** only surviving legitimate child of Henry I, b Feb 1102; d 10 Sep 1167. Married at 12 to the elderly German Emperor, widowed at 23 and remarried against her will at 28 to a boy, Geoffrey of Anjou, Matilda became an obstinate woman. Between 1139 and 1148, with her half-brother Robert of Gloucester as commander, she challenged Stephen for her throne which she secured in Apr 1141 being proclaimed 'Lady of England'. Forced to flee London, which she had alienated by her manner and heavy taxation, her brief supremacy ended when forced to exchange Stephen for Robert (Nov 1141), and when the latter died her campaign collapsed. She returned to England in her son's reign.

HOUSE OF BLOIS
STEPHEN   Nov 1141-25 Oct 1154.

HOUSE OF ANJOU
HENRY II   19 Dec 1154-6 Jul 1189, eldest son of Matilda, b 5 Mar 1133. Henry II inherited England, Normandy, Anjou and Maine from his parents and Aquitaine from his wife, Eleanor. Well educated, he was responsible for important legal reforms; modest, he lived frugally but was generous to the poor. It is unfortunate that this just King should be chiefly remember for the death of Becket for which he was not directly responsible. Henry's health was broken by the rebellions of his Queen and his treacherous sons. (HENRY the Young King (14 Jun 1170-11 Jun 1183), second son of Henry II, b 28 Feb 1155. King of England in his father's lifetime, Henry the Young King - who predeceased Henry II - rewarded his father's gift of association in the Royalty with revolt.)
RICHARD I   3 Sep 1189-6 Apr 1199 wounded at the siege of Chalus, he died of gangrene, third son of Henry II, b 8 Sep 1157. To the detriment of his people, Richard became obsessed with the noble aim of freeing Jerusalem from the Saracens, and all but a few months of his reign were spent abroad. Brave and chivalrous, he won the name 'Lion-Heart' but the Crusades failed. Journeying home he was captured and held for ransom by Leopold of Austria, with whom he had quarrelled at the seige of Acre. A complex character, Richard was a popular hero, brilliant strategist, poet and musician but given to unnatural vice and neglectful of his Kingdom - the cost of the Crusade, his ransom and the French war bankrupted England.
JOHN   27 May 1199-18 or 19 Oct 1216, fifth son of Henry II, b 24 Dec 1167. In Richard's absence John deposed the tactless Norman regent and misruled like a Midas in reverse. The chroniclers presented this humorous rogue as an ogre, but they were clerics and he was a cynical agnostic. Although responsible for the death of his nephew Arthur, John was not a usurper as is often claimed for he was named heir by his dying brother. His indolence lost most of the French possessions; his stormy relations with the Church led to excommunication. The barons forced him to make concessions in the Magna Carta (1215), a document originally concerned with barons' rights but which gained importance when misinterpreted in Stuart times. His death, from dysentery, ended a short civil war in which those same barons treasonably involved the Dauphin.
HENRY III   28 Oct 1216-16 Nov 1272, elder son of John, b 1 Oct 1207. Henry III was a generous benefactor, a loyal husband, a great builder and an administrator who paid extraordinary attention to detail. The rebellion of the avaricious

barons led by de Montfort, notorious for his extortion, dominated the reign. It is a mistake to represent the barons as constitutional campaigners - the revolt was one against heavy taxes imposed to meet the King's extravagance - the nobles were guilty of the same offence against the peasants. The reforms won in the Statutes of Oxford and implemented in the Parliament of 1265 were intended to give the barons greater freedom of action and only gained constitutional importance much later.
EDWARD I   20 Nov 1272-7 Jul 1307, elder surviving son of Henry III, b c 17 Jun 1239. A just king, whose firm rule encouraged trade, Edward I wished to unite Britain. Invading Wales when Llywelyn refused to do homage, he conquered that country and secured it by building castles such as Caernarfon. There was to be little success, however, when he intervened in Scotland when the crown was contested. Selecting John Balliol, whom he expected to be a puppet, Edward became committed to the conquest of Scotland. Defeated by the campaigns of Wallace and Robert I, Edward I died when about to reinvade the northern Kingdom.
EDWARD II   8 Jul 1307-20 Jan 1327 when he was deposed, fourth but eldest surviving son of Edward I, b 25 Apr 1284; d 20 or 21 Sep 1327 when he was murdered by disembowelling at Berkeley Castle. Edward II was a lonely, introverted man of limited ability. He was dominated by his clever but sarcastic friend Gaveston, and later by the Despensers. The reign that saw the defeat of English ambition in Scotland at Bannockburn (1314) and considerable disorder at home ended savagely when he was deposed by the treachery of his Queen, Isabella, and Mortimer, her lover, and then brutally murdered.
EDWARD III   25 Jan 1327-21 Jun 1377, elder son of Edward II, b 13 Nov 1312. In founding the Order of the Garter and sponsoring tournaments, this chivalrous King sought to recreate Arthurian legends. When Philippe VI invaded English possessions in France, Edward claimed the throne of that country through his French mother - conveniently forgetting Salic law. Victories over France, by the Black Prince at Crécy, and over Scotland, when David II was taken prisoner, were won in 1346, but when Edward was elected Emperor he had to decline owing to his lack of capital. Further military success followed, including the battle of Poitiers (1356), but the French struggled to an eventual victory under du Guesclin. The great King was stricken by the loss of his heir and his beloved wife, and suffered a sad dotage dominated by a grasping mistress.
RICHARD II   22 Jun 1377-30 Sep 1399 when he was deposed, only surviving son of Edward the Black Prince, eldest son of Edward III, b 6 Jan 1367; d Feb? 1400 while imprisoned at Pontefract Castle. Still a boy, Richard showed bravery facing Wat Tyler's rebels, and it is likely that this

monarch of high ideals sympathised with the people. Richard II, a clever and cultured man, saw the need for peace to restore the economy but he was opposed by those who wished to continue the French war. The King tried to strengthen the crown's authority but, challenged by grasping disloyal relatives, he was deposed.

HENRY IV 30 Sep 1399-20 Mar 1413, son of John of Gaunt, fourth son of Edward III, b spring 1366. An unattractive figure, Henry, called Bolingbroke from his birthplace in Lincolnshire, usurped the crown but achieved little in a reign marked by war and rebellion, in particular Glyndwr's revolt in Wales.

HENRY V 21 Mar 1413-31 Aug 1422, eldest son of Henry IV, b c 16 Sep 1387. Popular for his great victories, including Agincourt (25 Oct 1415), Henry was a gifted King, extraordinarily conscientious in his duties. Claiming the French crown, he conquered the lands north of the Loire - helped by France's divisive factions. By the Treaty of Troyes, Henry was recognised as heir to Charles VI and married his daughter Catherine, but the peace was too humiliating to France to be expected to last.

HENRY VI 1 Sep 1422-4 Mar 1461 when he was deposed, only child of Henry V, b 6 Dec 1421; murdered in the Tower 21 May 1471. Infant-King to two Kingdoms, France was lost before his minority ended (1437). Meek and notoriously pious, Henry was nevertheless respected although he neglected the government and was more generous than he could afford to be. The War of the Roses broke out when the Duke of York, who had a better claim to the crown than Henry, was displaced in the order of succession by the birth of an heir to Henry's fiery Queen, Margaret. Suffering a breakdown (once interpreted as madness), Henry could not lead the Lancastrian fight but despite Margaret's spirited 'generalship' the king's armies were beaten and the King deposed. Briefly restored by Warwick, the 'King-Maker', Henry was murdered upon the return of Edward IV.

EDWARD IV 4 Mar 1461-6 Oct 1470 when he was deposed, eldest son of Richard, Duke of York, who was descended from Edward III's second and fourth sons, b 28 Apr 1442. Edward was a tall, good-looking philanderer and a capable but impetuous ruler whose firm rule restored prosperity and encouraged the first flowerings of the Renaissance in England. After his rash marriage to Elizabeth Woodville, whose avaricious relatives were resented, Warwick abandoned his protegé. Exiled, Edward soon reconquered his realm defeating Warwick at Barnet and Queen Margaret at Tewkesbury.

HENRY VI 6 Oct 1470-11 Apr 1471 deposed.

EDWARD IV 11 Apr 1471-9 Apr 1483.

EDWARD V 9 Apr-25 Jun 1483 when he was deposed, elder son of Edward IV, b 2 Nov 1470; d probably murdered in 1483, 1485, or 1486. Taking advantage of the unpopularity of the Woodvilles and of doubts concerning the legality of Edward IV's marriage, Richard of Gloucester usurped the throne of his nephew Edward V who was retired to the Tower and not seen again. It is impossible to say who murdered the 'Princes in the Tower' - Richard III, Buckingham and Henry VII have all been cast as the villain - but the most puzzling aspect of the affair is that the Bill of Henry VII attainting Richard III is silent on their fate.

RICHARD III 26 Jun 1483-22 Aug 1485, only surviving brother of Edward IV, b 2 Oct 1452. The ogre created by Tudor propaganda has obscured the real Richard III who was not a hunchback and who can neither be convicted nor cleared of the murder of his nephews. An able administrator and a brave soldier, Richard usurped the throne but was unable to win support from the most powerful nobles, including Buckingham, who attempted a coup in 1483, and the treacherous Stanley whose desertion cost Richard his crown and his life at the Battle of Bosworth.

HOUSE OF TUDOR

HENRY VII 21 Aug 1485-21 Apr 1509, son of Edmund Tudor, the son of Henry V's widow, and Margaret Beaufort, who was descended from John of Gaunt, b 27 Jan 1457. (Henry craftily dated his reign from the day before Bosworth to be able to treat those who had opposed him as traitors.) The hard-headed usurper who won the crown at Bosworth became an austere monarch who restored the Nation's solvency. His meanness is legendary but it was born out of necessity. He brought peace through the intelligent use of mercy, but recent research shows he was less conciliatory than used to be supposed. A parvenu with little real claim to the throne, Henry achieved 'respectability' through marriage to Elizabeth, daughter of Edward IV, and by matrimonial alliances with France, Aragon and Scotland. Despite the conspiracies of Lambert Simnel and 'Perkin Warbeck' (Pierre Osbecq), who claimed to be the Duke of York, Henry was able to leave a peaceful, stable Kingdom to his son.

HENRY VIII 22 Apr 1509-28 Jan 1547, only surviving son of Henry VII, b 28 Jun 1491. In a blood-stained reign Henry VIII degenerated from being a talented athletic youth to a gross cruel Bluebeard. Intolerant and suspicious, he used judical murder to remove opposition: judges, faithful servants, two wives (Anne Boleyn and Catherine Howard), the brilliant but unscrupulous Thomas Cromwell and those who opposed his religious settlement including the saintly More and Fisher. Disturbed at having no male heir and, besotted by Anne Boleyn, he tried to have his marriage to Catherine of Aragon annulled by the Pope. Frustrated in this, Henry, prompted by Thomas Cromwell, declared himself Head of the English Church - the Reformation, easily accomplished in an anti-clerical country at a time when the Church was rife with abuses, was not caused by 'The Divorce' but without the lead from the crown the break could not have happened. The early part of the reign was dominated by Wolsey who mismanaged the economy and pursued a futile foreign policy; the end of the reign saw Henry having to govern for himself - he produced debts and economic distress; the middle years belong to the extraordinary intellect of Thomas Cromwell who more than any other man created the modern nation state in England - despoiling the monasteries Cromwell used their wealth to restore england's finances; he formed recognisable government departments and achieved a revolution through Statute Law which he established as supreme. It is a fine irony that the genius of Thomas Cromwell by making the tyrant Henry VIII act through Parliament laid the foundations of constitutional monarchy.

EDWARD VI 28 Jan 1547-6 Jul 1553, only surviving son of Henry VIII, b 12 Oct 1537. An able but precocious child Edward VI played little part in his reign which was ended by the tolls of measles and smallpox upon a consumptive constitution. The first part of the reign, under Somerset, produced the beautiful Cranmerian Prayer Book and economic chaos; the later years belonged to Northumberland who tried to save his Protestant innovations by inducing Edward to will the crown to Jane Grey.

House of Grey

JANE (Queen) **10-19 Jul 1553,** Lady Jane Dudley, née Grey, grand-daughter of Henry VII's daughter Mary, b Oct 1537; executed after a rising in her favour 12 Feb 1554. Jane was not just the helpless puppet usually depicted: she firmly rejected the demands of her father-in-law, Northumberland, that her husband, Guilford Dudley, be made King.

House of Tudor

MARY I (Queen) **19 Jul 1553-17 Nov 1558,** elder daughter of Henry VIII, b 18 Feb 1516. Despite harsh treatment from her father, Mary remained generous, but her unpopular marriage to Philip of Spain (who became titular King of England) and her overzealous devotion to her religion alienated her subjects. Although reconciled to Rome, Protestant feeling remained strong in England and was strengthened by the burning of Latimer, Ridley, Cranmer, Hooper and others. She died still longing for a child and broken by the loss of Calais in a useless war in which she had felt obliged to support her Spanish husband.

ELIZABETH I (Queen) **17 Nov 1558-24 Mar 1603,** younger daughter of Henry VIII and half-sister of Mary I, b 7 Sep 1533. 'Gloriana' cast a spell over Court and subjects despite her unattractive jealousy and her extreme but enforced meanness. Politically gifted, she was lucky to have Burghley as chief minister and together they governed with great caution making the most of slight resources. The religious controversy was ended in a conciliatory manner, although Puritans and Catholics were persecuted. For political and personal reasons, she decided not to marry but she continued to encourage 'suitors' into the 1570s and was devoted to Robert Dudley.

The refugee Mary, Queen of Scots, was an embarrassment and the centre of plots. After being held captive for 19 years, she was finally executed. (Although Elizabeth's behaviour to her was shameful, it is difficult to see any alternative which would not have endangered the country.) After Mary's death and Elizabeth's military intervention in the Netherlands, England faced the Spanish Armada (Jul 1588) - Elizabeth's famous speech rallied her troops superbly at Tilbury, and the damage to the Armada begun by English guns at Gravelines was completed by storms. The great patroness of music and exploration became the legendary 'Faerie Queene' but her last years were marked by increasing Parliamentary defiance.

As she grew less like her portraits Elizabeth I painted her face and stuffed her cheeks to hide the wrinkles (Radio Times Hulton Picture Library)

House of Stuart

JAMES I 24 Mar 1603-27 Mar 1625, King of Scots, great-great-grandson of Henry VII, b 19 Jun 1566. Used to the tame Scottish Parliament, James I underestimated Westminster with which he was often in conflict. Coarse and slovenly, his behaviour was remarkable even by the standards of the day; conceited, his concept of the Divine Right of Kings alienated Parliament over which he lost control; extravagant, he lavished gifts on vicious young men particularly George Villiers; unpopular, even his escape from the Gunpowder Plot earned him little personal sympathy.

CHARLES I 27 Mar 1625-30 Jan 1649 when he was executed at Whitehall, second and only surviving son of James I, b 19 Nov 1600. A weakly child who had difficulty walking, he became a healthy but short, shy, lonely man with a stammer and a falsetto voice. Charles I was dignified and elegant, living a life remote from his subjects by whom he was not trusted having forfeited respect by making promises he could not keep. The Scottish Covenanters revolted against his attempts to impose an Anglican Prayer Book and they invaded England. The

King had to summon Parliament which he had dissolved after it overreached itself in 1629 and for 11 years Charles resorted to legal but dubious levies. The struggle between King and a Parliament of Puritans given to revolutionary excesses revived. Following Charles' attempt to seize Pym and his refusal to surrender command of the army which Parliament wished to deny him, the King had to leave hostile London. His vacillation lost the Civil War, but Parliament lost too for it became the captive of the army's radical republican leaders - Cromwell, etc. The military extremists purged Westminster, reducing it to a rubber-stamp and established the dictatorship that was to try and execute the King, who faced his death superbly.

THE COMMONWEALTH
Lords Protector of the Commonwealth

OLIVER CROMWELL 16 Dec 1653-3 Sep 1658, b 25 Apr 1599. Oliver Cromwell was a small farmer, Member of Parliament for Huntingdon, and the courageous captain of a troop of Parliamentary horse in the Civil War. Having won important victories with the New Model Army, he achieved supreme power under the Republic. The erstwhile defender of Parliament treated it with less respect than Charles I, excluding members who opposed him and then replacing it with a hand-picked radical assembly. He had himself proclaimed Lord Protector with sweeping dictatorial powers. Although he declined the title 'King' and his court was simple, it is possible to see ambition mixed with his higher motives. He effected a union of England, Scotland and Ireland, putting down civil war in the latter severely. He banned theatres, dancing and most pastimes, and, although he was sincere in his strict Puritanism, the dour religion of the Commonwealth and its thoughtless iconoclasm became unpopular. Perhaps the greatest success of his efficient administration was a foreign policy which restored England to the rank of a major power.

RICHARD CROMWELL 3 Sep 1658-25 May 1659 when he resigned, third but elder surviving son of Oliver Cromwell, b 4 Oct 1626; d 12 Jul 1712. An amiable but weak man, Richard Cromwell was not capable of exercising the powers of the Protector. After the Restoration he went into exile for 20 years.

THE KINGDOM OF ENGLAND
† Kings

House of Stuart

CHARLES II 30 Jan 1649-6 Feb 1685; his reign did not begin *de facto* until **29 May 1660,** eldest surviving son of Charles I, b 29 May 1630. After his ill-fated attempt on the throne (1650-1651) ending in defeat at Worcester and a dramatic escape, Charles II spent a decade as a poor exile.

Richard Cromwell was too weak to exercise the powers of Lord Protector and Parliament, its purged members restored by General Monk, negotiated the return of the King. This tactful monarch's character is hard to fathom - he treated friend and foe with the same cynical affability. A shrewd politician, he skilfully resisted attempts to exclude his Catholic brother James from the succession. The attention paid to his amorous adventures has obscured Charles' very real achievements in scientific and academic foundations and in patronising the Navy, architecture, painting and racing - he rode several winners at Newmarket himself.

JAMES II 6 Feb 1685-11 Dec 1688 when he fled - an act which legal fiction interpreted as abdication, only surviving brother of Charles II, b 14 Oct 1633. Humourless and stubborn, James initially had the support of his subjects, as the poor response to Monmouth's rebellion showed, but his manner and unwise policies lost him popularity. His suspension of penal legislation against Catholics and Protestant dissenters and his advancement of Catholics in administration was deeply resented. When seven bishops protested against the Declaration of Indulgence, the king overreacted and arrested them. The birth of the Prince of Wales, raising the prospect of a Catholic dynasty, brought ludicrous rumours of an imposture (the Warming Pan plot), and seven Anglican leaders invited William of Orange, James' son-in-law, to investigate. Deserted by his army and his family, the Dutch invasion panicked James to flight.

House of Orange and Stuart

WILLIAM III co-ruler **13 Feb 1689-28 Dec 1694**; sole ruler **28 Dec 1694-8 Mar 1702,** son-in-law and nephew of James II, b 4 Nov 1650. The elected Stadtholder of the United Provinces felt compelled to intervene in England to counter James II's pro-French policy which threatened the Dutch rather than to protect the dynastic interests of his wife. The Glorious Revolution was not a national movement but a constitutional change effected by Parliament and a small group of nobles. King at the invitation of Parliament (which had, however, little choice), William III's power was limited by the Bill of Rights. He achieved important army reforms, for which Marlborough is usually credited, and after quashing Jacobite revolts in Scotland and Ireland, he continued his Continental wars spending five months a year abroad.

MARY II (Queen) co-ruler **13 Feb 1689-28 Dec 1694,** wife of William III and elder surviving daughter of James II, b 30 Apr 1662. A woman of charm and good sense, Mary was deeply upset by the deposition of her father and only accepted the crown, which she insisted William should share, because she believed the Warming Pan story. Her presence on the throne gave the Revolution the support of many who were opposed to William.

HOUSE OF STUART

ANNE (Queen) **8 Mar 1702-1 Aug 1714,** younger sister of Mary II, b 6 Feb 1665. A small-minded, stout woman, Queen Anne suffered constant pain in her legs (possibly gout), and was often unable to walk. She had twelve miscarriages and five children, only one of whom survived infancy - but then died aged 12 - and interpreted this tragedy as divine retribution for her betrayal of her father. A devout Anglican, conscientious in her duties, Anne formed her policies almost entirely upon personalities. At first dominated by the bullying Sarah Churchill, she callously dismissed Marlborough, the victor of Blenheim, after quarrelling with his wife.

HOUSE OF HANOVER

GEORGE I 1 Aug 1714-11 Jun 1727, grandson of Elizabeth who was eldest daughter of James I - succeeded as the Act of Settlement excluded Catholics; b 28 May 1660. A shy, lonely man who left Hanover reluctantly, George I patronised Handel but his court was lacklustre - his wife had been imprisoned for adultery since 1694 and the King's unattractive mistresses seemed to emphasise the absence of a Queen Consort. Two crises rocked the throne: the Jacobite rebellion (1715) and the more serious South Sea Bubble which brought financial ruin to many. His command of English was poor, making his presence at Cabinet meetings difficult, and it is no accident that Walpole emerged in this reign eventually to occupy a position recognisable as Premier.

GEORGE II 11 Jun 1727-25 Oct 1760, only son of George I, b 30 Oct 1683. The last British monarch to lead his troops into battle (Dettingen 1743), George II longed for military glory and regarded the victories in Canada, the Caribbean and India in 1759 as the crowning glory of his reign. A brave, conscientious man, he remained calm throughout the 45 Rebellion and there is no evidence to support the claim that he packed his bags. He had a truly German passion for military history and uniforms and became increasingly intolerant of things English. His alarming temper was most often vented on his heir Frederick whom he hated.

GEORGE III 25 Oct 1760-29 Jan 1820, eldest son of George II's eldest son Frederick, b 4 Jun 1738. A popular King whose personal integrity strengthened the monarchy, 'Farmer George' wrote agricultural pamphlets under the name Ralph Robinson. George III over-protected his 15 children and his high-spirited spendthrift sons rebelled against the unpretentious domesticity of Kew. Much criticised for his political actions, his behaviour was in fact constitutional for he took no new powers upon himself and two of the premiers he chose enjoyed the confidence of Parliament for long periods: North for 10 years and Pitt the Younger for 21. George III and North have been held responsible for the loss of America and represented as tyrants whereas both reflected public opinion and neither acted

illegally. In 1788, 1801 and 1804 he suffered attacks of porphyria, a rare but particularly distressing and painful disease, which asserted itself permanently in 1810 when he lost his sight and reason (symptoms of the illness).

GEORGE IV 29 Jan 1820-26 Jun 1830, eldest son of George III, b 12 Aug 1762. George IV, who was Prince Regent during his father's illness (1810-1820), was a man of great taste and a leader of fashion who helped popularise the seaside resort. 'Prince Charming' became a gross wastrel and philanderer with a streak of cruelty that let him publicly mimic his father's insanity. His marriage to Maria Fitzherbert was invalid under the Royal Marriages Act and, in order that Parliament might cancel his debts, he wed the unattractive and unwashed Caroline of Brunswick. After the birth of Princess Charlotte they parted, Caroline going to Italy where she lived scandalously. Returning as Queen, she was turned away from the coronation but saved George further embarassment and controversy by dying soon afterwards.

WILLIAM IV 26 Jun 1830-20 Jun 1837, third son of George III, b 21 Aug 1765. A naval career, then years of enforced inactivity, left William IV untrained to rule, but then no one had expected him to succeed. Honest to the point of tactlessness, he enjoyed being King and his popularity increased at his request for a simple coronation and his initial support for the Reform Bill.

VICTORIA (Queen) **20 Jun 1837-22 Jan 1901,** daughter of Edward, Duke of Kent, fourth son of George III, b 24 May 1819. The young Queen relied on Melbourne; the old Queen trusted Disraeli and Salisbury but did not give Gladstone her confidence. The main influence on her was Prince Albert and together their strict morality had a great effect on society. Queen Victoria was often amused and had a rich sense of the ridiculous. The Prince Consort encouraged trade (The Great Exhibition), and had a moderating influence on foreign policy (eg The 'Trent' Incident). His early death prostrated her with grief and the seclusion of the 'Widow of Windsor' momentarily stirred a republicanism which was strengthened by a misunderstanding of her dependence on Brown, a servant whom Albert had valued. Enjoying the longest reign in British history, she saw her Golden and Diamond Jubilees celebrated with a very real affection throughout her Empire. Politically conservative and imperialist, she was never narrowly jingoistic and had a genuine concern for her colonial subjects, abhorring racialism and counselling restraint during the Indian mutiny.

HOUSE OF SAXE-COBURG AND GOTHA

EDWARD VII 22 Jan 1901-6 May 1910, eldest son of Victoria, b 9 Nov 1841. Even his tutors thought he was subjected to a too rigid education in a childhood which lacked affection. Later, denied a useful role by his mother, he led a life of

Queen Victoria with Albert Edward, Prince of Wales (later Edward VII), with whom she refused to share her onerous duties (Popperfoto)

pleasure, and though his ladies attracted little scandal his appearance in court as a witness in the Tranby Croft baccarat case did. It says much for his character that he emerged a loyal and warm-hearted man. In a short reign 'Edward the Peacemaker' influenced foreign affairs - his European tours improved relations, eg The Entente Cordiale - and he played an important role encouraging Fisher's work for the navy.

HOUSE OF WINDSOR

GEORGE V 6 May 1910-20 Jan 1936, only surviving son of Edward VII, b 3 Jun 1865. Prince George pursued a naval career until his elder brother's death made him eventual heir, but he remained a forthright naval officer all his life. Very English, he led the nation ably in World War I and turned the Germanic Saxe-Coburg Dynasty into the House of Windsor. A serious monarch, George V earned a popularity he never courted.

EDWARD VIII 20 Jan-11 Dec 1936 when he abdicated, eldest son of George V, b 23 Jun 1894; d 28 May 1972. Feted as Prince of Wales, much was expected from King Edward VIII, but he wished to escape the publicity that attends kingship in a way that is not possible in England. Abdicating to marry an American divorcee, Mrs Simpson, he became Duke of Windsor.

GEORGE VI 11 Dec 1936-6 Feb 1952, second son of George V, b 14 Dec 1895. A shy man whose health was never strong, George VI was horrified at the thought of reigning. Aided by Queen Elizabeth his inspiring leadership had an important effect upon the country at war.

ELIZABETH II Queen since 6 Feb 1952, elder daughter of George VI, b 21 Apr 1926.

PRIME MINISTERS OF GREAT BRITAIN

Sir **ROBERT WALPOLE** (later 1st Earl of ORFORD) **3 Apr 1721-8 Feb 1742**; he did not control the Cabinet in a manner recognisable as 'Prime Ministerial' until May 1730, b 26 Aug 1676; d 18 Mar 1745. Tolerant and worldly, Walpole was a financial genius whose greatest service was probably the restoration of confidence after the South Sea Bubble. By his example he set the pattern for future Premiers and, pursuing a policy of peace and low taxes, he became indispensable to the first two Georges and respected by the kindred spirit of Queen Caroline. He enjoyed the exercise of power but was not always scrupulous, having been found guilty of corruption in 1710 while Treasurer of the Navy, and after retiring was accused of bribery.

Sir **SPENCER COMPTON** (1st Earl of WIL-MINGTON) **16 Feb 1742-2 Jul 1743,** b 1673 or 1674; d in office 2 Jul 1743.

Hon **HENRY PELHAM 27 Aug 1743-10 Feb 1746,** b c 1695; d 6 Mar 1754.

William Ewert Gladstone of whom Queen Victoria wrote 'I never could have the slightest particle of confidence in Mr Gladstone' (Radio Times Hulton Picture Library)

Sir William Pulteney, 1st Earl of **BATH 10-12 Feb 1746,** b 22 Mar 1684; d 7 Jul 1764. The shortest premiership in British history, the Earl of Bath was unable to form a ministry.

Hon, **HENRY PELHAM 12 Feb 1746-6 Mar 1754** when he died in office.

The 1st Duke of **NEWCASTLE upon Tyne** (the Hon Sir Thomas Pelham-Holles) **16 Mar 1754-26 Oct 1756.**

The 4th Duke of **DEVONSHIRE** (Sir William Cavendish) **16 Nov 1756-May 1757,** b 1720; d 2 Oct 1764.

JAMES WALDEGRAVE (2nd Earl of WALDEG-RAVE) **8-12 Jun 1757**; unable to form a ministry, b 14 Mar 1715; d 28 Apr 1763.

The 1st Duke of **NEWCASTLE upon Tyne** (the Hon Sir Thomas Pelham-Holles) **2 Jul 1757-25 Oct 1760,** brother of Hon Henry Pelham, b 21 Jul 1693; d 17 Nov 1768. In two ministries this powerful aristocrat wielded enormous political influence through the control of patronage. His second ministry was dominated by the Seven Years' War with France, but Newcastle was a man of no great ability and the war and the

Government were directed by William Pitt the Elder, Leader of the Commons, who had almost brought complete victory when Newcastle had to resign on the death of George II.

The 3rd Earl of **BUTE** (the Hon. Sir John Stuart) **26 May 1762-8 Apr 1763,** b 25 May 1713; d 10 Mar 1792. A scholarly man who was a father figure to George III, he was resented by the Establishment as a Scottish outsider, and became most unpopular because of the poor terms that Britain obtained at the peace ending the Seven Years' War. Satirised by Wilkes, burnt in effigy and the subject of scurrilous ballads, Bute resigned rather than face a hostile Parliament.

Hon. **GEORGE GRENVILLE 16 Apr 1763-10 Jul 1765,** b 14 Oct 1712; d 13 Nov 1770. An unhappy ministry: his Revenue and Stamp Acts provoked the American colonists and his prosecution of the irresponsible Wilkes increased his unpopularity. Grenville's tactless handling of the Regency Bill led to his dismissal by George III who regarded him as a bore.

The 2nd Marquess of **ROCKINGHAM** (Lord Charles Watson-Wentworth) **13 Jul 1765-Jul 1766.**

The 1st Earl of **CHATHAM** (WILLIAM PITT the Elder) **30 Jul 1766-14 Oct 1768,** b 15 Nov 1708; d 11 May 1788. The 'Great Commoner' became Premier when his health was too poor to allow him to govern effectively. He had been virtual Prime Minister in Newcastle's second ministry, directing the war against France with brilliance and by his vigorous foreign policy he laid the foundations of Britain's imperial power. One of the finest orators the Commons has ever seen, he was dignified if haughty; a great patriot and war leader, he understood strategy and the integration of land and sea power in a way that perhaps only two others have in British history - Marlborough and Churchill.

The 3rd Duke of **GRAFTON** (Sir Augustus Henry FitzRoy) **Oct 1768-28 Jan 1770,** b 28 Sep 1735; d 14 Mar 1811.

Baron **NORTH** (the Hon Sir Frederick North, later succeeded as 2nd Earl of Guildford) **28 Jan 1770-20 Mar 1782,** b 13 Apr 1732; d 5 Aug 1792. Rather unfairly, Lord North is remembered as the man who lost the American colonies. A childhood friend of George III, North was an able speaker and an adequate peace-time Premier who retained the confidence of the Commons for over a decade, but his vacillation made him totally unsuited to be a war leader. The loss of America discredited North and he resigned after Yorktown, but it was his gradual loss of sight that made him quit politics.

The 2nd Marquess of **ROCKINGHAM** (Lord Charles Watson-Wentworth) **27 Mar 1782-1 Jul 1782** when he died, b 13 May 1730; d 1 Jul 1782. An elder statesman but an uninspiring speaker who relied, in his second ministry, upon the skills of Edmund Burke to present his policies.

The 2nd Earl of **SHELBURNE** (the Hon Sir William Petty) **4 Jul 1782-24 Feb 1783,** b 20 May 1737; d 7 May 1805.

The 3rd Duke of **PORTLAND** (Sir William Henry Cavendish Bentinck) **2 Apr 1783-Dec 1783.**

Hon **WILLIAM PITT 19 Dec 1783-14 Mar 1801,** second son of William Pitt, Earl of Chatham, b 28 May 1759; d in office 23 Jan 1806. A gifted classicist, he became Chancellor at 23 and a precocious Premier at 24. Courageously he fought an initially hostile Commons and effected important financial and commercial legislation. Although a withdrawn and lonely man Pitt had considerable influence in strengthening the Premiership. He did not have his father's understanding of war and many of his campaigns were ill-conceived. Believing that the French revolutionary wars would be short, he mismanaged their finance through the expensive sinking fund. In 1801 Pitt resigned as the King would not consider Catholic emancipation. His second ministry was disappointing: apart from Trafalgar there was little success in the war. Pitt's health broke and he died in office.

HENRY ADDINGTON (later 1st Viscount Sidmouth) **17 Mar 1801-30 Apr 1804,** b 30 May 1757; d 15 Feb 1844. Honest but lacking in ideas, he was unable to conduct the Napoleonic wars. Later as Home Secretary he became unpopular because of his stern measures against political and economic dissenters.

Hon **WILLIAM PITT 10 May 1804-23 Jan 1806** when he died.

The 1st Baron **GRENVILLE** (William Wyndham Grenville) **10 Feb 1806-Mar 1807,** son of Hon George Grenville, b 25 Oct 1759; d 12 Jan 1834. Grenville was head of a coalition 'Ministry of All Talents' whose most important Act outlawed the slave trade.

The 3rd Duke of **PORTLAND** (Sir William Henry Cavendish Bentinck) **31 Mar 1807-Oct 1809,** b 14 Apr 1738; d 30 Oct 1809. In both his ministries the Duke was but the nominal head of the Government: the first ministry was dominated by the rather strange alliance of Fox and North; the second by Canning and Castlereagh, who quarrelled, then duelled, over the Walcheren expedition - their disagreement and Portland's poor health ended the ministry.

The Hon. **SPENCER PERCEVAL 4 Oct 1809-11 May 1812** when he was assassinated, b 1 Nov 1762. The only British Premier to be murdered, he was shot in the lobby of the Commons by a madman, Bellingham, who believed he had a grievance against the Government.

The 2nd Earl of **LIVERPOOL** (Sir Robert Banks Jenkinson) **8 Jun 1812-17 Feb 1827,** b 7 Jun 1770; d 4 Dec 1828. Overshadowed by Canning and Castlereagh, Liverpool is sometimes underestimated. He succeeded in uniting the Tories in a way that Wellington and Canning did not; his financial policies were largely sound; he appointed upon merit rather than influence. Much criticised for coercive methods and for supporting the Metternich settlement in Europe, his government became more liberal after 1822. A paralytic stroke forced him to retire.

GEORGE CANNING 10 Apr 1827-8 Aug 1827 when he died, b 11 Apr 1770. Canning was nearly lost to British politics: opposing the campaign against Queen Caroline, he resigned the Board of Control and accepted the governorship of Bengal, but Castlereagh's suicide gave him the Foreign Office. A patriotic, able Foreign Secretary (1822-1827) he tried to counter the illiberal 'Holy Alliance'; at home, he fought Parliamentary reform through conviction rather than fear. By the time he became Premier his legendary energy was failing and, as an outsider, he had to face bitter prejudice from the Tory aristocracy, though it must be recalled that his clever sarcastic tongue earned him enemies.

The 1st Viscount **GODERICH** (Hon Frederick John Robinson, later the 1st Earl of Ripon) **31 Aug 1827-8 Jan 1828,** b 1 Nov 1782; d 28 Jan 1859.

The 1st Duke of **WELLINGTON** (Hon Sir Arthur Wellesley, originally Wesley) **22 Jan 1828-21 Nov 1830,** b 1 May 1769; d 14 Sep 1852. A cautious soldier, Wellington was known for his care for his men, his attention to detail and his simple commonsense. His extraordinary military career began in India where he was greatly helped by his brother Richard, the viceroy; success in the Peninsula war, in which he tied down important numbers of French troops, was followed by the final defeat of Napoléon at Waterloo (18 Jun 1815). Showered with honours, Wellington retained his attractive modesty. As a staunch Tory he opposed the reform of Parliament, and lost a wing of his party by his inflexibility (he only accepted Grey's Bill eventually rather than see the Lords packed with new Whig creations to carry the measure). His second ministry was a caretaker Government for the absent Peel. The Great Duke ended his days universally respected and a personal friend of the Royal Family.

The 2nd Earl **GREY** (Hon Sir Charles Grey) **22 Nov 1830-Jul 1834,** b 13 Mar 1764; d 17 Jul 1845. The advocate of peace, retrenchment and reform, Grey was capable of brilliant eloquence if a subject interested him. He saw the need for reform but wished only for enough change to remove the worst abuses and end discontent. He was surprised by Parliament's opposition and the country's determination, but supported by William IV, whose initial enthusiasm waned, reform was achieved. The Act was more radical than Grey had envisaged although it did little more than enfranchise the upper middle classes and suppress rotten boroughs.

The 3rd Viscount **MELBOURNE** (Hon Sir William Lamb) **16 Jul 1834-Nov 1834.**

The 1st Duke of **WELLINGTON 17 Nov-9 Dec 1834.**

Sir **ROBERT PEEL 10 Dec 1834-8 Apr 1835.**

The 3rd Viscount **MELBOURNE** (Hon Sir William Lamb) **18 Apr 1835-Aug 1841,** b 15 Mar 1779; d 24 Nov 1848. Despite his somewhat irregular private life, Melbourne became Queen Victoria's close friend and political adviser in her early years as sovereign. A poor speaker and a reluctant politician, he was more interested in theology than politics which he believed to be of little benefit to the world. He introduced Victoria to government by endeavouring to make affairs of state interesting and he tactfully persuaded her to share her work with Prince Albert.

Sir **ROBERT PEEL 30 Aug 1841-29 Jun 1846,** b 5 Feb 1788; d 2 Jul 1850 following a fall from his horse. As Secretary for Ireland (1812-1818) his lack of impartiality earned him the nickname 'Orange Peel' but later at the Home Office he introduced the Catholic Relief Act; he founded the Metropolitan Police and effected a major review of the criminal code. After propounding his political philosophy in the Tamworth Manifesto, usually regarded as the birth of the Conservative Party, he became Premier in 1834 but the Government was short-lived as he lacked support. His important second Ministry encouraged trade, ruled Ireland firmly but in a conciliatory manner, repealed the Corn Laws and in the Bank Charter Act set up the basis for the modern banking system.

Lord **JOHN RUSSELL** (in his second ministry the 1st Earl **RUSSELL**) **30 Jun 1846-Feb 1852,** b 18 Aug 1792; d 28 May 1878. Serving under Melbourne, Russell reformed the boroughs, established the registration of births, deaths and marriages and obtained concessions for Dissenters. Russell's first ministry, which was troubled by Chartist agitation, failed to gain the support of the Whig aristocracy. A notable writer of history, poetry and biography, he was not a gifted administrator and this noble liberal, in many ways ahead of his time, was unable to translate his ideals into legislation.

The 14th Earl of **DERBY** (Hon Sir Edward Geoffry Smith-Stanley) **23 Feb-18 Dec 1852.**

The 4th Earl of **ABERDEEN** (Sir George Hamilton Gordon) **19 Dec 1852-5 Feb 1855,** b 28 Jan 1784; d 14 Dec 1860. Aberdeen was reluctant to begin the Crimean War and his indecision contributed to the mismanagement of the campaign. He resigned when the Commons decided to investigate the conduct of the war in which he had been gravely hampered by the poor reports he received from the front.

The 3rd Viscount **PALMERSTON** (Hon Sir Henry John Temple) **6 Feb 1855-19 Feb 1858.**

The 14th Earl of **DERBY** (Hon Sir Edward Geoffry Smith-Stanley) **20 Feb 1858-11 Jun 1859.**

The 3rd Viscount **PALMERSTON** (Hon Sir Henry John Temple) **12 Jun 1859-18 Oct 1865** when he died, b 20 Oct 1784. Brusque, witty, irrepressible 'Firebrand' Palmerston is best remembered as Foreign Secretary: under Melbourne, he helped secure Belgian independence and the thrones of the Spanish and Portuguese Queens; under Russell, his 'gunboat diplomacy' provoked controversy in his reactions to the Swiss civil war, the Spanish marriages, the 1848 revolutions and the Don Pacifico affair. It is fitting that his ministries should be dominated by foreign affairs: the Crimean War, which he vigorously pursued; Italian unity; the American Civil War, involving him in the delicate Trent and Alabama affairs and the Schleswig-Holstein dispute whose ·complexities he claimed to understand. Palmerston was a British nationalist, more responsible than he is usually given credit for, who gained great popularity at home through the establishment of 'Pax Britannica' (largely deceptive for, though economically dominant, Britain had moderate military resources) and who won enmity abroad.

The 1st Earl **RUSSELL** (formerly Lord JOHN RUSSELL) **29 Oct 1865-Jun 1866.**

The 14th Earl of **DERBY** (Hon Sir Edward Geoffry Smith-Stanley) **28 Jun 1866-26 Feb 1868** b 19 Mar 1799; d 23 Oct 1869. Derby was a scholar and a patron of the turf who was overshadowed by Disraeli and hence underestimated. An aristocrat who found government irksome, he was nevertheless a considerable orator who reformed Parliament (1867) and handed over India from the East India Company to the Crown.

BENJAMIN DISRAELI (from 1876 1st Earl of BEACONSFIELD) **27 Feb-Nov 1868.**

WILLIAM EWART GLADSTONE 3 Dec 1868-Feb 1874.

BENJAMIN DISRAELI (from 1876 1st Earl of BEACONSFIELD) **20 Feb 1874-Apr 1880,** b (Benjamin D'Israeli) 21 Dec 1804; d 19 Apr 1881. This flamboyant politician is an enigma - he was courageous, an efficient administrator, a sparkling debater and master of Parliamentary tactics, but his character remains hidden. Many have doubted his sincerity but he understood the people and his social reforms (public health, trade union, slum clearance and factory Acts) were more practical than those of idealistic Gladstone. He secured the Suez Canal shares (1875); he made his Queen, who was particularly susceptible to his flattery, Empress of India (1876) and received his peerage in the same year. At the Berlin Congress, he won for himself praise as an arbiter and for Britain 'peace with honour' and Cyprus. A debter, he openly married for money; a writer, his political novels are entertaining.

WILLIAM EWART GLADSTONE 23 Apr 1880-12 Jun 1885.

The 3rd Marquess of **SALISBURY** (Robert Arthur Talbot Gascoyne-Cecil) **23 Jun 1885-28 Jan 1886.**

WILLIAM EWART GLADSTONE 1 Feb-20 Jul 1886.

The 3rd Marquess of **SALISBURY** (Robert Arthur Talbot Gascoyne-Cecil) **25 Jul 1886-Aug 1892.**

WILLIAM EWART GLADSTONE 15 Aug 1892-3 Mar 1894, b 29 Dec 1809; d 19 May 1898. Gladstone, a humanitarian with an overwhelming moral sense, was influenced by Christianity and John Stuart Mill's Utilitarianism. A fine orator he could be too fluent, carried away with his own eloquence - Queen Victoria, who disliked him,

complained that he treated her like a 'public department'. An able writer, he ranged from political pamphlets to brilliant Homeric studies; an able Chancellor, perhaps his greatest achievements were in finance. His first ministry began Army reform and a national system of primary education; it reformed the Civil Service, instituted the secret ballot and ended religious discrimination at the universities. After this fruitful administration he retired, but Disraeli's indifference to the Bulgarian atrocities made him return. Swept to power in the Midlothian campaign, his second ministry passed the third Reform Bill but fell on failing to rescue Gordon. Gladstone's two last ministries were dominated by Ireland: a conciliatory policy included a Land Act, fair rents, security of tenure and the disestablishment of the Church of Ireland, but the Home Rule Bill failed, split the Liberals and the country.

The 5th Earl of **ROSEBERY** (Sir Archibald Philip Primrose; after 1911 Earl of Midlothian - a title he did not adopt) **5 Mar 1894-21 Jun 1895,** b 7 May 1847; d 21 May 1921.

The 3rd Marquess of **SALISBURY** (Robert Arthur Talbot Gascoyne-Cecil) **25 Jun 1895-11 Jul 1902,** b 3 Feb 1830; d 22 Aug 1903. The last Premier to lead the Government from the Lords, this shy Marquess, a botanist, was a practical reformer and skilled diplomat whose policies led to a great development of the Empire.

ARTHUR JAMES BALFOUR (later the 1st Earl of Balfour) **12 Jul 1902-4 Dec 1905,** b 25 Jul 1848; d 19 Mar 1930. Balfour is best remembered as Foreign Secretary (1916-1919) in which capacity he made his 'Declaration' in favour of a Jewish homeland in Palestine.

Sir **HENRY CAMPBELL-BANNERMAN 5 Dec 1905-5 Apr 1908,** b 7 Sep 1836; d 22 Apr 1908.

HERBERT HENRY ASQUITH (later 1st Earl of OXFORD and ASQUITH) **7 Apr 1908-5 Dec 1916,** b 12 Sep 1852; d 15 Feb 1928. Asquith introduced the Parliament Act, restricting the powers of the Lords, after that House rejected the 'People's Budget' and precipitated a constitutional crisis. His war leadership lacked decision and he was much criticised by the Press after the Dardenelles expedition and the lack of progress on the Western Front. He resigned after Lloyd George schemed with Opposition members behind his back.

DAVID LLOYD GEORGE (later 1st Earl Lloyd-George) **7 Dec 1916-19 Oct 1922,** b 17 Jan 1863; d 26 Mar 1945. Jocular and charming, the 'Welsh Wizard', brought up in poverty, was also injudicious and incapable of loyalty either to his political allies or his ladies. His ruthlessness in ousting Asquith was not forgiven by many. As Chancellor he laid the foundations of the 'welfare state' (health and unemployment insurance); as Premier he advocated a peace treaty acceptable to Germany and he negotiated Irish Home Rule.

ANDREW BONAR LAW 23 Oct 1922-20 May 1923, b (a Canadian) 16 Sep 1858; d 30 Oct 1923.

STANLEY BALDWIN (later 1st Earl Baldwin) **22 May 1923-22 Jan 1924.**

JAMES RAMSAY MACDONALD 22 Jan-4 Nov 1924.

STANLEY BALDWIN (later 1st Earl Baldwin) **4 Nov 1924-4 Jun 1929.**

JAMES RAMSAY MACDONALD 5 Jun 1929-7 Jun 1935, b 12 Oct 1866; d 9 Nov 1937. The first Labour Premier played an important role in developing the relationship between his party and the trade unions. His first ministry fell because of its factionalism and the electoral influence of the forged Zinoviev letter. When his second ministry was unable to cope with the economic crisis of the Slump, Macdonald headed a National Government (1931-1935), an action regarded as treacherous by most of his colleagues.

STANLEY BALDWIN (later 1st Earl Baldwin) **7 Jun 1935-28 May 1937,** b 3 Aug 1867; d 14 Dec 1947. A modest Premier who, bored by foreign affairs, neglected the growing menace of Nazi Germany. His actions remain controversial: refusing to negotiate during the General Strike (4-12 May 1926), he proclaimed a state of emergency; he offered Edward VIII no compromise in the Abdication crisis; he did not rearm.

ARTHUR NEVILLE CHAMBERLAIN 28 May 1937-10 May 1940, b 18 Mar 1869; d 9 Nov 1940. Chamberlain, reluctant to enter a 'quarrel in a faraway country between people of whom we know nothing' (Hitler's threat to Czechoslovakia), claimed he had brought 'peace in our time': all that can be said for his appeasement is it gained Britain a little time to rearm before the inevitable war.

WINSTON LEONARD SPENCER-CHURCHILL (after 1953 Sir) **10 May 1940-26 Jul 1945,** b 30 Nov 1874; d 24 Jan 1965. In a distinguished Parliamentary career Churchill occupied many posts: the Board of Trade, where he attacked sweated labour; the Home Office, where he effected prison reform and did not send troops to Tonypandy - he stopped them and sent unarmed police; the Admiralty, which he resigned after Gallipoli but was reinstated after being exonerated of blame; the Colonial Office; and the Exchequer, where he had little success. Politically in the wilderness in the 1930s, Churchill warned of the ambitions of Germany and advocated rearmament, but few heeded the Rhineland, Abyssinia and Spain. Chamberlain's half-hearted war leadership gave way in May 1940 to a new spirit when Churchill becoming Premier offered Britain 'nothing but blood, toil, tears and sweat'. He provided inspired leadership to the nation, directing the war effort with consummate skill. Though he won the war, he was less successful in winning the peace - Churchill was overruled by Roosevelt at Tehran and so East Europe passed from German to Russian occupation. He was a great debater, a memorable wit, a distinguished painter and a fine writer who won the Nobel Prize in 1953.

CLEMENT RICHARD ATTLEE (later 1st Earl Attlee) **26 Jul 1945-26 Oct 1951,** b 3 Jan 1883; d 8 Oct 1967. Attlee presided over the Labour Government which nationalised the railways, the Bank of England and the mines, instituted the 'welfare state', and began the dismantling of the Empire - India became independent in 1947.

WINSTON LEONARD SPENCER-CHURCHILL (after 1953 Sir) **26 Oct 1951-5 Apr 1955.**

Sir **ROBERT ANTHONY EDEN** (later 1st Earl of Avon) **6 Apr 1955-9 Jan 1957** b 12 Jun 1897; d 14 Jan 1977. Sir Anthony had a distinguished career as Foreign Secretary and was Churchill's 'right-hand man' during the war. His Premiership was dominated by the controversial Suez campaign.

MAURICE HAROLD MACMILLAN 10 Jan 1957-18 Oct 1963, b 10 Feb 1894.

Sir **ALEXANDER FREDERICK DOUGLAS-HOME** (formerly the 14th Earl of HOME; since 1974 Baron Home - life peerage) **19 Oct 1963-16 Oct 1964,** b 2 Jul 1903.

JAMES HAROLD WILSON (from 1976 Sir) **16 Oct 1964-17 Jun 1970,** b 11 Mar 1916.

EDWARD RICHARD GEORGE HEATH 18 Jun 1970-3 Mar 1974, b 7 Jul 1916.

JAMES HAROLD WILSON (from 1976 Sir) **4 Mar 1974-5 Apr 1976.**

LEONARD JAMES CALLAGHAN since 5 Apr 1976, b 27 Mar 1912.

Scotland

The formation of Scotland began in 843 when Kenneth MacAlpin, King of the Scots, became King of the Picts. In early times, the sovereign was usually succeeded by the eldest member of a collateral branch of the Royal House - a system which generally produced a King of age but which led to dynastic squabbles and assassinations. Primogeniture, introduced through English influence at the time of Malcolm III, cannot be said to have been established firmly until the reign of David I. The Scottish sovereign was styled 'King of Scots' rather than 'King of Scotland', a title used only by the Balliols.

† Kings of Scots

HOUSE OF MACALPIN OR ALBA
Before Kenneth II they were called 'Kings of Alba'.

KENNETH I (MacAlpin) King of Dalriada from 841; King of Picts and Scots **843-858 or 859.** Kenneth, who may have been related to the Pictish Kings through his mother, was able to bring the Picts under his rule as they had been seriously weakened by Danish attacks.

DONALD I 858 or 859-862 or 863, brother of Kenneth I.

Mary, Queen of Scots, who in death lies near Elizabeth I who in life consistently denied her rival a meeting (Radio Times Hulton Picture Library)

CONSTANTINE I   862 or 863-877 killed in battle by the Danes, son of Kenneth I.

AEDH (Whitefoot) **877-878** murdered by Giric of Strathclyde; son of Kenneth I.

EOCHAID 878-889 deposed by Donald II; nephew of Aedh. Eochaid, whose mother was Aed's sister, was King of Strathclyde, and probably a minor, for whom Giric acted as Regent.

GIRIC   878-889, Regent of Strathclyde, and possibly a relative of Eochaid. Giric, guardian of Eochaid, seems to have been co-ruler of the Scots and may have usurped the crown completely - his name is present and Eochaid's is missing on early lists of Scottish Kings.

DONALD II   889-900, son of Constantine I.

CONSTANTINE II   900-942 abdicated to become Abbot of St Andrews, son of Aedh; d 952. Constantine was defeated by Athelstan at Brunanburh (937).

MALCOLM I   942-954 murdered, son of Donald II.

INDULF   954-962 killed by Vikings, son of Constantine II.

DUBH 962-966 or 967 murdered, Malcolm I's elder son.

CULEN (or CUILEAN) **966 or 967-971** murdered, son of Indulf.

KENNETH II   971-995 murdered, Malcolm I's younger son. Kenneth received Lothian from Edgar of England.

CONSTANTINE III   995-997 killed by Kenneth III; son of Culen.

KENNETH III   997-25 Mar 1005 killed at Monzievaird by Malcolm II; son of Dubh.

MALCOLM II   Mar 1005-25 Nov 1034, son of Kenneth II, b *c*954. Beating the Northumbrians at Carham (1016 or 1018) Malcolm II confirmed his rule over Lothian; obtaining Strathclyde (for his grandson Duncan) he established a Kingdom roughly the same in extent as modern Scotland.

DUNCAN I   Nov 1034-14 Aug 1040, grandson of Malcolm II, b *c*1001. Malcolm II arranged that Duncan, son of his daughter Bethoc, should succeed him, but this unorthodox settlement was challenged by the representative of a collateral branch of the Royal House, Macbeth, who killed the King at Pitgaveny near Elgin.

MACBETH   Aug 1040-15 Aug 1057 slain by the future Malcolm III at Lumphanan near Aberdeen, husband of Gruoch who was the granddaughter of Kenneth III; Macbeth may have been descended from Kenneth II. Shakespeare's character has hidden the real Macbeth, who had a claim to the throne - though not a good one - and who seems to have been a good ruler and, like his maligned wife, was a lavish patron of the Church.

LULACH (called the Simple) **Aug 1057-17 Mar 1058** killed at Essie (Strathbogie) by Malcolm III; stepson of Macbeth and great-grandson of Kenneth III, b *c*1032.

MALCOLM III (CANMORE meaning 'Great Chief') **Mar 1058-13 Nov 1093,** son of Duncan I, b *c*1031. Malcolm III's long reign was marked by border wars and he was slain near Alnwick while invading England. Canmore was much influenced by his Saxon wife, St Margaret who encouraged reforms in the Scottish 'Culdee' church and who introduced resented English customs.

DONALD III (DONALD BANE) **Nov 1093-May 1094** when he was deposed by Duncan II; brother of Malcolm III, b *c*1033; d 1099 having been deposed and blinded by Edgar.

DUNCAN II   May-Nov 1094 murdered at the command of Edmund his half-brother; son of Malcolm III by his first marriage, b *c*1060. In designating Duncan as his heir Malcolm III introduced primogeniture to Scotland, but Donald Bane took advantage of Duncan's absence in England to seize the throne. With Norman help Duncan gained the crown.

EDMUND   Nov 1094-Oct 1097 deposed by Edgar and became a monk, son of Malcolm III by his second marriage. Co-ruler with Donald III.

DONALD III (DONALD BANE) **12 Nov 1094-Oct 1097** deposed. Co-ruler with Edmund.

EDGAR   Oct 1097-8 Jan 1107, seventh son of Malcolm III by his second marriage, b *c*1074. Accepting the position of a vassal King, Edgar won the crown with English aid.

ALEXANDER I Jan 1107-25? Apr 1124, eighth son of Malcolm III and St Margaret, b *c* 1077. A patron of the Church, he strove to free the Scottish sees from the archdiocese of York. A vassal of Henry I he wed the English King's natural daughter Sybilla.

DAVID I (David the Saint) **Apr 1124-24 May 1153,** ninth and youngest son of Malcolm III, b *c* 1080. English influence was greatly increased under David I who gave lands to a new Norman aristocracy who played an important role establishing a more efficient administration. He granted large estates to the Church; founded abbeys, several sees, at least 15 burghs and the first sheriffdoms to implement the law. His coinage can be said to have introduced the money economy to Scotland.

MALCOLM IV May 1153-9 Dec 1165, son of David I's second son Henry, b 20 Mar 1142. Malcolm IV was obliged to cede Cumbria and Northumberland to England.

WILLIAM I ('The Lion') **Dec 1165-4 Dec 1214,** brother of Malcolm IV, b 1143. In campaigns in the north, William put down a serious revolt by the MacWilliams - descendants of Duncan II with a good claim to the throne - and secured Caithness, Ross and Sutherland. Allied to Henry 'the Young King', he invaded England and was taken prisoner at Alnwick (Jul 1174). Released as a subject of Henry II (1175), the independence of Scotland was not restored until Richard I's quitclaim of 1189.

ALEXANDER II Dec 1214-8 Jul 1249, son of William I, b 24 Aug 1198. Alexander renounced Scotland's claim to Cumbria and Northumberland.

ALEXANDER III Jul 1249-19 Mar 1286 when he died accidentally falling from his horse over the cliffs at Kinghorn, Fife; son of Alexander II by his second marriage, b 4 Sep 1241. He obtained the Western Isles from Norway.

House of Norway

MARGARET (Queen) **Mar 1286-*c* 26 Sep 1290** when she died in Orkney either in a shipwreck or from severe sea-sickness. Only child of Alexander III's daughter Margaret who had married Eirik II of Norway, b Apr? 1283. The child Queen of Scots sailed from Norway (Sep 1290) but never reached her Kingdom.

Sep 1290-17 Nov 1292 First Interregnum. The throne was contested by 13 claimants. Edward I, who took advantage of the situation, was referred to as arbitrator, and having extracted promises of acknowledgement of his feudal overlordship from all candidates, chose in favour of John Balliol whom he hoped would be a puppet.

House of Balliol

JOHN (Balliol, styled King of Scotland not King of Scots) **17 Nov 1292-10 Jul 1296** when he was forced to abdicate, great-great-great-grandson of David I, b *c* 1250; d Apr 1313. When Balliol refused Edward I's demands as 'overlord', the English King invaded. Deserted by both sides in the War of Independence, John Balliol deserves some sympathy, being trapped between a provocative 'overlord' and the force of Scottish nationalism.

10 Jul 1296-27 Mar 1306 Second Interregnum. Scotland fought without a recognised government against the attempts of Edward I to conquer the country. At first led by William Wallace, who used terrorist tactics, from 1306 the struggle was under Robert Bruce, who had himself crowned to provide a rallying point for the nation.

House of Bruce

ROBERT I 27 Mar 1306-7 Jun 1329, great-great-great-great-grandson of David I, b 11 Jul 1274. A great King and patriot, Robert I's early defeat nearly ended his cause, but the accession of the incompetent Edward II decided the war in Scotland's favour. The English were totally crushed at Bannockburn (24 Jun 1314) and in 1328 England renounced all claims over Scotland - papal recognition was more difficult to obtain and Robert was excommunicated for killing Comyn in sanctuary. His firm rule restored order and Robert II moulded a nation. He died from a painful and unknown disease - possibly leprosy.

DAVID II Jun 1329-22 Feb 1371, only surviving son of Robert I, b 5 Mar 1324. A selfish and extravagant King who lacked his father's ability and character. Much of his reign was spent in exile: deposed by Edward Balliol (1332) he took refuge in France; invading England (1346) he was captured, imprisoned for 11 years and then ransomed.

House of Balliol

EDWARD (Balliol, styled King of Scotland not King of Scots), son of John Balliol; d 1363. It is not possible to date the 'reign' of Edward Balliol. Invading with English support, Edward Balliol deposed David II and was crowned on 24 Sep 1332. In six years of civil war Balliol acknowledged Edward III as overlord and ceded to him all the Border counties. Unable to rule without English aid, he finally fled in 1338 and David II returned two years later.

House of Stewart (later Stuart)

ROBERT II Feb 1371-19 Apr 1390, half-nephew of David II and first King of the Stewart dynasty, b Mar 1316. An elderly, weak and incompetent ruler in whose reign law and order collapsed.

ROBERT III Apr 1390-4 Apr 1406, eldest son of Robert II by Elizabeth Mure, he was born *c* 1337 - 10 years before his parents' marriage, but was held to be legitimised *per subsequens matrimonium*. Christened John, he changed his name (Aug 1390) to avoid being known as John II - the heirs of Bruce could not recognise that Balliol had reigned. Robert III left his own epitaph: 'Here lies the worst of Kings and the most miserable of men'. Totally unfitted to rule, he was a shy and nervous man, physically and mentally weakened by a horse's kick. The nobles misruled unhindered and in the anarchy Robert's heir was imprisoned by Albany and starved to death.

JAMES I Jun 1406-21 Feb 1437 assassinated at Perth by Atholl, his uncle, and Sir Robert Graham; youngest and only surviving son of Robert III, b Dec (or possibly Jul) 1394. Sent abroad for his own safety by Robert III, James fell into English hands and was imprisoned until ransomed in 1424 when he returned to reform Scotland. A poet, a musician and a determined if acquisitive ruler, James restored justice and order and introduced county representatives to Parliament in an attempt to curb the power of the nobles, who resisted his heavy but necessary taxation - Scotland's finances were chaotic.

JAMES II Feb 1437-3 Aug 1460, only surviving son of James I, b 16 Oct 1430. Dispossessing the overmighty Douglas family James II eventually made himself master of his Kingdom. He was killed by the bursting of a cannon while attempting to retake Roxburgh from England.

JAMES III Aug 1460-11 Jun 1488 murdered after a battle against rebellious lords near Stirling, eldest son of James II, b May 1452. A superstitious, incompetent King who preferred music and his witty favourites to government. His neglect, coupled with the famine and inflation of the day, fed discontent.

JAMES IV Jun 1488-9 Sep 1513, eldest son of James III, b 17 Mar 1473. He encouraged trade and education, upheld the law and tried to subdue the Highlands. Scotland became involved in European politics, renewed the 'auld alliance' with France and inevitably went to war with England. James IV, a popular King and a brave warrior, perished at Flodden Field when the 'Flowers of the Forest' were cut down.

JAMES V Sep 1513-14 Dec 1542, third but eldest surviving son of James IV, b 10 Apr 1512. Troubled by the 'English' and 'French' parties, James lacked the ability to control his nobles.

MARY (Queen of Scots) **Dec 1542-24 Jul 1567** when she was forced to abdicate, only surviving child of James V, b 6 or 7 Dec 1542; executed at Fotheringhay (near Peterborough) 8 Feb 1587. Taken to France to wed the Dauphin (Francois II) after England's 'rough wooing', she was widowed in 1560 and returned to be the Catholic, almost foreign, Queen of a turbulent Protestant country. Initially popular, but she showed remarkable religious toleration, but her Catholic marriage to the despised Darnley (in whose murder she may have been implicated), her unwise choice of favourites, eg Riccio, and her inexplicable marriage to Bothwell, regarded as the murderer of Darnley, lost her sympathy and the throne. Taking refuge in England, she became a prisoner following a hearing at which the incriminating but suspect 'casket letters' were produced. An embarassment to Elizabeth, to whose throne she was the Catholic candidate, Mary was the centre of plots which she eventually became desperate enough to condone.

JAMES VI 24 Jul 1567-27 Mar 1625, only child of Mary. Became King of England - 24 Mar 1603.

Wales

WELSH SOVEREIGNS

Wales was divided into about half a dozen small Kingdoms of which two (Gwynedd and Deheubarth) were usually dominant. When forced to accept the King of England as overlord, the Welsh sovereigns changed their title of 'King' to 'Prince', but only three Welsh rulers - the last two of Gwynedd and Owain Glyndwr - styled themselves 'Prince of Wales'.

Gwynedd

† KINGS
For most of its history, the Kingdom of Gwynedd was smaller than the present county of the same name. From its mountain fastness of Snowdonia, Gwynedd was to offer strong resistance to England in the 13th century.

MAELGWN GWYNEDD (or MAELGWN HIR) **?-547.** Maelgwn the Tall.

RHUN ap MAELGWN GWYNEDD 547-?, illegitimate son of Maelgwn Gwynedd.

BELI ap RHUN fl. late 6th century, son of Rhun ap Maelgwn Gwynedd.

IAGO ap BELI ?-616, son of Beli ap Rhun.

CADFAN ab IAGO 616-c625, son of Iago ap Beli.

CADWALLON ap CADFAN c625-633, son of Cadfan ab Iago. Cadwallon was allied to Penda with whom he defeated and killed Edwin of Deira. The King of Gwynedd was himself slain by Oswald of Bernicia the following year.

CADAFAEL ap Cynfedw CADOMEDD 633-654. A usurper who fled after his defeat at the Battle of the Winwaed (Nov 654).

CADWALADR ap CADWALLON (or CADWALADR FENDIGAID - Cadwaladr the Blessed) **654-664,** son of Cadwallon ap Cadfan.

IDWAL IWRCH ap CADWALADR 664-?, son of Cadwaladr ap Cadwallon.

RHODRI MOLWYNOG ?-754, son of Idwal Iwrch ap Cadwaladr.

HYWEL ap RHODRI MOLWYNOG 754-825, son of Rhodri Molwynog. Hywel and his brother Cynan contested the throne of Gwynedd from 754 to 816 when Cynan died.

CYNAN TINDAETHWY ap RHODRI MOLWYNOG Rival King **754-816,** son of Rhodri Molwynog.

MERFYN (FRYCH, which means 'freckled') **825-844,** great-nephew of Hywel ap Rhodri Molwynog and grandson of Cynan Tindaethwy.

Merfyn Frych greatly extended the area of Gwynedd.

RHODRI MAWR (Rhodri the Great) **844-878** killed in battle by the English, son of Merfyn Frych. The ruler of most of northern and central Wales, succeeding his father to Gwynedd (844), his maternal uncle to Powys (855) and his brother-in-law to Seisyllwg - Ceredigion and the Twyi valley - (872).

ANARAWD ap RHODRI MAWR 878-916, elder son of Rhodri Mawr. Anarawd was obliged to acknowledge Alfred of Wessex as his overlord.

IDWAL FOEL (Idwal the Bald) **916-942** killed in battle by the English, son of Anarawd.

HYWEL DDA 942-950, King of Deheubarth and cousin of Idwal Foel.

IDWAL (IEUAF) **950-969** deposed and exiled by Iago; third son of Idwal Foel; d 985. Idwal reigned with his brother Iago.

IAGO 950-979 deposed and imprisoned by his nephew Hywel ap Ieuaf; brother of Idwal and second son of Idwal Foel. He submitted to Edgar of England (973).

HYWEL ap IEUAF 979-985, son of Idwal.

CADWALLON ap IEUAF 985-986, younger brother of Hywel ap Ieuaf.

MAREDUDD ab OWAIN ap HYWELDDA 986-999, King of Deheubarth.

LLYWELYN ap SEISYLL 999-1023, King of Deheubarth.

RHYDDERCH ab IESTYN 1023-1033, King of Deheubarth.

IAGO ab IDWAL ap MEURIG   1033-1039 murdered, grandson of Idwal Foel.

GRUFFYDD ap LLYWELYN 1039-1063 murdered, son of Llywelyn ap Seisyll. Having succeeded to Gwynedd (1039), he took Deheubarth (1042 or 1043) expelling Hywel ab Edwin. Gruffydd briefly lost South Wales when Hywel returned with a Danish force (1044), but in killing his rival at the Battle of the Tywi Gruffydd became ruler of all Wales again.

BLEDDYN ap CYNFYN 1063-1075, half-brother of Gruffydd ap Llywelyn.

TRAHAEARN ap CARADOG 1075-1081 murdered, cousin of Bleddyn.

GRUFFYDD ap CYNAN 1081-1137, grandson of Iago ab Idwal ap Meurig, b c 1055. Gruffydd was imprisoned by the Normans in England from 1081 to 1093.

† PRINCES

OWAIN GWYNEDD King of Gwynedd **1137-1152;** Prince of Gwynedd **1152-28 Nov 1170,** second son of Gruffydd ap Cynan. Owain submitted to Henry II as his overlord and changed his style from King to Prince.

IORWERTH DRWYNDWN   Nov 1170-c 1174, eldest son of Owain Gwynedd.

DAFYDD I c 1174-1194 driven from the throne he had usurped, half-brother of Iorwerth Drwyndwn; d c May 1203.

LLYWELYN I (LLYWELYN FAWR - the Great) **1194-11 Apr 1240,** son of Iorwerth Drwyndwn, b

1173. Defeating Dafydd I, he won his father's throne and by 1203 had reconquered all Gwynedd to be recognised as overlord by the other Welsh rulers. Llywelyn, who styled himself Prince of Aberffraw and Lord of Snowdon, was a character who entered folk-lore, eg the tale of Gelert, his dog - an 18th century invention.

DAFYDD II Apr 1240-25 Feb 1246, only legitimate son of Llywelyn I, b c 1208. Dafydd submitted to his uncle Henry III as his overlord.

LLYWELYN II (Llywelyn the Last) **Feb 1246-11 Dec 1282,** illegitimate son of Llywelyn Fawr. Uniting North Wales, he adopted the style 'Prince of Wales' (1258) and received the allegiance of the other Welsh rulers. Llywelyn refused to submit to Edward I who invaded taking all Wales except Anglesey, for which Llywelyn had to do homage (1277). Fighting to recapture his Principality, he was killed near Builth Wells.

DAFYDD III   Dec 1282-Jun 1283, brother of Llywelyn II, b c 1235. Continuing the fight against Edward I, Dafydd was taken prisoner and was hanged, drawn and quartered at Shrewsbury (some maintain that this was the first instance of this punishment in England).

(MADOG attempted to continue the struggle, but cannot be considered to have reigned.)

1283-1400 English rule.

Deheubarth

† KINGS

The Kingdom of Deheubarth began as a personal union of the territories of Hywel Dda: Seisyllwg (Ceredigion and the Twyi valley) and Dyfed. Brycheiniog, Gwent and Morgannwg were usually subject to Deheubarth.

CADELL ap RHODRI King of Seisyllwg **878-909,** younger son of Rhodri Mawr, King of Gwynedd.

HYWEL DDA (Hywel the Good) King of Dyfed **904-950;** King of Seisyllwg **909-950;** King of Gwynedd **942-950,** elder son of Cadell ap Rhodri. He inherited Dyfed from his wife and Seisyllwg from his father while Gwynedd was usurped on the basis of his descent from Rhodri Mawr. Pious, he went on pilgrimage to Rome; just, Hywel codified the laws of Wales (920).

RHODRI ap HYWEL DDA 950-953, son of Hywel Dda. Co-ruler of Deheubarth.

EDWIN ap HYWEL DDA 950-954, son of Hywel Dda. Co-ruler of Deheubarth.

OWAIN ap HYWEL DDA 950-988, son of Hywel Dda. Co-ruler of Deheubarth.

MAREDUDD ab OWAIN 988-999, son of Owain ap Hywel Dda. Having usurped the throne of Gwynedd, Maredudd was ruler of all Wales.

LLYWELYN ap SEISYLL 999-1023, son-in-law of Maredudd ab Owain. King of Deheubarth and Gwynedd.

RHYDDERCH ab IESTYN   1023-1033. Usurped Gwynedd and Deheubarth.

HYWEL ab EDWIN 1033-1042 or 1043; 1044, son of Edwin ap Hywel Dda. Expelled by Gruffydd ap Llywelyn, Hywel returned with a Danish army (1044) but was killed at the Battle of the Tywi.

MAREDUDD ab EDWIN 1033-1035, brother of Hywel ab Edwin with whom he reigned.

GRUFFYDD ap LLYWELYN 1042 or 1043-1044 when he was deposed; **1044-1063,** son of Llywelyn ap Seisyll; King of Gwynedd.

MAREDUDD ab OWAIN ab EDWIN 1063-1072 killed on the banks of the Rhymney, grandson of Edwin ap Hywel Dda. He died while unsuccessfully fighting Norman invaders, to whom he ceded Gwent.

RHYS ab OWAIN ab EDWIN 1072-1078 murdered, brother of Maredudd ab Owain ab Edwin.

RHYS ap TEWDWR 1078-1093 murdered at Brecon, second cousin of Rhys ab Owain.

1093-1135 Interregnum.

† Princes

GRUFFYDD ap RHYS 1135-1137, son of Rhys ap Tewdwr, b c 1090. Taken to Ireland after the death of his father, Gruffydd was eventually able to return to Deheubarth to found a Principality.

ANARAWD ap GRUFFYDD 1137-1143, illegitimate son of Gruffydd ap Rhys.

CADELL ap GRUFFYDD 1143-1153 abdicated, brother of Anarawd ap Gruffydd; d 1175 having become a monk following his mutilation at the hands of a robber band.

MAREDUDD ap GRUFFYDD 1153-1155, elder legitimate son of Gruffydd ap Rhys, b c 1130.

RHYS ap GRUFFYDD 1153-28 Apr 1197, younger legitimate son of Gruffydd ap Rhys. Rhys' daughter Gwenllian was the great-great-great-grandmother of Owain Tudor who married Catherine, widow of Henry V, and became the grandfather of Henry VII (Henry Tudor).

GRUFFYDD ap RHYS ap GRUFFYDD 1197-25 Jul 1201, eldest son of Rhys ap Gruffydd. In the early 13th century South Wales was gradually absorbed by the English, and Deheubarth ceased to exist.

1201-1400 English rule.

Powys

† Kings

The early kingdom of Powys, founded in the 5th century, was joined to Gwynedd by Rhodri Mawr until the end of the 11th century when it was inherited by the sons of Bleddyn ap Cynfyn.

BLEDDYN ap CYNFYN 1063-1075 murdered, half-brother of Gruffydd ap Llywelyn. King of Gwynedd and Powys, b c 1025.

RHIWALLON 1063-1070, brother of Bleddyn. Co-ruler of Powys.

† Princes

Upon the re-establishment of the independence of Powys, the rulers of that district used the style 'Prince' rather than 'King'.

CADWGAN ap BLEDDYN 1075-?, son of Bleddyn ap Cynfyn. Co-Prince of Powys.

LLYWARCH ap BLEDDYN, son of Bleddyn ap Cynfyn. Co-Prince of Powys.

MADOG ap BLEDDYN 1075-1088 when he was killed at Llech-y-crau by Rhys ap Tewdwr; son of Bleddyn ap Cynfyn. Co-Prince of Powys.

RHIRYD ap BLEDDYN 1075-1088 killed with Madog, son of Bleddyn ap Cynfyn. Co-Prince of Powys.

MAREDUDD ap BLEDDYN 1075-1132, son of Bleddyn ap Cynfyn. He survived his brothers and reunited Powys.

IORWERTH ap BLEDDYN 1075-1103 deposed, son of Bleddyn ap Cynfyn. Given substantial territory by Henry I (1102), he was deprived of his lands in 1103, imprisoned at Shrewsbury until 1110 and killed at Caereinion in 1111.

LLYWELYN ap BLEDDYN (or RHIWALLON ap BLEDDYN), son of Bleddyn ap Cynfyn. Co-Prince of Powys.

MADOG ap MAREDUDD 1132-c 9 Feb 1160, eldest son of Maredudd ap Bleddyn. Upon the death of Madog ap Maredudd, Powys was divided into two lordships - North Powys and South Powys.

† Lords of South Powys (Powys
Wenwynwyn)

OWAIN CYFEILIOG Feb 1160-1195 when he abdicated, nephew of Madog ap Maredudd, b c 1125. Abdicating in 1195, Owain retired to a monastery - the date of his death is not certain.

GWENWYNWYN ab OWAIN 1195-1208 when he was deprived by King John; restored **1210-1215** when he swore allegiance to Llywelyn of Gwynedd; elder son of Owain Cyfeiliog; d in exile 1216.

† Lords of North Powys (Powys Fadog)

GRUFFYDD MAELOR I 1160-1191, son of Madog ap Maredudd.

MADOG ap GRUFFYDD 1191-1236, son of Gruffydd Maelor I.

GRUFFYDD MAELOR II 1236-1269, son of Madog ap Gruffydd.

1269-1400 English rule.

† Prince of Wales

OWAIN GLYNDWR 1400-c 1410 or later, self-proclaimed Prince of Wales, great-great-grandson of Gruffydd Maelor II of Powys Fadog, b c 1354; d after 1416. Henry IV took no action when Owain Glyndwr protested to him at the seizure of part of his estate by Lord Grey. Glyndwr resorted to arms, attracting support from many Welsh who resented English rule. Raising most of Wales in revolt and declaring himself Prince, he planned a Parliament at Machynlleth, allied himself to the disaffected Percys and received aid from France. After the English victory at Grosmont (1405) Welsh resistance faded.

(English rule was restored over most of Wales **from 1405** and over all of Wales **from c 1410.**)

United Provinces, The *see* The Netherlands

United States of America

The eastern seaboard of America was explored by Europeans in the 16th century but permanent colonies were not established until 1607 when Virginia was founded. By 1733 thirteen English colonies, later the first states, had been set up. On 4 Jul 1776 the thirteen colonies unilaterally declared their independence.

Presidents

Before 1937 the presidential term of office began on 4 March, although George Washington's first term began on 30 April; since 1937 the inauguration of the President has taken place on 20 January.

GEORGE WASHINGTON 30 Apr 1789-Mar 1797, b 22 Feb 1732; d 14 Dec 1799. Gaining military experience in the French and Indian wars, he became commander of the American army (1775), largely because of the influence of his powerful home state of Virginia. An unyielding leader, he forced the British to surrender Boston, and he ended the War of Independence by the capture of Yorktown (1781). His was the only name considered in the first presidential election, and, in many ways, he defined the nature of the presidency by his exemplary tenure of that office. He earned the epithet 'Father of His Country'.

JOHN ADAMS Mar 1797-Mar 1801, b 30 Oct 1735; d 4 Jul 1826. Adams was one of the leading political theorists responsible for the American constitution.

THOMAS JEFFERSON Mar 1801-Mar 1809, b 13 Apr 1743; d 4 Jul 1826. A most learned man, distinguished in diplomacy and sciences, Jefferson was one of the main authors of the Declaration of Independence (1776). During his presidency, he strove to keep America out of the Napoleonic wars and was responsible for the Louisiana Purchase.

JAMES MADISON Mar 1809-Mar 1817, b 16 Mar 1751; d 28 Jun 1836. Called the 'Father of the American Constitution', Madison was the major architect of the federal constitution. He was Commander-in-Chief during the war of 1812.

JAMES MONROE Mar 1817-Mar 1825, b 28 Apr 1758; d 4 Jul 1831. He is best remembered for the Monroe Doctrine, a major part of American

Abraham Lincoln who rose from being in turn farm labourer, boat-hand, log-chopper and storekeeper to be President (Radio Times Hulton Picture Library)

foreign policy, which does not tolerate European involvement in the New World.

JOHN QUINCY ADAMS Mar 1825-Mar 1829, b 11 Jul 1767; d 23 Feb 1848. The son of John Adams, he was one of America's greatest diplomats. He took a major role in the early development of the Mid-West, but his presidency was a disappointment with few achievements owing to a quarrel with Andrew Jackson. In his last years, he vigorously embraced the cause of anti-slavery.

ANDREW JACKSON Mar 1829-Mar 1837, b 15 Mar 1767; d 8 Jun 1845.

MARTIN VAN BUREN Mar 1837-Mar 1841, b 5 Dec 1782; d 24 Jul 1862.

WILLIAM HENRY HARRISON 4 Mar-4 Apr 1841, b 9 Feb 1773; d 4 Apr 1841, having caught pneumonia after delivering his long inaugural address in bitter weather and having stubbornly refused to wear a hat or coat.

JOHN TYLER Apr 1841-Mar 1845, b 29 Mar 1790; d 18 Jan 1862. Vice-president Tyler succeeded on the death of President Harrison.

JAMES KNOX POLK Mar 1845-Mar 1849, b 2 Nov 1795; d 15 Jun 1849. A man who succeeded despite having had no schooling, Polk conducted war against Mexico, resulting in large gains of territory including Texas and California. A great President, his dedication to work ruined his health.

ZACHARY TAYLOR Mar 1849-9 Jul 1850, b 24 Nov 1784; d in office 9 Jul 1850. Taylor was elected as the victorious general of the Mexican War in which he won the important battle of Buena Vista.

MILLARD FILLMORE Jul 1850-Mar 1853, b 7 Jan 1800; d 8 Mar 1874. Vice-president Fillmore succeeded on the death of President Taylor.

FRANKLIN PIERCE Mar 1853-Mar 1857, b 23 Nov 1804; d 8 Oct 1869.

JAMES BUCHANAN Mar 1857-Mar 1861, b 23 Apr 1791; d 1 Jun 1868. Unassuming and indecisive, this brilliant lawyer could not stop the Civil War. Although opposed to slavery, he would not support anti-slavery legislation which he regarded as interference in state affairs. When South Carolina seceded, to be followed by other states, he maintained the federal forts in the Confederacy - the immediate cause of the war.

ABRAHAM LINCOLN Mar 1861-15 Apr 1865, b 12 Feb 1809; assassinated 15 Apr 1865. A self-taught, humane and gentle man of lowly pioneer origins, Lincoln's presidency was dominated by the Civil War. In 1863 he emancipated the southern slaves, and later that year he delivered, in superb English, the Gettysburg Address, a lament for the dead and a moving personal commitment to democracy. Acclaimed for preserving the Union and as the liberator of the slaves, he was assassinated, in Ford's Theatre, Washington, a few days after the North's military victory.

ANDREW JOHNSON Apr 1865-Mar 1869, b 29 Dec 1808; d 31 Jul 1875. An unpopular President, who never lived down having taken alcohol to 'steady' himself before his vice-presidential inauguration. Succeeding Lincoln as President, he suffered by comparison and, having fallen out with Congress in the strained atmosphere after the Civil War, he suffered an unsuccessful trial of impeachment based on a technicality.

ULYSSES SIMPSON GRANT Mar 1869-Mar 1877, b (Hiram Ulysses Grant) 27 Apr 1822; d 23 Jul 1885.

RUTHERFORD BIRCHARD HAYES Mar 1877-Mar 1881, b 4 Oct 1822; d 17 Jan 1893.

JAMES ABRAM GARFIELD 4 Mar-19 Sep 1881, b 19 Nov 1831; d 19 Sep 1881 having been mortally wounded by an assassin at Washington station (2 Jul 1881).

CHESTER ALAN ARTHUR Sep 1881-Mar 1885, b 5 Oct 1831; d 18 Nov 1886. Vice-president Arthur succeeded on the death of President Garfield.

STEPHEN GROVER CLEVELAND Mar 1885-Mar 1889, b 18 Mar 1837; d 24 Jun 1908. The only President to serve two non-consecutive terms.

BENJAMIN HARRISON Mar 1889-Mar 1893, b 20 Aug 1833; d 13 Mar 1901. The grandson of William Henry Harrison.

STEPHEN GROVER CLEVELAND Mar 1893-Mar 1897.

WILLIAM McKINLEY Mar 1897-14 Sep 1901, b 29 Jan 1843; d 14 Sep 1901 having been shot by an anarchist on 6 Sep 1901.

THEODORE ROOSEVELT Sep 1901-Mar 1909, b 27 Oct 1858; d 6 Jan 1919. 'Teddy' Roosevelt, the vice-president who succeeded on McKinley's death, greatly expanded the powers of his office, intervening between business and labour and interfering, somewhat high-handedly, in the internal affairs of several Latin American states. He was a soldier (his volunteer cavalry achieved dramatic victories in Cuba in the Spanish War of 1898), explorer, author, hunter and rugged sportsman who believed in much physical exercise - in all, a popular hero who enjoyed being President.

WILLIAM HOWARD TAFT Mar 1909-Mar 1913, b 15 Sep 1857; d 8 Mar 1930.

THOMAS WOODROW WILSON Mar 1913-Mar 1921, b 28 Dec 1856; d 23 Feb 1924. Wilson brought America into World War I and then tried to impose his great ideals, summarised in the Fourteen Points, on the victors at the Versailles conference. His was the concept of a League of Nations to preserve world peace, and he was physically broken by his vigorous, but fruitless, campaign to persuade an isolationist America to join.

WARREN GAMALIEL HARDING Mar 1921-2 Aug 1923, b 2 Nov 1865; d in office.

JOHN CALVIN COOLIDGE Aug 1923-Mar 1929, b 4 Jul 1872; d 5 Jan 1933.

HERBERT CLARK HOOVER Mar 1929-Mar 1933, b 10 Aug 1874; d 20 Oct 1964. A controversial figure, Hoover was a Quaker humanitarian whose belief in personal dignity and responsibilities prevented him from granting federal aid during the Great Depression.

FRANKLIN DELANO ROOSEVELT Mar 1933-12 Apr 1945, b 30 Jan 1882; d in office. Few Americans excite such mixed feelings as Franklin Roosevelt who transformed the activities of the US Government, involving it deeply in welfare and social affairs, and provoking much criticism of 'interference'. His New Deal was an effective policy of relief and economic recovery after the Depression. A successful President and an able war leader, this distant relative of Theodore Roosevelt was the only President to be re-elected three times.

HARRY S. TRUMAN Apr 1945-Jan 1953, b 8 May 1884; d 26 Dec 1972. The Marshall Plan, the establishment of NATO, the Berlin Airlift and American involvement in Korea were the main items of Truman's successful foreign policy. He had been Roosevelt's vice-president.

DWIGHT DAVID EISENHOWER Jan 1953-Jan 1961, b 14 Oct 1890; d 28 Mar 1969. The distinguished general (Commander-in-Chief in North Africa 1942-1944 and West Europe 1944-1945) strengthened the Western Alliance during his presidency.

JOHN FITZGERALD KENNEDY Jan 1961-22 Nov 1963, b 29 May 1917; assassinated at Dallas 22 Nov 1963.

LYNDON BAINES JOHNSON Nov 1963-Jan 1969, b 27 Aug 1908; d 22 Jan 1973. Johnson, Kennedy's vice-president, accomplished an important domestic reform programme, but divided America by further involvement in the war in Vietnam.

RICHARD MILHOUS NIXON Jan 1969-9 Aug 1974, b 9 Jan 1913. The only President to have resigned, Nixon left office after admitting he had attempted to conceal evidence about the Watergate affair.

GERALD RUDOLPH FORD Aug 1974-Jan 1977, b (Leslie Lynch King - he was adopted and renamed by his step-father) 14 Jul 1913. Gerald Ford was Nixon's second vice-president.

JAMES EARL CARTER since 20 Jan 1977, b 1 Oct 1924.

The Confederate States of America

President

JEFFERSON DAVIS Feb 1861-May 1865 when captured by northern troops, b 3 Jun 1808; d 6 Dec 1889. He was President of the eleven secessionist states during the American Civil War and although charged with treason afterwards he was never brought to trial.

Hawaii

Hawaii was an independent Kingdom and then a Republic before it was annexed by the United States in 1900.

† Kings

KAMEHAMEHA I 1810-1819, b 1758.
KAMEHAMEHA II 1819-Jul 1824, son of Kamehameha I, b 1797.
KAMEHAMEHA III Jul 1824-1854, b 1814.
KAMEHAMEHA IV 1854-Nov 1863, b 1834.
KAMEHAMEHA V Nov 1863-Jan 1873, brother of Kamehameha IV, b 1830.
LUNALILO Jan 1873-Feb 1874, b 1835.
KALAKAUA Feb 1874-1891, b 1836.
LILIUOKALANI (Queen) 1891-1893 deposed, b 1838; d 1917. Queen Liliuokalani was deposed in a revolution, the people seeking constitutional reform after the misrule of two non-Royal Kings - the Royal House having become extinct in Jan 1873.

President

SANFORD BALLARD DOLE 1893-1898; 1898-1900 under American control.

Upper Peru see Bolivia

Upper Volta

The colonial territory of Upper Volta which existed between 1919 and 1932 was reconstituted by the French authorities in 1947, and was granted independence on 5 Aug 1960.

Presidents

MAURICE YAMÉOGO Head of State 5 Aug-8 Dec 1960; President 8 Dec 1960-3 Jan 1966 when he was deposed in a coup, b 31 Dec 1921.
Lieut-Col SANGOULE LAMIZANA (later Gen) since 3 Jan 1966.

Prime Ministers

MAURICE YAMÉOGO 5 Aug 1960-3 Jan 1966; see President Yaméogo.
Lieut-Col SANGOULE LAMIZANA (later Gen) 7 Jan 1966-13 Feb 1971, b 1916; see President Lamizana.
GÉRARD KANGO OUEDRAOGO 13 Feb 1971-11 Feb 1974.
Lieut-Col SANGOULE LAMIZANA (later Gen) since 11 Feb 1971; also President.

Ur and Urnanshe see Babylonia

Urartu

A Kingdom of the ancient world, Urartu was situated in eastern Asia Minor and Armenia.

† Kings

ARRAMU fl.850 BC.
SARDURI I c840-c830 BC.
ISHPUINI c830-c810 BC, son of Sarduri I.
MEINUA c810-781 BC, son of Ishpuini.
ARGISHTI I (or ARGISTIS I) c780-756 BC, son of Meinua.
SARDURI II c755-c735 BC probably deposed, grandson of Meinua; date of death uncertain.
RUSAS I (or UEDIPRIS-RUSAS) c735-c713 BC, son of Sarduri II.

ARGISHTI II (or ARGISTIS II) *c*712-685 BC, son of Rusas I.

RUSAS II sole ruler *c*685-*c*650 BC; co-ruler *c*650-*c*645 BC, kinsman of Rusas I.

SARDURI III co-ruler *c*650-*c*645 BC; sole ruler *c*645-*c*640 BC, son of Rusas II.

SARDURI IV *c*640-? BC, son of Sarduri III.

ERIMENA fl. after *c*640 BC, probably kinsman of Sarduri IV.

RUSAS III ?-609 BC when the Urartian state was overthrown by the Scythian invasion, son of Erimena; date of death uncertain.

(Some sources maintain that Urartu lingered as an independent Kingdom until *c*593 BC.)

Uruguay

Spanish from 1516, Portuguese for a brief period up to 1762, Spanish from 1762, Uruguay - then known as Banda Oriental - attempted to obtain independence between 1813 and 1820. A Brazilian province from 1821 to 1825 the country was fought over by that state and Argentina until both sides recognised its independence by the Treaty of Montevideo (27 Aug 1828).

BANDA ORIENTAL

Chief of the Orientals and Protector

JOSÉ GERVASIO ARTIGAS 1813-Sep 1820 deposed by Brazilian invasion, b 19 Jun 1764; d 23 Sep 1850. Heroic and resourceful he is regarded as the Father of Uruguay, but the brief independence of the state he created was ended by a Brazilian invasion before which he executed a remarkable withdrawal of the civilian population.

Sep 1820-1821 Brazilian occupation.

1821-1825 Uruguay formed the Cisplatine province of Brazil.

1825-1828 War over Uruguay between Argentina and Brazil.

THE ORIENTAL REPUBLIC OF URUGUAY

Presidents

Gen **JOSÉ FRUCTUOSO RIVERA** 22 Oct 1830-Mar 1835, b *c*1790; d 1854. One of the legendary 'Thirty Three' who led the revolt against Brazilian rule.

MANUEL ORIBE 1 Mar 1835-Oct 1838, b 1790; d 1857.

Gen **JOSÉ FRUCTUOSO RIVERA** 21 Oct 1838-1843.

JOAQUIN SUAREL 1843-Apr 1852. In the war against the Argentinian Rosas during Suarel's term Montevideo endured an eight month siege.

JUAN FRANCISCO GIRÓ 1 Mar 1852-Mar 1854, b 1781; d 1863.

Col **VENANCIO FLORES** Mar 1854-Oct 1855 deposed.

MANUEL BASILICO BUSTAMENTE acting President Oct 1855-Mar 1856, b 1785; d 1863.

GABRIEL ANTONIO PEREIRA 1 Mar 1856-Mar 1860, b 1794; d 1861.

BERNARDO PRUDENCIO BERRO 1 Mar 1860-Mar 1864, b 1803; d 1868.

ANASTASIO CRUZ AGUIRRE acting President 1 Mar 1864-Feb 1865.

Col **VENANCIO FLORES** acting President Feb 1865-1866, b 1808; assassinated 1868.

FRANCISCO ANTONIO VIDAL 1866-1868, b 1827; d 1889.

PEDRO VARELA acting President Feb 1868.

Col **LORENZO BATLLE y GRAU** 1 Mar 1868-Mar 1872, b 1810; d 1887.

TOMÁS GOMENSORO 1 Mar 1872-Mar 1873, b 1810; d 1900.

JOSÉ ELLAURI 1 Mar 1873-Mar 1875, b 1839; d 1897.

PEDRO VARELA 15 Mar 1875-Mar 1876 deposed.

Col **LORENZO LATORRE** 11 Mar 1876-Mar 1880, b 1844; d 1916.

FRANCISCO ANTONIO VIDAL 17 Mar 1880-Mar 1882.

Gen **MÁXIMO SANTOS** 1 Mar 1882-Nov 1886, b 1847; d 1889.

Gen **MÁXIMO TAJES** 19 Nov 1886-Mar 1890, b 1852; d 1912.

JULIO HERRERA y OBES Mar 1890-Mar 1894, b 1842; d 1912.

JUAN IDIARTE BORDA Mar 1894-23 Aug 1897, b 1844; d in office - assassinated.

JUAN LINDOLFO CUESTAS Aug 1897-Feb 1903, b 1837; d 1905.

JOSÉ BATLLE y ORDÓÑEZ Feb 1903-Feb 1907, son of Col Lorenzo Batllé y Grau, b 21 May 1856; d 20 Oct 1929. Uruguay's greatest President and the dominant political thinker of his country. He introduced democratic practices to Uruguay and advocated a collegiate system of government which was used from 1952 to 1967 during which time Uruguay was a real democracy.

CLAUDIO WILLIMAN Feb 1907-Mar 1911, b 1863; d 1934.

JOSÉ BATLLE y ORDÓÑEZ 1 Mar 1911-Mar 1915.

FELICIANO VIERA 1 Mar 1915-Mar 1919, b 1870; d 1929.

BALTASAR BRUM Mar 1919-Mar 1923, b 18 Jun 1883; d 31 Mar 1933 - committed suicide as a protest against Terra's coup.

JOSÉ SERRATO Mar 1923-Mar 1927.

JUAN CAMPISTEGUY Mar 1927-Mar 1931, b 1859; d 1937.

GABRIEL TERRA Mar 1931-Mar 1938, b *c*1873; d 15 Sep 1942. He undid the democratic reforms of Batlle, seized absolute power in a coup and instituted a dictatorship.

Gen **ALFREDO BALDOMIR 27 Mar 1938-Mar 1943,** brother-in-law of President Terra, b 1884; d 25 Feb 1948.

Dr **JUAN JOSÉ AMÉZAGA 1 Mar 1943-Mar 1947.**

Dr **TOMÁS BERRETA 1 Mar-2 Aug 1947,** b 1875; d in office.

LUIS BATLLE BERRES Aug 1947-Mar 1951, b 1897; d 1964.

ANDRES MARTINEZ TRUEBA 1 Mar 1951-Mar 1952.

Presidents of the National Council

Uruguay instituted a collegiate Presidential system of government based by Batlle on the Swiss constitution.

ANDRES MARTINEZ TRUEBA 1 Mar 1952-Mar 1955.

LUIS BATLLE BERRES 1 Mar 1955-Mar 1956.

Dr **ALBERTO F. ZUBIRÍA 1 Mar 1956-Mar 1957.**

ARTURO LEZAMA 1 Mar 1957-Mar 1958.

Dr **CARLO L. FISCHER 1 Mar 1958-Mar 1959.**

Dr **MARTIN R. ECHEGOYEN 1 Mar 1959-Mar 1960.**

BENITO NARDONE 1 Mar 1960-Mar 1961.

EDUARDO V. CRESPO 1 Mar 1961-Mar 1962.

FAUSTINO HARRISON 1 Mar 1962-Mar 1963.

DANIEL FERNÁNDEZ CRESPO 1 Mar 1963-Mar 1964.

LUIS GIANNATTASIO 1 Mar 1964-7 Feb 1965; d in office.

Dr **WASHINGTON BELTRÁN** acting President **7 Feb-1 Mar 1965;** President **1 Mar 1965-Mar 1966,** b 1914.

ALBERTO HEBER USHER 1 Mar 1966-Mar 1967.

In **1967** the 'Swiss' system was abolished.

Presidents

The presidential system of government was reintroduced in 1967.

Gen **OSCAR DANIEL GESTIDO 1 Mar-6 Dec 1967,** b 1901; d in office.

JORGE PACHECO ARECO 6 Dec 1967-Mar 1972, b 9 Apr 1920.

JUAN MARÍA BORDABERRY AROCENA 1 Mar 1972-12 Jun 1976 deposed, b 17 Jun 1928.

Dr **PEDRO ALBERTO DEMICHELL LIZASO** acting President **12 Jun-1 Sep 1976,** b 7 Aug 1896.

Dr **APARICIO MÉNDEZ since 1 Sep 1976,** b 24 Aug 1904.

Vatican City *see* The Papal State

Venezuela

The site of a landing by Columbus in Aug 1498, the Venezuelan coast was claimed and settled by the Spanish between 1502 and 1530. Three attempts were made to establish an independent Venezuelan state (1811, 1813 and 1815-1816) before the country formed part of an independent Greater Columbia in 1820. In Jan 1830 Venezuela seceded and its independence was recognised from 11 May 1830.

CONFEDERATION OF THE STATES OF VENEZUELA

Dictators

Jul 1811-Apr 1812 Provisional Government.

FRANCISCO de MIRANDA Apr-Jul 1812, b 28 Mar 1750; d in gaol in Spain 14 Jul 1816. His work for Venezuelan independence is largely ignored as he favoured an Empire uniting all Latin American states under a descendant of the Incas.

Jul 1812-Aug 1813 Spanish rule restored.

SIMÓN BOLIVAR Aug 1813-Jan 1814; see Colombia.

Jan 1814-Feb 1819 Spanish rule restored.

SIMÓN BOLIVAR Feb 1819-Dec 1820 when Venezuela joined New Granada in Greater Colombia; see Colombia.

Dec 1820-Jan 1830 Venezuela formed part of Greater Colombia.

PROVISIONAL GOVERNMENT OF VENEZUELA

Head

JOSÉ ANTONIO de PÁEZ 13 Jan-May 1830.

THE REPUBLIC OF VENEZUELA

Presidents

JOSÉ ANTONIO de PAEZ acting President **May 1830-Mar 1831;** President **Mar 1831-Feb 1835,** b 1790; d 1873.

Dr **JOSÉ MARÍA VARGAS Feb 1835-Apr 1836,** b 1786; d 1854.

ANDRES NAVARTE Apr 1836-Jan 1837.

JOSÉ ANTONIO de PÁEZ acting President **Jan-May 1837.**

CARLOS SOUBLETTE May 1837-Jan 1838, b 1795; d 1870.

JOSÉ ANTONIO de PAÉZ acting President **Jan 1838-Feb 1839;** President **Feb 1839-Feb 1843.**

CARLOS SOUBLETTE Feb 1843-Feb 1847.

JOSÉ TADEO MONAGAS Feb 1847-Feb 1851.

President Antonio Guzman Blanco, dictator of Venezuela, who achieved public works and economic progress and still reduced taxation (Radio Times Hulton Picture Library)

JOSÉ GREGORIO MONAGAS Feb 1851-Feb 1855, brother of José Tadeo Monagas, b 1795; d 1858.

JOSÉ TADEO MONAGAS Feb 1855-15 Mar 1858 deposed in coup, b 1784; d 1868. A dictator who reduced the powers of Congress in favour of the presidency.

Gen **JULIÁN CASTRO Mar 1858-Jun 1859.** Resigned at the start of a civil war.

MANUEL FELIPE TOVAR acting President **Jun 1859** - for one week.

Gen **JULIÁN CASTRO** acting President **Jun-Aug 1859.**

PEDRO GAUL acting President **Aug-Sep 1859,** b 1784; d 1862.

MANUEL FELIPE TOVAR Sep 1859-Mar 1861.

PEDRO GAUL Mar-Sep 1861 deposed.

JOSÉ ANTONIO de PÁEZ Sep 1861-Jun 1863.

Gen **JUAN CRISÓSTOMO FALCON** acting President **Jun-Dec 1863**; President **Dec 1863-Jun 1868** fled, b 1820; d 29 Apr 1870. He defeated Páez in the civil war and introduced a federalism that increased the instability of Venezuela.

JOSÉ TADEO MONAGAS acting President **Jun-Dec 1868.**

JOSÉ RUPERTO MONAGAS acting President **Dec 1868-Mar 1869**; President **Mar 1869-Jun 1870,** son of José Tadeo Monagas.

Gen **ANTONIO GUZMÁN BLANCO** acting President **Jun 1870-Feb 1873**; President **Feb 1873-Feb 1877,** b 28 Feb 1829; d 20 Jul 1899. 'The Regenerator', he dominated Venezuela for a generation and surrounded himself with very able ministers. This dictator achieved great public works, agricultural progress, the construction of a rail and road network and an increase in individual prosperity.

Gen **FRANCISCO LINARES ALCÁNTARA Feb 1877-Nov 1878**; d in office.

JACINTO GUTIÉRREZ acting President **Nov 1878-Feb 1879.**

Gen **ANTONIO GUZMÁN BLANCO 25 Feb 1879-May 1884.**

Gen **JOAQUÍN CRESPO May 1884-Sep 1886.**

Gen **ANTONIO GUZMÁN BLANCO 14 Sep 1886-Aug 1887**

HERMOGENES LOPEZ Aug 1887-Oct 1889, b 1828; d 1903.

JOSÉ PABLO ROJAS PAÚL acting President **Feb 1888-Feb 1890,** b 1829; d 1905.

Dr **RAIMUNDO ANDUEZA PALACIO Feb 1890-Oct 1892,** b 1852; d 1900.

Gen **JOAQUÍN CRESPO** acting President **Oct 1892-Feb 1894**; President **Feb 1894-Feb 1898,** b 1845; d in office - assassinated.

Gen **IGNACIO ANDRADE Feb 1898-22 Oct 1899** deposed in coup, b 1839; d 1925.

CIPRIANO CASTRO 22 Oct 1899-19 Dec 1908 deposed *in absentia,* b 14 Oct 1858; d 4 Dec 1924. Having seized power in a minor civil war he ruined the economy with amazing incompetence, and, having reneged on the state's debts, witnessed the seizure of the navy by the European powers.

JUAN VICENTE GOMÉZ acting President **19 Dec 1908-Feb 1910** President **Feb 1910-May 1915,** b 1864; d (in office) 17 Dec 1935. He used the growing oil revenue to achieve remarkable economic development and to make himself the richest man in Latin America. This Indian, with no formal education, proved a capable ruler who held the reigns of power personally or through puppets for 27 years in which peace was restored and the only violence was that frequently committed by the state.

VICTORINO MÁRQUEZ BUSTILLOS acting President **3 May 1915-May 1922.**

JUAN VICENTE GOMÉZ 3 May 1922-May 1929.

Dr **JUAN BAUTISTA PÉREZ 3 May 1929-Jun 1931,** b 1869; d 1952.

Dr **PEDRO ITRIAGO CHACIN 24 Jun-13 Jul 1931.**

JUAN VICENTE GOMÉZ 13 Jul 1931-17 Dec 1935.

Gen **ELEAZAR LÓPEZ CONTRERAS** acting President **18 Dec 1935-19 Apr 1936**; President **19 Apr 1936-May 1941,** b 1883.

Gen **ISAÍAS MEDINA ANGARITA 6 May 1941-18 Oct 1945** deposed in coup, b 1897; d 15 Sep 1953.

RÓMULO BETANCOURT **20 Oct 1945-Feb 1948,** b 22 Feb 1908.

RÓMULO GALLEGOS FREIRE **15 Feb-24 Nov 1948** deposed in coup, b 2 Aug 1884; d 4 Apr 1969. The distinguished author.

Lieut-Col **CARLOS DELGADO CHALBAUD** Head of military junta **24 Nov 1948-13 Nov 1950** when he was assassinated.

13-27 Nov 1950 Military junta.

Dr **GERMÁN SUAREZ FLAMERICH 27 Nov 1950-3 Dec 1952,** b 1908.

Col **MARCOS PÉREZ JIMÉNEZ 3 Dec 1952-23 Jan 1958** deposed in coup, b 25 Apr 1914.

Rear Admiral **WOLFGANG LARRAZÁBAL UGUETO** acting President **23 Jan-Nov 1958.**

From this term Venezuela has been one of the three Latin American states to enjoy a full democracy upon the West European model.

Dr **EDGARD SANABRIA** acting President **14 Nov 1958-Feb 1959,** b 1911.

RÓMULO BETANCOURT **13 Feb 1959-Mar 1964.**

RAÚL LEONI **11 Mar 1964-Mar 1969,** b 1905.

Dr **RAFAEL CALDERA RODRIGUEZ 9 Mar 1969-Mar 1974,** b 24 Jan 1916.

CARLOS ANDRÉS PÉREZ RODRIGUEZ **since 12 Mar 1974,** b 27 Oct 1922.

Venice *see* Italy

Vietnam

A Vietnamese Kingdom, ruled by the Le Dynasty, was founded in the 15th century and divided into two states in 1757. Reunited in 1802 under Gia Long, Vietnam was conquered by the French (1858-1883). The Emperors continued as monarchs of the French protected state of Annam. After World War II a Communist regime was established in the north, although it did not gain a clear territorial expression until the country was partitioned in 1954. In the south an independent Empire of Vietnam was formed in Jun 1954 but was replaced by a Republic in 1955. Communist forces gradually overran the south Saigon falling in Apr 1975. A reunited Vietnam - the Communist 'Socialist Republic of Vietnam' - came into existence on 2 Jul 1976.

THE EMPIRE OF VIETNAM

† Emperors

NGUYEN DYNASTY
GIA LONG (Nguyen Anh) **1802-1820.**
MINH MANG **1820-1841.**
THIEU TRI **1841-1847.**
TU DUC **1847-9 Jul 1883,** son of Thieu Tri.

25 Aug 1883 Annam - central Vietnam - became a French protectorate.

THE EMPIRE OF ANNAM

† Emperors
(under French protection)

THANH THAI **1889-1907** deposed.

DUY TAN **Sep 1907-13 May 1916,** son of Thanh Tri, b 1883; d (in an air accident) Dec 1945. He was exiled after an attempted revolt against French rule.

KHAI DINH **May 1916-6 Nov 1925,** son of Duy Tan.

BAO DIN **Nov 1925-Nov 1945** abdicated.

1940-45 Japanese rule.

1945-6 French rule restored.

1946-1954 Autonomy under French rule.

THE EMPIRE OF VIETNAM

† Emperor

BAO DIN **4 Jun 1954-26 Oct 1955** deposed, b (Nguyen Vinh Thuy) 1913.

Prime Ministers

Prince **BUU LOC 4 Jun 1954-16 Jun 1955.**

NGO DINH-DIEM **16 Jun-26 Oct 1955** when he became President.

THE REPUBLIC OF VIETNAM
(South Vietnam)

Presidents

NGO DINH-DIEM **26 Oct 1955-2 Nov 1963,** b 1 Jan 1901; d in office - assassinated in coup.

2-4 Nov 1963 Military Revolutionary Council.

Maj-Gen **DUONG VAN MINH** Head of State *ad interim* **4 Nov 1963-30 Jan 1964** deposed in coup.

Maj-Gen **NGUYEN KHANH 30 Jan-8 Feb 1964.**

Maj-Gen **DUONG VAN MINH 8 Feb-16 Aug 1964** deposed.

Gen **NGUYEN KHANH 16-25 Aug 1964,** b 1927.

26 Aug-8 Sep 1964 Three man Leadership Committee.

Gen **DUONG VAN MINH 8 Sep-24 Oct 1964.**

PHAN KHAC SUU **26 Oct 1964-11 Jun 1965.**

Gen **NGUYEN VAN THIEU** acting Head of State **11 Jun 1965-Oct 1967;** President **31 Oct 1967-Apr 1975,** b 5 Apr 1923.

TRAN VAN HUONG **21-28 Apr 1975.**

Gen **DUONG VAN MINH 28-30 Apr 1975** when Saigon fell to the Communists.

Prime Ministers

NGO DINH-DIEM **26 Oct 1955-2 Nov 1963.**

2-4 Nov 1963 Military Revolutionary Committee.
NGUYEN NGOC THO 4 Nov 1963-Feb 1964.
Maj-Gen **NGUYEN KHANH 8 Feb-24 Aug 1964.**
Dr **NGUYEN XUAN OANH 29 Aug-3 Sep 1964.**
Gen **NGUYEN KHANH 3 Sep-26 Oct 1964.**
TRAN VAN HUONG 30 Oct 1964-27 Jan 1965
deposed in coup, b 1 Dec 1903.
Dr **NGUYEN XUAN OANH** acting PM **28 Jan-16 Feb 1965.**
Dr **PHAN HUY QUAT 16 Feb-11 Jun 1965.**
11-19 Jun 1965 Committee for the Direction of the State.
Air Vice-Marshal **NGUYEN CAO KY 19 Jun 1965-Oct 1967,** b 8 Sep 1930.
NGUYEN VAN LOC 31 Oct 1967-18 May 1969, b 24 Aug 1922.
TRAN VAN HUONG 18 May-22 Aug 1969.
Gen **TRAN THIEN KHIEM 23 Aug 1969-Apr 1975,** b 15 Dec 1925.
NGUYEN BA CAN 4-22 Apr 1975.
VU VAN MAU 28-30 Apr 1975 when Saigon fell to the Communists.

THE DEMOCRATIC REPUBLIC OF VIETNAM
(North Vietnam)

Presidents

HO CHI MINH 28 Aug 1945-3 Sep 1969, b (Nguyen Ai-Quoc) 19 May 1890; d in office. A former steward, who once worked as a pastry-cook in the Carlton Hotel in London, this founder member of the French Communist party became a full-time agitator against French rule in Indochina. He founded the Communist northern Republic but was confined to rural areas until the French evacuated Hanoi in 1954. Violating international agreements and the neutrality of Laos and Cambodia he waged a constant campaign of war and subversion against the legal Government of the South.
TON DUC THANG Sep 1969-Jul 1976 when he became President of reunited Vietnam.

Prime Ministers

HO CHI MINH 28 Aug 1945-Sep 1955.
PHAM VAN DONG 20 Sep 1955-Jul 1976 when he became PM of reunited Vietnam.

Chairman of the Vietnamese Party of Labour
(Communist Party)

HO CHI MINH Mar 1951-3 Sep 1969.
LE DUAN Sep 1969-Jul 1976 when he became head of the Communist Party of reunited Vietnam.

THE PROVISIONAL REVOLUTIONARY GOVERNMENT OF THE REPUBLIC OF VIETNAM
(South Vietnam)

Head of Government

HUYNH TAN PHAT 30 Apr 1975-2 Jul 1976 when Vietnam was reunited.

THE SOCIALIST REPUBLIC OF VIETNAM

(The merger of North and South Vietnam)

President

TON DUC THANG since **2 Jul 1976,** b 20 Aug 1888.

Prime Minister

PHAM VAN DONG since **2 Jul 1976,** b 1 Mar 1906.

Chairman of the Vietnamese Party of Labour
(Communist Party)

LE DUAN since **2 Jul 1976.**

Vijayanagar *see* India

Visigoths, Kings of the *see* Spain

Vladimir, Grand Princes of *see* Union of the Soviet Socialist Republics

Waldeck *see* Germany

Wales *see* United Kingdom

Warsaw, Grand Duchy *see* Poland

Western Samoa

Western Samoa was a German protectorate (from 1900 until World War I), then a New Zealand Trust Territory until independence was achieved on 1 Jan 1962.

Heads of State

Chief **TUPUA TAMASESE MEA'OLE** Joint Head of State **1 Jan 1962-5 Apr 1963** when he died in office.
Chief **MALIETOA TANUMAFILI II** Joint Head of State **1 Jan 1962-5 Apr 1963**; sole Head of State **since 5 Apr 1963**, b 1913.

Prime Ministers

FIAME MATA'AFA FAUMUINA MULINU'U II 1 Jan 1962-1970.
TUPUA TAMASESE LEALOFI IV 1970-1973, b 1922.
FIAME MATA'AFA FAUMUINA MULINU'U II 1973-22 May 1975 when he died in office.
TUPUA TAMASESE LEALOFI IV May 1975-Mar 1976, b 1922.
TUPUOLA TAISI EFI since Mar 1976, b 1936.

West Germany *see* Federal Republic of Germany

Westphalia *see* Germany

West Saxons or Wessex *see* Anglo-Saxon Kingdoms, United Kingdom

Wurttemberg *see* Germany

Yapahuva Kingdom *see* Sri Lanka

Yemen

Part of the Ottoman Empire until 1916 Yemen became a Kingdom under an Imam until the revolution of 1962 which created the Yemeni Arab Republic.

THE KINGDOM OF YEMEN.

† Imams

ZAYDI OR HAMIDUDDIN DYNASTY
YAHIA 1916-1948. He had to virtually rebuild the country from scratch after the Turkish administrators were expelled.
AHMED 1948-18 Sep 1962.
MOHAMMED el BADR 18-27 Sep 1962 deposed.

Prime Ministers

Emir **SEIF el-ISLAM ABDULLAH el HASSAN Mar 1948-1958.**
Emir **MOHAMMED el-BADR 1958-Sep 1962**; see Imam Mohammed.

THE YEMENI ARAB REPUBLIC

Presidents

Col **ABDULLAH SALLAL** acting Head of State **29 Sep-31 Oct 1962**; President **31 Oct 1962-5 Nov 1967** deposed, b 1917.
Lieut-Col **MOHAMMED al IRIANI 5 Nov 1967-13 Jun 1974** deposed.
Col **IBRAHIM MOHAMMED al HAMADI 13 Jun 1974-11 Oct 1977,** b 1943; d in office - assassinated.
Lieut-Col **AHMED HUSSAIN al GHASMI 11 Oct 1977-24 Jun 1978**; died in office - assassinated.
QADI ABDUL KARIM al ARSHI since 24 Jun 1978.

Prime Ministers

Col **ABDULLAH SALLAL 28 Sep 1962-Apr 1963**; see President Sallal.
ABDEL LATIF DHAIFALLAH 26 Apr 1963-May 1964.
Maj-Gen **MAMOUD al-JAIFI 4 May 1964-Jan 1965.**
Maj-Gen **HASSAN al-AMRI 5 Jan-15 Apr 1965.**
AHMED MOHAMMED NOOMAN 15 Apr-6 Jul 1965.
Col **ABDULLAH SALLAL 6-18 Jul 1965**; see President Sallal.
Maj-Gen **HASSAN al-AMRI 18 Jul 1965-Sep 1966.**
Col **ABDULLAH SALLAL 9 Sep 1966-5 Nov 1967** deposed; see President Sallal.
MUHSIN al AINI 5 Nov-18 Dec 1967.
Maj-Gen **HASSAN al-AMRI 18 Dec 1967-Sep 1969.**
ABDULLAH al KHORSHUMI 2 Sep 1969-Feb 1970.
MUHSIN al AINI 2 Feb 1970-Feb 1971.
ABDEL SALAM SABRA acting PM **26 Feb-3 May 1971.**
AHMED MOHAMMED NOOMAN 3 May-20 Jul 1971; acting PM **Jul-Aug 1971.**
Maj-Gen **HASSAN al-AMRI 24 Aug-16 Sep 1971.**
MUHSIN al AINI 16 Sep 1971-Dec 1972.
QADI ABDULLAH al HIJRI 30 Dec 1972-11 Feb 1974; assassinated in London 10 Apr 1977.
HASSAN MAKKI 11 Feb-22 Jun 1974.
MUHSIN al AINI 22 Jun 1974-Jan 1975, b 1932.
Col **ABDEL LATIF DHAIFALLAH** PM ad interim **16-23 Jan 1975.**
ABDEL AZIZ ABDEL GHANI since 23 Jan 1975.

Yemen, People's Democratic Republic of *see* South Yemen

York, Kings of *see* Anglo-Saxon Kingdoms, United Kingdom

Yugoslavia

A Kingdom of the Serbs, Croats and Slovenes was formed during the period of pan-Slavic euphoria that swept the Balkans at the end of World War I. The Kingdom - a union of the former Kingdoms of Serbia and Montenegro plus Bosnia-Hercegovina, Croatia, Carniola, and Voivodina (all previously part of the Austro-Hungarian Empire) - was proclaimed on 24 Nov 1918 and adopted the name Yugoslavia on 3 Oct 1929. A Communist Republic was established in Nov 1945.

THE KINGDOM OF YUGOSLAVIA

† Kings

Prior to 3 Oct 1929 styled 'of the Serbs, Croats and Slovenes'.

PETER I King of Serbia from Jun 1903; **24 Nov 1918-16 Aug 1921,** son of Alexander I, Prince of Serbia, b 11 Jul 1844.

ALEXANDER I **Aug 1921-9 Oct 1934** assassinated, son of Peter I, b 16 Dec 1888. As the conflicting interests of the various peoples of the new Kingdom made Yugoslavia virtually ungovernable, Alexander assumed dictatorial powers.

PETER II **Oct 1934-29 Nov 1945** when a Republic was declared, son of Alexander I, b 6 Sep 1923; d in exile 3 Nov 1970.

Prime Ministers

Dr **NICOLA PASIC Nov-Dec 1918,** b 31 Dec 1845; d 10 Dec 1926. The dominating figure in Serbian politics from 1891.

STOJAN PROTIC Dec 1918-Aug 1919, b 1857; d 1923.

LJUBOMIR DAVIDOVIC Aug 1919-Feb 1920, b 24 Dec 1863; d 19 Feb 1940.

STOJAN PROTIC Feb-May 1920.

MILENKO VESNIC May 1920-Jan 1921, b 1862; d 1921.

Dr **NICOLA PASIC 1 Jan 1921-Jul 1924.**

LJUBOMIR DAVIDOVIC Jul-Nov 1924.

Dr **NICOLA PASIC Nov 1924-Apr 1926.**

Dr **NICOLA UZONOVIC Apr 1926-Apr 1927,** b 1873; d 1954?

Dr **VELJA VUKICIVIC Apr 1927-Jul 1928,** b 1871; d 1930.

Dr **ANTON KOROSEC 28 Jul 1928-Jan 1929,** b 12 May 1872; d 14 Dec 1940. A Catholic priest.

Gen **PETAR ZIVKOVIC 6 Jan 1929-Apr 1932,** b 1879; d 3 Feb 1947. With King Alexander he established a dictatorship.

Dr **VOYISLAV MARINKOVIC 11 Apr-Jul 1932,** b 1876; d 18 Sep 1935.

Dr **MILAN SERSKIC 11 Jul 1932-Jan 1934,** b 1880; d ?

Dr **NICOLA UZONOVIC 27 Jan-Dec 1934.**

BOGOLYUB YEVTIC 21 Dec 1934-Jun 1935, b 1886; d in exile 1960.

Dr **MILAN STOYADINOVIC 25 Jun 1935-Feb 1939,** b 1888; d in exile 1961.

Dr **DRAGISA CVETKOVIC 5 Feb 1939-27 Mar 1941** deposed in coup, b 1893; d in exile 1969.

Gen **DUSAN SIMOVIC 27 Mar-17 Apr 1941; from Apr 1941** in exile.

Prime Ministers of the Royal Yugoslav Government in Exile.

Gen **DUSAN SIMOVIC Mar 1941-Jan 1942,** b 1882; d 1962.

Prof **SLOBODAN JOVANOVIC Jan 1942-Jun 1943,** b 1870; d in exile 1959.

MILOS TRIFUNOVIC 27 Jun-7 Aug 1943, b c 1877; d 1957.

Dr **BOZIDAR PURIC 7 Aug 1943-1 Jun 1944,** b 1891.

Dr **IVAN SUBASIC 1 Jun 1944-Feb 1945** when he returned to Belgrade.

CROATIA

A puppet Republic, later a Kingdom, of Croatia was created in 1941 sponsored by the Axis powers.

† King

TOMISLAV **18 May 1941-1943** renounced all claims, Duke of Spoleto and great-grandson of King Vittorio Emanuele II of Italy, b (Prince AIMONE of Savoy) 9 Mar 1900; d 30 Jan 1948.

Head of Government

ANTE PAVELIC **10 Apr 1941-May 1945,** b 14 Jul 1889; d 28 Dec 1959. He was the leader of the Ushtashe terrorists who were the murderers of King Alexander.

THE PROVISIONAL GOVERNMENT OF YUGOSLAVIA

Formed underground in Nazi occupied Yugoslavia in 1943.

Head of Government

Gen **JOSIP BROZ TITO** (later Marshal) **30 Nov 1943-Mar 1945.**

THE YUGOSLAV GOVERNMENT OF NATIONAL UNITY

Prime Minister

Marshal **JOSIP BROZ TITO 7 Mar-29 Nov 1945.**

THE PEOPLE'S REPUBLIC OF YUGOSLAVIA

From 7 Apr 1963 styled **The Socialist Republic of Yugoslavia.**

Presidents

Styled President of the Presidium of the National Assembly before Jan 1953; President from Jan 1953 to Jul 1971; President of the Presidency Council from 7 Jul 1971.

Dr **IVAN RIBAR 2 Dec 1945-14 Jan 1953,** b 21 Jan 1881; d 2 Feb 1968.
Marshal **JOSIP BROZ TITO since 14 Jan 1953,** b (Josip Broz) 7 May 1892.

Prime Ministers

From 1963 styled President of the Federal Executive Council.

Marshal **JOSIP BROZ TITO 29 Nov 1945-14 Jan 1953** when the post of Premier was abolished by constitutional amendment.
Jan 1953-7 Apr 1963 Premiership in abeyance until the post was revived by constitutional amendment.
PETAR STAMBOLIC 30 Jun 1963-May 1967, b 12 Jul 1912.
MIKA SPILJAK 18 May 1967-May 1969 , b 28 Nov 1916.
MITJA RIBICIC 17 May 1969-30 Jul 1971, b 1919.
DZEMAL BIJEDIC 30 Jul 1971-18 Jan 1977, b 1917; d in office (killed in an air accident).
VESELIN DJURANOVIC since 14 Feb 1977, b 1925.

Montenegro

The fighting Montenegrins in their mountain fastnesses were able to maintain a degree of independence of the Ottoman Turks though the sovereignty of the little state was not recognised until 1878. Montenegro was ruled by a Vladika, or Prince-Bishop, from 1696 a member of the

Marshal Josip Broz Tito who since his quarrel with Moscow has maintained an independence of the Soviet block (Radio Times Hulton Picture Library)

Petrovic family, until the establishment of the Principality in 1852. Declared a Kingdom in 1910, Montenegro ceased to exist *de facto* in 1918, *de jure* in 1922, annexed to neighbouring Yugoslavia.

† Vladikas

DANILO I Jul 1696-21 Jan 1735, b 20 Dec 1675.
SAVA II Jan 1735-9 Mar 1782, cousin of Danilo I, b 18 Jan 1702.
PETAR I Mar 1782-31 Oct 1830, cousin of Sava II, b 4 May 1747. A formidable Prince-Bishop who fought the Turks and secured Montenegro's autonomy.
PETAR II Nov 1830-31 Oct 1851, nephew of Petar I, b 13 Jul 1813. Recognised as the greatest writer in his language.
DANILO II Oct 1851-Jan 1852 when he became Prince.

† Princes

DANILO I (formerly Danilo II, Vladika of Montenegro) **8 Jan 1852-13 Aug 1860** when he was assassinated, nephew of Petar II, b 2 Jun 1826. Unattracted by celibacy, Danilo refused to be consecrated Bishop and abolished the position of Vladika.
NIKOLA I Aug 1860-28 Aug 1910 when he became King.

† King

NIKOLA I   Prince from Aug 1860; King **28 Aug 1910-Nov 1918** when Montenegro was incorporated in the enlarged Serbian Kingdom, nephew of Danilo I, b 7 Oct 1841; d 1 Mar 1921.

Serbia

Serbia threw off allegiance to the Byzantine Empire *c*1180 and flourished as an independent state until 1389 when the Ottoman Turks invaded. Ottoman rule lasted from 1389 to 1804 *de facto* (except for a brief spell of Austrian control in the 18th century). Independent Serbia merged with the other South Slav peoples to form what became known as Yugoslavia after World War I (see Yugoslavia).

MEDIEVAL SERBIA

† Grand Zupans of Serbia

NEMANYA DYNASTY
STEPAN I NEMANYA   Ruler under Byzantine Empire from *c*1165; independent Grand Zupan *c*1180-1196 abdicated; d 1200 having retired to the monastery he founded with his son, St Sava.
STEPAN II   Grand Zupan **1196-1217** when he became King.

† Kings

NEMANYA DYNASTY
STEPAN II   Grand Zupan from 1196; King **1217-1227 or 1228**, son of Stepan I Nemanya.
STEPAN III RADOSLAV   **1227 or 1228-1234.**
STEPAN IV VLADISLAV   **1234-1243.**
STEPAN V UROS I   **1243-1276.**
STEPAN VI DRAGUTIN   **1276-1282.**
STEPAN VII UROS II MILUTIN   **1282-1321,** son of Stepan V Uros I.
STEPAN VIII UROS III DECANSKI   **1321-1331.**
STEPAN IX UROS IV DUSAN   **1331-1345 or 1346** when he became Emperor.

† Emperors

NEMANYA DYNASTY
STEPAN IX UROS IV DUSAN   (or STEPAN DUSAN) King from 1331; Emperor **1345 or 1346-1355,** b 1308. Stepan's realm included all Serbia plus Bosnia, Albania and Macedonia, but the Empire he created did not prove strong enough to withstand the growing threat of the Turks.
STEPAN X UROS V   **1355-1371,** son of Stepan IX.
1371-1389 Period of anarchy.
1389-1804 Ottoman rule *de facto*, except for an interlude of Austrian rule from 1718-1739.

THE PRINCIPALITY OF SERBIA

Gospodar (National Leader) of Serbia

HOUSE OF KARADJORDJEVIC
DJORDJE PETROVIC (better known as KARADJORDJE) **4 Feb 1804-2 Sep 1813** fled, b 14 Sep 1752; assassinated 13 Jul 1817. Of peasant origin he led the 1804 revolt against the Turks and was 'elected' national leader but had to flee after being double-crossed by the Russians.
1813-1817 Period of Turkish rule.

† Princes

HOUSE OF OBRENOVIC
MILOS OBRENOVIC I   **6 Nov 1817-25 Jun 1839** abdicated.
MILAN OBRENOVIC II   **25 Jun-8 Jul 1839,** son of Milos Obrenovic I, b 21 Oct 1819.
MIHAILO OBRENOVIC III   **Jul 1839-6 Sep 1842** deposed.

HOUSE OF KARADJORDJEVIC
ALEXANDER I   **15 Sep 1842-12 Dec 1858** fled; *de jure* to 23 Dec 1858 when he was replaced or 3 Jan 1859 when he abdicated, son of Djorde Petrovic, b 11 Oct 1806; d 3 May 1885.

HOUSE OF OBRENOVIC
MILOS OBRENOVIC I   **23 Dec 1858-26 Sep 1860,** b 18 Mar 1780. Milos' stormy life illustrates Serbia's instability: elected Prince after leading the second revolt against Turkish rule he was obliged to abdicate having lost Russian support. He returned to oust the rival Karadjordjevic Prince.
MIHAILO OBRENOVIC III   **Sep 1860-10 Jun 1868** when he was assassinated, son of Milos Obrenovic I, b 16 Sep 1823.
MILAN OBRENOVIC IV   **Jun 1868-6 Mar 1882** when he became King.

THE KINGDOM OF SERBIA

Under the terms of the Treaty of Berlin Serbia was recognised as independent (22 Aug 1878). In 1882 Milan declared himself to be King.

† Kings

HOUSE OF OBRENOVIC
MILAN I (formerly Milan Obrenovic IV) **6 Mar 1882-6 Mar 1889** when he abdicated, cousin of Mihailo Obrenovic III, b 22 Aug 1854; d 11 Feb 1901. A devious man whose stormy relations with his Queen (Natalie) gravely weakened the throne, Milan contributed much to Serbia, enlarging the state and establishing it as an independent Kingdom. However, he made many enemies and was obliged to abdicate when his position became untenable.

ALEXANDER I Mar 1889-10 Jun 1903, son of Milan I, b 15 Aug 1876. Alienated from the military by temperament and from his people by a disastrous marriage, Alexander and his Queen (Draga) were savagely murdered in a coup.

HOUSE OF KARADJORDJEVIC
PETER I 15 Jun 1903-Nov 1918 when he became King of the Serbs, Croats and Slovenes; see Yugoslavia.

Zaire

The Congo Free State was founded in 1885 under the patronage of Léopold II, King of the Belgians, who ceded the state to Belgium in 1908. On 30 Jun 1960 independence was gained and in Oct 1971 the country was renamed Zaïre.

Presidents

JOSEPH KASAVUBU 1 Jul 1960-25 Nov 1965 when he was deposed in a coup, b 1917; d 24 Mar 1969.
Gen **MOBUTU SÉSÉ SÉKO KUKU NGBENDU WA ZABANGA** (before 1972 known as Gen Joseph-Desiré Mobutu) **since 25 Nov 1965**; since 26 Oct 1966 Head of Government as well as Head of State, b 14 Oct 1930.

Prime Ministers

PATRICE HEMERY LUMUMBA 1 Jul-10 Sep 1960 although he continued to regard himself as Premier after his dismissal, b 2 Jul 1925; murdered 17 Jan 1961. An ambitious radical, distrusted in the West, Lumumba strove to end the tribal anarchy and the secession of Katanga which followed independence. Dismissed by Kasavubu, he was shamefully handed to his Katangan enemies and murdered. Regarded as a national hero in Zaire, his importance is in his stand against tribalism and for an infant nationalism.
JOSEPH ILEO 10-14 Sep 1960 when he was suspended upon the intervention of the military, b 1922.
14 Sep 1960-9 Feb 1961 The powers of the premiership were exercised by a College of Commissioners.
JOSEPH ILEO 9 Feb-1 Aug 1961.
CYRILLE ADOULA 1 Aug 1961-30 Jun 1964; caretaker PM **30 Jun-6 Jul 1964**, b 1923; d 31 May 1978.
MOÏSE KAPENDA TSHOMBE 6 Jul 1964-12 Oct 1965, b 10 Nov 1919; d 29 Jun 1969. The leader of secessionist Katanga (1960-63), Tshombe was an able politician but has been accused of being the pawn of business interests - his choice of ally was not always tactful. Becoming national Premier,

Moise Tshombe, leader of Katanga (Shaba) and later Premier of the Congo (Zaire), remains after death a controversial figure (Popperfoto)

he crushed the Gizenga revolt, but was dismissed for using white mercenaries. Exiled he died in Algeria to which country he had been abducted in 1967.
EVARISTE KIMBA 12 Oct-25 Nov 1965 when he was deposed in a coup, b 16 Jul 1926; d 2 Jul 1966.
Gen **LÉONARD MULAMBA 28 Nov 1965-26 Oct 1966,** b 1928.
(The duties of Premier have been taken over by the President and the office of Prime Minister abolished.)

Zambia

Northern Rhodesia was created as a separate territory by the British South Africa Company in 1911, was passed to the Crown in 1924, was part of the Federation of Rhodesia and Nyasaland (1953-1963) and finally achieved independence as the Republic of Zambia on 24 Oct 1964.

President

Dr **KENNETH DAVID KAUNDA since 24 Oct 1964,** b 28 Apr 1924.

Prime Ministers

Dr **KENNETH DAVID KAUNDA   24 Oct 1964-3
  Dec 1973.**
MAINZA CHONA 3 Dec 1973-27 May 1975.
ELIJAH MUDENDA 27 May 1975-Jul 1977.
MAINZA CHONA since 21 Jul 1977.

Zanzibar *see* Tanzania

Index

ABADIA MÉNDEZ, Dr MIGUEL   52
ABAHAI   47
ABAS   7
ABBAS, FERHAT   4
ABBAS HILMI I   72
ABBAS HILMI II   72
ABBIYAH   140
ABBOTT, Sir JOHN JOSEPH CALDWELL   39
ABBOUD, Gen FERIK IBRAHIM   229
ABD ALLAH   219
ABDALLAH, AHMED   52
'ABD al-MALIK ibn MARWAN   35
ABD-ar-RAHMAN I ad Dakkil   219
ABD-ar-RAHMAN II   219
ABD-ar-RAHMAN III   219
ABDOR RAHMAN KHAN   2
ABDULAZIZ   242
ABDUL AZIZ ibn SAUD Abdur Rahman
  al-Faisal   211, 212
ABDUL HALIM MU'AZZAM SHAH ibni Al-Marhum
  Sultan Badishah   167
ABDULHAMID I   242
ABDULHAMID II   243
ABDULLAH es-SALEM es-SABAH   159
ABDULLAH ibn HUSSEIN   157
ABDULMECID   242, 243
ABE, Gen NOBUYUKI   156
ABEL   62
ABEL SMITH, Sir HENRY   11
ABERDEEN, Sir John Campbell Gordon, 7th Earl
  of   39
ABERDEEN, The 4th Earl of   263
ABERDEEN and TEMAIR 1st Marquess of   39
ABIESHU   17
d'ABIN, Gen GANIER   64
ABIRATTASH   17
ABISARE   16
ABU BAKR   35
ABULHUDA, TEWFIK   157
ABULHUDA, TEWFIK PASHA   157
ABU SA'ID (Iran)   135
ABU SA'ID (Timurid Empire)   239
ACAMAPICHTLI   170
ACEVAL, EMILIO   194
d'ACHA, JOSÉ MARIA   24
ACHAB   140
ACHAEMENES   133
ACHEAMPONG, Lieut-Gen IGNATIUS KUTU
  110
ACHES   67
ACHORIS   70
ACHTHOES   67
ACHYUTA   129
ACOSTA, Gen SANTOS   51
ACOSTA GARCIA, JULIO   54
ACROTATUS   114
ADADNIRARI I   9
ADADNIRARI II   9
ADADNIRARI III   10
ADADSHUMIDDIN   17
ADADSHUMUSUR   17
ADALBERT   12
ADALOALD   142
ADAMS, JOHN   271
ADAMS, JOHN MICHAEL GODFREY   20
ADAMS, JOHN QUINCY   271
ADASI   8
ADDA .   252
ADDINGTON, HENRY   262
ADENAUR, KONRAD   109
ADHUR-NARSEH   134
ADLY PASHA   73
ADOLF (Holy Roman Empire)   120
ADOLF (Nassau)   103
ADOLF (The Rhine)   103
ADOLF I   108

ADOLF II   108
ADOLF FREDRIK   232
ADOLF FRIEDRICH II   102
ADOLF FRIEDRICH III   102
ADOLF FRIEDRICH IV   102
ADOLF FRIEDRICH V   103
ADOLF FRIEDRICH VI   103
ADOLPH (Holy Roman Empire) see Adolf
ADOLPH FREDERICK (German states) see Adolf
  Friedrich
ADOLPH FREDERICK (Sweden) see Adolf Fredrik
ADOLPHE I   165
ADOR, GUSTAVE   234
ADOULA, CYRILLE   283
ADRIAN (Papal State) see Hadrianus
AEACIDES   75
AEDH   266
AEDILRIC   252
AELFWALD   250
AELLA   249
AELLE (Northumbria)   253
AELLE (Sussex)   249
AELLI   252
AEMILIANUS   207
AESCWINE   250
AETHELBALD (Mercia)   251
AETHELBALD (Wessex)   250
AETHELBERT (East Anglia)   251
AETHELBERT (Sussex)   249
AETHELBERT (Wessex)   250
AETHELBERT I   249
AETHELBERT II   249
AETHELFRITH   252
AETHELHEARD   250
AETHELHERE   251
AETHELRED (East Anglia)   251
AETHELRED (Mercia)   251
AETHELRED (Wessex)   250
AETHELRED I   252
AETHELRED II   252, 253
AETHELSTAN   249
AETHELWALCH   249
AETHELWALD (Deira)   252
AETHELWALD (York)   253
AETHELWALD MULL   252
AETHELWALH   249
AETHELWEARD   251
AETHELWOLD   251
AETHELWULF   250
AFONSO   201
AFONSO I   202
AFONSO II   202
AFONSO III   202
AFONSO IV   202
AFONSO V   202
AFONSO VI   202
AFRIFA, Brig AKWASI AMANKWA   110
AGAPETUS I   188
AGAPETUS II   189
AGATHO   188
AGATHOCLES   235
AGESILAUS II   113
AGESIPOLIS I   113
AGESIPOLIS II   113
AGESIPOLIS III   114
AGGABODHI I   227
AGGABODHI II   227
AGGABODHI III   227
AGGABODHI IV   227
AGGABODHI V   227
AGGABODHI VI   227
AGGABODHI VII   227
AGGABODHI VIII   227
AGGABODHI IX   227
AGHA MOHAMMAD KHAN   136
AGILA   219

AGILULF   142
AGIS I   113
AGIS II   114
AGIS IV   114
AGNES   98
AGRON   126
AGUILAR, EUGENIO   74
AGUILAR, FRANCISCO   121
AGUILAR BARQUERO, FRANCISCO   54
AGUIRRE, ANASTASIO CRUZ   274
AGUIRRE CERDA, PEDRO   43
AGUIRRE SALINAS, OSMIN   75
AGUIYI-IRONSI, Gen JOHNSON T.U.   182
AGUM I   17
AGUM II   17
AGUM III   17
AHA   66
AHAZ   140
AHAZARIYAH   140
AHAZIYAH   140
  AHIDJO, AHMADOU   38
AHMAD bin ALI al THANI   204
AHMAD ebn BUYEH   36
AHMAD FUAD   72
AHMAD II   128
AHMAD SHAH   131
AHMAD SHAH DURRANI   1
AHMED   279
AHMED, AHMED DINI   63
AHMED bin Said   185
AHMED I   242
AHMED II   242
AHMED III   242
AHMED MIRZA SHAH   136
AHMED, TAJUDDIN   20
AHMOSE   68, 70
AHOMADEGBE, JUSTIN   23
AHOMADEGBE, JUSTIN   23
AHUITZOTL   170
AI-TI   44
AIMONE   150
al AINI, MUHSIN   279
AISTULF   142
AJATASATRU   127
AKBAR   130
AKBAR KHAN   2
AKBAR SHAH II   131
AKEL, FRIEDRICH   76
AKENKHERES   68
AKHENATON   68
AKHERRE   69
AKHTOY   67
AKKARI, NAZIM   161
AKUFFO, Lieut-Gen FRED   110
AKUFO-ADDO, EDWARD   110
ALA, HUSSEIN   137
'ALA-ud-DIN II   128
'ALA-ud-DIN AHMAD II   128
'ALA-ud-DIN HASAN BAHMANI SHAH   128
'ALA-ud-DIN KHALJI   128
'ALA-ud-DIN MUJAHID   128
ALAIN III   90
ALAIN IV   90
ALAIN V   90
ALAIN VI   90
ALAM, ASSADOLLAH   137
'ALAMGIR II   131
ALARICO   219
ALAUNGPAYA   30
ALBERHT   251
ALBERT (Austria and German states) see
  Albrecht
ALBERT (Holland)   179
ALBERT (Lorraine)   92
ALBERT I (Belgium)   21
ALBERT I (Monaco)   174

ALBERTUS   189
ALBINUS   207
ALBOIN   142
ALBRECHT (Hungary)   122
ALBRECHT (Saxony)   108
ALBRECHT (Schwarzburg)   108
ALBRECHT (Sweden)   231
ALBRECHT I (Austria)   12
ALBRECHT I (Holy Roman Empire)   120
ALBRECHT II (Austria)   12
ALBRECHT II (Holy Roman Empire)   120
ALBRECHT III (Austria)   13
ALBRECHT III (Bavaria)   98
ALBRECHT III (Brandenburg)   100
ALBRECHT III (Saxony)   106, 107
ALBRECHT IV (Austria)   13
ALBRECHT IV (Bavaria)   99
ALBRECHT V (Austria)   13
ALBRECHT V (Bavaria)   99
ALBRECHT VI   13
ALBREKT   60
ALCALA ZAMORA, NICETO   226
ALCALA ZAMORA y TORRES, NICETO   226
ALCHRED   252
ALCORTA, JOSÉ FIGUEROA   6
ALDWULF   251
ALEKSANDER Jagiellonczyk   198
ALEKSANDR I (Georgia)   95
ALEKSANDR I (Novgorod)   244
ALEKSANDR I Pavlovich   246
ALEKSANDR II   244
ALEKSANDR II Nikolayevich   247
ALEKSANDR III Aleksandrovich   247
ALEKSEY Mikhailovich   245
ALESSANDRI PALMA, ARTURO   43
ALESSANDRI RODRIGUEZ, JORGE   44
ALESSANDRO   149
ALESSANDRO de 'MEDICI   145
ALEXANDER (Epirus) see Alexandros
ALEXANDER (Ethiopia) see Eskender
ALEXANDER (Georgia and Russia) see Aleksandr
ALEXANDER (Greece and Greek states) see
   Alexandros
ALEXANDER (Poland) see Aleksander
ALEXANDER (Romania) see Alexandru Ioan
ALEXANDER   102
ALEXANDER I (Bulgaria)   28
ALEXANDER I (Papal State)   187
ALEXANDER I (Scotland)   267
ALEXANDER I (Serbia)   282, 283
ALEXANDER I (Yugoslavia)   280
ALEXANDER II (Papal State)   189
ALEXANDER II (Scotland)   267
ALEXANDER II ZABINAS   213
ALEXANDER III (Papal State)   190
ALEXANDER III (Scotland)   267
ALEXANDER IV   190
ALEXANDER V   191
ALEXANDER VI   191
ALEXANDER VII   192
ALEXANDER VIII   192
ALEXANDER BALAS   213
ALEXANDER of Tunis, Harold Rupert Leofric
   George Alexander, Field Marshal 1st
   Viscount   39
ALEXANDER YANNAI   141
ALEXANDROS I (Greece)   111
ALEXANDROS I (Macedonia)   112
ALEXANDROS II (Epirus)   75
ALEXANDROS II (Macedonia)   112
ALEXANDROS III   113
ALEXANDROS IV   113
ALEXANDROS V   113
ALEXANDRU IOAN I   209
ALEXIS (Russia) see Aleksey
ALEXIS I   240
ALEXIS II   240
ALEXIS III   240
ALEXIS IV   240
ALEXIUS I COMNENUS   33
ALEXIUS II COMNENUS   33
ALEXIUS III   33
ALEXIUS IV   33
ALEXIUS V   33
ALFARO, ELOY   65
ALFARO, JOSÉ MARIA   53
ALFARO, RICARDO   186
ALFONS   120
ALFONSO I (Aragon)   221
ALFONSO I (Asturias)   220
ALFONSO I (Modena)   147
ALFONSO I (Naples)   147
ALFONSO I (Navarre)   222
ALFONSO I (Sicily)   151
ALFONSO II (Asturias)   220
ALFONSO II (Modena)   147
ALFONSO II (Naples)   148
ALFONSO II RAMON   221

ALFONSO III (Aragon)   221
ALFONSO III (Asturias)   220
ALFONSO III (Modena)   147
ALFONSO IV (Aragon)   221
ALFONSO IV (Leon)   220
ALFONSO IV (Modena)   147
ALFONSO V (Aragon)   222
ALFONSO V (Leon)   220
ALFONSO VI   220
ALFONSO VII   220
ALFONSO VIII   220
ALFONSO IX   220
ALFONSO X   221
ALFONSO XI   221
ALFONSO XII   225
ALFONSO XIII   226
ALFONSO FROILAZ   220
ALFRED (Saxe-Coburg)   106
ALFRED (Wessex)   250
ALFWOLD   251
ALGIRDAS   163
ALI, MOHAMMED   185
ALI II   129
ALI ADIL SHAH I   129
ALI ADIL SHAH II   129
ALI AHMED, FAKHRUDDIN   132
ALI ibn ALI TALIB   35
ALI ibn Husayn   212
ALI KHAN, LIAQUAT   185
ALLENDE GOSSENS, SALVADOR   44
ALLEY, Lieut-Col ALPHONSE   23
ALLON, Gen YIGAL   141
ALLUWAMNAS (?)   118
de ALMEIDA, Dr ANTONIO JOSÉ   203
ALOYS I   163
ALOYS II   163
ALP-ARSLAN, Muhammad ibn Da'ud   213
ALPHONSE (Holy Roman Empire) see Alfons
ALPHONSE (Italian states) see Alfonso
ALPHONSE (Portugal) see Afonso
ALPHONSE (Spain) see Alfonso
ALPHONSE-JOURDAIN   54
ALSINA, Dr VALENTINO   5, 7
ALTAMIRANO, LUIS   43
ALUSIANUS   28
d'ALVA, LEONEL MARIO   211
ALVAREZ, Gen JUAN   171
ALVAREZ CRUZ, GEN DOMINGO   121
ALVES, Dr FRANCISCO da PAULA
   RODRIGUES   26
ALYATTES   166
AMADEO   225
AMADEUS (Italian states) see Amedeo
AMALARICO   219
AMALASUNTHA   142
AMALRIC   57
AMALRIC (Jerusalem) see Amaury
AMANOLLAH KHAN   2
AMAURY   57
AMAURY I   55
AMAURY II   55
AMAZIYAH   140
AMBROISE   173
AMDA SION I   76
AMDA SION II   76
AMEDEO I   150
AMEDEO II   150
AMEDEO III   150
AMEDEO IV   150
AMEDEO V   150
AMEDEO VI   150
AMEDEO VII   150
AMEDEO VIII   150
AMEDEO IX   150
AMENEMHET I   68
AMENEMHET II   68
AMENEMHET III   68
AMENEMHET IV   68
AMENEMOPE   69
AMENHOTEP I   68
AMENHOTEP II   68
AMENHOTEP III   68
AMENHOTEP IV   68
AMENMESSE   69
AMENMOSE   69
AMENOPHATH   69
AMENOPHIS   68
AMENSIS   68
AMEZAGA, Dr JUAN JOSÉ   275
al-AMIN, MUHAMMAD   35
AMIN, NURUL   186
AMIN DADA, Maj-Gen Al-Hajji IDI   244
AMINI, Dr ALI   137
AMITROCHATES   127
AMMENEMES   68
AMMIDITANA   17
AMMIZADUQA   17
AMMUNAS I   118

AMOGHAVARSA   127
AMON   140
AMONMESES   69
AMOSIS   68
AMOUZEGAR, Dr JAMSHID   137
al-AMRI, Maj-Gen HASSAN   279
AMYNTAS I   112
AMYNTAS III   112
AMYNTAS IV   112
AMYRTAEUS   70
ANACLETUS II   189
ANANDA MAHIDOL   238
ANARAWD ap GRUFFYDD   270
ANARAWD ap RHODRI MAWR   269
ANASTASIUS   187, 188
ANASTASIUS I   31
ANASTASIUS II   32
ANASTASIUS III   189
ANASTASIUS IV   189
ANAXANDRIDES   113
ANAYA, PEDRO MARIA   171
ANDHUN   249
ANDOM, Lieut-Gen AMAN MIKHAIL   77
ANDRADE, Gen IGNACIO   276
ANDRAS I   121
ANDRAS II   122
ANDRAS III   122
ANDREI   244
ANDREOTTI, GIULIO   145
ANDREW (Hungary) see Andras
ANDREW (Russia) see Andrei
ANDRIAMAHAZO, Brig-Gen GILLES   166
ANDRONICUS I   240
ANDRONICUS I COMNENUS   33
ANDRONICUS II   240
ANDRONICUS II PALAEOLOGUS   34
ANDRONICUS III   240
ANDRONICUS III PALAEOLOGUS   34
ANDRONICUS IV PALAEOLOGUS   34
ANDROUTSOPOULOS, ADAMANTIOS   112
ANDUEZA PALACIO, Dr RAIMUNDO   276
ANG CHAN   37
ANG DUONG   37
ANGELESCU, GHEORGHE   209
de ANGULO, EUCLIDES   51
ANICETUS   187
ANIKANGA   228
ANKAN   154
ANKO   154
ANKRAH, Maj-Gen JOSEPH A.   110
ANLAF GUTHFRITHSON   253
ANLAF SIHTRICSON   253
ANNA (East Anglia)   251
ANNA (Trebizond)   240
ANNA Ivanovna   246
ANNE (Brittany)   90
ANNE (England)   259
ANNE (Trebizond) see Anna
ANTERUS   187
ANTHEMIUS   208
ANTHONY (France) see Antoine
ANTHONY (German states) see Anton
ANTHONY (Portugal) see Antonio
ANTIGONUS I   8
ANTIGONUS II   113
ANTIOCHUS I SOTER   212
ANTIOCHUS II THEOS   212
ANTIOCHUS III   212
ANTIOCHUS IV EPIPHANES   213
ANTIOCHUS V EUPATOR   213
ANTIOCHUS VI EPIPHANES DIONYSIUS   213
ANTIOCHUS VII SIDETES   213
ANTIOCHUS VIII PHILOMETOR   213
ANTIOCHUS IX CYZICENUS   213
ANTIOCHUS X EUSEBES PHILOPATOR   213
ANTIOCHUS XI EPIPHANES PHILADELPHUS
   213
ANTIOCHUS XII DIONYSUS   213
ANTIOCHUS XIII   213
ANTIPATER I   113
ANTIPATER II   113
ANTOINE (Lorraine)   92
ANTOINE (Monaco)   173
ANTOKU   155
ANTON (Luxembourg)   165
ANTON (Saxony)   107
ANTONESCU, Gen ION   210
ANTON FLORIAN   163
ANTONINUS PIUS   206
ANTONIO (Parma and Piacenza)   149
ANTONIO (Portugal)   202
ANUND   230
APILSIN   17
APITHY, SOUROU MIGAN   23
APOSTOL, GHEORGHE   210
APRIES   70
APTIDON, HASSAN GOULED   63
ARAMBURU, Gen PEDRO EUGENIO   6

ARANA-OSORIO, Col CARLOS MANUEL 115
ARAP MOI, DANIEL T. 158
ARAUJO, ARTURO 74
ARAUJO, MANUEL ENRIQUE 74
ARBENZ-GUZMAN, Lieut-Col JACOBO 115
ARBOLEDA, JULIO 51
ARBULU GALLIANI, Gen GUILLERMO 196
ARCADIUS 31
ARCE, ANICETO 24
ARCE, MANUEL JOSÉ 42
ARCE, PEDRO 74
ARCHELAUS 112
ARCHELAUS SISINES 40
ARCHIDAMUS II 113
ARCHIDAMUS III 113
ARCHIDAMUS IV 114
ARCHIDAMUS V 114
ARCISZEWSKI, TOMASZ 200
ARDASHIR I 134
ARDASHIR II 135
ARDASHIR III 135
ARDEN-CLARKE, Sir CHARLES 110
ARECO, JORGE PACHECO 275
AREF, Col ABDUL SALAM MOHAMMED 138
AREF, Maj-Gen ABDUL RAHMAN 138
ARENAS, ANTONIO 195
AREUS I 114
AREUS II 114
AREVALO, Dr JUAN JOSÉ 115
ARGETOIANU, CONSTANTIN 209
ARGISHTI I 273
ARGISHTI II 274
ARGISTIS I 273
ARGISTIS II 274
ARGUELLO, Dr LEONARDO 181
ARGYLL, 9th Duke of 38
ARIARAMNES 133
ARIARATHES EUSEBES PHILOPATOR 40
ARIARATHES III 40
ARIARATHES IV EUSEBES 40
ARIARATHES V EUSEBES PHILOPATOR 40
ARIARATHES VI 40
ARIARATHES VIII 40
ARIARATHES VII PHILOMETOR 40
ARIAS, CELIO 121
ARIAS ESPINOSA, RICARDO 187
ARIAS, HARMODIO 186
ARIAS MADRID, Dr ARNULFO 186
ARIAS NAVARRO, CARLOS 226
ARIBERT I 142
ARIBERT II 142
ARIKDENILI 9
ARIOBARZANES 201
ARIOBARZANES I PHILOROMAIOS 40
ARIOBARZANES II PHILOPATOR 40
ARIOBARZANES III EUSEBES PHILOROMAIOS 40
ARISTA, Gen MARIANO 171
ARISTOBULUS II 141
ARISTON 113
ARKURGAL 15
ARNOLPHE I 22
ARNOLPHE II 22
ARNOLPHE III 22
ARNULF (Bavaria) 98
ARNULF (Holy Roman Empire) 119
ARNULF I 22
ARNULF II 22
ARNULF III 22
ARNUWANDAS I 118
ARNUWANDAS II 118
AROSEMENA, ALCIBIADES 186
AROSEMENA, Dr JUAN DEMOSTENES 186
AROSEMENA, FLORENCIO HARMODIO 186
AROSEMENA GOMEZ, Dr OTTO 66
AROSEMENA, JUSTO 186
AROSEMENA MONROY, Dr CARLOS JULIO 66
AROSEMENA, PABLO 186
AROSEMENA TOLA, CARLOS JULIO 66
ARRAMU 273
de ARRIAGA, Dr MANUEL JOSÉ 203
ARRON, HENCK ALFONSIUS EUGENE 230
ARROYO del RIO, Dr CARLOS ALBERTO 65, 66
ARSACES I 133
ARSACES II 134
ARSES 133
ARSHAKAN 134
al ARSHI, QADI ABDUL KARIM 279
ARSINOE 70
ARSLAN, Emir ABDEL 236
ARTABANUS I 134
ARTABANUS II 134
ARTABANUS III 134
ARTABANUS IV 134
ARTABANUS V 134
ARTAKHSHATHRA I 133
ARTAKHSHATHRA II 133

ARTAKHSHATHRA III 133
ARTAKHSHATHRA V 134
ARTATAMA 173
ARTAVASDES 134
ARTAXERXES 70
ARTAXERXES I 133
ARTAXERXES II 133
ARTAXERXES III 133
ARTESEANU, Gen 209
ARTHUR, CHESTER ALAN 272
ARTHUR I 90
ARTHUR II 90
ARTHUR III de Richemont 90
ARTHUR of CONNAUGHT, Prince 216
ARTHUR William Patrick Albert,, Prince 39
ARTIGAS, JOSÉ GERVASIO 274
ARUNWANDAS III 118
ASA 140
ASANDER 201
ASFA WOSSEN 77
ASGEIRSSON, ASGEIR 125
ASHARIDAPALEKUR 9
ASHIDA, HITOSHI 156
ASHOT I 7
ASHOT II 7
ASHOT III 7
ASHRAF KHAN 1
ASHURAKHEDDINA 10
ASHURBANIPAL (Assyria) 10
ASHURBANIPAL (Babylonia) 18
ASHURBELKALA I 9
ASHURBELNISHESHU 9
ASHURDAN I 9
ASHURDAN II 9
ASHURDAN III 10
ASHURDANINAPAL 10
ASHURETILILANI 10
ASHURNADINAHHE I 9
ASHURNADINAHHE II 9
ASHURNADINAPLI 9
ASHURNADINSHUM 18
ASHURNASIRPAL I 9
ASHURNASIRPAL II 9
ASHURNIRARI I 9
ASHURNIRARI II 9
ASHURNIRARI III 9
ASHURNIRARI IV 9
ASHURNIRARI V 10
ASHURRABI I 9
ASHURRABI II 9
ASHURRESHISHI I 9
ASHURRESHISHI II 9
ASHURUBALLIT I 9
ASHURUBALLIT II 10
ASOKA 127
ASOT I and V 7
ASOT II and VI 7
ASOT III and VII 7
ASOT IV and VIII 7
ASPARUKH 27
ASQUITH, HERBERT HENRY 264
al ASSAD, Lieut-Gen HAFEZ 236
ASSALI, SABRY 236
ASSEN I 28
as-SHAABI, ABDUL LATIF 218
as-SHAABI, QAHTAN 218
ASTYAGES 133
ATAHUALLPA (Inca Empire) see Ataw Wallpa 'Inka
ATANAGILDO 219
al-ATASSI, HASHEM 236
ATASSI, Maj-Gen LOUAY 236
ATASSI, Dr NUREDDIN 236
ATATURK, KEMAL 243
ATAULFO 219
ATAW WALLPA 'INKA 127
ATHALARIC 142
ATHALIYAH 140
ATHANASIADIS-NOVAS, GIORGIOS 112
ATHELSTAN (East Anglia) 251
ATHELSTAN (England) 253
ATHELSTAN (Wessex) 250
ATHLONE, Alexander Augustus Frederick William Alfred George, Earl of 39, 216
ATHOTHIS 66
ATTALUS III PHILOMETOR EUERGETES 194
ATTALUS II PHILADELPHUS 194
ATTALUS I SOTER 194
ATTHOUMANI, SAID 52
ATTLEE, CLEMENT RICHARD 265
AUGUST (Oldenburg) 103
AUGUST (Poland) 199
AUGUST I 107
AUGUST II 199
AUGUST III 199
AUGUSTE, TANCREDE 117
AUGUSTIN 170
AUGUSTIN 173

AUGUSTUS (German states and Poland) see August
AUGUSTUS 205
AURANZEB ALAMGIR I 130
AURA, TEUVO ENSIO 79
AURELIAN (Roman Empire) see Aurelianus
AURELIANUS 207
AURELIO 220
AURIOL, VINCENT 88
AUTHARI 142
AVELINO CACERES, Gen ANDRÉS 195
AVELLANEDA, NICOLAS 6
AVERESCU, Marshal ALEXANDRU 209
AVITUS 208
AWADALLA, BABIKAR 229
AWIL-MARDUK 19
AXAYACATL 170
AY 69
AYALA, ELIGIO 194
AYALA, Dr EUSEBIO 194
AYCINENA, PEDRO 114
AYORA, ISIDRO 65
AYUBI, SAYED ALI JAWDAT 137
AYUB KHAN, Gen MOHAMMED 186
al-AYYOUBI, MAHMOUD BEN SALEH 236
el-AZAM, Dr KHALED 236
AZANA, MANUEL 226
AZANA y DIAZ, MANUEL 226
al AZHARI, ISMAIL 229
AZIKIWE, Dr NNAMDI 182
el AZMEH, Dr AHMED BASHIR 236
AZNAR, Admiral JUAN BAUTISTA 226
AZZAN bin Qais 185
AZZO 146

BA SWE, U 30
BA U, Dr 30
BAASHA 140
BAATOR, SUKHE 175
BABA-AHI-IDDIN 18
BABAN, AHMED MUKHTAR 137
BABUR 130
BACCIOCHI, FELIX (Italy) see Felice, Duke of Lucca
BA'DA MARYAM 76
BADAR bin Seif 185
BADOGLIO, Marshal PIETRO 144
BADRAN, MUDAR 158
al BADRI, ABDEL KADER 162
BAEZ, BUENAVENTURA 64
BAEZ, CECILIO 194
BAEZ, RAMON 64
BAGAZA, Lieut-Col JEAN-BAPTISTE 30
BAGRAT III 94
BAGRAT IV 94
BAGRAT V 95
BAGRAT VI 95
BAGRIANOV, IVAN 29
BAGYIDAW 30
BAHADUR SHAH I Mu'azzam 130
BAHADUR SHAH II 131
BAHLUL LODI 128
BAHNINI, Hadj AHMED 176
BAHRAM I 134
BAHRAM II 134
BAHRAM III 134
BAHRAM IV CHUBIN 135
BAHRAM V 135
BAHRAM VI CHUBIN 135
BAJI RAO I 131
BAJI RAO II 131
BAKAFFA 77
BAKKOUCHE, ABDEL HAMID 162
BAKR, Maj-Gen AHMED HASSAN 138
BAKR, RASHID al TAHIR 229
BALAFREJ, AHMED 175
BALAGUER, Dr JOAQUIN 64
BALAJI RAO 131
BALAJI VISVANATH 131
BALBINUS 207
BALCARCE, JUAN RAMON 5
BALDOMIR, Gen ALFREDO 275
BALDRED 249
BALDWIN (Flanders) see Boudewijn
BALDWIN (Jerusalem and Belgium) see Baudouin
BALDWIN, STANLEY 265
BALEWA, Alhaji Sir ABUBAKAR TAFAWA 182
BALFOUR, ARTHUR JAMES 264
BALLIVIAN, Lieut-Col ADOLFO 24
BALLIVIAN, JOSÉ 24
BALLIVIAN ROJAS, Gen HUGO 25
BALMACEDA, JOSÉ MANUEL 43
BALTA, Col JOSÉ 195
BAMINA, JOSEPH 30
BANDA, Dr HASTINGS KAMUZU 167

BANDARANAIKE, Mrs SIRIMAVO RATWATTE DIAS 229
BANDARANAIKE, SOLOMON WEST RIDGEWAY DIAS 229
BANZER SUARÉZ, Col HUGO 25
BAO DIN 277
BAPTISTA, MARIANO 24
BAQUERIZO MORENA, ALFREDO 65
BARAONA, MIGUEL PAZ 121
BARAZI, Dr MOHSEN BEY 236
BARBARIGO, AGOSTINO 153
BARBARIGO, MARCO 153
BARCIA, AUGUSTO 226
BARCLAY, ARTHUR 162
BARCLAY, EDWIN 162
BARDIYA 19
BARDOSSY, LASZLO 124
BARIYA 133
BARNET y VINAGERAS, Dr JOSÉ 56
BAROM REACHEA I 37
BAROM REACHEA II 37
BAROM REACHEA III 37
BAROM REACHEA IV 37
de la BARRA, FRANCISCO LEON 172
BARRAGAN, Gen MIGUEL 171
BARRE, RAYMOND 89
BARREH, Maj-Gen MOHAMMED SIYAD 216
BARREIRO, CANDIDO 193
BARRIENTOS ORTUNO, Gen RENÉ 25
BARRIOS, GERARD 74
BARROETA, RAFAEL 53
BARROS, Dr PRUDENTE de MORAES 26
BARROS BORGONO, LUIS 43
BARROS LUCO, RAMON 43
BARROW, ERROL WALTON 20
BARRUNDIA, JOSÉ F. 42
BARTON, Sir EDMUND 11
BASIL (Byzantine Empire and Trebizond) see Basilius
BASIL (Russia) see Vasily
BASILISCUS 31
BASILIUS I (Byzantine Empire) 32
BASILIUS I (Trebizond) 240
BASILIUS II 32
BATH, Sir William Pulteney, 1st Earl of 261
BATISTA y ZALDIVAR, Gen FULGENCIO 56
BATLINER, Dr GERARD 163
BATLLE BERRES, LUIS 275
BATLLE y GRAU, Col LORENZO 274
BATLLE y ORDONEZ, JOSÉ 274
BATMOUNKI I, JAMBYN 175
BATU KHAN 174
BAUDOUIN I (Belgium) 21
BAUDOUIN I (Edessa) 55
BAUDOUIN I (Flanders) 22
BAUDOUIN I (Jerusalem) 55
BAUDOUIN I (Latin Empire) 34
BAUDOUIN II (Edessa) 55
BAUDOUIN II (Flanders) 22
BAUDOUIN II (Jerusalem) 55
BAUDOUIN II de Courtenay 34
BAUDOUIN III (Flanders) 22
BAUDOUIN III (Jerusalem) 55
BAUDOUIN IV (Flanders) 22
BAUDOUIN IV (Jerusalem) 55
BAUDOUIN V (Flanders) 22
BAUDOUIN V (Jerusalem) 55
BAUDOUIN VI 22
BAUDOUIN VII 22
BAUDOUIN VIII 22
BAUDOUIN IX 22
BAUER, GUSTAV ADOLF 97
BAUMANN, JOHANNES 234
BAUNSGAARD, HILMAR TORMOD INGOLF 63
BAVIER, SIMEON 234
BAYDU 135
BAYER, MAHMUD CELAL 243
BAYEZID I 241
BAYEZID II 242
BAYINNAUNG 30
BAZAIJU 8
al BAZZAZ, Dr ABDUL RAHMAN 138
BEACONSFIELD, 1st Earl of 264
BEATRICE (Portugal) see Beatriz
BEATRIZ 202
BEAUHARNAIS EUGENE de see also Eugen, Grand Duke of Frankfurt 143
BEAVOGUI, Dr LOUIS LANSANA 115
BECERRA de la FLOR, Dr DANIEL 196
BECH, JOSEPH 165
BEEL, Dr LOUIS JOSEPH MARIA 179
BEGIN, MENAHEM 141
BÉLA I 121
BÉLA II 121
BÉLA III 122
BÉLA IV 122
BELAUNDE TERRY, FERNANDO 196
BELBANI 8

BELI ap RHUN 268
BELIBNI 18
BELL, Sir FRANCIS HENRY DILLON 180
BELLINI, FRANCISCO G. 64
BELSHARUSUR 19
BELSHIMMANI 19
BELTRAN, Dr WASHINGTON 275
BELZU, MANUEL ISIDORO 24
BEMBO, GIOVANNI 153
BEN AMMAR, TAHAR 241
BEN BELLA, AHMED 4
BEN GURION, DAVID 141
BEN KHEDDA, YOUSSEF 4
BEN-ZVI, ISHVAK 141
BENAVIDES, Marshal OSCAR RAIMUNDO 196
BENEDICT (Papal State) see Benedictus
BENEDICTUS I 188
BENEDICTUS II 188
BENEDICTUS III 188
BENEDICTUS IV 188
BENEDICTUS V 189
BENEDICTUS VI 189
BENEDICTUS VII 189
BENEDICTUS VIII 189
BENEDICTUS IX 189
BENEDICTUS X 189
BENEDICTUS XI 191
BENEDICTUS XII 191
BENEDICTUS XIII 191, 192
BENEDICTUS XIV 192
BENEDICTUS XV 193
BENEDIKTSSON, Dr BJARNI 125
BENES, EDVARD 58
BENHIMA, Dr MOHAMMAD 176
BENNETT, RICHARD BEDFORD 40
BENOIT, Col PEDRO 64
BENSON, STEPHEN ALLEN 162
BENTI, Brig-Gen TEFERI 77
BEONNA 251
BEONRED 251
BEORHTRIC 250
BEORHTWULF 252
BEORNA 251
BEORNWULF 252
BERAN, RUDOLF 58
BERCHTOLD 98
BEREGFAY, Col-Gen KAROLY 124
BERENGARIUS I 143
BERENGARIUS II 143
BÉRENGER 90
BERENGUER, Gen DAMASO 226
BERENICE 71
BERGE, ABRAHAM 184
BERHTWALD 251
BERK-YARUQ 213
BERMUDO (Asturias) see Vermudo
BERNABO 146
BERNARDES, Dr ARTUR da SILVA 26
BERNARDUS 143
BERNHARD II 106
BERNHARD III 106
BERRETA, Dr TOMAS 275
BERRO, BERNARDO PRUDENCIO 274
BERTHARITUS 142
BERTHUN 249
BERTRAND 54
BERTRAND, FRANCISCO 121
BESSBOROUGH, Vere Brabazon Ponsonby, 9th Earl of 39
BETANCOURT, ROMULO 277
BETHLEN, Count ISTVAN 124
von BETHMANN-HOLLWEG, THEOBALD THEODOR FRIEDRICH ALFRED 96
BEY, ALI JAUDAT 137
BHAVAVARMAN I 36
BHAVAVARMAN II 36
BHUMIPOL ADULYADEJ 238
BHUTTO, ZULFIQAR ALI 166
BHUVANAIKA BAHU I 228
BHUVANAIKA BAHU II 228
BHUVANAIKA BAHU III 228
BHUVANAIKA BAHU IV 228
BHUVANAIKA BAHU V 228
BHUVANAIKA BAHU VI 228
BIDATSU 154
BIDAULT, GEORGES 88
BIENEKHES 66
BIERUT, BOLESLAW 200
BIESHEUVEL, BAREND WILLEM 179
BIHA, LÉOPOLD 30
BIJEDIC, DZEMAL 281
BILLINGHURST, GUILLERMO ENRIQUE 196
BIMBISARA 127
bin ONN, Datuk HUSSEIN 167
BINDUSARA 127
BINOTHRIS 66
BIRENDRA BIR BIKRAM SHAH DEVA 176
BIRGER 231

BIRGER Jarl 231
von BISMARCK-SCHONHAUSEN, OTTO, Prince 96
BISTA, KIRTINIDI 177
BITAR, SALAH ed DIN 236
BIYA, PAUL 38
BJORNSSON, SVEINN 125
BLACKBURNE, Sir KENNETH 153
BLANCHE 222
BLANCHE, Gen BARTOLOMÉ 43
BLANCO, PEDRO 24
BLANCO GALINDO, Gen CARLOS 25
BLEDDYN ap CYNFYN (Gwynedd) 269
BLEDDYN ap CYNFYN (Powys) 270
BLEDISLOE, Sir Charles Bathurst, 1st Viscount 180
BLEHR, OTTO 184
BLODNIEKS, ADOLFS 161
BLOTSVEN (?) 230
BLUM, LÉON 88
BLUNDELL, Sir EDWARD DENIS 180
de BOCANEGRA, JOSÉ MARIA 171
BOCCHORIS 70
BODAWPAYA 30
BODJOLLÉ, EMMANUEL 239
BOETHOS 66
BOGRAN, Gen LUIS 121
BOHEMOND I 54
BOHEMOND I and IV 55
BOHEMOND II 54
BOHEMOND II and V 55
BOHEMOND III 54
BOHEMOND III and VI 55
BOHEMOND IV 54
BOHEMOND IV and VII 55
BOHEMOND V 54
BOHEMOND VI 54
BOJILOV, Prof DOBRI 29
BOKASSA I 42
BOLESLAV I 59
BOLESLAV II 59
BOLESLAV III 59
BOLESLAW I 197
BOLESLAW II 197
BOLESLAW III 197
BOLESLAW IV 197
BOLESLAW V 198
BOLIVAR, SIMON 50, 195, 275
BOMILCAR 41
BONAPARTE, ELISE see ELISA
BONAPARTE, JEROME (Westphalia) see Hieronymus Napoleon
BONAPARTE, JOSEPH see Giuseppe, King of Naples and Jose, King of Spain
BONAPARTE, LOUIS (Netherlands) see Lodewijk I, King of Holland
BONAPARTE, NAPOLÉON 84
BONAPARTE, NAPOLÉON-LOUIS (Netherlands) see Lodewijk II, King of Holland
BONAPARTE, NAPOLÉON-LOUIS 178
BONAPARTE, PAULINE (Italy) see Pauline, Duchess of Guastalla
BONAPARTE, Prince LOUIS-NAPOLÉON 86
BONAR LAW, ANDREW 264
BONG SOUVANNAVONG 160
BONGO, OMAR 93
BONIFACE (Papal State) see Bonifacius
BONIFACIO 150
BONIFACIUS I 187
BONIFACIUS II 188
BONIFACIUS III 188
BONIFACIUS IV 188
BONIFACIUS V 188
BONIFACIUS VI 188
BONIFACIUS VII 189
BONIFACIUS VIII 191
BONIFACIUS IX 191
BONIFAZ, NAFTALIO 65
BONILLA, MANUEL 121
BONILLA, POLICARPO 121
BONNELLY, Dr RAFAEL F. 64
BONOMI, IVANOE 144
BONVIN, ROGER 234, 235
BORDA, JUAN IDIARTE 274
BORDABERRY AROCENA, JUAN MARIA 275
BORDAS VALDES, JOSÉ 64
BORDEN, Sir ROBERT LAIRD 39
BORGONO, JUSTINIANO 195
BORIL 28
BORIS I 27
BORIS I MIHAIL 27
BORIS II 28
BORIS III 29
BORIS Godunov 245
BORIVOJ II 60
BORRERO, ANTONIO 65
BORRERO, Dr MANUEL MARIA 65
BORSO 147

BORTEN, PER 184
BOSCH, Prof JUAN 64
BOSHOFF, JACOBUS NICOLAAS 217
BOSON 91
BOSQUE, PIO ROMERO 74
BOTHA, Gen LOUIS 217
BOUDEWIJN I 22
BOUDEWIJN II 22
BOUDEWIJN III 22
BOUDEWIJN IV 22
BOUDEWIJN V 22
BOUDEWIJN VI 22
BOUDEWIJN VII 22
BOUDEWIJN VIII 22
BOUDEWIJN IX 22
BOUISSON, FERNAND 88
BOUMEDIENNE, HOUARI 4
BOUN OUM NA CHAMPASSAK, Prince 160
BOURGES-MAUNOURY, MAURICE
    JEAN-MARIE 89
BOURGUIBA, HABIB ibn ALI 241
BOWELL, Sir MACKENZIE 39
BOYD, Dr AUGUSTO SAMUEL 186
BOYER, JEAN-PIERRE 116
BRAGA, Dr JOAQUIM TÉOFILO FERNANDES
    203
BRAND, Sir JOHANNES HENDRICUS 217
BRAND van ZYL, Major GIDEON 216
BRANDT, Dr WILLY 109
BRANTING, KARL HJALMAR 233
BRATIANU, IONEL 209
BRATTELI, TRYGVE 184
BRAVO, Gen NICOLAS 170, 171
BRENNER, ERNST 234
BRETISLAV I 59
BRETISLAV II 60
BREZHNEV, LEONID ILICH 248
BRIAND, ARISTIDE 87
BROOKE, CHARLES VYNER de WINDT 211
BROOKE, JAMES 211
BROOKS, Sir REGINALD ALEXANDER DALLAS
    11
de BROQUEVILLE, CHARLES Count 21
BRUCE, STANLEY MELBOURNE 11
BRUGGER, ERNST 235
BRUM, BALTASAR 274
BRUNHART, HANS 163
BRUNING, Dr HEINRICH 97
BRUNO 92
BUCHAN, JOHN 39
BUCHANAN, JAMES 272
BUCKLEY, DONAL 138
BUDDHADASA 227
BUHL, VILHELM 63
BUITRAGO, PABLO 181
BUKKA I 129
BUKKA II 129
BULGANIN, Marshal NIKOLAI
    ALEKSANDROVICH 248
BULNES, Gen MANUEL 43
von BULOW, BERNHARDT HEINRICH MARTIN
    KARL, Prince 96
BUONAPARTE, NAPOLEONE 143
BURESCH, Dr KARL 14
BURETSU 154
BURGERS, THOMAS FRANCOIS 217
BURGRED 252
BURHRED 252
BURNABURIASH I 17
BURNABURIASH II 17
BURNHAM, LINDEN FORBES SAMPSON 116
BURSIN 16
BUSCH, Col GERMAN 25
BUSIA, Dr KOFI ABREFA 110
BUSTAMENTE, Sir ALEXANDER 153
BUSTAMENTE, Gen ANASTASIO 171
BUSTAMENTE, MANUEL BASILICO 274
BUSTAMENTE RIVERO, Dr JOSÉ LUIS 196
BUTE, The 3rd Earl of 262
BUTLER, Sir MILO BOUGHTON 19
BUTTIGIEG, Dr ANTON 169
BUU LOC, Prince 277
BUXTON, Sydney Charles Buxton, 1st Earl 216
BYNG of Vimy, Gen Julian Hedworth George
    Byng, 1st Viscount 39

CAAMANO, Col FRANCISCO 64
CAAMANO, JOSÉ MARIA PLACIDO 65
CABALLERO, Gen BERNARDINO 194
CABANAS, Gen TRINIDAD 121
CABECADAS, Commander JOSÉ MENDES 203
CABRAL, JOSÉ MARIA 64
CABRAL, LUIS 115
CACAMA 170
CACERES, RAMON 64
CADAFAEL ap Cynfedw CADOMEDD 268

CADELL ap GRUFFYDD 270
CADELL ap RHODRI 269
CADFAN ab IAGO 268
CADWALADR ap CADWALLON 268
CADWALADR FENDIGAID 268
CADWALLON ap CADFAN 268
CADWALLON ap IEUAF 269
CADWGAN ap BLEDDYN 270
CAEDWALLA 250
CAELESTINUS 189
CAELESTINUS I 187
CAELESTINUS II 189
CAELESTINUS III 190
CAELESTINUS IV 190
CAELESTINUS V 190
CAESAR (Italian states) see Cesare
CAETANO, Prof MARCELO JOSÉ das NEVES
    204
CAFE FILHO, Dr JOAO 26
CAIUS 187
CAJANDER, Prof AINO KAARLO 78
CAKA 28
CAKOBAU, Ratu Sir GEORGE 77
CALDERA RODRIGUEZ, Dr RAFAEL 277
CALDERON, CLIMACHO 51
CALDERON, GUILLERMO QUINTERO 51
CALDERON, SERAPIO 196
CALDERON GUARDIA, Dr RAFAEL ANGEL 54
CALIGULA 205
CALINESCU, ARMAND 209
CALLAGHAN, LEONARD JAMES 265
CALLES, Gen PLUTARCO ELIAS 172
CALLISTUS I 187
CALLISTUS II 189
CALLISTUS III 190, 191
CALONDER, FELIX LUDWIG 234
CALS, Dr JOSEPH MARIA LAURENS THEO 179
CALVO, Gen BARTOLOMEO 186
CAMACHO, Gen MANUEL AVILA 172
CAMARGO, SERGIO 53
de CAMBACERES, JEAN-JACQUES 84
CAMBYSES (Babylonia) 19
CAMBYSES (Egypt) 70
CAMBYSES I 133
CAMBYSES II 133
CAMORRA, PEDRO JOAQUIN 181
CAMPBELL, Sir CLIFFORD CLARENCE 153
CAMPBELL-BANNERMAN, Sir HENRY 264
CAMPERO, Gen NARCISO 24
CAMPISTEGUY, JUAN 274
CAMPO, RAFAEL 74
CAMPO SERRANO, JOSÉ MARIA 51
CAMPORA, Dr HECTOR JOSE 6
CANAL, Gen BOISROND 117
CANAS, ANTONIO 74
CANDAMO, MANUEL 195, 196
CANDRA GUPTA I 127
CANDRA GUPTA II 127
CANDRAGUPTA MAURYA 127
CANMORE 266
CANNING, GEORGE 263
CANSECO, PEDRO DIEZ 195
CANTAVE, Gen LEON 117
CANTILLO, Maj-Gen EULALIO 56
CANUTE (Denmark) see Knud
CANUTE (Norway) see Knut
CANUTE (Sweden) see Cnud
CANUTE 254
CAPAC YUPANQUI (Inca Empire) see Qhapaq
    Yupanki
CAPODISTRIAS, AGOSTINO 110
CAPODISTRIAS, IOANNIS ANTONIOS 110
von CAPRIVI, GEORG LEO, Count 96
CARACALLA 207
CARACCIOLI Col HECTOR 121
CARAFFA, GREGORIO 168
CARAZO, EVARISTO 181
CARAZO, RODRIGO 54
CARBAJAL, FRANCISCO 172
CARDENAS, ADAN 181
CARDENAS, Gen LAZARO 172
CARIAS ANDINO, Gen TIBURCIO 121
CARIBERT 80
CARILLO, BRAULIO 53
CARINUS 207
CARL 106
CARL VII Sverkerssen 230
CARL VIII 231
CARL IX 232
CARL X GUSTAF 232
CARL XI 232
CARL XII 232
CARL XIII 232
CARL XIV JOHAN 233
CARL XV 233
CARL XVI GUSTAF 233
CARL ALEXANDER 106
CARL AUGUST 106

CARL FRIEDRICH 106
CARLO 149
CARLO I (Naples) 147
CARLO I (Parma and Piacenza) 149
CARLO I (Savoy) 150
CARLO I (Sicily) 151
CARLO II (Naples) 147
CARLO II (Parma and Piacenza) 149
CARLO II (Savoy) 150
CARLO II (Sicily) 151
CARLO III (Naples) 147
CARLO III (Parma and Piacenza) 149
CARLO III (Savoy) 150
CARLO III (Sicily) 152
CARLO IV (Naples) 148
CARLO IV (Sicily) 152
CARLO V 148
CARLO VI 148
CARLO VII 148
CARLO ALBERTO 149
CARLO EMANUELE I 150
CARLO EMANUELE II 150
CARLO EMANUELE III 149
CARLO EMANUELE IV 149
CARLO FELICE 149
CARLO LODOVICO 146
CARLOMAN (France) 81
CARLOMAN (Italy) 143
CARLOS, Prof ADELINO da PALMA 204
CARLOS 203
CARLOS I 224
C ARLOS II 224
CARLOS III 225
CARLOS IV 225
CARMONA, Gen ANTONIO OSCAR de
    FRAGOSA 203
CARNOT, MARIE-FRANCOIS SADI 87
CARO, MIGUEL ANTONIO 51
CAROL I 209
CAROL II 209
CAROLUS 142, 143
CARRANZA, BRUNO 53
CARRANZA, VENUSTIANO 172
CARRERA, JOSÉ MIGUEL 43
CARRERA, MARTIN 171
CARRERA, RAFAEL 114
CARRERO BLANCO, Admiral LUIS 226
CARRION, GERONIMO 65
CARTER, JAMES EARL 273
CARTON de WIART, HENRI VICTOR Count 21
CARUS 207
CARVALLO, HECTOR 194
CASARES QUIROGA, SANTIAGO 226
CASEY, Sir Richard Gardiner Casey, Baron 11
CASH, GERALD 19
CASIMIR (Poland) see Kazimierz
CASIMIR-PÉRIER, JEAN PAUL PIERRE 87
CASSANDER 113
de la CASSIERE, JEAN LEVESQUE 168
CASTELAR y RIPOLI, EMILIO 225
CASTELLANOS, VITTORIANO 121
CASTELO BRANCO, Marshal HUMBERTO de
    ALENCAR 27
CASTILLA, Gen RAMON 195
CASTILLO, Col MIGUEL 75
CASTILLO, Dr RAMON S. 6
CASTILLO-ARMAS, Col CARLOS 115
CASTREN, KAARLO 78
CASTREN, URHO 78
CASTRO, CIPRIANO 276
CASTRO, JOSÉ MARIA 53
CASTRO, Gen JULIAN 276
CASTRO JIJON, Cpt RAMON 66
CASTRO RUZ, Dr FIDEL 56
CASTRO SILVA ANTUNES, Admiral JOAO de
    CANTO e 203
CATALAN 173
CATANEDA CASTRO, SALVADOR 75
CATHERINE (Cyprus) 57
CATHERINE (Navarre) 222
CATHERINE (Russia) see Ekaterina
CAVAIGNAC, Gen LOUIS EUGENE 86
CEAUSESCU, NICOLAE 210
CEAWLIN 250
CEBELLOS, JUAN BAUTISTA 171
CELAYA, Lieut-Gen AMILCAR 121
CELESTINE (Papal State) see Caelestinus
CELIO, ENRICO 234
CELIO, NELLO 235
CELMAN, MIGUEL JUAREZ 6
CELMINS, HUGO 161
CENFUS 250
CENTURIONI, FRANCESCO 153
CENTURIONI, NICOLO 153
CENTWINE 250
CENWALH 250
CEOL 250
CEOLRED 251

CEOLWULF *(Northumbria)* 252
CEOLWULF *(Wessex)* 250
CEOLWULF I 252
CEOLWULF II 252
CERDIC 250
CERESOLE, PAUL 234
CERNA, Gen VICENTE 114
CERNIK, OLDRICH 59
CERNIUS, Gen JONAS 164
CERNY, Dr JAN 58
CESARE 147
de CESPEDES y QUESADA, CARLOS MANUEL
    56
CHABAN-DELMAS, JACQUES PIERRE MICHEL
    89
CHABRYES 67
CHACIN, Dr PEDRO ITRIAGO 276
CHACON, LAZARO 115
CHAGATAI 174
CHAKSTE, JAN 160
CHAMBERLAIN, ARTHUR NEVILLE 265
CHAMORRO, DIEGO MANUEL 181
CHAMORRO, Gen FRUTOS 181
CHAMOUN, CAMILLE 161
CHANDRA GUPTA (India) *see* Candra Gupta
CHANG CHUN, Gen 48
CHANG DO YUNG, Lieut-Gen 159
CHANG, Dr JOHN MYUN 159
CHANG PAIK SONG 159
CHANG TSO-LIN 48
CHANG HUANG TI 47
CHANG-TI 45
CHANIS, Dr DANIEL 186
CHANN AK 37
CHAO CHI 46
CHAO K'UANG-YIN 46
CHAO-TI 44
CHAPAPRIETA, JOAQUIN 226
CHARIBERT (France) *see* Caribert
CHARLEMAGNE (France) *see* Charles I
CHARLEMAGNE 81
CHARLES (Austria and German states) *see* Karl
CHARLES (Bohemia) *see* Karel
CHARLES (Holy Roman Empire) *see* Karl
CHARLES (Hungary) *see* Karoly
CHARLES (Italian states) *see* Carlo
CHARLES (Norway) *see* Karl
CHARLES (Spain and Portugal) *see* Carlos
CHARLES (Sweden) *see* Carl
CHARLES 165
CHARLES I *(Achaea)* 1
CHARLES I *(Burgundy)* 92
CHARLES I *(England)* 258
CHARLES I *(Flanders)* 22
CHARLES I *(France)* 81
CHARLES I *(Monaco)* 173
CHARLES I *(Navarre)* 222
CHARLES II *(Achaea)* 1
CHARLES II *(Burgundy)* 92
CHARLES II *(England)* 258
CHARLES II *(France)* 81
CHARLES II *(Lorraine)* 92, 93
CHARLES II *(Monaco)* 173
CHARLES II *(Navarre)* 222
CHARLES III *(France)* 81
CHARLES III *(Lorraine)* 93
CHARLES III *(Monaco)* 174
CHARLES III *(Navarre)* 222
CHARLES IV *(France)* 82
CHARLES IV *(Lorraine)* 93
CHARLES IV *(Navarre)* 222
CHARLES V *(France)* 82
CHARLES V *(Lorraine)* 93
CHARLES V, HOLY ROMAN EMPEROR (Spain)
    see Carlos I
CHARLES VI 82
CHARLES VII 82
CHARLES VIII 82
CHARLES IX 83
CHARLES X 86
CHARLES ALBERT (German states) *see* Karl
    Albrecht
CHARLES ALBERT (Italian states) *see* Carlo
    Alberto
CHARLES ALEXANDER (German states) *see* Karl
    Alexander
CHARLES d'Anjou
CHARLES EDWARD, DUKE OF ALBANY
    (Germany) *see* Karl Eduard, Duke of
    Saxe-Coburg
CHARLES EMMANUEL (Italian states) *see* Carlo
    Emanuele
CHARLES EUGENE (German states) *see* Karl
    Eugen
CHARLES FELIX (Italian states) *see* Carlo Felice
CHARLES FREDERICK (German states) *see* Karl
    Friedrich

CHARLES LOUIS (German states) *see* Karl
    Ludwig
CHARLES LOUIS (Italian states) *see* Carlo
    Lodovico
CHARLES PHILIP (German states) *see* Karl
    Philipp
CHARLES THEODORE (German states) *see* Karl
    Theodor
CHARLOTTE *(Cyprus)* 57
CHARLOTTE *(Luxembourg)* 165
CHATHAM, The 1st Earl of 262
CHAUDET, PAUL 234
CHAUDHRI, FAZAL ELAHI 186
CHUAI 154
CHAUTEMPS, CAMILLE 87
CHAVES, Dr FEDERICO 194
CHAVEZ, CORONADO 120
CHE-TSUNG 46
CHEBAB, KHELAB 161
CHEESEMAN, JOSEPH 162
CHEHAB, Gen FUAD 161
CHEN CHENG, Gen 50
CHEN-TSUNG 46
CHENG HENG 37, 38
CH'ENG HUA 46
CH'ENG HUANG TI 47
CHENG-TE 46
CH'ENG-TI 44
CH'ENG TSU 46
CH'ENG-T'UNG 46
CHEOPS 67
CHERES 67
CHERVENKOV, VALKO 29
CHEY CHETTA II 37
CHIA-CHING 46
CHIA-CH'ING 47
CHIANG CHING-KUO 50
CHIANG KAI-SHEK 48
CHIARI, Dr ROBERTO FRANCISCO 186, 187
CHIARI, RODOLFO 186
CH'IEN-LUNG 47
CHIEN-WEN 46
CHIFLEY, JOSEPH BENEDICT 11
CHILDEBERT 80
CHILDEBERT I 79
CHILDEBERT II 80
CHILDEBERT III 80
CHILDÉRIC I 79
CHILDÉRIC II 80
CHILDÉRIC III 80
CHILDERS, ERSKINE 139
CHILPÉRIC 91
CHILPÉRIC I 80
CHILPÉRIC II 80
CHIMALPOPOCA 170
CH'IN-TSUNG 46
CHINDAVINTO 219
CHING HUANG TI 47
CHING-T'AI 46
CHING-TI 44
CHING TI 46
CHINTILA 219
CHIRAC, JACQUES RENÉ 89
CHOI DOO SUN, Dr 159
CHOI KYU HAH 159
CHOI YONG KUN 159
CHOKEI 155
CHOM KLOA 238
CHONA, MAINZA 284
CHONG MING-SHU 48
CHOU EN-LAI 49
CHOWDHURY, ABU SAYEED 20
CHOYBOLSAN, Marshal KHORLOGIN 175
CHRISTIAN I *(Denmark)* 62
CHRISTIAN I *(Saxony)* 107
CHRISTIAN I *(Sweden)* 231
CHRISTIAN II *(Denmark)* 62
CHRISTIAN II *(Saxony)* 107
CHRISTIAN II *(Sweden)* 231
CHRISTIAN III 62
CHRISTIAN IV 62
CHRISTIAN V 62
CHRISTIAN VI 63
CHRISTIAN VII 63
CHRISTIAN VIII 63
CHRISTIAN IX 63
CHRISTIAN X 63
CHRISTIAN FREDERICK (Norway) *see* Kristian
    Fredrik
CHRISTIAN LUDWIG II 102
CHRISTINA 232
CHRISTOPH 109
CHRISTOPHE, HENRI 116
CHRISTOPHER (German states) *see* Christoph
CHRISTOPHER 231
CHRISTOPHER I 62
CHRISTOPHER II 62
CHRISTOPHER III 62

CHRISTOPHORUS 189
CHU CHAN-CHI 46
CHU CH'ANG-LO 47
CHU CH'I-CHEN 46
CHU CHIEN-SHEN 46
CHU CH'I-YU 46
CHU HOU-CHAO 46
CHU HOU-TSUNG 46
CHU I-CHUN 46
CHU KAO-CHIH 46
CHU TEH, Marshal 49
CHU TI 46
CHU TSAI-KOU 46
CHU YU-CHIAO 47
CHU YU-CHIEN 47
CHU YU-T'ANG 46
CHU YUAN-CHANG 46
CHU YUN-WEN 46
CHUAI 154
CHUANG-LIEH-TI 47
CHUARD, ERNEST 234
CHUKYO 155
CHULA CHOM KLAO 238
CHULALONGKORN 238
CH'UN HUANG-TI 47
CHUNDRIGAR, ISMAEL IBRAHIM 186
CHUNG IL KWON, Gen 159
CHUNG, RAYMOND ARTHUR 116
CH'UNG-CHEN 46
CHUNG PREI 37
CHUNG-TSUNG 45
CHURCHILL, WINSTON LEONARD SPENCER-
    265
CICOGNA, PASQUALE 153
CINNAMUS 134
CISSA 249
CLAPPA 252
CLARENDON, George Herbert Hyde Villiers, 6th
    Earl of 216
CLARKE, Sir ELLIS EMMANUEL INNOCENT 240
CLAUDE 90
CLAUDINE 173
CLAUDIUS (Ethiopia) *see* Galawdewos
CLAUDIUS I 205
CLAUDIUS II 207
CLEMENCEAU, GEORGES 87
CLEMENS I 187
CLEMENS II 189
CLEMENS III 189, 190
CLEMENS IV 190
CLEMENS V 191
CLEMENS VI 191
CLEMENS VII 191
CLEMENS VIII 192
CLEMENS IX 192
CLEMENS X 192
CLEMENS XI 192
CLEMENS XII 192
CLEMENS XIII 192
CLEMENS XIV 192
CLEMENT (Papal State) *see* Clemens
CLEOMBROTUS II 113
CLEOMBROTUS III 114
CLEOMENES I 113
CLEOMENES II 113
CLEOMENES III 114
CLEOPATRA I 70
CLEOPATRA II 70
CLEOPATRA III 71
CLEOPATRA IV BERENICE 71
CLEOPATRA VI TRYPHAENA 71
CLEOPATRA VII 72
CLEOPATRA THEA 213
CLEPH 142
de CLERMONT, ANNET 168
CLETUS 187
CLEVELAND, STEPHEN GROVER 272
CLODOMIR 79
CLOTAIRE I 79
CLOTAIRE II 80
CLOTAIRE III 80
CLOTAIRE IV 80
CLOVIS I 79
CLOVIS II 80
CLOVIS III 80
CLOVIS IV 80
CNUD I Ericssen 230
CNUD II 230
CNUT *(England)* 254
CNUT *(York)* 253
COATES, JOSEPH GORDON 180
COBHAM, Sir Charles John Lyttelton, 10th
    Viscount 180
CODAGANGA 228
COENRED *(Mercia)* 251
COENRED *(Northumbria)* 252
COENWULF 252
COHEN, Sir ZELMAN 11

COLE, Justice CHRISTOPHER OKORO 214, 215
COLEMAN, WILLIAM 162
COLIJN, Dr HENDRIKUS 178, 179
COLLINS, MICHAEL 138
COLOMAN (Hungary) see Kalman
COLOMBO, EMILIO 145
COMMODUS 207
COMONFORT, Gen IGNACIO 171
COMPTON, Sir SPENCER 261
COMTESSE, ROBERT 234
CONAN I 90
CONAN II 90
CONAN III 90
CONAN IV 90
CONCHA, JOSÉ VICENTE 52
CONGACOU, TAIROU 23
CONNAUGHT and STRATHEARN, Duke of 39
CONON 188
CONRAD (German states) see Konrad
CONRAD (Holy Roman Empire) see Konrad
CONRAD (Italian states) see Corrado
CONRAD I (Burgundy) 91
CONRAD I (Luxembourg) 164
CONRAD I de Montferrat 55
CONRAD II (Burgundy) 91
CONRAD II (Jerusalem) 56
CONRAD II (Luxembourg) 165
CONRAD III 56
CONRADIN 56
CONSTANCE (Antioch) 54
CONSTANCE (Brittany) 90
CONSTANCE (Sicily) 151
CONSTANS I 208
CONSTANS II 32
CONSTANTINE (Armenia and Georgia) see Konstantin
CONSTANTINE (Byzantine Empire) see Constantinus
CONSTANTINE (Greece) see Konstantinos
CONSTANTINE (Papal State and Roman Empire) see Constantinus
CONSTANTINE I 266
CONSTANTINE II 266
CONSTANTINE III 266
CONSTANTINE ASSEN TIKH (Bulgaria) see Konstantin Assen Tikh
CONSTANTINE BERENG SEFISO (Lesotho) see Motlotlehi Moshoeshoe II
CONSTANTINUS I (Papal State) 188
CONSTANTINUS I (Roman Empire) 208
CONSTANTINUS 'II' 188
CONSTANTINUS II 208
CONSTANTINUS III 32
CONSTANTINUS IV 32
CONSTANTINUS V 32
CONSTANTINUS VI 32
CONSTANTINUS VII 32
CONSTANTINUS VIII 32
CONSTANTINUS IX 32
CONSTANTINUS X DUCAS 33
CONSTANTINUS XI PALAEOLOGUS 34
CONSTANTIUS I 208
CONSTANTIUS II 208
CONSTANTIUS III 208
CONTARINI, ALVISO 153
CONTARINI, CARLO 153
CONTARINI, DOMENICO 153
COOBAR, ABDUL MAJID 162
COOK, Sir JOSEPH 11
COOLIDGE, JOHN CALVIN 272
CORDERO, LUIS 65
CORDOBA, GONZALO 65
CORDOBA, Gen JORGE 24
de CORDOBA, Col MANUEL 75
CORDON CEA, Dr EUSEBIO RODOLFO 75
CORDOVA, ANDRÉS 66
CORNARI I, GIOVANNI 153
CORNARI II, GIOVANNI 153
CORNELIUS 187
CORRADO I 151
CORRADO II 151
CORRO, JOSÉ JUSTO 171
CORTÉS CASTRO, LÉON 54
COSGRAVE, LIAM 139
COSGRAVE, WILLIAM THOMAS 138
COSIMO de 'MEDICI 145
COSIMO I 152
COSIMO II 152
COSIMO III 152
da COSTA, ALFREDO NOBRE 204
de COSTA, Gen MANOEL de OLIVEIRA GOMES 203
COSTA. Commander VASCO ALMEIDA e 204
COSTANZA 151
COSTELLO, JOHN ALOYSIUS 139
COTONER, NICOLAS 168
COTONER, RAPHAEL 168

COTY, RENÉ 88
COUTTS, Sir WALTER 244
COUVE de MURVILLE, JACQUES MAURICE 89
CRASSUS (Roman Empire) see Marcus Licinius Crassus
CRESPO, EDUARDO V. 275
CRESPO, Gen JOAQUIN 276
CRISTEA, Dr MIRON 209
CROESUS 166
CROMWELL, OLIVER 258
CROMWELL, RICHARD 258
CSIA, Dr SANDOR 124
CUADRA, VICENTE 181
CUAUHTÉMOC 170
CUESTAS, JUAN LINDOLFO 274
CUILEAN 266
CUITLAHUAC 170
CULEN 266
CUNIBERT 142
CUNO, WILHELM CARL JOSEF 97
CURTIN, JOHN JOSEPH 11
CUTHRED (Kent) 249
CUTHRED (Wessex) 250
CVETKOVIC, Dr DRAGISA 280
CWICHELM 250
CYAXARES 133
CYNAN TINDAETHWY ap RHODRI MOLWYNOG 268
CYNEGILS 250
CYNEWULF 250
CYNRIC 250
CYRANKIEWICZ, JOZEF 200
CYRUS 19
CYRUS I 133
CYRUS II 133

DACKO, DAVID 42
DADEF-RE 67
DADJO, Col KLÉBER 239
DAFYDD I 269
DAFYDD II 269
DAFYDD III 269
DAGOBERT I 80
DAGOBERT II 80
DAGOBERT III 80
DAHANAYAKE, WIJEYANANDA 229
DAIGO 155
DALADIER, ÉDOUARD 87
DAMASKINOS, Archbishop 111
DAMASUS 187
DAMASUS II 189
DAMBA, DASHIN 175
DAMIQILISHU 16
DAMYANOV, GEORGI 29
DANILO I 281
DANILO II 281
da PONTE, NICOLO 153
DAPPULA I 227
DAPPULA II 227
DAPPULA III 227
DAPPULA IV 227
von DARANYI, Dr KALMAN 124
DARAYAVAUSH III MOREIRA 133
DARAYAVAUSH I (Babylonia) 19
DARAYAVAUSH I (Iran) 133
DARAYAVAUSH II 133
DARIUS 201
DARIUS I (Egypt) 70
DARIUS I (Iran) 133
DARIUS II (Egypt) 70
DARIUS II (Iran) 133
DARIUS III (Egypt) 70
DARIUS III (Iran) 133
DARLAN, Admiral FRANCOIS 88
DASARATHA 127
DATHAPAHUTI 227
DATHOPATISSA I 227
DATTA 227
DA'UD 128
DAVID (Ethiopia) see Dawit
DAVID (Georgia) see Dawith
DAVID (Israel and Judah) see Dawid
DAVID 240
DAVID I 267
DAVID II 267
DAVID SOSLAN (Georgia) see Dawith Soslan
DAVIDOVIC, LJUBOMIR 280
DAVILA, FAUSTO 121
DAVILA, MIGUEL 121
DAVILA ESPINOZA, CARLOS 43
DAVIS, JEFFERSON 273
DAWALIBI, Dr MAAROUF 236
DAWAR BAKHSH 130

DAWID 139
DAWIT I 76
DAWITH III or II 94
DAWITH IV or III 94
DAWITH VIII or VII 95
DAWITH VII or VI 94
DAWITH VI or V 94
DAWITH V or IV 94
DAWITH SOSLAN 94
DAZA, Gen HILARION 24
DEAKIN, ALFRED 11
DEBRÉ, MICHEL JEAN-PIERRE 89
DECIUS 207
DECOPPET, CAMILLE 234
DEDKERE ISESI 67
de GEER, Baron LOUIS 233
DEIDAMEIA 75
DEIOCES 133
DELGADO CHALBAUD, Lieut-Col CARLOS 277
DE L'ISLE, 1st Viscount 11
DEMARATUS 113
DEMERDJIS, KONSTANTINOS 111
DEMETRIOS I 113
DEMETRIOS II 113
DEMETRIUS (Greece) see Demetrios
DEMETRIUS I SOTER 213
DEMETRIUS II NICATOR 213
DEMETRIUS III EUKAIROS PHILOPATOR SOTER 213
DEMICHELL LIZASO, Dr PEDRO ALBERTO 275
DEMIREL, SULEYMAN 243
DEN 66
DEN SEMTI 66
de NICOLA, ENRICO 144
DENIS (Portugal) see Dinis
DENKTASH, RAUF 57
DENMAN, Thomas Denman, 3rd Baron 10
DEORIC 252
DERBY, The 14th Earl of 263
DERBY, 16th Earl of 38
DERQUI, SANTIAGO 6
DESAI, SHRI MORARJI RANCHODJI 132
DESCHANEL, PAUL 87
DESIDERIUS 142
DESSALINES, JEAN JACQUES 116
DEUCHER, ADOLF 234
DEUSDEDIT I 188
DEUSDEDIT II 188
de VALERA, EAMON 138
DEVA RAYA 129
DEVARAYA I 129
DEVARAYA II 129
DEVESI, B 215
DEVONSHIRE, The 4th Duke of 261
DEVONSHIRE, Victor Christian William Cavendish, Duke of 39
de WET, NICOLAS JACOBUS 216
DHAIFALLAH, Col ABDEL LATIF 279
DHARANINDRAVARMAN I 36
DHARANINDRAVARMAN II 36
DHARMASOKA 228
DHATUSENA 227
DHRUVA 127
DIA, MAMADOU 214
DIAKITÉ, Captain YORO 168
DIAS, Col CARLOS ENRIQUE 115
DIAZ, ADOLFO 181
DIAZ, MANUEL MARIA 186
DIAZ, Gen PORFIRIO 172
DIAZ AROSEMENA, Dr DOMINGO 186
DIAZ de la VEGA, ROMULO 171
DIAZ ORDAZ, Dr GUSTAVO 172
DIDIUS JULIANUS 207
DIEDERICH, Dr NICOLAAS 217
DIEFENBAKER, JOHN GEORGE 40
DIMITROV, GEORGI 29
DINIS 202
DINNYÉS, LAJOS 124
DIOCLETIAN (Roman Empire) see Diocletianus
DIOCLETIANUS 207
DIOMEDES, ALEXANDROS 112
DION 235
DIONYSIUS 187
DIONYSIUS I 235
DIONYSIUS II 235
DIORI, HAMANI 181
DIOSCORUS 188
DIOUF, ABDOU 214
DIRK I 22
DIRK III 179
DIRK IV 179
DIRK V 179
DIRK VI 179
DIRK VII 179
DISRAELI, BENJAMIN 264
DJER 66
DJORDJE PETROVIC 282
DJOSER 67

DJURANOVIC, VESELIN 281
DLAMINI, Prince MAKHOSINI 230
DLAMINI, Col MAPHEVU 230
DMITRI 245
DMITRI I *(Georgia)* 94
DMITRI I *(Novgorod)* 244
DMITRI II *(Georgia)* 94
DMITRI II *(Novgorod)* 244
DMITRI III 95
DMITRI Ivanovich Donskoy 244
DMITRI Shemyaka 245
DOBI, ISTVAN 124
DOLE, SANFORD BALLARD 273
DOLLFUSS, Dr ENGELBERT 14
DOMINGUE, Gen MICHEL 117
DOMITIAN (Roman Empire) *see* Domitianus
DOMITIANUS 206
DOMITIEN, ÉLISABETH 42
DONALD I 265
DONALD II 266
DONALD III 266
DONALD BANE 266
DONA, NICOLO 153
DONATO, FRANCESCO 153
DONATO, LEONARDO 153
DONITZ, Admiral KARL 97
DONUS 188
DONUS II 189
DORMAN, Sir MAURICE HENRY 169, 214
DORTICOS TORRADO, OSVALDO 56
DOST MOHAMMAD KHAN 1, 2
DOUGLAS-HOME, Sir ALEXANDER
    FREDERICK 265
DOUMER, PAUL 87
DOUMERGUE, GASTON 87
DOVAS, Gen KONSTANTINOS 112
DOVYDAITIS, PRANAS 164
DOWIYOGO, BERNARD 176
DREES, Dr WILLEM 179
DROGO 90
DROZ, NUMA 234
DRUEY, DANIEL-HENRI 233
DUARTE 202
DUBCEK, ALEXANDER 59
DUBH 266
DUBS, JAKOB 233, 234
DUCA, ION G. 209
DUCOS, ROGER 84
DUDLEY, William Humble Ward, 2nd Earl of 10
DUDU 16
DUENAS, FRANCISCO 74
DUFFERIN and AVA, Frederick Temple
    Hamilton-Temple-Blackwood, 1st Marquess
    of 38
DUGAN, Sir WINSTON J 10
DUHALE, ALFREDO 44
DUNCAN, Sir PATRICK 216
DUNCAN I 266
DUNCAN II 266
DUNROSSIL, 1st Viscount 11
DUONG VAN MINH, Gen 277
DUPONG, PIERRE 165
DUPONT, CLIFFORD 204
DUTRA, Gen EURICO GASPAR 26
DUVALIER, Dr FRANCOIS 117
DUVALIER, JEAN-CLAUDE 117
DUVIEUSART, Prof JEAN PIERRE 22
DUY TAN 277

EADBALD 249
EADBERT *(Kent)* 249
EADBERT *(Northumbria)* 252
EADBERT PRAEN 249
EADRIC 249
EADWALD 249
EADWULF 252
EALDFRITH 252
EALDWULF 250
EALHMUND 249
EAMUKINSHUMI 18
EANES, Gen ANTONIO RAMALHO 203
EANFRITH 252
EANNATUM 15
EANRED 252
EARCONBERT 249
EARDWULF *(Kent)* 249
EARDWULF *(Northumbria)* 252
EARPWALD 251
EATHELRIC 252
EBERHARD I 109
EBERHARD II 109
EBERHARD III 109
EBERHARD LUDWIG 109
EBERT, FRIEDRICH 97
ECEVIT, BULENT 243
ECGBRIHT I 249

ECGBRIHT II 249
ECGRIC 251
ECHANDI JIMÉNEZ, MARIO 54
ECHEGOYEN, Dr MARTIN R. 275
ECHEVERRIA, JAVIER 171
ECHEVERRIA ALVAREZ, LUIS 173
ECHINEQUE, Gen JOSÉ RUFINO 195
EDEN, Prof NILS 233
EDEN, Sir ROBERT ANTHONY 265
EDGAR *(England)* 253, 254
EDGAR *(Scotland)* 266
EDMUND *(East Anglia)* 251
EDMUND *(Scotland)* 266
EDMUND I 253
EDMUND II 253
EDRED 253
EDUARD 98
EDUARDO 150
EDWALD (Anglo-Saxon Kingdoms) *see* Eadwald
EDWARD *(German states) see* Eduard
EDWARD *(Portugal) see* Duarte
EDWARD 267
EDWARD the Confessor 254
EDWARD the Elder 250
EDWARD the Martyr 253
EDWARD I 255
EDWARD II 255
EDWARD III 255
EDWARD IV 256
EDWARD V 256
EDWARD VI 257
EDWARD VII 261
EDWARD VIII 261
EDWIN 252
EDWIN ap HYWEL DDA 269
EDWY 253
EENPALU, KAAREL 76
EGAL, MOHAMMED HAJI IBRAHIM 215, 216
EGBERT 250
EGBERT I *(Kent)* 249
EGBERT I *(Northumbria)* 253
EGBERT II *(Kent)* 249
EGBERT II *(Northumbria)* 253
EGFRITH *(Mercia)* 252
EGFRITH *(Northumbria)* 252
EGGERZ, SIGURDUR 125
EGHBAL, Dr MANOUCHEHR 137
EGICA 219
EGUSQUIZA, JUAN BAUTISTA 194
EINAUDI, LUIGI 144
EINBUND, KARL 76
EIRIK I 182
EIRIK II 183
EIRIK III 183
EISENHOWER, DWIGHT DAVID 272
EKATERINA I Alekseyevna 246
EKATERINA II Alekseyevna 246
EKHTAI II . 67
EKMAN, CARL GUSTAV 233
ELAGABALUS 207
ELAH 140
ELDJARN, Dr KRISTJAN 125
ÉLÉONORE 222
ELEUTHERIUS 187
ELFWALD I 252
ELFWALD II 252
ELIAS, RICARDO LEONICIO 196
ELISA 146, 152
ELISABETH 165
ELISAVETA Petrovna 246
ELIZABETH I 257
ELIZABETH II 261
ELLAURI, JOSÉ 274
ELULU 16
EMAMI, Dr JAFAR SHARIF 137
EMANUELE FILIBERTO 150
EMI 16
EMISUM 16
EMMANUEL I 240
EMMANUEL I COMNENUS 33
EMMANUEL II 240
EMMANUEL II PALAEOLOGUS 34
EMMANUEL III 240
EMMANUEL PHILIBERT (Italian states) *see*
    Emanuele Filiberto
EMUND 230
ENANNATUM I 15
ENANNATUM II 15
ENCALADA, MANUEL BLANCO 43
ENETARZI 15
ENEZIB MERPEBA 66
ENGELBREKTSSEN, ENGELBREKT 231
ENLILBANI 16
ENLILKUDURUSUR 9
ENLILNADINAHHE 17
ENLILNADINAPLI 17
ENLILNADINSHUMI 17
ENLILNASIR I 9

ENLILNASIR II 9
ENLILNIRARI 9
ENRICO 151
ENRIQUE I 220
ENRIQUE II 221
ENRIQUE III 221
ENRIQUE IV 221
ENRIQUEZ, Gen ALBERTO 65
EN?TAR-SIN 8
ENTEMENA 15
EN-YU 155
EOCHAID 266
EORMENRIC 249
EOWA 251
EOWILS 253
ERARIC 142
ERCOLE I 147
ERCOLE II 147
ERCOLE III 147
ERH SHIH 44
ERHARD, Prof LUDWIG 109
ERIBA-ADAD I 9
ERIBA-ADAD II 9
ERIBAMARDUK 18
ERIC (Denmark) *see* Erik
ERIC (Norway) *see* Eirik
ERIC, St 230
ERIC *(Sweden)* 231
ERIC *(East Anglia)* 251
ERIC *(York)* 253
ERIC IX 230
ERIC X 230
ERIC XI Ericssen 230, 231
ERIC XII 231
ERIC XIII 231
ERIC XIV 232
ERICH, RAFAEL 78
ERIK I 61
ERIK II 61
ERIK III 61
ERIK IV 61
ERIK V 62
ERIK VI 62
ERIK VII 62
ERIKSEN, ERIK 63
ERIM, Prof NIHAT 243
ERIMENA 274
ERISPOË 90
ERIZZO, FRANCESCO 153
ERLANDER, TAGE 233
ERMESINDE 165
ERNEST (Austria and German states) *see* Ernst
ERNEST AUGUSTUS (German states) *see* Ernst
    August
ERNEST LOUIS (German states) *see* Ernst
    Ludwig
ERNST *(Austria)* 12, 13
ERNST *(Bavaria)* 98
ERNST *(Saxony)* 106
ERNST I *(Saxe-Altenburg)* 105
ERNST I *(Saxe-Coburg)* 105
ERNST II *(Saxe-Altenburg)* 105
ERNST II *(Saxe-Coburg)* 105
ERNST AUGUST *(Brunswick)* 100
ERNST AUGUST *(Hanover)* 100, 101
ERNST AUGUST I 106
ERNST AUGUST II 106
ERNST LUDWIG 101
ERRAIMITTI 16
ERRAZURIZ ECHAURREN, FEDERICO 43
ERRAZURIZ ZANARTU, FEDERICO 43
ERVIGIO 219
ESARHADDON *(Assyria)* 10
ESARHADDON *(Babylonia)* 18
ESC 249
ESCALON, PEDRO JOSÉ 74
ESCOBAR, BERNARDO 114
ESCOBAR, Gen PATRICIO 194
ESCURRA, JUAN BAUTISTA 194
ESHKOL, LEVI 141
ESKENDER 76
ESMA'IL I 135
ESMA'IL II 135
ESMA'IL III 136
ESPAILLAT, ULISES FRANCISCO 64
ESPINOSA, JAVIER 65
ESQUIVEL, ANICETO 53
ESQUIVEL, ASCENSION 53
ESSAD PASHA 3
ESTEBAN MONTERO, JUAN 43
de ESTELLA, Marquess 226
ESTIGARRIBA, Gen JOSÉ F. 194
ESTIMÉ, DUMARSAIS 117
ESTRADA, EMILIO 65
ESTRADA, JOSÉ 181
ESTRADA, JOSÉ MARIA 181
ESTRADA, JUAN 181
ESTRADA CABRERA, MANUEL 115

ESTRADA PALMA, TOMAS **56**
ESTRELLA URENA, RAFAEL **64**
ETEMADI, NOUR AHMAD **2**
ETHELBALD (Anglo-Saxon Kingdoms) see
 Aethelbald
ETHELBERT (Anglo-Saxon Kingdoms) see
 Aethelbert
ETHELFRITH (Anglo-Saxon Kingdoms) see
 Aethelfrith
ETHELRED (Anglo-Saxon Kingdoms) see
 Aethelred
ETHELWALD (Anglo-Saxon Kingdoms) see
 Aethelwald
ETHELWOLD (Anglo-Saxon Kingdoms) see
 Aethelwold
ETHELWULF (Anglo-Saxon Kingdoms) see
 Aethelwulf
ETIENNE **93**
ETTER, PHILIPP **234**
EUDAMIDAS I **114**
EUDAMIDAS II **114**
EUDES (Brittany) **90**
EUDES (France) **81**
EUDES I **91**
EUDES II **91**
EUDES III **91**
EUDES IV **91**
EUGEN **100**
EUGENE (Papal State) see Eugenius
EUGENIUS **208**
EUGENIUS I **188**
EUGENIUS II **188**
EUGENIUS III **189**
EUGENIUS IV **191**
EULMASHSHAKINSHUMI **18**
EUMENES I **194**
EUMENES II **194**
EURICO **219**
EURYDAMIDAS **114**
EUSEBIUS **187**
EUTYCHIAN (Papal State) see Eutychianus
EUTYCHIANUS **187**
EVARISTUS **187**
EYADEMA, ETIENNE **239**
EYADEMA, Lieut-Col GNASSINGBE **239**
EYSKENS, GASTON **22**
EYSTEIN I **183**
EYSTEIN II **183**
EZETA, CARLOS **74**

FABIAN (Roman Empire) see Fabianus
FABIANUS I **187**
FACTA, LUIGI **144**
FADDEN, Sir ARTHUR WILLIAM **11**
FAGERHOLM, KARL-AUGUST **78, 79**
FAISAL (Iraq) see Faysal
FAISAL ibn Abdul Aziz ibn Saud **211**
FAISAL ibn Abdul Aziz ibn SAUD **212**
FAISAL ibn Abdul Aziz ibn Saud, Prince **212**
FALCON, Gen JUAN CRISOSTOMO **276**
FALLDIN, NILS OLOF THORBJORN **233**
FALLIERES, CLEMENT ARMAND **87**
FANFANI, AMINTORE **144**
FARAMURZ, Ala'ad-Din **214**
FARHAD I **134**
FARHAD II **134**
FARHAD III **134**
FARHAD IV **134**
FARHAD V **134**
FARKAS, Gen MIHALY **125**
FAROUK (Egypt) see Faruq
FAROUK **73**
FARRELL, Gen EDELMIRO J. **6**
FARRUKHSIYAR **130**
FARUQ **73**
FASILADAS **77**
FATH 'ALI SHAH **136**
FAURE, EDGAR **88, 89**
FAURE, FRANCOIS FÉLIX **87**
FAUSTIN I **117**
FAVILA **220**
FAWZI, Dr MAHMOUD **74**
FAYSAL **235**
FAYSAL I **137**
FAYSAL II **137**
FEDERIGO **148**
FEDERIGO I RUGGIERO **151**
FEDERIGO III **151**
FEDERIGO IV **151**
FEHRENBACH, KONSTANTIN **97**
FEISAL bin Turki **185**
FEKINI, Dr MOHIEDDINE **162**
FELDMANN, MARKUS **234**
FELICE **146**
FELIPE I **223**
FELIPE II **224**

FELIPE III **224**
FELIPE IV **224**
FELIPE V **224**
FELIPPE I **202**
FELIPPE II **202**
FELIPPE III **202**
FELIX I **187**
FELIX II **187**
FELIX III or II **188**
FELIX IV or III **188**
FELIX V **191**
FENG KUO-CHANG **48**
FERDINAND (Flanders) **22**
FERDINAND (Hesse-Homburg) **102**
FERDINAND (Italian states) see Ferrante
FERDINAND (Italian states) see Ferdinando
FERDINAND (Portugal) see Fernando
FERDINAND (Spain) see Fernando
FERDINAND I (Austria) **13, 14**
FERDINAND I (Bohemia) **60**
FERDINAND I (Bulgaria) **28**
FERDINAND I (Holy Roman Empire) **120**
FERDINAND I (Hungary) **123**
FERDINAND I (Romania) **209**
FERDINAND II (Austria) **13**
FERDINAND II (Bohemia) **60, 61**
FERDINAND II (Holy Roman Empire) **120**
FERDINAND II (Hungary) **123**
FERDINAND III (Austria) **13**
FERDINAND III (Holy Roman Empire) **120**
FERDINAND III (Hungary) **123**
FERDINAND IV **123**
FERDINAND V **123**
FERDINAND MARIA **99**
FERDINANDO **149**
FERDINANDO I (Naples) **148**
FERDINANDO I (Sicily) **151, 152**
FERDINANDO I (Tuscany) **152**
FERDINANDO II (Naples) **148**
FERDINANDO II (Sicily) **151, 152**
FERDINANDO II (Tuscany) **152**
FERDINANDO III (Naples) **148**
FERDINANDO III (Sicily) **152**
FERDINANDO III (Tuscany) **152**
FERDINANDO IV (Naples) **148**
FERDINANDO IV (Tuscany) **152**
FERENC I **123**
FERENC JOSZEF I **123**
FERGUSSON, Brig Sir BERNARD EDWARD **180**
FERGUSSON, Sir CHARLES **180**
FERGUSSON, Sir RONALD **10**
FERNANDEZ, PROSPERO **53**
FERNANDEZ ALBANO, ELIAS **43**
FERNANDEZ ALONSO, SERGIO **24**
FERNANDEZ CRESPO, DANIEL **275**
FERNANDEZ MALDONADO, Gen JORGE **196**
FERNANDO I (Aragon) **221**
FERNANDO I (Castile) **220**
FERNANDO I (Portugal) **202**
FERNANDO II (Aragon) **222**
FERNANDO II (Castile) **220**
FERNANDO II (Portugal) **203**
FERNANDO III **221**
FERNANDO IV **221**
FERNANDO V **223**
FERNANDO VI **225**
FERNANDO VII **225**
FERRANTE I (Naples) **148**
FERRANTE I (Tuscany) **152**
FERRANTE II (Naples) **148**
FERRANTE II (Tuscany) **152**
FERREIRA, BENIGNO **194**
FERRERA, FRANCISCO **120**
FERRERO REBAGLIATI, RAUL **196**
FERRIER, Dr JOHAN HENRI ELIZA **230**
FERRI I **92**
FERRI II **92**
FERRI III **92**
FERRI IV **92**
FIAME MATA'AFA FAUMUINA MULINU'U II **279**
von FIEANDT, Dr RAINER **79**
FIERLINGER, ZDENEK **59**
FIGL, LEOPOLD **15**
FIGNOLE, Prof DANIEL **117**
FIGUERAS Y MORAGAS, ESTANISLAO **225**
FIGUEREO, JUAN WENCESLAO **64**
FIGUERES FERRER, JOSÉ **54**
FIGUEROA, EMILIANO **43**
FIGUEROA, FERNANDO **74**
FIGUEROS LARRAIN, EMILIANO **43**
FILIBERTO I **150**
FILIBERTO II **150**
FILIPPO **149**
FILIPPO I (Naples) **148**
FILIPPO I (Savoy) **150**
FILIPPO I (Sicily) **151**
FILIPPO II (Naples) **148**
FILIPPO II (Savoy) **150**

FILIPPO II (Sicily) **151**
FILIPPO III (Naples) **148**
FILIPPO III (Sicily) **151**
FILIPPO IV (Naples) **148**
FILIPPO IV (Sicily) **151**
FILIPPO MARIA **146**
FILLMORE, MILLARD **272**
FILOV, Prof BOGDAN **29**
FIROZ KHAN NOON, MALIK **186**
FIRUZ **130**
FIRUZ I **135**
FIRUZ II **135**
FIRUZ SHAH ibn RAJAH **128**
FISCHER, Dr CARLO L. **275**
FISHER, ANDREW **11**
FLANDIN, PIERRE-ÉTIENNE **87**
FLAVIUS VICTOR **208**
FLORENT **1**
FLORES, ANTONIO **65**
FLORES, Gen JUAN JOSE **65**
FLORES-AVENDANO, GUILLERMO **115**
FLORESTAN **174**
FLORES, Col VENANCIO **274**
FLORIAN (Roman Empire) see Florianus
FLORIANUS **207**
FLORIS I **179**
FLORIS II **179**
FLORIS III **179**
FLORIS IV **179**
FLORIS V **179**
FOCK, JENO **125**
FONSECA, Maj-Gen DEOGRACIAS **52**
da FONSECA, Marshal HERMES RODRIGUES
 26
da FONSECA, Marshal MANUEL DEODORO **26**
de FONSECA, MANUEL PINTO **169**
FORBES, GEORGE WILLIAM **180**
FORD, GERALD RUDOLPH **273**
FORDE, FRANCIS MICHAEL **11**
FORMOSUS **188**
FORNEROD, CHARLES -EMMANUEL
 -CONSTANT **233**
FORRER, LUDWIG **234**
FORSTER, Dr ALBERT **61**
FORSTER of Lepe, Sir Henry William Forster, 1st
 Baron **10**
FOSCARINI, MARCO **153**
FOSTER, Sir ROBERT **77**
FOUCHÉ, JACOBUS JOHANNES **217**
FOULQUES **55**
FOULQUES I **89**
FOULQUES II **89**
FOULQUES III **89**
FOULQUES IV **89**
FOULQUES V **89**
FRANCESCO (Milan) **146**
FRANCESCO (Parma and Piacenza) **149**
FRANCESCO I (Modena) **147**
FRANCESCO I (Sicily) **152**
FRANCESCO I (Tuscany) **152**
FRANCESCO II (Milan) **147**
FRANCESCO II (Modena) **147**
FRANCESCO II (Tuscany) **152**
FRANCESCO II d'ASSISI **152**
FRANCESCO III **147**
FRANCESCO IV **147**
FRANCESCO V **147**
FRANCESCO GIACINTO **150**
FRANCIS (Austria and German states) see Franz
FRANCIS (France) see Francois
FRANCIS (Holy Roman Empire) see Franz
FRANCIS (Italian states) see Francesco
FRANCIS HYACINTH (Italian states) see
 Francesco Giacinto
FRANCIS JOSEPH (Austria) see Franz Joseph
FRANCO, Gen GUILLERMO **65**
FRANCO, MANUEL **194**
FRANCO, Col RAFAEL **194**
FRANCO y BAHAMONDE, Generalissimo Don
 FRANCISCO **226**
FRANCOIS I (Brittany) **90**
FRANCOIS I (France) **82**
FRANCOIS I (Lorraine) **92**
FRANCOIS I Phoebus **222**
FRANCOIS II **90**
FRANCOIS II **82**
FRANCOIS II **93**
FRANCOIS III (Brittany) **90**
FRANCOIS III (Lorraine) **93**
FRANCOIS-MARSAL, FRÉDÉRIC **87**
F RANJIEH, SULEIMAN **161**
FRANZ **163**
FRANZ I **14**
FRANZ I STEPHAN **120**
FRANZ II (Austria) **14**
FRANZ II (Holy Roman Empire) **120**
FRANZ JOSEPH I (Austria) **14**
FRANZ JOSEPH I (Liechtenstein) **163**

FRANZ JOSEPH II   163
FRASER, JOHN MALCOLM   11
FRASER, PETER   180
FRÉDÉRIC   56
FRÉDÉRIC I   92
FRÉDÉRIC II   92
FRÉDÉRIC III   92
FRÉDÉRIC IV   92
FREDERICK (Austria and German states) see Friedrich
FREDERICK (Holy Roman Empire) see Friedrich
FREDERICK (Italian states) see Federigo
FREDERICK (Jerusalem) see Frederic
FREDERICK (Sweden) see Fredrik
FREDERICK AUGUSTUS (German states) see Friedrich August
FREDERICK CHRISTIAN (German states) see Friedrich Christian
FREDERICK EUGENE (German states) see Friedrich Eugen
FREDERICK FRANCIS (German states) see Friedrich Franz
FREDERICK HENRY (Netherlands) see Frederik Hendrik
FREDERICK WILLIAM (German states) see Friedrich Wilhelm
FREDERIK   60
FREDERIK I   62
FREDERIK II   62
FREDERIK III   62
FREDERIK IV   62
FREDERIK V   63
FREDERIK VI   63
FREDERIK VII   63
FREDERIK VIII   63
FREDERIK IX   63
FREDERIK HENDRIK , Prince of Orange   177
FREDRIK   232
FREI MONTALVA, EDUARDO   44
FREIRE, Gen RAMON   43
FREYBERG, Lieut-Gen Sir Bernard Cyril Freyberg, 1st Baron   180
FREY, EMIL   234
FREY-HEROSEE, FRIEDRICH   233
FRIAS, TOMAS   24
FRICK, Dr ALEXANDER   163
FRIDUUALD   252
FRIEDEN, PIERRE   165
FRIEDRICH (Holy Roman Empire)   120
FRIEDRICH (Mecklenburg-Schwerin)   102
FRIEDRICH (Saxe-Altenburg)   105
FRIEDRICH (Waldeck)   108
FRIEDRICH (Wurttemberg)   109
FRIEDRICH I (Anhalt)   97
FRIEDRICH I (Austria)   12
FRIEDRICH I (Baden)   98
FRIEDRICH I (Brandenburg)   99
FRIEDRICH I (Hesse-Cassel)   101
FRIEDRICH I (Holy Roman Empire)   119
FRIEDRICH I (Prussia)   104
FRIEDRICH I (Saxony)   106
FRIEDRICH I (The Rhine)   103
FRIEDRICH I (Wurttemberg)   109
FRIEDRICH II (Anhalt)   97
FRIEDRICH II (Austria)   12
FRIEDRICH II (Baden)   98
FRIEDRICH II (Brandenburg)   100
FRIEDRICH II (Hesse-Cassel)   101
FRIEDRICH II (Holy Roman Empire)   119
FRIEDRICH II (Prussia)   104
FRIEDRICH II (Saxony)   106
FRIEDRICH II (The Rhine)   103
FRIEDRICH II (Wurttemberg)   109
FRIEDRICH III (Austria)   13
FRIEDRICH III (Brandenburg)   100
FRIEDRICH III (Germany)   96
FRIEDRICH III (Holy Roman Empire)   120
FRIEDRICH III (Prussia)   104
FRIEDRICH III (Saxony)   106
FRIEDRICH III (The Rhine)   103
FRIEDRICH IV   103
FRIEDRICH V   103
FRIEDRICH V LUDWIG   102
FRIEDRICH VI   102
FRIEDRICH AUGUST   103
FRIEDRICH AUGUST I   107
FRIEDRICH AUGUST II   107
FRIEDRICH AUGUST III   107, 108
FRIEDRICH CHRISTIAN   107
FRIEDRICH EUGEN   109
FRIEDRICH FRANZ I   102
FRIEDRICH FRANZ II   102
FRIEDRICH FRANZ III   102
FRIEDRICH FRANZ IV   102
FRIEDRICH GUNTHER   108
FRIEDRICH WILHELM (Brandenburg)   100
FRIEDRICH WILHELM (Brunswick)   100
FRIEDRICH WILHELM (Hesse-Cassel)   102

FRIEDRICH WILHELM (Mecklenburg-Strelitz)   103
FRIEDRICH WILHELM I   104
FRIEDRICH WILHELM II   104
FRIEDRICH WILHELM III   104
FRIEDRICH WILHELM IV   104
FRITHEWLF   252
FROILA I   220
FROILA II   220
FRONDIZI, Dr ARTURO   6
FRUTOS, Dr MANUEL   194
FRYCH   269
FU-LIN   47
FUAD I   72
FUAD II   73
FUKUDA, TAKEO   157
FULK (Jerusalem and Anjou) see Foulques
FURANGHI, ALI   136
FURGLER, KURT   235
FURRER, JONAS   233
FUSHIMI   155
FYODOR I Ivanovich   245
FYODOR II Godunov   245
FYODOR III Alekseyevich   245

GABRIEL RADOMIR   28
al-GADDAFI, Col MU'AMMAR MUHAMMAD   162
GAGIK I   7
GAGIK II   7
el GAILANI, SAYID RASHID ALI   137
GAILLARD, FÉLIX   89
GAIRY, Sir ERIC MATTHEW   114
GAIUS CAESAR   205
GAJABAHU II   227
GALAWDEWOS   77
GALBA   206
GALEAZZO I   146
GALFAZZO II   146
GALEAZZO MARIA   146
GALERIUS   208
de GALE, Sir LEO   114
de GALLEGOS, JOSÉ RAFAEL   53
GALLEGOS FREIRE, ROMULO   277
GALLIENUS   207
GALLUS   207
GALVEZ, Dr JUAN MANUEL   121
GALWAY, George Vere Arundell Monckton-Arundell, 8th Viscount   180
GAMARRA, Gen AGUSTIN   195
GANDASH   17
GANDHI, Mrs INDIRA   132
GANEV, DIMITER   29
GAONA, JUAN   194
GARCIA, CARLOS POLESTICO   196
GARCIA, JAEN   186
GARCIA, LIZARDO   65
GARCIA, Gen POLICARPO PAZ   121
GARCIA I   220
GARCIA I SANCHEZ   222
GARCIA II   222
GARCIA III   222
GARCIA IV RAMIREZ   222
GARCIA CALDERON, FRANCISCO   195
GARCIA-GODOY, Dr HECTOR   64
GARCIA GRANADOS, MIGUEL   114
GARCIA MENOCAL, Gen MARIO   56
GARCIA MORENA, GABRIEL   65
GARCIA RAMIREZ   222
GARDINER, ANTHONY   162
GARDINER ROSE, Sir DAVID JAMES   116
GARFIELD, JAMES ABRAM   272
GARIBALD   142
GARRASTAZU, Gen EMILIO   27
de GARZEZ, MARTIN   168
de GASPERI, ALCIDE   144
GAUL, PEDRO   276
de GAULLE, Gen CHARLES ANDRÉ MARIE JOSEPH   88, 89
GAYKHATU   135
GAZI, Marshal SHAH MAHMUD KHAN   2
al GEDDAFI, WANIS   162
GEDIMINAS   163
de GEER, Jonkheer Dr DIRK JAN   178, 179
GEFFRARD, Gen NICOLAS FABRE   117
GEISEL, Gen ERNESTO   27
GEISELICO   219
GELASIUS I   188
GELASIUS II   189
GELON   235
GEMMEI   154
GENDA, Lieut-Col AMBROSE PATRICK   215
GENGHIS KHAN   174
GENSHO   154
GEOFFREY (France) see Geoffroi
GEOFFROI   93
GEOFFROI I (Anjou)   89

GEOFFROI I (Brittany)   90
GEOFFROI I de Villehardouin   1
GEOFFROI II   89
GEOFFROI II or III   90
GEOFFROI II de Villehardouin   1
GEOFFROI III   89
GEOFFROI IV   89
GEOFFROI V   89
GEOFFROI VI   89
GEOFFROI of Anjou   90
GEORG (Mecklenburg-Strelitz)   103
GEORG (Saxe-Altenburg)   105
GEORG (Saxony)   107, 108
GEORG (Schwarzburg)   108
GEORG I (Hanover)   100
GEORG I (Hesse)   101
GEORG I (Saxe-Meiningen)   106
GEORG I (Schaumberg-Lippe)   108
GEORG I (Waldeck)   108
GEORG II (Hanover)   100
GEORG II (Hesse)   101
GEORG II (Saxe-Meiningen)   106
GEORG II (Schaumberg-Lippe)   108
GEORG II (Waldeck)   108
GEORG III   101
GEORG V   101
GEORG VIKTOR   108
GEORG WILHELM   100
GEORGE, DAVID LLOYD   264
GEORGE (Bohemia) see Jiri
GEORGE (Georgia) see Giorgi
GEORGE (German states) see Georg
GEORGE (Greece) see Giorgios
GEORGE (Trebizond) see Georgius
GEORGE I   259
GEORGE I TERTER (Bulgaria) see Georgi I Terter
GEORGE II   259
GEORGE III   259
GEORGE IV   259
GEORGE V   261
GEORGE VI   261
GEORGE PETROVICH (Serbia) see Djordje Petrovic
GEORGE TUPOU I   239
GEORGE TUPOU II   239
GEORGE WILLIAM (German states) see Georg Wilhelm
GEORGI I TERTER   28
GEORGI II TERTER   28
GEORGIUS I   240
GÉRARD   92
GERBRANDY, Prof PIETER SJOERD   179
GERHARDSEN, EINAR HENRY   184
GERO, ERNO   125
GESTIDO, Gen OSCAR DANIEL   275
GETA   207
GÉZA   121
GÉZA I   121
GÉZA II   121
GHANI, ABDEL AZIZ ABDEL   279
al GHASMI, Liet-Col AHMED HUSSAIN   279
GHAZI   137
GHAZZI, SAID   236
GHEORGHE MAURER, ION   210
GHEORGHIEV, Col KIMON   29
GHEORGHIU-DEJ, GHEORGHE   210
GHIYAS-ud-DIN   128
GHIYAS-ud-DIN BALBAN   128
GHIYAS-ud-DIN TUGHLUQ   128
GIACOMO   151
GIA LONG   277
GIAN GALEAZZO I   146
GIAN GALEAZZO II   146
GIAN GASTONE   152
GIANNATTASIO, LUIS   275
GIBSON, GARRETT   162
GIEREK, EDWARD   201
GIGURTU, ION   209
GIL, JUAN BAUTISTA   193
GIOACCHINO NAPOLEONE   148
GIOLITTI, GIOVANNI   144
GIORGAKOPOULOS, KONSTANTINOS   112
GIORGI I   94
GIORGI II   94
GIORGI III   94
GIORGI IV   94
GIORGI V   95
GIORGI VI   95
GIORGI VII   95
GIORGI VIII   95
GIORGI IX   95
GIORGI XIII   95
GIORGIOS I   111
GIORGIOS II   111
GIOVANNA   151
GIOVANNA I   147
GIOVANNA II   147
GIOVANNA III   148

GIOVANNI *(Milan)* 146
GIOVANNI *(Sicily)* 151
GIOVANNI MARIA 146
GIRAL, JOSÉ 226
GIRI, Dr TULSI 177
GIRI, VARAHGIRI VENKATA 132
GIRIC 266
GIRO, JUAN FRANCISCO 274
GIRVAN JUDDHA VIKRAM 176
GISCARD d'ESTAING, VALÉRY 89
GISCO 41
GISELBERT *(Lorraine)* 92
GISELBERT *(Luxembourg)* 164
GIULIANO I de 'MEDICI 145
GIULIANO II de 'MEDICI 145
GIUSEPPE *(Naples)* 148
GIUSEPPE *(Sicily)* 151
GIUSTINIANI, MARCANTONIO 153
GIZIKIS, Gen PHAEDON 112
GLADSTONE, Herbert John Gladstone, 1st
  Viscount 216
GLADSTONE, WILLIAM EWART 264
GLAPPA 252
GLASSPOLE, FLORIZEL AUGUSTUS 153
GLENDOWER, OWEN (Wales) *see* Owain
  Glyndwr
GLOUCESTER, Prince HENRY, DUKE OF 10
GLYCERIUS 208
GNAGI, RUDOLF 234, 235
GOBAZYE 77
GODAIGO 155
GODARZ I 134
GODARZ II 134
GODEFROI de Bouillon 55
GODERICH, The 1st Viscount 263
GODFREY (Jerusalem) *see* Godefroi
GOFUKAKUSA 155
GOFUSHIMI 155
GOGA, Dr OCTAVIAN 209
GOHANAZONO 155
GO-ICHIJO 155
GOKAMEYAMA 155
GOKASHIWABARA 155
GOKOMATSU 155
GOKOMYO 155
GOMA, Major LOUIS SYLVAIN 53
von GOMBOS, Gen GYULA 124
GOMENSORO, TOMAS 274
GOMES, Gen FRANCISCO da COSTA 203
GOMES, MANOEL TEIXEIRA 203
GOMES Dr WENCESLAU BRAZ PEREIRA 26
GOMEZ, Gen JOSÉ MIGUEL 56
GOMEZ, JUAN VICENTE 276
GOMEZ CASTRO, Dr LAUREANO ELEUTERIO
  52
GOMEZ FARIAS, Gen VALENTIN 171
GOMEZ PEDRAZA, Gen MANUEL 170, 171
GOMEZ y ARIAS, Dr MIGUEL MARIANO 56
GOMIZUNO-O 155
GOMOMOZONO 155
GOMULKA, WLADYSLAW 201
GOMURAKAMI 155
GONARA 155
GONCALVES, Lieut-Col VASCO dos SANTOS
  204
GONDEBAUD 91
GONDEMAR 91
GONDIBERT 142
GONDRA, MANUEL 194
GONIJO 155
GONORIKAWA 155
GONZALES, Gen SAN JUAN 74
GONZALEZ, IGNACIO MARIA 64
GONZALEZ, Dr J. NATALICIO 194
GONZALEZ, JUAN 194
GONZALEZ, Gen MANUEL 172
GONZALEZ, SALVADOR 53
GONZALEZ GARZA, ROQUE 172
GONZALEZ-LOPEZ, LUIS ARTURO 194
GONZALEZ NAVARO, EMILIANO 194
GONZALEZ VALENCIA, RAMON 51
GONZALEZ VIQUEZ, CLETO 53
GOONETILLEKE, Sir OLIVER ERNEST 228
GOPALLAWA, WILLIAM 228, 229
GORBACH, Dr ALFONS 15
GORDIANUS I 207
GORDIANUS II 207
GORDIANUS III 207
GOREIZEI 155
GORGEY, ARTUR 123
GORM 61
GORTON, JOHN GREY 11
GOSAGA 155
GOSAI 155
GOSAKURAMACHI 155
GOSANJO 155
GOSHIRAKAWA 155
GOSUZAKU 155

GOTARZES I 134
GOTARZES II 134
GOTHELON I 92
GOTHELON II 92
GOTO, Count FUMIO 156
GOTOBA 155
GOTSUCHAMIKADO 155
GOTTWALD, KLEMENS 59
GO-UDA 155
GOUIN, FÉLIX 88
GOULART, JOAO BELCHIOR MARQUES 26
GOVINDA III 127
GOWON, Liout-Col YAKUBU 182
GOWRIE, Brig-Gen Sir Alexander Gore Arkwright
  Hore-Ruthven, 1st Baron 10
GOYOZEI 155
GRABER, PIERRE 235
GRAFTON, The 3rd Duke of 262
GRANT, ULYSSES SIMPSON 272
GRATIAN (Roman Empire) *see* Gratianus
GRATIANUS 208
GRAU SAN MARTIN, Dr RAMON 56
GREGORIUS I 188
GREGORIUS II 188
GREGORIUS III 188
GREGORIUS IV 188
GREGORIUS V 189
GREGORIUS VI 189
GREGORIUS VII 189
GREGORIUS VIII 189, 190
GREGORIUS IX 190
GREGORIUS X 190
GREGORIUS XI 191
GREGORIUS XII 191
GREGORIUS XIII 191
GREGORIUS XIV 192
GREGORIUS XV 192
GREGORIUS XVI 192
GREGORY (Papal State) *see* Gregorius
GREISER, Dr ARTHUR CARL 61
GRENVILLE, Hon. GEORGE 262
GRENVILLE, The 1st Baron 262
GRÉVY, FRANCOIS PAUL JULES 87
GREY, Albert Henry George Grey, 4th Earl 39
GREY, The 2nd Earl 263
GRIFFITH, ARTHUR 138
GRIMANI, ANTONIO 153
GRIMANI, MARINO 153
GRIMANI, PIETRO 153
GRIMOALD 142
GRINIUS, Dr KAZYS 164
GRITTI, ANDREA 153
GRONCHI, GIOVANNI 144
GROTEWOHL, OTTO 95
GROZA, Dr PETRU 210
GRUFFYDD ap CYNAN 269
GRUFFYDD ap LLYWELYN *(Deheubarth)* 270
GRUFFYDD ap LLYWELYN *(Gwynedd)* 269
GRUFFYDD ap RHYS 270
GRUFFYDD ap RHYS ap GRUFFYDD 270
GRUFFYDD MAELOR I 270
GRUFFYDD MAELOR II 270
GRUNITZKY, NICOLAS 239
GUADALUPE VICTORIA, Gen MANUEL 170
de la GUARDIA, ERNESTO 187
GUARDIA, Gen TOMAS 53
de la GUARDIA, RICARDO ADOLFO 186
de la GUARDIA, SANTIAGO 186
GUARDIOLA, Gen SANTOS 121
GUDFRED 61
GUÉROC 90
GUERRERO, JOSÉ 181
GUERRERO, MANUEL AMADOR 186
GUERRERO, Gen VICENTE 170
GUERRERO GUTIERREZ, LORENZO 181
GUERRIER, PHILIPPE 116
GUGGIARI, JOSÉ PATRICIO 194
GUI de Dampierre 22
GUI de Lusignan *(Armenia)* 8
GUI de Lusignan *(Cyprus)* 57
GUI de Lusignan *(Jerusalem)* 55
GUIDO, Dr JOSÉ MARIA 6
GUIDO 143
GUILARTE, EUSEBIO 24
GUILIO de 'MEDICI 145
GUILLAUME 164
GUILLAUME I *(Belgium)* 22
GUILLAUME I *(Luxembourg)* 165
GUILLAUME I *(Normandy)* 93
GUILLAUME I *(Sicily)* 151
GUILLAUME I de Champlitte 1
GUILLAUME II *(Achaea)* 1
GUILLAUME II *(Luxembourg)* 165
GUILLAUME II *(Normandy)* 93
GUILLAUME II *(Sicily)* 151

GUILLAUME III *(Luxembourg)* 165
GUILLAUME III *(Sicily)* 151
GUILLAUME IV 165
GUILLAUME de Poitou 90
GUILLAUME-JOURDAIN 54
GUILLÉN, Dr NÉSTOR 25
GUILLERMO, Gen CAESARIO 64
GUIMARAES, Dr BERNARDINO LUIS
  MACHADO 203
GUISE, Sir JOHN 193
GUISEPPE 148
GUIZADO, JOSÉ RAMON 187
GULKISHAR 17
GUNALTAY, SEMSEDDIN 243
GUNDEMARO 219
GUNDERIC 91
GUNDICAR 91
GUNGUNUM 16
GUNTHER *(Burgundy)* 91
GUNTHER *(Schwarzburg)* 108
GUNTHER FRIEDRICH KARL I 108
GUNTHER FRIEDRICH KARL II 108
GURMALLION 90
GURSEL, Gen CEMAL 243
GURVAN 90
GUSTAF I 232
GUSTAF II ADOLF 232
GUSTAF III 232
GUSTAF IV ADOLF 232
GUSTAF V 233
GUSTAF VI ADOLF 233
GUSTAV (Sweden) *see* Gustaf
GUSTAV 102
GUSTAVUS II ADOLPHUS (Sweden) *see* Gustaf II
  Adolf
GUTHFRITH I 253
GUTHFRITH II 253
GUTHRUM 251
GUTIÉRREZ, Gen EULALIO MARTIN 172
GUTIÉRREZ, JACINTO 276
GUTIÉRREZ, RAFAEL 74
GUTIÉRREZ, Gen SANTIAGO 51
GUTIÉRREZ, SILVESTRO 195
GUTIÉRREZ GUERRA, JOSÉ 24
GUY (Jerusalem and France) *see* Gui
GUYUK 174
GUZMAN, FELIPE 24
GUZMAN, FERNANDO 181
GUZMAN, JUAN JOSÉ 74
GUZMAN BLANCO, Gen ANTONIO 276
GWENWYNWYN ab OWAIN 270
GYANENDRA 176
GYGES 166

HAAB, ROBERT 234
HAAKON 230, 231
HAAKON I 182
HAAKON II 183
HAAKON III 183
HAAKON IV 183
HAAKON V 183
HAAKON VI 183
HAAKON VII 184
HABERLIN, HEINRICH 234
HABIBOLLAH 2
HABIBOLLAH KHAN 2
HABTE WOLD, AKLILOU 77
HABYALIMANA, Maj-Gen JUVENAL 210
HACHA, Dr EMIL 58
HACKZELL, ANTTI 78
al-HADI, MUSA 35
HADI PASHA, IBRAHIM ABDUL 73
HADRIAN (Roman Empire) *see* Hadrianus
HADRIANUS 206
HADRIANUS I 188
HADRIANUS II 188
HADRIANUS III 188
HADRIANUS IV 190
HADRIANUS V 190
HADRIANUS VI 191
el HAFEZ, Gen AMIN 236
HAFEZ, Dr AMIN 161
HAFSTEIN, JOHANN 125
HAILE SELASSIE 77
HAILE SELASSIE, LIJ MIKHAIL IMRU 77
HAINISCH, Dr MICHAEL ARTHUR JOSEF
  JAKOB 14
HAITHEM, MOHAMMED ALI 218
HAJIR, ABDUL HUSSEIN 136
al-HAKAM I 219
al-HAKAM II 219
el-HAKIM, HASSAN BEY 236
HAKIMI, Dr IBRAHIM 136
HALABY, MOHAMMED ALI 236
HALFDAN I 253
HALFDAN II 253

HALIM, MUSTAFA   162
HALLGRIMSSON, GEIR   125
HALSTAN   230
HALVORSEN, OTTO   184
HAMAD bin Said   185
al HAMADI, Col IBRAHIM MOHAMMED   279
HAMADI, Sheikh MUHAMMED SHAMTE   237
HAMAGUCHI, OSACHI   156
HAMARUD, CHRISTOPHER   184
HAMILCAR   40, 41
HAMILCAR BARCA   41
HAMMARSKJOLD, Dr KNUT HJALMAR   233
HAMMER, BERNHARD   234
HAMMURABI   17
HAMRIN, FELIX TEODOR   233
HANAZONO   155
HANG THUN HAK   38
HANGA, Sheikh ABDULLAH KASSIM   237
HANNIBAL   41
HANNO   41
HANS   62
HANSEN, HANS CHRISTIAN SVANE   63
HANSSON, PER ALBIN   233
HANTILIS I   118
HANTILIS II (?)   118
HANZEI   154
HARAHAP, BURHANUDDIN   132
HARALD I   182
HARALD II (Denmark)   61
HARALD II (Norway)   182
HARALD III (Denmark)   61
HARALD III (Norway)   183
HARALD IV (Denmark)   61
HARALD IV (Norway)   183
HARA, TAKASHI   156
HARDING, WARREN GAMALIEL   272
HAREMHAB   69
HARIHARA I   129
HARIHARA I   129
HARMAIS   69
HARMEL, PIERRE CHARLES JOSÉ MARIE   22
HAROLD (Norway) see Harald
HAROLD I   254
HAROLD II   254
HARRIS, LAGUMOT   176
HARRISON, BENJAMIN   272
HARRISON, FAUSTINO   275
HARRISON, WILLIAM HENRY   271
HARSHAVARMAN I   36
HARSHAVARMAN II   36
HARSHAVARMAN III   36
HARTHACNUT   254
HARTHAKNUD   61
HARTHAKNUD II   61
HARTLING, POUL   63
al-HASAN   35
HASDRUBAL   41
HASDRUBAL I   40
HASDRUBAL II   41
HASHIM, IBRAHIM   157
HASHIM KHAN, SARDAR MUHAMMAD   2
el HASHIMI, Gen YASIN PASHA   137
HASLUCK, Sir PAUL MEERNAA CAEDWALLA   11
al-HASSAN, Mulay   175
HASSAN II   175, 176
HATOYAMA, ICHIRO   156
HATSHEPSUT   68
HATTA, Dr MOHAMMED   132
HATTHADATHA I   227
HATTHADATHA II   227
HATTUSILIS I   118
HATTUSILIS II   118
HATTUSILIS III   118
HAUSER, WALTER   234
HAXAMANISH   133
HAYASHI, Gen SENJURO   156
HAYES, RUTHERFORD BIRCHARD   272
HAYTON I   8
HAYTON II   8
HEABERHT   249
HEALY, TIMOTHY MICHAEL   138
HEATH, EDWARD RICHARD GEORGE   265
HEBER USHER, ALBERTO   275
HEDTOFT HANSEN, HANS CHRISTIAN   63
HEER, JOACHIM   234
HEGAZY, Dr ABDUL AZIZ MUHAMMED   74
HEGEDUS, ANDRAS   125
HEINEMANN, Dr GUSTAV   109
HEINRICH (Saxony)   107
HEINRICH (Sicily)   151
HEINRICH I (Austria)   12
HEINRICH I (Bavaria)   98
HEINRICH I (Holy Roman Empire)   119
HEINRICH II (Austria)   12
HEINRICH II (Bavaria)   98
HEINRICH II (Holy Roman Empire)   119
HEINRICH III (Bavaria)   98

HEINRICH III (Holy Roman Empire)   119
HEINRICH IV (Bavaria)   98
HEINRICH IV (Holy Roman Empire)   119
HEINRICH V (Bavaria)   98
HEINRICH V (Holy Roman Empire)   119
HEINRICH VI (Bavaria)   98
HEINRICH VI (Holy Roman Empire)   119
HEINRICH VII (Bavaria)   98
HEINRICH VII (Holy Roman Empire)   120
HEINRICH VIII   98
HEINRICH IX   98
HEINRICH X   98
HEINRICH XI (Bavaria)   98
HEINRICH XI (Reuss zu Greiz)   105
HEINRICH XII   98
HEINRICH XIII   105
HEINRICH XIV   105
HEINRICH XIX   105
HEINRICH XX   105
HEINRICH XXII   105
HEINRICH XXIV   105
HEINRICH XXVII   105
HEINRICH XLII   105
HEINRICH LXII   105
HEINRICH LXVII   105
HEIZEI   155
HEKMAT, SARDAR FAKHER   136
HELIODORUS   212
HÉLOU, CHARLES   161
HEMMING   61
HENGIST   249
HENRI (Anjou)   90
HENRI (Latin Empire)   34
HENRI I (Burgundy)   91
HENRI I (Cyprus)   57
HENRI I (France)   81
HENRI I (Haiti)   116
HENRI I (Lorraine)   92
HENRI I (Luxembourg)   164
HENRI I (Navarre)   222
HENRI I (Normandy)   93
HENRI I de Champagne   55
HENRI II (Burgundy)   91
HENRI II (Cyprus)   57
HENRI II (France)   82
HENRI II (Jerusalem)   56
HENRI II (Lorraine)   93
HENRI II (Luxembourg)   164
HENRI II (Navarre)   223
HENRI II (Normandy)   93
HENRI III (France)   83
HENRI III (Luxembourg)   164
HENRI III (Navarre)   223
HENRI IV (France)   83
HENRI IV (Luxembourg)   165
HENRI V (France)   86
HENRI V (Luxembourg)   165
HENRI VI   165
HENRI VII   165
HENRIQUE   201
HENRIQUEZ y CARVAJAL, FRANCISCO   64
HENRY (Austria and German states) see Heinrich
HENRY (France, Luxembourg and Jerusalem) see Henri
HENRY (Holy Roman Empire) see Heinrich
HENRY (Italian states) see Enrico
HENRY (Poland) see Henryk
HENRY (Portugal) see Henrique
HENRY (Spain) see Enrique
HENRY the Young King   255
HENRY I   254
HENRY II   255
HENRY III   255
HENRY IV   256
HENRY V   256
HENRY VI   256
HENRY VII   256
HENRY VIII   256
HENRY PU YI   47
HENRYK   199
HERACLEONAS   32
HERACLES (Georgia) see Irakli
HERACLIUS   32
HÉRARD, CHARLES   116
HERCELLES, Dr OSVALDO   196
HERCULE   173
HERCULES (Italian states) see Ercole
HERMANN   12
HERNANDEZ MARTINEZ, Gen MAXIMILIANO   75
HEROD   141
HEROD AGRIPPA I   141
HEROD AGRIPPA II   141
HEROD ANTIPAS   141
HEROD ARCHELAUS   141
HERRAN, PEDRO ALCANTARA   51
HERRERA, Gen ALBERTO   56
HERRERA, CARLOS   115

HERRERA, Gen JOSÉ JOAQUIN   171
HERRERA, LEON   54
HERRERA, VICENTE   53
HERRERA y OBES, JULIO   274
HERRIOT, ÉDOUARD   87
HERTENSTEIN, WILHELM FRIEDRICH   234
HERTZOG, Dr ENRIQUE   25
HERTZOG, JAMES BARRY MUNNIK   217
HETUM I   8
HETUM II   8
HEUREAUX, Gen ULISES   64
HEUSS, Prof THEODOR   109
HEVIA, CARLOS   56
HIDETADA TOKUGAWA   156
HIERON I   235
HIERON II   235
HIERONYMUS   235
HIERONYMUS NAPOLEON   109
HIGASHIKUNI, Prince NARUHIKO   156
HIGASHIYAMA   155
al HIJRI, QADI ABDULLAH   279
HIKETAS   235
HILALY PASHA, AHMED NAGUIB   73
HILARIUS   187
HILARY (Papal State) see Hilarius
HILBE, Dr ALFRED   163
HILDEBRAND   142
HILLERY, Dr PATRICK JOHN   139
HILTUNEN, ONNI   79
HIMILCO I   41
HIMILCO II   41
von HINDENBURG, Marshal PAUL von BENECKENDORFF und   97
HINNAWI, Col SAMI   235, 236
HIPPOLYTE, LOUIS FLORÉAL   117
HIPPOLYTUS   187
HIRANUMA, Count KIICHIRO   156
HIROHITO   156
HIROTA, KOKI   156
HISAMUDDIN ALAM SHAH   167
HISHAM I (Caliphate)   35
HISHAM I (Moorish Spain)   219
HISHAM II   219
HITLER, ADOLF   97
HIZQIYYA   140
HLOTHERE   249
HO CHI MINH   278
HO-TI   45
HO YING-CHIN, Gen   48
HOCHOY, Sir SOLOMON   240
HODZA, Dr MILAN   58
HOEL V   90
HOEL VI   90
HOFFMAN, JOSIAS PHILIPPUS   217
HOFFMANN, ARTHUR   234
von HOHENLOHE-SCHILLINGSFURST, CHLODWIG KARL VICTOR, Prince   96
HOLENSTEIN, THOMAS   234
HOLGUIN, CARLOS   51
HOLGUIN, Gen JORGE   51, 52
HOLLAND, Sir SIDNEY GEORGE   180
HOLT, HAROLD EDWARD   11
HOLYOAKE, Sir KEITH JACKA   180
HOME, 14th Earl of   265
d' HOMEDES, JEAN   168
von HOMPESCH, FERDINAND   169
HONECKER, ERICH   95
HONORÉ I   173
HONORÉ II   173
HONORÉ III   173
HONORÉ IV   174
HONORÉ V   174
HONORIUS   208
HONORIUS I   188
HONORIUS II   189
HONORIUS III   190
HONORIUS IV   190
HOOVER, HERBERT CLARK   272
HOPETOUN, 7th Earl of   10
HOPHRA   70
HOREMHEB   69
HORIKAWA   155
HORMISDAS   188
HORMIZD I   134
HORMIZD II   134
HORMIZD III   135
HORMIZD IV   135
HORMIZD V   135
HOROS   68
HORSA   249
HORTHY de NAGYBANYA, Admiral MIKLOS   124
HOSHEA   140
al-HOSS, Dr SELIM   161
HOSTILIANUS   207
HOSTLIAN (Roman Empire) see Hostilanus
HOTEPSEKHEMUI   66
HOUPHOUET-BOIGNY, FÉLIX   153

HOVEIDA, AMIR ABBAS   137
HOWARD, DANIEL   162
HOXHA, Gen ENVER   4
HSEKIU   66
HSI TSUNG   47
HSIAO-TSUNG   46
HSIAO TSUNG   46
HSIEN-FENG   47
HSIEN HUAN TI   47
HSIEN-TSUNG   45
HSIEN TSUNG   46
HSINBYUSHIN   30
HSU SHIH CH'ANG   48
HSUAN-TE   46
HSUAN-TI   44
HSUAN-TSUNG   45
HSUAN TSUNG   46, 47
HSUAN-TUNG   47, 48
HSUAN-YEH   47
HU HAN-MIN   48
HUA KUO-FENG   49
HUAI-TI   45
HUAI TSUNG   47
HUASCAR (Inca Empire) see Washkar 'Inka
HUAYNA CAPAC (Inca Empire) see Wayna
   Qhapaq
de la HUERTA, ADOLFO   172
HUERTA, Gen VICTORIANO   172
HUGH (France and Jerusalem) see Hugues
HUGHES, WILLIAM MORRIS   11
HUGO   143
HUGUES (Burgundy)   91
HUGUES (France)   81
HUGUES (Jerusalem)   56
HUGUES I (Burgundy)   91
HUGUES I (Cyprus)   57
HUGUES II (Burgundy)   91
HUGUES II (Cyprus)   57
HUGUES III (Burgundy)   91
HUGUES III (Cyprus)   57
HUGUES IV (Burgundy)   91
HUGUES IV (Cyprus)   57
HUGUES V   91
HUH CHUNG   159
HUI-TI   44, 45
HUI TI   46
HUI-TSUNG   46
HUITZILHUITL   170
HUMAYAN   130
HUMAYUN   128
HUMBERT (Italy) see Umberto
HUN   251
HUNDSEID, JENS   184
HUNG-CHIH   46
HUNG-HSI   46
HUNG-LI   47
HUNG-WU   46
HUNI   67
HURTADO, EZEQUIEL   51
HUSAK, Dr GUSTAV   59
al-HUSAYN   35
HUSAYN ibn Ali   212
HUSAYN KAMIL   72
HUSSA   252
HUSSAIN, Dr ZAHIR   132
HUSSEIN, ABDIRIZAK HAJI   216
HUSSEIN, Sheikh MUKHTAR MOHAMMED   216
HUSSEIN ibn TALAL   157
HUSZAR, KAROLY   124
HUYNH TAN PHAT   278
HUYSMANS, CAMILLE   22
HUZEFA   67
HUZZIYAS I   118
HYDE, Dr DOUGLAS   138
HYGINUS   187
HYWEL ab EDWIN   270
HYWEL ap IEUAF   269
HYWEL ap RHODRI MOLWYNOG   268
HYWEL DDA (Deheubarth)   269
HYWEL DDA (Gwynedd)   269

I HUANG-TI   47
I TSUNG   47
IAGO   269
IAGO ab IDWAL ap MEURIG   269
IAGO ap BELI   268
IBANEZ del CAMPO, Gen CARLOS   43, 44
IBBISIN   16
IBN SAUD (Saudi Arabia) see Abdul Aziz ibn
   Saud
IBRAHIM (Caliphate)   35
IBRAHIM (Egypt)   72
IBRAHIM (India)   128, 130
IBRAHIM (Turkey)   242
IBRAHIM, MOULAY ABDALLAH   175
IBRAHIM ADIL SHAH I   129

IBRAHIM ADIL SHAH II   129
ICHIJO   155
IDA   252
IDDINDAGAN   16
IDRIS I   162
IDWAL   269
IDWAL FOEL   269
IDWAL IWRCH ap CADWALADR   268
IEHARU TOKUGAWA   156
IEMITSU TOKUGAWA   156
IEMOCHI TOKUGAWA   156
IENARI TOKUGAWA   156
IENOBU TOKUGAWA   156
IESADA TOKUGAWA   156
IESHIGE TOKUGAWA   156
IETSUGU TOKUGAWA   156
IETSUNA TOKUGAWA   156
IEUAF   269
IEYASU TOKUGAWA   156
IEYOSHI TOKUGAWA   156
IGIGI   16
IGLESIAS, Gen MIGUEL   195
IGLESIAS, RAFAEL   53
IKEDA, HAYATO   157
ILEO, JOSEPH   283
ILLIA, Dr ARTURO UMBERTO   6
ILTUTMISH   128
IMBERT, Gen ANTONIO   64
IMMADI   129
IMMADI NARASIMHA   129
IMRE   122
IMRÉDY, Dr BÉLA   124
IN TAM   38
INAROS   70
INCHE ROCA (Inca Empire) see 'Inka Roq'a 'Inka
INDRA III   127
INDRAJAYAVARMAN   37
INDRAVARMAN I   36
INDRAVARMAN II   37
INDRAVARMAN III   37
INDULF   266
INE   250
INGE I   230
INGE II   230
INGELGER   89
INGI I   183
INGI II   183
INGMAN, LAURI JOHANNES   78
INGYO   154
'INKA ROQ'A 'INKA   126
'INKA 'URQON   126
INNOCENS I   187
INNOCENS II   189
INNOCENS III   190
INNOCENS IV   190
INNOCENS V   190
INNOCENS VI   191
INNOCENS VII   191
INNOCENS VIII   191
INNOCENS IX   192
INNOCENS X   192
INNOCENS XI   192
INNOCENS XII   192
INNOCENS XIII   192
INNOCENT (Papal State) see Innocens
INONU, Gen ISMET   243
INTEF I   68
INTEF II   68
INUKAI, TSUYOSHI   156
IOANNES   188
IOANNES I (Papal State)   188
IOANNES I (Trebizond)   240
IOANNES I TZIMISCES   32
IOANNES II (Papal State)   188
IOANNES II (Trebizond)   240
IOANNES II COMNENUS   33
IOANNES III (Papal State)   188
IOANNES III (Trebizond)   240
IOANNES III DUCAS VATATZES   34
IOANNES IV (Papal State)   188
IOANNES IV (Trebizond)   240
IOANNES IV LASCARIS   34
IOANNES V   188
IOANNES V PALAEOLOGUS   34
IOANNES VI   188
IOANNES VI CANTACUZENUS   34
IOANNES VII   188
IOANNES VII PALAEOLOGUS   34
IOANNES VIII   188
IOANNES VIII PALAEOLOGUS   34
IOANNES IX   188
IOANNES X   189
IOANNES XI   189
IOANNES XII   189
IOANNES XIII   189
IOANNES XIV   189
IOANNES XV   189
IOANNES XVI   189

IOANNES XVII   189
IOANNES XVIII   189
IOANNES XIX   189
IOANNES XXI   190
IOANNES XXII   191
IOANNES 'XXIII'   191
IOANNES XXIII   193
IORWERTH ap BLEDDYN   270
IORWERTH DRWYNDWN   269
IPPOLITO de 'MEDICI   145
IRAKLI II   95
IRENE (Byzantine Empire)   32
IRENE (Trebizond)   240
al IRIANI, Lieut-Col MOHAMMED   279
IRIGOYEN, Dr HIPOLITO   6
IRINA   245
IRISHUM   8
IRMAK, Prof SADI   243
ISA bin SULMAN al KHALIFAH   19
ISAAC I COMNENUS   32
ISAAC II ANGELUS   33
ISAACS, Sir ISAAC ALFRED   10
ISABEL (Armenia)   7
ISABEL (Castile)   221
ISABEL I   223
ISABEL II   225
ISABELLA (Spain) see Isabel
ISABELLE (Achaea)   1
ISABELLE (Lorraine)   92
ISABELLE I   55
ISABELLE II   55
ISANAVARMAN   36
ISHBAAL   139
ISHBI-IRRA   16
ISHBOSETH (Israel and Judah) see Ishbaal
ISHIBASHI, TANZAN   156
ISHMEDAGAN   16
ISHMEDAGAN I   8
ISHMEDAGAN II   9
ISHPUINI   273
ISLAM SHAH   130
ISLAM, SYED NAZRUL   20
ISLINGTON, John Poynder Dickson-Poynder, 1st
   Baron   180
ISMA'IL   72
ISMAIL NASIRUDDIN SHAH ibni Al-Marhum
   Sultan Zainal Abidin   167
ISMAIL SHAH   129
ISSA, ABDULLE   216
ISTVAN   121
ISTVAN I   121
ISTVAN II   121
ISTVAN III   121
ISTVAN IV   122
ISTVAN V   122
ITERPISHA   16
ITTIMARDUKBALATU   17
de ITURBIDE, Generalissimo AUGUSTIN   170
ITZCOATL   170
IVAILO   28
IVAN I Danilovich   244
IVAN II Ivanovich   244
IVAN III Vasilyevich   245
IVAN IV Vasilyevich   245
IVAN V Alekseyevich   245
IVAN VI Antonovich   246
IVAN ALEXANDER   28
IVAN ASSEN II   28
IVAN ASSEN III   28
IVAN SHISHMAN   28
IVAN VLADISLAV   28
IVAR   253
IXTLILXOCHITL   170
IYASU I   77
IYASU II   77
IYO'AS   77
'IZZ ad-DIN KAY-KAUS II   214

JAAKSON, JURI   76
JABIR al-AHMED al-JABIR ES-SABAH, SHAIKH
   159
JABIR al-AHMED al-JABIR es-SABAH, Shaikh
   160
JABLONSKI, Prof HENRYK   200
JABR, SALEH   137
JABRY, SAADULLAH   236
JACKSON, ANDREW   271
JACOB (Ethiopia) see Ya'qob
JACQUELINE   179
JACQUES   173
JACQUES I (Cyprus)   57
JACQUES I (Haiti)   116
JACQUES I des Baux   1
JACQUES II   57
JACQUES III   57
JADWIGA   198

JAFFAR, Prince SAID MOHAMMED   52
JAHAN SHAH   135
JAHANDAR SHAH   130
JAHANGIR   130
al-JAIFI, Maj-Gen MAMOUD   279
JAIME I   221
JAIME II   221
JALAL-ud-DIN FIRUZ KHALJI   128
JALLUD, Maj ABDUL SALAM AHMED   162
JAMALI, Dr MOHAMMED FADIL   137
JAMASP   135
JAMES (Cyprus) see Jacques
JAMES (Italian states) see Giacomo
JAMES (Spain) see Jaime
JAMES I (England)   257
JAMES I (Scotland)   268
JAMES II (England)   258
JAMES II (Scotland)   268
JAMES III   268
JAMES IV   268
JAMES V   268
JAMES VI   268
JAMSHID   130
JAN   60
JAN I   179
JAN I OLBRACHT   198
JAN II   179
JAN II KAZIMIERZ Wasa   199
JAN III Sobieski   199
JANE   257
JANOS   123
JANSEN, Dr ERNEST GEORGE   216
JANSON, PAUL-ÉMILE   21
JANUS   57
JARA, ALBINO   194
JAROSZEWICZ, PIOTR   201
JARQUIN, Dr CARLOS BRENES   181
JASPAR, MARCEL-HENRI   21
JATTI, BASAPPA DANAPPA   132
JAUNUTIS   163
JAWARA, DAUDA KAIRABA   94
JAYABAHU I   227
JAYABAHU II   228
JAYAVARMAN I   36
JAYAVARMAN II   36
JAYAVARMAN III   36
JAYAVARMAN IV   36
JAYAVARMAN V   36
JAYAVARMAN VI   36
JAYAVARMAN VII   37
JAYAVARMAN VIII   37
JAYAVARMAN PARAMESVARA   37
JAYAWARDENE, JUNIUS RICHARD   229
JEAN (Anjou)   90
JEAN (Armenia)   8
JEAN (Burgundy)   92
JEAN (Normandy)   93
JEAN I (Achaea)   1
JEAN I (Brittany)   90
JEAN I (Cyprus)   57
JEAN I (France)   82
JEAN I (Lorraine)   92
JEAN I (Luxembourg)   165
JEAN I (Monaco)   173
JEAN I (Navarre)   222
JEAN I de Brienne   55
JEAN II (Brittany)   90
JEAN II (Cyprus)   57
JEAN II (France)   82
JEAN II (Jerusalem)   56
JEAN II (Lorraine)   92
JEAN II (Luxembourg)   165
JEAN II (Monaco)   173
JEAN II (Navarre)   222
JEAN III (Brittany)   90
JEAN III (Navarre)   223
JEAN IV de Montfort   90
JEAN V de Montfort   90
JEAN VI de Montfort   90
JEANNE   22
JEANNE I   222
JEANNE II   222
JEANNE III   223
JEANNE de Penthievre   90
JEBTSUNDAMBA KHUTUKHTU   174, 175
JEFFERSON, THOMAS   271
JEHOAHAZ (Israel and Judah) see Ahaz
JEHOIACHIN (Israel and Judah) see Yehoiachin
JEHOIAKIM (Israel and Judah) see Yehoiakim
JEHORAM (Israel and Judah) see Yehoram
JEHOSHAPHAT (Israel and Judah) see
    Yehoshaphat
JEHU (Israel and Judah) see Yehu
JELLICOE of Scapa, John Rushworth Jellicoe, 1st
    Viscount, later 1st Earl,   180
JEN HUANG-TI   47
JEN-TSUNG   46
JEN TSUNG   46, 47

JEROBOAM (Israel and Judah) see Yeroboam
JETTHATISSA II   227
JETTHATISSA III   227
JIGME DORJI WANGCHUK   23
JIGME SINGHI WANGCHUK   23
JIGME WANGCHUK   23
JIMÉNES, JÉSUS   53
JIMÉNEZ, ENRIQUE ADOLFO   186
JIMÉNEZ, JUAN ISIDRO   64
JIMÉNEZ, MANUEL   64
JIMÉNEZ FLORES, ALFREDO ME   53
JIMÉNEZ OREAMUNO, RICARDO   53, 54
JIMINEZ, Col GUSTAVO   196
JINNAH, MOHAMMED ALI   185
JIRÍ Z PODEBRAD   60
JITO   154
JOACHIM I   100
JOACHIM II   100
JOACHIM ERNST   98
JOACHIM FRIEDRICH   100
JOAN (France) see Jeanne
JOAN (Italian states) see Giovanna
JOAN (Spain) see Juana
JOAO   25
JOAO I   202
JOAO II   202
JOAO III   202
JOAO IV   202
JOAO V   202
JOAO VI   203
JOASH (Israel and Judah) see Yoash
JOBST   165
JOCHI   174
JOGAILA   163
JOHAN   98
JOHAN I Sverkerssen   230
JOHAN II   231
JOHAN III   232
JOHANN   107
JOHANN I   163
JOHANN II   163
JOHANN ADAM   163
JOHANN CICERO   100
JOHANN FRIEDRICH (Saxony)   107
JOHANN FRIEDRICH (Wurttemberg)   109
JOHANN GEORG   100
JOHANN GEORG I   107
JOHANN GEORG II   107
JOHANN GEORG III   107
JOHANN GEORG IV   107
JOHANN KARL   163
JOHANN SIGISMUND   100
JOHANN WILHELM   104
JOHANNESSON, OLAFUR   125
JOHN (Bohemia) see Jan
JOHN (Byzantine Empire) see Ioannes
JOHN   (England)   255
JOHN (Ethiopia) see Yohannes
JOHN (France, Luxembourg and Jerusalem) see
    Jean
JOHN (German states) see Johan
JOHN (German states) see Johann
JOHN (Italian states) see Giovanni
JOHN (Papal State and Trebizond) see Ioannes
JOHN (Poland) see Jan
JOHN (Portugal and Brazil) see Joao
JOHN (Scotland)   267
JOHN (Spain) see Juan
JOHN (Sweden) see Johan
JOHN I ALBERT (Poland) see Jan I Olbracht
JOHN II CASIMIR (Poland) see Jan II Kazimierz
JOHN CICERO (German states) see Johann
    Cicero
JOHN FREDERICK (German states) see Johann
    Friedrich
JOHN GEORGE (German states) see Johann
    Georg
JOHN HYRCANUS I (Israel) see Yehokhanan
    Hyrcanus I
JOHN HYRCANUS II (Israel and Judah) see
    Hyrcanus II
JOHN WILLIAM (German states) see Johann
    Wilhelm
JOHNSON, ANDREW   272
JOHNSON, HILLARY   162
JOHNSON, LYNDON BAINES   273
JOHNSON BROOKE, CHARLES ANTHONI   211
JOLANTHE   92
JOMEI   154
JONAS, Dr FRANZ   15
JONASSON, HERMANN   125
JONATHAN, Chief JOSEPH LEBUA   162
JONES, Sir GLYN SMALLWOOD   167
de JONG, PETRUS J.S.   179
JONSSON, EMIL   125
JORDANIA, NOE   95
JORGA, Prof   209
JORGENSEN, ANKER   63

JOSCELIN I   55
JOSCELIN II   55
JOSÉ (Portugal)   202
JOSÉ (Spain)   225
JOSEPH (Italian states) see Giuseppe
JOSEPH (Spain) see Jose
JOSEPH   105
JOSEPH I (Austria)   13
JOSEPH I (Holy Roman Empire)   120
JOSEPH II (Austria)   14
JOSEPH II (Holy Roman Empire)   120
JOSEPH JOHANN   163
JOSEPH WENZEL   163
JOSIAH (Israel and Judah) see Yoshiyah
JOSZEF I   123
JOSZEF II   123
JOTHAM (Israel and Judah) see Yotham
JOUNDI, Dr   236
JOVANOVIC, Prof SLOBODAN   280
JOVELLANOS, SALVADOR   193
JOVIAN (Roman Empire) see Jovianus
JOVIANUS   208
JUAN I (Aragon)   221
JUAN I (Castile)   221
JUAN II (Aragon)   222
JUAN II (Castile)   221
JUAN CARLOS   226
JUANA   223
JUAREZ, Gen BENITO PABLO   171, 172
JUDICAEL   90
JUDITH (Empress) see Zauditu
JUI-TSUNG   45
JULIAN (Roman Empire) see Julianus
JULIANA   178
JULIANUS   208
JULIUS I   187
JULIUS II   191
JULIUS III   191
JULIUS CAESAR, GAIUS   205
JULIUS NEPOS   209
JUMAA, SAAD   157
JUNNA   155
JUNNIN   154
JUNTOKU   155
JUSTIN (Byzantine Empire) see Justinus
JUSTINIAN (Byzantine Empire) see Justinianus
JUSTINIANUS I   32
JUSTINIANUS II   32
JUSTINUS I   31
JUSTINUS II   32
JUSTO, Gen AGUSTIN PEDRO   6
JUXON-SMITH, Lieut-Col ANDREW J.   214, 215

KA-RA   67
KA SEN   66
KACHAZNUNI, R   8
KADAR, JANOS   125
KADASHMANENLIL I   17
KADASHMANENLIL II   17
KADASHMANKHARBE I   17
KADASHMANKHARBE II   17
KADASHMANTURGU   17
KADHAFI, MU'AMMAR (Libya) see al-Gaddafi,
    Mu'ammar Muhammad
KADIR, Gen DAGARWAL ABDUL   2
KAIEKHOS   66
KALAKAUA   273
KALININ, MIKHAIL IVANOVICH   247, 248
KALLAI, GYULA   125
KALLAV, MIKLOS   124
de KALLAY, MIKLOS   124
KALLIO, KYOSTI   78
KALMAN   121
KALOYAN   28
KALYANAVATI   228
KAMARA-TAYLOR, CHRISTIAN A.   215
KAMBUJIA I   133
KAMBUJIA II   133
KAMEHAMEHA I   273
KAMEHAMEHA II   273
KAMEHAMEHA III   273
KAMEHAMEHA IV   273
KAMEHAMEHA V   273
KAMEYAMA   155
KAMIL, ABDALLAH MOHAMED   63
KAMMU   154
KAMOSE   68
KAMPMANN, VIGGO   63
KANDALANU   19
KANELLOPOULOS, PANAYOTIS   111, 112
K'ANG   46
K'ANG HSI   47
K'ANG-TE (China)   47
K'ANG-TE (Manchuria)   50
KAO TSU   44
KAO-TSUNG   45, 46

KAO TSUNG 47
KARADJORDJE 282
KARAINDASH 17
KARAKHARDASH II 17
KARAMANLIS, KONSTANTINOS 112
KARAMI, ABDUL HAMED 161
KARAMI, RASHID ABDUL HAMID 161
KARDAM 27
KAREL 60
KAREL I 22
KARJAI AINEN, Dr AHTI 79
KARL (Baden) 98
KARL (Brandenburg) 99
KARL (Hesse-Cassel) 101
KARL (Mecklenburg-Strelitz) 103
KARL (Norway) 183
KARL (Schwarzburg) 108
KARL (Wurttemberg) 109
KARL I (Austria) 13, 14
KARL I (Brunswick) 100
KARL I (Holy Roman Empire) 118
KARL I (Norway) 184
KARL II (Austria) 13
KARL II (Brunswick) 100
KARL II (Holy Roman Empire) 119
KARL II (Norway) 184
KARL II (The Rhine) 104
KARL III (Brunswick) 100
KARL III (Holy Roman Empire) 119
KARL III (Norway) 184
KARL IV 120
KARL V 120
KARL VI 120
KARL VII 120
KARL ALBRECHT 99
KARL ALEXANDER 109
KARL EDUARD 106
KARL EUGEN 109
KARL FRIEDRICH 98
KARL LEOPOLD 102
KARL LUDWIG 104
KARL PHILIPP 104
KARL THEODOR (Bavaria) 99
KARL THEODOR (The Rhine) 104
KAROLY I 122
KAROLY II 122
KAROLY III 123
KAROLY IV 123
KAROLYI, Count MIHALY 123
KARTAWIDJAJA, Dr DJUANDA 132
KARUME, Sheikh ABEID AMANI 237
KASAVUBU, JOSEPH 283
KASBARI, Dr 236
KASHTA 70
KASHTILIASH I 17
KASHTILIASH II 17
KASHTILIASH III 17
KASHTILIASH IV 17
KASHUNADINAHHE 18
KASSAPA II 227
KASSAPA III 227
KASSAPA IV 227
KASSAPA V 227
KASSEM, Brig ABDUL KARIM 138
KASYAPA I 227
KATAYAMA, TETSU 156
KATHAY DON SASORITH 160
KATO, Viscount TAKAAKIRA 156
KATO, Baron TOMO SABURO 156
KATZIR, Prof EPHRAIM 141
KAUNDA, Dr KENNETH DAVID 283, 284
KAVADH I 135
KAVADH II SHIRUYE 135
KAWAWA, RASHIDI MFAUME 237
KAYIBANDA, GRÉGOIRE 210
KAY-KA'US I 214
KAY-KHUSRAW I 213, 214
KAY-KHUSRAW II 214
KAY-KHUSRAW III 214
KAY-QUBADH, Ala'ad-Din 214
KAYSONE PHOMVIHAN 160
KAZAN 155
KAZIMIERZ I Karol Odnowiciel 197
KAZIMIERZ II 197
KAZIMIERZ III Wielki 198
KAZIMIERZ IV JAGIELLONCZYK (Lithuania) 164
KAZIMIERZ IV JAGIELLONCZYK (Poland) 198
KEBREAU, ANTOINE 117
KEIKI TOKUGAWA 156
KEIKO 154
KEITA, MODIBO 168
KEITAI 154
KEKKONEN, Dr URHO KALEVA 78
KENILOREA, PETER 215
KENKENES 66
KENNEDY, JOHN FITZGERALD 273
KENNETH I 265

KENNETH II 266
KENNETH III 266
KENYATTA, JOMO 158
KENZO 154
KEREKOU, Maj MATHIEU 23
KERENSKY, ALEKSANDR FYODOROVICH 247
KERPHERES 67
KERR, Sir JOHN ROBERT 11
KERRY, 6th earl of 38
KESTUTIS 163
KHABA 67
KHABABASHA 70
KHAFRE 67
KHAI DINH 277
KHAKAURE SENUSRET III 68
KHALED ibn Abdul Aziz ibn Saud 211
KHALED ibn Abdul Aziz ibn SAUD 212
KHALIDI, Dr HUSSEIN 157
KHALIFA, SERR al KHATIM 229
KHALIFA bin HAMAD al THANI 204
al KHALIFAH, Shaikh KHALIFA bin SULMAN 20
KHALIL, ABDULLAH 229
KHAMA, Sir SERETSE 25
KHAN KRUM 27
KHAN KUBRAT 27
KHANEFERRE 67
KHARBASHIKHU 17
KHASEKHEM 67
KHASEKHEMUI 67
KHATIB, AHMED 236
KHEBRES 69
KHEBRON 68
KHENERES 67
KHIEU SAMPHAN 38
KHIM TIT 37
KHLEIFAWI, Gen ABDEL RAHMAN 236
KHOJA, HAMID 236
al KHORSHUMI, ABDULLAH 279
KHOSROW I 135
KHOSROW II PARVIZ 135
KHOSROW III 135
KHOUPRASITH ABHAY, Gen 160
el-KHOURY, FARIS 236
al-KHOURY, FAYEZ 236
KHRUSCHEV, NIKITA SERGEYEVICH 248
KHUBILAI 46
KHUBILAI KHAN 174
KHUFU 67
al-KHURI, BISHARA 161
KIEBER, Dr WALTER 163
KIESINGER, Dr KURT GEORG 109
KIM CHONG PIL 159
KIM DU BON 159
KIM HYUN CHUL 159
KIM IL 159
KIM IL SUNG, Marshal 159
KIMBA, EVARISTE 283
KIMMEI 154
KING, CHARLES 162
KING, WILLIAM LYON MacKENZIE 39
KIOSSEIVANOV, Dr GEORGI 29
KIOUSSOPOULOS, DEMETRIOS 112
KIRCHENSTEINS, Prof AUGUSTUS 161
KIRCHSCHLAGER, Dr RUDOLF 15
KIRK, NORMAN ERIC 180
KISHI, NOBUSUKE 156
KITTISENA 227
KITTISIRIMEGHA 227
KIVIMAKI, TOIVO MIKAEL 78
KLAUS, Dr JOSEF 15
KLERIDES, GLAFKOS 57
KNUD I 61
KNUD III 61
KNUD IV 61
KNUD V 61
KNUD VI 61
KNUSEL, MELCHIOR JOSEPH MARTIN 233
KNUT 183
KNUTSSEN, CARL 231
KOBELT, KARL 234
KOBUN 154
KOGYUKU 154
KOISO, Gen KUNIAKI 156
KOIVISTO, Dr MAUNO HENRIK 79
KOJONG 158
KOKAKU 155
KOKEN/SHOTOKU 154
KOKO 154
KOL (?) 230
KOLAROV, VASSIL 29
KOLLIAS, KONSTANTINOS V. 112
KOLOMAN I 28
KOLSTAD, PEDER 184
KOMEI 155
KONDILIS, Gen GIORGIOS 111
KONDORIOTIS, Admiral PAVLOS 111
KONIN 154
KONOE 155

KONOYE, Prince FUMINARO 156
KONRAD I (Bavaria) 98
KONRAD I (Holy Roman Empire) 119
KONRAD I (Sicily) 151
KONRAD II (Bavaria) 98
KONRAD II (Holy Roman Empire) 119
KONRAD II (Sicily) 151
KONRAD III 119
KONRAD IV 119
KONRAD V 119
KONSTANTIN I (Armenia) 7
KONSTANTIN I (Georgia) 95
KONSTANTIN II or I 8
KONSTANTIN III or II 8
KONSTANTIN IV or III 8
KONSTANTIN ASSEN TIKH 28
KONSTANTIN Pavlovich 247
KONSTANTINOS I 111
KONSTANTINOS II 111
KORIZIS, ALEXANDROS 111
KORMISOSH 27
KORNER, Dr THEODOR 15
KOROMA, SORIE IBRAHIM 215
KOROSEC, Dr ANTON 280
KORUTURK, FAHRI 243
KORVALD, LARS 184
KOSSOMAK 37
KOSSUTH, LAJOS 123
KOSYGIN, ALEXEI NIKOLAIEVICH 248
KOTELAWALA, Sir JOHN LIONEL 228
KOTOKU 154
KOU ABHAY 160
KOUANDETE, Maj MAURICE 23
KOUNTCHE, Lieut-Col SEYNI 181
KOZLOWSKI, M.L. 200
KRAG, JENS OTTO 63
KRAMAR, Dr KAREL 58
KREISKY, Dr BRUNO 15
KRIANGSAK CHANANAND, Gen 238
KRISHNA (India) see Krsna II
KRISTENSEN, KNUD 63
KRISTIAN FREDRIK 183
KRISTOFER 183
KRSNA II 127
KRSNADEVARAYA 129
KRUGER, STEPHANUS JOHANNES PAULUS 217
KUANG APHAIWONGSE 238
KUANG-HSU 47
KUANG-TSUNG 46
KUANG TSUNG 47
KUANG WU-TI 45
KUBABA 15
KUBITSCHEK de OLIVEIRA, JUSCELINO 26
el-KUDSI, Dr NAZIM 236
KUDURENLIL 17
KUDURMABUK 16
KUKK, JOHAN 76
K UKRIT PRAMOJ 238
KUMARA DHATUSENA 227
KUMARA GUPTA 127
KUN, BELA 124
KUNALA 127
KUNG HSIANG-HSI, Dr 48
KURASH I 133
KURASH II 133
KURIGALZU I 17
KURIGALZU II 17
KUUSKOSKI, Dr REINO 79
al-KUWATLY, SAYED SHUKRI 235, 236
KUZBARI, Dr MAMOUN 236
KVIESIS, ALBERT 161
KY, Air Vice-Marshal NGUYEN CAO 278
KYOURA, Viscount KEIGO 156
KYPRIANOU, SPYROS 57

LABARNAS I 118
LABARNAS II 118
LABASHIMARDUK 19
LACHENAL, ADRIEN 234
LADGHAM, BAHDI 241
LADISLAUS 13
LAGOS CHAZARO, FRANCISCO 172
LAJOS I (Hungary) 122
LAJOS I (Poland) 198
LAJOS II 123
LAKAS BAHAS, DEMETRIO BASILIO 187
LAKATOS, Col-Gen K. 124
LAKHARES 68
LAMARIS 68
LAMBERT 173
LAMBERTUS 143
LAMIZANA, Lieut-Col SANGOULE 273
LAMRANI, KARIM 176
LANDO 189
LANDO, PIETRO 153

LANIEL, JOSEPH   89
LANSANA, Brig DAVID   215
LANSDOWNE, Henry Charles Keith
  Petty-Fitzmaurice, 5th Marquess of   38
LANUSSE, Gen ALEJANDRO AGUSTIN   6
la PUERTA, LUIS   195
LARAKI, Dr AHMED   176
LAREDO BRU, Dr FEDERICO   56
LARGARCHA, FROILAN   51
LARRAZABAL UGUETO, Rear Admiral
  WOLFGANG   277
LARREA ALBA, Col LUIS A.   65
LASCARIS CASTELLARD, PAUL   168
LASCURAIN, PEDRO   172
LASLO   147
LASTIRI, Dr RAUL   6
LASZLO   122
LASZLO I   121
LASZLO II   121
LASZLO III   122
LASZLO IV   122
LASZLO V   122
LATORRE, Col LORENZO   274
LAUGERUD-GARCIA, Gen KJELL EUGENIO
  115
LAURENTIUS   188
LAURIER, Sir WILFRID   39
de la VALETTE, JEAN PARISOT   168
LAVAL, PIERRE   87, 88
LAZAR, GYORGY   125
LE DUAN   278
LEBNA DENGEL   77
LEBRUN, ALBERT   87
LEBRUN, CHARLES FRANCOIS   84
LEBURTON, EDMOND JULES ISIDORE   22
LECONTE, SIMON MICHEL CINCINNATUS   117
LEE BUM SUK, Gen   159
LEFEVRE, ERNESTO   186
LEFEVRE, THÉO   22
LEGER, JULES   39
LEGITIME, FRANCOIS DENIS   117
LEGUIA y SALCEDO, AUGUSTO BERNADINO
  196
LEHTO, Dr REINO RAGNAR   79
LEIVA, PARIANO   121
LEMASS, SEAN   139
LEMUS, Lieut-Col JOSÉ MARIA   75
LENART, JOSEF   59
LENG NGETH   37
LENIN, VLADYMIH ILIČH ULYANOV   247, 248
LEO I (Armenia)   7
LEO I (Byzantine Empire)   31
LEO I (Papal State)   187
LEO II (Armenia)   7
LEO II (Byzantine Empire)   31
LEO II (Papal State)   188
LEO II and I   7
LEO III (Byzantine Empire)   32
LEO III (Papal State)   188
LEO III or II   8
LEO IV (Byzantine Empire)   32
LEO IV (Papal State)   188
LEO IV or III   8
LEO V (Byzantine Empire)   32
LEO V (Papal State)   189
LEO V or IV   8
LEO VI (Byzantine Empire)   32
LEO VI (Papal State)   189
LEO VI or V de Lusignan   8
LEO VII   189
LEO VIII   189
LEO IX   189
LEO X   191
LEO XI   192
LEO XII   192
LEO XIII   193
LEONE, GIOVANNI   144, 145
LEONI, RAUL   277
LEONIDAS I   113
LEONIDAS II   114
LEONTIUS   32
LEOPOLD (Italian states) see Leopoldo
LEOPOLD (Austria)   13
LEOPOLD (Baden)   98
LEOPOLD (Bavaria)   98
LEOPOLD (Lorraine)   93
LEOPOLD I (Austria)   12
LEOPOLD I (Belgium)   21
LEOPOLD I (Holy Roman Empire)   120
LEOPOLD I (Hungary)   123
LEOPOLD I (Lippe)   102
LEOPOLD II (Austria)   12, 14
LEOPOLD II (Belgium)   21
LEOPOLD II (Holy Roman Empire)   120
LEOPOLD II (Hungary)   123
LEOPOLD II (Lippe)   102
LEOPOLD III (Anhalt)   97
LEOPOLD III (Austria)   12, 13

LEOPOLD III (Belgium)   21
LEOPOLD III (Lippe)   102
LEOPOLD IV (Anhalt)   97
LEOPOLD IV (Austria)   12, 13
LEOPOLD IV (Lippe)   102
LEOPOLD V   12
LEOPOLD VI   12
LEOPOLDO I   152
LEOPOLDO II   152
LEOTYCHIDES   113
LEOVIGILDO   219
LEPIDUS (Roman Empire) see Marcus Aemilius
  Lepidus
LEPIDUS, MARCUS AEMILIUS   205
LERDO de TEJADA, SEBASTIAN   172
LERROUX, ALEJANDRO   226
LESCAYO-SACASA, BENJAMIN   181
LESCOT, ÉLIE   117
LESTKO   197
LESZEK   197
LESZEK I   197
LESZEK II   198
LEVAUD, Col FRANK   117
LEVINGSTON, Brig-Gen ROBERTO MARCELO
  6
LEYGUES, GEORGES   87
LEZAMA, ARTURO   275
LI JONG OK   159
LI LUNG-CHI   45
LI SHIH-MIN   45
LI-TSUNG   46
LI TSUNG-JEN, Gen   48, 50
LI TZU-CH'ENG   47
LI YUAN   45
LI YUAN-HUNG   48
LIAPCHEV, ANDREI   29
LIBAIJU   9
LIBERIUS   187
LIBIUS SEVERUS   208
LICINIUS   208
LICINIUS CRASSUS, MARCUS   205
LIDJ IYASU   77
LIEBE, OTTO   63
LIGHTFOOT-BOSTON, Sir HENRY JOSIAH   214
LIINAMAA, KEIJO   79
LILAVATI   228
LILIUOKALANI   273
LIN SEN   48
LINARES ALCANTARA, Gen FRANCISCO   276
LINARES, JOSÉ MARIA   24
LINCOLN, ABRAHAM   272
LINDLEY LOPEZ, Gen NICOLAS   196
LINDMAN, ARVID   233
LINDO, JUAN (El Salvador)   74
LINDO, JUAN (Honduras)   120
LINHARES, Chief Justice Dr JOSÉ   26
LINKOMIES, Prof EDWIN   78
LINLITHGOW, John Adrian Louis Hope, 1st
  Marquess of   10
LINUS   187
LIPITENLIL   16
LIPITISHTAR   16
LISGAR, John Young, 1st Baron   38
LISNADRO BARILLAS, MANUEL   115
LISSOUBA, PASCAL   53
LISTOWEL, WILLIAM FRANCIS HARE, 5th Earl
  of   110
LIU HENG   44
LIU HSIU   45
LIU PANG   44
LIU SHAO-CHI   49
LIUVA I   219
LIUVA II   219
LIVERPOOL, Arthur William de Brito Savile
  Foljambe, 2nd Earl of   180, 263
LLERAS CAMARGO, Dr ALBERTO   52
LLERAS RESTREPO, Dr CARLOS   52
LLESHI, Maj-Gen HADJI   4
LLOQ'E YUPANKI   126
LLOQUE YUPANQUI (Inca Empire) see Lloq'e
  Yupanki
LLYWARCH ap BLEDDYN   270
LLYWELYN I   269
LLYWELYN II   269
LLYWELYN ap BLEDDYN   270
LLYWELYN ap SEISYLL (Deheubarth)   269
LLYWELYN ap SEISYLL (Gwynedd)   269
LLYWELYN FAWR   269
LOBO CORDERO, Gen ALFONSO   181
LODEWIJK I   178
LODEWIJK II   178
LODOVICO (Milan)   147
LODOVICO (Savoy)   150
LODOVICO (Sicily)   151
LODOVICO I   145
LODOVICO II   145
LOE THAI   238
LOES LA NABHALAI   238

LOKESVARA   228
LOKOLOKO, Sir TORE   193
LOMBARDINI, MANUEL   171
LON NOL, Gen   37
LONARDI, Gen EDUARDO   6
LONG BARET   38
LOPES, Marshal FRANCISCO HIGINO
  CRAVEIRO   203
LOPES, HENRI   53
LOPEZ, CARLOS ANTONIO   193
LOPEZ, FRANCISCO SOLANO   193
LOPEZ, HERMOGENES   276
LOPEZ, JOSÉ HILARIO   51
LOPEZ, VENANCIO   114
LOPEZ ARELLANO, Col OSWALDO   121
LOPEZ CONTRERAS, Gen ELEAZAR   276
LOPEZ de ROMANA, EDUARDO   196
LOPEZ de SANTA ANNA, Gen ANTONIO   171
LOPEZ GUTIÉRREZ, RAFAEL   121
LOPEZ MATEOS, ADOLFO   172
LOPEZ MICHELSEN, Dr ALFONSO   52
LOPEZ PORTILLO, JOSÉ   173
LOPEZ PUMAREJO, Dr ALFONSO   52
LOPEZ y PLANES, VICENTE   5
LOREDANO, FRANCESCO   153
LOREDANO, LEONARDO   153
LOREDANO, PIETRO   153
LORENZO I de 'MEDICI   145
LORENZO II de 'MEDICI   145
LORNE, John Douglas Sutherland Campbell,
  Marquess of   38
LOSONCZI, PAL   125
de los SANTOS, Dr EMILIO   64
LOTHAIRE   81
LOTHAIRE (Holy Roman Empire) see Lothar
LOTHAR I   118
LOTHAR II   119
LOTHARIO   143
LOTHARIO II   143
LOTHERE   249
de LOUBENS, HUGO VERDALE   168
LOUBET, ÉMILE FRANCOIS   87
LOUIS (Bohemia) see Ludvik
LOUIS (German states) see Ludwig
LOUIS (German states) see Ludewig
LOUIS (Hungary) see Lajos
LOUIS (Italian states) see Lodovico
LOUIS (Netherlands) see Lodewijk
LOUIS (Portugal) see Luis
LOUIS (Spain) see Luis
LOUIS   91
LOUIS I (France)   81
LOUIS I (Monaco)   173
LOUIS I (Navarre)   222
LOUIS I de Nevers   22
LOUIS II (Flanders)   22
LOUIS II (France)   81
LOUIS II (Monaco)   174
LOUIS II (Navarre)   223
LOUIS III   81
LOUIS IV   81
LOUIS V   81
LOUIS VI   81
LOUIS VII   81
LOUIS VIII   81
LOUIS IX   81
LOUIS X   82
LOUIS XI   82
LOUIS XII   82
LOUIS XIII   83
LOUIS XIV   83
LOUIS XV   83
LOUIS XVI   84
LOUIS XVII   84
LOUIS XVIII   84
LOUIS XIX   86
LOUIS EUGENE (German states) see Ludwig
  Eugen
LOUIS-PHILIPPE   86
LOUISE-HIPPOLYTE   173
L'OUVERTURE, FRANCOIS DOMINIQUE
  TOUSSAINT   116
LOUZI, AHMED   158
LOZANO DIAZ, Dr JULIO   121
LU   44
LU THAI   238
LUANG DHAMRONG NAWASASAT   238
LUANG PIBUL SONGGRAM, Marshal   238
LUBKE, Dr HEINRICH   109
LUCAS GARCIA, Gen FERNANDO ROMEO   115
LUCCHINO   146
LUCIE   55
LUCIEN   173
LUCIUS I   187
LUCIUS II   189
LUCIUS III   190
LUCIUS DOMITIUS ALEXANDER   208
LUCIUS VERUS   207

LUCKHOO, Sir EDWARD 116
LUDECAN 252
LUDER, ITALO ARGENTINO 6
LUDEWIG I 101
LUDEWIG X 101
LUDOVICUS 143
LUDVIK 60
LUDWIG (Brandenburg) 99
LUDWIG (Hesse-Homburg) 102
LUDWIG I (Baden) 98
LUDWIG I (Bavaria) 98, 99
LUDWIG I (Holy Roman Empire) 118
LUDWIG II (Baden) 98
LUDWIG II (Bavaria) 98, 99
LUDWIG II (Hesse) 101
LUDWIG II (Holy Roman Empire) 119
LUDWIG III (Bavaria) 98, 99
LUDWIG III (Hesse) 101
LUDWIG III (Holy Roman Empire) 119
LUDWIG III (The Rhine) 103
LUDWIG III (Wurttemberg) 109
LUDWIG IV (Hesse) 101
LUDWIG IV (Holy Roman Empire) 120
LUDWIG IV (The Rhine) 103
LUDWIG V (Hesse) 101
LUDWIG V (The Rhine) 103
LUDWIG VI (Hesse) 101
LUDWIG VI (The Rhine) 103
LUDWIG VII 101
LUDWIG VIII 101
LUDWIG IX 101
LUDWIG EUGEN 109
LUGALANDA 15
LUGALSHAGENGUR 15
LUGALZAGGISI 15
LUIDPRAND 142
LUIS (Portugal) 203
LUIS (Spain) 224
LUITBERT 142
LULACH 266
LULLAIJU 8
LUMUMBA, PATRICE HEMERY 283
LUNALILO 273
LUNG-CH'ING 46
LUPÉRON, GREGORIO 64
LUTHER, Dr HANS 97
LUVSAN, SONOMYN 175
LUYT, Sir RICHARD 116
da LUZ, CARLOS COIMBRA 26
LVOV, Prince GEORGY YEVGENYEVICH 247
LYCURGUS 114
LYKKE, IVAR 184
LYNCH, JACK 139
LYNCH, JOHN MARY 139
LYNG, JOHAN 184
LYONS, JOSEPH ALOYSIUS 11
LYSIMACHUS (Macedonia) 113
LYSIMACHUS (Thrace) 114

MACAPAGAL, DIOSDADO 196
MACBETH 266
MACDONALD, JAMES RAMSAY 265
MacDONALD, Sir JOHN ALEXANDER 39
MacDONALD, MALCOLM 158
McEWEN, Sir JOHN 11
MACHADO y MORALES, Gen GERARDO 56
MACHEL, SAMORA MOISES 176
MACIAS NGUEMA FRANCISCO, (Equatorial
  Guinea) see Masie Nguema Biyogo Negue
  Ndong
MACIAS NGUEMA, FRANCISCO 75
McKELL, Sir WILLIAM JOHN 10
MacKENZIE, ALEXANDER 39
MACKENZIE, THOMAS 180
McKINLEY, WILLIAM 272
McMAHON, WILLIAM 11
McNEILL, JAMES 138
MAC-MAHON, MARIE EDME PATRICE
  MAURICE 87
MACMILLAN, MAURICE HAROLD 265
MACRINUS 207
MADERNO, FRANCISCO INDALECIO 172
MADHAV RAO I 131
MADHAV RAO II 131
MADISON, JAMES 271
MADOG ap BLEDDYN 270
MADOG ap GRUFFYDD 270
MADOG ap MAREDUDD 270
MADRIZ, JOSÉ 181
MADSEN-MYGDAL, THOMAS 63
MAELGWN GWYNEDD 268
MAELGWN HIR 268
MAGA, HUBERT 23
MAGHA 228
al MAGHRABI, Dr MAHMOUD SULAIMAN 162
MAGLOIRE, Gen PAUL E. 117

MAGNUS 61
MAGNUS I 183
MAGNUS I Ladulas 231
MAGNUS II 183
MAGNUS II Ericssen 231
MAGNUS III 183
MAGNUS IV 183
MAGNUS V 183
MAGNUS VI 183
MAGNUS VII 183
MAGNUS MAGNENTIUS 208
MAGNUS MAXIMUS 208
MAGNUSSON, JON 125
MAGO I 40
MAGO II 40
MAGSAYSAY, RAMON 196
MAHANAGA 227
MAHANAMA 227
MAHASENA 227
al-MAHDI, MUHAMMAD 35
al MAHDI, Dr SAYED SADIQ 229
MAHENDRA, King 177
MAHENDRA, Prince 177
MAHENDRA BIR BIKRAM SHAH DEVA 176
MAHENDRAVARMAN 36
MAHER, ALY PASHA 73
MAHER PASHA, Dr AHMED 73
MAHGOUB, MOHAMMED AHMED 229
MAHINDA I 227
MAHINDA II 227
MAHINDA III 227
MAHINDA IV 227
MAHINDA V 227
MAHMUD 128
MAHMUD I 242
MAHMUD II 242
MAHMUD GHAZAN 135
MAHMUD KHAN 1
MAHMUD PASHA, MOHAMMED 73
MAHMUD SHAH 1
MAIWANDWAL, MOHAMMED HASHIM 2
el-MAJALI, HAZZA 157
MAJORIAN (Roman Empire) see Majorianus
MAJORIANUS 208
MAKARIOS III, Archbishop 57
MAKKI, HASSAN 279
MAKONNEN, LIJ ENDALKATCHEW 77
al MAKTOUM, Shaikh MAKTOUM bin RASHID
  248
al MAKTOUM, Shaikh RASHID bin SA'ID 248
MALAMIR 27
MALAN, DANIEL FRANCOIS 217
MALCHUS 40
MALCOLM I 266
MALCOLM II 266
MALCOLM III 266
MALCOLM IV 267
MALENKOV, GEORGY MAKSIMILIANOVICH
  248
MALESPIN, FRANCISCO 74
MALIETOA TANUMAFILI II, Chief 279
MALIK-SHAH I 213
MALIK-SHAH II 213
MALINKOV, ALEKSANDR 29
MALLARINO, MANUEL MARIA 51
MALLIKARJUNA 129
MALLOUM, Brig-Gen FÉLIX 43
MALLU SHAH 129
MALYPETR, MILAN J. 58
MAMO, Sir ANTONY J. 169
al-MAMUN, ABDOLLAH 35
MANAVAMMA 227
MANCHAM, JAMES 214
MANCHENO, Col CARLOS 66
MANCO CAPAC (Inca Empire) see Manqo
  Qhapaq
MANCO INCA YUPANQUI (Inca Empire) see
  Manqo 'Inka Yupanki
MANESCU, MANEA 210
MANFRED 151
MANGOPE, Chief LUCAS 218
MANIN, LODOVICO 153
MANISHTUSU 16
MANIU, Dr IULIU 209
MANLEY, MICHAEL N. 154
MANNERHEIM, Marshal Baron CARL GUSTAV
  EMIL 78
MANOEL I 202
MANOEL II 203
MANQO 'INKA YUPANKI 127
MANQO QHAPAQ 126
MANSOOR ALI, M. 20
al-MANSUR, ABU-DJAFAR 35
MANSUR, ALI 137
MANSUR, HASSAN ALI 137
MANTERE, OSKARI 78
MANUEL (Byzantine Empire and Trebizond) see
  Emmanuel

MANUEL (Portugal) see Manoel
MAO TSE-TUNG 49
de la MAR, Gen JOSÉ 195
MARA, Ratu Sir KAMISESE K.T. 77
MARBITAHHEIDDIN 18
MARBITIAPALUSUR 18
MARCELLINUS 187
MARCELLUS I 187
MARCELLUS II 191
MARCIANUS 31
MARCOS, FERDINAND EDRALIN 196
MARCUS 187
MARCUS ANTONIUS 205
MARCUS AURELIUS 207
MARCUS AURELIUS ANTONINUS I 207
MARCUS AURELIUS ANTONINUS II 207
MARDAM BEY, JAMIL 236
MARDUK-? 18
MARDUKAHHE-ERIBA 18
MARDUKAPALIDDINA I 17
MARDUKAPALIDDINA II 18
MARDUKAPALIDOINA II. 18
MARDUKBALATSUIQBI 18
MARDUKBELUSATE 18
MARDUKELZERI . 18
MARDUKKABITAHHESHU 17
MARDUKNADINAHHE 17
MARDUKSHAPIKZERI 17
MARDUKZAKIRSHUMI I 18
MARDUKZAKIRSHUMI II 18
MAREDUDD ab EDWIN 270
MAREDUDD ab OWAIN 269
MAREDUDD ab OWAIN ab EDWIN 270
MAREDUDD ab OWAIN ap HYWELDDA 269
MAREDUDD ap BLEDDYN 270
MAREDUDD ap GRUFFYDD 270
MARGAI, Dr ALBERT MICHAEL 215
MARGAI, Sir MILTON 215
MARGARET (Flanders) see Margaretha
MARGARET (Norway) see Margrete
MARGARET 267
MARGARETHA 231
MARGARETHA I 22
MARGARETHA II 22
MARGARETHA III 23
MARGARETHE 179
MARGRETE 183
MARGRETHE I 62
MAHGRETHE II 63
MARGUERITE I 22
MARGUERITE II 22
MARGUERITE III 23
MARIA (Brazil) 25
MARIA (Hungary) 122
MARIA (Sicily) 151
MARIA I 202
MARIA II da GLORIA 203
MARIA CRISTINA 225
MARIA LUISA (Lucca) 146
MARIA LUISA (Parma and Piacenza) 149
MARIA TERESA 149
MARIA THERESA (Austria) see Maria Theresia
MARIA THERESIA (Austria) 13
MARIA THERESIA (Hungary) 123
MARIE 92
MARIE-ADÉLAIDE 165
MARIE, ANDRÉ 88
MARIE de Bourbon 1
MARIE de Montferrat 55
MARIE LOUISE (Italian states) see Maria Luisa
MARIJNEN, Dr VICTOR GERARD MARIE 179
MARIN, ESCOLASTICO 74
MARINKOVIC, Dr VOYISLAV 280
MARINUS I 188
MARINUS II 189
MARK (Papal State) see Marcus
MARK ANTONY (Roman Empire) see Marcus
  Antonius
MARKEZINIS, SPYROS 112
de MARQUEZ, JOSÉ IGNACIO 51
MARQUEZ BUSTILLOS, VICTORINO 276
MARROQUIN, JOSÉ MANUEL 51
MARSHALL, Sir JOHN ROSS 180
MARTIN (Italy) see Martino
MARTIN (Papal State) see Martinus
MARTIN (Papal State) see Marinus
MARTINEZ, BARTOLOMÉ 181
MARTINEZ, JUAN 114
MARTINEZ, Gen TOMAS 181
MARTINEZ BARRIO, DIEGO 226
MARTINEZ LACLAYO, Gen ROBERTO 181
MARTINEZ MERA, JUAN de DIOS 65
MARTINEZ TRUEBA, ANDRES 275
MARTIN I 221
MARTINO I 151
MARTINO II 151
MARTINUS I 188
MARTINUS IV 190

MARTINUS V   191
MARWAN I ibn al-HAKAM   35
MARWAN II   35
MARX, WILHELM   97
MARY   268
MARY I   257
MARY II   258
MASARYK, TOMAS GARRIGUE   58
MASIE NGUEMA BIYOGO NEGUE NDONG   75
MASSEMBA-DÉBAT, ALPHONSE   53
MASSEY, CHARLES VINCENT   39
MASSEY, WILLIAM FERGUSSON   180
MASSIMILIANO   147
MAS'UD I   213
MAS'UD II   214
MATANZIMA, Chief KAISER   218
MATEJ   60
MATEJ II   60
MATHILDA (Normandy) see Mathilde
MATHILDE (Achaea)   1
MATHILDE (Normandy)   93
MATILDA   255
MATTEO I   146
MATTEO II   146
MATTHAEUS CANTACUZENUS   34
MATTHEW (Byzantine Empire) see Matthaeus
   Cantacuzenus
MATTHEW (Lorraine) see Matthieu
MATTHIAS (Bohemia) see Matej
MATTHIAS (Austria)   13
MATTHIAS (Holy Roman Empire)   120
MATTHIAS I CORVINUS (Hungary) see Matyas I
MATTHIEU I   92
MATTHIEU II   92
MATTIWAZA   173
MATYAS I Corvinus   122
MATYAS II   123
MAUNG MAUNG KHA, U   30
MAUREGATO   220
MAURER, ION GHEORGHE   210
MAURICE (Byzantine Empire) see Mauricius
MAURICE (German states) see Moritz
MAURICE (Netherlands) see Maurits
MAURICIUS   32
MAURITS , Prince of Orange   177
MAVROMIHALIS, STYLOS   112
MAXENTIUS   208
MAXIMIAN (Roman Empire) see Maximianus
MAXIMIANUS   208
MAXIMILIAN (Bohemia)   60
MAXIMILIAN (Hungary)   123
MAXIMILIAN I (Austria)   13
MAXIMILIAN I (Bavaria)   99
MAXIMILIAN I (Holy Roman Empire)   120
MAXIMILIAN I (Mexico)   172
MAXIMILIAN II (Austria)   13
MAXIMILIAN II (Bavaria)   99
MAXIMILIAN II (Holy Roman Empire)   120
MAXIMILIAN II EMANUEL   99
MAXIMILIAN III JOSEPH   99
MAXIMILIAN IV JOSEPH   99
MAXIMILIAN of Baden, Prince   97
MAXIMINUS   207
MAXIMINUS DAIA   208
MAXIMOS, DEMETRIOS   111
MAXTLA   170
MAYTA CAPAC (Inca Empire) see Mayta Qhapaq
MAYTA QHAPAQ   126
MAZIQ, HUSAIN   162
MAZZILLI, PASCOAL RANIERI   26, 27
M'BA, LÉON   93
M'BAREK MOSTAPHA el BEKKI, Si   175
MÉBIAME, LÉON   94
MEDINA ANGARITA, Gen ISAIAS   276
MEDINA, Gen JOSÉ MARIA   121
MEHMED I   241
MEHMED II   242
MEHMED III   242
MEHMED IV   242
MEHMED V Resad   243
MEHMED VI Vahideddin   243
MEIEROVICS, ZIGFRIDS   160
MEIGHEN, ARTHUR   39
MEIJI   155
MEINUA   273
MEIR, Mrs GOLDA   141
MEISHO   155
MEJIA COLINDRES, VICENTE   121
MELBOURNE, The 3rd Viscount   263
MELEAGER   113
MELÉNDEZ, CARLOS   74
MELÉNDEZ, JORGE   74
MELEN, FERIT   243
MELGAR CASTRO, Col JUAN ALBERTO   121
MELGAREJO, Gen MARIANO   24
MELISENDE   55
MELISHIKHU   17
MELZI d'ERIL, FRANCESCO   143

MEMO, MARCANTONIO   153
MENASSEH   140
MENCHERES   67
MENDERES, ADNAN   243
MENDES-FRANCE, PIERRE   89
MENDES, FRANCISCO   115
MÉNDEZ, Dr APARICIO   275
MÉNDEZ, GÉRONIMO   44
MENDEZ, JUAN   172
MÉNDEZ-MONTENEGRO, Dr JULIO CÉSAR
   115
MENDIETA, Col CARLOS   56
MENDOZA, CARLOS ANTONIO   186
MENDOZA AZURDIA, Col OSCAR   115
MENELIK II   77
MENÉNDEZ, Gen ANDRES IGNACIO   75
MENÉNDEZ, Gen FRANCISCO   74
MENÉNDEZ, MANUEL   195
MENES   66
MENGISTU HAILE MARIAM, Lieut-Col   77
MENKAUHOR   67
MENKAURE   67
MENOCHEM   140
MENOPHRES   69
MENTHESOUPHIS   67
MENTUHOTEP I   68
MENTUHOTEP II   68
MENTUHOTEP IV   68
MENZIES, Sir ROBERT GORDON   11
MEPHRES   68
MERCADO JARRIN, Gen EDGARDO   196
MERENRE   67
MERENRE MEHTIMSAF I   67
MERENRE MEHTIMŞAF II   67
MERFYN   269
MERIEBRE EKHTAI   67
MERIKARE .   67
de MERINO, FERNANDO ARTURO   64
MERINO BIELECH, Vice-Admiral VICENTE   44
MERKYS, Dr ANTONAS̄   164
MERNEPTAH   69
MERPEBA   66
MESOCHRIS   67
MESSMER, PIERRE AUGUSTE JOSEPH   89
METAXAS, Gen IOANNIS   111
METHESOUPHIS   67
MEYER, ALBERT   234
MICHAEL (Portugal) see Miguel
MICHAEL (Romania) see Mihai
MICHAEL (Russia) see Mikhail
MICHAEL   240
MICHAEL I   32
MICHAEL II   32
MICHAEL III   32
MICHAEL IV   32
MICHAEL V   32
MICHAEL VI   32
MICHAEL VII DUCAS   33
MICHAEL VIII PALAEOLOGUS   34
MICHAEL OBRENOVICH (Serbia) see Mihai
   Obrenovic
MICHAEL SHISHMAN (Bulgaria) see Mihail
   Shishman
MICHAELIS, Dr GEORG   97
MICHENER, DANIEL ROLAND   39
MICO   28
MICOMBERO, Lieut-Gen MICHEL   31
MIDFAI, JAMIL   137
MIEBIS   66
MIECZYSLAW I   197
MIECZYSLAW II   197
MIECZYSLAW III   197
MIETTUNEN, MARTTI   79
MIGUEL   203
MIHAI I   209
MIHAIL II ASSEN   28
MIHAILO OBRENOVIC III   282
MIHAIL SHISHMAN   28
MIKHAIL Fyodorovich Romanov   245
MIKHAIL II   244
MIKI, TAKEO   157
MIKLAS, Dr WILHELM   14
MIKLOS, Col-Gen BÉLA   124
MIKOLA Korybut Wisniowiecki   199
MIKOLAJCZYK, STANISLAW   200
MIKOYAN, ANASTAS IVANOVICH   248
MILAN I   282
MILAN OBRENOVIC II   282
MILAN OBRENOVIC IV   282
MILLERAND, ALEXANDRE   87
MILOSH OBRENOVICH (Serbia) see Milos
   Obrenovic
MILOS OBRENOVIC I   282
MILTIADES   187
MIN-NING   47
MIN-TI   45
MINAS   77
MINDAUGAS   163

MINDAUGAS II   164
MINDON MIN   30
MINGER, RUDOLF   234
MING HUANG   45
MING-TI   45
MINH MANG   277
MINTO, Gilbert John Elliot-Murray-Kynynmound,
   4th Earl of   39
MINTOFF, DOMINIC   169
MIR VEYS KHAN   1
MIRAMON, Gen MIGUEL   171
de MIRANDA, FRANCISCO   275
MIRANSHAH   239
MIRJAN, ABDUL WAHAB   137
MIRO CARDONA, Dr JOSÉ   56
MIRONAS, Fr VLADAS   164
MIRZA, Maj-Gen ISKANDER   185
MITHRADATES   201
MITHRADATES I (Iran)   134
MITHRADATES I (Pontus)   201
IV IITHRADATES II (Iran)   134
MITHRADATES II (Pontus)   201
MITHRADATES III (Iran)   134
MITHRADATES III (Pontus)   201
MITHRADATES IV PHILOPATOR
   PHILADELPHUS   201
MITHRADATES V EUERGETES   201
MITHRADATES VI EUPATOR   201
MITHRADATES VII CHRESTOS   201
MITHRADATES VIII   201
MITRE, Gen BARTOLOMÉ   6
MLEH   7
MOBUTU SÉSÉ SÉKO KUKU NGBENDU WA
   ZABANGA, Gen   283
MOCENIGO, GIOVANNI   153
MOCENIGO I, ALVISO   153
MOCENIGO II, ALVISO   153
MOCENIGO III, ALVISO   153
MOCENIGO IV, ALVISO   153
MOCTEZUMA I ILHUICAMINA   170
MOCTEZUMA II XOCOYOTZIN   170
MOGGALLANA I   227
MOGGALLANA II   227
MOGGALLANA III   227
M OHAMMAD   135
MOHAMMAD 'ALI SHAH   136
MOHAMMAD AZIM KHAN   2
MOHAMMAD REZA SHAH PAHLAVI   136
MOHAMMAD SHAH   136
MOHAMMAD UFZUL KHAN   2
MOHAMMED, ABDALLAH   52
MOHAMMED, Brig MURTALA RAMAT   182
MOHAMMED, Gen NUREDDIN   137
MOHAMMED ALI, CHAUDHRI   185
MOHAMMED ALI, CHAUDRI   186
MOHAMMED el BADR   279
MOHAMMED el-BADR, Emir   279
MOHAMMED HASSANIYA, ALI NASSER   218
MOHIEDDIN, ZAKARIA   74
MOJMIR I   59
MOJMIR II   59
MOLAS LOPEZ, Dr FELIPE   194
MOLIN, FRANCESCO   153
MOLINA BARRAZA, Col ARTURO ARMANDO
   75
MOLINA PALLOCHIA, Gen OSCAR   196
MOLLET, GUY   89
MOLOTOV, VYACHESLAV MIKHAYLOVICH   248
MOMMU   154
MOMOZONO   155
MONAGAS, JOSÉ GREGORIO   276
MONAGAS, JOSÉ RUPERTO   276
MONAGAS, JOSÉ TADEO   275, 276
MONCADA, Gen JOSÉ MARIA   181
MONCK, Charles Stanley, 4th Viscount   38
MONGKE   174
MONGKUT   238
MONGKUT KLAO   238
MONIVONG   37
MONJE GUTIÉRREZ, Chief Justice TOMAS   25
MONROE, JAMES   271
MONTAGNE SANCHEZ, Gen ERNESTO   196
MONTALVO, ABELARDO   65
· da MONTÉ, PIETRO   168
MONTEALEGRA, JOSÉ MARIA   53
de MONTENEGRE, RAIMON DESPUIZ   168
MONTERO, JOSÉ   194
MONTERO, LIZARDO   195
MONTES, Gen ISMAEL   24
MONTES, JOSÉ FRANCISCO   121
MONTOKU   155
MONTT, JORGE   43
MONTT, MANUEL   43
MONTT, PEDRO   43
MONZON, Col ELFEGO   115
MOORE, Sir HENRY MONCK-MASON   228
von MOOS, LUDWIG   234
MORA, JUAN RAFAEL   53

MORALES, Col AGUSTIN   24
MORALES BERMUDEZ, Gen FRANCISCO   196
MORALES BERMUDEZ, Col REMIGIO   195
MORALES LAUGUASCO, CARLOS   64
MORAZAN, FRANCISCO   42, 53
MORENO, JULIO   66
MORINIGO, Gen HIGINIO   194
MORINIGO, MARCOS   194
MORITZ (Hesse-Cassel)   101
MORITZ (Saxony)   107
MORO, ALDO   145
MOROSINI, FRANCESCO   153
MORRISON, WILLIAM SHEPHERD   11
MOSCICKI, Prof IGNACY   200
MOSHTAQUE AHMED, KHANDAKER   20
MOSQUERA, JOAQUIN   51
MOSQUERA NARVAEZ, AURELIO   65
de MOSQUERA, Gen TOMAS CIPRIANO   51
MOSSADEQ, Dr MOHAMMED   137
MOTLOTLEHI MOSHOESHOE II, Constantine
   Bereng Seeiso   162
MOTTA, GIUSEPPE   234
MOUNLA, SAADI   161
MOUNTBATTEN of Burma, LOUIS, 1st Earl   131
MOWINCKEL, JOHAN LUDWIG   184
MOYA, RAFAEL   53
MOZAFFAR od-DIN SHAH   136
MU TSUNG   46, 47
MU'AWIYAH I   35
MU'AWIYAH II   35
al-MU'AYYAD   219
MUDENDA, ELIJAH   284
el-MUFTI, SAYED PASHA   157
MUHAMMAD, GHULAM   185
MUHAMMAD (Seal of the Prophets)   35
MUHAMMAD (Seljuq Empire)   213
MUHAMMAD (Turkey) see Mehmed
MUHAMMAD I (India)   128
MUHAMMAD I (Moorish Spain)   219
MUHAMMAD II   128
MUHAMMAD III   128
MUHAMMAD V   175, 176
MUHAMMAD 'ADIL SHAH   130
MUHAMMAD ALI   72
MUHAMMAD ibn TUGHLUQ   128
MUHAMMAD IBRAHIM   131
MUHAMMAD NADER SHAH   2
MUHAMMAD QULI   130
MUHAMMAD SHAH   129, 131
MUHAMMAD SHAH I   128
MUHAMMAD ULLAH   20
MUHAMMAD ZAHIR SHAH   2
MUHIRA, ANDRE   30
al-MUHTADI, MUHAMMAD   35
MUJICA GALLO, MIGUEL   196
al-MUKTAFI, ALI   35
MULAMBA, Gen LEONARD   283
Mulay ABD al-AZIZ   175
Mulay ABD al-HAFID   175
Mulay ABD ar-RAHMAN   175
Mulay YUSUF   175
MULDOON, ROBERT DAVID   180
el-MULKI, Dr FAWZI   157
MULLER, EDUARD   234
MULLER, HERMANN   97
al-MUNDHIR   219
MUNNICI I, Dr FFRENC   125
al-MUNSTANSIR   36
al-MUNTASIR, MUHAMMAD   35
MUNTASSER, MAHMUD   162
MUNZINGER, MARTIN JOSEPH   233
al-MUQTADI   36
al-MUQTADIR, DJAFAR   35
al-MUQTAFI   36
MURAD I   241
MURAD II   242
MURAD III   242
MURAD IV   242
MURAD V   242
MURAKAMI   155
MURAT, JOACHIM (Naples) see Gioacchino
   Napoleone, King of Naples
MURAVIEV, KOSTA   29
MURILLO TORO, MANUEL   51
MURSILIS I   118
MURSILIS II   118
MURSILIS III   118
MURUMBI, JOSEPH   158
MUSHANOV, NIKOLAI   29
MUSHEZIBMARDUK   18
MUSSADEQ, Dr MOHAMMED   137
MUSSOLINI, BENITO AMILCARE ANDREA   144
al-MUSTADI   36
MUSTAFA I   242
MUSTAFA II oglu Mehmed   242
MUSTAFA III   242
MUSTAFA IV   242
al-MUSTA'IN, AHMAD   35

al-MUSTAKFI   36
al-MUSTANJID   36
al-MUSTANSIR   219
MUSTAPHA (Turkey) see Mustafa
al-MUSTARSHID   36
al-MUSTA'SIM   36
al-MUSTAZHI   36
MUSY, JEAN-MARIE   234
al-MU'TADID, AHMAD   35
MUTAKKILNUSKU   9
al-MU'TAMID, AHMAD   35
al-MU'TASIM   35
al-MUTAWAKKIL, DJAFAR   35
al-MU'TAZZ, MUHAMMAD   35
MUTESA II   244
MUTESA, Sir EDWARD   244
al-MUTI   36
MUTSUHITO   155
al-MUTTAQI, IBRAHIM   36
MUWATALLIS   118
MUZQUIZ, MELCHOR   171
MWAMBUTSA IV   30
MYERS, Sir MICHAEL   180
MYKERINOS   67

NABONIDUS   19
NABOPOLASSAR   19
NABUAPALIDDIN   18
NABUKUDURRIUSUR I   17
NABUKUDURRIUSUR II   19
NABULSI, SULIMAN   157
NABUMUKINAPLI   18
NABUMUKINZER   18
NABUMUKINZERI   18
NABUNADINZERI   18
NABUNA'ID   19
NABUNASIR   18
NABUSHUMILIBUR   18
NABUSHUMISHKUN I   18
NABUSHUMISHKUN II   18
NABUSHUMUKIN   18
NADAB   140
NADER SHAH   136
NAEFF, WILHELM MATHIAS   233
NAGY, FERENC   124
NAGY, IMRE   125
NAHAS PASHA, MUSTAFA   73
al NAHAYYAN, Shaikh ZAYED bin SULTAN   248
NAI PRIDI PHANOMJONG   238
NAI THAWI BUNYAKAT   238
NAKAMIKADO   155
NANDA, GULZARILAL   132
NANG KLAO   238
NANUM   16
NA'OD   76
NAPLANUM   16
NAPOLEON I   84
NAPOLEON II   84
NAPOLEON III   86
NAPOLEONE   143
NARAMSIN   16
NARDONE, BENITO   275
NARMER   66
NARMERZA   66
NARSEH   134
NARUTOWICZ, GABRIEL   200
do NASCIMENTO, LOPO FORTUNATO
   FERREIRA   4
NASER od-DIN SHAH   136
NASH, Sir WALTER   180
NASIR, Amir IBRAHIM   168
an-NASIR (Caliphate)   36
an-NASIR (Moorish Spain)   219
NASIR-ud-DIN MAHMUD   128
NASSER, Col GAMAL ABDEL   73
NASSER, Sherif HUSSEIN bin   157
NATSIR, Dr MOHAMMED   132
NAUDE, JOZUA FRANCOIS T.   217
NAVARTE, ANDRES   275
NAVAS PARDO, Brig RAFAEL   52
NAVOM, YGZHAK   141
al NAYEF, Col ABDUL RAZZAK   138
NAZIBUGASH   17
NAZIMARUTTASH   17
NAZIMUDDIN, KHWAJA   185
NE WIN, U   30
NEBUCHADNEZZAR I   17
NEBUCHADNEZZAR II   19
NEBUCHADNEZZAR III   19
NEBUCHADNEZZAR IV   19
NECHEROPHES   67
NECHO   70
NECTANEBO I   70
NECTANEBO II   70
NEERGAARD, NIELS   63
NEFEREFRE SHEPSESKERE   67

NEFERIRIKERE KAKAU   67
NEFERKA   67
NEFERKERE   67
NEFERKESOKARI   67
NEGRETI, Gen   170
NEGUIB, Gen MOHAMED   73
NEHRU, JAWAHARLAL   131, 132
NEITH-AQERT   67
NEITSEV, MINTSO   29
NEKHTHAREHBE   70
NEKHTNEBEF   70
NEL OSPINA, Gen PEDRO   52
NEMAATHE AMONEMHAT   68
NENETER   66
NEOPTOLEMUS   75
NEPHERCHERES   67
NEPHERITES   70
NEPHERKERES   67
NEPOTIANUS   208
NERGALUSHEZIB   18
NERIGLISSAR   19
NERO   206
NERVA   206
NESSIM PASHA, MOHAMMED TEWFIK   73
NESUBANEBDED   69
NETERI-MU   66
NETERKERE   67
NETO, Dr AGOSTINHO   4
NEUSERRE   67
NEWALL, Air Chief Marshal Sir Cyril Louis Norton
   Newall, 1st Baron   180
NEWAYA MARYAM   76
NEWCASTLE upon Tyne, The 1st Duke of   261,
   262
NEZAHUALCOYOTL   170
NEZAHUALPILLI   170
NGENDANDUMWE, PIERRE   30
NGO DINH-DIEM   277
NGOUABI, Major MARIEN   53
NGUYEN BA CAN   278
NGUYEN KHANH, Gen   277, 278
NGUYEN NGOC THO   278
NGUYEN VAN LOC   278
NGUYEN VAN THIEU, Gen   277
NGUYEN XUAN OANH, Dr   278
NICEPHORUS I   32
NICEPHORUS III BOTANEIATES   33
NICEPHORUS II PHOCAS   32
NICHANI, Dr OMER   4
NICHOLAS (France) see Nicolas
NICHOLAS (Montenegro) see Nikola
NICHOLAS (Papal State) see Nicholaus
NICHOLAS (Poland) see Nikolai
NICHOLAS (Russia) see Nikolai
NICHOLAS FRANCIS (France) see Nicolas
   Francois
NICHOLAUS I   188
NICHOLAUS II   189
NICHOLAUS III   190
NICHOLAUS IV   190
NICHOLAUS V   191
NICOLAS   92
NICOLAS FRANCOIS   93
NICOLE   93
NICOMEDES I   23
NICOMEDES II EPIPHANES   23
NICOMEDES III EPIPHANES PHILOPATOR   24
NICOMEDES IV   24
NIEDRA, ANDRIEVS   160
NIELS   61
NIJO   155
NIKOLA I   281, 282
NIKOLAI I Pavlovich   247
NIKOLAI II Aleksandrovich   247
NIKUSIYAR   131
NIMMYO   155
NIMR, Dr   157
NINAN CUYUCHI   126
NING-TSUNG   46
NINKEN   154
NINKO   155
NINTOKU   154
NINURTA-APALEKUR I   9
NINURTAKUDURUSUR I   18
NINURTAKUDURUSUR II   18
NINURTANADINSHUM   17
NINURTATUKULTIASHUR   9
NISSANKA MALLA   228
NITOKRIS   67
NITTI, FRANCESCO   144
NIXON, RICHARD MILHOUS   273
NIZAM   128
NIZAM-ud-DIN AHMAD III   128
NKRUMAH, Dr KWAME   110, 115
NOBOA, DIEGO   65
NOBS, ERNST   234
NOKRASHY PASHA, MAHMOUD FAHMY   73
NOMINOE   90

NOOMAN, AHMED MOHAMMED   279
NORD, ALEXIS   117
NORDLI, ODVAR   184
NORIEGA, Gen ZENON   196
NORODOM   37
NORODOM KANTOL, Prince   37
NORODOM SIHANOUK   37
NORODOM SURAMARIT   37
NORRIE, Gen Sir Charles Willoughby Moke
   Norrie, 1st Baron   180
NORTH, Baron   262
NORTHCOTE, Henry Stafford Northcote, 1st
   Baron   10
NOTHELM   249
NOUEL, Archbishop ADOLFO   64
NOUIRA, HEDI   241
NOUMAZALAY, AMBROISE   53
NOVAR of Raith, 1st Viscount   10
NOVATIANUS   187
NOVOTNY, ANTONIN   59
NTARE V   30
NU, U   30
NUMERIAN (Roman Empire) see Numerianus
NUMERIANUS   207
al NUMERY, Maj-Gen JAAFER MOHAMMED
   229
NUNEZ, Gen RAFAEL   51
NUNNA   249
NUON CHEA   38
NURADAD   16
NURHACHU   47
NURILI   9
el NUS, Dr IZZAT   236
NYAMOYA, ALBIN   30, 31
NYERERE, Dr JULIUS KAMBARAGE   237
NYGAARDSVOLD, JOHAN   184
NYSA   40
NZAMBIMANA, Lieut-Col ÉDOUARD   31

de OBALDIA, JOSÉ   186
de OBALDIA, JOSÉ DOMINGO   186
OBANDO, Gen JOSÉ MARIA   51
OBASANJO, Lieut-Gen OLUSEGUN   182
OBEIDI, ABDULLAH   162
OBLIGADO, Pastor   7
OBOTE, Dr APOLLO MILTON   244
OBREGON, Gen ALVARO   172
OCHAB, EDWARD   200, 201
OCTA   249
OCTAVIAN   205
OCTAVIANUS, GAIUS JULIUS CAESAR   205
O'DALAIGH, CEARBHALL   139
ODDONE   150
ODINGA, OGINGA   158
ODO (France) see Eudes
ODOACER   142
ODOARDO   149
ODRIA, Gen MANUEL   196
ODUBER QUIROS, DANIEL   54
OFFA (Essex)   251
OFFA (Mercia)   251
OGIMACHI   155
OGODEI   174
O'HIGGINS, Gen BERNARDO   43
OISC   249
OJIN   154
OKADO, Admiral KEISUKE   156
O'KELLY, SEAN THOMAS   138
OKYAR, FETHI   243
OLAF I   61
OLAF II   62
OLAF SIHTRICSON   253
OLAV (Sweden) see Olof
OLAV I Tryggvesson   183
OLAV II Haraldsson   183
OLAV III   183
OLAV IV   183
OLAV V   134
OLAV MAGNUSSON   183
OLAYA HERRERA, Dr ENRIQUE   52
OLIVIER, GEORGE BORG   169
OLJEITU   135
OLOF Skotkonung   230
OLYBRIUS   208
OLYMPIO, SYLVANUS   239
OMAR (The Caliphate) see 'Umar
OMRI   140
OMURTAG   27
ONGANIA, Gen JUAN CARLOS   6
ONNOS   67
OPAZO, PEDRO   43
ORANTES, JOSÉ MARIA   114
de ORBEGOSO, LUIS JOSÉ   195
ORDONO I   220
ORDONO II   220
ORDONO III   220

ORDONO IV   220
OREAMUNO, FRANCISCO MARIA   53
OREAMUNO FLORES, ALBERTO   54
ORELLANA, Gen JOSE MARIA   115
ORELLANA, Gen MANUEL   115
ORESTE, MICHEL   117
ORFORD, 1st Earl of   261
ORHAN   241
ORIBE, MANUEL   274
ORIZU, Dr NWAFOR   182
ORKHAN (Turkey) see Orhan
ORKHAN   241
ORLICH BOLMARICH, JOSÉ FRANCISCO   54
ORODES I   134
ORODES II   134
ORODONES III   134
OROPHERNES   40
OROSCO, JUAN de DIOS   181
ORTIZ, Dr ROBERTO M.   6
ORTIZ RUBIO, PASCUAL   172
OSAHITO   155
OSBALD   252
OSBERT   253
OSCAR (Norway) see Oskar
OSCAR I   233
OSCAR II   233
OSHIN   8
OSIN   8
OSKAR I   184
OSKAR II   184
OSLAC   250
OSMAN, ADAN ABDULLE   216
OSMAN, AHMED   176
OSMAN I   241
OSMAN II oglu Ahmed   242
OSMAN III   242
OSMAN, Sir RAMAN   169
OSMUND   249
OSOBKA-MORAWSKI, EDWARD BOLESLAW
   200
OSORIO, Major OSCAR   75
OSORKON I   69
OSORKON III   69
OSPINA PÉREZ, Dr MARIANO   52
OSPINA RODRIGUEZ, MARIANO   51
OSRED I   252
OSRED II   252
OSRIC (Deira)   252
OSRIC (Northumbria)   252
OSROES   134
OSULF   252
OSWALD (Bernicia)   252
OSWALD (East Anglia)   251
OSWALD (Sussex)   250
OSWINE   252
OSWINI   249
OSWIU   252
OSWULF   252
OTALORA, JOSÉ EUSEBIO   51
OTHMAN (The Caliphate) see Uthman
OTHMAN (Turkey) see Osman I
OTHMAN   241
OTHO   206
OTHOES   67
OTHO HENRY (German states) see Otto Heinrich
OTHON   110
OTHONAIOS, Gen ALEXANDROS   111
OTLAS   66
OTTAVIO   149
OTTO (Austria)   12
OTTO (Bavaria)   99
OTTO (Brandenburg)   99
OTTO (Greece) see Othon
OTTO (Hungary)   122
OTTO (Italy)   143
OTTO I (Bavaria)   98
OTTO I (Holy Roman Empire)   119
OTTO II (Bavaria)   98
OTTO II (Holy Roman Empire)   119
OTTO III   119
OTTO IV   119
OTTO HEINRICH   103
OTTO von Nordheim   98
OTTOKAR   12
OTTON   91
OTTONE   146
OUEDRAOGO, GÉRARD KANGO   273
OUENI, HUSSEIN   161
OULD DADDAH, MOKHTAR   169
OULD SALEK, Col MUSTAFA   169
OUN CHEANG SUN   37
OUSAPHAIS   66
OUSERCHERES   67
OVANDO CANDIA, Gen ALFREDO   25
OWAIN ap HYWEL DDA   269
OWAIN CYFEILIOG   270
OWAIN GLYNDWR   271
OWAIN GWYNEDD   269

OXFORD and ASQUITH, 1st Earl of   264
OYANEDEL, ABRAHAM   43
OZDILEK, Gen FAHRI   243

PAASIKIVI, JUHO KUSTI   78
PAASIO, KUSTAA RAFAEL   79
el-PACHACHI, HAMDI   137
PACHACUTI INCA YUPANQUI (Inca Empire) see
   Pachakuti 'Inka Yupanki
PACHAKUTI 'INKA YUPANKI   126
PACHECO, GREGORIO   24
el-PACHICHI, MUZAHIM   137
PACORUS   134
PAEZ, FEDERICO   65
de PAEZ, JOSÉ ANTONIO   275
PAGAN MIN   30
PAGE, Sir EARLE CHRISTMAS GRAFTON   11
PAIK TOO CHIN   159
PAINLEVÉ, PAUL   87
PAIS, Major SIDONIO BERNARDINO CARDOSO
   da SILVA   203
PAIVA, Dr FELIX   194
PALACIO, FRANCISCO   74
PALECKIS, Dr   164
PALMA, BAUDILLO   115
PALME, OLOF   233
PALMERSTON, The 3rd Viscount   263, 264
PAMAY,   69
PANDO, Col JOSÉ MANUEL   24
PANGALOS, Gen THEODOROS   111
PAPADOPOULOS, GIORGIOS   112
PAPAGOS, Marshal ALEXANDROS   112
PAPANDREOU, GIORGIOS   111, 112
von PAPEN, FRANZ   97
PAPUAGA IRIAS, EDMONDO   181
PARAKRAMA BAHU I   227
PARAKRAMA BAHU II   228
PARAKRAMA BAHU III   228
PARAKRAMA BAHU IV   228
PARAKRAMA BAHU V   228
PARAKRAMA BAHU VI   228
PARAKRAMA BAHU VII   228
PARAKRAMA BAHU VIII   228
PARAKRAMA PANDU   228
PARANTAKA I   128
PARASKEVOPOULOS, IOANNIS   112
PARDO, MANUEL   195
PARDO y BARREJA, JOSÉ   196
PAREDES, MARIANO   114
PAREDES y ARRILLAGA, Gen MARIANO   171
PARHON, Prof CONSTANTIN   210
PARIS, Gen GABRIEL   52
PARK CHUNG HI, Gen   159
PARK SUNG CHUL   159
PARRA, AQUILEO   51
PARRI, FERRUCCIO   144
PASCAL (Papal State) see Paschalis
PASCHALIS   188
PASCHALIS I   188
PASCHALIS II   189
PASCHALIS III   190
PASIC, Dr NICOLA   280
PASQUITO   90
PASTRANA BORRERO, Dr MISAEL   52
PATASSÉ, ANGE   42
PATS, KONSTANTIN   75, 76
PAUL (Greece) see Pavlos
PAUL (Papal State) see Paulus
PAUL (Russia) see Pavel
PAUL-BONCOUR, JOSEPH   87
de PAULE, ANTONIO   168
PAUL FREDERICK (German states) see Paul
   Friedrich
PAUL FRIEDRICH   102
PAULINE   146
PAULLA TOPA INCA (Inca Empire) see Paullu
   Thupa 'Inka
PAULUS I   188
PAULUS II   191
PAULUS III   191
PAULUS IV   191
PAULUS V   192
PAULUS VI   193
PAVEL Petrovich   246
PAVELIC, ANTE   280
PAVLOS I   111
PAWLLU THUPA 'INKA   127
PAYAN, ELISEO   51
PAYNE, JAMES SPRIGG   162
PAZ ESTENSSORO, Dr VICTOR   25
PEARSON, LESTER BOWLES   40
PECANHA, Dr NILO   26
PEDERNERA, JUAN ESTEBAN   6
PEDRO I (Aragon)   221
PEDRO I (Brazil)   26
PEDRO I (Castile)   221

PEDRO I *(Navarre)*   222
PEDRO I *(Portugal)*   202
PEDRO II *(Aragon)*   221
PEDRO II *(Brazil)*   26
PEDRO II *(Portugal)*   202
PEDRO III *(Aragon)*   221
PEDRO III *(Portugal)*   202
PEDRO IV *(Aragon)*   221
PEDRO IV *(Portugal)*   203
PEDRO V   203
PEDUBAST .   69
PEEL, Sir ROBERT   263
PEHRSSON-BRAMSTORP, AXEL   233
PEIXOTO, Marshal FLORIANO   26
PEKAH   140
PEKAHIYAH   140
PEKER, RECEP   243
PEKKALA, MAUNO   78
PELAGIUS I   188
PELAGIUS II   188
PELAYO   220
PELHAM, Hon, HENRY   261
PELLA, GUISEPPE   144
PELLEGRINI, CARLOS   6
PELLETIER, ÉMILE   174
PENA, LUIS SAENZ   6
PENA, PEDRO   194
PENA, ROQUE SAENZ   6
de la PENA y PENA, MANUEL   171
PENARANDA, Gen ENRIQUE   25
PENDA   251
PENNA, Dr AFFONSO AUGUSTO MOREIRA   26
PEPI I   67
PEPI II   67
PÉPIN   80
PEPIN   143
PERADA ASBUN, Gen JUAN   25
PERALTA-AZURDIA, Col CARLOS ENRIQUE   115
PERCEVAL, The Hon. SPENCER   262
PERDICCAS II   112
PERDICCAS III   112
PEREIRA, ARISTIDES   40
PEREIRA, GABRIEL ANTONIO   274
PEREIRA, TOMAS ROMERO   194
PEREIRA de SOUZA, Dr WASHINGTON LUIZ   26
PERELLOS y ROCCAFOL, RAIMON   168
PÉREZ, JOSÉ JOAQUIN   43
PÉREZ, Dr JUAN BAUTISTA   276
PÉREZ, SANTIAGO   51
PÉREZ GODOY, Gen RICARDO   196
PÉREZ JIMÉNEZ, Col MARCOS   277
PÉREZ RODRIGUEZ, CARLOS ANDRÉS   277
PERIBSEN   66
de PERON, ISABEL   6
PERON, Gen JUAN DOMINGO   6
de PERON, Senora MARIA ESTELA MARTINEZ   6
PERSEUS   113
PERTINAX   207
PERTINI, ALESSANDRO   144
PESARO, GIOVANNI   153
PESCENNIUS NIGER   207
PESSOA, Dr EPITACIO da SILVA   26
PÉTAIN, PHILIPPE   88
PETAR I   281
PETAR II   281
PETER (Bulgaria) *see* Petur
PETER (Cyprus) *see* Pierre
PETER (Italian states) *see* Pietro
PETER (Montenegro) *see* Petar
PETER, SAINT (Papal State) *see* Petrus
PETER (Portugal and Brazil) *see* Pedro
PETER (Spain) *see* Pedro
PETER   121
PETER I *(Oldenburg)*   103
PETER I *(Serbia)*   283
PETER I *(Yugoslavia)*   280
PETER I Alekseyevich *(Muscovy)*   245
PETER I Alekseyevich *(Russia)*   246
PETER II *(Oldenburg)*   103
PETER II *(Yugoslavia)*   280
PETER II Alekseyevich   246
PETER II Fyodorovich   246
PETER ASSEN (Bulgaria) *see* Petur Assen
PETER DELYAN (Bulgaria) *see* Petur Delyan
PETERSEN FRIIS, MICHAEL   63
PÉTION, ALEXANDRE SABES   116
PETITPIERRE, MAX   234
PETRONILLA   221
PETRONIUS MAXIMUS   208
PETRUS   187
PETUR   27
PETUR ASSEN   28
PETUR DELYAN   28
PEYNADO, JACINTO B.   64
PEZET, Gen JUAN ANTONIO   195

PFLIMLIN, PIERRE   89
PHAM VAN DONG   278
PHAN HUY QUAT, Dr   278
PHAN KHAC SUU   277
PHARNACES I   201
PHARNACES II   201
PHILIBERT (Italian states) *see* Filiberto
PHILIP (France) *see* Philippe
PHILIP (Greece) *see* Philippos
PHILIP (Holy Roman Empire and German states) *see* Philipp
PHILIP (Italian states) *see* Filippo
PHILIP (Portugal) *see* Felipe
PHILIP (Roman Empire) *see* Philippus
PHILIP (Spain) *see* Felipe
PHILIP   230
PHILIP I   22
PHILIP WILLIAM (German states) *see* Philipp Wilhelm
PHILIPP *(Hesse-Homburg)*   102
PHILIPP *(Holy Roman Empire)*   119
PHILIPP *(The Rhine)*   103
PHILIPP WILHELM   104
PHILIPPE   7
PHILIPPE I *(Achaea)*   1
PHILIPPE I *(Belgium)*   22
PHILIPPE I *(France)*   81
PHILIPPE I *(Navarre)*   222
PHILIPPE I de Rouvres   91
PHILIPPE II *(Achaea)*   1
PHILIPPE II *(Burgundy)*   92
PHILIPPE II *(Navarre)*   222
PHILIPPE II AUGUSTE   81
PHILIPPE III *(Achaea)*   1
PHILIPPE III *(Burgundy)*   92
PHILIPPE III *(France)*   81
PHILIPPE III *(Navarre)*   222
PHILIPPE IV *(Burgundy)*   92
PHILIPPE IV *(France)*   82
PHILIPPE V   82
PHILIPPE VI   82
PHILIPPICUS   32
PHILIPPOS II   112
PHILIPPOS III   113
PHILIPPOS IV   113
PHILIPPOS V   113
PHILIPPUS *(Israel)*   141
PHILIPPUS *(Papal State)*   188
PHILIPPUS *(Roman Empire)*   207
PHILIPPUS I EPIPHANES PHILADELPHUS   213
PHILIPPUS II   213
PHIOPS   67
PHIOS   67
PHO PROEUNG   37
PHOCAS   32
PHOLIEN, JOSEPH   22
PHOUI SANANIKONG   160
PHOUMI NOSAVAN, Gen   160
PHRA POK KLAO   238
PHRAATES I   134
PHRAATES II   134
PHRAATES III   134
PHRAATES IV   134
PHRAATES V   134
PHRAORTES   133
PHRAYA TAKSIN   238
PI y MARGALL, FRANCISCO JOSÉ   225
PIANKHY   70
PIANKHY II   70
PIAST   197
PICADO MICHALSKI, TEODORO   54
PIECK, WILHELM   95
PIEDRA, Judge CARLOS   56
PIEDRAHITA, Rear-Admiral RUBEN   52
PIER-LUIGI   149
PIERCE, FRANKLIN   272
PIERLOT, HUBERT   21
PIERO I de 'MEDICI   145
PIERO II de 'MEDICI   145
de PIEROLA, NICOLAS   196
PIERRE   8
PIERRE de Courtenay   34
PIERRE I *(Brittany)*   90
PIERRE I *(Cyprus)*   57
PIERRE II *(Brittany)*   90
PIERRE II *(Cyprus)*   57
PIERRE-LOUIS, JOSEPH   117
PIERROT, LOUIS   116
PIETRO I *(Savoy)*   150
PIETRO I *(Sicily)*   151
PIETRO II *(Savoy)*   150
PIETRO II *(Sicily)*   151
PIIP, ANTS   76
PILET-GOLAZ, MARCEL   234
PILSUDSKI, Marshal JOZEF   200
PIMENTEL, PEDRO   64
PINAY, ANTOINE   89
PINDLING, LYNDEN O.   19

PINEAU, CHRISTIAN   89
PINEDA, LAUREANO   181
P'ING-TI   44
PINHEIRO de AZEVEDO, Admiral JOSÉ BAPTISTA   204
PINILLA FABREGA, Col JOSÉ MANUEL   187
PINNES   126
PINOCHET UGARTE, Gen AUGUSTO   44
PINTO, Gen   5
PINTO, ANIBAL   43
PINTO, FRANCISCO   43
PINTO da COSTA, Dr MANUEL   211
PIPINELIS, PANAYOTIS   112
PIRES, Major PEDRO   40
PISANI, ALVISO   153
PITT, Hon WILLIAM   262
PITT the Elder, WILLIAM   262
PIUS I   187
PIUS II   191
PIUS III   191
PIUS IV   191
PIUS V   191
PIUS VI   192
PIUS VII   192
PIUS VIII   192
PIUS IX   193
PIUS X   193
PIUS XI   193
PIUS XII   193
PLASTIRAS, Gen NIKOLAOS   111
de la PLAZA, Dr VICTORINO   6
PLAZA GUTIÉRREZ, LEONIDAS   65
PLAZA LASSO, GALO   66
PLEISTARCHUS   113
PLEISTOANAX   113
PLEVEN, RENÉ   88
PLUNKET, William Lee Plunket, 5th Baron   180
PODGORNY, NIKOLAI VIKTOROVICH   248
POHER, ALAIN   89
POINCARE, RAYMOND   87
POL POT   38
POLK, JAMES KNOX   271
POMPEIUS MAGNUS, GNAEUS   205
POMPEY (Roman Empire) *see* Pompeius Magnus, Gnaeus
POMPEY   205
POMPIDOU, GEORGES JEAN RAYMOND   89
PONCE ENRIQUEZ, Dr CAMILO   66
PONCE, Gen MANUEL   196
PONCE-VAIDES, Gen FEDERICO   115
PONS   54
PONS, ANTONIO   65
da PONTE, PIETRO   168
PONTIAN (Papal State) *see* Pontianus
PONTIANUS   187
PORRAS, BELISARIO   186
PORRITT, Sir ARTHUR   180
PORTELA VALLADARES, MANUEL   226
PORTES GIL, EMILIO   172
PORTLAND, The 3rd Duke of   262
POTE SARASIN   238
POULITSAS, PANAYOTIS   111
POULLET, PROSPER Viscount   21
POVEDA BURBANO, Vice-Admiral ALFREDO   66
PRADO, Gen MARIANO IGNACIO   195
PRADO, MARIANO   195
PRADO y UGARTECHE, Dr MANUEL   196
PRAJADHIPOK   238
PRASAD ACHARYA, TANKA   177
PRASAD, Dr RAJENDRA   131
PRASAD KOIRALA, BISWESWAR   177
PRASAD KOIRALA, MATRIKA   177
PRASAD RAIJAL, NAGENDRA   177
PRAUDHADEVARAYA   129
PREMADASA, RANASINGHE   229
PREMYSL OTAKAR I   60
PREMYSL OTAKAR II   60
PRESSIAN   27
PRETORIUS, ANDRIES WILHELMUS JACOBUS   217
PRETORIUS, MARTHINUS WESSELS   217
PRIAPATIUS   134
PRIETO, Gen JOAQUIN   43
PRIMO de RIVERO y ORBANEJA, Gen MIGUEL   226
PRIO SOCARRAS, Dr CARLOS   56
PRITHVI BIR VIKRAM   176
PRITHVI NARAYAN SHAH   176
PRIULI, ANTONIO   153
PRIULI, GIROLAMO   153
PRIULI, LORENZO   153
PROBUS   207
PROCOPIUS   208
PROTIC, STOJAN   280
PRUSIAS I   23
PRUSIAS II   23
PRZEMYSL   198

PSAMTIK I   70
PSAMTIK II .   70
PSAMTIK III .   70
PSAMTIK IV   70
PSIBKHENNO I   69
PSIBKHENNO II   69
PSUSENNES I   69
PSUSENNES II   69
PTOLEMAEUS (Epirus)   75
PTOLEMAEUS (Thrace)   114
PTOLEMAIOS   113
PTOLEMY (Epirus) see Ptolamaeus
PTOLEMY (Greek states) see Ptolemaeus
PTOLEMY I SOTER   70
PTOLEMY II PHILADELPHUS   70
PTOLEMY III EUERGETES I   70
PTOLEMY IV PHILOPATOR   70
PTOLEMY V EPIPHANES   70
PTOLEMY VI PHILOMETOR   70
PTOLEMY VII EUERGETES II   70
PTOLEMY VIII EUPATOR   71
PTOLEMY IX APION   71
PTOLEMY X SOTER II   71
PTOLEMY XI ALEXANDER I   71
PTOLEMY XII ALEXANDER II   71
PTOLEMY XIII NEOS DIONYSOS   71
PTOLEMY XIV   71
PTOLEMY XV   71
PTOLEMY XVI CAESAR   72
PTOLEMY NEOS PHILOPATOR   70
P'U-I   47
PU-SARRUMAS   118
PU YI   49
PULCHERIA   31
PULU   18
PUPIENUS MAXIMUS   207
PURANDOKHT   135
PURIC, Dr BOZIDAR   280
PUZURASHUR   9
PUZURSIN   15
PYRRHUS I   75
PYRRHUS II   75
PYUN YUNG TAI   159

QA   66
QABOOS bin Said   185
QADHAFI, MU'AMMAR (Libya) see al-Gaddafi,
    Mu'ammar Muhammad
al-QADIR   36
al-QAHIR, MUHAMMAD   36
al-QA'IM   36
QHAPAQ YUPANKI   126
QILICH ARSLAN I   213
QILICH ARSLAN II   213
QILICH ARSLAN III   214
QILICH ARSLAN IV, Rukn ad-Din   214
QOBAD I   135
QUADRA, VICENTE   53
QUADROS, JANIO da SILVA   26
QUALIKHAN BAYATT, NURTEZA   136
de QUAY, Prof JAN EDUARD   179
QUEUILLE, HENRI   88
QUINONEZ, ALFONSO   74
QUINTANA, MANUEL   6
QUINTANILLA, Gen CARLOS   25
QUINTILLUS   207
QUIRINO, ELPIDIO   196
QUIROS, JUAN   74
QUIROS, JUAN BAUTISTA   54
QULI QUTB SHAH   130
QUTB-ud-DIN AYBAK   128
QUTB-ud-DIN MUBARAK SHAH   128

RA-NEB   66
RAAB, Dr JULIUS   15
RABIN, Gen ITZHAK   141
RACHIS   142
RACZKIEWICZ, WLADYSLAW   200
RADAMA I   166
RADAMA II   166
RADESCU, Gen NICOLAE   210
RADHAKRISHNAN, Dr SARVAPALLI   132
ar-RADI, AHMAD   36
RAFI-ud-DARAJAT   131
RAFI-ud-DAULAT   130
RAGIMBERTUS   142
RAGNALD   253
RAGNALD GUTHFRITHSON   253
RAHMAN, TUANKU ABDUL   167
RAHMAN, ABDUL   167
RAHMAN, Shaikh MUJIBUR   20
RAHMAN, Maj-Gen ZIAUR   20
RAIMOND I   54
RAIMOND II   54

RAIMOND III   54
RAIMOND de POITIERS   54
RAIMOND-ROUPEN   54
RAINIER I   173
RAINIER II   173
RAINIER III   174
RAJA RAM   131
RAJAGOPALACHARI, CHAKRAVARTI   131
RAJARAJA   128
RAJENDRA   128
RAJENDRAVARMAN I   36
RAJENDRAVARMAN II   36
RAJENDRA VIKRAM   176
RAJNISS, Dr FERENC   124
RAKOSI, MATYAS   125
RAKOTOMALALA, Col JOEL   167
RAKOTONIAINA, JUSTIN   167
RAMA I   238
RAMA II   238
RAMA III   238
RAMA IV   238
RAMA V   238
RAMA VI   238
RAMA VII   238
RAMA DEVA RAYA   129
RAMA RAYA   129
RAMANANTSOA, Maj-Gen GABRIEL   166
RAMADIER, PAUL   88
RAMCHANDRA   129
RAMESSES   69
RAMGOOLAM, Sir SEEWOOSAGUR   169
RAMIREZ, Gen PEDRO P.   6
RAMIREZ, NOBERTO   181
RAMIRO I (Aragon)   221
RAMIRO I (Asturias)   220
RAMIRO II (Aragon)   221
RAMIRO II (Leon)   220
RAMIRO III   220
RAMISHVILI, NOE   95
RAMKHAMHAENG   238
RAMON RAMON, Col JOSE ANTONIO   186
RAMOS, NEREU de OLIVEIRA   26
RAMSES I   69
RAMSES II   69
RAMSES III HIKON   69
RAMSES IV   69
RAMSES V   69
RAMSES VI   69
RAMSES VII   69
RAMSES VIII   69
RAMSES IX   69
RAMSES X   69
RAMSES XI   69
RAMSES XII   69
RAMSES-SIPTAH   69
RANA BAHADUR   176
RANA PRATAP SINGH   176
RANAVALONA I   166
RANAVALONA II   166
RANAVALONA III   166
RANGA I   129
RANGA II   129
RANGA III   129
RANGELL, JOHAN WILHELM   78
RANUCCIO I   149
RANUCCIO II   149
RAOUL, Major ALFRED   53
RAOUL (France)   81
RAOUL (Lorraine)   92
al-RASCHID   36
ar-RASHID, HARUN   35
RASHTIKIS, Gen   164
RASOAHERINA   166
RATHOURES   67
RATOISES   67
RATSIMANDRAVA, Col RICHARD   166
RATSIRAKA, Lieut-Commander DIDIER   166,
    167
RAUSCHNING, Dr HERMAN   61
RAWSON, Gen ARTURO   6
RAYES, RAFAEL   43
RAZAK bin Dato Hussein, Tuanku ABDUL   167
RAZMARA, Gen ALI   137
RAZZAK, Brig AREF ABDUL   138
RECAREDO I   219
RECAREDO II   219
RECESVINTO   219
REDDY, NEELAM SANJIVA   132
de REDIN, MARTIN   168
REDJEDEF   67
REDWALD   251
REDWULF   252
REGALADO, TOMAS   74
de REGLA-MOTTA, MANUEL   64
REHOBOAM   140
REI, AUGUST   76
REID, Sir GEORGE HOUSTON   11
REID CABRAL, Dr DONALD J.   64

REIG, JULIA   4
REIGEN   155
REINA-ANDRADE, JOSE MARIA   115
REINA-BARRIOS, JOSE MARIA   115
REITZ, FRANCIS WILLIAM   217
REIZEI   155
RELANDER, LAURI KRISTIAN   78
RENE, FRANCE ALBERT   214
RENE   147
RENE I   92
RENE II   92
RENEB   66
RENIER, PAOLO   153
RENKIN, JULES   21
RENNER, Dr KARL   15
RENNIE, Sir JOHN SHAW   169
RESTREPO, CARLOS E.   52
REYES, PRIETO RAFAEL   51
REYMOND, JEAN   174
REYNAUD, PAUL   88
REYNAUD de Chatillon   54
REZA SHAH PAHLAVI   136
RHEE, Dr SYNGMAN   159
RHIRYD ap BLEDDYN   270
RHIWALLON   270
RHIWALLON ap BLEDDYN   270
RHODRI ap HYWEL DDA   269
RHODRI MAWR   269
RHODRI MOLWYNOG   268
RHUN ap MAELGWN GWYNEDD   268
RHYDDERCH ab IESTYN (Deheubarth)   269
RHYDDERCH ab IESTYN (Gwynedd)   269
RHYS ab OWAIN ab EDWIN   270
RHYS ap GRUFFYDD   270
RHYS ap TEWDWR   270
RIART, LUIS   194
RIBAR, Dr IVAN   281
RIBEIRO, Dr DELFIM MOREIRA da COSTA   26
RIBICIC, MITJA   281
RIBOT, ALEXANDRE   87
RICHARD (Anjou)   90
RICHARD (Holy Roman Empire)   120
RICHARD I (England)   255
RICHARD I (Normandy)   93
RICHARD II (England)   256
RICHARD II (Normandy)   93
RICHARD III (England)   256
RICHARD III (Normandy)   93
RICHARD IV   93
RICHE, JEAN-BAPTISTE   116
RICHU   154
RICSIGE   253
RIESCO, GERMAN   43
RIFAI, ABDUL MONEIM   157
RIFAI, Brig NOUREDDIN   161
RIFAI, SAMIR PASHA   157
RIFAI, ZAID   158
RIMSIN   16
RIMUSH   16
RINALDO (Modena)   147
RINALDO (Naples)   147
RIOS, JUAN ANTONIO   44
RITSCHARD, WILLI   235
de la RIVA AGUERO, JOSE   195
RIVADAVIA, BERNARDINO   5
RIVAROLA, CIRILO ANTONIO   193
RIVAS, PATRICIO   181
RIVERA, Gen JOSE FRUCTUOSO   274
RIVERA, Col JULIO ADALBERTO   75
RIVERA PAZ, MARIANO   114
RO   66
ROBERT (Italian states) see Roberto
ROBERT I (Achaea)   1
ROBERT I (Burgundy)   91
ROBERT I (Flanders)   22
ROBERT I (France)   81
ROBERT I (Normandy)   93
ROBERT I (Scotland)   267
ROBERT II (Achaea)   1
ROBERT II (Burgundy)   91
ROBERT II (France)   81
ROBERT II (Normandy)   93
ROBERT II (Scotland)   267
ROBERT II of Jerusalem   22
ROBERT III (Flanders)   22
ROBERT III (Normandy)   93
ROBERT III (Scotland)   268
ROBERT III or II   91
ROBERT de Courtenay   34
ROBERTO (Naples)   147
ROBERTO (Parma and Piacenza)   149
ROBERTS, JOSEPH JENKINS   162
ROBERTSON, Sir JAMES   182
ROBLES, Gen FRANCISCO   65
ROBLES, MARCO AURELIO   187
de ROBURT, HAMER   176
ROCA, Gen JULIO A.   6
ROCA, VICENTE RAMON   65

ROCAFUERTE, VICENTE   65
ROCKINGHAM, The 2nd Marquess of   262
RODOALD   142
RODOLF II   120
RODOLPHE   92
RODOLPHE I   91
RODOLPHE II   91
RODOLPHE III   91
RODRIGO   219
RODRIGUEZ, Gen ABELARDO   172
RODRIGUEZ, JOSÉ JOAQUIN   53
RODRIGUEZ de FRANCIA, JOSÉ GASPAR   193
RODRIGUEZ LARA, Brig-Gen GUILLERMO   66
RODULFUS   143
ROGER   54
ROGER I   150
ROGER II   151
de ROHAN, EMMANUEL   169
ROJAS GARRIDO, JOSÉ MARIA   51
ROJAS, LIBERATO MARCIAL   194
ROJAS PAUL, JOSÉ PABLO   276
ROJAS PINILLA, Gen GUSTAVO   52
ROKUJO   155
ROLLO (France) see Robert
ROLLON   93
ROLON, Gen RAIMUNDO   194
ROMAN y REYES, Dr VICTOR M.   181
ROMANUS (Italy)   142
ROMANUS (Papal State)   188
ROMANUS I   32
ROMANUS II   32
ROMANUS III   32
ROMANUS IV DIOGENES   33
ROMERO, Gen CARLOS HUMBERTO   75
ROMULUS AUGUSTUS   209
RONAI, SANDOR   124
ROOSEVELT, FRANKLIN DELANO   272
ROOSEVELT, THEODORE   272
de ROSAS, Gen JUAN MANUEL   5
ROSEBERY, The 5th Earl of   264
ROSTISLAV   59
ROTHARI   142
ROUPEN I   7
ROUPEN II   7
ROUPEN III   7
ROWLING, BILL   180
ROWLING, WALLACE EDWARD   180
ROXAS y ACUNA, Brig-Gen MANUEL   196
ROYE, EDWARD JAMES   162
RUBAI, Gen MUHAMMAD NAJIB   138
RUBATTEL, RODOLPHE   234
RUBAYYI ALI, SALEM   218
RUBEN (Armenia) see Roupen
RUCHET, MARC-EMILE   234
RUCHONNET, LOUIS   234
RUDOLF   60
RUDOLF (France) see Raoul
RUDOLF I (Austria)   12
RUDOLF I (Holy Roman Empire)   120
RUDOLF I (The Rhine)   103
RUDOLF II (Austria)   12, 13
RUDOLF II (The Rhine)   103
RUDOLF III   12
RUDOLF IV   12
RUDOLPH (Holy Roman Empire) see Rudolf
RUDOLPH (Bavaria)   98
RUDOLPH (Hungary)   123
RUFFY, EUGENE   234
RUFINO BARRIOS, JUSTO   114, 115
RUGGIERO I   150
RUGGIERO II   151
RUIZ CORTINES, ADOLFO   172
RUMOR, MARIANO   145
RUPERT (German states) see Rupprecht
RUPERT CLEMENT (Holy Roman Empire) see
   Emperor Rupprecht Klem
RUPPRECHT I   103
RUPPRECHT II   103
RUPPRECHT III KLEM   103
RUPPRECHT KLEM   120
RUSADAN   94
RUSAS I   273
RUSAS II   274
RUSAS III   274
RUSSELL, ALFRED   162
RUSSELL, Lord JOHN   263, 264
RUSSELL, 1st Earl   263, 264
RUYS de BEERENBROUCK, Jonkheer Dr
   CHARLES JOSEPH MARIE   178
RUZZINI, CARLO   153
RYKOV, ALEKSEY IVANOVICH   248
RYTI, RISTO HEIKKI   78

SAAD al-AHMED es-SABAH, Shaikh   160
SAAVEDRA, JUAN BAUTISTA   24
SABAH al-SALEM al-SABAH   159

SABINIANUS   188
SABIUM   17
SABRA, ABDEL SALAM   279
SABRY, HASSAN PASHA   73
SABRY, Wing Commander ALI   74
SACASA, JUAN BAUTISTA   181
SACASA, ROBERTO   181
SADASIVA   129
SADAT, ANWAR   73, 74
el-SADR, MOHAMMED   137
SADR, MUHSIN   136
SADYATTES   166
SAEBERHT   250
SAED, MOHAMMED   136
SAELRED   251
SAEWEARD   250
al-SAFFAH, ABU' al-ABBAS   35
SAGA   155
SAGET, Gen NISSAGE   117
SAGREDO, NICOLO   153
SAGUIER, ADOLFO   194
SAHASSAMALLA   228
SAHM, Dr HEINRICH   61
SAHURE   67
es-SAID, Gen NURI PASHA   137
SA'ID   72
SAID bin Ahmed   185
SAID bin Sultan   185
SAID bin Taimur   185
al SAID, MOHAMMED bin-OTHMAN   162
SAIFA AR'AD   76
SAIMEI   154
de SAINT-JAILE, DESIDERIUS   168
St LAURENT, LOUIS STEPHEN   40
St-MLEUX, ANDRÉ   174
SAITO, Admiral Viscount MAKOTO   156
SAKA, HASAN   243
SAKURAMACHI   155
SALAM, MAMDOUH MOHAMMED   74
SALAM, SAEB   161
SALAMANCA, DANIEL   25
SALAMON   121
SALAS, JOSÉ MARIANO   171
SALAVERRY, FELIPE SANTIAGO   195
SALAZAR, Dr ANTONIO de OLIVEIRA   203, 204
SALAZAR y BAQUIJANO, MANUEL   195
SALGAR, Gen EUSTORJIO   51
SALIM bin Thwaini   185
SALISBURY, The 3rd Marquess of   264
SALLAL, Col ABDULLAH   279
SALLES, Dr MANUEL FERRAZ de CAMPOS   26
SALMERON, NICOLAS   225
SALNAVE, Gen SYLVAIN   117
SALOMON   90
SALOMON, Gen LOUIS ÉTIENNE FÉLICITÉ   117
SALOTE TUPOU III   239
SALUVA NARASIMHA   129
SAM, TIRESIAS SIMON   117
SAMAMEZ OCAMPO, DAVID   196
SAMBHAJI   185
SAMBUU, ZHAMSARANGIN   175
SAMDECH PENN NOUTH   37
SAMGHATISSA II   227
SAMIUM   16
SAMPER, RICARDO   226
SAMPSON, NICOS   57
SAMSUDITANA   17
SAMSUILUNA   17
SAMUDRA GUPTA   127
SAMUEL (Bulgaria)   28
SAMUEL (Hungary)   121
de SAN MARTIN, JOSÉ   194
SAN MARTIN, JOSÉ MARIA   74
de SAN RAMON, Marshal MIGUEL   195
de SAN SUPERANO, PEDRO BORDO   1
SAN YUN   37
SANABRIA, Dr EDGARD   277
SANAKHT   67
SANATESCU, Gen CONSTANTIN   210
SANATRUCES   134
SANCHEZ CERRO, Col LUIS M.   196
SANCHEZ HERNANDEZ, Col FIDEL   75
SANCHO I (Leon)   220
SANCHO I (Portugal)   202
SANCHO I GARCÉS   222
SANCHO I RAMIREZ   221
SANCHO II (Castile)   220
SANCHO II (Portugal)   202
SANCHO II GARCÉS   222
SANCHO III   220
SANCHO III GARCÉS   222
SANCHO IV (Castile)   221
SANCHO IV (Navarre)   222
SANCHO V RAMIREZ   222
SANCHO VI   222
SANCHO VII   222
SANCLEMENTE, MANUEL ANTONIO   51
SANDLER, RICHARD   233

SANDOVAL, JOSÉ LEON   181
SANFUENTES, JUAN LUIS   43
SANGSTER, Sir DONALD BURNS   153
SANJAR   213
SANJO   155
SANKHARE MENTUHOTEP III   68
SANTA ANNA, Gen ANTONIO LOPEZ de   171
SANTA CRUZ, ANDRÉS   195, 24, 51, 195
SANTA MARIA, DOMINGO   43
SANTANA, PEDRO   64
SANTANDER, FRANCISCO de PAULA   51
SANTIN del CASTILLO, MIGUEL   74
SANTOS, Dr EDUARDO   52
de los SANTOS Dr EMILIO   64
SANTOS, Gen MAXIMO   274
SANYA DHARMASAKTI, Dr   238
SANYA THAMMASAK   238
SAO SHWE THAIK   30
SAQIZLY, MOHAMMED   162
SARACOGLU, SUKRU   243
SARAGAT, GIUSEPPE   144
SARDURI I   273
SARDURI II   273
SARDURI III   274
SARDURI IV   274
SARGON I   16
SARGON II (Assyria)   10
SARGON II (Babylonia)   18
SARIT THANARAT, Marshal   238
SARKIS, ELIAS   161
SARMIENTO, Col DOMINGO FAUSTINO   6
SARRAUT, ALBERT   87, 88
SARSA DENGEL   77
SARTONO, Dr   132
SARWAT PASHA, ABDUL   73
SASTROAMIDJOJO, Dr ALI   132
SATHA   37
SATO, EISAKU   157
SAUD ibn Abdul Aziz ibn Saud   211, 212
SAUKHAM KHOY, Maj-Gen   38
SAUL (Israel and Judah) see Shaul
SAUSTATAR   173
SAVA II   281
SAVAGE, MICHAEL JOSEPH   180
SAVANG VATTHANA   160
SAVONAROLA, GIROLAMO   145
SAYDAM, Dr REFIK   243
SAYEM, Justice ABUSADAT MOHAMMED   20
SCAVENIUS, ERIK   63
SCELBA, MARIO   144
SCHAERER, EDUARDO   194
SCHAFFNER, HANS   234
SCHARF, Dr ADOLF   15
SCHEEL, WALTER   109
SCHEIDEMANN, PHILIPP   97
SCHERER, JAKOB   234
SCHERMERHORN, Prof WILLEM   179
SCHEURER, KARL   234
SCHICK GUTIERREZ, RENÉ   181
SCHINK, KARL   233, 234
von SCHLEIDER, Gen CURT   97
SCHMIDT, HELMUT   109
SCHULTHESS, EDMUND   234
SCHUMAN, ROBERT   88
SCHUSCHNIGG, Dr KURT   14
SCHWALE, Dr FERNANDO   196
SCOTT, Sir WINSTON   20
SCULLIN, JAMES HENRY   11
SEAXBURH   250
SEBASTAO   202
SEBASTIAN (Portugal) see Sebastao
SEBBI   250
SEBEK-KA-RE   67
SEBEK-NEFRU   68
SEBERCHERES   67
SEGNI, ANTONIO   144
SEHERTOWY INTEF   68
SEHETEPIBRE AMONEMHAT   68
SEIF el-ISLAM ABDULLAH el HASSAN, Emir   279
SEIMU   154
SEIN WIN, U   30
SEINEI   154
SEITZ, Dr KARL   14
SEIWA   155
SEKHEMKHET   67
SEKOU TOURÉ, AHMED   115
SELEUCUS   113
SELEUCUS I NICATOR   212
SELEUCUS II CALLINICUS   212
SELEUCUS III SOTER   212
SELEUCUS IV PHILOPATOR   212
SELEUCUS V   213
SELEUCUS VI EPIPHANES NICATOR   213
SELIM I   242
SELIM II   242
SELIM III   242
SELO, Col FAWZI   236

SEMBAT I   7
SEMBAT II   7
SEMBAT III   7
SEMEMPSES   66
SEMERKHET NEKHT   66
SENA I   227
SENA II   227
SENA III   227
SENA IV   227
SENA V   227
SENANAYAKE, DONALD STEPHEN   228
SENANAYAKE, DUDLEY SHELTON   228, 229
SENEDI   67
SENGHOR, LEOPOLD SEDAR   214
SENI PRAMOJ   238
SENKA   154
SENNACHERIB (Assyria)   10
SENNACHERIB (Babylonia)   18
SENUSRET I   68
SENUSRET II   68
SEOANE CORRALES, EDGARDO   196
SEPHRES   67
SEPTIMUS SEVERUS   207
SEQENENRE I   68
SEQENENRE II   68
SEQENENRE III   68
SERGIUS I   188
SERGIUS II   188
SERGIUS III   189
SERGIUS IV   189
SERRANO y DOMINGUEZ, Marshal
   FRANCISCO   225
SERRATO, JOSE   274
SERSKIC, Dr MILAN   280
SESOKHRIS   67
SESONKHOSIS   68
SESOSTRIS I   68
SESOSTRIS II   68
SESOSTRIS III   68
SETEKHY I   69
SETEKHY II   69
SETHENES   67
SETHOS   69
SETI I   69
SETI II   69
SETNAKHT   69
SEVAR   27
SEVERINUS   188
SEVERUS   208
SEVERUS ALEXANDER   207
SEXRED   250
SEYSS-INQUART, Dr ARTHUR   14
SEYYID JAMSHID bin-ABDULLAH
   bin-KHALIFAH   237
SEZES   67
SHABAKA   70
SHABATAKA   70
SHAFIQ, Dr MOHAMMED MUSA   2
SHAGARAKTISHURIASH   17
SHAH ABBAS I   136
SHAH ABBAS II   136
SHAH ABBAS III   136
SHAH ALAM I   130
SHAH 'ALAM II   131
SHAH JAHAN   130
SHAH ROKH   136
SHAH ROKH SHAH   239
SHAH SAFI I   136
SHAH SAFI II SULEYMAN   136
SHAH SHOJA   1, 2
SHAH SOLTAN HOSEYN   136
SHAHJAHAN II   131
SHAHJAHAN III   131
SHAHRBARAZ   135
SHAHU   131
SHALLUM   140
SHALMANESER I   9
SHALMANESER II   9
SHALMANESER III   9
SHALMANESER IV   10
SHALMANESER V (Assyria)   10
SHALMANESER V (Babylonia)   18
SHALOM ALEXANDRA   141
SHAMASHERA   19
SHAMASHMUDAMMIQ   18
SHAMASHSHUMKIN   18
SHAMS-ud-DIN   128
SHAMSHIADAD I   8
SHAMSHIADAD II   9
SHAMSHIADAD III   9
SHAMSHIADAD IV   9
SHAMSHIADAD V   10
SHAPUR I   134
SHAPUR II   135
SHAPUR III   135
SHARETT, MOSHE   141
SHARKALISHARRI   16
SHARMA-ADAD I   8

SHARMA-ADAD II   8
SHARRU-KIN II   10
SHARRUM-KIN   16
SHARU   67
SHASTRI, LAL BAHADUR   132
SHATTUARA (?).   173
SHAUL   139
SHAZAR, ZALMAN   141
SHEARER, HUGH LAWSON   153
SHEARES, Prof BENJAMIN HENRY   215
SHEBITKU   70
SHEHU, Col-Gen MEHMET   4
SHELBURNE, The 2nd Earl of   262
SHELOMOH   140
SHEN-TSUNG   46
SHEN TSUNG   46
SHENG-TSU   47
SHEPSESKAF   67
SHER SHAH   130
SHERMAKE, Dr ABDELRASHID ALI   216
SHESHONK I .   69
SHESHONK II .   69
SHESHONK III .   69
SHESHONK IV .   69
SHIBAB-ud-DIN AHMAD I   128
SHIDEHARA, Baron KIJURO   156
SHIH HUANG-TI   44
SHIH TSU   47
SHIH TSUNG   46, 47
SHIHAB-ud-DIN MAHMUD   128
SHIJO   155
SHIMON   141
SHIR 'ALI KHAN   2
SHIRAKAWA   155
SHIRIQTUSHUQAMUNA   18
SHISHAKLI, Col ADIB   236
SHOKO   155
SHOMU   154
SHOWA   156
SHUDURAL   16
SHUILISHU   16
SHULGI   16
SHUMSHERE, Gen SUBARNA   177
SHUMSHERE JUNG BAHADUR RANA, Gen
   MOHAN   177
SHUMSHERE JUNG BAHADUR RANA, Maharaja
   JOODHA   177
SHUMSHERE JUNG BAHADUR RANA, Maharaja
   PADMA   177
SHUN-CHIH   47
SHUN-TSUNG   45
SHUSIN   16
SHUTTARA I   173
SHUTTARNA II   173
SHVERNIK, NIKOLAI   248
SIAMON   69
SIBYLLE (Jerusalem)   55
SIBYLLE (Tripoli)   55
SIDI LAMINE   240
SIDI MOHAMMAD ibn ARAFA   175
SIDI MUHAMMAD   175
SIDI MUHAMMAD ben YUSUF   175
SIDKY, Dr AZIZ   74
SIDKY PASHA, ISMAIL   73
SIDNEY, Sir WILLIAM PHILIP   11
SIEFRED   253
SIERRA, TERENCIO   121
SIEYES, EMMANUEL JOSEPH   84
SIGCAU, Chief BOTHA JONGILIZWE   218
SIGEBERHT (East Anglia)   251
SIGEBERHT (Wessex)   250
SIGEBERHT I   250
SIGEBERHT II   250
SIGEBERT I   80
SIGEBERT II   80
SIGEBERT III   80
SIGEFROI   164
SIGEHEARD   251
SIGERED (Essex)   251
SIGERED (Kent)   249
SIGERIC   251
SIGERICO   219
SIGFRID (Luxembourg) see Sigefroi
SIGHERE   250
SIGISMOND   91
SIGISMOND I   92
SIGISMOND II   92
SIGISMUND (Bavaria)   99
SIGISMUND (Bohemia)   60
SIGISMUND (Brandenburg)   99
SIGISMUND (Holy Roman Empire)   120
SIGISMUND (Hungary)   122
SIGISMUND (Poland) see Zygmunt
SIGISMUND   232
SIGURD I   183
SIGURD II   183
SIHANOUK (Cambodia) see Norodom Sihanouk
SIHTRIC CAOCH   253

SIKANDER   128
SIKANDER SHAH   129
SIKORSKI, Gen WLADYSLAW   200
SILAKALA   227
SILAMEGHAVANNA   227
SILES, Dr HERNAN   25
SILES, HERNANDO   24
SILES SALINAS, Dr LUIS ADOLFO   25
SILO   220
SILVA, Marshal ARTUR da COSTA e   27
SILVERIUS   188
SILVESTER I   187
SILVESTER II   188
SILVESTER III   189
SILVESTER IV   189
SIM VAR   37
SIMEON I   27
SIMEON II   29
SIMEON Ivanovich   244
SIMMASHSHIHU   18
SIMON, ANTOINE   117
SIMON, RENE JOEL   89
SIMON (Israel and Judah) see Shimon
SIMON   150
SIMONE   150
SIMOVIC, Gen DUSAN   280
SIMPLICIUS   187
SINAKHKHE-ERIBA   10
SINCHI ROCA (Inca Empire) see Zinchi Roq'a
SINDERMANN, HORST   95
SINERIBAM   16
SINGH, Dr K.I.   177
SINGHATEH, Alhaji Sir FARIMANG   94
SINIBALDI, ALEJANDRO   115
SINIDINNAM   16
SINIQISHAM   16
SINMAGIR   16
SINMUBALLIT   17
SINSHARISHKUN   10
SIPTAH   69
SIRICIUS   187
SIRIMEGHAVANNA   227
SIROKY, VILIAM   59
SIROVY, Gen JAN   58
SIRRY PASHA, HUSSEIN   73
SISAVANG VONG   160
SISEBUTO   219
SISENANDO   219
SISINNIUS   188
SISIRES   67
SISOWATH   37
SISOWATH SIRIK MATAK, Lieut-Gen   38
SIVA   227
SIVAJI   131
SKANDA GUPTA   127
SKEMIOPHRIS   68
SKUJENIEKS, MARGERS   161
SLAWEK, Col VALERIAN   200
SLAWOJ-SKLADKOWSKI, Gen FELICJAN   200
SLEZEVICIUS, MYKOLAS   164
SLIM, Field Marshal Sir William Joseph Slim, 1st
   Viscount   10
SMBAT   8
SMBAT I and IX   7
SMBAT II and X   7
SMBAT III and XI   7
SMENDES   69
SMENKHARE   68
SMETONA, ANTONAS   164
SMILETS   28
SMILITZ   28
SMITH, IAN DOUGLAS   204
SMITH, JAMES   162
SMUTS, Field Marshal JAN CHRISTIAAN   217
SNEFERU   67
SNEFRU   67
SNEPHOURIS   67
SOARES, Dr MARIO ALBERTO NOBRE LOPES
   204
SOBHUZA II   230
SOBJISLAV   60
SODERINI, PIERO   145
SOFOULIS, THEMISTOCLES   111, 112
SOGLO, Gen CHRISTOPHE   23
SOHL, RASHID   161
SOHL, RIAD   161
SOHL, SAMI   161
SOHL, TAKIEDDINE   161
SOILIH, ALI   52
SOKOINE, EDWARD M.   237
SOLAIMAN, MOHAMMED SIDKI   74
SOLHEILY, ALI   136
SOLOMON (Hungary) see Salamon
SOLOMON   140
SOLORZANO, CARLOS   181
SOMARE, MICHAEL   193
SOMERS, Arthur Herbert Tennyson Cocks, 6th
   Baron   10

SOMOZA DEBAYLE, Gen ANASTASIO   181
SOMOZA DEBAYLE, LUIS ANASTASIO   181
SOMOZA GARCIA, Gen ANASTASIO   181
SON NGOC THANH   38
SON SANN   37
SONG YO CHAN, Maj-Gen   159
SOONG CHING-LING, Madame   49
SOONG TZU-WEN, Dr   48
SORIS   67
SORSA, TAISTO KALEVI   79
SÓSISÍRATUS   235
SOTERUS   187
SOTO, Gen BERNARDO   53
SOTO, MARCO AURELIO   121
SOUBLETTE, CARLOS   275
SOULBURY, Herwald Ramsbotham, 1st
   Viscount   228
SOULOUQUE, FAUSTIN-ELIE   117
SOUPHANOUVONG   160
SOUPHIS   67
SOUVANNA PHOUMA, Prince   160
de SOUZA, Lieut-Col EMILE   23
SOYPHIS   67
SPAAK, PAUL-HENRI   21
SPILJAK MIKA   281
de SPINOLA, Gen ANTONIO SEBASTIAO
   RIBEIRO   203
SPITHNJEV   59
SPRINGZAK, Dr JOSEPH   141
SPUHLER, WILLY   234
SPYCHALSKI, Marshal MARIAN   200
SRAMEK, Msgr JAN   58, 59
SRIRANGA   129
SSU TSUNG   47
STAHLBERG, Dr KAARLO JUHO   78
STALIN, JOSIF VISSARIONOVICH
   DJUGASHVILI   247 248
STAMBOLIC, PETAR   281
STAMBOLIYSKI, ALEKSANDR   29
STAMPFLI, JAKOB   233
STAMPFLI, WALTER   234
STANISLAS   93
STANISLAS II AUGUSTUS (Poland) see Stanislaw
   II August
STANISLAW I Leszczynski   199
STANISLAW II AUGUST Poniatowski   199
STANLEY of Preston, Frederick Arthur Stanley, 1st
   Baron   38
STARHEMBERG, ERNST RUDIGER , Prince   14
STASSINOPOULOS, MIKAEL   112
STAUNING, THORVALD   63
STAURACIUS   32
STEEG, THEODORE   87
STEFAN I Batory   199
STEFANSSON, STEFAN JOHANN   125
von STEIGER, EDUARD   234
STEINTHORSSON, STEINGRIMUR   125
STENKIL Ragnvaldssen   230
STEPAN I NEMANYA   282
STEPAN II   282
STEPAN III RADOSLAV   282
STEPAN IV VLADISLAV   282
STEPAN V UROS I   282
STEPAN VI DRAGUTIN   282
STEPAN VII UROS II MILUTIN   282
STEPAN VIII UROS III DECANSKI   282
STEPAN IX UROS IV DUSAN   282
STEPAN X UROS V   282
STEPAN DUSAN   282
STEPHANOPOULOS, STEPHANOS   112
STEPHANUS I   187
STEPHANUS II   188
STEPHANUS II or III   188
STEPHANUS III or IV   188
STEPHANUS IV or V   188
STEPHANUS V or VI   188
STEPHANUS VI or VII   188
STEPHANUS VII or VIII   189
STEPHANUS VIII or IX   189
STEPHANUS IX   189
STEPHEN   254, 255
STEPHEN (France) see Etienne
STEPHEN (Papal State) see Stephanus
STEPHEN (Poland) see Stefan
STEPHEN (Serbia) see Stepan
STEVENS, SIAKA PROBYN   215
STEYN, Dr LUCAS CORNELIUS   216
STEYN, MARTHINUS THEUNIS   217
STIRBEY, Prince   210
STOICA, CHIVU   210
STONEHAVEN, Sir John Lawrence Baird, 1st
   Baron   10
STOPH, WILLI   95
STOUT, Sir ROBERT   180
STOW, Sir JOHN MONTAGUE   20
STOYADINOVIC, Dr MILAN   280
STRANDMAN, OTTO   75, 76
STRESEMANN, Dr GUSTAV   97

STREULI, HANS   234
STRIJDOM, JOHANNES GERHARDHUS   217
STROESSNER, Gen ALFREDO   194
STROUGAL, LUBOMIR   59
STULGINSKIS, ALEKSANDRAS   164
STURE the Elder, STEN   231
STURE the Younger, STEN   231
STURE, SVANTE   231
SU-TSUNG   45
SUAEBHARD   249
SUAREL, JOAQUIN   274
SUAREZ, MARCO FIDEI   52
SUAREZ FLAMERICH, Dr GERMAN   277
SUAREZ GONZALEZ, ADOLFO   226
SUAREZ VEINTIMILIA, MARIANO   66
SUBASIC, Dr IVAN   280
de SUCRE, Gen ANTONIO JOSÉ (Peru)   24
de SUCRE, Gen ANTONIO JOSÉ (Bolivia)   24
SUHARTO, Gen RADEN   132
SUHRAWARDY, HUSSEIN SHAHEED   186
SUIKO   154
SUININ   154
SUINTILA   219
SUJIN   154
SUJONG   158
SUKARNO, Dr MOHAMED ACHMAD   132
SUKIMAN, Dr   132
SUKSELAINEN, Dr VEINO JOHANNES   79
SULAIMAN, SEYYID HIKMAT   137
SULAYMAN   35
SULAYMAN I ibn Qutalmish   213
SULEIMAN (Caliphate) see Sulayman
SULEYMAN I   242
SULEYMAN II Ibrahim   242
SULTAN bin Ahmed   185
es-SULTANEH, QAVAM   136
SULYAMAN II, Rukn ad-Din   214
SUMUABUM   17
SUMUEL   16
SUMULAEL   17
SUN FO, Dr   48
SUN YAT-SEN   47
SUNAY, Gen CEVDET   243
SUNILA, JUHO EMIL   78
SUPPILULIUMAS I   118
SUPPILULIUMAS II   118
SURENDRA   176
SURYAVARMAN I   36
SURYAVARMAN II   36
SHUNINUA   8
SUSENYOS   77
SUSHUN   154
SUTOKU   155
SUTSAKHAN, Gen   38
SUWAIDI, TEWFIQ   137
el-SUWEIDI, TEWFIQ   137
SUWIRJO, Dr   132
SUZAKU   155
SUZUKI, Admiral Baron KANTARO   156
SVARTOPLUK   60
SVATOPLUK   59
SVELHA, Dr ANTONIN   58
SVEN   253
SVEN I   61
SVEN II Estrithsson   61
SVEN III   61
SVERDLOV, YAKOV MIKHAYLOVICH   247
SVERKER I   230
SVERKER II Carlssen   230
SVERRE   183
SVERRIR Sigurdsson   183
SVINHUFVUD, Dr PEHR EVIND   78
SVOBODA, Gen LUDVIK   59
SWAEFBERHT   251
SWAEFRED   251
SWART, CHARLES ROBBERTS   216, 217
SWARTZ, CARL GUSTAV JOHAN   233
SWEGN   253
SWEYN (Denmark) see Sven
SWITHELM   250
SWITHRED   251
von SYDOW, OSKAR FREDRIK   233
SYED PUTRA ibni Almarhum Syed Hassan
   Jamalullail   167
SYLVAIN, FRANCK   117
SYMMACHUS   188
SZAKASITS, ARPAD   124
SZALASI, Maj FERENC   124
SZTOJAY, Maj-Gen DOEME   124

TABINSHWEHTI   30
TACHOS   70
TACITUS   207
TAFT, WILLIAM HOWARD   272
TAGLE, JOSÉ BERNARDO   195
TAHARKA   70

TAHMASP I   135
TAHMASP II   136
al-TA'I   36
T'AI-CH'ANG   47
T'AI-TSU   46
T'AI TSU   46
T'AI-TSUNG   45
TAI-TSUNG   45
T'AI-TSUNG   46
T'AI TSUNG   47
T AIMUR bin Feisal   185
TAISHO   155
TAJ-ud DIN FIRUZ   128
TAJES, Gen MAXIMO   274
TAKAHASHI, Count KOREKIYO   156
TAKAKURA   155
TAKELOTH I .   69
TAKELOTH II .   69
TAKELOTH III .   70
TALAL ibn ABDULLAH   157
TALEB, Maj-Gen NAJI   138
TALHOUNI, BAHJAT   157
TALU, NAIM   243
TAMARA   94
TAMAYO, JOSÉ LUIS   65
TAMBRONI, FERNANDO   145
TAMERLANE (Timurid Empire) see Timur
TANAKA, GIICHI   156
TANAKA, KAKEUI   157
TANCHERES   67
TANCRED   54
TANCREDE   151
TANNER, VAINO ALFRED   78
TANUTAMON . Fled when the Assyrians sacked
   Thebes.   70
T'AN YEN-K'AI   48
TAO-KUANG   47
TARA BAI   131
TARAKI, NOOR MOHAMMED   2
TARDIEU, ANDRE   87
TATARESCU, GHEORGHE   209
TAUFA'AHAU TUPOU I   239
TAUFA'AHAU TUPOU IV   239
TAUSERT   69
TAWFIQ   72
TAYLOR, ZACHARY   272
TAYMURAZI II   95
TE TSUNG   45
TE TSUNG   47
TEEMANT, JAAN   76
TEIA   142
TEISPES   133
TEJADA SORZANO, JOSÉ LUIS   25
TEJAN-SIE, Chief Justice BANJA   214
TEKLA GIYORGIS II   77
TEKLA HAYMANOT   77
TELEKI, Count PAL   124
TELERIG   27
TELESPHORUS   187
TELETS   27
TELIPINUS   118
al-TELL, WASFI   157
TEMMU   154
TEMUJIN   174
TENJI   154
TENNYSON, Hallam Tennyson, 2nd Baron   10
TENOCH   170
TENZING GYATSO   239
TEODOREDO I   219
TEODOREDO II   219
TERRA, GABRIEL   275
TERVEL   27
TETHMOSIS   68
TETI   67
TEUDIS   219
TEUDISCULUS   219
de TEXADA, FRANCISCO XIMENES   169
TEZOZOMOC   170
THAKIN NU   30
THAMAR   94
THAMPHTHIS   67
THANH THAI   277
al THANI, KHALIFA bin HAMAD   204
THANIN KRAIVICHIEN   238
THANOM KITTIKACHORN, Gen   238
THAPA, SURYA BAHADUR   177
THARRAWADDY MIN   30
THEOBALD (France) see Thibaut
THEOBALD (Navarre) see Thibaut
THEODAHAD   142
THÉODEBALD   80
THEODEBALD   142
THEODELINDA   142
THEODOR SVETOSLAV (Bulgaria) see Todor
   Svetoslav
THEODOR   77
THEODOR I   76
THEODORA (Byzantine Empire)   32

THEODORA (Trebizond) 240
THÉODORE, DAVILMARE 117
THEODORE (Armenia) see Thoros
THEODORE (Byzantine Empire and Papal State) see Theodorus
THEODORE (Russia) see Fyodor
THEODORIC 142
THEODORICUS 189
THEODORUS 188
THEODORUS I 188
THEODORUS I LASCARIS 34
THEODORUS II 188
THEODORUS II LASCARIS 34
THEODOSIUS I 208
THEODOSIUS II 31
THEODOSIUS III 32
THEODRIC 252
THEONON 235
THEOPHILUS 32
THEOTOKIS, IOANNIS 112
THESH , King of Lower Egypt. 66
THEUDEBERT (France) see Thibert
THEUDERIC (France) see Thierry
THEUDERIC I 79
THEUNIS, GEORGES 21
THIBAUT I (Lorraine) 92
THIBAUT I (Navarre) 222
THIBAUT II (Lorraine) 92
THIBAUT II (Navarre) 222
THIBAW 30
THIBERT I 79
THIBERT II 80
THIERRY I (Belgium) 22
THIERRY I (France) 79
THIERRY I (Lorraine) 92
THIERRY II (France) 80
THIERRY II (Lorraine) 92
THIERRY III 80
THIERRY IV 80
THIERS, LOUIS ADOLPHE 87
THIEU TRI 277
THOMPSON, Sir JOHN SPARROW DAVID 39
THORDARSON, BJORN 125
THORHALLSSON, VIGFUS 125
THORLAKSSON, JON 125
THORN, GASTON 165
THOROS I 7
THOROS II 7
THOROS III or I 8
THORS, OLAFUR 125
THOTHMES I 68
THOTHMES II 68
THOTHMES III 68
THOTHMES IV 68
THOUORIS 69
THRASYBULUS 235
THUPA 'AMARU 127
THUPA 'INKA YUPANKI 126
THUPA WALLPA 127
THUSTEN GYATSO 238
THUTMOSE I 68
THUTMOSE II 68
THUTMOSE III 68
THUTMOSE IV 68
THWAINI bin Said 185
TIAO SOMSANITH, Prince 160
TIBERIUS 205
TIBERIUS II CONSTANTINUS 32
TIBERIUS III ASPIMAR 32
TIBINI 140
T'IEN-CH'I 47
T'IEN-SHUN 46
TIGLATHPILESER I 9
TIGLATHPILESER II 9
TIGLATHPILESER III (Assyria) 10
TIGLATHPILESER III (Babylonia) 18
TIGRAN II 7
TIGRANES 213
TIGRANES II 7
TILDY, ZOLTAN 124
TIMOLEON 235
TIMUR 239
TIMUR SHAH 1
TINDEMANS, LÉO 22
TINOCO GRANADOS, Gen FEDERICO 53
TIPTAKZI 17
TIRIDATES I 134
TIRIDATES II 134
TIRIDATES III 134
TIRUMALA 129
TISO, Dr JOSEF 58
TISO, STEFAN 58
TITO, Marshal JOSIP BROZ 281
TITUS 206
TIU , King of Lower Egypt. 66
TIZOC 170
TLACTOZIN 170
TOBA 155

TODOR SVETOSLAV 28
TODOROV, STANKO 29
TOGHRIL BEG 213
TOJO, Lieut-Gen HIDEKI 156
TOLBERT, WILLIAM RICHARD 162
TOLUI 174
TOMAS, Rear-Admiral AMÉRICO DEUS RODRIGUES 203
TOMBALBAYE, FRANCOIS 42
TOMBALBAYE, NGARTA 42, 43
TOMISLAV 280
TOMMASO 150
TON DUC THANG 278
TONISSON, JAAN 75, 76
TOPA HUALLPA (Inca Empire) see Thupa Wallpa
TOPA INCA YUPANQUI (Inca Empire) see Thupa 'Inka Yupanki
TORCUATO de ALVEAR, Dr MARCELO 6
TORISMUNDO 219
TORNGREN, RALF 78
TORO, Col DAVID R. 24, 25
TORP, OSCAR 184
TORRES, Gen JUAN JOSÉ 25
TORRIJOS HERRERA, Brig-Gen OMAR 187
TOSERTASIS 67
TOSHEV, ANDREI 29
TOSORTHROS 67
TOSTA, VICENTE 121
TOTILA 142
TOUKAN, AHMED 158
TOUTHMOSIS 68
TOVAR, MANUEL FELIPE 276
TRAHAEARN ap CARADOG 269
TRAIKOV, GEORGI 29
TRAJANUS 206
TRAN THIEN KHIEM, Gen 278
TRAN VAN HUONG 277, 278
TRAORE, Lieut MOUSSA 168
TRDAT I 134
TRDAT II 134
TRDAT III 134
TREJOS FERNANDEZ, Dr JOSÉ JOAQUIN 54
TRELLES MONTES, Dr OSCAR 196
TREVISANO, MARCANTONIO 153
TRIBHUVANA 177
TRIBHUVANA BIR VIKRAM SHAH 176
TRIBHUVANADITYAVARMAN 36
TRIFUNOVIC, MILOS 280
TRONCOSO de la CONCHA, MANUEL JESUS 64
TROUVOADA, MIGUEL 211
TRUCCO, MANUEL 43
TRUDEAU, PIERRE ELLIOTT 40
TRUJILLO, JULIAN 51
TRUJILLO MOLINA, Generalissimo RAFAEL LEONIDAS 64
TRUJILLO MOLINA, Gen HÉCTOR BIENVENIDO 64
TRUMAN, HARRY s. 272
TRYGGER, ERNST 233
TSAI-CH'UN 47
TSAI T'IEN 47
TSALDARIS, KONSTANTINOS 111
TSALDARIS, PANAGIOTES E. 111
TSANKOV, ALEKSANDR 29
TS'AO K'UN 48
TSATSOS, KONSTANTINOS 112
TSCHUDI, HANS-PETER 234
TSEDENBAL, Marshal YUMZHAGIYN 175
TSENG-TSUNG 46
TSHOMBE, MOISE KAPENDA 283
TSIDQIYAH 140
TSIRANA, PHILIBERT 166
TSIRIMOKOS, ELIAS 112
TSOUDEROS, Dr EMMANUEL 111
TSUCHIMIKADO 155
TSUNAYOSHI TOKUGAWA 156
TU DUC 277
TU-TSUNG 46
TUAN CHI-JUI, Marshal 48
TUBELIS, Dr JUOZAS 164
TUBMAN, WILLIAM VACANARARAT SHADRACH 162
TUDHALIYAS I 118
TUDHALIYAS II 118
TUDHALIYAS III 118
TUDHALIYAS IV 118
TU'IPELEHAKE, Prince 239
TUKA, Dr BELA 58
TUKULTIAPALESHARRA I 9
TUKULTIAPALESHARRA II 9
TUKULTIAPALESHARRA III 10
TUKULTININURTA I (Assyria) 9
TUKULTININURTA I (Babylonia) 17
TUKULTININURTA II 9
TULENHEIMO, ANTTI AGATON 78
TULGA 219
T'UNG CHIH 47

TUNG PI-WU 49
TUOMIOJA, Dr SAKARI 78
TUPPER, Sir CHARLES 39
TUPUA TAMASESE LEALOFI IV 279
TUPUA TAMASESE MEA'OLE, Chief 279
TUPUOLA TAISI EFI 279
TURBAY, Dr JULIO CESAR 52
TURKI bin Said 185
TURNBALL, Sir RICHARD 237
TUSAR, VLASTIMIL 58
TUSHRATTA 173
TUTANHKAMEN 69
TUTANKHATON 69
TWEEDSMUIR, 1st Baron 39
TYLER, JOHN 271
TYREIS 67

UAZKERE 67
UAZNAR 66
UBICO CASTANEDA, Gen JORGE 115
UCHIDA, Count YASUYA 156
UCLÉS, RAMON ERNESTO CRUZ 121
UDA 155
UDAYA I 227
UDAYA II 227
UDAYA III 227
UDAYA IV 227
UDAYADITYAVARMAN I 36
UDAYADITYAVARMAN II 36
UDRZAL, FRANTISEK 58
UDY-M IU 66
UEDIPRIS-RUSAS 273
UGYEN WANGCHUK 23
ULARTE, OTILIO 54
ULASZLO I 122
ULASZLO II 123
ULBRICHT, WALTER 95
ULMANIS, KARLIS 160
ULPIA SEVERINA 207
ULRICH VI 109
ULRIKA ELEONORA 232
ULUGH BEG 239
ULULAI 18
ULUMBURIASH 17
ULUOTS, JURI 76
'UMAR I 35
el-UMARI, ARSHAD 137
el-UMARI, SAYED MUSTAFA 137
'UMAR II ibn 'Abd al-Aziz 35
UMBERTO I (Italy) 143
UMBERTO I (Savoy) 150
UMBERTO II (Italy) 144
UMBERTO II (Savoy) 150
UMBERTO III 150
UNAS 67
UNGERN STERNBERG, Baron 174
UPATISSA I 227
UPATISSA II 227
URBAN (Papal State) see Urbanus
URBANUS I 187
URBANUS II 189
URBANUS III 190
URBANUS IV 190
URBANUS V 191
URBANUS VI 191
URBANUS VII 192
URBANUS VIII 192
URBINA, JOSE MARIA 65
URBSYS, Dr 164
URCO (Inca Empire) see 'Inka 'Urqon
URDUKUGA 16
URGUPLU, SUAT HAYRI 243
URHI-TESHUB 118
URIARTE, HIGINIO 193
URIBURU, Dr JOSÉ EVARISTO 6
URIBURU, Gen JOSÉ FELIX 6
URICOECHEA, JUAN AGUSTIN 51
URNAMMU 16
URNANSHE 15
URNINURTA 16
de URQUIZA, Gen JUSTO JOSÉ 5, 6
URRACA 220
URRIOLA, CIRO LUIS 186
URRIOLAGOITIA, Dr MAMERTO 25
URRUTIA LLEO, Dr MANUEL 56
URSICINUS 187
URUKAGINA 15
URZABABA 16
URZIGURUMASH 17
    USERKAF 67
USERKERE 67
UTHMAN ibn 'AFFAN 35
UTUHEGAL 16
UVAKHSHATRA 133
den UYL, Dr JOHANNES MARTEN 179
den UYL, Dr JOOP 179

UZONOVIC, Dr NICOLA   **280**
UZUN HASAN   **135**
UZZIAH (Israel and Judah) see Ahazariyah
UZZIYAH   **140**

VACLAV   **59**
VACLAV I   **60**
VACLAV II   **60**
VACLAV III   **60**
VACLAV IV   **60**
VAHARAN I   **134**
VAHARAN II   **134**
VAHARAN III   **134**
VAHARAN IV   **135**
VAHARAN V   **135**
VAHARAN VI   **135**
VAIDA VOEVOD, Dr ALEXANDRU   **209**
VAJIRAVUDH   **238**
VALAKHSH   **135**
VALDEMAR   **231**
VALDEMAR I   **61**
VALDEMAR II   **61**
VALDEMAR III   **61**
VALDEMAR IV Atterdag   **62**
VALDES, MIGUEL ALEMAN   **172**
VALDEZ, RAMON   **186**
VALENCIA, Dr GUILLERMO-LEON   **52**
VALENS   **208**
VALENTINE (Papal State) see Valentinus
VALENTINIAN (Roman Empire) see Valentinianus
VALENTINIANUS I   **208**
VALENTINIANUS II   **208**
VALENTINIANUS III   **208**
VALENTINUS   **188**
VALERIAN (Roman Empire) see Valerianus
VALERIANUS   **207**
VALIER, BERTUCCIO   **153**
VALIER, SILVESTRO   **153**
VALLADARES, TOMAS   **181**
VALLE, ANDRES   **74**
del VALLE, MAX   **187**
VALVERDE, JOSE DESIDERIO   **64**
van ACKER, ACHILLE   **21, 22**
van AGT, ANDREAS A.M.   **179**
VAN BUREN, MARTIN   **271**
VAN DEN BOEYNANTS, PAUL   **22**
van de VIJVERE, ALOIS Burgrave   **21**
van HOUTTE, JEAN   **22**
VANIER, Maj-Gen GEORGES PHILIAS   **39**
van ZEELAND, PAUL   **21**
VARDANES   **134**
VARELA, PEDRO   **274**
VARGAS, EMILIANO CHAMORRO   **181**
VARGAS, Dr GETULIO DORNELLES   **26**
VARGAS, Dr JOSE MARIA   **275**
VARGAS PRIETO, Gen OSCAR   **196**
VARRE, JOHANNES   **76**
de VASCONCELLOS, LUIZ MENDEZ   **168**
VASCONCELOS, DOROTEO   **74**
VASILY   **244**
VASILY I Dmitriyevich   **244**
VASILY III Ivanovich   **245**
VASILY II Vasilyevich   **244, 245**
VASILY IV Ivanovich Shuysky   **245**
VASQUEZ, DOMINGO   **121**
VASQUEZ, HORACIO   **64**
VAXTANG II   **94**
VAXTANG III   **94**
VAXTANG IV   **95**
de VEINTEMILLA, IGNACIO   **65**
de VELASCO, Gen JOSE MIGUEL   **24**
VELASCO ALVARADO, Gen JUAN   **196**
VELASCO IBARRA, Dr JOSE MARIA   **65, 66**
VENCESLAS I   **165**
VENCESLAS II   **165**
VENIER, FRANCESO   **153**
VENIER, SEBASTIANO   **153**
VENIZELOS, ELEUTHERIOS   **111**
VENIZELOS, SOPHOCLES   **111, 112**
VENKATA I   **129**
VENKATA II   **129**
VENNOLA, JUHO HEIKKI   **78**
VERMUDO I   **220**
VERMUDO II   **220**
VERMUDO III   **220**
VERWOERD, HENDRIK FRENSCH   **217**
VESNIC, MILENKO   **280**
VESPASIAN (Roman Empire) see Vespasianus
VESPASIANUS   **206**
VETRANIO   **208**
VICINI BURGOS, JUAN BAUTISTA   **64**
VICTOR I   **187**
VICTOR II   **189**
VICTOR III   **189**
VICTOR IV   **189**

VICTOR AMADEUS (Italian states) see Vittorio
   Amadeo
VICTOR EMMANUEL (Italy) see Vittorio Emanuele
VICTORIA, ALFREDO   **64**
VICTORIA   **259**
VIDAL, FRANCISCO ANTONIO   **274**
VIDELA, GABRIEL GONZALEZ   **44**
VIDELA, Gen JORGE RAFAEL   **6**
VIERA, FELICIANO   **274**
VIGILIUS   **188**
VIJAYABAHU I   **227**
VIJAYABAHU II   **227**
VIJAYABAHU III   **228**
VIJAYABAHU IV   **228**
VIJAYABAHU V   **228**
VIKRAMABAHU I   **227**
VIKRAMABAHU II   **228**
VIKRAMABAHU III   **228**
VILBRUN-GUILLAUME, JOSEPH   **117**
de VILHENA, ANTONIO MANUEL   **168**
VILLAROEL, Major GUALBERTO   **25**
VILLAZON, ELIODORO   **24**
VILLEDA MORALES, JOSE RAMON   **121**
VINCENT, STENIO JOSEPH   **117**
VINEKH   **27**
VIRA NARASIMHA   **129**
VIRA VIJAYA   **129**
VIRACOCHA (Inca Empire) see Wiraqocha 'Inka
VIROLAINEN, Dr JOHANNES   **79**
VIRUPAKSA   **129**
VIRUPAKSHA   **129**
VITALIAN (Roman Empire) see Vitalianus
VITALIANUS   **188**
VITELLIUS   **206**
VITTORIO AMEDEO   **152**
VITTORIO AMEDEO I   **150**
VITTORIO AMEDEO II (Sardinia)   **149**
VITTORIO AMEDEO II (Savoy)   **150**
VITTORIO AMEDEO III   **149**
VITTORIO EMANUELE I   **149**
VITTORIO EMANUELE II (Italy)   **143**
VITTORIO EMANUELE II (Sardinia)   **149**
VITTORIO EMANUELE III   **3, 144**
VIVIANI, RENE   **87**
VLADIMIR   **27**
VLADISLAV I   **60**
VLADISLAV II   **60**
VLADISLAV III   **60**
VLADIVOJ   **59**
VOLDEMARAS, AUGUSTINAS   **164**
VOLOGASES I   **134**
VOLOGASES II   **134**
VOLOGASES III   **134**
VOLOGASES IV   **134**
VOLOGASES V   **134**
VONONES I   **134**
VONONES II   **134**
VOROSHILOV, Marshal KLIMENT
   EFREMOVICH   **248**
VORSTER, BALTHAZAR JOHN   **217**
VOULGARIS, Admiral PETROS   **111**
VRATISLAV I   **59**
VRATISLAV II   **59**
VU VAN MAU   **278**
VUKICIVIC, Dr VELJA   **280**
VYTAUTAS   **163**
VYTENIS   **163**

WACLAW I   **198**
WACLAW II   **198**
WAHLEN, FRIEDRICH TRAUGOTT   **234**
WAKATSUKI, Baron REIJIRO   **156**
WALDEGRAVE, JAMES   **261**
WALDEGRAVE, 2nd Earl of   **261**
WALDEMAR (Denmark) see Valdemar
al-WALID I   **35**
al-WALID II   **35**
WALKER, WILLIAM   **181**
WALLIA   **219**
WALPOLE, Sir ROBERT   **261**
WAMBA   **219**
WAN-LI   **46**
WANG CHING-WEI, Dr   **48**
WANG MANG   **44**
WARADSIN   **16**
WARBURTON PAUL, Sir JOHN   **94**
WARD, Sir DEIGHTON   **20**
WARD, Sir JOSEPH GEORGE   **180**
WARNER, DANIEL   **162**
WASASHATTA (?).   **173**
WASHINGTON, GEORGE   **271**
WASHKAR 'INKA   **126**
al-WATHIQ, HARUN   **35**
WATSON, JOHN CHRISTIAN   **11**
WATT, HUGH   **180**
WATT   **249**

WAYNA QHAPAQ   **126**
WEBHERD   **249**
WEI   **45**
WEIZMANN, Dr CHAIM AZRIEL   **141**
WELF I   **98**
WELF II   **98**
W ELLINGTON, The 1st Duke of   **263**
WELTI, EMIL   **234**
WEN-TI   **44**
WEN TSUNG   **47**
WENCESLAUS (Bohemia) see Vaclav
WENCESLAUS (Holy Roman Empire) see Wenzel
WENCESLAUS (Hungary) see Laszlo
WENCESLAUS (Luxembourg) see Venceslas
WENCESLAUS (Poland) see Waclaw
WENIS   **67**
WENZEL   **120**
WERNER, PIERRE   **165**
WETTER, ERNST   **234**
WHITLAM, EDWARD GOUGH   **11**
WIGLAF   **252**
de WIGNACOURT, ALOF   **168**
de WIGNACOURT, ADRIEN   **168**
WIHTRED   **249**
WILHELM (Austria)   **13**
WILHELM (Brunswick)   **100**
WILHELM (Hanover)   **101**
WILHELM (Nassau)   **103**
WILHELM I (Albania)   **3**
WILHELM I (Germany)   **96**
WILHELM I (Hesse-Cassel)   **101**
WILHELM I (Prussia)   **104**
WILHELM I (Wurttemberg)   **109**
WILHELM II (Germany)   **96**
WI LHELM II (Hesse-Cassel)   **101**
WILHELM II (Prussia)   **104**
WILHELM II (Wurttemberg)   **109**
WILHELM IV (Bavaria)   **99**
WILHELM IV (Hesse-Cassel)   **101**
WILHELM V (Bavaria)   **99**
WILHELM V (Hesse-Cassel)   **101**
WILHELM VI   **101**
WILHELM VII   **101**
WILHELM VIII   **101**
WILHELM IX   **101**
WILHELM ERNST   **106**
WILHELM LUDWIG   **109**
WILHELMINA   **178**
WILLEM I (Flanders)   **22**
WILLEM I (Holland)   **179**
WILLEM I (Netherlands)   **176**
W ILLEM I , Prince of Orange   **177**
WILLEM II (Holland)   **179**
WILLEM II (Netherlands)   **178**
WILLEM II Prince of Orange   **177**
WILLEM III (Holland)   **179**
WILLEM III (Netherlands)   **178**
WILLEM III , Prince of Orange   **177**
WILLEM IV   **179**
WILLEM IV Friso , Prince of Orange   **177**
WILLEM V   **179**
WILLEM V , Prince of Orange   **178**
WILLEM VI   **179**
WILLEM VI , Prince of Orange   **178**
WILLIAM (NETHERLANDS and FLANDERS) see
   willem
WILLIAM (France) see Guillaume
WILLIAM (German states and Germany) see
   Wilhelm
WILLIAM I (England)   **254**
WILLIAM I (Scotland)   **267**
WILLIAM II   **254**
WILLIAM III   **258**
WILLIAM IV   **259**
W ILLIAM IV (Netherlands) see Willem IV Friso
WILLIAM LOUIS (German states) see Wilhelm
   Ludwig
WILLIAMS, Dr ERIC EUSTACE   **240**
WILLIAMS, Sir ARTHUR LEONARD   **169**
WILLIMAN, CLAUDIO   **274**
WILLINGDON, Freeman Freeman-Thomas, 1st
   Viscount of   **39**
WILMINGTON, 1st Earl of   **261**
WILOPO, Dr   **132**
WILSON, JAMES HAROLD   **265**
WILSON, THOMAS WOODROW   **272**
WIN MAUNG, U   **30**
WIRAQOCHA 'INKA   **126**
WIRTH, KARL JOSEPH   **97**
WITERICO   **219**
WITIGIS   **142**
WITIZA   **219**
WLADYSLAW (Hungary) see Ulaszlo
WLADYSLAW I   **198**
WLADYSLAW I Herman   **197**
WLADYSLAW II   **197**
WLADYSLAW II Jagiello   **163**
WLADYSLAW III Jagiello   **198**

WLADYSLAW IV Wasa   199
WLGS I   134
WLGS II   134
WLGS III   134
WLGS IV   134
WLGS V   134
WOJCIECHOWSKI, STANISLAW   200
WOLDEMAR   102
WONG WEN-HAO, Dr   48
WONGSONEGORO, Dr   132
WOSS y GIL, ALEJANDRO   64
WRATHALL, JOHN J.   204
WU   45
WU-TI   44, 45
WU TSUNG   46
WULFHERE   251
WYRWY I   134
WYRWY II   134

XERXES (Babylonia)   19
XERXES (Egypt)   70
XERXES I   133
XERXES II   133
XYSTUS I   187
XYSTUS II   187
XYSTUS III   187
XYSTUS IV   191
XYSTUS V   191

al-YAFI, Dr ABDULLAH AREF   161
YAGODA, GENRIKH GRIGORYEVICH   248
YAHIA   279
YAHYA, Lieut-Gen TAHER   138
YAHYA KHAN, Gen AGHA MUHAMMAD   186
YAHYA PUTRA ibni Al Marhum Sultan Ibrahim
   167
YAMAMOTO, Admiral Count GOMBEI   156
YAMEOGO, MAURICE   273
YANES URIAS, Col CESAR   75
YANG CHIEN   45
YANG-TI   45
YA'QOB   77
YA'QUB   135
YA'QUB KHAN   2
YASOVARMAN I   36
YASOVARMAN II   36
YAWAR WAQAQ   126
YAZDEGERD I   135
YAZDEGERD II   135
YAZDEGERD III   135
YAZID I   35
YAZID II   35
YAZID III   35
YDIGORAS-FUENTES, Gen MIGUEL   115
YEH CHIEN-YING, Marshal   49
YEHIA PASHA, ABDEL FATTAH   73
YEHOIACHIN   140
YEHOIAKIM   140
YEHOKHANAN HYRCANUS I   141
YEHOKHANAN HYRCANUS II   141
YEHORAM   140
YEHOSHAPHAT   140
YEHU ben-NIMSHI   140
YEHUDAH ARISTOBULUS I   141
YEN CHIA-KAN, Dr   50
YEN HSI-SHAN, Marshal (China)   48
YEN HSI-SHAN, Marshal (Taiwan)   50
YEROBOAM I   140
YEROBOAM II   140
YEROVI INDABURU, CLEMENTE   66
YESHAQ   76
YEVTIC, BOGOLYUB   280
YEW, LEE KUAN   215
YHOMBI-OPANGO, Col JOACHIM   53
YIN-CHEN   47
YING-TI   44
YING-TSUNG   46
YING TSUNG   46
YI T'AE WANG   158
YOASH   140
YOHANNES I   77
YOHANNES II   77
YOHANNES IV   77
YOLANDE (Jerusalem)   55
YOLANDE (Latin Empire)   34
YOMEI   154
YONAI, Admiral MITSUMASA   156
YOON BO SUN   159
YOSHIDA, SHIGERU   156
YOSHIHITO   155
YOSHIMUNE TOKUGAWA   156
YOSHIYAH   140
YOTHAM   140
YOULOU, Abbot FULBERT   52, 53

YOZEI   155
YUAN CHIN-KAI, Gen   49
YUAN SHIH-K'AI, Gen   48
YUAN-TI   44
YUGOV, ANTON   29
YUI, O.K.   50
YUNG-CHENG   47
YUNG-LO   46
YUNG-YEN   47
YURI   244
YURI Vasilyevich   245
YURYAKU   154
YUSSUF, Dr MOHAMMED   2
YUSUF ADIL KHAN   129
YUSUF ADIL SHAH   129
YUSUF bin ISHAK, INCHE   215
YZDKRT I   135
YZDKRT II   135
YZDKRT III   135

ZA   66
ZA-DENGEL   77
ZABABASHUMIDDIN   17
ZABAYA   16
ZABEL   7
ZACCARIA, CENTURIONE   1
ZACHARIAH (Israel and Judah) see Zekariyah
ZACHARIAS   188
ZACHARY (Papal State) see Zacharias
ZAGHLUL PASHA, SAAD   73
ZAHEDA, Gen FAZULLA   137
ZAHIR, Dr ABDUL   2
az-ZAHIR   36
ZAHLE, CARL THEODOR   63
ZAHREDDIN, Maj-Gen   236
ZAIM, Col HUSNI   235, 236
ZAIMIS, ALEXANDROS   111
ZALDIVAR y LAZO, RAFAEL   74
ZALDUA, FRANCISCO JAVIER   51
ZAMAM MIRZA SHAH   1
ZAMBIA   16
ZAMOR, ORESTE   117
ZAMUELS, VOLDEMARS   160
ZAPOTOCKY, ANTONIN   59
ZAR'A YA'QOB   76
ZAUDITU   77
ZAVALA, JOAQUIN   181
ZAWADSKI, ALEKSANDER   200
ZAYAS y ALFONSO, Dr ALFREDO   56
ZEAYEN, Dr YOUSSEF   236
ZEDEKIAH (Israel and Judah) see Tsidqiyah
ZEKARIYAH   140
ZELAYA, JOSE SANTOS   181
ZEMGALS, GUSTAVS   160
ZEMP, JOSEPH   234
ZENO   31
ZEPHYRINUS   187
ZER ATOTI   66
ZET   66
ZHIVKOV, TODOR   29
ZIAELAS   23
ZIA ul-HAQ, Gen MOHAMMED   186
ZIBOETES   23
ZIDANTAS I   118
ZIDANTAS II (?)   118
ZIEHM, Dr E.   61
ZIEMOMYSL   197
ZIEMOWIT   197
ZIJLSTRA, Prof JELLE   179
ZIMRI   140
ZINCHI ROQ'A   126
ZINSOU, Dr EMILE DERLIN   23
ZIVKOVIC, Gen PETAR   280
ZIWER PASHA, AHMED   73
ZLATEV, Gen PENCHO   29
ZOE   32
ZOG I SKANDERBEG III   3
ZOGU, AHMED BEY   3
ZOLI, ADONE   144
ZONDONARI, MICHELE ANTONIO   168
ZOSER   67
ZOSER-NETERKHET   67
ZOSERTETI   67
ZOSIMUS   187
ZSEDENYI, Prof BELA   124
ZUBIRIA, Dr ALBERTO F.   275
ZULOAGA, Gen FELIX   171
ZYGMUNT I   198
ZYGMUNT II AUGUST   198
ZYGMUNT III Wasa   199
ZYNDRAM-KOSCIALKOWSKI, MARIAN   200